MICROSOFT CERTIFIED SOLUTION DEVELOPER

MCSD Visual Basic 6 Distributed Applications Study Guide

MICROSOFT CERTIFIED SOLUTION DEVELOPER

MCSD Visual Basic 6 Distributed Applications Study Guide

(Exam 70-175)

Syngress Media, Inc.

Osborne/McGraw-Hill

Berkeley   New York   St. Louis   San Francisco   Auckland   Bogotá   Hamburg   London   Madrid   Mexico City
Milan   Montreal   New Delhi   Panama City   Paris   São Paulo   Singapore   Sydney   Tokyo   Toronto

Osborne/**McGraw-Hill**
2600 Tenth Street
Berkeley, California 94710
U.S.A.

For information on translations or book distributors outside the U.S.A., or to arrange bulk purchase discounts for sales promotions, premiums, or fund-raisers, please contact Osborne/**McGraw-Hill** at the above address.

**MCSD Visual Basic 6 Distributed Applications Study Guide
(Exam 70-175)**

34567890 AGM AGM 90198765432109

ISBN 0-07-211932-2

Publisher
Brandon A. Nordin

Editor-in-Chief
Scott Rogers

Acquisitions Editor
Gareth Hancock

Project Editor
Jennifer Wenzel

Editorial Assistant
Stephane Thomas

Technical Editors
Michael Lane Thomas
Julie U. Davis

Copy Editor
Nancy Sixsmith

Proofreader
Rhonda Holmes

Indexer
Valerie Robbins

Computer Designers
Jean Butterfield
Michelle Galicia
Ann Sellers

Illustrators
Beth Young
Brian Wells

Series Design
Peter Hancik

Cover Design
Regan Honda

From Global Knowledge Network

At Global Knowledge Network we strive to support the multiplicity of learning styles required by our students to achieve success as technical professionals. In this series of books, it is our intention to offer the reader a valuable tool for successful completion of the MCSD Certification Exam.

As the world's largest IT training company, Global Knowledge Network is uniquely positioned to offer these books. The expertise gained each year from providing instructor-led training to hundreds of thousands of students worldwide has been captured in book form to enhance your learning experience. We hope that the quality of these books demonstrates our commitment to your lifelong learning success. Whether you choose to learn through the written word, computer-based training, Web delivery, or instructor-led training, Global Knowledge Network is committed to providing you the very best in each of those categories. For those of you who know Global Knowledge Network, or those of you who have just found us for the first time, our goal is to be your lifelong competency partner.

Thank you for the opportunity to serve you. We look forward to serving your needs again in the future.

Warmest regards,

Duncan Anderson
President and Chief Operating Officer, Global Knowledge Network

January 12, 1998

Dear Osborne/McGraw-Hill Customer:

Microsoft is pleased to inform you that Osborne/McGraw-Hill is a participant in the Microsoft® Independent Courseware Vendor (ICV) program. Microsoft ICVs design, develop, and market self-paced courseware, books, and other products that support Microsoft software and the Microsoft Certified Professional (MCP) program.

To be accepted into the Microsoft ICV program, an ICV must meet set criteria. In addition, Microsoft reviews and approves each ICV training product before permission is granted to use the Microsoft Certified Professional Approved Study Guide logo on that product. This logo assures the consumer that the product has passed the following Microsoft standards:

- The course contains accurate product information.
- The course includes labs and activities during which the student can apply knowledge and skills learned from the course.
- The course teaches skills that help prepare the student to take corresponding MCP exams.

Microsoft ICVs continually develop and release new MCP Approved Study Guides. To prepare for a particular Microsoft certification exam, a student may choose one or more single, self-paced training courses or a series of training courses.

You will be pleased with the quality and effectiveness of the MCP Approved Study Guides available from Osborne/McGraw-Hill.

Sincerely,

Becky Kirsininkas

Becky Kirsininkas
ICV Program Manager
Microsoft Training & Certification

The Global Knowledge Network Advantage

Global Knowledge Network has a global delivery system for its products and services. The company has 28 subsidiaries, and offers its programs through a total of 60+ locations. No other vendor can provide consistent services across a geographic area this large. Global Knowledge Network is the largest independent information technology education provider, offering programs on a variety of platforms. This enables our multi-platform and multi-national customers to obtain all of their programs from a single vendor. The company has developed the unique CompetusTM Framework software tool and methodology which can quickly reconfigure courseware to the proficiency level of a student on an interactive basis. Combined with self-paced and on-line programs, this technology can reduce the time required for training by prescribing content in only the deficient skills areas. The company has fully automated every aspect of the education process, from registration and follow-up, to "just-in-time" production of courseware. Global Knowledge Network, through its Enterprise Services Consultancy, can customize programs and products to suit the needs of an individual customer.

Global Knowledge Network Classroom Education Programs

The backbone of our delivery options is classroom-based education. Our modern, well-equipped facilities staffed with the finest instructors offer programs in a wide variety of information technology topics, many of which lead to professional certifications.

Custom Learning Solutions

This delivery option has been created for companies and governments that value customized learning solutions. For them, our consultancy-based approach of developing targeted education solutions is most effective at helping them meet specific objectives.

Self-Paced and Multimedia Products

This delivery option offers self-paced program titles in interactive CD-ROM, videotape and audio tape programs. In addition, we offer custom development of interactive multimedia courseware to customers and partners. Call us at 1 (888) 427-4228.

Electronic Delivery of Training

Our network-based training service delivers efficient competency-based, interactive training via the World Wide Web and organizational intranets. This leading-edge delivery option provides a custom learning path and "just-in-time" training for maximum convenience to students.

ARG

American Research Group (ARG), a wholly-owned subsidiary of Global Knowledge Network, one of the largest worldwide training partners of Cisco Systems, offers a wide range of internetworking, LAN/WAN, Bay Networks, FORE Systems, IBM, and UNIX courses. ARG offers hands on network training in both instructor-led classes and self-paced PC-based training.

Global Knowledge Network Courses Available

Network Fundamentals

- Understanding Computer Networks
- Telecommunications Fundamentals I
- Telecommunications Fundamentals II
- Understanding Networking Fundamentals
- Implementing Computer Telephony Integration
- Introduction to Voice Over IP
- Introduction to Wide Area Networking
- Cabling Voice and Data Networks
- Introduction to LAN/WAN protocols
- Virtual Private Networks
- ATM Essentials

Network Security & Management

- Troubleshooting TCP/IP Networks
- Network Management
- Network Troubleshooting
- IP Address Management
- Network Security Administration
- Web Security
- Implementing UNIX Security
- Managing Cisco Network Security
- Windows NT 4.0 Security

IT Professional Skills

- Project Management for IT Professionals
- Advanced Project Management for IT Professionals
- Survival Skills for the New IT Manager
- Making IT Teams Work

LAN/WAN Internetworking

- Frame Relay Internetworking
- Implementing T1/T3 Services
- Understanding Digital Subscriber Line (xDSL)
- Internetworking with Routers and Switches
- Advanced Routing and Switching
- Multi-Layer Switching and Wire-Speed Routing
- Internetworking with TCP/IP
- ATM Internetworking
- OSPF Design and Configuration
- Border Gateway Protocol (BGP) Configuration

Authorized Vendor Training

Cisco Systems

- Introduction to Cisco Router Configuration
- Advanced Cisco Router Configuration
- Installation and Maintenance of Cisco Routers
- Cisco Internetwork Troubleshooting
- Cisco Internetwork Design
- Cisco Routers and LAN Switches
- Catalyst 5000 Series Configuration
- Cisco LAN Switch Configuration
- Managing Cisco Switched Internetworks
- Configuring, Monitoring, and Troubleshooting Dial-Up Services
- Cisco AS5200 Installation and Configuration
- Cisco Campus ATM Solutions

Bay Networks

- Bay Networks Accelerated Router Configuration
- Bay Networks Advanced IP Routing
- Bay Networks Hub Connectivity
- Bay Networks Accelar 1xxx Installation and Basic Configuration
- Bay Networks Centillion Switching

FORE Systems

- FORE ATM Enterprise Core Products
- FORE ATM Enterprise Edge Products
- FORE ATM Theory
- FORE LAN Certification

Operating Systems & Programming

Microsoft

- Introduction to Windows NT
- Microsoft Networking Essentials
- Windows NT 4.0 Workstation
- Windows NT 4.0 Server
- Advanced Windows NT 4.0 Server
- Windows NT Networking with TCP/IP
- Introduction to Microsoft Web Tools
- Windows NT Troubleshooting
- Windows Registry Configuration

UNIX

- UNIX Level I
- UNIX Level II
- Essentials of UNIX and NT Integration

Programming

- Introduction to JavaScript
- Java Programming
- PERL Programming
- Advanced PERL with CGI for the Web

Web Site Management & Development

- Building a Web Site
- Web Site Management and Performance
- Web Development Fundamentals

High Speed Networking

- Essentials of Wide Area Networking
- Integrating ISDN
- Fiber Optic Network Design
- Fiber Optic Network Installation
- Migrating to High Performance Ethernet

DIGITAL UNIX

- UNIX Utilities and Commands
- DIGITAL UNIX v4.0 System Administration
- DIGITAL UNIX v4.0 (TCP/IP) Network Management
- AdvFS, LSM, and RAID Configuration and Management
- DIGITAL UNIX TruCluster Software Configuration and Management
- UNIX Shell Programming Featuring Kornshell
- DIGITAL UNIX v4.0 Security Management
- DIGITAL UNIX v4.0 Performance Management
- DIGITAL UNIX v4.0 Intervals Overview

DIGITAL OpenVMS

- OpenVMS Skills for Users
- OpenVMS System and Network Node Management I
- OpenVMS System and Network Node Management II
- OpenVMS System and Network Node Management III
- OpenVMS System and Network Node Operations
- OpenVMS for Programmers
- OpenVMS System Troubleshooting for Systems Managers
- Configuring and Managing Complex VMScluster Systems
- Utilizing OpenVMS Features from C
- OpenVMS Performance Management
- Managing DEC TCP/IP Services for OpenVMS
- Programming in C

Hardware Courses

- AlphaServer 1000/1000A Installation, Configuration and Maintenance
- AlphaServer 2100 Server Maintenance
- AlphaServer 4100, Troubleshooting Techniques and Problem Solving

ABOUT THE CONTRIBUTORS

Syngress Media

Syngress Media creates books and software for Information Technology professionals seeking skill enhancement and career advancement. Its products are designed to comply with vendor and industry standard course curricula, and are optimized for certification exam preparation. You can contact Syngress via the Web at http://www.syngress.com.

The Contributors

Michael Cross is a MCSE, MCPS, and MCP + Internet, computer programmer, and network support specialist. He works as an instructor at private colleges, teaching courses in hardware, software, programming, and networking. He is the owner of KnightWare, a company that provides consulting, programming, network support, Web page design, computer training, and various other services. In his spare time, he has been a freelance writer for several years, in genres of fiction and non-fiction. He currently lives in London, Ontario.

John Fuex is an MCP and an MCSD, and works as a programmer for InfoEdge Technology, Inc. (http://www.nfo.com) in Austin, Texas, where he writes custom litigation support applications and consults on the use of technology in law offices. His development work centers primarily on document management and imaging systems written in Visual Basic and Access. Prior to his position at InfoEdge technology he worked as a database analyst and LAN administrator at Tracor Aerospace, Inc., where he wrote and maintained contract management systems in Microsoft Access. John has also done database consulting and training as an independent consultant. In 1998, he finished the WinArch track to become an MCSD. His formal education was in Computer Science at the University of Texas, and in Computer Information Systems at Austin Community College. His current pet projects are Active Server Pages, Visual C++, and SQL Server. John lives in Webberville, Texas, with his wife Athene and son Julian (resident Webmaster and football star for the Elgin Wildcats). When he has some free time, he is an avid basketball fanatic and confirmed number one fan of the Houston Rockets. John can be contacted via e-mail at jfuex@nfo.com.

Terry Knaul, a MCSD, and MCSE, presently works for a national IT consulting firm. He has worked in the IT field for more than nine years with such companies as Procter & Gamble, Fidelity Investments, and Ernst & Young LLP. He is currently on assignment as regional IT manager with a global insurance company. Terry also freelances as an application developer and Web designer. In his free time he is an avid runner (having finished a marathon) and cycling wanna-be who competes in triathlons.

Venkatarama Uppugunduri, a MCSD, is an Internet/Intranet developer with Reed Elsevier, in New Providence, NJ. He specializes in Visual Studio environment, COM/DCOM, ADO, ASP, MTS, and CGI development on both UNIX and Windows. Before joining Reed Elsevier, he worked as a senior intranet consultant at Merrill Lynch. Venkatarama has also done graphics software development, including 3D-object generation and rendering and customizing AutoCAD and other CAD tools. He can be reached at vruppugunduri@msn.com.

Mike Almond, a MCSD, has been an IT developer/consultant in the area of distributed/networked computer systems for over 20 years. He has developed wide and local area network solutions involving the integration of multiplatform and multiprotocol systems for a variety of firms. He helped pioneer a mainframe capacity planning discipline in the early 1980s and has experience developing in COBOL, FORTRAN, ASM, SAS, PASCAL, C, and C++. Most recently, Mike has been involved in designing and developing multitier strategies in the insurance, banking, and financial services areas—and living the COM lifestyle whenever possible!

Mick Porter works as a development consultant in Sydney, Australia, developing distributed intranet applications. He has many years' experience developing Windows and Web applications, and is a Microsoft Certified Professional and a Sun Certified Java Programmer. Mick can be contacted at porter@pragma.com.au.

Technical Reviewer and From the Classroom Contributor

Michael Lane Thomas (MCSE+I, MCSD, MCT, MCSS, A+) is a consultant, trainer, developer, and all-around technology slave who has spent eight years in the fields of computers and training. Michael has written for many computer trade publishers and magazines, including *Microsoft Certification Professional* magazine. Michael has also served as guest speaker at assorted users groups and at the 1998 MCP TechMentor Conference. Having earned his MCSE+I by passing the IEAK exam in beta, Michael has the distinction of being tied as the first MCSE+I recipient in the world.

Additionally, Michael is one of the top 20 Microsoft certified computer professionals in the world, having passed approximately 25 Microsoft certification exams, holding seven Microsoft certification titles, and being certified to teach 28 Microsoft Official Curriculum courses. Michael graduated from the University of Kansas with two bachelor's degrees in mathematics. He is currently working on an M.S. in Engineering Management at the University of Kansas. Occasionally known by his online name of Shiar, Michael can be reached at mlthomas@winning-edge.com, but only if his beautiful wife of three years, Jennifer, gives permission.

Technical Reviewer

Julie U. Davis (MCP) has been working as a developer of client/server systems for over three years. Julie does most of her work with Visual Basic front ends running on a Windows NT or Windows 95 platform, with SQL Server or Access backends. She has a B.S. degree in Data Processing Management. She is currently working as a computer consultant creating a VB/SQL Server data-mining tool. She also does technical reviews and/or small projects for small businesses.

ACKNOWLEDGMENTS

We would like to thank the following people:

- Richard Kristof of Global Knowledge Network for championing the series and providing us access to some great people and information, and to Shelley Everett, Marty Young, Patrick Faison, Brenda Thistle, Stacey Cannon, and Chuck Terrien.

- All the incredibly hard-working folks at Osborne/McGraw-Hill: Brandon Nordin, Scott Rogers, and Gareth Hancock for their help in launching a great series and being solid team players. In addition, Steve Emry and Jennifer Wenzel for their help in fine-tuning the book.

- Becky Kirsininkas and Karen Cronin at Microsoft Corporation for being patient and diligent in answering all our questions.

CONTENTS AT A GLANCE

CONTENTS

PREFACE

This book's primary objective is to help you prepare for and pass the required MCSD exam, so you can begin to reap the career benefits of certification. We believe the only way to do this is to help you increase your knowledge and build your skills. After completing this book, you should feel confident that you have thoroughly reviewed all of the objectives that Microsoft has established for the exam.

In This Book

This book is organized around the actual structure of the Microsoft exam administered at Sylvan Testing Centers. Microsoft has let us know all the topics we need to cover for the exam. We've followed their list carefully, so you can be assured you're not missing anything.

In Every Chapter

We've created a set of chapter components that call your attention to important items, reinforce important points, and provide helpful exam-taking hints. Take a look at what you'll find in every chapter:

- Every chapter begins with the **Certification Objectives**—what you need to know in order to pass the section on the exam dealing with the chapter topic. The Certification Objective headings identify the objectives within the chapter, so you'll always know an objective when you see it!

- **Exam Watch** notes call attention to information about, and potential pitfalls in, the exam. These helpful hints are written by MCSDs who have taken the exams and received their certification—who better to tell you what to worry about? They know what you're about to go through!

EXERCISE

- **On the Job** notes point out procedures and techniques important for coding actual applications for employers or contract jobs.

- **Certification Exercises** are interspersed throughout the chapters. These are step-by-step exercises that mirror vendor-recommended labs. They help you master skills that are likely to be an area of focus on the exam. Don't just read through the exercises; they are hands-on practice that you should be comfortable completing. Learning by doing is an effective way to increase your competency with a product.

- **From the Classroom** sidebars describe the issues that come up most often in the training classroom setting. These sidebars give you a valuable perspective into certification- and product-related topics. They point out common mistakes and address questions that have arisen from classroom discussions.

- **Q & A** sections lay out problems and solutions in a quick-read format. For example:

QUESTIONS AND ANSWERS

I want to add menus to my program, but don't want to go through the hassle of creating them at runtime.	Use the Menu Editor that comes with VB. Menu Editor allows you to create custom menus in Design time for your application.

- The **Certification Summary** is a succinct review of the chapter and a re-statement of salient points regarding the exam.

- The **Two-Minute Drill** at the end of every chapter is a checklist of the main points of the chapter. It can be used for last-minute review.

- The **Self Test** offers questions similar to those found on the certification exams, including multiple choice, true/false questions, and fill-in-the-blank. The answers to these questions, as well as explanations of the answers, can be found in Appendix A. By taking the Self Test after completing each chapter, you'll reinforce what you've learned from that chapter, while becoming familiar with the structure of the exam questions.

Some Pointers

Once you've finished reading this book, set aside some time to do a thorough review. You might want to return to the book several times and make use of all the methods it offers for reviewing the material:

1. *Re-read all the Two-Minute Drills,* or have someone quiz you. You also can use the drills as a way to do a quick cram before the exam.

2. *Re-read all the Exam Watch notes.* Remember that these are written by MCSDs who have taken the exam and passed. They know what you should expect—and what you should be careful about.

3. *Review all the Q & A scenarios* for quick problem solving.

4. *Re-take the Self Tests.* Taking the tests right after you've read the chapter is a good idea, because it helps reinforce what you've just learned. However, it's an even better idea to go back later and do all the questions in the book in one sitting. Pretend you're taking the exam. (For this reason, you should mark your answers on a separate piece of paper when you go through the questions the first time.)

5. *Complete the exercises.* Did you do the exercises when you read through each chapter? If not, do them! These exercises are designed to cover exam topics, and there's no better way to get to know this material than by practicing.

6. *Check out the Web site.* Global Knowledge Network invites you to become an active member of the Access Global Web site. This site is an online mall and an information repository that you'll find invaluable. You can access many types of products to assist you in your preparation for the exams, and you'll be able to participate in forums, online discussions, and threaded discussions. No other book brings you unlimited access to such a resource. You'll find more information about this site in Appendix C.

A Brief History of MCSD Certification

Although the MCSD certification for software developers was introduced in the same year as the MCSE certification for system engineers, there are currently many more MCSEs than MCSDs. There are several reasons for this discrepancy:

- The MCSE was immediately understood as similar to the Novell's CNE (Certified Network Engineer), but there was no popular credential competing with the MCSD.

- The learning curve is traditionally steeper for system engineers than it has been for software developers, and the consequences of error are usually much more severe. (A software developer who has an off day might end up working late every day the next week, but a system engineer who has an off day might end up working at Burger King.) Consequently, there has been more demand from companies for a network certification, and more willingness to invest in their employees receiving the appropriate training.

- The MCSD was considered by some to be more difficult than the MCSE. Although the MCSE required passing six tests (as opposed to the four required for the MCSD) there was significant overlap in the content covered on the MCSE tests. By contrast, the content learned for one MCSD test was of little value on other MCSD tests.

- While a network engineer would encounter most of the MCSE test concepts in their day-to-day work, even an experienced developer would have to deal with new material when preparing for a MCSD test. For example, on the original WOSSA 2 exam, a level of understanding of ODBC was required that far exceeded the needs of almost all developers.

- Finally, while MCSE study resources were plentiful, there were few classes and fewer books covering the MCSD curriculum.

However, the popularity of the MCSD is starting to reach a critical mass. As the number of organizations dependent on custom-developed Microsoft applications increases, so does the desire of these organizations to be able to objectively measure the skills of developers, and the willingness of these organizations to use these certifications as a factor in determining compensation. According to *Microsoft Certified Professional* magazine, developers with the MCSD certification reported a median salary of $71,500, while developers lacking any certifications reported a median salary of $56,500. (More information is available by viewing their Web site at http://www.mcpmag.com/members/98feb/fea1pmain.asp.)

To Microsoft's credit, they have continually surveyed developers and employees and used this feedback to align their certification tracks with market needs. In June 1998, Microsoft revamped the MCSD program, providing new requirements and tests required to achieve this status. However, they did not discontinue the existing path, which leaves developers with the challenge of determining which to pursue.

Original and New MCSD Tracks Compared

The primary difference between the two tracks concerns the emphasis on architecture. The new track reduces the number of generalized architecture tests, but requires at least one test that covers distributed application development. A test-by-test comparison of the exams required is presented in the following table:

Test	Original Track Requirements	New Track Requirements
1	Core: Microsoft Windows Architecture 1 (70-160).	Core: Analyzing Requirements and Defining Solutions Architectures (70-100).
2	Core: Microsoft Windows Architecture 2 (70-161).	Core: Desktop Application Development (in C++ 6, VB 6, FoxPro, or J++).
3	Elective: One elective from the following table.	Core: Distributed Application Development (in C++ 6, VB 6, FoxPro, or J++).
4	Elective: One elective from the following table.	Elective: One elective from the following table.
	Tests 3 and 4 must cover different Microsoft products. For example, you cannot use Programming with Microsoft Visual Basic 4.0 for Test 3 and Developing Applications with Microsoft Visual Basic 5.0 for Test 4.	Although the test choices for Test 2 and Test 3 are available as electives, the same test cannot be used to fill both a core and an elective test requirement.

Note that the Microsoft Windows Architecture exams were introduced to replace the original Windows Operating System and Services

Architecture exams used for MCSD certification. Microsoft has already retired these, so they are excluded from the preceding list.

Tests Available for MCSD Certification

As of this writing, there are 27 exams that can be used to achieve the MCSD certification (although some of these will be retired soon). These tests are listed below, sorted by the subject they cover:

Subject	Test Number	Full Test Name	Original	New
Architecture	70-160*	Microsoft Windows Architecture I	C	
Architecture	70-161*	Microsoft Windows Architecture II	C	
Architecture	70-100	Analyzing Requirements and Defining Solution Architectures		C
Visual Basic	70-065*	Programming with Microsoft Visual Basic 4.0	E	E
Visual Basic	70-165	Developing Applications with Microsoft Visual Basic 5.0	E	E
Visual Basic	70-176	Designing and Implementing Desktop Applications with Microsoft Visual Basic 6.0	E	C, E
Visual Basic	70-175	Designing and Implementing Distributed Applications with Microsoft Visual Basic 6.0	E	C, E
FoxPro	70-054*	Programming in Microsoft Visual FoxPro 3.0 for Windows	E	
FoxPro	(none)	Designing and Implementing Desktop Applications with Microsoft Visual FoxPro	E	C
FoxPro	(none)	Designing and Implementing Distributed Applications with Microsoft Visual FoxPro	E	C

Subject	Test Number	Full Test Name	Original	New
C++	70-024	Developing Applications with C++ Using the Microsoft Foundation Class Library	E	E
C++	70-025	Implementing OLE in Microsoft Foundation Class Applications	E	E
C++	70-016	Designing and Implementing Desktop Applications with Microsoft Visual C++ 6.0	E	C, E
C++	70-015	Designing and Implementing Distributed Applications with Microsoft Visual C++ 6.0	E	C, E
J++	(none)	Designing and Implementing Desktop Applications with Microsoft Visual J++	E	C
J++	(none)	Designing and Implementing Distributed Applications with Microsoft Visual J++	E	C
Access	70-051*	Microsoft Access 2.0 for Windows-Application Development	E	
Access	70-069	Microsoft Access for Windows 95 and the Microsoft Access Developer's Toolkit	E	E
Access	(none)	Designing and Implementing Database Design on Microsoft Access	E	E
Office	70-052*	Developing Applications with Microsoft Excel 5.0 Using Visual Basic for Applications	E	
Office	70-091	Designing and Implementing Solutions with Microsoft Office 2000 and Microsoft Visual Basic for Applications	E	E
SQL Server	70-021*	Microsoft SQL Server 4.2 Database Implementation	E	E

Subject	Test Number	Full Test Name	Original	New
SQL Server	70-027	Implementing a Database Design on Microsoft SQL Server 6.5	E	E
SQL Server	70-029	Designing and Implementing Databases with Microsoft SQL Server 7.0	E	E
Internet	70-055	Designing and Implementing Web Sites with Microsoft FrontPage 98	E	E
Internet	70-152	Designing and Implementing Web Solutions with Microsoft Visual InterDev 6.0	E	E
Internet	70-057	Designing and Implementing Commerce Solutions with Microsoft Site Server 3.0, Commerce Edition	E	E

Notes:

■ An "E" means that a test can be used as an elective, while a "C" means that a test can be used as a core requirement. "Original" refers to the Original MCSD track, while "New" refers to the New MCSD track.

■ Exams with no number are not scheduled to be available until 1999.

■ Test numbers with an asterisk are scheduled to be retired by Microsoft. (Note that after Microsoft retires an exam, it usually remains valid for certification status, but only for a limited time.)

Note that this test list is adapted from the content available at http://www.microsoft.com/mcp/certstep/mcsd.htm. This content frequently changes, so it would be wise to check this site before finalizing your study plans.

Choosing a Track

So which track should you choose? Good question! Although Microsoft is obviously providing more support for the New track, there are legitimate reasons for considering both options. Some of these reasons are described below.

Advantages of the Original Track

■ *You may already be partway there.* If you already have, or are close to obtaining, the Windows Architecture 1 or 2, you should pursue the Original track. These tests are of no value in the New track. Similarly, if you have already passed an exam such as Access 2 or FoxPro 3, that is a valid elective for the Original track but not for the New track (though of course, these exams will be retired soon).

■ *You cover more architecture.* The system architecture exams are excellent overviews to client/server development. The Original track consists of two architecture tests, but the New track only has one.

■ *You don't have to use the most recent versions of the tools.* If your current job responsibilities make it unlikely that you will be working with the newest versions of C++, Visual Basic, FoxPro, or J++, you should pursue the Original track. The New track requires that you pass two tests on one of these four environments, and it seems very unlikely that these tests will be adapted to support prior versions. In other words, if you are an expert in VB version 5 but won't have an opportunity to significantly use VB version 6 for at least a year, it will be very difficult for you to use the New track.

■ *You can start now.* As of this writing, some of the tests used for the New track (Desktop and Distribution for FoxPro and J++, for example) are scheduled to be available in 1999, and haven't even been released in beta yet.

Advantages of the New Track

■ *Your credentials will last longer.* The Architecture 1 and 2 exams required for the original track will be retired more quickly than any of the New track core exams. However, this may not be as much of a disadvantage as it may originally seem. After all, all of the exams you take will be retired within a few years. The certification process is designed not just to determine which developers have achieved a base level of competency, but to identify which developers are doing the best job of keeping their skills current.

■ *You can become more of a specialist in your chosen tool.* Arguably, because the New track offers more exams for each product, the Original track encourages product breadth while the New track encourages depth. Therefore, if you're selling yourself as a specialist, the New track may be an advantage. (Specialists often can have higher salaries, though sometimes generalists have more continuous employment.)

■ *You'll be more closely aligned with Microsoft's strategies.* If you are just beginning to consider certification and haven't already invested time pursuing the Original track, you should probably pursue the New track. The changes made by Microsoft are a product of their research into the needs of the marketplace, and it couldn't hurt for you to leverage their investment. In addition, if Microsoft revises the MCSD requirements again, the transition would probably be easiest for those who used the New track.

■ *You'll be "New and Improved!"* Works for laundry detergent…

Of course, the best choice may be not to choose at all, at least not yet. As the tables in this chapter have shown, many of the exams are equally applicable to both tracks. For example, the Designing and Implementing Desktop Applications with Microsoft Visual Basic 6.0 exam counts not only as a core requirement for the New track, but also an elective for either track. You do not need to declare to Microsoft which track you are pursuing, so you can delay that decision until after you have passed your first test.

And with this book at your side, you're well on your way to doing just that.

The CD-ROM Resource

This book comes with a CD-ROM that contains test preparation software, and provides you with another method for studying for the exam. You will find more information on the testing software in Appendix C.

How to Take a Microsoft Certification Examination

Good News and Bad News

If you are new to Microsoft certification, we have some good news and some bad news. The good news, of course, is that Microsoft certification is one of the most valuable credentials you can earn. It sets you apart from the crowd and marks you as a valuable asset to your employer. You will gain the respect of your peers, and Microsoft certification can have a wonderful effect on your income.

The bad news is that Microsoft certification tests are not easy. You may think you will read through some study material, memorize a few facts, and pass the Microsoft examinations. After all, these certification exams are just computer-based, multiple-choice tests, so they must be easy. If you believe this, you are wrong. Unlike many "multiple guess" tests you have been exposed to in school, the questions on Microsoft certification examinations go beyond simple factual knowledge.

The purpose of this introduction is to teach you how to take a Microsoft certification examination. To be successful, you need to know something about the purpose and structure of these tests. We will also look at the latest innovations in Microsoft testing. Using simulations and adaptive testing, Microsoft is enhancing both the validity and security of the certification process. These factors have some important effects on how you should prepare for an exam, as well as your approach to each question during the test.

We will begin by looking at the purpose, focus, and structure of Microsoft certification tests, and examine the effect these factors have on the kinds of questions you will face on your certification exams. We will define the structure of examination questions, and investigate some common formats. Next, we will present a strategy for answering these questions.

Finally, we will give some specific guidelines on what you should do on the day of your test.

Why Vendor Certification?

The Microsoft Certified Professional program, like the certification programs from Lotus, Novell, Oracle, and other software vendors, is maintained for the ultimate purpose of increasing the corporation's profits. A successful vendor certification program accomplishes this goal by helping to create a pool of experts in a company's software, and by "branding" these experts so that companies using the software can identify them.

We know that vendor certification has become increasingly popular in the last few years because it helps employers find qualified workers, and because it helps software vendors like Microsoft sell their products. But why should you be interested in vendor certification rather than a more traditional approach like a college or professional degree in computer science? A college education is a broadening and enriching experience, but a degree in computer science does not prepare students for most jobs in the IT industry.

A common truism in our business states, "If you are out of the IT industry for three years and want to return, you have to start over." The problem, of course, is *timeliness*; if a first-year student learns about a specific computer program, it probably will no longer be in wide use when he or she graduates. Although some colleges are trying to integrate Microsoft certification into their curriculum, the problem is not really a flaw in higher education, but a characteristic of the IT industry. Computer software is changing so rapidly that a four-year college just can't keep up.

A marked characteristic of the Microsoft certification program is an emphasis on performing specific job tasks rather than merely gathering knowledge. It may come as a shock, but most potential employers do not care how much you know about the theory of operating systems, testing, or software design. As one IT manager put it, "I don't really care what my employees know about the theory of our network. We don't need someone to sit at a desk and think about it. We need people who can actually do something to make it work better."

You should not think that this attitude is some kind of anti-intellectual revolt against book learning. Knowledge is a necessary prerequisite, but it is not enough. More than one company has hired a computer science graduate as a network administrator only to learn that the new employee has no idea how to add users, assign permissions, or perform the other everyday tasks necessary to maintain a network. This brings us to the second major characteristic of Microsoft certification that affects the questions you must be prepared to answer. In addition to timeliness, Microsoft certification is also job task–oriented.

The timeliness of Microsoft's certification program is obvious, and is inherent in the fact that you will be tested on current versions of software in wide use today. The job task orientation of Microsoft certification is almost as obvious, but testing real-world job skills using a computer-based test is not easy.

Computerized Testing

Considering the popularity of Microsoft certification, and the fact that certification candidates are spread around the world, the only practical way to administer tests for the certification program is through Sylvan Prometric testing centers. Sylvan Prometric provides proctored testing services for Microsoft, Oracle, Novell, Lotus, and the A+ computer technician certification. Although the IT industry accounts for much of Sylvan's revenue, the company provides services for a number of other businesses and organizations, such as FAA preflight pilot tests. In fact, most companies that need secure test delivery over a wide geographic area use the services of Sylvan Prometric. In addition to delivery, Sylvan Prometric also scores the tests and provides statistical feedback on the performance of each test question to the companies and organizations that use their services.

Typically, several hundred questions are developed for a new Microsoft certification examination. The questions are first reviewed by a number of subject matter experts for technical accuracy, and then are presented in a beta test. The beta test may last for several hours, due to the large number of questions. After a few weeks, Microsoft certification uses the statistical feedback from Sylvan to check the performance of the beta questions.

Questions are discarded if most test takers get them right (too easy) or wrong (too difficult), and a number of other statistical measures are taken of each question. Although the scope of our discussion precludes a rigorous treatment of question analysis, you should be aware that Microsoft and other vendors spend a great deal of time and effort making sure their examination questions are valid. In addition to the obvious desire for quality, the fairness of a vendor's certification program must be legally defensible.

The questions that survive statistical analysis form the pool of questions for the final certification examination.

Test Structure

The kind of test we are most familiar with is known as a *form* test. For Microsoft certification, a form usually consists of 50–70 questions and takes 60–90 minutes to complete. If there are 240 questions in the final pool for an examination, then four forms can be created. Thus, candidates who retake the test probably will not see the same questions.

Other variations are possible. From the same pool of 240 questions, *five* forms can be created, each containing 40 unique questions (200 questions) and 20 questions selected at random from the remaining 40.

The questions in a Microsoft form test are equally weighted. This means they all count the same when the test is scored. An interesting and useful characteristic of a form test is that you can mark a question you have doubts about as you take the test. Assuming you have time left when you finish all the questions, you can return and spend more time on the questions you have marked as doubtful.

Microsoft may soon implement *adaptive* testing. To use this interactive technique, a form test is first created and administered to several thousand certification candidates. The statistics generated are used to assign a weight, or difficulty level, for each question. For example, the questions in a form might be divided into levels one through five, with level-one questions being the easiest and level-five questions the hardest.

When an adaptive test begins, the candidate is first given a level-three question. If it is answered correctly, a question from the next higher level is presented, and an incorrect response results in a question from the next lower level. When 15–20 questions have been answered in this manner, the scoring algorithm is able to predict, with a high degree of statistical certainty, whether the candidate would pass or fail if all the questions in the form were answered. When the required degree of certainty is attained, the test ends and the candidate receives a pass/fail grade.

Adaptive testing has some definite advantages for everyone involved in the certification process. Adaptive tests allow Sylvan Prometric to deliver more tests with the same resources, as certification candidates often are in and out in 30 minutes or less. For Microsoft, adaptive testing means that fewer test questions are exposed to each candidate, and this can enhance the security, and therefore the validity, of certification tests.

One possible problem you may have with adaptive testing is that you are not allowed to mark and revisit questions. Since the adaptive algorithm is interactive, and all questions but the first are selected on the basis of your response to the previous question, it is not possible to skip a particular question or change an answer.

Question Types

Computerized test questions can be presented in a number of ways. Some of the possible formats are used on Microsoft certification examinations, and some are not.

True/False

We are all familiar with true/false questions, but because of the inherent 50 percent chance of guessing the correct answer, you will not see questions of this type on Microsoft certification exams.

Multiple Choice

The majority of Microsoft certification questions are in the multiple-choice format, with either a single correct answer or multiple correct answers. One interesting variation on multiple-choice questions with multiple correct answers is whether or not the candidate is told how many answers are correct.

Example:

Which two of the following controls can be used on a MDI form? (Choose two.)

Or

Which of the following controls can be used on a MDI form? (Choose all that apply.)

You may see both variations on Microsoft certification examinations, but the trend seems to be toward the first type, where candidates are told explicitly how many answers are correct. Questions of the "choose all that apply" variety are more difficult, and can be merely confusing.

Graphical Questions

One or more graphical elements are sometimes used as exhibits to help present or clarify an exam question. These elements may take the form of a database diagram, flow charts, or screen shots from the software on which you are being tested. It is often easier to present the concepts required for a complex performance-based scenario with a graphic than with words.

Test questions known as hotspots actually incorporate graphics as part of the answer. These questions ask the certification candidate to click on a location or graphical element to answer the question. As an example, you might be shown the diagram of a three-tiered application and asked to click on a tier described by the question. The answer is correct if the candidate clicks within the hotspot that defines the correct location.

Free Response Questions

Another kind of question you sometimes see on Microsoft certification examinations requires a *free response* or type-in answer. An example of this type of question might present a complex code sample including loops and error trapping and ask the candidate to calculate and enter the final value of a variable.

Knowledge-Based and Performance-Based Questions

Microsoft certification develops a blueprint for each Microsoft certification examination with input from subject matter experts. This blueprint defines the content areas and objectives for each test, and each test question is created to test a specific objective. The basic information from the examination blueprint can be found on Microsoft's Web site in the Exam Prep Guide for each test.

Psychometricians (psychologists who specialize in designing and analyzing tests) categorize test questions as knowledge-based or performance-based. As the names imply, knowledge-based questions are designed to test knowledge, while performance-based questions are designed to test performance.

Some objectives demand a knowledge-based question. For example, objectives that use verbs like *list* and *identify* tend to test only what you know, not what you can do.

Example:

Objective: Identify the ADO Cursor Types that support read and write operations.

Which two of the following ADO Cursor Types support write access? (Choose two.)

    A. adOpenStatic

    B. adOpenDynamic

    C. adOpenForwardOnly

    D. adOpenKeyset

Correct answers: B and D

Other objectives use action verbs like *connect, configure*, and *troubleshoot* to define job tasks. These objectives can often be tested with either a knowledge-based question or a performance-based question.

Example:

Objective: Connect to a data source appropriately using ADO Cursor Type properties.

Knowledge-based question:

What is the correct Cursor Type to allow users to view new records created by other users?

   A. adOpenStatic

   B. adOpenDynamic

   C. adOpenForwardOnly

   D. adOpenKeyset

Correct answer: B

Performance-based question:

Your company supports several travel agents using a common data store, and each agent needs to be able to see the reservations taken by all the other agents. What is the best application development strategy to allow users to be able to see records modified and created by other users?

   A. Use an adOpenKeyset Cursor Type to create the record set, and keep the same Recordset object open continuously.

   B. Use an adOpenDynamic Cursor Type to create the record set, and keep the same Recordset object open continuously.

   C. Use an adOpenStatic Cursor Type to create the record set, but destroy and create the Recordset object after every data update.

   D. Use an adOpenForwardOnly Cursor Type create the record set, but destroy and create the Recordset object after every data update.

Correct answer: B

Even in this simple example, the superiority of the performance-based question is obvious. Whereas the knowledge-based question asks for a single fact, the performance-based question presents a real-life situation and requires that you make a decision based on this scenario. Thus, performance-based questions give more bang (validity) for the test author's buck (individual question).

Testing Job Performance

We have said that Microsoft certification focuses on timeliness and the ability to perform job tasks. We have also introduced the concept of performance-based questions, but even performance-based, multiple-choice questions do not really measure performance. Another strategy is needed to test job skills.

Given unlimited resources, it is not difficult to test job skills. In an ideal world, Microsoft would fly MCP candidates to Redmond, place them in a controlled environment with a team of experts, and ask them to design, author, debug, and revise a Windows application. In a few days at most, the experts could reach a valid decision as to whether each candidate should or should not be granted MCSD status. Needless to say, this is not likely to happen.

Closer to reality, another way to test performance is by using the actual software, and creating a testing program to present tasks and automatically grade a candidate's performance when the tasks are completed. This *cooperative* approach would be practical in some testing situations, but the same test that is presented to MCP candidates in Boston must also be available in Bahrain and Botswana. Many Sylvan Prometric testing locations around the world cannot run 32-bit applications, much less provide the complex networked solutions required by cooperative testing applications.

The most workable solution for measuring performance in today's testing environment is a *simulation* program. When the program is launched during a test, the candidate sees a simulation of the actual software that looks, and behaves, just like the real thing. When the testing software presents a task, the simulation program is launched and the candidate performs the required task. The testing software then grades the candidate's performance on the required task and moves to the next question. In this way, a 16-bit simulation program can mimic the look and feel of 32-bit operating systems, a complicated network, or even the entire Internet.

Microsoft has introduced simulation questions on the certification examination for Internet Information Server version 4. Simulation questions provide many advantages over other testing methodologies, and simulations are expected to become increasingly important in the Microsoft Certification Program. For example, studies have shown that there is a very high correlation between the ability to perform simulated tasks on a computer-based test and the ability to perform the actual job tasks. Thus, simulations enhance the validity of the certification process.

Another truly wonderful benefit of simulations is in the area of test security. It is just not possible to cheat on a simulation question. In fact, you will be told exactly what tasks you are expected to perform on the test. How can a certification candidate cheat? By learning to perform the tasks? What a concept!

Study Strategies

There are appropriate ways to study for the different types of questions you will see on a Microsoft certification examination.

Knowledge-Based Questions

Knowledge-based questions require that you memorize facts. There are hundreds of facts inherent in every content area of every Microsoft certification examination. There are several keys to memorizing facts:

- *Repetition.* The more times your brain is exposed to a fact, the more likely you are to remember it.

- *Association.* Connecting facts within a logical framework makes them easier to remember.

- *Motor Association.* It is often easier to remember something if you write it down or perform some other physical act, like clicking a practice test answer.

We have said that the emphasis of Microsoft certification is job performance, and that there are very few knowledge-based questions on

Microsoft certification exams. Why should you waste a lot of time learning filenames, property values, and other minutiae? Read on.

Performance-Based Questions

Most of the questions you will face on a Microsoft certification exam are performance-based scenario questions. We have discussed the superiority of these questions over simple knowledge-based questions, but you should remember that the job task–orientation of Microsoft certification extends the knowledge you need to pass the exams; it does *not* replace this knowledge. Therefore, the first step in preparing for scenario questions is to absorb as many facts relating to the exam content areas as you can. In other words, go back to the previous section and follow the steps to prepare for an exam composed of knowledge-based questions.

The second step is to familiarize yourself with the format of the questions you are likely to see on the exam. You can do this by answering the questions in this study guide, by using Microsoft assessment tests, or by using practice tests. The day of your test is not the time to be surprised by the convoluted construction of Microsoft exam questions.

For example, one of Microsoft's favorite formats of late takes the following form:

Scenario: You have an application with . . .
Primary Objective: You want to . . .
Secondary Objective: You also want to . . .
Proposed Solution: Do this . . .

What does the proposed solution accomplish?

    A. Satisfies the primary and the secondary objective

    B. Satisfies the primary but not the secondary objective

    C. Satisfies the secondary but not the primary objective

    D. Satisfies neither the primary nor the secondary objective

This kind of question, with some variation, is seen on many Microsoft certification examinations.

At best, these performance-based scenario questions really do test certification candidates at a higher cognitive level than knowledge-based questions. At worst, these questions can test your reading comprehension and test-taking ability rather than your ability to use Microsoft products. Be sure to get in the habit of reading the question carefully to determine what is being asked.

The third step in preparing for Microsoft scenario questions is to adopt the following attitude: Multiple-choice questions aren't really performance-based. It is all a cruel lie. These scenario questions are just knowledge-based questions with a little story wrapped around them.

To answer a scenario question, you have to sift through the story to the underlying facts of the situation, and apply your knowledge to determine the correct answer. This may sound silly at first, but the process we go through in solving real-life problems is quite similar. The key concept is that every scenario question (and every real-life problem) has a fact at its center, and if we can identify that fact, we can answer the question.

Simulations

Simulation questions really do measure your ability to perform job tasks. You *must* be able to perform the specified tasks. There are two ways to prepare for simulation questions:

- Get experience with the actual software. If you have the resources, this is a great way to prepare for simulation questions.

- Use official Microsoft practice tests. Practice tests are available that provide practice with the same simulation engine used on Microsoft certification exams. This approach has the added advantage of grading your efforts.

Signing Up

Signing up to take a Microsoft certification examination is easy. Sylvan operators in each country can schedule tests at any testing center. There are, however, a few things you should know:

■ If you call Sylvan during a busy time period, get a cup of coffee first, because you may be in for a long wait. Sylvan does an excellent job, but everyone in the world seems to want to sign up for a test on Monday morning.

■ You will need your Social Security number or some other unique identifier to sign up for a Sylvan test, so have it at hand.

■ Pay for your test by credit card if at all possible. This makes things easier, and you can even schedule tests for the same day you call, if space is available at your local testing center.

■ Know the number and title of the test you want to take before you call. This is not essential, and the Sylvan operators will help you if they can. Having this information in advance, however, speeds up the registration process and reduces the risk that you will accidentally register for the wrong test.

Taking the Test

Teachers have always told you not to try to cram for examinations, because it does no good. Sometimes they lied. If you are faced with a knowledge-based test requiring only that you regurgitate facts, cramming can mean the difference between passing and failing. This is not the case, however, with Microsoft certification exams. If you don't know it the night before, don't bother to stay up and cram.

Instead, create a schedule and stick to it. Follow these guidelines on the day of your exam:

1. Get a good night's sleep. The scenario questions you will face on a Microsoft certification examination require a clear head.

2. Remember to take two forms of identification—at least one with a picture. A driver's license with your picture, and Social Security or credit cards are acceptable.

3. Leave home in time to arrive at your testing center a few minutes early. It is not a good idea to feel rushed as you begin your exam.

4. Do not spend too much time on any one question. If you are taking a form test, take your best guess and mark the question so you can come back to it if you have time. You cannot mark and revisit questions on an adaptive test, so you must do your best on each question as you go.

5. If you do not know the answer to a question, try to eliminate the obviously wrong answers and guess from the rest. If you can eliminate two out of four options, you have a 50 percent chance of guessing the correct answer.

6. For scenario questions, follow the steps outlined earlier. Read the question carefully and try to identify the facts at the center of the story.

Finally, I would advise anyone attempting to earn Microsoft MCSD certification to adopt a philosophical attitude. Even if you are the kind of person who never fails a test, you are likely to fail at least one Microsoft certification test somewhere along the way. Do not get discouraged. If Microsoft certification were easy to obtain, more people would have it, and it would not be so respected and so valuable to your future in the IT industry.

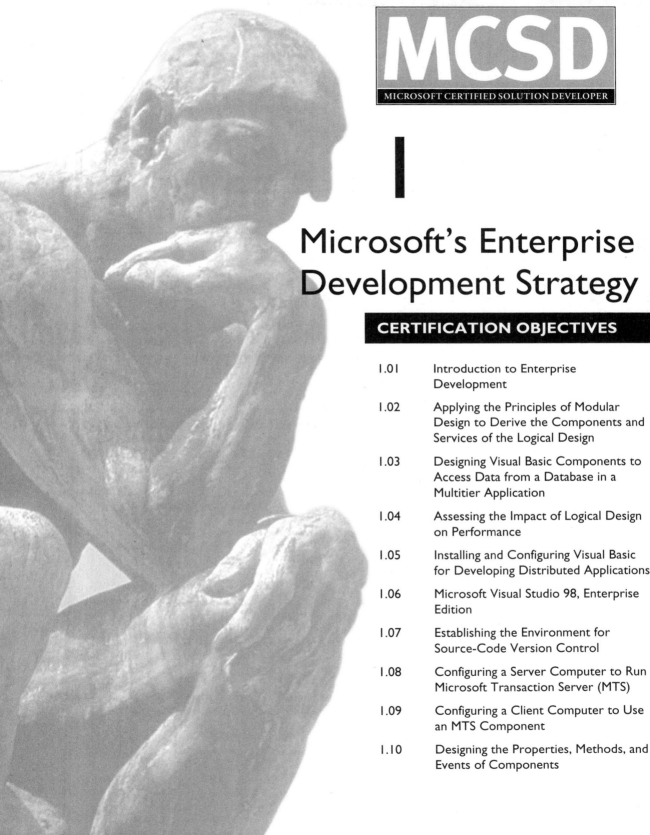

MCSD
MICROSOFT CERTIFIED SOLUTION DEVELOPER

1

Microsoft's Enterprise Development Strategy

CERTIFICATION OBJECTIVES

Considering the number of developers who are Trekkies, the term "enterprise development" can invoke some strange images in a new programmer's head. An enterprise is a business, such as a corporation, which uses computers in a network or an interconnected group of networks that can span different geographical areas. Usually, the network will consist of a variety of platforms, operating systems, protocols, and/or network architectures. Due to the increased number of technologies and users you're dealing with, developing applications for the enterprise can require you *to boldly program as no one has before.*

Introduction to Enterprise Development

When developing applications for the enterprise, you experience technologies and circumstances that rarely come into play when developing desktop applications. Your application may need to access a network, a corporate intranet, or the Internet. Rather than dealing with a single user, such as with a desktop application, enterprise applications can be split so part of it resides on a server and another part resides on client computers. Hundreds or thousands of requirements may need to be addressed by the application as users use it to access data on the server application. Because of these and other factors, enterprise development is far more complex than building desktop applications.

In learning how to develop enterprise applications, you don't need to trash any knowledge you've gained from building desktop applications. Enterprise development requires expanding the scope of your knowledge to deal with a larger environment. An application in the enterprise usually has these common attributes:

- It's big ... very big!
- It's business-oriented.
- It's mission-critical.

To understand how these attributes affect an enterprise application, we'll discuss each attribute individually.

Saying that an enterprise application is big covers a number of items. Not only does this describe size, but also the number of machines and users who use the application. Generally, teams of developers will create such an application, which will be used by multiple users and on multiple machines. Parts of the application will reside on different computers, distributed across the network. ActiveX components can be used, allowing the software to communicate and interact across the network. The application can use these computers to handle more than one event at a time (by using parallel processing and/or multiprocessing) and manipulate enormous amounts of data.

An enterprise application encodes the policies, rules, entities, and processes of a business, and is deployed to meet the needs of a business. If you have created a legal program, and the laws this application deals with change, it is no longer business-oriented because it no longer meets the business's needs. Similarly, if you were creating a human resources database program, you wouldn't want to include fields that require the input of an employee's gender. In short, it must function in accordance to the practices and procedures of the enterprise.

When an enterprise application is called "mission-critical," it means that the application is vital to the operation of an enterprise. For example, insurance companies use applications that store policy information in a database. If this application stopped working, none of the insurance agents could input new policy information or process existing policies. This would affect the operation of the enterprise. As such, enterprise applications need to be robust, so they can function in unexpected situations and thereby sustain continuous operations. It must also allow for scalability, which means that it can be expanded to meet future needs, and has the capability to be maintained and administered.

The reason these features need to appear in an enterprise application is due to their importance to an organization. Because of the cost of creating an enterprise application, it usually has the attribute of being mission-critical. Even though a properly designed three-tier enterprise application can be written at a fraction of the cost of client/server applications, it still costs money to pay developers and other project team members. Few enterprises would be able to justify paying for the creation of such applications if they weren't essential to the operation of the business.

Applying the Principles of Modular Design to Derive the Components and Services of the Logical Design

Design seems to be one of the most talked-about, and least-used area of application development. It is most talked about because everyone endorses it, and for good reason. The design of an application involves finding what the customer requires from a program, and hammering out the details needed to take it from a conceived idea to a physical product. You will generally spend more than half the time of creating a project in analysis and design. The value of design becomes apparent when you consider that a change or error in design is faster to fix than one that's already been programmed. When an error appears in the programming code of an application or if a change needs to be made, it can take ten times longer to fix than if it had been made during design. Despite its benefit, many programmers either know little about design, or are too lazy to use it. In interviewing developers for positions, Microsoft found that only a surprising minority of programmers could accurately explain the most fundamental of design. When dealing with enterprise applications, you can't do without it.

Enterprise applications are too complex and too large not to design first. Although you might be able to fly by the seat of your pants on a small desktop application, there is no way to avoid designing an enterprise application before coding it.

A recommended approach to designing applications is modular design, which involves breaking a large project into smaller chunks. Each of these manageable chunks is called a *module.* They are designed to perform a different function or task; and can be developed and tested independently of one another, and then combined into the final project. By designing these modules as stand-alone components of a project, they can be reused in other projects that require the same functionality. This saves you the trouble of having to rewrite the same code over and over in different projects or in different areas of the same program.

Using modular design requires implementing stored procedures, class modules, ActiveX components, and so forth. Such components allow you to split an application so that parts are spread across a network or a computer. These components are reusable and accessible to other programs. Using this method of design, you can split application design into two main tasks: creating reusable components (ActiveX, stored procedures, and so forth), and integrating those components into your application.

To design an application in this manner, you must organize or separate the requirements of an application. This means you must decide what each component will do and determine what each component requires. This process results in a conceptual design. Although there are numerous conceptual models available to help with designing an application, the one that Microsoft recommends is the three-tiered "services model."

The services model is also known as the "application model." It organizes an application's requirements into specific services. Generally, the requirements of an application fall into one of three tiers or categories: user services, business services (and other middle tier services), and data services. In the following paragraphs, each of these tiers will be discussed.

The top tier of this model, user services, is also known as the presentation layer. This tier is associated with the user interface, which presents data to the end user. It is through this tier that the user is able to view and manipulate data. The user interface can be the executable program that a user starts on a workstation or a separate component that's placed on a container object like a form, which, in Visual Basic, is a container for other controls. When you compile your program, the form object appears as a Window to the end user. An example of using a separate component in this fashion would be using an ActiveX control to view or manipulate data in a database.

The middle tier of the service model contains a number of services, but it is primarily associated with business services. Business services apply business rules to tasks that an application performs. An example of this is a banking program that allows the withdrawal of money from an account. Before the money can be withdrawn, the application checks to see if there is enough money in the account to make the withdrawal. If there is, the transaction continues; if not, it is canceled. In such an application, there is a business rule of needing to have more than the amount withdrawn. When business rules are added to a program, they are done so at this layer.

The middle tier is also known as the "application-server tier," which is the layer between the user interface and a database. Generally, this is where a Web server will reside in Internet applications, and where business objects (COM components that retrieve and process data) are instantiated. Because business rules change more often than the actual tasks a program needs to perform, they are prime candidates for being a component of a program. By having such rules incorporated into components, the entire program doesn't need to be changed; just the component of that application.

The bottom tier of the service model is data services, which is also called the "data-source tier." This tier defines, maintains, and updates data. When a request is made for data, data services manages and satisfies the request. This capability to manage and satisfy requests can be implemented as part of the database management system (DBMS) or as components.

Although the services model clarifies the way applications fall into one of three tiers of service, it doesn't explain the stages of the design process. The steps in creating an application can be broken into four stages: conceptual design, logical design, physical design, and deployment. While there are many models for designing an application, they can all be mapped to these four stages.

These four stages aren't completed in one pass. It's not a matter of moving from step one to step two, and so on. One stage may be revised or refined when a later stage is being worked on. In doing this, you keep a certain amount of flexibility to your design.

The first stage we'll discuss is conceptual design, which addresses what needs to be included in the application. This involves taking information that's been gathered about the needs of users, and addressing these needs in the application. The conceptual design is ideally non-technical, but details the functionality of a proposed solution, how it will interact with the end user, the criteria for performance, and how the existing technology infrastructure will react to the new functionality. While this sounds simple enough, it can be one of the most frustrating design stages because many customers and end users will forget to tell you certain things that they consider essential. Such essentials need to be added to the design, even if it has reached a later stage in the design process.

Logical design is a process that's made up of five activities:

- Identifying business objects and services
- Defining interfaces
- Identifying business object dependencies
- Validating the logical view
- Revision and refining

Like the design stages, each of these activities can be refined and revised as later stages are being worked on.

The first of the five parts that make up logical design is the identification of business objects and services. Business objects are abstract representations of real-world things or concepts (such as orders, customers, and so on). You can consider something to be a business object if one or both of the following are true:

- It is something (or someone) that the system is required to know about.
- It is something (or someone) that the system gets information from, or provides information to.

It's important to identify business objects because they are what define the data to appear in your application. For example, let's say an insurance agency requires a program for inputting policy information. The customer's policy number and name would be something and someone that the system is required to know. The agent's employee number would be required to access this data, so this person would be someone the system gets information from. The agent, customer, and policy number would thus be business objects implemented into the system.

Once you've identified the business objects and services, you then need to define the interfaces to be used in the application. An interface in this case is simply a statement of preconditions and conventions (syntax, input, and output parameters) that are needed to call the service. It outlines what is needed to call on that particular component.

When one business object calls on services in another business object, it is called a "business object dependency." One business object depends on the services of another business object. An example of this is an order that depends on the existence of a customer in a database. Such dependencies need to be identified.

It's useless if the logical design work done to this point doesn't match the requirements in the original conceptual view. This is where validation comes into play. Validation requires a comparison of the logical design to the conceptual view of a project. If these requirements in the conceptual design aren't met, the logical design is invalid.

Revision and refining of the logical design deals with any problems, and also improves the design. This is the final activity of logical design, and it can occur several times before moving from logical design to the physical deployment stage. As mentioned earlier, application design isn't done in a single pass, but goes through multiple iterations.

When the logical design stage is finished, the next step is physical design. This takes the business objects and services that were identified in logical design, and maps them to software components. In doing so, the actual program is physically built.

Once the components have been established and the application is built, the deployment stage comes into effect. It is here that decisions are made about how components are or aren't distributed across the network. Once this stage is completed and no further work needs to be done by going back to previous stages, the application itself is finished.

FROM THE CLASSROOM

Enterprise Evolution

Microsoft's strategy for Enterprise-level-distributed application development is centered around the three-tier application architecture. This methodology splits distributed application development into three distinctly defined tiers: presentation tier, business tier, and data services tier. The Microsoft Solution Framework lists several application development models, such as the application model. This model corresponds to the three-tier, or n-tier, as it is sometimes referred to by developers and is espoused by Microsoft. According to Microsoft, the concept of an n-tier-distributed application is simply a distributed extension of the basic three-tier-model that conforms to the separation of services.

Although it is easy to discuss the distinct tiers, the actual separation between the components and functions that should be placed in each tier is somewhat fuzzy at times. The middle or business tier is often subdivided into business logic components and data access components. Occasionally, an overt decision to violate the clear separation of tiers can yield optimized benefits in application performance, as the denormalization of a database can achieve optimized data-retrieval performance.

Application design can be broken into five types of processes: analysis, design, development, deployment, and maintenance. Microsoft defines seven steps to follow, beginning with Analyzing Business Requirements.

The conceptual, logical, and physical models are a series of application models that progressively move the developer from the abstract to the concrete design and implementation phases of application design.

Being aware of the core design issues, questions, and concerns is vital in passing what will probably be some of the more difficult areas of the exam.

— *By Michael Lane Thomas, MCSE+I, MCP+SB, MCSD, MCT, A+*

Designing Visual Basic Components to Access Data from a Database in a Multitier Application

Most applications access some form of data, whether it is internal to the application or from a database. This can get a little bit more difficult when designing components that will access data from databases in a multitier application. As mentioned in the previous section, multitier applications are made up of user services, business (and other middle tier) services, and data services. When designing such applications, consideration must be given to each of these services.

Creating a multitier database application is made up of several parts. There must be a client application, which can be a standard EXE program. This is an executable that the end user will use to interact with an application. Other clients, such as Web-clients, can be used, which also provide user services to the end user. An ActiveX DLL server component must also be created. The DLL is written in Visual Basic (or another programming language, such as C++). We will cover creating DLLs in the next chapter, and build on that knowledge throughout this book. The server component can then be installed into a Microsoft Transaction Server package, which acts as the middle-tier. (Using Microsoft Transaction Server isn't a requirement, just highly recommended by developers and Microsoft.) A database would then be created, which could be placed on a SQL Server to provide data services for the multitier application. When this is done, the client computers (on which the standard EXE program resides) would be set up. Setting up client computers and installing server components into Microsoft Transaction Server package is covered later in this chapter.

As you can see, creating a three-tier application is a four-step process. In the case of using Visual Basic 6.0 and Microsoft Transaction Server, the following steps are used to access a database on a SQL Server:

1. Create a client application using Visual Basic 6.0. This will be a standard EXE application.
2. Create a server component using Visual Basic 6.0. This will be an ActiveX DLL.
3. Install your server components into a Microsoft Transaction Server package.
4. Set up the client computers.

Although this outlines the tactics for creating the multitier application, we still need to explore the tools used to design and create this application. In this chapter and those that follow, we will cover the tools and technologies that enable you to create multitier applications with Visual Basic 6.0.

CERTIFICATION OBJECTIVE 1.04

Assessing the Impact of Logical Design on Performance

Imagine spending hundreds of hours coding an enterprise application, and then discovering that it runs sluggishly because an hour or two wasn't spent considering the impact of the design. Also, imagine the headache of going over hundreds or thousands of lines of code to find a security problem that should have been taken care of in the design! Although testing an application after it is complete is important, it is equally (if not more) important to consider what an application will do before coding has begun.

While there are no definitive rules on how much time should be spent on each phase of an application's life cycle, more time is generally spent on analysis and design. On average, you should spend 25% in analysis, 38% in design, 13% coding, 19% testing, and 7% in integration, with time to assess your application included in the design phase. Doing this will improve an application and shorten the amount of time it takes to get your application to the end user. These estimates are more of a suggestion than hard statistics. How much time you actually spend in each phase will depend on what the project entails.

No matter how much time you spend on each phase, a certain amount of time should be incorporated into your design schedule for assessment. In assessing the impact of your design, you should consider the following areas:

- Performance
- Maintainability
- Extendibility
- Scalability
- Availability
- Security

When all these factors have been considered, you are then (and only then) ready to do one of the following: revise your design to improve certain factors in your design or start coding your program.

Performance

If every user had incredibly fast processors, networks that transferred information faster than the speed of light, and unlimited hard drive space, there would be no performance issues. It would also be a relatively pointless issue if every user used the same computer or network system. In the real world, however, companies have trouble keeping up with technology, hard drive space is limited, networks are slow, and numerous users work on older equipment.

A lot of programmers forget that many (if not most) end users will run an application on a system that isn't as good as the one the developer uses. While there are ways to optimize your application at the end of the development cycle, performance really comes into effect during the design stage.

One area in which you can improve the design of an application is with variables. These are named storage locations that can hold certain types of data. The way you create this storage location is by declaring it in code, as shown in the following example:

```
Dim intNum as Integer
```

In this example, we told the computer to create a storage location called "intNum," which will hold data of the integer type. There are many different types of data that can be stored in a variable, and the type you choose can affect the performance of your application. These data types are shown in Table 1-1.

TABLE 1-1	Data Type	Description
Variable Data Types	Boolean	Can accept values of "True" or "False." Storage space: 2 bytes
	Byte	Numbers ranging in value from 0-255 Storage space: 1 byte
	Currency	-922,337,203,685,477.5808 to 922,337,203,685,477.5807 Storage space: 8 bytes
	Date	Represents dates ranging from 1 January 100 to 31 December 9999 Storage space: 8 bytes
	Double	-1.79769313486232E308 to -4.94065645841247E-324 for negative values and from 4.94065645841247E-324 to 1.79769313486232E308 for positive values Storage space: 8 bytes

TABLE 1-1

Variable Data Types
(continued)

Data Type	Description
Integer	-32,768 to 32,767 Storage space: 2 bytes
Long	-2,147,483,648 to 2,147,483,647 Storage space: 4 bytes
Object	Used to refer to objects. By using the Set statement, a variable declared as an Object can then have any object reference assigned to it Storage space: 4 bytes
Single	-3.402823E38 to -1.401298E-45 for negative values and from 1.401298E-45 to 3.402823E38 for positive values Storage space: 4 bytes
String	Codes in the ASCII character set (the first 128 characters on a keyboard) and special characters (such as accents and international symbols, which make up the remaining 128)
Variant	Default data type. This is used when no data type has been specified, and takes up 16 bytes of storage space. It represents numeric values ranging from 1.79769313486231 5E308 to -4.94066E-324 for negative values and from 4.94066E-324 to 1.79769313486231 5E308 for positive values

By putting some thought into the data types you'll use for variables, you can increase the speed of an application and lower the amount of memory required by your application. Different data types use different amounts of memory. A variant uses more than an integer, for example. Also, you can use data types that provide a larger range of numbers than you could possibly need. In the case of a variable used to store a person's age, you would use an integer rather than a long. Performance increases when consideration is given to the data types used in an application.

Each time you use a variable in your code, the computer has to resolve it. In other words, it must look up the value of a variable each time it's used. To expand on the example we used earlier, let's look at the following example:

```
Dim intNum As Integer
intNum=10
MsgBox intNum
```

In this code, we first declare the variable intNum as an integer type. In the second line, we assign the value of 10 to the variable. This is done with the "assignment operator," which is the equal sign. Anything to the right of the assignment operator is placed in the variable on the left of the assignment operator. As such, intNum now contains the value of 10. When we use the code on the third line, a message box displays the value of intNum. To do this, the computer must look at intNum, determine its value, and then apply that value to display the value. To speed up this process, constants should be used whenever it is useful.

Constants are resolved when an application is compiled. By using a constant for something like minimum wage, the application doesn't have to look up what the value of minimum wage is. The value is always the same, so the program's performance increases.

```
Const strName as String
strName="Hello World"
```

By using the Const statement, the value of the variable is constant throughout the code. As such, this variable doesn't need to be looked up each time it's used.

If a number of modules are loaded at startup, it can significantly slow the startup time of an application. You should only load modules on an "as-needed" basis. If you can't avoid having a number of modules loaded at startup, you may want to incorporate a splash screen in your application. You've seen splash screens when you start Visual Basic 6.0 (it's the form that first starts, and it has no controls, min, or max button). Splash screens let the user know that the application is actually starting, and masks the amount of time it takes to load the program. While this does nothing to improve the speed at which an application starts up, it makes it appear faster by having something appear on the screen, and thereby hides the slow startup time.

Performance is often a matter of give and take. In a number of cases, increasing performance in one area is done by decreasing it in another. This becomes apparent when dealing with forms: If all forms are loaded at startup, the application will run faster as it switches from one form to another. However, when an application uses a lot of forms, loading them all into memory can gobble up memory. A rule of thumb is to determine which forms will commonly be used during the design stage, and then have the commonly used forms loaded into memory when the application starts. Less commonly used forms (such as those used for configuring preferences, or "About this Program" forms) should not be loaded at startup.

Controls are another area that requires some thought. You can greatly improve performance by carefully choosing what controls should appear on a form. Controls take up memory, so reduce the number of controls to the minimum amount needed. If you have a number of controls that will be used by advanced users or that aren't commonly used, you can have them accessed by expanding the form. By adding a "More Information" or "Advanced" command button, you can have the form expand to show additional controls or information. An example of this is a personnel application that allows you to move through information on each employee in a firm. Although it would be nice to have a picture of each employee appear on-screen, graphics are well known for eating up memory. By designing the application with a command button that brings up a form with additional information and adding a "View Picture" command button that brings up the employee's picture, performance is dramatically increased.

A similar method involves having a drop-down style dialog box appear when a user clicks a button that says something like "Details>>." An example of this is when you use a dial-up connection in Windows 98. Once connected, the Connected to dialog box displays how long you've been connected, bytes received and sent, and your connection speed. By clicking the Details>> button, the dialog box expands (via a dialog box that drops down from the original) to show additional information. Because the additional information doesn't need to be commonly accessed, the drop-down box allows the information to be displayed on demand.

Other suggestions for improving performance are shown in Table 1-2. Each of these is a proven method suggested by Microsoft. For additional design stage tips, refer to Visual Basic 6.0's Help.

TABLE 1-2	Coding Suggestion	Reason
Suggestions for Improving Performance during the Design of an Application	Reduction of dialog boxes	Dialog boxes require memory, whether they're visible or not. Reducing the number in your application will reduce the amount of memory your application uses.
	Early binding of COM objects	Late binding causes extra work for the processor because you don't get compile-time type checking. This means that reference at runtime must be checked, slowing the performance.
	Use variables instead of arrays	It takes longer to access an array than it does to access a variable
	Remove "dead code"	Remove all unused code from your application before compiling. This does not mean comments, but code that is no longer used by your application.

Maintainability

In designing an application, it is important to incorporate ways that allow the program to be maintained. Without maintainability, problems can arise when changes need to be made to the application. Although we will cover a few methods here, various methods of maintainability will be covered throughout this book.

An important aspect of making your source code maintainable involves documentation. This means writing down the objectives of your application, what different aspects of your application do, creating flow charts, and so forth. Throughout the design process, it is important to create documentation that can be utilized in later stages of design, and in the creation of Help documentation.

An area of the design process that can't be stressed enough is the adding of comments to source code. Comments are a way of explaining what is going on in the code. A comment might explain what a procedure does, why a variable is included, and so on. There are two ways of adding comments to source code: by using REM or by putting an apostrophe before a statement. Anything typed on a line that starts with REM, or anything on a line that is typed after an apostrophe, is ignored. When an apostrophe is used, anything after the apostrophe is ignored. The following shows two examples of comments:

```
' This is a comment
REM This is a comment as well
```

Adding comments allows you to remember why a line of code exists or what a procedure is for. While this is apparent when you're typing the code, it is less evident months or years down the road. In addition, someone else may have to alter the code if you leave the company for another job, or work on a different project.

on the job

The Year 2000 (Y2K) issue shows the need for comments in source code. Many of the original programmers who wrote the code that still runs today's programs are no longer in the business or are no longer working for the company they worked for decades ago. New programmers must look at comments to quickly determine what the original programmer was doing in a section of code. Considering the impact and time-sensitive nature of Y2K, a lack of comments can determine whether a company will be ready for the new millennium.

Consistent naming conventions are another issue for maintainability. Naming conventions allow programmers in a company to quickly determine the data type of a variable, what the variable is for, its scope, and much more information. Appendix D covers naming conventions in great detail, and shows why they should be used in your programs. If you don't use the standards and conventions detailed in the appendix, you should implement some sort of convention for your company.

Extensibility

Extensibility allows an application to go beyond its original design. In other words, you can add stuff that wasn't there before. A good example of extensibility is Visual Basic 6.0 itself: you can add "Add-Ins," which extend the abilities of the development environment.

In addition, you can allow an added method of upgrading your application. Rather than having to create a complete upgrade with new features for a product, the features can be added through options like an Add-in Manager that's available as a menu item.

Availability

Availability has to do with how well your application deals with failures. Error-handling is an important feature of any program, and is a necessary implementation. People won't be too thrilled with a program that crashes when a file can't be found or when another user is accessing the same file on a network. In later chapters, we will deal with implementing error-handling in greater depth. The important thing to remember is that availability is a design issue, it is added during the design stage, and incorporated into the code. It is not something that's added as an afterthought.

Security

In a secure application, only authorized users can access its components, services, files, and data; unauthorized users are kept from viewing, modifying, or tampering with them.

Microsoft recommends using the built-in services of Windows NT and BackOffice products like SQL Server or Internet Information Server. By implementing Windows NT operating system security, Windows NT can prevent unauthorized use through user access control, audibility, and resource and service protection. It can also protect data transmissions by using encryption and digital signatures. SQL Server and Internet Information Server can likewise be configured to control both access and process privileges. This allows the tightest protection for your application.

Installing and Configuring Visual Basic for Developing Distributed Applications

After all of this discussion on design and planning, you're probably more than ready to install your copy of Visual Basic 6.0 (VB6). The steps for installing VB6 depend on how you purchased it. Visual Basic 6.0 is available as a stand-alone program, or it can be installed as part of the Visual Studio 6.0 suite of products (which is explained in detail later in this chapter). Although it's the same program in either installation, the methods of installation are slightly different. In this section, we'll cover how to install Visual Basic 6.0, both as part of Visual Studio and as a stand-alone program.

As with any installation, you should check that the computer you're performing the installation on meets the system requirements for the program. If your machine does not meet the requirements for Visual Basic 6.0, the installation will fail. The system requirements for VB6 are listed in Table 1-3.

TABLE 1-3 System Requirements for Visual Basic 6.0	**Operating System**	**Microsoft Windows 95, Microsoft Windows 98, or Microsoft Windows NT Workstation 4.0 (Service Pack 3 recommended) or later**
	Processor	486DX/66 MHz or higher processor. A Pentium or higher processor is recommended. Any Alpha processor running Microsoft Windows NT Workstation.
	Memory	16 MB of RAM for Windows 95 or Windows 98. 32 MB of RAM is required for Windows NT Workstation.
	Display	VGA or higher resolution.

TABLE 1-3	Operating System	Microsoft Windows 95, Microsoft Windows 98, or Microsoft Windows NT Workstation 4.0 (Service Pack 3 recommended) or later
System Requirements for Visual Basic 6.0 (continued)	Other Devices	CD ROM disk drive (used to install VB6), and a mouse or other suitable pointing device
	Disk Space	Standard Edition: typical installation 48MB; full installation 80MB.
		Professional Edition: typical installation 48MB; full installation 80MB.
		Enterprise Edition: typical installation 128MB; full installation 147MB.

Notice in the Disk Space section that Visual Basic 6.0 comes in three flavors: Standard Edition, Professional Edition, and Enterprise Edition. The differences between these are the tools, templates, utilities, and other items contained in the package. While any edition can be used for desktop programming, you should buy the Enterprise Edition for enterprise development. It is designed for this type of development.

exam
ⓦatch

Installation failures often occur because the system requirements aren't met. Knowing this, Microsoft commonly puts questions on exams that deal with the system requirements for an application. You should memorize the system requirements for Visual Basic 6.0 before taking the exam.

Installing Visual Basic 6.0

Whether you're installing Visual Basic 6.0 as a stand-alone program or through Visual Studio 6.0, both come with an Installation Wizard. A wizard is a program that walks you through the process of creating something or the performance of a task. In this case, the Installation Wizard takes you step-by-step through the process of installing Visual Basic 6.0.

In this section, we will first cover the process of installing VB6 through Visual Studio, and then cover installing it through the Enterprise Edition package. We will also go through an exercise that you can follow when installing Visual Basic 6.0.

Installing VB6 through Visual Studio

The first step in the installation process is to start the setup program from your installation CD-ROM. Once this is done, an opening screen will appear to welcome you and tell you that you'll be walked through the setup of Visual Studio. Click Next and you'll see a screen filled with the babbling of lawyers (also called the End User License Agreement). Agreeing to be a good boy or girl with the program, click the "I accept the agreement" option button, and then click Next. If you don't accept the agreement, you will only have the option of exiting the installation. All other command buttons are disabled, except the Exit button, until you accept the agreement.

The screen following this gives the option of uninstalling previous installations of Visual Basic, as well as other programs that come with the Visual Studio suite. This screen is illustrated in Figure 1-1. If you have Visual Studio 97 on your computer, or a previous stand-alone version of these products, they will be checked off. In other words, if you've never owned Visual Studio 97 and have a copy of VB5 on your system, Visual Basic will appear checked. If you wish to keep your previous version of VB, simply uncheck the box beside the program's name.

Clicking Next brings you to the screen that determines what kind of installation you want to perform. This screen has three options: Custom, Products, or Server Applications. This may be a little different from some of the options given by other suites. Visual Studio offers different options for servers, workstations, and stand-alone computers. Server Applications skips over workstation programs and installs server tools. Products installs programs used on workstations and stand-alone computers, such as the Visual Basic program. Custom allows the installation of server and workstation/stand-alone products. To install Visual Basic 6.0, choose either Products or Custom.

FIGURE 1-1

The Uninstall Visual Studio 97 screen gives the option of removing previous versions

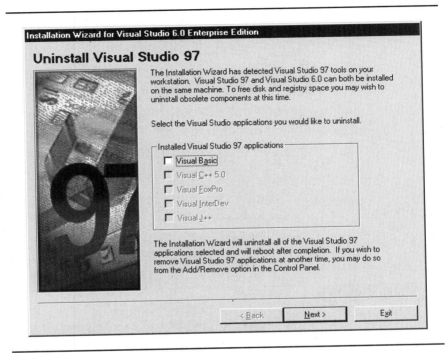

After clicking Next, you are required to enter your Name and Company information, which the Wizard will obtain from the operating system. Check to see whether this information is correct. If not, edit the information in these two fields. You are also required to enter the CD-Key that comes with your installation package. You will not be able to continue without a valid CD-Key.

After inputting and verifying this information, click Next again and you'll see a Product ID screen. This is the same information that will appear in the About Microsoft Visual Basic screen in VB6's Help menu. Microsoft occasionally requests the Product ID when you call its support number. It is a good idea to write this number down. Its appearance in the About this Product screen is of no help to you if you're unable to load Visual Basic!

The next screen will ask you if you want to install other client products, such as InstallShield. This version of InstallShield is designed for Visual C++. Click Install if you're also installing Visual C++ or Next if you're not.

The following screen offers you a choice of changing the install directory, exiting the install, or customizing the install. This is different from the previous option screen because this customization deals with choosing the programs you want to install. If the current directory to install to is okay, just click the Custom button. You'll then be faced with a listing of different programs and tools, as shown in Figure 1-2. If you just want to install VB, deselect everything except Microsoft Visual Basic 6.0 and Data Access. Parts of Visual Basic won't run properly without the Data Access components installed. After selecting the components you wish to install, click the Continue button.

Visual Basic 6.0 (and any other components you selected) will now install onto your hard drive. No further interaction is required until after all files have been transferred and your system files have been updated. Once this is done, a screen offering you to exit setup or restart your computer

FIGURE 1-2

Custom installation screen of Visual Studio 6.0 Setup

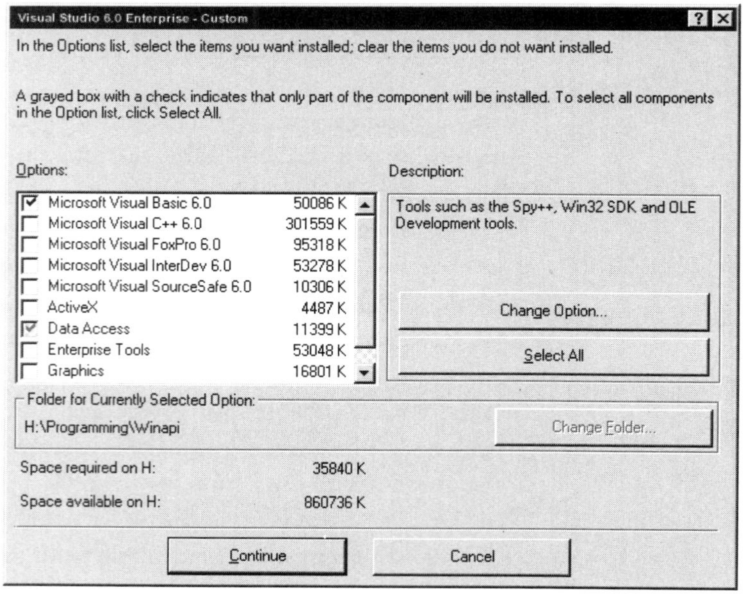

appears. Clicking Restart Windows will reboot the computer; upon loading Windows, your system files will finish being updated. Upon entering Windows, you can start Visual Basic 6.0 and begin programming.

Installing Visual Basic 6.0 Enterprise Edition

Although this installation deals with installing the Enterprise Edition of Visual Basic 6.0, the installation procedure is the same for any edition of VB6. However, as you are creating enterprise applications, you will need the extra tools Enterprise carries to create robust network and stand-alone applications.

Once you've determined that your system will support Visual Basic 6.0, start the installation by clicking the setup executable on your installation CD-ROM. Once the setup program starts, you'll be greeted with a Welcome screen. Click Next and you'll see a screen that outlines the End User License Agreement. Information on this screen outlines your agreement to use the product. Select the option to accept the agreement to continue. If you disagree with the agreement, you will not be able to continue with the installation.

Click Next and you will see a screen that requires you to enter your Name and Company information, as well as proof that this is a legal installation. Your Name and Company name will appear in the fields from information obtained from the Windows Registry. The third field requires the CD-Key. This is the registration number for your installation, which is found on the package containing your installation CD-ROM. Its purpose is to determine that this is a legitimate install, and that you haven't gotten a pirate copy of the software from a buddy or the Internet. After confirming that your Name and Company information is correct, enter the CD-Key and click Next to continue with the installation.

The Product ID screen appears next, containing an identification number that's been made from the CD-Key you entered in the previous screen and information coded in the setup program. This number can be viewed, after your installation is complete, by clicking "About Microsoft Visual Basic" on the Help menu. However, it is important to write this number down during the installation process. Microsoft may request the number if you call its support number for help. If the reason you call

Microsoft is because VB6 won't start or install properly, you won't be able to access the number from the Help menu. Once the number is written down, store it in a handy and safe place.

The remaining screens involve choosing the type of installation you wish to perform and where you want the files to be installed. If you don't want VB to install to the default C: drive and directory, this is when you should change the default settings. However, if Setup detects that not enough room is available on a drive you've chosen, you will be given another chance to choose a different target path. Of the installation types available, Typical installation will install the main components required to run Visual Basic 6.0 on your system. Full installation will fully install Visual Basic and all of its components and documentation from the CD-ROM to your hard drive. Custom installation allows you to fit the installation to suit your needs. If you choose Custom, you will also have to choose which components of Visual Basic you want to install. For most installations, Full is all that is required.

Following this, files will be transferred from the install CD-ROM to your hard disk. This can be a long process, depending on the components or type of installation you've chosen, and the speed of the system itself. Information will be displayed about Visual Basic throughout the installation. Also, a bar will display the progress of the installation. If for some reason this freezes, and no hard drive activity occurs for some time, you may need to reboot your computer. Depending on when the problem occurred, VB will either automatically continue from the point of failure or you may be forced to run Setup again.

When all of the files have been successfully transferred, you will be informed that Windows needs to be restarted and asks whether you want to reboot the computer. Choose Yes, your computer will restart, and the Windows system files will be updated. When Windows reloads, a submenu named "Microsoft Visual Basic 6.0" will appear on the Start | Programs menu. This is where you can start VB and begin programming.

Installing Visual Basic 6.0

1. From the installation disk, start the setup program.

2. You will be met with an initial welcome screen. Click Next to continue.

3. Accept the End User License Agreement. Click Next to continue to an information screen.

4. The information screen will already have your Name and Company Name information filled in. It acquires this information from Windows. If the information is incorrect, change it. Enter your CD-Key, which is located on the back of the Visual Basic's installation CD-ROM's cover. Click Next.

5. The next screen is a Product ID screen, which includes an ID number that should be written down.

6. Follow the remaining screens, choosing the type of installation you want to perform. If you choose Custom, you will also have to choose the components of Visual Basic you wish to install.

7. When prompted, reboot the computer. Your system files will be updated when Windows reloads.

8. Upon installation, Visual Basic 6.0 will be available from the Start | Programs menu

CERTIFICATION OBJECTIVE 1.06

Microsoft Visual Studio 98, Enterprise Edition

Visual Studio 98 (version 6.0) is a suite of Microsoft products suited for enterprise and desktop application development. Like Visual Basic, Visual Studio comes in Professional and Enterprise Editions. The difference between them is that the Enterprise Edition comes with additional features which make it the must-have choice for enterprise development.

Table 1-4 shows what's included with the Enterprise Edition of both Visual Studio 6.0 and Visual Basic 6.0. In looking through these features, note that Visual Studio offers considerably more for enterprise development than Visual Basic. Any development systems listed in the table are Enterprise Editions of the product.

TABLE 1-4   Comparison of Features in Visual Studio 98 and Visual Basic 6.0

Visual Studio 98 (version 6.0)	Visual Basic 6.0	Description
Visual Basic 6.0	Visual Basic 6.0	Development system
Visual C++ 6.0		Development system
Visual FoxPro 6.0		Database development system
Visual InterDev 6.0		Web development system
Visual J++ 6.0		Java development system
Microsoft Developer Network Library, Single Edition		Used as an information reference
Windows NT 4.0 Option Pack		Used for application, communication, and Web services, it includes Microsoft Transaction Server 2.0 and Microsoft Internet Information Server 4.0
Included in NT Option Pack	Microsoft Transaction Server 2.0, Developer Edition	Transaction server
Included in NT Option Pack	Microsoft Internet Information Server 4.0, Developer Edition	Web server
Visual SourceSafe 6.0	Visual SourceSafe 6.0	Source code version control system
Application Life Cycle Support		Includes tools for application and database design, component management, and performance analysis
Enterprise Visual Database Tools	Enterprise Visual Database Tools	Includes tools for designing SQL Server and Oracle databases
Team Development Support		Includes Visual Component Manager, Visual SourceSafe 6.0, and Microsoft Repository

TABLE 1-4	Comparison of Features in Visual Studio 98 and Visual Basic 6.0 (continued)

Visual Studio 98 (version 6.0)	Visual Basic 6.0	Description
Microsoft BackOffice Server 4.5 Developer Edition		Includes BackOffice programs like Microsoft SQL Server, Microsoft SNA Server, Microsoft Exchange Server, Microsoft Site Server, Microsoft Systems Management Server, and so forth
Included in BackOffice Server 4.5	Microsoft SQL Server 6.5, Developer Edition	Database server
	Learn Visual Basic Now	Instruction CD-ROM

on the
job

For the most part, Visual Studio 6.0 includes everything Visual Basic 6.0 does, but it has much more. Because Visual Studio is a suite of products, if you need any of the products included in Visual Studio, it is more cost-effective to buy the suite than to purchase each product individually. It will also prevent having a pile of boxes in the corner of your office!

CERTIFICATION OBJECTIVE 1.07

Establishing the Environment for Source-Code Version Control

Enterprise development can't avoid the need for source-code version control because such applications are considerably more complex than desktop applications, and they are generally worked on by teams of developers. Imagine that you and another developer unknowingly begin working on the same source code, making changes and saving as you go. After a time, you realize you've been destroying each other's work and both wish you could go back to a previous version. That's the importance of version control.

Sometimes changes are made that don't work, changes need to be made but aren't, and the need for tracking (and sometimes returning to a previous version) becomes apparent. In addition, large projects also usually mean large groups of files that can be difficult to manage. To help you with this problem, Microsoft Visual SourceSafe 6.0 is included with the Enterprise Editions of Visual Studio 98 and Visual Basic 6.0.

Visual SourceSafe (VSS) keeps a record of changes made to your source code. Changes to source code are saved to a database, and can then be edited and restored. Once you've installed VSS from your Visual Basic 6.0 or Visual Studio 6.0 installation disk), you will be able invoke VSS from the SourceSafe submenu on the Tools menu.

In the SourceSafe submenu, you can also configure the way VB will interact with VSS. Opening "Options" from this submenu, you can configure the options shown in the illustration below. For each of these options, you have three choices: Yes, No, and Ask. Setting these options will determine whether VB will open and save files to the VSS database, or if it should ask you each time you attempt to open or save a file. The final option on this dialog box determines whether deleted forms from your VB project should also be deleted from the VSS database.

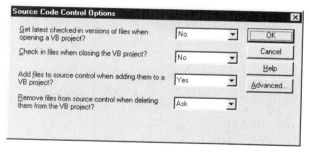

Once VSS is integrated into Visual Basic 6.0, you will be asked each time you start a new project whether you want to add it to Visual SourceSafe. Similarly, each time you close your project, you will be asked if the project should be saved to the VSS database. In using VSS, very little interaction is required by the developer. Most of the work is performed by the VSS Administrator, explained next.

Visual SourceSafe 6.0 Administrator Utility

To use VSS, a user must have a valid user account. Accounts are created with SourceSafe's Admin utility. If a user does not have a valid account, he or she won't be able to access the database. Instead, the user will receive a message stating that the user in question wasn't found.

From the developer's point of view, using Visual Basic 6.0 with VSS is almost transparent and is easy to use. Most of the work for SourceSafe is done by the Admin utility. A person in the role of VSS Administrator should have the responsibility of controlling this utility. It is here that you control user accounts for VSS, add and delete databases, and so forth. To open this utility, select "Visual SourceSafe 6.0 Admin" from the Visual SourceSafe menu of your Windows Start menu.

The first time you start the Admin utility, no password will be set for the Admin account, which belongs to the person acting as the VSS Administrator. This will cause you to go directly into the utility. Once here, the first thing you should do is set a password for the Admin account. This will keep other users from being able to access the utility and alter settings. To change a password, select the account you want to alter, and select "Change Password" from the Users menu. A dialog box will appear, with a field for your new password and a second field to verify it. Type the same password in each field. If you attempt to change the password later, a third field will appear on this dialog box that requires you to enter the old password. If you don't know the existing password, you won't be able to change it. Once a password is set for the Admin account, a password dialog box will appear each time you open the utility. You must enter the correct password before the screen shown below will appear.

To create a new Visual SourceSafe database, you need to select "Create Database" from the Tools menu. When this is selected, a dialog box appears, allowing you to enter the path to your new database. Clicking the

Browse button on this dialog box allows you to browse the local hard drive or network for an existing folder for the database. You can also click the New Folder button to create a new folder for your database.

After more than one database has been created, you are able to switch between databases to administer with the "Open SourceSafe Database" item on the Users menu. A dialog box appears with a listing of existing databases. If you have no further need for a particular database, select it from the list and click Remove to delete it. To administer a new database, select the one you want from this list, and then click Open. You will be prompted for your password before the database will be opened.

Once you've selected a database, you'll be able to archive and restore projects and files from the Archive menu. Selecting "Archive Projects" from this menu allows you to save a file or a project to a compressed file. Selecting this menu item also starts the Archive Wizard. The first screen of this Wizard has you select the files or projects to compress. After clicking Next, you are able to select one of the following options for your archive:

- Save data to file (archives project or file to a compressed file)
- Save data to file, then delete from database to save space
- Delete data permanently

Selecting either of the first two options requires you to enter the path for the compressed file. Compressed files have the extension of .SSA. Once the path is set, clicking Next brings up a screen that allows you to specify the data to be archived. Clicking Finish archives the files or project to the compressed file.

To restore this data, select Restore Project Files from the Tools menu, which will bring up the Restore Wizard. The first screen of this Wizard requires you to enter the path and filename of an archive file. After doing this, you can click Next and select the files or projects to restore from the compressed file. Finally, clicking Next brings you to a screen that allows you to specify where to restore the files. You can restore to the original location of the files or project, or enter a new path to restore the files or project to. Clicking Finish has the Wizard restore the files or project, based on the settings you've chosen.

To modify the accounts of VSS users, use the menu items under the Users menu. The Add User item brings up a dialog box in which you can enter a to name and password. Remove User allows you to remove any user except the Admin account, while Edit User allows you to modify the account name of every user except Admin. Under no circumstances can the Admin account be removed or modified because this is the account that has the power to modify databases and accounts. Finally, as mentioned earlier in this section, the Change password item allows you to alter the password of a user.

Visual SourceSafe Explorer

The VSS Explorer is a graphical user interface for Visual SourceSafe. It is accessed from the SourceSafe submenu under the Tools menu of Visual Basic 6.0. After clicking Run SourceSafe from this submenu, the Explorer (shown in Figure 1-3) appears. The Explorer is made up of three panes. The left pane is the Project pane, which displays a listing of all projects in a particular database. The right pane is the File pane, which shows a list of all files in a particular project. Finally, the bottom pane is the Results pane. This shows the results of operations performed by VSS.

FIGURE 1-3

Visual SourceSafe Explorer

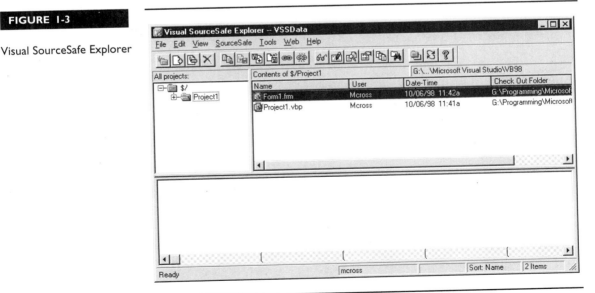

The Explorer allows you to navigate through a project, view status information, and even view the history of a project. To open a particular database and view its contents, you must click the File menu and select Open SourceSafe Database. This brings up a listing of databases that currently exist, which you can open or delete from this dialog box (which is the same as the Admin utility). To add files to a project in this database, select Add File from the Files menu. You can also delete and rename files and projects from this menu.

To record changes to a project, you must choose to Check In or Check Out files and projects from the SourceSafe menu of the VSS Explorer or through the SourceSafe submenu under Tools in Visual Basic 6.0. This process is like checking books in and out from a library. When a file or project is checked in, changes in your work are stored in the database. When a file or project is checked out, a writable copy of the project or file is placed in your working folder.

CERTIFICATION OBJECTIVE 1.08

Configuring a Server Computer to Run Microsoft Transaction Server (MTS)

Earlier in this chapter, we discussed the three tiers of the application model: user services, business services, and data services. The middle-tier is where business logic can be encapsulated into components and Microsoft Transaction Server (MTS) can be used to provide the platform for running these components. MTS can be installed on Windows 9x, NT Workstation, or NT Server, and provides the following features:

■ MTS runtime environment, which serves as the middle-tier platform for running these components.

■ MTS Explorer, which is used for managing and deploying components.

■ Application Programming Interfaces (APIs) and Resource Dispensers, which enable you to make scalable and robust applications. APIs are sets of commands used in an application to request services performed by the operating system, while Resource Dispensers are used to access shared information.

Each of these features is available in MTS for all platforms. Together, they make it easier to build, deploy, and maintain complex three-tier applications.

Although MTS is available for Windows 9x, NT Workstation, and NT Server, the capabilities of MTS on these various platforms are quite different. The version of MTS offered in the NT Option Pack and the Developer Edition is meant for developing packages. It is limited in its abilities to administer installations of MTS on other computers, and certain features aren't available to computers running Windows 9x. These limitations are discussed later, in the meantime it is important to remember that the platform running MTS will affect what features are offered.

As its name states, Microsoft Transaction Server allows you to use *transactions*, which can simplify your work in developing components. A transaction is a set of actions, or processing steps, that's treated as a single unit of work. You've probably heard the word "transaction" in a banking context. For example, you might go to an ATM machine to withdraw some cash. After entering the amount to withdraw from your account, the program in the bank machine checks to see if there's enough money in your account. If there isn't, the program responds with an "Insufficient Funds" message. If there is enough money, it adjusts the account balance, gives you your money, and returns your bank card. This is a transaction which is treated as a single action, even though it requires many processing steps.

Transactions provide protection from system failures or concurrent updates because transactions have four basic properties:

■ Atomicity

■ Consistency

■ Isolation

■ Durability

To understand how transactions work, it is important to understand each of the basic properties that make up a transaction.

Atomicity is an "all-or-nothing" feature of transactions: either all of the steps in a transaction succeed or nothing happens. If any of the processing steps in the transaction fail, the transaction is aborted, and the data is rolled back to its previous state.

Consistency means that when data is modified, it matches the state that's expected. When business rules in your application modify data, it is important that the data is correctly modified.

Isolation is used to keep transactions from seeing that transactions are also running. This keeps the other transactions from seeing the partial or uncommitted results of the other transactions. In other words, when two or more transactions are occurring on the same data, isolation makes it appear that only one transaction is running at a time.

Durability refers to a transaction's ability to survive failures. Imagine how infuriated you'd be if you deposited your paycheck into that ATM machine mentioned above and the system failed, causing the record of the transaction to be forever lost! When an update is committed to data, it must be able to survive such crises as communication failures, process failures, and server failures.

exam
ⓦatch
An easy way to remember the properties of a transaction is to think of the acronym "ACID:" atomicity, consistency, isolation, durability.

For the developer, using transactions ensures that all of the steps in a procedure succeed before changes are committed to data. By creating components that run on MTS, you are able to focus on developing the components without worrying about complex server issues. This is done by creating ActiveX DLLs (Dynamic Link Libraries) with Visual Basic 6.0, and adding them to packages that are installed and run on MTS. Creating and working with ActiveX components is introduced in the next chapter. In this chapter, we'll discuss Microsoft Transaction Server so you can see how these components can be used. While this may seem like putting the cart before the horse, it is important to understand where components can be used before actually taking steps to create them.

Like everything else in computers, MTS has certain system requirements that must be met before it can be installed and run on a machine. In addition to a minimum of 30 megabytes of free hard drive space, and 32 megabytes of memory, other requirements are necessary. Windows 95 and higher must have DCOM enabled. If you are using a version of Windows NT previous to version 4.0 or don't have DCOM enabled on Windows 9x, the following message will display when you try to install MTS:

```
"Setup library mtssetup.dll could not be loaded or the
function MTSSetupProc could not be found."
```

To enable DCOM (or to ensure that its already enabled), follow the steps in Exercise 1-2. (An NT Server 4.0 installation requires that Windows NT Service Pack 3 already be installed on the machine. If you don't have Service Pack 3 installed on your NT Server, you can download it from Microsoft's Web site: http://www.microsoft.com/support.)

exam
ⓦatch

One of the big innovations of MTS 2.0 is its integration with Internet Information Server (IIS) 4.0. IIS is a Web server. Using Visual Basic 6.0, you can create three-tier applications that can be used with IIS and MTS on the Internet or an intranet.

EXERCISE 1-2

Enabling DCOM on a Windows 9.x Machine

1. Select the Network applet from Control Panel on your Windows Start menu. When the Network applet opens, click the Access Control tab and ensure that you have the "User-level access control" option selected. If this option isn't selected, select it, and then click OK to exit the Network applet. If you've changed to user-level access control, you'll be prompted to restart your machine. Restart it and continue to the next step upon re-entering Windows.

2. From the Windows Start menu, click Run. When the Run dialog box appears, type **dcomcnfg** and click OK. This starts the Distributed COM Configuration Properties.

3. Click the Default Properties tab, and ensure that the "Enable Distributed COM on this computer" check box is checked. If it is not, click this check box to enable DCOM and click OK to save your settings. DCOM is now enabled on your machine.

Installing MTS

Like many of the products Microsoft is putting out these days, Microsoft Transaction Server is installed with an easy-to-use wizard. You simply follow the instructions on each screen and click a Next button to move from one step to the next. After specifying where you want MTS to be installed, you are required to reboot your computer so the installation can complete.

Microsoft Transaction Server is available on both the Visual Basic 6.0 and Visual Studio 6.0 installation disks. For Visual Basic, the installation disk includes Microsoft Transaction Server 2.0, Developer Edition. If you're using Visual Studio 6.0, you can install MTS as part of the NT Option Pack (for Windows 9x).

If you don't have your installation disk handy and require a copy of MTS, it is available for download from http://backoffice.microsoft.com, as part of the NT Option Pack. By going to the Download section from this Web site, you can obtain a copy of the NT Option Pack for Windows 9x and other platforms as well, including NT Server 4.0, NT Server 4.0 alpha, NT Workstation 4.0, and NT Workstation 4.0 alpha. Upon selecting the platform you are using (and providing some statistical information about yourself), select a Web site location to download the installation program from.

If you are installing from the Internet, the next screen you'll see is an End User License Agreement screen. Click the Yes button to agree to it. (Clicking No cancels your installation.) You will then be given two options: install the Option Pack or save the installation program so it can be used for additional installations on other computers. If you're installing on multiple computers that run the same operating system, it will save time if you select Download. Select Install if this is the only computer you are installing to, and then click Next.

If you're installing NT Option Pack for Windows 9x, Personal Web Server 4.0 comes as part of the installation package. Don't be dismayed when you reach the next screen, which offers three choices for installing Personal Web Server. You haven't picked the wrong program to install, it's supposed to be here. Your three installation options, Typical, Minimum, and Full, determine which components for Personal Web Server will be installed on your computer.

The next screen offers you a choice about where the installation files should be stored on your hard drive. Accept the default location that appears on this screen or type in a new location. Clicking Next starts the download of installation files and brings up the Personal Web Server welcome screen.

If you're installing NT Option Pack (for Windows 9x) from Visual Studio's installation disks, there are only a couple of steps to take to reach the Personal Web Server welcome screen. Upon starting the setup program from Visual Studio's installation CD-ROM, select Server Applications and Tools (Add Only). After clicking Next, a listing of server components that includes NT Option Pack (for Windows 9x) appears. Select this from the listing and click the Install button. The welcome screen for Personal Web Server then appears.

on the **job**

The NT Option Pack included with Visual Studio is for Windows 95 and above. If you need to install MTS on an NT Workstation or NT Server, you'll have to obtain the appropriate NT Option Pack from Microsoft's Web site.

If you're installing from the Visual Studio CD-ROM, clicking the Next button displays an End User License Agreement. Accept the agreement to continue. (If you don't accept the agreement, you won't be able to continue.) Move to the next screen, which allows three installation types: Minimum, Typical, and Custom. Minimum installs the bare-ones components of Personal Web Server, Typical installs additional components for building and deploying Web applications, and Custom allows you to pick and choose what you want installed.

If you already have components of Personal Web Server installed, you'll see two buttons after the welcome screen: Add/Remove and Remove All. Remove All is used to remove components added in a previous installation. To remove only certain components or to install MTS on a computer, select Add/Remove, which will bring up a listing of components available in the NT Option Pack. This is the same information that displays when you click Custom the first time you install NT Option Pack.

A check box appears beside each name in the listing. To install a component, click its check box so that a check mark appears in it. Clicking to remove a check mark from the check box will remove components or not have them installed. For MTS to function, these minimum components need to be checked:

- Common Program Files
- Microsoft Data Access Components 1.5
- Transaction Server

If these three items aren't checked in the list, MTS won't run properly on your computer.

Once you're sure the proper items are checked, click Next. Because NT Option Pack includes Personal Web Server (PWS), the next screen allows you to specify the directory PWS will use for publishing Web pages. This directory is used as the root directory for Web pages that other people on your network can access over an intranet. Any Web pages you create can be placed in this folder and viewed on the intranet.

The screen following this allows you to specify the directory into which MTS will be installed. If you are concerned about hard disk space or want to use a different directory for MTS, type a new path in the MTS Install Folder field. You can also click the Browse button to navigate through your hard drive or the network for a folder to install to.

Click Next and the installation program will begin transferring files onto your computer. Depending on the components you've checked, this can take several minutes. At the end of transferring files, you'll be prompted to restart your computer. Click Yes to restart your computer, so that the installation can update system settings.

Installing MTS with the NT Option Pack

1. Start the Setup program on your Visual Studio installation disk, select Server Applications and Tools (Add Only), and then click Next. From the listing of server components, select NT Option Pack (for Windows 9x) and click Install.

2. A welcome screen for Personal Web Server appears. Click the Next button and click Accept to accept the End User License Agreement.

3. If you don't have Personal Web Server installed, click the Custom button. If Personal Web Server is already installed, click the Add/Remove button to bring up a screen that allows you to select components to install from the NT Option Pack. To ensure that Microsoft Transaction Server is installed correctly, be sure to check:

   ■ Common Program Files

   ■ Microsoft Data Access Components 1.5

   ■ Transaction Server

   Once you see that these are selected, click Next.

4. Because NT Option Pack includes Personal Web Server, you need to specify the directory for publishing Web pages. Accept the default and click Next.

5. The Microsoft Transaction Server screen allows you to specify where MTS will be installed. Click Next if the default directory is acceptable. Otherwise, enter a new path in the MTS Install Folder field, and click Next.

6. Click Next, and MTS is installed on your computer. Wait for all files to be transferred. When prompted, restart your computer to complete the installation.

MTS Explorer

MTS Explorer is a graphical user interface (GUI : pronounced "goo-ee") that allows you to create, manage, and deploy MTS packages. MTS packages are components that perform related functions and are grouped together (packaged) so they can be run together on Microsoft Transaction Server. Depending on the platform used to run MTS, the Explorer will have a different functionality and appearance.

On NT Server, an MTS Explorer plug-in is added to Microsoft Management Console (MMC). This interface consists of a left and right pane, which makes it appear similar to Windows Explorer. The left pane shows a hierarchy of items as they are organized in the MTS runtime environment.

From highest to lowest in the hierarchy, these items are as follows:

- Computers
- Packages
- Components
- Roles
- Interfaces
- Methods

By double-clicking items in the left pane, you can navigate through the hierarchy and tunnel down into items beneath. This is the same as navigating from folders to subfolders in Windows Explorer. When you click an item in the left pane, its contents are displayed in the right pane of MMC.

As shown in Figure 1-4, the MTS Explorer that runs in Windows 9x has only a single pane and has a similar appearance to My Computer. To navigate down the hierarchy, you double-click folders or listed items. To move back up the hierarchy, you must click the Up one level button on the toolbar.

When you start MTS Explorer on computers running Windows NT 4.0 or above, you see a Computers folder in the left pane. Opening this folder by double-clicking it allows you to see the computers that you can administer. If nothing else, My Computer will be displayed, representing

FIGURE 1-4

MTS Explorer as seen in Windows 98

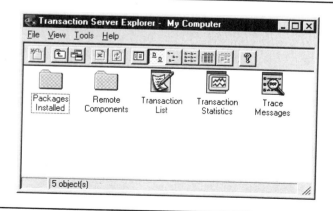

the computer you're currently working on. To add other computers to this folder, you must do one of the following actions:

- Right-click the Computers folder, and then select New and Computer
- Select the Computers folder, and click the Create new object icon in the right pane toolbar
- Select the Computers folder, open the Action menu in the left pane, and select New

The Add Computer dialog box opens, in which you can enter the name of the server you want to administer. The new server will be added to the Computers folder.

When you start MTS Explorer, you first see My Computer in the pane of the Explorer. To add additional computers, select New from the File menu, and enter the name of the computer you'd like to administer. When using MTS Explorer on Windows 9.x, you can't administer remote Windows 9.x computers running MTS. This is a limitation of the Windows 95/98 installation. When you double-click the My Computer icon (or the icon of another computer you've added), a listing similar to that in Figure 1-4 will appear.

The Packages Installed folder lists all packages that have been installed on a particular computer. By double-clicking this folder, you can see all of the packages currently installed on the computer you're managing with MTS Explorer. To add new packages, select New from the File menu. The Package Wizard appears, which allows you to create empty packages (to which you can later add COM components) or install existing MTS packages. By following the instructions offered by the Wizard, you are able to create or add new packages easily.

The Remote Components folder contains components, registered on the local computer (the one you're using), which will run remotely on other computers. If you haven't added additional computers to MTS Explorer, nothing will appear when this folder is opened. In addition, MTS must be installed on the client computers you wish to configure through this folder. To add components that are accessed by remote computers, select New from the File menu when you're in the Remote Components folder, and then choose the component to add.

The remaining icons shown in Figure 1-4 are tools for administering MTS. Double-clicking the Transaction List icon allows you to view the current transactions that the computer is participating in. Information displayed here allows you to view the status of a transaction and the units of work being performed. Double-clicking Transaction Statistics allows you to view status bars that show the statistical information on transactions that have occurred on your computer. Some of the information displayed here reflects the current performance of transactions, while others are cumulative. Finally, Trace Messages allows you to view the trace messages that have currently been issued by Microsoft Distributed Transaction Coordinator (MS DTC). MS DTC is a transaction manager that coordinates multiple resource managers. Resource managers are services, such as SQL Server, that maintain durable data. In using Trace Messages, you can see messages that indicate the status of MTS activities.

Setting Up Security on a System Package

Using MTS on Windows NT allows you to administer security properties and roles. Roles are symbolic names that represent the groups of users that are able to use a package of components on MTS. This is done through the Roles, Role Membership, and Users folders in MTS Explorer. If you are using MTS on Windows 9x, you won't be able to see these folders because administration on this platform doesn't support security properties and roles.

After MTS has been installed on a computer, and you're familiar with the MTS Explorer, you must make certain configurations and set up security for the System package. The System package contains components used by MTS for internal functions. You can view the System package by opening the Installed Packages folder. After right-clicking the System package contained within and selecting Properties, a tabbed property sheet appears, which displays properties of the System package. If you were to double-click the package in MTS Explorer, select a component, and right-click it, you would bring up a similar property sheet for components. On these tabs, you can view, but not set, the properties of components in the System package.

When MTS is first installed, security for the System package is disabled because no user or group accounts have been mapped to the Administrator role of a System package. Mapping a user or group to the Administrator role enables a user to perform administrative tasks on the System package. Before security is enabled, any user is able to modify MTS packages. After you map an account to the Administrator role, only those accounts mapped to this role can delete and modify packages appearing in MTS Explorer.

To map a user or group to the Administrator role, you must follow these steps:

1. Select the Security package from the left pane of MTS Explorer.

2. Open the Roles folder and double-click the Administrator role.

3. Open the Users folder. Click New from the Action menu.

4. When the dialog box appears, add the usernames and groups you want to map to the Administrator role. If you need to locate a user account, use the Show Users and Search buttons. Click OK, and the user or group will be mapped to the Administrator role.

Once a user or group has been mapped to a role, MTS can check the role of any user or group attempting to modify a package. If the accounts haven't been mapped to this role, they won't be allowed to modify or delete packages.

Limitations of who can be mapped to the Administrator role exist if MTS is installed on either a primary or backup domain controller. Primary and backup domain controllers are servers that are used to authenticate accounts in a Windows NT domain. If MTS is installed on such a server, a user must be a domain administrator to manage packages in the MTS Explorer. If you've installed MTS on a computer that isn't a primary or backup domain controller, any user can be mapped to this role.

Once the Administration role has been configured, you must enable authorization checking, which enables MTS to check whether a user or group is authorized to make changes to a package. To make this configuration, you must first have mapped your user account to the Administrator role. Once this is done, you can perform the following steps:

1. Select the System package, and choose Properties from the Action menu.

2. When the tabbed property sheet appears, click the Security tab. Click the "Enable authorization" check box, so that it appears with a check mark inside of it.

3. Select My Computer from the left pane of MTS Explorer. From the Action menu, select Shut Down Server Processes, which will shut down all server packages.

When you restart the server packages, authorization checking is enabled. MTS will check users and groups to see if they are authorized (assigned to the proper role) before packages can be modified.

In addition to the Administrator role, which can use all MTS Explorer functions, the System package also has a Reader role. When you map users and groups to a Reader role, they have the ability to view the objects in MTS Explorer. Although they can view these objects in the hierarchy, they can't install, create, change, or delete any objects, nor can they shut down server processes or export packages. To have these capabilities, users and groups must be mapped to the Administrator role.

CERTIFICATION OBJECTIVE 1.09

Configuring a Client Computer to Use an MTS Package

MTS Explorer allows you to do more than install, delete, and monitor packages on a server computer. With the Explorer, you can also create application executables that install to, and configure, client computers. The executable enables the client computer to access a remote server application. By using the Explorer, you can configure the client computer not only to access applications on the local computer, but also to access other computers on your network.

Before delving into configuring client computers to use MTS packages, it is important to understand how to create and modify one. The first step is to decide where the package will be created. As mentioned previously, you can add computers to MTS Explorer and then administer them. Once a computer has been added to the Computers folder, you can create packages that will be installed on that particular computer. To review how to add a computer, refer to the "MTS Explorer" section of this chapter.

Once you've decided whether you will create a package on the local My Computer or on another computer, double-click the computer icon you'll use. You'll then see the Installed Packages folder. Opening this folder reveals all of the packages currently installed on that computer. To create a new package or install an existing one, select New from the File menu, which will start the Package Wizard. Two buttons appear on the first screen of the Wizard: "Install pre-built packages" and "Create an empty package." Clicking the first button makes the Wizard present you with a screen that allows you to install existing packages. By clicking the Add button you can select packages on your hard disk, which have the extension .PAK.

The Next button then brings you to a screen that allows you to specify the path where the package will be installed. Creating a new package is equally easy. After clicking "Create an empty package," you are presented with a screen that allows you to enter the name for your new package. Clicking Finish creates the package, which is displayed in the Installed Packages folder.

Once an empty package has been created, you must add components to it. Double-clicking your new package's icon displays a Components folder. After opening the Components folder (by double-clicking it), you are ready to add components. To do this, select New from the File menu to start the Component Wizard. The first screen of the Wizard has two buttons: "Install new component(s)" and "Import component(s) that are already registered." Clicking the first of these buttons brings up the Install Components screen. By clicking the Add Files button, you can select files from your hard disk to add to the package. Clicking Finish adds the files to the package. Selecting "Import component(s) that are already registered" makes the Wizard build a listing of every component that's been registered with the Windows Registry of the computer. After selecting the components to add from this list, click Finish to add the components to your package. This is the same procedure as adding components to an existing package. To delete components from a package, simply select the component you want to remove and press Delete on your keyboard.

Creating Packages that Install or Update MTS Components on a Client Computer

As mentioned, MTS Explorer allows you to create application executables, which install and configure client computers, to access applications on remote MTS servers. A requirement for this is that the client computer has DCOM (which does not require any MTS server files other than the application executable) enabled. Once you've established that DCOM is enabled on the client computer, you are ready to go through the process of generating the executable.

By default, any executables generated in MTS Explorer configure a client computer to access the server that the executable was created on. In other words, when you create an executable on your server computer, the executable will configure the client computer (by default) to access packages on your server. If you want to configure the client computer to access another server, you must use the Options tab of the Computer property sheet. This is done by right-clicking the My Computer icon, selecting Properties, and then clicking the Options tab from the dialog box that appears. On the Options tab, enter the name of a remote server in the "Remote server name" field in the Replication section. When this is done, you can export your package, which creates the executable that can be run on the client computer.

To export a package, you must first select the icon of the package to export from the Installed Packages folder. Having done this, select Export Package from the File menu. In the dialog box that appears, enter the path and filename for the package file. Clicking the Browse button displays a dialog box that allows you to navigate through your local hard disk and the network. Click the Export button to finish.

When a package is exported, MTS automatically creates an executable for the client application on the MTS server. A subdirectory will be created in the folder to which you exported your package. This new subdirectory is named Clients, and contains an executable file with the name of your exported package. When this file is executed on a client computer that supports DCOM, it installs information that enables the client to access the server application.

Because this executable file installs information onto the client computer, it makes changes to the Windows Registry of that computer. Thus, you should never run this executable on the server computer because it will overwrite and remove Registry settings that are needed to run the server application. If you do this by mistake, you'll have to use Add/Remove Programs to remove the application, and then delete and reinstall the package in MTS Explorer.

CERTIFICATION OBJECTIVE 1.10

Designing the Properties, Methods and Events of Components

After all the discussion of different programs, you probably feel like you're working toward your MCSE rather than your MCSD. Although it's vital that you know the tools and issues covered so far in this chapter, this section deals with the meat and potatoes of programming. Here, we will introduce you to the three basic parts of any component: properties, methods, and events.

A property is an attribute of a control or object. For example, the color of text is a property, while the visible property of a control determines whether it can be seen or not when the program runs. Properties should have a default value, and can be changed programmatically or through an interface (such as a property sheet).

Methods are actions that an object can perform. An example of this is the PrintForm method of a form object. A form is a container in Visual Basic that can contain other objects and controls. Basically, it's like the canvas on which you create part of your application. When you run your program, the form appears as a Window on the user's screen. When you use the PrintForm method in your programming code, the form you specify will be printed. For example, let's say you have a form named Form1 that you want to print. The following code prints it to the local printer:

```
Form1.PrintForm
```

By using this code, you invoke the PrintForm method of the object Form1, and a depiction of your form will be printed.

Events are actions that are recognized by an object. Examples of events include a form loading into memory (load event) or a user clicking a button (click event). As you can see, some events are triggered by user interaction; others are triggered by the application itself.

To understand how properties, methods, and events work together, we'll look at an ActiveX DLL project. Starting Visual Basic 6.0 and selecting ActiveX DLL from the New Project dialog box creates an ActiveX DLL project. This dialog box appears whenever you start Visual Basic 6.0. As illustrated in Figure 1-5, after you start a new ActiveX DLL project, a project with a class module appears. A class module is a template for creating objects programmatically, which we will begin using extensively in the next chapter.

Figure 1-5 also illustrates a number of tools used to view, create, and modify properties, methods, and events. We will introduce you to them here, then go into greater depth in the Chapter 2. The Project window, shown in the top right of Figure 1-5, allows us to navigate through various forms and modules that make up our project. Below this is the Properties window, in which we can modify the value of certain properties at Design time. Design-time is where you create your application, while runtime is when the application is loaded into memory and running. In the center of the figure is the Code window, in which you write your actual programming code. The Code window has two ListBoxes (which are fields that display a list of various items that you select by clicking). The left ListBox contains a listing of objects, and the right ListBox contains a list of

FIGURE 1-5

An ActiveX project in Visual Basic 6.0

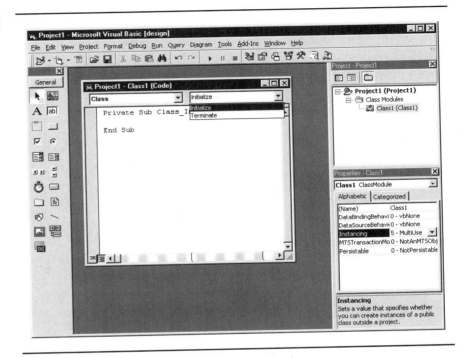

events associated with those objects. When creating Visual Basic applications, you will use each of these extensively.

The class object of a class module it has two events associated with it: Initialize and Terminate. The Initialize event occurs when an instance of a class is created and before any properties are set. It is used to initialize any data used by the class and can be used to load forms used by the class. Terminate occurs when the object variable is set to nothing, or when it goes out of scope. To destroy an object use the following syntax in your code, where "Object" is the name of the object you wish to destroy:

```
Set Object = Nothing
```

The Terminate event is used to save information, unload forms, and perform any other tasks required when the class ends. Initialize is the first event that occurs and Terminate is the last.

Events are handled in class modules as they are in built-in objects (like forms). By referring to Chapter 2, you can see that the Initialize and Terminate events in a form are identical to what occurs when dealing with these same events in a class. By adding code to such events, you can manipulate the way your class module will act, just as you would manipulate the actions of a form.

Adding events is first done by declaring it in the class module's General Declaration section. To do this, select General from the object ListBox and Declaration from the event ListBox. Use the following syntax to add your new event:

```
Public Event Eventname (argument list)
```

"Eventname" is the name you've chosen to call the event, and "argument list" is a list of arguments that are declared by name and type. The argument list is similar to a list of parameters that you use in a regular procedure. If you were going to use an event called LoginName with an argument of the current user's username, you might declare the following event in the General Declaration section of your class:

```
Public Event LoginName (UserName as String)
```

The code that raises the event (as we'll see next) would then pass the value to the argument UserName.

To trigger an event to run, use the RaiseEvent keyword. Assigning a value to a variable, and then using the RaiseEvent keyword to call the event and pass the variable's value does this. To use our previous example, the LoginName event we created would be raised with the following code:

```
StrName="Guest"
RaiseEvent LoginName (strName)
```

Once a class is created, you can create methods. Adding methods is done by creating Public procedures in the class module. You can create either subprocedures or functions. Once these procedures are added, other parts of your application, or ActiveX controllers, can call the procedures as methods of the object class.

In addition to creating methods, you can also create properties. Custom properties are implemented as either Public variables of the class, or by using the procedures Property Let, Property Set, and Property Get.

Public variables in a class become the properties of the object. Declaring Public variables is done the same way as declaring them in standard modules and forms. If you were going to add a property called UserName to the class, you would add the following code to your class module's General Declaration section:

```
Public UserName as String
```

Once you declare the Public variable it becomes a property of the object. When the object has been instantiated, your calling code can then manipulate the properties. You can then assign and manipulate values, and get the values returned to your program. To expand on the previous UserName example, the following code assigns the value "Michael" to the UserName property of an object called Object1:

```
Object1.UserName = "Michael"
```

After doing this, we can create a message box to display the UserName property of our object:

```
MsgBox Object1.UserName
```

The other way to create properties is by using property procedures. Using property procedures allows you to execute a procedure when a value is changed or read, have a property constrained to a small set of values, or expose properties that are read-only. Property procedures are created in two parts: one part assigns values to the property and the other returns its value.

Property Set and Property Let both assign values to a property. The difference between them is that Property Set is used when setting the value of an object property. If the property is a reference to an object, Property Set is always used. Property Let is used for non-objects like variables.

You can assign object references to an object variable by using the Set command. In the following syntax, Property Set is used to Set x as a New Class object:

```
Dim x as Class1
Set x = New Class1
```

Property Set is thus used to set the value of an object property.

At this point, you've seen the Property Let statement used without even realizing it. In the early days of Visual Basic, you assigned a value to a variable by using the following syntax:

```
Let x=5
```

Although this is still supported in VB, the common way to assign a value to a variable is with the following syntax:

```
x=5
```

The reason that this occurs is that the Let statement is always called, except in cases in which a Set statement is used. Visual Basic will call the property procedure that goes with the type of assignment being used: Let for variables, and Set for object properties.

There may be times when both Property Let and Property Set are used. This is done when you set a property that is a reference to an object, and then use Property Let to assign values to its properties. This is seen in the following example:

```
Private Amnt As Integer
Dim x As Class1

Set x =New Class1
x.Amnt=13
```

In this example, a class module is created, setting x as a new Class1 object. There is also a property called Amnt that has an integer value. By using Property Let, the value of 13 is assigned to the Amnt.

Property Get, as its name suggests, executes when the calling code reads the property. Because Property Set and Property Let write to the property, you can create read-only properties by using Property Get without a matching Property Set or Property Let.

To fully understand property procedures, let's work through the following example of code. Don't get too stressed-out about what you see here because we will go through it, line-by-line afterward.

```
Private gstrUser As String

Public Property Let UserName (strInput As String)
     gstrUser=Lcase(strInput)
End Property
Public Property Get UserName () As String
     UserName = gstrUser
End Property
```

In the first line, we declare gstrUser as a string (a group of characters not longer than 255 characters in length). We then create our first property procedure. Notice that the Property Let and Property Get procedures both have the same name. You are able to do this because Property Let is writing to the property and Property Get reads the property. They are not duplicates of one another; they are performing different tasks. In the example, Property Let takes the value that our user has input and assigns the value to the variable gstrUser. In the example, it is also converting the characters to lowercase. In the next procedure, Property Get UserName is reading the value of gstrUser and returning it. While Property Let assigns a value of UserName, Property Get is reading and returning the value.

QUESTIONS AND ANSWERS

How do I map users to Roles through MTS Explorer on a computer running Windows 95?	You can't. Users and groups can only be mapped to roles through MTS Explorer on computers running Windows NT 4.0 or higher.
I am trying to install Microsoft Transaction Server on a Windows 95 machine, and keep getting a message stating that MTSSETUP.DLL can't load. Why?	When you receive a message stating "Setup library mtssetup.dll could not be loaded or the function MTSSetupProc could not be found," it means that you haven't enabled DCOM on your Windows 9x machine.
What are the three tiers of the application model?	User services, business (and other middle-tier) services, and data services.
What are the basic properties of a transaction?	Atomicity, consistency, isolation, and durability.
I want to create custom properties, but don't want to implement them as Public variables of a Class. What can I do?	Use the procedures Property Let, Property Set, and Property Get.

CERTIFICATION SUMMARY

The first step to a good distributed application is a good design. The application model breaks an application into three tiers: user services, business (and other middle-tier) services, and data services. By using this model, you are able to create robust applications.

Microsoft Transaction Server (MTS) works on the middle-tier of the application model. It is component-based and shields developers from many of the complex server issues of developing distributed applications.

Due to the complexity of distributed applications, source-code version control is of great importance. Visual SourceSafe allows you save and restore versions of your source code, and provides numerous features that aid in the effective development of distributed applications.

Visual Basic is available in the Visual Basic 6.0 package or the Visual Studio suite of products. The differences between these are the tools, utilities, and development applications available in each package.

To program components, you must master the use of properties, methods, and events. In this chapter, we introduced some of the basic and more advanced issues with these. We will build on this knowledge in following chapters.

TWO-MINUTE DRILL

❑ An enterprise application is business oriented, and it is required to meet the business requirements of an organization.

❑ A recommended approach to designing applications is modular design, which involves breaking a large project into smaller chunks.

❑ Multitier applications are made up of user services, business (and other middle tier) services, and data services.

❑ Before a developer begins coding an application, time should be spent assessing the impact of the initial design.

❑ On average, you should spend 25% in analysis, 38% in design, 13% coding, 19% testing, and 7% in integration, with time to assess your application included in the design phase.

❑ In assessing the impact of your design, you should consider performance, maintainability, extendibility, scalability, availability, and security

❑ One area in which you can improve the design of an application is with variables. These are named storage locations that can hold certain types of data.

❑ An important aspect of making your source code maintainable involves documentation.

❑ Comments are a way of explaining what is going on in the code. A comment might explain what a procedure does, why a variable is included, and so on.

❑ By incorporating extensibility into your design, you are able to benefit from third-party programmers developing added features to your application.

❑ Visual SourceSafe (VSS) keeps a record of changes made to your source code. Changes to source code are saved to a database, and can then be edited and restored.

❑ The VSS Explorer is a graphical user interface for Visual SourceSafe. It is accessed from the SourceSafe submenu under the Tools menu of Visual Basic 6.0.

❑ Microsoft Transaction Server allows you to use *transactions*, which can simplify your work in developing components. A transaction is a set of actions, or processing steps, that's treated as a single unit of work.

❑ For MTS to function, these minimum components need to be checked: Common Program Files, Microsoft Data Access Components 1.5, and Transaction Server.

❑ Using MTS on Windows NT allows you to administer security properties and roles. Roles are symbolic names that represent the groups of users that are able to use a package of components on MTS.

SELF TEST

The following Self-Test questions will help you measure your understanding of the material presented in this chapter. Read all the choices carefully, as there may be more than one correct answer. Choose all correct answers for each question.

1. You are attempting to install Microsoft Transaction Server on a Windows 98 machine, and receive the following message: "Setup library mtssetup.dll could not be loaded or the function MTSSetupProc could not be found." What is most likely the problem?

   A. Microsoft Transaction Server doesn't run on Windows 98 (you must use Windows 95

   B. Microsoft Transaction Server will only run on Windows NT Server 4.0 or higher

   C. Microsoft Transaction Server will only run on Windows NT Workstation 4.0 or higher

   D. DCOM hasn't been enabled on the computer

2. Which of the following is an attribute of a control or object that can be manipulated programmatically or through a window at Design time?

   A. Event

   B. Property

   C. Method

   D. Form

3. Which of the following features of a transaction determine that if any of the processing steps in the transaction fail, the transaction is aborted, and the data is rolled back to its previous state?

   A. Acidity

   B. Atomicity

   C. Consistency

   D. Durability

   E. Integrity

4. Which of the following serves as a middle-tier platform for running components?

   A. MTS Explorer

   B. Application Programming Interfaces (APIs)

   C. Resource Dispensers

   D. MTS runtime environment

5. Which of the following is proper use of commenting code? (Choose all that apply.)

   A. Dim x As Integer REM My Comment

   B. Dim x As Integer 'My Comment

   C. REM My Comment

   D. 'My Comment

6. You are attempting to install Visual Basic 6.0 on a Windows 98 machine that has 12 MB of memory. The installation fails. Why?

A. Visual Basic 6.0 won't run on Windows 98 because you need Windows NT 4.0 or higher, or Windows 95.

B. You require 32 MB of RAM

C. You require 16 MB of RAM

D. You require 16 GB of RAM

7. You are using MTS Explorer on an NT Server 4.0 machine and want to add a computer to the Computers folder. Which of the following methods will allow you to add a computer? (Choose all that apply.)

A. Right-click the Computers folder, and then select New and Computer

B. Select the Computers folder, and then click the Create new object icon in the right pane toolbar

C. Select the Computers folder, open the Action menu in the left pane, and select New

D. None of the above. There is no Computers folder in MTS Explorer.

8. You have decided to declare a variable that will contain a user's first name. Which of the following data types is the best to declare this variable as?

A. Integer

B. Variant

C. String

D. Text

9. Which tier of the application model is associated with the user interface?

A. User services

B. Business services

C. Data services

D. Middle-tier services

10. You have declared a variable called intNum with the data type of integer. How will you assign a value of 13 to this variable?

A. Dim intNum As Integer

B. 13=intNum

C. intNum=13

D. Dim intNum As 13

11. Which event is used to save information, unload forms, and perform any other tasks required when the class ends?

A. Load

B. Initialize

C. Terminate

D. End

E. Unload

12. Which of the following is used for managing and deploying components?

A. VSS Explorer

B. MTS Explorer

C. VSS Admin utility

D. MTS Admin utility

13. Which of the following can be used to assign values to a property? (Choose all that apply.)

A. Dim

B. Property Set

C. Property Let

D. Property Get

14. Which of the following keeps a record of changes made to your source code?

    A. Visual Studio

    B. Visual SourceSafe

    C. Microsoft Transaction Server

    D. Microsoft SourceCode

15. You have exported a package, and notice that a subdirectory named Clients has been created on your server computer. Inside this subdirectory, you find an executable. Executing it, you find that it has overwritten and removed settings from the Windows Registry for the server application you just exported. What must you do to restore these settings?

    A. Shut down MTS Explorer and restart it

    B. Shut down the package and restart it

    C. Reinstall MTS on your server machine

    D. Use Add/Remove Programs to remove the application, and then delete and reinstall the package in MTS Explorer

16. You need to create a new account so a user can save changes to source code to a database. What tool will you use to create the account?

    A. VSS Explorer

    B. MTS Explorer

C. VSS Admin utility

D. NT Admin utility

17. You are installing the Enterprise Edition of Visual Basic 6.0. How much disk space is required for the full installation?

    A. 48 MB

    B. 80 MB

    C. 128 MB

    D. 147 MB

18. Which of the following refers to concurrent transactions not being able to see another when they are running?

    A. Atomicity

    B. Concurrency

    C. Consistency

    D. Isolation

    E. Durability

19. You are using MTS Explorer and find that the Roles, Role Membership, and Users folders are missing. What is most likely the problem?

    A. Installation of MTS has failed, so you must remove MTS and reinstall

    B. You are using MTS on a Windows NT 4.0 machine

    C. You are using MTS on a Windows 95 machine

    D. You have Hide Roles selected on the View menu

MICROSOFT CERTIFIED SOLUTION DEVELOPER

2

Creating User Services

T he bulk of information presented in this chapter deals with making the end user's life easier. There is nothing more frustrating than not being able to get around in an application. If you don't have proper navigational design, a user won't get very far. If they do have a problem and no help is available, then you're literally risking your life with some users. Finally, if you don't implement some code to deal with errors, then you might as well tighten your own noose. Quite simply, users get irate with bad applications and bad programmers. A deciding factor of how well they rate both you and your program is ease of use and how well your application handles problems.

In addition to these issues, this chapter deals with the meat of programming—adding code to manipulate events and data. Sections in this chapter include using COM components, Data Input forms and dialog boxes, and using ActiveX. By being able to create and code such controls, components, and documents, you will be able to create robust applications.

CERTIFICATION OBJECTIVE 2.01

Implementing Navigational Design

One of my favorite cartoons deals with "making a left turn at Albuquerque" and winding up in hell. While it's great fun to watch this happen to cartoon rabbits, it is less fun when the equivalent happens to you. Good navigational design allows the user to get from point A to point B. Bad navigational design can confuse users, and take them where they have no intention of being.

Implementing navigation into your application is done with controls and menus. After adding these to a form, code is then added to the control or menu item. With these a user is able to navigate through an application, and get to other forms, dialog boxes, or applications. In this section, we will cover adding controls and menu items to an application for navigational purposes.

Menu Editor is a tool included with Visual Basic version 6 that makes implementing menus easier. Like controls, menus belong to individual forms. This means you can create different menus for each form in your application, and must specify each form's menu interface separately. By using Menu Editor, you can add, view, and delete a list of menu items for an individual form.

To use Menu Editor, you must be in Design mode and have a form open. If you are viewing code in the Code window, or have no open Forms, Menu Editor will be disabled on the menu and toolbar, and won't start if you use a shortcut key. If these conditions are met, you can then start Menu Editor in one of three ways:

- Selecting Menu Editor from the Tools menu
- Pressing CTRL-E
- Clicking the Menu icon from the toolbar

Performing any of these actions will bring up the dialog box shown in Figure 2-1.

FIGURE 2-1

The Menu Editor
dialog box

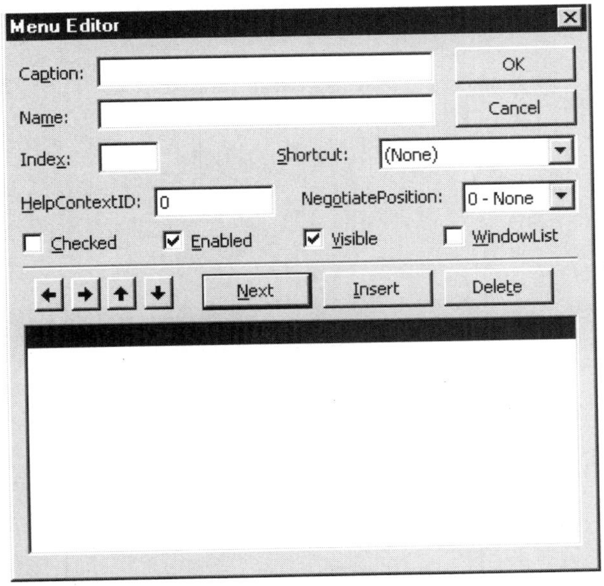

The top section of the dialog box allows you to configure menu items that will appear on your menu. Typing information into a blank menu will make a new item appear in the listbox at the very bottom of Menu Editor. If you were to select an existing item from the listbox, its properties would fill the fields in the top section. Below this upper section are four arrow buttons, along with Next, Insert, and Delete buttons. Insert allows you to add new menu items, and Delete removes existing items. Next allows you to navigate down a list of existing menu items. By clicking Next, you move to the next menu item appearing in the listbox. Finally, the four arrow buttons allow you to configure the structure of your menu.

As you build a menu interface, it takes on a hierarchical structure, similar to that seen in directories and subdirectories viewed in Windows Explorer.

The Menu Editor filled with menu items

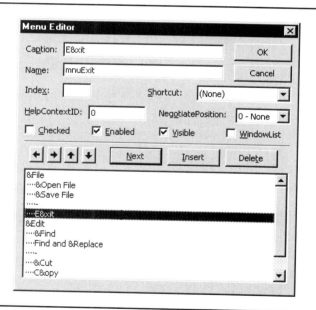

As seen in Figure 2-2, this structure consists of menu and submenu items. The left-most menu items in the listbox are what will appear at the top of your application. Examples of how this will appear are the File, Edit, View, and other menus that appear in VB. Submenus and menu items (which will appear within the menu) are indented. The right arrow button in Menu Editor is used to demote a menu item to being a submenu or menu item. If it is indented once, it becomes an item in the menu; indenting twice makes it a submenu. The left arrow button is used in a similar manner, promoting items from being items to submenus or menus. If you don't like where an item appears in the menu, the up and down arrow buttons allow you to change an item's placement in a menu. By using the arrow buttons, you are able to change the structure of your menu interface, thereby improving its appearance to the user.

In designing menu navigation, you need to plan out your menu interface and be consistent with menus. For example, it would be confusing to have an Options item appear under Edit on one form, under View on another, and under Tools on a third. A user should be able to access an item from the same menu, no matter which form is being used. In addition, you should follow patterns of menu design that have become standard for Windows applications. In every Windows application, Exit appears under File, Find appears under Edit, and a vanity screen telling "About this Program" should appear under Help. Users have become used to finding certain items under certain menus. Following a different pattern of where items appear under menus will confuse your users.

The first field on the Menu Editor is Captions. Captions are what a user sees on a menu. When you put an ampersand (&) before a letter in the caption, the user will be able to press the ALT key to access a menu item. For example, if a menu item is called File and you want the user to press ALT-F to access it, the caption would be &File. When this is viewed on the form, it will appear with the F underlined (that is, File). By using an ampersand, you are specifying the *access key* for that particular menu item.

An access key is different from a shortcut key, which you specify with the Shortcut ListBox. Shortcut keys allow a user to access a menu item at any time. An access key can only be used while a menu item is showing, and affects the appearance of a menu item by underlining a letter in the caption. However, shortcut keys will still affect the appearance of a menu item, by adding what the shortcut key is. For example, if you added a shortcut key of CTRL-A to a menu item, CTRL-A would appear beside the menu item.

The Name field is used to specify a name for your menu item. Like everything else in VB, items in your menu system must have a name. To signify that this is a menu item, you should use the prefix (called Hungarian notation) of *mnu*. In other words, if you had a menu item called File, you should use the name mnuFile. (For more information on naming conventions, refer to Appendix D of this book.) By using this naming convention, you'll be able to identify code for a menu item when you're looking through your code.

Each item in a menu system must have a different name. Menu Editor won't allow you to exit if an item is unnamed or has the same name as another item. You should also name your menu item something meaningful, as it is used for referencing in code. This is what you will use to identify and manipulate the menu item programmatically. If you want two or more menu items to share the same name, you can use the Index field.

The Index field allows you to have two or more items with the same name, but a different Index number. When the Index field is used, each item with this name becomes an element of an array. Each element is accessed through its Index number, which can be set at either 0 (zero) or 1 (one) to start the array. The largest number you can set the Index property to is 32,767, giving you up to 32,768 index numbers to work with. If you had five menu items named mnuServer, these items would become mnuServer(0), mnuServer(1), and so on up to mnuServer(32767).

The HelpContextID field allows you to set the help topic associated with this item. The value of this field is numeric, and is used to find the appropriate help topic in a help file. Using HelpContextID is explained in greater detail later in this chapter.

The NegotiatePosition listbox allows you to determine how a menu item shares menu bar space with the menus of an active object. This is used in things such as ActiveX documents (explained further in Chapter 12), which are loaded into container applications. If the ActiveX document has its own menus, it must negotiate how its menus will be displayed with those of the container application. By setting the listbox to 1-Left, 2-Middle, or 3-Right, your menu will appear on the menu along with menus from an active object. Leaving it at the default setting (0-None) will cause an item to not appear. The NegotiatePosition listbox pertains only to top-level menu items (that is, menu items that will appear at the top of your form). You cannot use NegotiatePosition to manipulate submenus or lower-level menu items, which appear under top-level items.

Below these settings are four check boxes that set the Checked, Enabled, Visible, and WindowList properties. To enable or disable any of these properties, simply click the check box. Unchecking them will disable the property, while checking them will cause the property to be enabled. The Checked property determines whether a check mark will appear beside the menu item. This property only applies to lower-level menu items, such as submenus and items that appear within a top-level menu item.

The Enabled property allows you to set whether a menu item will respond to events. If this property is unchecked, the menu item will appear grayed out and will not respond when the user clicks it. The default setting for this property is to be selected, so users can use the menu item.

Many people confuse the Visible property with the Enabled property. While the Enabled property determines if the item will be grayed out or not, the Visible property determines if the user can even see this menu element at all. If the Visible property is unselected, the menu item won't appear on the menu.

The WindowList property is used to specify that the menu control contains a list of open Multiple Document Interface (MDI) child forms in an MDI application. MDI child forms are windows that appear within your main application (such as multiple spreadsheets being open in Excel). When the WindowList property is checked, any MDI child forms will be displayed under this menu control. It will appear on the menu as a submenu, with MDI child forms displayed under it.

After you've used Menu Editor to set up your menu system, you must add code to the menu items, which will execute when the item is clicked. After closing Menu Editor, you can click on a menu item to bring up the Code window. This allows you to enter code that will execute when the user clicks an item. You'll notice that while each item has its own methods and properties, it only has one event procedure: Click. When an application is running, code will only execute when you click that menu item (or programmatically call the click code, which simulates a user clicking the menu item). No other event can execute the code associated with a menu item.

EXERCISE 2-1

Creating a Menu Interface

1. Select Menu Editor from the Tools menu.

2. Type **mnuFile** in the Name field, and **&File** in the Caption field. Click the Next button.

3. Click the right arrow button to indent this menu item. This will make this entry appear as an item under mnuFile. Type **mnuExit** in the Name field, and E**&**xit in the Caption field.

4. Close Menu Editor. On your form, click the Exit menu item under the File menu. This will bring up the Code window. Type the following code:

```
Unload Me
```

5. Press the F5 key on your keyboard to run your application. Click Exit under the File menu, and your application will exit.

In the above exercise, you'll note that we didn't specify the name of the form that we wanted to unload when the Click event of mnuExit was executed. Instead we used the Me keyword. This keyword acts as an implicitly declared variable, allowing us to unload the form without referring to its name. It will always refer to the current form, but because it was the only form in our program, when it unloaded, our program was completely shut down.

Dynamically Modifying the Appearance of a Menu

Toggling the value of properties can dynamically modify the appearance of a menu. This is useful if you don't want users to view or access a particular menu item at runtime. By setting the Visible or Enabled properties to False, you can make a menu item respectively disappear or be grayed out on a menu.

To see how this is done, let's look at the Checked property. You can toggle this property within your code, so that the check mark appears or disappears as an item is selected. For example, if you had a menu item called mnuCheck, you would use the following code to turn the check mark on or off:

```
If mnuCheck.Checked=True Then
     mnuCheck.Checked=False
Else
     mnuCheck.Checked=True
End If
```

In this code, If...Then...Else structure is used to determine if the Checked property of mnuCheck is checked. If it is, then it changed the value to False, causing the check mark to disappear. The Else statement allows mnuCheck to make a check mark appear if the value of the Checked property is anything other than True (that is, False). Similar code can be used to toggle the other three property check boxes, as each has a Boolean value (that is, True or False).

The properties for Checked, Visible, WindowList, and Enabled can be toggled by using the code: *Object.Property*=True or *Object.Property*=False. In addition to this, you can change the Caption that will appear in your menu with the syntax *Object.Caption*="New Name". By altering the property values, the menu's appearance is modified.

Adding a Pop-Up Menu to an Application

Users of Microsoft applications will be familiar with pop-up menus (sometimes called contextual menus), that appear in almost every product that Microsoft has put out. Pop-up menus are menus that appear when a user right-clicks the mouse over something on the screen, such as a command button. Many new programmers think that it takes elaborate coding skills to use this in an application. Users think that this functionality is either fairly impressive or have come to expect this in programs. The fact is, adding pop-up menus is one of the simplest and handiest procedures you'll ever use.

To add a pop-up menu, add code to the MouseDown or MouseUp event of a form or control. Both of these events take an argument called Button, which allows the procedure to determine which mouse button has been clicked. The MouseDown event is used when the mouse button is pressed, and the MouseUp event is run when the button is released. In other words, the event that runs depends on whether the button is depressed or released.

By using an If…Then statement, you specify that if the mouse button pressed is the right button, then a particular menu as a pop-up menu is shown. You can determine if the button is the right button using vbRightButton, and bring up the menu using the PopupMenu method. This is seen in the following example, which brings up the form named mnuFile:

```
If Button = vbRightButton Then
    Me.PopupMenu mnuFile
End If
```

Creating an Application that Adds and Deletes Menus at Runtime

Dynamically adding and deleting menu items is done by creating a menu control array. An array is like an expanding file folder, to which you add elements, which are like files in the file folder. Because elements can be added and deleted from an array, we are able to add and remove items to and from a menu system.

A simple way to create a menu control array starts by using Menu Editor and creating a menu item with an index number of zero. A useful item to do this to is a menu separator bar, which is created in Menu Editor by placing a hyphen in the Caption of a new menu item. A separator bar is a line that appears on a menu that separates a menu item(s) from other items on the menu. A common use of a separator bar in applications is seen above Exit on the File menu. Because the separator bar isn't as important as other menu items, you needn't worry about the array affecting other aspects of your program. As such, it is perfectly suited for use in creating a menu control array.

Once the array has been created from a menu item, new menu items can be added or removed through your code. This is made possible by first declaring a variable whose assigned value, as it is increased or decreased, will be used as the Index value of the menu array's index. A variable is used for temporary storage of the Index value, and its value is referenced by using the assigned variable's name. You create a variable by declaring it with the Dim keyword. Declaring a variable is basically telling your code, "Hey, I'm creating a temporary storage for something I'll be using later." The following code shows a variable being declared, a value being assigned to it, and its value being accessed through use of its name:

```
Dim intNum as Integer
intNum=0
Msgbox intNum
```

In the first line we declare a variable called intNum, and specify that the value it contains will be of the Integer data type. (For more information on data types, see Appendix D.) The next line assigns the value of zero to the variable. The final line of code uses the value of the variable by way of a named reference to its assigned variable name. The value of intNum is retrieved, and its value is displayed in a message box.

In using arrays, we can use a variable in place of the value of the Index. Referring to the Index number can access an element of an array. For example, if we wanted to access the fourth element of an array called MyArray, we would type MyArray(3). This assumes that the array is zero-based or that its first member has an index of zero. If the value of a variable called intNum was 3, we could access this same element by typing MyArray(intNum). By using a variable in place of the actual Index number, we can access and manipulate the elements of the array.

Since the value of a variable is accessed by invoking its name, you can manipulate the data in a variable (depending on its data type) arithmetically. As such, we can add or subtract from its value. This is seen in the following code:

```
Dim intNum As Integer
intNum=intNum+1

Load mnuItem(intNum)
mnuItem(intNum).Caption = "Menu Item" & intNum
mnuItem(intNum).Enabled = True
```

In the first line of code, the variable intNum is declared. Because it is of the Integer data type, and no value has been assigned to it, it has a default value of zero. The next line sets a new value to intNum, adding one to its current value. The following lines of code show the variable being used to create a new menu item. The Load keyword is used to load a new menu item to a menu control array called mnuItem(). Putting intNum within the parentheses passes the value (which will be the index) of this menu item. The lines of code that follow this set what caption this menu item will have, and sets the enabled property of the new menu item to True.

By passing the variables value, and using the Load command to load a new menu item called mnuItem, we have added a new menu item to the menu. By subtracting a value from the variable, we could just as easily remove a menu item by using the Unload keyword. This enables us to dynamically add and remove menu items during runtime.

Dynamically Adding and Removing Menus at Runtime

1. Create a new project by selecting New Project from the File menu. Select Standard EXE.

2. Open the Menu Editor. Since a form exists and is opened in the appropriate mode when the new project is created, the Menu Editor is available immediately. Create a new menu named mnuArray with the caption of Array. Click Next.

3. Click the right arrow button to create a menu item that will appear under the Array menu. Create a menu item named mnuAdd, with the caption of **Add Menu Item**.

4. Click Next, and create a menu item named mnuRemove, with the caption of **Remove Menu Item**. Click Next.

5. Create a separator bar. This is done by typing a single hyphen in the Caption field. Name your separator bar mnuSep, and type **0** in the Index field. Close the Menu Editor.

6. In the Code window, go to the General Declarations section of your form. To do this, click General from the left listbox (which is called the Object listbox) of the Code window, and select

Declarations from the right listbox (called the Procedure listbox). Type the following code:

```
Option Explicit
Dim intNum As Integer
```

7. By typing Option Explicit, the programmer is forced to explicitly declare variable names by using the Dim keyword and specifying what data type a variable is. If you didn't type this, misspelling a variable (such as typing inNum rather than intNum) would create a new variable of the variant type.

8. In the Code window, go to the Form Load section of your code. Choose Form from the Object listbox, and Load from the Procedure listbox. We will now assign the value of zero to intNum, so it will have the value of zero when the application starts. In the Form_Load procedure, type the following:

```
IntNum=0
```

9. In the Code window, go to the Click event of mnuAdd and type the following code:

```
intNum = intNum + 1
Load mnuSep(intNum)
mnuSep(intNum).Caption = "Menu Item " & intNum
mnuSep(intNum).Enabled = True
```

10. The first line of this code increments the counter by one. This adds one element to our array. We then tell our program to load the menu item so we can use it. The third line gives our new menu a caption (with the counter number added to make it distinct). The fourth line enables the menu so that we can use it.

11. In the Code window, go to the Click event of mnuRemove and add the following code, which will remove a menu item from the menu:

```
Unload mnuSep(intNum)
intNum = intNum - 1
```

12. Press the F5 key to run the application. As you click Add Menu Item on the Array menu, a new menu item will be added to the Array menu. Clicking Remove Menu Item will remove the last menu item added.

Adding Controls to Forms

The VB development environment includes a Toolbox that contains commonly used controls (see Figure 2-3). You can see the control's name by holding your mouse pointer over an icon in the Toolbox, and a ToolTip will appear. To add any of these controls to a form, you must be in Design mode (as opposed to viewing the Code window). To switch to Design mode, click the View Objects button located at the top of the Projects window, or select Object from the View menu. After switching to the proper view, simply double-click the icon depicting the control you want to add. The control will automatically be added to your form.

Adding a control in this fashion will create a default-sized control in the center of the currently displayed form. If you want to create a custom-sized control, simply select the control you want to use by clicking the proper icon in the Toolbox. After selecting the control, hold down your left mouse button and drag your mouse across the form.

FIGURE 2-3

Toolbox showing standard controls

Whether you've double-clicked to add the control, or drawn it with your mouse, there will be times when you want to edit the size or shape of a control. When you add a control, or select it by clicking on a control on the form, it will be surrounded by a number of colored squares called handles (as shown in Figure 2-4). By clicking on one of these handles, you can adjust the size and shape of a control. For example, after adding a command button to a form, you may want it to appear wider. By clicking the center-left or center-right handle of the control and holding down the mouse button, you can drag the control to a different width. Top- and bottom-centered handles control height, while the corner handles are used to adjust height and width simultaneously.

Adding a control inside of a frame, which is used for grouping controls that have a related purpose, is a similar procedure. By first selecting the frame in which you want a control to appear, you select a control from the Toolbox and draw it within the frame. The difference between placing a

FIGURE 2-4

Handles appear around a selected object, allowing you to adjust its size

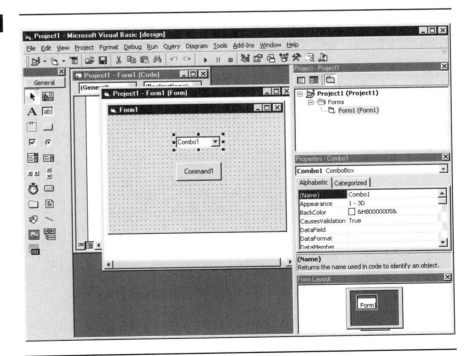

control on a form or in a frame becomes evident when you attempt moving or resizing a control within the frame. A control in a frame can be larger than the frame itself, but any areas larger than the frame aren't visible. Also, when you move a control (or part of one) outside the edge of a frame, any areas moved outside of the edge disappear from view. As such, you will have to resize the frame, then resize or move the control.

By clicking within a control and holding down your mouse, you are able to move a control anywhere on the form. This is useful when designing controls on your form, to place them in a manner that best suits conveying information to a user. For example, a TextBox control that displays first names should be moved before one that displays surnames. Being able to move controls around a form allows you to make such design changes.

on the ! Job

When arranging controls on a form, it is important to balance functionality with an aesthetically pleasing appearance. Do not cram numerous controls together, as they are difficult to follow on a screen, and be sure to use labels to explain the purpose of controls. In addition, don't make controls so big that they're unpleasing to the eye, or so small that data can't be read properly or controls are difficult to click. The best way to learn this is by looking at how applications you like are arranged and follow the way those forms are arranged.

Setting Properties for Command Buttons, Text Boxes, and Labels

Controls that you add to a form have properties that can be set programmatically at runtime, or set at Design time with the Properties window. When you add a control or select an existing one on a form, its properties appear automatically in the Properties window. If this window isn't already open, it can be accessed by selecting Properties window from the View menu, or by pressing F4.

When viewing a control's properties in this window, you'll notice that many of the properties for different controls are similar. For example, each control must have a name. It is through this window that you can alter the name, color, and other aspects of each control (see Figure 2-5). To change the value of a property, simply click the property you want to change. You will then be required to either select a property from a listbox, type in a new property (such as a name), or a dialog box will appear providing other options.

You can also change an object's property with code that will execute at runtime. This is something that we saw in Exercise 2-2, when we changed the Caption and Enabled properties of a new menu item. You can change a property by using the following syntax:

```
object.property = new value
```

If the Auto List Members feature is enabled (a feature that is found on the General tab of the Options dialog box) properties of an object will be displayed as you type. For example, let's say you added a command button named Command1 to your form. If you typed Command1 in the Code window, all properties of this object would be listed when you typed a period after the name. These properties would appear in a small pop-up listbox. After typing an equals sign (=) at the end of a property with a

FIGURE 2-5

The Properties window

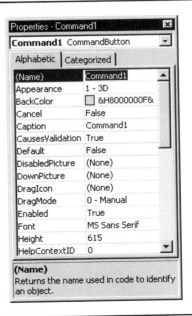

Boolean value, you would then see a small box with True and False. These members will only appear if the Auto List Members check box is checked.

Command Buttons

Command buttons have the appearance of push buttons. They are used to begin, end, or interrupt a process through code, which is added to the control. When the command button is clicked, code associated with that event is executed. The Click event is the default event for this control, meaning that it is the event that will be triggered unless another is specified. Of the various properties associated with command buttons, the Name property is that which is most commonly changed at Design time. It cannot be changed at runtime because it has a read-only value at that time. When naming command buttons, you should always add the prefix cmd to the name. This naming convention allows you to see in your code that you're dealing with a command button, and not some other type of object. The naming convention mentioned here, and explained further in Appendix D, is strongly suggested as it is most commonly used. However, if you don't use this naming convention, your and other programmers you work with should use some sort of standard naming convention.

The properties most commonly manipulated on this control at runtime are Caption and Enabled. The value of the Caption property is what appears to the user on the button face, while the Enabled property determines whether the object is dimmed. When dimmed, the caption of the control appears grayed out and can't be used by the end user. The Enabled property has a Boolean value (True or False), and can be changed in Design mode through the Properties window, or during runtime with code.

Text Boxes

Text boxes are used to obtain input from users, and return information to them. Their default behavior is to only return and accept data on a single line. This can, however, be changed. The MultiLine property allows you to configure a text box to accept text on a single line or on multiple lines. MultiLine has a Boolean value of either True or False. By default it is set to False, allowing text to appear on a single line. If MultiLine is set to True, word-wrapping will be performed and will break text into paragraphs when hard returns are used.

If you set the MultiLine property to True, you should also change the ScrollBars property during Design mode. The default value for this property is None, but you can set this to Vertical, Horizontal, or Both, allowing users to scroll down and across long pieces to text.

The first property you should change, when adding a text box to a form, is the Name property. As seen in Appendix D, the prefix for this control is txt. This will allow you to determine that the control is a text box, and not some other control. This is especially important with text boxes, as they will usually be appear with Label controls beside them. The label is often used to inform the user of the purpose of the text box. It is common to name such paired controls with similar names. Using the txt prefix will allow you to give the text box a name that's similar to its accompanying label. As such, deciphering which control is which and what they are for will be made easier.

As with other controls, the TextBox control has a default property, which in its case is Text. The value of the Text property is what appears inside of the text box. The Text property can be set at both runtime and Design time. The value of the Text property can be read at runtime by reading data from a Data control or a value set at Design time. This value can also be manipulated or set by the user at runtime, by typing in the text box itself.

Labels

Label controls are used to display alphanumeric text to a user. In other words, it can display numbers, letters, or any other kind of text-based data. Labels are commonly used to provide information about another control, such as explaining its purpose (for example, displaying what information to input into a text box). A user can't directly alter the text contained in a label, although its contents can be manipulated at runtime through code.

The Label control is depicted in the Toolbox with a capital A. As previously mentioned, the Name property is the first property you should change when adding any control. The prefix used for labels is lbl. In doing so, you can then use similar names to show the relationship between the label and another control. For example, you might have a label that states "Enter Name" placed beside a text box on a form. In naming these controls, you could have lblName and txtName. This allows you to see what type of control each is, and that they are related on the form.

The text displayed in a label is set through its Caption property. This can be set at Design time through the Properties window. As seen previously in Exercise 2-2, you can manipulate a Caption property at runtime. To change the value of the Caption property programmatically, use the following syntax:

```
label.Caption = "new caption"
```

When changing the value of the Caption property at runtime, remember to place the new value of the caption in quotes or use a variable. Failing to enclose the actual text you want in the caption within quotes will cause a runtime error, as VB will assume you want to place the contents of a nonexistent variable in the caption.

Assigning Code to a Control to Respond to an Event

You can add controls and manipulate their properties, but without code behind a control, it is little more than decoration. When an event occurs, code for that particular event procedure executes. For example, when you click on a command button, code placed in the Click event executes. This is what allows you to navigate with command buttons, run a procedure, interrupt code currently running, or stop execution of code. Clicking on the command button triggers the event procedure, and code associated with that event performs the action.

Different controls can have different events associated with them. While the CommandButton control has a Click event, the Drive control has none. The reasoning behind this is that not all events apply to all controls. For example, while a ListBox control has a Scroll event, there is no reason to have such an event in a CommandButton—no one would ever have the need to scroll down the length of a command button.

As mentioned earlier in this chapter, you can view different events through the Procedure listbox of the Code window. This is the top right listbox of the Code window. The listbox located at the top left of the Code window is called the Object listbox, which allows you to navigate through the different controls on your form. Using these listboxes together, you can go to a specific control and then assign code to a specific event procedure.

The process of assigning code to a control is virtually the same as assigning code to menu events. You assign code to a control to respond to an event through the Code window (see Figure 2-6). This window can be accessed by either clicking the View Code button on the Project window, selecting Code from the View menu, or by double-clicking a control. When you double-click a control, the Code window opens with the default event for that control. If there is no code in the default event, but another event has code in it, the Code window will open to the event containing code. Once you've gone to the event to which you want to assign code, simply type in the code you wish to use for the event.

FIGURE 2-6

The Code window

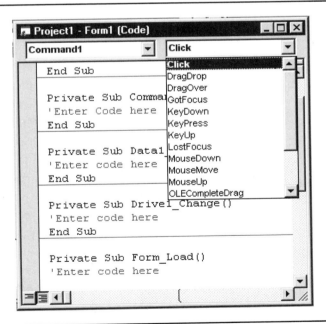

Creating Data Input Forms and Dialog Boxes

Data input forms and dialog boxes are created by combining various controls on a form. To create a data input form, you must include controls that accept some form of data input from a user. As such, you must include such things as text boxes, which accept and return data to a user. You must also include command buttons, which are used when input is completed to save or manipulate data, or to allow a user to cancel an operation. Data input forms are commonly used in database applications or programs that require users to type in data that the application saves or manipulates.

Dialog boxes are similar to data input forms in that they are also created by combining various controls on a form. Dialog boxes allow a program to interact with a user and obtain information to perform such tasks as opening and saving files, setting print options, selecting fonts, and so forth. You've seen dialog boxes whenever you've attempted to open a file in any Windows application. Because the same dialog boxes are commonly used throughout an application, you only need to create one for each task (that is, opening files, closing files, and so on) and then invoke the dialog box through controls and menus.

Because there are a number of dialog boxes you'll commonly use repeatedly in applications, VB includes different methods to quickly add certain kinds of dialog boxes to your application. The first way to add one is by adding a new form to your application. From the Project menu, select Add Form. In the Add Form dialog box that appears, you'll see several different dialog box templates that you can add to your project.

The About Dialog template allows you to add a form for telling users about the application they are using. Like all of the dialog boxes you can add to your project, the form contains a number of controls. These controls have code already assigned to them, which you can leave as is or edit. This saves you the trouble of completely coding the dialog box. Information appearing on this dialog box informs users about the application name, version number, and so on. The information appearing here is obtained from information you add to Project Properties.

The template called Dialog that appears in the Add Form dialog box adds a form that has OK and Cancel buttons. To this, you can add controls and code that will enable the user to perform a task. For example, you could add Drive, DirListBox, and FileListBox controls to the form, and add code so your user can open a file.

The Login template allows you to add a simple login screen to your application. When the user clicks the OK button, the text entered in the Password field is compared to a value in your code. If successful, an action (that you've determined) is executed through code in the OK CommandButton. If the password doesn't match, a message box appears instructing the user to try again.

The ODBC Log In enables you to add a dialog box that is used to connect to an ODBC database. This dialog box contains a number of controls, which a user configures. If you are creating a database program that connects to an ODBC database located on a server, you should use this dialog box.

Finally, the Options Dialog template adds a form to your project that contains a TabStrip control. Incorporating this in a project allows you to provide a dialog box in which users can configure the application, set preferences, and so on. By right-clicking on the tabs and selecting Properties, you will see a dialog box appear that allows you to set what each tab will represent, and various other settings.

Another way to add dialog boxes to a project is with the CommonDialog control. By adding this control to a form, you can then invoke standard dialog boxes used in Windows applications. To use CommonDialog, you must first add the Microsoft Common Dialog Control 6 to your project by selecting it from the list that appears when you select Components under the Project menu. When this is done, you can use the syntax shown in Table 2-1. For the syntax shown here to work, replace "CommonDialog" with the actual name of your CommonDialog control.

	Syntax	Description
TABLE 2-1	CommonDialog.ShowOpen	Displays an Open dialog box, used to open files.
CommonDialog syntax	CommonDialog.ShowSave	Displays a Save As dialog box, used to save files.
	CommonDialog.ShowFont	Displays a Font dialog box, for setting fonts and font styles.
	CommonDialog.ShowColor	Displays a Color dialog box, which has a color well for selecting colors.
	CommonDialog.ShowPrinter	Displays a Print dialog box, for configuring printer and print options.
	CommonDialog.ShowHelp	Used to invoke the Windows Help engine.

EXERCISE 2-3

Creating Data Input Forms and Dialog Boxes

1. Create a new project. From File, select New Project and then choose Standard EXE.

2. Add a Data control to your form. In the Properties window, select DatabaseName, and click the ellipsis button that appears in the field. The DatabaseName dialog box appears. Select the NWWIND.MDB database from your hard disk. Under RecordSource in the Properties window, select Employees.

3. On the form, create a label with the caption First Name. Beside this, create a text box. In the Properties window, erase the value of the Text property. Under DataSource, select Data1. Under DataField, select FirstName.

4. On the form, create a label with the caption Last Name. Beside this, create a text box. In the Properties window, erase the value of the Text property. Under DataSource, select Data1. Under DataField, select LastName.

5. On the form, create a label with the caption Age. Beside this, create a text box. In the Properties window, erase the value of the Text property. Under DataSource, select Data1. Under DataField, select BirthDate.

6. Add a command button to the form with the caption Add New. Double-click this control to bring up the Code window. The event in the Procedure listbox should read Click, which is the default event of the command button. In this procedure, type the following code:

```
Data1.Recordset.AddNew
```

7. From the Project menu, select Add Form. From the dialog box that appears, select About Dialog.

8. Using the Menu Editor, create a menu with the caption &Help and the name mnuHelp. Create a menu item under this menu named mnuAbout, with the caption &About. Exit from Menu Editor

9. Click on the new menu item you just created for your application, and select the About menu item. When the Code window appears, add the following code:

```
frmAbout.Show
```

10. Run the application by pressing F5. Click the Add New command button. Notice that a new record appears. Input your name and age. Click the arrow buttons on the data control to move to other records. Notice that your new record is permanently added to the database. Click the File menu, and select About. Notice that your new dialog box appears showing information about the application.

Displaying and Manipulating Data by Using Custom Controls

The controls you'll commonly use in creating an application appear on the Toolbox every time you start a new project. While these are the controls you'll use most, there may be times when you'll need special controls for certain applications. When occasions like this arise, custom controls, such as ActiveX controls, can be used.

Custom controls are stored in OCX files, and can provide all sorts of features to an application. VB comes with a wide variety of custom controls, but other OCX files can be purchased or created for your projects. For example, if you were creating an application that would be enhanced by controls that look like a car's dashboard or a plane's cockpit, you could purchase an OCX file and incorporate the controls in your project. When you use such custom controls, you must include the OCX files with the application's install disks. If you don't include them when you distribute your application to users, the custom control won't appear on any forms that use them. Since the code for custom control is contained in the OCX file, forgetting to include these files will cause runtime errors.

In the last section, you saw how to add custom components when we talked about the CommonDialog control. Custom controls are added by selecting Components from the Project menu. When this is selected, a dialog box will appear showing a list of available components that can be added to your project. In this section, we will cover custom controls which are part of Microsoft Windows Common Controls 6 (MSCOMCTR.OCX). By checking the check box beside this item and clicking OK, the controls will appear in the toolbar.

As with other controls, you can add a custom control to a form by either double-clicking a control's icon (found on the Toolbox), or selecting the icon and drawing the control on the form. Custom controls have properties that appear in the Properties window, just like other controls we've used. However, custom controls often have Property Pages as well. By right-clicking on a custom control that's been added to a form, you can view the Property Page and alter various properties of the custom control.

ListView

The ListView control enables your application to display items in one of four different views: list, large (standard) icons, small icons, and report. After it has been configured, the ListView control looks at runtime like the right pane in Windows Explorer. The way you configure the view style and other properties is through this control's Property Page. As with properties of other controls, you can set the properties and view style with either the Property window, Property Pages, or programmatically.

When using the Property Page, the General tab is where most configurations are made to the ListView control. It is here that you can set which view is used to display list items, how they will be sorted, and how they appear in the list. You can also use this tab to set whether the labels for items use single or multiple lines. If you want text in a label to be displayed over several lines, configure the ListView for multiple lines.

ImageList

Many new developers often confuse the ImageList control with the ListView control, which allows you to view a list of items as icons. ImageList isn't used to view lists in an image format, but acts as a storehouse for images you'll use in your application. The ImageList control is a repository for image files, which can be bitmaps, GIFs, JPGs, icons, or cursors. It allows you to store such files in one or more ImageList control, rather than scattering them throughout an application. By using this control, you can then provide the images it stores to other controls.

When you add one or more ImageList controls to a form at Design time, it appears as a group of squares on a button. You can add images to the control through its Property Page (see Figure 2-7). This is done by right-clicking on the control and selecting Properties from the pop-up menu. After adding the images you want, you can then call the images through your code, so they appear during runtime. Unlike many controls in

FIGURE 2-7

Images tab of the ImageList Property Page

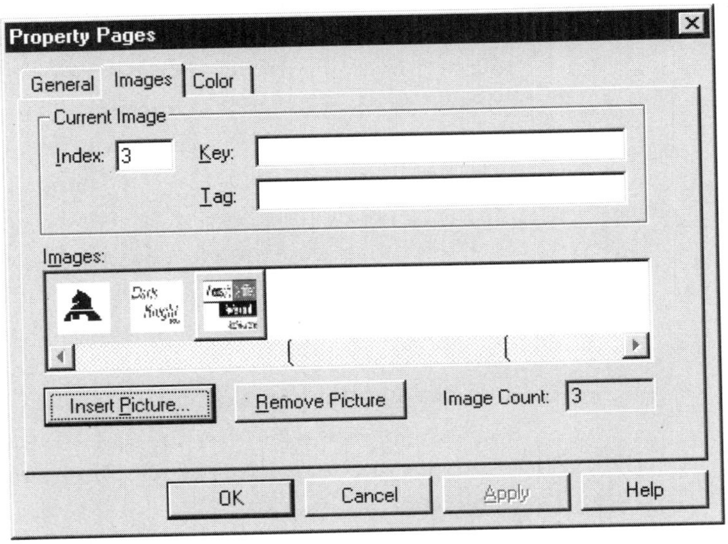

VB, ImageList isn't visible during runtime. It is a repository used by your code to call images, but is not meant for interaction with the user.

After opening the Property Page, you can add images through the Images tab. Clicking the Insert Picture button allows you to add images. When you add an image, it will have an Index number associated with it. Each image you add gets a new Index number that's incrementally advanced by one. To remove a picture from the ImageList, click the Remove Picture button. Each of the images following that image will have its index renumbered. If you removed image 1 from the ImageList, image 2 would have its index number decreased to 2. Because of this, you would need to edit your code so that instead of calling image 2, the code now calls image 1.

Toolbar

The Toolbar control allows you to add toolbars to a Form. Toolbars contain buttons that execute code when they are clicked. After adding this control to a form, you can right-click it, select Properties, and bring up its Property Page. It is here that you configure the Toolbar in Design time.

Using the Property Page for this control, you can add as many or as few buttons as you want to your toolbar. Adding and removing buttons is done from the Buttons tab. To add a new button, click the Insert Button command button. You must then type in the text you want to appear on the button during runtime in the Caption property. The ToolTip property allows you to set text that will appear when the mouse is held over the button. This allows you to give a brief description of what the button does. The Value property enables you to configure the appearance of the button, defining whether it appears sunken or raised.

Code can be associated to a button through the Code window, allowing code to be executed when a button on the toolbar is clicked. To associate code with a particular button, double-click the toolbar on your form, or navigate in the Code window to the toolbar's code. The default event for this control is ButtonClick, and it receives Button (which is the caption of the button) as an argument. By using an If...Then...Else or Select Case structure, you can set what code will run based on the value of the Button argument.

StatusBar

Anyone who's used a Microsoft product has had some experience with status bars. Status bars provide a standardized way of displaying status information to a user. It is made up of panels that display such things as what the program is doing, time and date information, whether particular keys (such as Insert, Num Lock, Caps Lock, and so on) are on or off, and so forth. The StatusBar control places a bar on a form that displays this information in different panels of the bar.

As with the other custom controls we've covered, you can set a number of properties through the Property window, but many of the important settings are done through the Property Page. After adding this control to a form, right-click it and select Properties to bring up the Property Page. Here, you can change settings that alter the form's behavior and appearance. Of the different tabs available from this page, the most important one is the Panels tab.

As mentioned earlier, a status bar is made up of various panels that display different kinds of information. As each panel in the status bar displays different information, each panel must be configured and/or programmed to display the information. These changes are made through the Panels tab of the StatusBar Property Page.

Before configuring the information you want displayed, you must add panels to your status bar. This is done with the Insert Panel button. Each panel has an Index number associated with it, and as panels are added, you can navigate from one panel's options to another by clicking the arrow buttons beside the Index number. To remove a panel, click the Remove Panel button. As was mentioned with the ImageList property, when one is removed the indexes are renumbered. Therefore, if you have three panels and the second is removed, the third panel will have its index decreased incrementally by one.

As naming a control is the first thing you do upon adding it, it follows the first property we'll cover after adding a panel is naming it. The Key property is used for this, and allows you to identify a particular panel in your code. This property is textual, and allows you to name a panel. The key should be descriptive and different from other panels.

The Text property allows you to specify what text will appear in the status bar's panel, but your text will only appear if the Style property is set to sbrText. As this setting suggests, Style isn't used to define whether the text will be bold, italic, and so on. Rather, it is used to determine what a panel's contents will be. Of the choices that appear in the Style listbox, sbrText is used to assign textual information from the panel's Text property. When this is set, anything typed in the Text property will be appear in that panel.

sbrText isn't the only Style setting to choose from. sbrCaps, sbrNum, sbrIns, and sbrScrl will display the toggle status of the Caps Lock, Num lock, Insert, and Scroll lock keys, respectively. sbrTime and sbrDate will show the time and date in a panel, respectively. The final setting that appears in the Style listbox is often confusing to Western programmers. That's because sbrKana is only used on Japanese computers that have a Kana Lock key, which toggles the display into Kanji mode. Needless to say, unless you're programming for Japanese customers, you'll probably never use this setting.

The ToolTipText property allows you to specify text that will display when a user holds their mouse pointer over a panel. You should add some description as to what the panel does, so the purpose of the panel is clear to users. At the very least, you should type the full name of the action, such as Scroll Lock. When the mouse is held over the panel at runtime, a small box appears displaying the ToolTip text.

To change the appearance of a panel, use the Alignment and Bevel properties. The Bevel property allows you to change the appearance of the border surrounding a panel. You are provided with three options for Bevel: sbrNoBevel, sbrInset, and sbrRaised. sbrNoBevel removes the appearance of a border, sbrInset gives it the appears of being sunken into the StatusBar, and sbrRaised makes it appear raised. The Alignment property determines the alignment of the contents of a panel. With this property, you can set a panel's contents to be justified left, right, or centered.

Creating an Application that Adds and Deletes Controls at Runtime

The process of adding and deleting controls at runtime is very similar to what we've already done with adding and deleting menu items. Just as we manipulated an array with menu items, you can effectively add and delete controls with an array of controls.

The first step to creating a control array is adding one control to a form in Design mode. In the Properties window, you must then select the Index property for this control and input a value (zero or one). While you must create at least one control in Design mode, you're not limited to creating only one. In creating a controls array, you can create several controls, give them all the same name, and give each an Index number that is incrementally advanced by a value of one. Another way of doing this is by copying and pasting. You add one control, such as a command button to your form, select it, and choose Copy from the Edit menu. After this is done, go back to the Edit menu and select Paste. You can do this as many times as you want to add more controls. Because they are all copies of the first control, each has the same name and will have an Index number that is automatically advanced by one. In doing either of these methods, you have created a control array.

While copying and pasting the same control or manually advancing the Index of controls that have the same name will create a control array, none of these can be deleted at runtime. They are the foundation on which new controls can be added during runtime, but it is important to remember that controls created in Design mode can't be deleted at runtime. Only controls created at runtime can be removed from an array.

To add controls at runtime, use the Load statement. You use this statement with the name of a control array, and by incrementally advancing the Index associated with the control. For example, let's say we had one command button on a form with an Index value of zero. If you wanted to add another command button to the array, so it appears on the form at runtime, you would use the following code:

```
Load cmdMyControl(1)
```

Similarly, you can remove controls from a control array using the Unload statement. If you wanted to remove the command button we just added with the above code, you would use the following code:

```
Unload cmdMyControl(1)
```

By creating one (or more) controls in Design mode that have an Index property set, you are then able to add more of these kinds of controls at runtime. If you experience any problems with removing a control at runtime, you should first ensure that you aren't trying to remove a control that was created during Design mode. Only controls added to an array at runtime can be removed.

When you add controls to an array, each of the properties for each new control are identical. If you have a label with the caption of Name and you add new labels at runtime, all of the new labels will have the caption Name. Because of this, there is a need to manipulate the controls in the array, and alter the properties for each new control.

Fortunately, there is very little difference between manipulating controls that are part of an array and manipulating independent controls that aren't part of an array. When manipulating an individual control, you state the name of the control and property you wish to change, followed by the property's new value. For example:

```
cmdOK.Caption="OK"
```

When manipulating a control that's a member of an array, you merely specify the index of the control in the array. Each control in an array has an identical name, but is distinguished from other controls by its Index number. As such, the Index is specified in parentheses after the name of the control. For example, in the following code, the fifth element of the array cmdOK is to be manipulated, and its new Caption property will have a value of Fifth Element:

```
cmdOK(4).Caption="Fifth Element"
```

But wait, if we're changing the fifth element of the array, why then does it say cmdOK(4)? Remember that an array can start with a zero or one. By starting a control array with an Index of zero, the fifth element of the array will be four.

As you can see, the difference between manipulating independent controls and controls that are part of the control array is specifying the Index. Failing to specify the Index will generate a runtime error because the program has no idea which element you want to manipulate.

Using the Controls Collection to Manipulate Controls at Runtime

Another method of manipulating controls is with the Controls collection. A collection is an object containing other objects, and in this case, represents the controls of a component. By using the Controls collection, you are able to count, access, and manipulate the controls appearing on your form.

The Count method of the Controls collection allows you to see how many controls are members of the collection. This is done with the following syntax:

```
Controls.Count
```

This is useful if you need to know how many controls you are actually dealing with.

Because the Controls collection is basically one big array of everything on a component, you can access individual members of the collection by name or index. If you wish to specify a single member, called cmdOK, that is to be the only control added to a form, either of the following code lines would access that particular member:

```
Controls("cmdOK")
```

```
Controls(1)
```

By being able to specify a collection member by name or index, you thereby have more control over which control you want to manipulate.

After specifying which control you want to manipulate, you must then specify which properties you want to change. This is the same as programmatically changing properties for other controls, and is seen in the following example:

```
Controls(1).Text="OK"
```

In the above example, we simply use the Index number (or you could use the control's name) to specify which control we want to change. We then assign a new value to the property.

Where the Controls collection really comes in handy is when you are changing the same property on large groups of objects. If you wanted to change the background color of each control on a form, you could use a For Each...Next loop to move through each control in the Controls collection. In the following example, each control is looked at and its BackColor property is changed to blue:

```
For Each Control In Controls
Control.ForeColor = RGB(255, 0, 0)
Next
```

The RGB function stands for red, green, and blue. Each number that follows in the brackets is between zero and 255 and represents the intensity of each color. Zero is no color, while 255 is the strongest intensity of that particular color. In using the Controls collection, you can set each color to blue by looping through each member of the collection.

EXERCISE 2-4

Using the Controls Collection to Manipulate Controls

1. Start a new project. In the Load Event of the form, add the following code:

```
Dim x As Integer
x = Controls.Count
MsgBox x
```

2. Press F5 to run the application. Notice that while Controls.Count counts all controls on the form, it doesn't include the form itself because it is the component in which all our controls will reside.

3. Stop the application and return to Design mode. Add a command button, label, and text box to the form. Don't change any of the default properties for these controls

4. In the Code window, go to the Click event of the command button. We will now add error handling (covered later in this chapter) to our code. By typing the following code, if an error occurs during the execution of any code in the Click event, it will ignore it and move to the next line of code:

```
On Error Resume Next
```

5. Below the error-handling statement, type the following code:

```
Controls(1).Caption = "Start"
Controls("Command1").MousePointer = 2
```

6. The first line of this code will change the caption of our command button to Start, while the second line will have the cursor appear as a cross while it is over the command button. Despite the two different ways of identifying the control, both represent the command button.

7. Below the code added in Step 5, type code that will loop through each control and change its foreground color (the color of the text) to red. The following code will perform this action:

```
For Each Control In Controls
Control.ForeColor = RGB(255, 0, 0)
Next
```

8. Press F5 again to run the application. Notice that the message box now tells us that there are three controls counted in our collection. Press the COMMAND button. Notice that by using the Controls collection, the command button's caption changes, and the mouse pointer changes to a cross. The color of text in the text box and label should now appear red, as our code loops through the various controls.

Using the Forms Collection to Manipulate Forms at Runtime

Just like using the Controls collection to manipulate controls at runtime, you can use the Forms collection to manipulate forms. Elements of the Forms collection are made up of every loaded form in the application. Its members do not include forms that haven't yet been loaded into memory.

Like the Controls collection, the Forms collection also has a Count property. This is in fact the only property that this object has, and it allows you to count how many members are part of the collection. For example, if you had an application with four forms, and three of the forms were loaded into memory, the value of Forms.Count would be three.

The Forms collection particularly comes in handy when you want to loop through all forms loaded in memory and have something done to each one. As seen in the following example, a For Each...Next loop is used to go through each loaded form. For every form encountered in the loop, an instruction is given to minimize that form.

```
For Each Form In Forms
Form.WindowState = 1
Next
```

We could have just as easily had our code perform some other action, such as changing its appearance or behavior.

CERTIFICATION OBJECTIVE 2.03

Writing Code that Validates User Input

Humans aren't perfect, but they expect their applications to be. To a point we're justified in expecting this. After all, a primary reason that computers became so popular was that software could catch mistakes made by users. Let's say a person taking customer orders in a store fails to input a credit card number, meaning the company won't be paid for goods that were ordered. While the employee may catch the boss's wrath, the application should have had some code incorporated to catch the error.

on the **!** **()** o b

The importance of validating user input is often overlooked and considered unimportant until a problem arises. An example of this is a program that was used by medical technicians to record information and walk them through procedures involving medical treatment. The original programmer hadn't bothered adding code to validate user input. As such, a day came when human error resulted in a procedure being missed. While the error was caught and no one was hurt, it could have easily resulted in a major lawsuit and medical complications. Who was at fault? The answer is clear when you consider that humans get overworked, tired, and busy. Software, on the other hand, doesn't suffer from these human frailties, and should include code that deals with mistakes, failure to input proper data, and other validation code.

Creating an Application that Verifies Data Entered by a User at the Field Level and the Form Level

There may be times when you want to determine if a user has entered the correct data into a field. This is particularly important when creating programs that require certain data to function properly. If you were creating a program that stores customer information, a required field would be the customer's name. Failing to enter such data could cause vast problems when the user tries to retrieve information and vital information isn't there.

Field Level

To verify data entered by a user, you must add code that analyzes the field's contents and determines if the input matches what you expected. For example, let's say you are creating a form that searches a database for entries containing certain words. This search engine would require the user to enter words to search for in a text box. Obviously, if nothing is entered, it can't search for anything, so you must ensure that something has been entered in the text box. In this case, you would add code to determine if the text box is empty, and then perform an action (such as a message box telling the user to enter something).

As you are analyzing the contents of a field and performing actions based on certain conditions, you must use code that executes conditionally. The common way to do this is with an If…Then structure. To look at the example stated above, you could use the following If…Then statement to perform an action, or continue processing:

```
If txtWords.Text= "" Then
    MsgBox "You must enter search criteria"
End If
```

In the first line, the Text property of a text box called txtWords is analyzed. If it equals nothing (that is, if it's empty) then the next line is processed. If something is entered, and the If…Then criteria isn't matched, then it will automatically go to code following the End If, and resume processing. The End If statement signifies where the end of this conditional code ends.

If you should require the conditions to be more elaborate, you can expand the If…Then statement to perform different actions based on several requirements. For example, if you needed to determine if a value entered was between 100 and 200, then you could use the following code:

```
If txtWords.Text < 100 Then
    MsgBox "Enter a value equal or greater than 100"
ElseIf txtWords.Text >200 Then
    MsgBox "Enter a value equal or less than 200"
Else
    'Some other action
End If
```

As with the previous example of code, the first line evaluates the contents of txtWords and performs an action if the criteria of the If…Then statement is met. However, if the criterion for the first line is not met, the ElseIf statement further analyzes the field's contents. If the criterion here is met, then it executes the next line. If neither of these previous analyses meets the criteria to execute code, then the code residing in the line following Else is used. Basically, what you are saying in your code is that if this is true then do this, or else if this is true do that, or if nothing else is true do this.

In addition to using conditional code, you can also verify user input through keystroke events. VB has three keystroke events that can be used for this purpose: KeyDown, KeyPress, and KeyUp. They occur in that order—on a keystroke, the KeyDown event executes first, then KeyPress, and finally KeyUp.

KeyPress executes when a key that's pressed represents an ASCII character. ASCII is an acronym for American Standard Code for Information Interchange. It uses numbers ranging from zero to 255 to represent keyboard characters like numbers, letters, and special characters such as ! @ # $ % ^ & * ( ). The KeyPress event has a single parameter of KeyASCII that has an integer value that relates to the ASCII value of zero to 255.

By adding code to the KeyPress event of a control, you are able to analyze which key was pressed, and then perform an action based on the key used. The following example of code is often used when creating applications that use e-mail. Since UNIX computers expect lowercase letters and the Internet is based on and still uses UNIX servers, e-mail addresses are lowercase. By adding this code to the KeyPress event of a text box, the ASCII value of a pressed key will be analyzed as being upper- or lowercase. If it is uppercase, it is automatically converted to lowercase.

```
Char=Chr(KeyAscii)
KeyAscii=Asc(Lcase(Char))
```

KeyDown occurs when a user depresses a key, while KeyUp occurs when that key is released. The reason for separating one keystroke into these two separate events is to give the programmer greater flexibility as to when code is executed. Both of these events look at KeyCodes, which are constants in VB that represent certain keys. The reason a KeyCode is used to look at a key rather than an ASCII value (as done with KeyASCII), is to allow events to occur when navigation and function keys are used. Such keys aren't recognized by the KeyPress event, and are only detected by KeyUp and KeyDown.

Each of the KeyCode constants can be viewed in VB's Help documentation, and can be identified by their prefix, vbKey. Each of these constants start with this prefix. By using KeyCode constants, you can control what occurs when certain keystrokes occur. An example of its use is seen in the following code:

```
If KeyCode = vbKeyF5 Then
    MsgBox "You pressed F5"
End If
```

When the F5 key is pressed or released—depending on whether you place the code in KeyDown or KeyUp, respectively—code is executed. In this case a message box is displayed, but a number of actions could be executed. The important thing to remember about KeyCode constants is that you are able to verify input by the key a user presses.

In addition to keystroke events, you can use the Validate event to verify that data has been input correctly. This event is triggered when a record pointer moves off the current record. It is at that time when changes to the copy buffer are written to data, and improper data input can cause problems. Because the Validate event occurs at this time, you can add code to this event to stop the control from losing focus.

When a control's CausesValidation has its property set to True, the Validation event causes the event to keep focus. In other words, a user cannot move from one control to another until certain criteria is met. The syntax for using the Validate event is as follows:

```
Private Sub object_Validate(KeepFocus As Boolean)
```

When the argument KeepFocus is set to True, the current control keeps the focus, thereby disallowing the user to move to another control. By adding code within this event, you can control the user's ability to move to another control.

Form Level

In addition to verifying input at the field level, you can verify input at the form level. This allows you to verify data input regardless of which control on the form is used. Rather than having to place code in every text box, combo box, and other control that accepts input, you are able to organize verification code. This saves a procedure from becoming incredibly long and confusing.

The first step to verifying input at the form level is adding code to the General Declarations section of your form. You will declare a variable and assign the value of a property here such as the Text property of a text box. You then invoke a procedure that takes this variable and does the actual verification. An example of this is seen in the following code:

```
Dim strName as String
strName = txtName.Text
VerifyText
```

Since you've called a procedure, you must create it. In the General section, the new procedure is created and ended with the following code

```
Private Sub VerifyText()
End Sub
```

Between this, you add the code that will evaluate the variable (in this case, strName), and perform some action based on its value. For example, if we wanted to determine if a field was blank, and inform the user to enter something, we could add the following code:

```
If strName = "" Then
    MsgBox "Please type your name"
End If
```

Creating an Application that Enables or Disables Controls Based on Input in Fields

When you installed VB, you saw a screen where you had the choice of accepting the end user agreement or exiting. You weren't able to continue if you disagreed with the license—because your lawyer wasn't handy or some other reason—because controls were disabled based on a negative response. Just as Microsoft had this feature in their setup program, VB allows you to enable and disable controls in your own applications.

Enabling Controls Based on Field Input

When a control is enabled, it will react to actions such as mouse clicks or data input. For example, if you have a text box that's enabled, you can enter text in it. By manipulating the Enabled property of a control, you can configure a control to be enabled.

To use the example of the VB setup program, let's say you had an application with two option buttons, and a command button that has its enabled property set to False. If the user clicks on the first button and accepts your agreement, the command button is enabled. This is done through the following code:

```
Private Sub optAccept_Click()
cmdNext.Enabled = True
End Sub
```

In this code, when the option button called optAccept is clicked, the command button called cmdNext is enabled.

Disabling Controls Based on Field Input

Just as you can enable controls based on field input, you can also disable controls by manipulating the value of the Enabled property. Setting the Enabled property to False does this. When this property is set to False, it appears grayed out and doesn't accept any user input. In the case of a command button, the user can click it, but nothing will happen. Similarly, a disabled text box won't accept any data input.

Using the previous example, if the user clicked a second option button that declined your agreement, the command button would be disabled through the following code:

```
Private Sub optDecline_Click()
cmdNext.Enabled = False
End Sub
```

In this example, when the option button called optDecline is clicked, the command button called cmdNext has its Enabled property set to False. As a result, it appears grayed out and won't react when clicked.

CERTIFICATION OBJECTIVE 2.04

Writing Code that Processes Data Entered on a Form

In this chapter, we've seen that you can add code to a form, and controls on a form. We've also seen that there are a number of events associated with both controls and Form objects that determine when code is processed. In writing code that processes data entered on a form, it is important to understand when such events are used and how to use them.

While each of the following Form events are covered in greater detail in the next section, it is important to understand the relative timing of these Form events. Adding code in the wrong order can cause all sorts of problems with your code. If you want one piece of code to be executed before code is executed in another event, it is important to understand when these events are triggered. Table 2-2 shows the order in which events are triggered as a form is loaded and then unloaded from memory.

TABLE 2-2	Events that occur when a form is loaded into memory	
Order of events when a form loads in and out of memory	Initialize	Occurs when an instance of a form is created.
	Load	Occurs when a form is loaded into memory.
	GotFocus	Occurs when there are no enabled or visible controls on the form. This is the case when implementing splash screens in your application.
	Events that occur when a form becomes the active form	
	Activate	Occurs when the form becomes the active window, or when it becomes visible with the Show or Visible property.
	GotFocus	Occurs when there are no enabled or visible controls on a form.

TABLE 2-2

Order of events when a form loads in and out of memory (*continued*)

Events that occur when another form becomes the active form	
LostFocus	Occurs when there are no enabled or visible controls on a form.
DeActivate	Occurs when the user switches from one form or window to another.
Events that occur when a form is unloaded from memory	
QueryUnload	Used to prompt user to save changes or cancel the Unload event.
Unload	Occurs when a form is unloaded from memory.
Terminate	Occurs when all variables in a form have been set to nothing.

exam
ⓦatch

Questions may arise on your exam that deal with the order in which a form's events occur. Review Table 2-2 before going into your exam.

Adding Code to the Appropriate Form Event

After understanding when an event is triggered, it is important to place code in the appropriate Form event. While you may realize that the Load event occurs before Activate, it does no good to you if your code is in the Load event and a user is switching from one window to another using ALT-TAB. Because the form is already loaded, any code you wanted executed wouldn't be triggered by this action since the form is already in memory. As such, it is just as important to understand why an event is triggered, as it is to understand when it is triggered.

Initialize

Initialize is triggered when an instance of a form is created. The only time this event occurs is when a form is created by an application.

Terminate

The Terminate event is the last event triggered in a form, and occurs when all variables in a form are set to nothing.

Load

Load, as its name suggests, is triggered when the form loads into memory. It is usually used to set form-level variables, properties, and other startup code.

Unload

Unload is where code is usually placed that unloads any other forms that are still open, cleans up variables, and clears other memory space used by an application. It is used for such cleanup code so that memory isn't used for data that's no longer needed.

QueryUnload

QueryUnload is commonly used for prompting the user to save changes or asking if they *really* want to leave your lovely application. This is useful for giving the user a chance to cancel the unload because this event takes place before the unload event. As such, no cleanup code has been triggered at this point, and data still resides in memory.

Activate

Activate is an event that occurs when a form becomes the current window. For example, if the user uses ALT-TAB or the Show or Visible property is used to make the window visible, the Activate event is triggered. It is particularly useful for graphic programs that require code to redraw an image when the window becomes visible.

Deactivate

While Activate triggers when a window becomes active, Deactivate is an event that occurs when the form is no longer the active window. When a user uses ALT-TAB, or clicks on another window, this event is triggered. It can be used for code that you want to execute in the background, when the user is working in another window.

Adding an ActiveX Control to the Toolbox

Adding an ActiveX control to the Toolbox is as easy as adding any other custom control. By selecting Components from the Project menu, or pressing CTRL-T, the Components dialog box will appear. This contains a listing of all the components you can add. Check boxes beside available component names are used to select a particular component.

If the component you want to add isn't listed in the dialog box, click the Browse button and the Add ActiveX Control dialog box will appear. This allows you to search through folders on your local hard disks and the network for the component you wish to add.

Upon selecting the components you want to add to the Toolbox, click the OK button. An icon, or icons, representing the control(s) you've added will appear in the Toolbox. To use a new control, simply double-click its icon, or select the icon and draw your control on a form.

Creating Dynamic Web Pages by Using Active Server Pages (ASP)

Web pages are written using the Hypertext Markup Language (HTML). A new innovation to Web pages has been Dynamic HTML, which provides the ability to dynamically change the content of a Web page. For example, with Dynamic HTML, you can manipulate text, add stock tickers to a Web page, or read, process, and respond to a user's input on a form. By using Active Server Pages (ASP), you can create dynamic Web pages and build Web applications.

ASP is a scripting environment in which processing of scripts takes place on a network or Web server. In using ASP, you can use scripting languages such as VBScript to create dynamic Web pages. ASP files have the extension .ASP. These files contain HTML tags, text, and script, and can call ActiveX components to perform various tasks. For example, by using ASP you can create Web pages that connect to databases, perform calculations, and return various results to the user.

When you create an Internet Information Server (IIS) application (by selecting New Project from the File menu, then choosing IIS Application), you create Web classes. These are components that reside on a server and service requests from browsers. For each Web class you create, an ASP file is created during compilation that is associated with the Web class. It is through these Web classes that you can create .DLL programs, which are stored on IIS to service browser requests.

After starting a new IIS application, you can add new Web classes to your project by clicking on the Project menu and selecting Add WebClass. By selecting the Web class you wish to work on from the Project window and clicking View Code, you are then able add code to it. It is here that you actually program the Web class. When you compile or run the project, an ASP file is created for each Web class automatically.

CERTIFICATION OBJECTIVE 2.07

Using Data Binding to Display and Manipulate Data from a Data Source

Before you can use data in a data source, such as an Access database, controls on your form must be *bound* to the data source. Binding means that your control is linked or tied to a data source, so it can access data contained within it. Once it can access this data, you can manipulate the data contained within.

The first step to binding a data consumer (that is, a TextBox, DBCombo, or some other control) to a data source, is to add to a form the controls you require. Deciding which controls to add takes some forethought, taking into consideration design issues for determining which parts of the database you wish to display which forms. In addition to adding text boxes and other controls to display the data, you must also add a Data control to the form. This is the control you will use to connect to a particular data source.

The Data control takes a bit of configuration before you can start binding data to controls. Select the Data control on your form and go to the Properties window. Here you will start configuring the Data control by setting the Connect field. The Connect field lists a number of types and versions of data sources, including Access, Dbase, FoxPro, text, and so on. You need to specify the type of database to which you're connecting before continuing. Having done this, select the DatabaseName property, click the button that appears with an ellipsis. You are then able to browse your local hard disk or network for the database you want to use. Once you select the appropriate database, select the RecordSource property. This allows you to select a table or query from the database, which you then use to bind to data consumers.

Once you've added the necessary controls, you are ready to configure these data consumers so they are bound to the data source. Selecting a control, you then go to the Properties window and set the DataSource field. This field allows you to set which data control you wish to use for this particular control. This field is useful when you are using several Data controls to access various information, and bind it to different controls on a form. In addition, you must also set the DataField property and select which field of data you want to appear in your control. Having done this, your data control is bound to a data source, and you are ready to run and use the application.

In addition to binding a data consumer to a data source at Design mode, VB also enables you to set the DataSource during runtime. This is new to VB version 6 and wasn't available in previous versions. Previously, you could only set the DataSource in Design mode.

exam
⚙atch

Microsoft likes touting the new features of a product in their exams. Remember that in versions previous to VB version 6, you were unable to set the DataSource during runtime. You were only able to set this at Design mode in previous versions.

Data binding at runtime is similar to setting the value of other properties programmatically. The following code shows how this is done:

```
Text1.DataMember="Employees"
Text1.DataField="LastName"
Set Text1.DataSource=Data1
```

Each property of the data consumer called Text1 is assigned a value. The DataSource is set using the Set keyword, to assign the Data control as the DataSource of the control. The ability to do this enables you to change the DataSource programmatically and gives you the ability to switch data sources at runtime.

Instantiating and Invoking a COM Component

COM is an acronym for *component object model* and allows different objects to interact with one another. It is a standard that defines how different objects can communicate with one another and how separate components can manipulate each other.

Not only does it allow you to employ reusable components, but enables you to use objects that are exposed by existing programs (such as Microsoft Excel). An exposed object is an object (such as a control in a different program) that your program can "see." Since it can see the object, it can manipulate it. Exposing objects is covered in more detail later in this book.

COM is a specification on which both ActiveX technology and OLE are based. *OLE* is an acronym for object linking and embedding, and it is an older form of COM. It has been replaced by ActiveX components, which have increased functionality, but you will still find elements of OLE around. This is seen in control events like OLECompleteDrag, OLEDragDrop, OLEDragOver, and others. These names are leftovers of OLE, while the events themselves are still used when dealing with ActiveX components.

ActiveX components have an object structure that is visible to the ActiveX client application. Objects that are visible to other programs are known as exposed objects. However, for an object to be exposed, it must be listed in the Windows Registry.

In documentation prior to 1996, ActiveX components were referred to as OLE Automation Servers; this term occasionally pops up today. It is a term that often leads to confusion, as many people new to ActiveX think that the server portion must reside on an actual network server. This is not the case. ActiveX components expose objects to other applications, and it doesn't matter if these components are on the local machine or a network server. The important thing to remember is that it exposes or serves up objects for other programs to use.

Creating a VB Client Application that Uses a COM Component

When using COM components in an application, you must set a reference to the application that will expose objects to your application. This is done by selecting References from the Project menu, and then selecting a library from the list of references that appears. Each of the libraries in the reference list have been registered with the Windows Registry.

After selecting the library you want to use from the list, your next step is using the ActiveX component name and classes. This means using the objects available in the library. Since it is difficult at best, and nearly impossible the rest of the time, to know each of the objects available in a library, pressing the F2 button on your computer will bring up the Object Manager. The Object Manager displays all objects in your current project, VB, and any objects exposed to it through the library you selected from References.

In using ActiveX components in your code, you must create and instantiate object variables for the ActiveX component classes. To do this, you use standard object declarations, with the CreateObject and GetObject functions or the As New keyword. To declare an ActiveX component as an object, use the following syntax:

```
Dim variable As New Object
```

To be more specific, using the following syntax would declare a variable called objX as a new instance of the Microsoft Excel application:

```
Dim objXL As New Excel.Application
```

In addition to using the standard Dim to declare an ActiveX component, you can also use the Set keyword to return a reference by returning its value to a variable. This is done using CreateObject and GetObject. GetObject is used when an instance of an object provided by an ActiveX component is running. If no instance of an object is running, use CreateObject. This will create an instance of an object provided by an ActiveX component and return a reference to it. Using the same variable and application as above, you would use the following syntax to perform this action:

```
Set objXL = GetObject ("Excel.Application")
```

or

```
Set objXL = CreateObject ("Excel Application")
```

Though the above code does exactly the same thing as the As New example, there is a reason why these two variations exist. Many ActiveX components don't support As New, and in such cases must use CreateObject or GetObject.

After declaring the variable in your code, you are ready to evoke an exposed object in your code. This is straightforward and consists of tunneling down to the procedure you want to use. In other words, you start by stating the name of the COM component, then stating the class you want to use, and finally the procedure. The following shows the syntax to use:

```
Servername.classname.procedure
```

To show a more specific example, the following example affects the Access application and evokes the Quit procedure. When running this snippet of code, you would shut down Access:

```
Access.Application.Quit
```

Creating a Visual Basic Application that Handles Events from a COM Component

Handling events from a COM component is done with the WithEvents keyword. WithEvents can be used in the context of Private, Public or Dim, and is best understood by looking at an example:

```
Public WithEvents AccRep As Access.Report
```

After typing this in, you can check the object section of your Code window (the left combo box), and see that it is now listed as an object of the form. You'll also see that the right combo box lists all events associated with that object. You can now handle events of the ActiveX component as if it were an object you created as part of your own application.

Creating Call-Back Procedures to Enable Asynchronous Processing Between COM Components and Visual Basic Client Applications

Asynchronous processing allows code to execute separately from other events or processes. In other words, it is what allows code to be processed, and allows the user to do something else. Without asynchronous processing, a client application might make a method call to an ActiveX component, but would have to wait for the component to return the call. This is what's called *synchronous processing*. Asynchronous processing frees the application so other code can be executed while it waits for a COM component to finish processing. Using asynchronous processing makes for more robust applications because the client can do several things at once.

An example of asynchronous processing is when a COM component is used to query a database located on a server. If a query was made for all customers with the first name of John, a significant amount of time might pass before a result is returned. If synchronous processing is used, a significant amount of time may be wasted waiting for a result. This decreases productivity.

If asynchronous processing is used, the user is able to continue work using the client application while waiting for a result to be returned.

There are several steps asynchronous processing must go through to complete a task. The first step occurs when the client application makes a method call, which initiates the task, but doesn't instantly return a result. Since asynchronous processing is being used, the client is able to perform other tasks while the COM component works on its task and return a result. As it is asynchronous and takes an unknown time to return a result, the COM component must provide some notification that it has finished and returned as result.

Asynchronous notifications are vital to the effectiveness of asynchronous processing. If no notification is given, a user may never realize that a result has been returned. To provide such notifications, you can use events or call-back methods. Between these methods, it is easier to provide notification by raising an event.

Raising an event for asynchronous notification is a dual responsibility: the first part is the responsibility of the COM component's author, and the second part is the responsibility of the developer (who writes applications that use the COM component). The reason for this is that the author of a COM component has to define which tasks and notifications will be performed and provide externally creatable classes for managing notifications. The class or classes have to be provided with methods that a developer can call on. Without these methods, there is no way to initiate various tasks of the components or provide a way to request notifications. Events handled by clients must also be declared so that these clients can receive notification. Code is then written that starts tasks and watches for things that the component will find meaningful. Finally, code is written to raise the event when a task is complete or when something meaningful has occurred. When this is all done, the author's job is finished, and the client developer's job begins.

When you use the COM component, you create a WithEvents variable. This variable contains a reference to the object that provides notification. Event procedures associated with this variable will contain code to handle notification events. Code must also be written that makes a request of the COM component and calls the methods that perform the required tasks.

Implementing asynchronous processing has two parts; it starts at the component side and is completed on the side of the client application. When the COM component's author and the developer using the component follow procedures correctly, asynchronous processing can be achieved. For more information pertaining to this and other Advanced Client/Server Technologies, see Chapter 9.

Implementing Online User Assistance in a Distributed Application

One of the biggest mistakes that developers often make is forgetting what it was like the first time they logged on to a network or used an application. It can be frightening when a new user (or *newbie*, as they're often affectionately called) experiences a problem. When a newbie finds that there is no online user assistance or the Help provided is poor, it's even worse. While experienced users may attempt trudging through an application with little or no assistance, a newbie may give up and uninstall the application you've worked so hard to create. To a point, they're completely justified. Inadequate or nonexistent online user assistance is a sign of a poor application and a lazy developer.

There are many different kinds of online user assistance, and VB includes features and tools that allow you to implement help into your application. What's This Help, Messages, HTML documents, and other forms of help can aid a user when they're having difficulties. By implementing these, you will enhance a user's experience with a program and develop applications that are more functional and robust.

Setting Appropriate Properties to Enable User Assistance

For user assistance to be enabled in a project, you must set certain properties so help files can be accessed and help can be displayed. Help files contain organized information that can be displayed when a user presses F1, selects a Help feature from the Help menu, or performs some other action that invokes Help. Standard help files are written with programs like Microsoft Word, then compiled with a special compiler and stored in a binary format. In addition, there are HTML help files that are written and compiled in (you guessed it) HTML. To display this information in a project, you must set certain properties to invoke the help files.

Help can be added to your project in Design mode or runtime. Adding help in Design mode is done through the Project Properties and the Properties window of each control and form. After adding such things as help files to your project in Design mode, you can change these properties programmatically, so their values alter at runtime. In doing so, you can change such things as the help file your project uses.

HelpFile

Setting which help file a project will use is done through Project Properties, which is located on the Project menu. After clicking this menu item, a tabbed screen will appear. Most of the setting for help is done on the General tab of this dialog box. On this tab there is a field titled Help File Name. By inputting the path and filename of your help file, you can set which help file your project will use.

When you implement help files into your VB project, it is important to remember that you can only use one help file at a time. This is not to say that you can only use one help file throughout your project, just that your application is unable to point to multiple files at any given point. If you need your project to switch from one help file to another, you can change the file used during runtime via code.

Assigning a Help file during runtime is done programmatically. By using the following example of code, you can change which help file is associated with the program:

```
App.Helpfile= "C:\Win98\Helpfile.hlp"
```

In this line of code, the application's help file points to a file called HELPFILE.HLP, which is located in the Win98 directory. By using such code, you can to switch from one help file to another throughout your application as needed.

HelpContextID

HelpContextID is a property that you can configure to provide context-sensitive help in your application. When this has been set, a user can press F1 (or some other method of invoking context-sensitive help) and view help that deals directly with a specific item. For example, if a user had a specific control selected and pressed F1, information pertaining to that control would appear in a Help window. To configure HelpContextID for an object, you need to set the HelpContextID property in either the Properties window or in your code. If you wish to set the HelpContextID programmatically, you can use the following syntax in your code:

```
Object.HelpContextID=number
```

HelpContextID is initially set to a value of zero (0). When it has this default value, it signifies that no help is associated with that object. If the user should invoke help for a control that has the HelpContextID set to zero, help for the container or parent object (such as the form) will be displayed.

Because accidents and errors can happen anywhere, it is wise to understand what will happen when an invalid value is entered for the HelpContextID. An invalid number is a value of the HelpContextID that doesn't exist or can't be found. If this is encountered, the request for help is ignored. In other words, the user can press F1 until the cows come home, but there is no context sensitive help with that particular HelpContextID, so nothing will happen.

WhatsThisHelp

WhatsThisHelp is a property that enables "What's This" help in your application. When a user invokes What's This, a pop-up screen is displayed that provides context-sensitive help for an object. The value of WhatsThisHelp is Boolean (that is, True or False), and can be set in the Properties window. It has a default setting of False, so if you wish to enable What's This–style help for a form, you will need to set it to True.

The WhatsThisHelp property is used to turn on the ability to use What's This help. After enabling this ability, you must still set an ID number for each object on the form. This ID is set through an object's

WhatsThisHelpID property. The purpose of WhatsThisHelpID is similar to that of HelpContextID, which was covered in the previous section. It is used to associate an object with a particular help topic.

Creating HTML Help for an Application

VB has always used standard help files, which have the extension of .HLP. These are text files that have been compiled into a binary format. VB version 6 has taken this a step further by allowing developers to incorporate help created with HTML, which is commonly used to create Web pages. HTML help is created from HTML documents, which have been compiled into files with a .CHM extension.

The first step to creating HTML help for an application is creating HTML documents. These can be created with any text editor, such as Notepad, or programs that are specially designed for creating Web pages, such as FrontPage. When you have created your help documentation, you compile them into a CHM file. To do this, you need to use a special program like HTML Help Workshop, which is part of Visual Studio 6.0.

HTML Help Workshop allows you to create new HTML files, import existing HTML documents, and compile them into the format used for help. Using the program is relatively simple, but it requires the user to have existing HTML documents or a knowledge of HTML.

After compiling the HTML documents into help files, you must then configure your project to use that help file. From the Project menu, select Project Properties, then go to the General tab. In the Help File Name field, type in the path and filename of the CHM file your project will use.

Should you wish to change from the help file set in Project Properties to another HTML Help file, you must do so programmatically. As is the case with standard help files, only one help file can be set for the project, although switching from one help file to another can be done via code. In the following example, the help file is set to an HTML Help file.

```
App.Helpfile= "C:\Win98\HTMLHelp.chm"
```

Except for the extension being .CHM, the process of setting which help file is used is identical to that seen with standard HLP files.

Implementing Messages from a Server Component to a User Component

Help is important in every area of programming, and ActiveX components are no different. When creating ActiveX servers, you can associate help files just as you would a desktop or client application. After selecting Project Properties from the Project menu, click the General tab and enter the projects help file in the Help File Name field. You can also specify a context ID by setting an ID number in the Project Help Context ID field. This help can be accessed when creating a client application that uses the ActiveX server.

When an ActiveX server has been registered with the Windows Registry, it can be included in other projects. This is done by selecting References from the Project menu, and selecting the server component from a listing of available references. When the reference to the ActiveX server has been set, you are ready to access its help.

If you require help on an ActiveX component when writing the client application, you can press F2 to bring up the Object Browser (see Figure 2-8). The Object Browser allows you to view the classes, events, methods, properties, and constants in a project. It is used to find objects you've created and those in other applications. In addition to these functions, you can also get help on an ActiveX server component.

Under the Project/Libraries listbox (located in the top left corner), select the server component you are using. Selecting <All Libraries> will show everything available to Object Browser, but it can be somewhat confusing to browse through due to the sheer number of objects available. After selecting your server component, the classes and modules of the component will be listed in the left pane. By selecting a class from the left pane, the right pane will display all of the class's methods, properties, and events. When you choose a method, property, or event from the right pane, a brief description of the object appears at the bottom of the Object browser. If you require help beyond that offered by the description, you can click the ? button to view extended help on that object. This extended help is retrieved from the help file of the server component.

FIGURE 2-8

The Object Browser

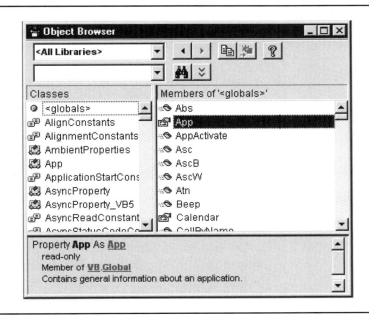

The information provided in the description field at the bottom of the Object Browser can also be edited. This is particularly useful when dealing with items that have no description. By right-clicking on an object and selecting Properties, you will see a Member Options dialog box, shown in Figure 2-9. In the description field for this item, you can enter a new

FIGURE 2-9

The Member Options dialog box

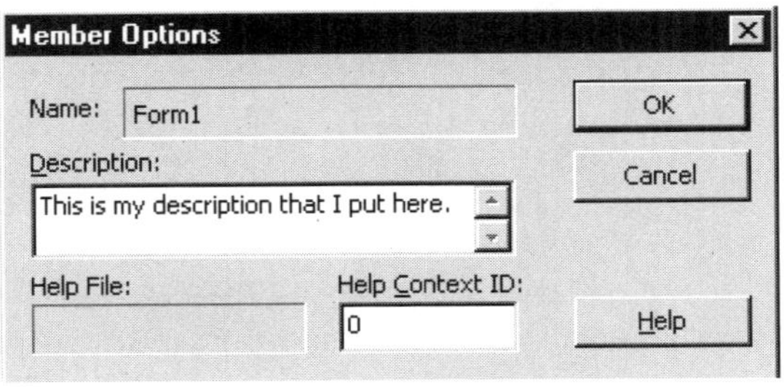

description. After exiting the dialog box, you will see this new description at the bottom of the Object Browser each time the item is selected.

To provide extended help for a server component's objects, you must have a help file with help topics for each item you want to provide extended help for, and valid context ID numbers that point to a topic. If you don't know the context IDs or possess the help file, you won't be able to implement help for the component in your project. If you have this, you can then go to the General tab of Project Properties (accessed from the Project menu) and enter the path and filename for the help file in the Help File Name field. This will allow the client application to access the help file.

Having done this, you can then attach a help file topic to an item in your project, and thereby provide context-sensitive help. By right-clicking on the item you wish to apply extended help to—either the class from the left pane, or the method, property, or class from the right—you must then select properties to bring up the Member Options dialog box. It is here that you will enter the context ID in the Help Context ID field.

Notifications

When an ActiveX client makes a call to an ActiveX server that cannot service a request, the server component will send one of two notifications to the client. A Component Busy notification rejects a request, while Request Pending informs the client that the request has been received but can't be serviced immediately.

When an ActiveX server sends a Component Busy notification to a client, VB attempts retrying the request. The request is resent until a timeout interval is reached, at which time the request is canceled and a Component Busy dialog box is displayed. This timeout interval can be set through the OLEServerBusyTimeout property of the App object. This property has a Long value, and is used to set the number of milliseconds before a request times out. By default, the value of this property is 10,000, which equals to 10 seconds. By setting the property to a value greater than 86,400,000—the number of milliseconds in a day—requests to the server component will continue indefinitely.

Two other properties of the App object allow you to change the text that appears in the Component Busy dialog box. OLEServerBusyMsgTitle allows you to set the text that will appear in the title bar of this dialog box. OLEServerBusyMsgText allows you to set the message text appearing in this dialog box. Both of these properties have string values and are set programmatically.

When a request can't be performed right away, a Request Pending notification can be sent to the client application. This notification is sent if a request is pending and the user attempts to close or minimize the ActiveX server or client application. Like the Component Busy notification, properties of the App object can be used to alter the Request Pending dialog box and the timeout interval.

The OLERequestPendingMsgTitle property of the App object alters the text that appears in the title bar of the Request Pending dialog box. In addition, you can programmatically change the OLERequestPendingMsgText to modify the message text that appears in this dialog. Both properties have a String value.

You can also change the amount of time before the Request Pending dialog box is displayed to a user. OLERequestPendingTimeout is a property of the App object; it defines how long before the Request Pending dialog box is shown to a user. It has a Long value, and its default value is 5,000 milliseconds, or five seconds. By setting this property to a value greater than 86,400,000, or one day, the request will continue to be made indefinitely.

CERTIFICATION OBJECTIVE 2.10

Implementing Error Handling for the User Interface in Distributed Applications

Just as people occasionally need help, so does the code of an application. Error-handling routines are just what they sound like—they handle errors that occur during processing of code and provide solutions to problems that arise. For example, if a user lost his or her connection to the network, error-handling code could be used to inform the user that he or she is no longer on the network, and give the option of reconnecting. Another example would be if your program experiences a divide-by-zero error and attempts to close down, error-handling code can be implemented to allow a user to save changes to data before the program shuts down. When errors occur, these routines are what an application uses as a crutch. It relies on such code to provide a solution to what could be a disastrous problem.

Because of the importance of error-handling routines, you should thoroughly test this code to ensure that they are functioning properly. This code deals with problems occurring in other parts of your code. As such, they have great responsibility for making sure that an error doesn't cripple the application, or—if an error does cripple it—allows the user to save information before exiting. Remember that nobody's perfect, but your error handling routines should be as close to perfect as possible.

Identifying and Trapping Runtime Errors

In the old days of programming, names attributed to things were either inane or blatantly obvious. Runtime errors fall into the latter category. A runtime error is an error that occurs at the time an application is running. The reasons they occur are various . . . a user forgets to insert a floppy disk when saving, tries to open a file that doesn't exist, or tries to access a network server that's been shut off. These are often errors that can't be completely avoided, but they can be *trapped*. Trapping a runtime error involves writing code that catches errors when they occur. This allows error-handling routines to correct, or offer a chance to deal with, the error.

Error-handling routines are code that checks the error, handles the error in some way, and then exits the error handler so processing can continue. The first step of implementing error handling is to turn on an error trap. The On Error statement enables error trapping and redirects execution to code that deals with the error. Error traps stay enabled until one of two things happen: the error-handing procedure ends or the trap is disabled.

To redirect an error to the error handler, you must follow the On Error statement with the GoTo statement and the name of your error-handling routine. This is shown in the following example:

```
On Error GoTo ErrHandler
```

Because of this statement, when an error occurs, execution will be redirected to code preceded with the label ErrHandler. You can create a label by simply writing a name followed by a colon (:). Any code following this will deal with the errors encountered.

To trap and deal with errors, there must be some way to determine what the error is and return information about it. This is the purpose of the Err object. This object has three important properties, which you will regularly use in handling errors:

- Number, which is an integer indicating the error that occurred
- Description, which provides a description of the error
- Source, which is the name of the object that contains the error

In addition to these properties, Err also has two methods to help with error handling: Clear and Raise. Clear resets the Err.Number to zero, which represents that no error exists. Raise is used to cause a specific error to occur and is essential for testing code. The Err object, with its properties and methods, is what you will use more than any other object in error handling.

After your error-handling routine has dealt with an error in some way, there must be a way for it to exit the routine so the application can continue executing code. The Resume and Resume Next statements are used for this purpose. Resume is used to return execution to the statement that caused an error. Resume Next is used to return execution to the line immediately following the line that caused an error. To illustrate this, let's say an error occurred on line 20 of your code, and the error was passed to the error handler. Resume would return execution to line 20, while Resume Next would return execution to line 21. You could also return execution to a specific line by typing Resume followed by a line number. If no Resume statement is used, the procedure exits.

Now that we've covered the elements required for an error handler, let's look at an example of an error handler.

```
On Error GoTo ErrHandler
Exit Sub
ErrHandler:
    If Err.Number=7 Then
        MsgBox "Error: Out of Memory. I don't remember why"
        Resume Next
    Else
        MsgBox "User Error. Replace User Now"
        Resume
    End If
```

The first line of this code instructs that if an error occurs to go to an error handler called ErrHandler. If an error occurs, it will go to the line that states ErrHandler, which is the label named in the first line. Using an If...Then...Else structure, the error number is evaluated and, depending on what the value of Err.Number is, certain code is used to deal with the error. To exit the error handler, the Resume and Resume Next statements are used.

An error handler is disabled as soon as it exits a procedure, but there may be times when you want to disable error handling. To do so, use the following code:

```
On Error GoTo 0
```

By using the above line of code, error handling is turned off.

While you can create error-handling routines that are separatep rocedures, you can also have error-handling code that is part of a procedure. However, because code runs from line to line until the procedure ends, you need to add code that keeps the error handler from running every time the procedure runs. To keep your error handler from running each time the procedure runs, Exit statements are used.

The Exit Function or Exit Sub functions keep error-handling routines from running when no error has occurred. Exit Function is used when an error handler is contained in a Function. Exit Sub is used when the error-handling routine is contained in a subprocedure. The error handler is encased between the Exit Sub and End Sub statements, respectively, to separate it from the procedure's normal flow, as seen in the following example:

```
Sub MyProc()
     On Error GoTo ErrHand
. . .
Exit Sub
ErrHand:
        . . .
Resume Next
End Sub
```

If no error occurs in this example, execution will exit the procedure at Exit Sub. If an error does occur, execution jumps to the error handler, which deals with the error. A Resume Next statement is used to pass execution to the line following the one that caused the error. End Sub is used to signify where the subprocedure itself ends, so another procedure might begin afterward.

Handling Inline Errors

In using the methods previously mentioned, errors are redirected to error handlers. You can also set up error handling that deals with an error immediately after it occurs. When writing code where errors are more likely or suspected, such inline error handling can be a better method of dealing with errors.

Dealing with an error immediately after it occurs, implement the following code:

```
On Error Resume Next
```

When an error occurs, it is immediately dealt with because of the previous code. This makes a line causing an error to be automatically skipped over and execution to continue on the next line. Lines that follow the error can deal with an error, without having to pass an error to a separate error-handling procedure. There is no need to redirect it to a separate error handler because the error is handled where it occurs.

FROM THE CLASSROOM

Building User Services

Microsoft has made a recent push to standardize enterprise application development with Microsoft tools with an application framework known as the Microsoft Solution Framework. This conceptual view of an application breaks functionality into three services. User Services are the front-tier layer of the Microsoft Solution Framework. User Services are responsible for controlling all aspects of interaction between the user and the application. With this concept firmly in mind, the real question is…"Who should care?"

The answer to this question is simple…."everyone!" Dividing functionality into the three services (User, Business, and Data) of the MSF, during application design phase, allows a convenient and efficient division of the development process into three distinct, and distinguishable aspects. Development that adheres to this paradigm allows highly extensible, reusable, and distributable application components.

The exam taker must keep in mind that User Services involve more than graphical UI elements. Excel, for example, may provide an obvious graphical interface, but the Object library exposes a set of interfaces, providing OLE automation server capabilities which fall into the group of User Services.

Developers must ensure that they fully understand those elements which are a part of the User Services group. This includes knowledge of how to invoke or instantiate COM components, ostensibly written in Visual Basic, from both Visual Basic applications and from Active Server Pages. A look at the proper syntax for setting help context values and WhatsThisHelp properties would also be beneficial for some of those incidental questions.

Some of the more auxiliary tasks that are performed to support creating User Services should also be focused. For example, the Visual Basic Toolbox lists available controls, including custom ActiveX controls. Adding controls to the toolbox involves making a project reference to the component, if properly registered on the system. Keep in mind, that forgetting to remove component references prior to running the Package and Deployment Wizard may result in unnecessary controls being listed as used by your project.

Finally, for the exam, pay careful attention to the procedure for establishing a call-back function, ActiveX document procedures (although these are rapidly becoming the black sheep of the ActiveX technology family), and the common error handling routines syntax.

— By Michael Lane Thomas,
MCSE+I, MCSD, MCT, A+

Determining How to Send Error Information from a COM Component to a Client Computer

When one piece of code calls an object or another procedure, it is important to understand what occurs in the called procedure or object. When an error occurs and no error handling exists, the error is passed back to the calling procedure. When an error occurs in an external object, the same holds true. Let's say you have an ActiveX component that calls on an Excel worksheet. If the worksheet experiences an error that it can't handle, it passes the error to the ActiveX component that called it. If the ActiveX component has error handling, it will attempt to deal with the error. Since you are able to incorporate error-handling code into components, you should always add error handlers to your code.

Rather than letting an error pass back to a client in this way, you can use the Err object's Raise method to raise errors in the client application that call a component's methods. By calling Raise from a method's error handler or with error handling disabled, an error can be raised in the client application. When this error is then raised in the client, its error-handling routine can then deal with the error.

CERTIFICATION OBJECTIVE 2.11

Using an Active Document to Present Information Within a Web Browser

VB allows you to create ActiveX documents that act like forms that can integrate into ActiveX document containers such as Microsoft Binder, VB version 6, and Internet Explorer (version 3 or higher). ActiveX documents are designed as you would design forms, and they can be packaged in either in-process or out-of-process components. They offer built-in viewport scrolling, hyperlinks, and menu negotiation.

The first step in creating an ActiveX document is starting a new ActiveX document project. By selecting New Project from the File menu, you then select either ActiveX document DLL or ActiveX document EXE. No matter which of these you select, a new project appears in the Project window containing a folder called User documents. Within this folder is an object called UserDocument. When double-clicked, this object appears in its own window, and looks like a form that's missing its title bar, control box, and Min and Max buttons. It is on UserDocument that you can add command buttons, hyperlinks, and other objects, just as you would when designing a form.

After you add the controls you want to use on your UserDocument, you should save your project before running it. By doing so you won't lose your work should any problems arise. Unlike forms, when UserDocuments are saved, they are saved with the extension .DOB.

Starting the ActiveX document for testing is a standard EXE project; press F5, or select Start or Start with Full Compile from the Run menu. The first time you run an ActiveX document in VB, the Project Properties dialog box (shown in Figure 2-10) appears.

This dialog box has one tab on it labeled Debugging. By configuring this screen, you can set how the document will run. The first option on this screen is Wait for components to be created, which will have components created before running. Start Component allows you to set which UserDocument will be the first to run. It is similar to setting which form will be the startup form in a standard EXE project. Start Program allows you to specify which program will be launched as a document container. Start Browser with URL

FIGURE 2-10

Project Properties dialog box of an ActiveX document

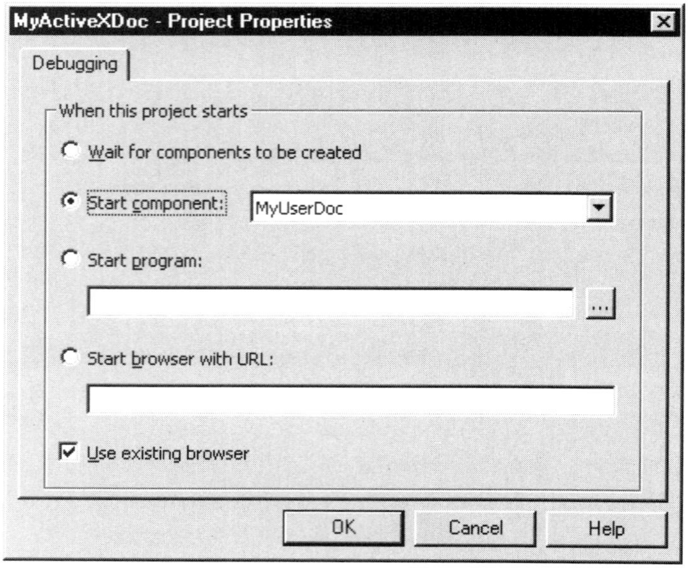

allows you to specify a specific Internet address or ActiveX document, which will take you to a Web site.

Based on how the Debug tab of Project Properties is configured, your ActiveX document will start in the ActiveX container. By using ActiveX documents, you can create form-like documents that display information in a browser, while having the functionality of a VB application.

CERTIFICATION SUMMARY

Navigation is an important part of creating an application. You can implement navigation through the use of menus, created with Menu Editor, or controls. In addition to the standard set of controls available in VB, you can also add custom controls to a project. However, when using controls or

QUESTIONS AND ANSWERS

I want to use dialog boxes in my application. How can I add them to my project?	To add a dialog box to an application, you can select Add Form from the Project menu, then select a dialog box template. You can also create one from scratch by adding the necessary controls to a form, or you can invoke a standard set of dialog boxes using the CommonDialog control.
I want to add controls like toolbars and status bars to my project, but these controls don't appear in the Toolbox. What can I do?	Select Components from the Project menu. When the list appears, select Microsoft Windows Common Controls 6.0, and then click OK. Icons for the toolbar, status bar, and other common custom controls will appear in the Toolbox.
For data binding, when can I set the DataSource?	Any time. Unlike previous versions of VB, you can now set the DataSource at either Design mode, runtime, or both.
I haven't set HelpContextID for every object in my application. What will happen when the user tries to access context-sensitive help for that particular object?	Help for the container or parent object will be displayed.
How can I view what error has occurred in my application, and where the error exits?	The Err object is used to view the number of an error, the description of an error, and the application that is the source of an error.

menus, you must also assign code to the control and set its properties before they will function in an application.

Data input forms and dialog boxes provide interfaces that allow a user to respectively input data and interact with the application. Data input forms are commonly used when developing database programs; dialog boxes allow a user to configure options, open and save files, and perform many other tasks.

By using control arrays, you are able to add and remove controls at runtime. You must remember that only those controls added at runtime can be removed. You can't remove a control from an array that was created in Design mode. After a control has been added, you can manipulate its properties programmatically as you would any other control.

COM stands for component object model, and is the specification on which OLE and ActiveX are based. OLE stands for object linking and embedding and is the predecessor of ActiveX technology.

Incorporating online user assistance into an application is essential for applications. Help files can be standard help files with the .HLP extension, or HTML help files with the .CHM extension. Context-sensitive help can be used to bring a user directly to a topic that deals with a specific object or control.

Error-handling routines deal with errors as they occur in an application. A cornerstone to error handling is the Err object. Its properties and methods allow error-handling code to determine the kind of error encountered, obtain a brief description of the error, and ascertain the source of the error. In addition, the Err object can be used to Raise and Clear errors.

TWO-MINUTE DRILL

- ❑ Menu Editor is a tool included with Visual Basic version 6 that makes implementing menus easier. Like controls, menus belong to individual forms. This means you can create different menus for each form in your application, and you must specify each form's menu interface separately.

- ❑ Menu items may be dynamically added or deleted using a menu control array. An array is like an expanding file folder, to which you add elements, which are like files in the file folder.

- ❑ The VB development environment includes a Toolbox containing commonly used controls. By holding your mouse pointer over an icon in the Toolbox, a ToolTip will appear. To add any of these controls to a form you must be in Design mode.

❑ Controls have properties that can be set programmatically at runtime, or set at Design time with the Properties window. When you add a control or select an existing one its properties appear automatically in the Properties window.

❑ Data input forms and dialog boxes are created by combining various controls on a form. To create a data input form, you must include controls that accept some form of data input from a user.

❑ Custom controls are stored in OCX files, and can provide all sorts of features to an application.

❑ The Forms collection is used to manipulate forms. The Forms collection is comprised of every form that is loaded in the application.

❑ Adding an ActiveX control to the Toolbox is done by selecting Components from the Project menu, or pressing CTRL-T, and using the Components dialog box.

❑ Web pages are written using the Hypertext Markup Language (HTML). Dynamic HTML is a new innovation that provides the ability to dynamically change the content of a Web page.

❑ Before you can use data in a data source, the controls on your form must be *bound* to the data source. Binding means that a control is linked or tied to a data source, so it can access data contained within it. Once a control can access this data, the data can then be manipulated.

❑ *COM* is an acronym for *component object model*, a standard that defines how different objects can communicate with one another and how separate components can manipulate each other.

❑ Handling events from a COM component is done using the WithEvents keyword.

❑ Asynchronous processing allows code to execute separately from other events or processes. Asynchronous processing frees the application, so that other code can be executed while it waits for a COM component to finish processing.

❑ VB includes features and tools that allow you to implement several types of help in your application. What's This Help, Messages, HTML documents, and other forms of help can aid a user when they're having difficulties.

SELF TEST

The following Self-Test questions will help you measure your understanding of the material presented in this chapter. Read all the choices carefully, as there may be more than one correct answer. Choose all correct answers for each question.

1. You specify CTRL-X as a shortcut key for a menu item called Exit. This menu item appears under the File menu. What effect will creating the shortcut key have on the menu?

   A. The x in Exit will be underlined.

   B. Exit will appear in bold.

   C. CTRL-X will appear beside the menu item.

   D. It will have no effect on the menu item.

2. You have added a menu item to your menu system. When naming this menu item, what prefix should you use?

   A. mnu

   B. menu

   C. m

   D. alt

3. You have decided to have a large number of menu items with the same name. How can you do this?

   A. Use the Index field to set a value starting at zero, and going up to 32,768.

   B. Use the Index field to set a value starting at zero or one, and going up to 32,767.

   C. Use the Index field to set any value.

   D. You can't have different menu items with the same name.

4. Which of the following events are associated with a menu item?

   A. Click

   B. Dragdrop

   C. GotFocus

   D. KeyUp

5. What are the possible values of the Checked, Enabled, Visible, and WindowList properties?

   A. True

   B. False

   C. Checked

   D. Unchecked

6. What will the following line of code do?

   ```
   Dim x As Integer
   ```

   A. Declare a variable named x as an integer.

   B. Declare an array named x that contains integer elements.

   C. Create a runtime error.

   D. None of the above.

7. Which of the following lines of code will load the first menu item in a menu control array?

A. mnuItem(0)

B. mnuItem()

C. mnuItem

D. Load mnuItem(0)

E. Load mnuItem(1)

8. Of the properties associated with command buttons, which are most commonly manipulated during runtime via code?

A. Caption

B. Name

C. Enabled

D. Text

9. You have decided that you want information displayed in a text box to appear on several lines. Which property will you set, and what value will you set the property to?

A. Set Text to True

B. Set Text to False

C. Set MultiLine to True

D. Set MultiLine to False

10. You have configured a text box to display text over several lines. Unfortunately, some of the data is disappearing below the bottom of the text box. What will you configure to see data below the bottom of the text box, and how will you configure it?

A. Set ScrollBars to True.

B. Set ScrollBars to False.

C. Set ScrollBars property to either Vertical, Horizontal, or Both.

D. Nothing, it will always allow you to view all data contained.

11. You want to change what appears in a label at runtime. Which syntax will you use to change this value?

A. *label*.Text = *new text*

B. *label*.Text = "*new text*"

C. *label*.Caption = "*new caption*"

D. *label*.Caption = *new caption*

12. You want to assign code that responds to a specific event of a control. Which window will you use?

A. Project

B. Code

C. Event

D. Object

13. You have added a CommonDialog control to a form, and want to use it to invoke a dialog box in which users can specify printer options. What syntax will you use to invoke such a dialog box?

A. CommonDialog.ShowOpen

B. CommonDialog.PrintOptions

C. CommonDialog.ShowPrinter

D. CommonDialog.ShowPrint

14. You want to add a custom control to a project. How will you add the control so it appears on the Toolbox from which you can then add it to a form?

   A. Select Components from the Project menu, then select the control from the list.

   B. Select Project Properties from the Project menu. Click the Components button, and select the control from the list.

   C. Select Components from the View menu, then select the control from the list.

   D. Select Components from the Add menu, then select the control from the list.

15. You want to add a control to a form that can act as a repository for images. You will then call the images you need for other controls through code. Which control will you add to act as a storehouse for graphics?

   A. GraphicList

   B. ImageList

   C. ListView

   D. Image

16. You have typed text into the Text property of a panel in the StatusBar control. When you run the application, this text doesn't appear in the status bar. Why?

   A. The Text property hasn't been set to sbrText.

   B. The Style property hasn't been set to sbrText.

   C. The text should have been typed in the Key property.

   D. The Alignment property hasn't been set.

17. You have added a two command buttons named cmdAccess to a form, and given them Index numbers of zero and one, respectively. At runtime your code adds the following buttons to the array: cmdAccess(2), cmdAccess(3), and cmdAccess(4). Which of these will you be able to remove programmatically using the Unload statement?

   A. cmdAccess(2), cmdAccess(2), cmdAccess(3), and cmdAccess(4)

   B. cmdAccess(2), cmdAccess(3), and cmdAccess(4)

   C. cmdAccess(3) and cmdAccess(4)

   D. cmdAccess(0), cmdAccess(1), cmdAccess(2), cmdAccess(3), and cmdAccess(4)

18. A text box is grayed out and doesn't accept any input. Why?

   A. The Enabled property is set to True.

   B. The Enabled property is set to False.

   C. The Disabled property has been set.

   D. The control has no code associated with it.

19. Of the following Form events, which will be triggered first?

    A. Activate

    B. Load

    C. Initialize

    D. GotFocus

20. You want to add a control to a form that will display a list of items as icons. Which control will you add to a form?

    A. ImageList

    B. ListView

    C. Toolbar

    D. Statusbar

21. When can you set the DataSource of a data consumer in VB?

    A. Runtime

    B. Design mode

    C. Any time

    D. Never. It must be done in the database application

22. A VB project uses help files for displaying online assistance. How many of these files can a project point to and use at any given time?

    A. One

    B. Two

    C. Unlimited

    D. As many as are configured in Project Properties

23. A user attempts invoking help for an object that has its HelpContextID set to zero. What help will be displayed to the user?

    A. Context-sensitive help for that control will be displayed.

    B. No help will be displayed.

    C. Help for the container or parent object will be displayed.

    D. An error will result.

24. Which object can provide the error number, a description of the error, and the source of an error encountered?

    A. Err

    B. Error

    C. ErrNum

    D. ErrHandler

25. An error occurs on line 10 of a procedure, and the error is passed to an error-handling routine. Resume Next is used to return execution to the original procedure. Where will execution resume?

    A. 10

    B. 11

    C. Execution will resume in the next called procedure

    D. It will exit the procedure

26. An error occurs on line 10 of a procedure, and the error is passed to an error-handling routine. Resume is used to

return execution to the original procedure. Where will execution resume?

A. 10

B. 11

C. Execution will resume in the next called procedure

D. It will exit the procedure

27. An error occurs on line 10 of a procedure, and the error is passed to an error-handling routine. No Resume statement is used in the error handler. Where will execution resume?

A. 10

B. 11

C. Execution will resume in the next called procedure

D. It will exit the procedure

28. You want to implement error-handling code that will deal with an error on the line it occurs. Which of the following lines of code will cause a line causing an error to be skipped, and execution to continue on the next line?

A. On Err Resume Next

B. On Error Resume Next

C. On Err Resume

D. On Error Resume

29. You want to configure the OLEServerBusyTimeout so a request is sent to an ActiveX server indefinitely. What will you set this property to so that this occurs?

A. A value greater than 10,000

B. A value greater than 86,400,000

C. True

D. False

30. A user presses the F1 key to invoke context-sensitive help for an object. The value of the HelpContextID is an invalid number. What happens when the user presses F1?

A. Help is searched, and help for the closest related object is displayed.

B. Help for the container or parent object is displayed.

C. The request for help is ignored.

D. A message explaining that an error has occurred is displayed

31. Which of the following can be used in your code to cause an error to occur?

A. Error.Raise

B. Raise

C. Err.Raise

D. None of the above.

32. You want to change the message text that appears in a dialog box, which is displayed when a request has been received but hasn't been serviced yet. Which property of the App object will you change?

A. OLEServerBusyMsgText

B. OLEServerBusyMsg

C. OLERequestPendingMsgText

D. OLERequestPendingMsg

33. What kind of object does an ActiveX document use so you can add command buttons, text boxes, and other controls that will display in a browser?

    A. Form
    B. UserDocument
    C. Document
    D. Hyperlink

34. Which of the following lines of code will disable an error handler?

    A. On Error GoTo Null
    B. On Error GoTo 0
    C. On Error Exit
    D. On Error Err

35. Which of the following is a valid label for an error handler?

    A. Err
    B. ErrHand
    C. MyErr
    D. MyErrHandler

36. Which property would you set to specify a specific topic for What's This help?

    A. WhatsThisHelp
    B. WhatsThis
    C. WhatsThisID
    D. WhatsThisHelpID

37. Which of the following lines of code will remove a control in a control array from a form?

    A. Unload cmdArray(1)
    B. Del cmdArray(1)

C. Load cmdArray(1)=False
D. Unload cmdArray(1)=True

38. You have Internet Explorer version 2 installed on your computer and find you can't display information from an ActiveX document in it. Why?

    A. ActiveX documents can only be displayed in containers like Microsoft Binder.
    B. ActiveX documents can only be displayed in version 3 or higher of Internet Explorer.
    C. ActiveX documents can only be displayed in browsers like Windows Explorer.
    D. ActiveX documents can only be displayed in version 5 or higher of Internet Explorer.

39. Which of the following occurs when there are no enabled or visible controls on a form?

    A. GotFocus
    B. Activate
    C. Focus
    D. Enable

40. Which of the following occurs when all variables in a form have been set to Nothing?

    A. LostFocus
    B. Terminate
    C. Deactivate
    D. Unload

MICROSOFT CERTIFIED SOLUTION DEVELOPER

3

Creating and Managing COM Components

Fasten your seat belts, folks — this chapter covers a lot of information. With each version, Microsoft adds more and more support for the Component Object Model (COM) to Visual Basic. Consequently, there is a lot to talk about on the topic of component programming in this third version of Visual Basic with support for components. I will start with a quick review on object-oriented programming and how classes fit into the Component Object Model. From there, I will present the different options available when designing and building COM-based components. I will then discuss how to register and manage the components you have on your development machine, and I will finish by talking about where COM components fit in the multitier programming model that everyone (most notably, Microsoft) is clamoring about.

Introduction: Classes Revisited

Remember class modules? Classes act as templates for creating objects in memory that can expose an interface via properties, methods, and events. Classes put the "Object" in the Component Object Model. Whether you define them in standard class modules or as the interface-centric UserDocument and UserControl classes, classes are the central part of every COM component. Before I get too far into this discussion, I want to clear up an issue that is often a source of confusion for Visual Basic programmers with respect to COM. Although COM is a standard for object oriented programming, it is not about the objects or components themselves, but rather, how those components and objects talk to each other. COM is a set of standard binary interfaces that define the way components should expose their functionality to other components. This allows communication between components that may have been developed by different developers or even in different programming languages.

If you are not comfortable with creating standard class modules in Visual Basic, you may find yourself hopelessly lost in this chapter. This chapter will focus on extending your understanding of classes to include compiling them into external packages (components) that other COM-based components and clients can communicate with.

CERTIFICATION OBJECTIVE 3.02

Selecting a Component Type

Visual Basic provides the capability to create several types of components. When you start a new project, Visual Basic prompts you to select a project type. The project types that are used to build COM components are the "ActiveX"-type projects in this dialog. Let's start off by discussing how to select the ActiveX component type that is the best fit for the component you are building. The following two questions are key for selecting a component type:

1. Where will the component be used? Will it be used on a form, from code, or maybe even inside an OLE Container application like Internet Explorer?

2. What are the performance, stability, and feature requirements for the component?

The answer to the first question will tell you what major category of control you will need to use (for example, ActiveX control, ActiveX code component, or ActiveX document). The second question will help you to determine whether the DLL or EXE type of the component will be most appropriate for your needs.

Types of ActiveX Components

In the New Project dialog box, you will see that there are five basic options for ActiveX components, which can be grouped into three major categories:

■ **ActiveX Control**   If you want a component that provides a user interface element that can be dropped into an application or Web page, an ActiveX control is the best fit.

■ **ActiveX Code Component**   If you want a component that runs behind the scenes through programmatic calls to methods and properties instead of user interaction with a visual element, an

ActiveX code component is usually the way to go. ActiveX code components come in two subtypes: DLL and EXE.

■ **ActiveX Document** This is another interface-centric type of component similar to the ActiveX control. These components were originally intended to run inside the Microsoft Binder application, which never really took off. Now they are used mostly in Internet Explorer in intranet environments. Unlike ActiveX controls that can also be used in Internet Explorer, an ActiveX document is not embedded in a Web page; it appears as the entire page. The advantage of using an ActiveX document instead of HTML for a Web page is that it is much easier to lay out a Visual Basic form. You also get most of the functionality of Visual Basic behind your page, a lot of which HTML cannot support. The downside of using ActiveX documents as Web pages is that they only work in Internet Explorer and they can be much slower to load than the equivalent HTML page. ActiveX documents also come in DLL and EXE subtypes.

In-Process (DLL) versus Out-of-Process (EXE) Components

Okay, now we know what type of component we want. What is with the EXE and DLL options for ActiveX code components and ActiveX documents? Well, the primary distinction between these types of components is how objects from the component are loaded into memory with respect to the client. As shown in Table 3-1, DLL components are always created in the client's process space (in-process), while objects created from an EXE-type component are loaded into a separate process space allocated to the component (out-of-process). Note: You don't get a choice with ActiveX controls, they are always compiled as in-process "OCX" files.

TABLE 3-1

A Sure Sign that a Component Runs an Out-of-Process Component Is the EXE Extension.

Component Type	In-Process	Out-of-Process
ActiveX Control	✓	
ActiveX DLL Code Component	✓	
ActiveX EXE Code Component		✓
ActiveX Document DLL	✓	
ActiveX Document EXE		✓

Be sure you know which types of components are created in-process, and which are created out-of-process. The Visual Basic exams always have questions about this in one form or another. Remember: EXE = out-of-process; DLL and OCX = in-process.

When I talk about a *process*, I am referring to the resources allocated by the operating system to a particular application. In the Windows implementation of multitasking, each application is compartmentalized into processes. Effectively, each process is as a virtual computer created for a particular application to run in. In this model, each application can act as if it has the entire machine to itself. Behind the scenes, the operating system intercepts all of the requests for memory and processor time from each process, prioritizes them, and passes them onto the actual hardware. When I talk about a component running *in-process*, I mean that the objects that the component creates are loaded into the same virtual computer space as the client that is using it. By contrast, an *out-of-process* component gets its own virtual computer for its objects, and can be operating on a separate machine as far as the client is concerned. (In fact, with DCOM, it actually is running on a separate machine.) Because they run in a separate process, out-of-process servers must talk to the client application across process boundaries using a process called *marshalling*. For this reason, out-of-process components are sometimes referred to as *cross-process* components.

Now that you understand some of the underlying technical details of where a component runs and what it means to run in one process or another, why should you care? You should care because there are costs and benefits to both models that can make a real difference in the ways your component can be used and how it performs. Here are the key points:

- **Speed (Winner by a landslide: in-process)**   When an application has to make calls across process boundaries, an operation called marshalling must occur. *Marshalling* is where the operating system acts as a translator; it translates communication between applications and/or components that need to talk across process boundaries. Like using a translator in real life, these conversations can move very slowly. In-process components don't need to take this extra step and can be called from the client as if it were part of the client itself. Although it might seem like almost all of the following items favor out-of-process components, this speed advantage is huge and should weigh heavily in your decision about whether to use in-process or out-of-process components.

- **Stability (Winner: out-of-process)**   If you are writing an application that requires the utmost in robustness, sometimes an out-of-process server is a better choice if the component is running some "iffy" code that might make it prone to crashing. When code in a process causes a serious enough error (read as GPF), the operating system has the option of dumping the entire process and everything in it. This means that if the component is running in the same process space as the client and makes a fatal mistake, the client will go down with the ship. On the other hand, a client is fairly insulated from a component that bombs in another process, and if error handling is set up properly, the client can sometimes just create another instance of the object that died and recover gracefully.

- **Distributed Computing (Winner: out-of-process)**   Because an out-of-process component runs in a separate process, and the communication between the client and component are brokered by Windows, only Windows needs to know where the component is actually running. Through *remote procedure calls* and *Distributed COM* (DCOM), Windows can access the process of a component running on another machine and represent it to the client as if it were running locally. This gives components that have their own processes the distinct advantage of running on a separate physical machine from the client. This is very useful in building *multitier* applications.

- **Bitness (Winner: out-of-process)**   When a process is created for an application or component, Windows can simulate either a 16- or 32-bit virtual machine, depending on the *bitness* of the code that is going to be executed on it. Each process space can be either 16- or 32-bit, but never both. Following this logic, a 32-bit component (the only kind Visual Basic 6.0 creates) cannot be loaded in the same process as a 16-bit client. If you want your component to work with 16-bit clients, you must use an out-of-process component.

Although the EXE/DLL decision is commonly based on whether the in-process or out-of-process loading method is more appropriate, there is a situation in which you would select the EXE component type when using ActiveX code components. This is when you want the component to act as an *application server*. An application server is a component with a dual identity. It can be run like any standard EXE type application, but can also be used by a client as an *OLE server*. DLL-type components cannot be used in this fashion.

Selecting the Type of Component

Here are some sample scenarios with regard to selecting an ActiveX Project Type:

QUESTIONS AND ANSWERS

"I need a component that can operate as a Web page in Internet Explorer."	Use an ActiveX document project to create components that can simulate a Web page.
"My component is going to be used to add the capability to draw a digital signature in a box on a form in the client application by using the mouse."	An ActiveX control is the best choice when you want interface-centric functionality that can be used as a tool to drop onto a form.
"I need an application that can run stand-alone, but also exposes objects programmatically to Visual Basic and Visual FoxPro clients."	ActiveX EXE code components are the only types of components that can be designed to run as application servers. All COM-based objects can be used in all COM containers, including Visual Basic and Visual FoxPro.
"I want to encapsulate advanced math functions into a component. There will be a lot of information passed between the component and the client, and speed is essential."	ActiveX DLL code components run in-process, and therefore can pass data back and forth to the application much more quickly than out-of-process components can.
"I am creating a component that can be used to expose business logic to a mission-critical accounting application. The component does some tricky stuff that might cause it to crash badly and I don't want it to crash my accounting app with it."	ActiveX EXE components run in another process that insulates them from the client.

Creating an ActiveX Control

Let's give this technology a test drive by following the steps in Exercise 3-1 to create an ActiveX control to implement the signature box control, as described in the previous scenarios.

EXERCISE 3-1

Creating an ActiveX Control

1. Open Visual Basic and start a new ActiveX control project. At this point, you should see a project called Project1 in the project explorer window with an object called UserControl1 underneath it.

2. Let's start by setting up some of the properties of our new control. Bring up the Project Properties dialog box. The Project Type field should be set to **ActiveX Control** if you selected the proper project type in step 1. If not, you can correct that now by setting the project type manually. Next, we will set the Project Name field to **SignIt** and the Project Description to **Signature Processing Controls**. Your screen should now resemble Figure 3-1. Press OK to close the dialog box and save your changes.

3. Double-click the UserControl object to open it. You will notice that UserControl objects are very similar to the form objects that you should be very used to by now. The UserControl object you are looking at now is how the control will look when dropped on a form or Web page. The first thing you need to do is give the control a meaningful name. Open the Properties dialog box and set the Name property or the UserControl object to **SignatureBox**. The Name property is used to set what the control type is called and to generate the default name for this type of control as it is added to a form in the client application. In this case, the default control name is SignatureBox1 for the first control of this type added to a client form.

4. Because a plain gray control that does nothing is not very useful, let's add a visual element. Pull up the toolbox and drag a PictureBox control onto the UserControl, set the AutoRedraw property of the

FIGURE 3-1

The project description property for ActiveX controls is used in the components dialog box when listing availalable components. Be sure to make it descriptive so that you can tell your components apart by the description alone.

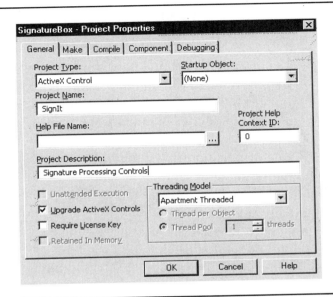

PictureBox to **False,** but leave the default name for the control as Picture1. This PictureBox will be used to hold the signature that the end user will draw using the mouse.

5. Because this will be the only visual element of the control, we want it to take up the entire area allocated to the control on the client form, even if the control on the client form changes size. Here we will set up the Resize event of the UserControl to handle sizing of the control on a form.

```
Private Sub UserControl_Resize
    `* Turn off Error handling or minimizing and Maximizing
    `* of the Container Form might trigger errors
    On Error Resume Next

    `* Set the left, top height and width of Picturebox1
    `* To hug the boundaries of the control.
    Picture1.Move 0, 0, ScaleWidth, ScaleHeight

    `* Note: The move method is a much quicker method
    `* to set the top, left, width and height properties.
    `* because setting all of these attributes in one
    `* call will only force only one redraw instead of four.
End Sub
```

6. At this point, you have an ActiveX control that displays a white box. Add the following code to allow the user to sign in the white box using the mouse.

```
'* Module level Variables
Private mDrawModeOn As Boolean

Private Sub Picture1_MouseDown(Button As Integer, Shift As
Integer, X As Single, Y As Single)

    If Button = VbLeftButton then
        'Switch To Draw Mode
        mDrawModeOn = True

        'Set the starting point for draw
        Picture1.CurrentX = X
        Picture1.CurrentY = Y
    End If
End Sub

Private Sub Picture1_MouseMove(Button As Integer,_
        Shift As Integer, X As Single, Y As Single)

    If mDrawModeOn Then
        'Draw from the last position to the current position
        Picture1.Line (Picture1.CurrentX, _
                        Picture1.CurrentY) -(X, Y), vbBlack

        'Save the current position for next draw
        Picture1.CurrentX = X
        Picture1.CurrentY = Y
    End If
End Sub

Private Sub Picture1_MouseUp(Button As Integer, _
        Shift As Integer, X As Single, Y As Single)
    If Button = vbLeftButton then
        'Turn off Draw Mode
        mDrawModeOn = False
    End If
End Sub
```

7. Now the control does what we set out to make it do. The user can now sign in the box.

Still, something is missing. What if the developer using our new control doesn't want the signature in black? Are we going to make them open up the source code and modify the ActiveX control each time they want a different pen color? Of course not; the idea behind

COM is reusability, and if the control isn't flexible, it isn't very reusable. While we are at it, that signature isn't very useful to the client if it isn't available outside of our control.

8. We will now set up a public property for PenColor. In this code, we will also add the capability to get a copy of the signature or save it out to a bitmap file:

```
'* Property implemented as a public variable
Public PenColor As Long

'* Property Implemented as a method
Public Property Get Signature() As Picture
    Set Signature = Picture1.Picture
End Property

'* Save Method
Public Sub Save(SignatureFile As String)
    SavePicture Picture1.Image, SignatureFile
End Sub

'* Update Drawing call in the MouseMove Sub to
'* use the new PenColor Property
    Picture1.Line (Picture1.CurrentX, _
              Picture1.CurrentY) -(X, Y), PenColor
```

9. Now we can customize the pen color, get a reference to the picture, and even save the picture out as a bitmap.

Implementing properties brings us to another issue. How do these properties get initialized? Also, when a developer using our control saves a form with our new control on it, it would be really nice (meaning the opposite of annoying) if the properties they set using the property sheet for our control would stick between sessions of Visual Basic.

There are three events associated with UserControl Objects that are included for just this reason: InitProperties, ReadProperties, and WriteProperties.

InitProperties—This event is called the first time a new instance of a control is added to a form to allow you to set the property values to their default values.

10. For our signature control, we will default our PenColor to black with the following code:

```
Private Sub UserControl_InitProperties()
    '* Initialize the PenColor
    PenColor = vbBlack

    '* Note: The Signature property need not be
    '* Initialized stored or read because
    '* it is calculated on the fly
End Sub
```

ReadProperties/WriteProperties—These events are raised when the client wants to restore (Read) or save (Write) persistent properties. These two events pass a property bag as a parameter. The *property bag* is an object, belonging to the client, which gives you a place to stick all of your property values for safekeeping. It makes a lot of sense for the client to take care of the property storage for the components it uses, because this allows each client to persist its own settings with respect to the component without stepping on the toes of other clients using the same component.

Including the following code will ensure that the PenColor setting on the property sheet for our control in the client application will stay set, even between sessions of Visual Basic:

```
Private Sub UserControl_ReadProperties(PropBag as PropertyBag)
    '* Restore the property from the property bag
    PropBag.ReadProperty"PenColor",vbBlack

    '* The second parameter is the default value if PenColor
    '* can not be read from the propertybag
End Sub

Private Sub UserControl_WriteProperties(PropBag as PropertyBag)
    '* Save the property out to the property bag object
    PropBag.WriteProperty "PenColor", vbBlack

    '* The second parameter specifies the default value
    '* If the default and the current value of the property
    '* Are the same, the property is not stored to save space
    '* because the property will automatically be set to the
    '* default anyway.
End Sub
```

11. The WriteProperties Event will not be raised unless at least one property has been marked dirty. A property is marked dirty whenever

it is changed in the client application through the property sheet. If you want to mark a property dirty from within your component, you can do so by calling the PropertyChanged method with the name of the property in a string parameter. For our control, we will just leave the property-changing up to the client developer.

on the
job

Although disabled by default, the InitProperties, ReadProperties, and WriteProperties events can be raised in public classes in ActiveX code components by setting the Persistable property to "1-Persistable." These events do not pass in a property bag object, so the component will need to have code in these procedures that stores and retrieves property values from a file, database, the Registry, or whatever custom solution you can come up with to stash properties away.

While we are on the topic of property sheets, the public properties you add to a UserControl object are automatically added to the standard property sheet in the client. However, sometimes the default property sheet doesn't allow for the flexibility to set some specialized property types, (for example, properties that allow multiple values). To make setting these properties easier for the consumer of your control, Visual Basic gives you the ability to add a custom property sheet to ActiveX controls. Follow the steps in Exercise 3-2 to add a property sheet to our SignatureBox Control.

EXERCISE 3-2

Adding a Property Sheet to the Signature Box Control

1. From the Project menu, select Add Property Page.

2. Select the Property Page Wizard from the dialog box. It is generally much easier to let the wizard do most of the work, and then go back and edit the results to your specific needs.

3. On the Select Property Pages page of the wizard, click the Add button and accept the default page name.

4. Make sure the Property Page1 item is clicked in the list box and click the Next button.

5. Add the PenColor property to the Property Page and click the Finish button.

6. Open the new PropertyPage1 object that was created by the wizard and modify it if you don't like the way it looks. Property Page objects work exactly like forms; they can even have ActiveX controls on them (with their own property sheets!). If you look at the code behind PropertyPage1, you will see that you can use the SelectedControls property of the Property Page to set the properties for selected instances of your control in the client application in the ApplyChanges event of the Property Page object.

7. Open the SignatureBox Control and bring up the Properties dialog box.

8. Bring up the Property Pages Property and make sure the PropertyPage1 property page is selected.

Now, when you choose the properties option with the SignatureBox control selected in the client application, the property page you just built will be displayed instead of Visual Basic's standard property sheet .

Testing and Debugging ActiveX Controls

Okay, now we have a working ActiveX control . I think. Well, how do we really know? The answer is, we don't. Let's find out. The very nature of an ActiveX control is that it doesn't run by itself; it runs inside a client application, so we are going to have to create a test client application to test our new control. Exercise 3-3 outlines the process for testing an ActiveX control.

EXERCISE 3-3

Testing an ActiveX Control

1. With the ActiveX control project open, select Add Project from the File menu of Visual Basic. When prompted, select a new Standard EXE type project.

2. Open the default form in your Test Project and make the control toolbox visible. You should see a new control added near the

bottom of the toolbox that will reveal itself as SignatureBox in the ToolTip if you hold the mouse pointer over it.

Note that we never registered this control or added a reference to its component, yet it still shows up in the toolbox. In order to allow you to debug ActiveX controls, they are temporarily registered and referenced in all projects in the same project group. This behavior is designed to let you set breakpoints and step through code in both the ActiveX control and the test. Even if you have compiled the control and registered it, the one in the current group is the one that will be used while in Visual Basic.

3. Add the SignatureBox control to the form in the test project. If the control is grayed-out in the toolbox, it means you still have the UserControl Object open in Design mode somewhere in the project group. If so, find the open copy of the UserControl Object and close the window. When you add the control to the form, it is immediately running, so you may get some errors if your ActiveX control code won't compile or if there is a bug in your Initialize or Initialize properties events in the control.

   This brings us to an interesting point. The control is indeed running, even when the client application is in Design mode. For this example, test Design mode by making sure you can add the control to a form in the test project without errors. Next, test the resize code by sizing the control on the form to make sure the white box grows to cover the whole control and no gray appears around the edges. Now right-click the control and select Properties from the right click menu. Our Property sheet should come up and let us type 255 (Red in RGB) for the PenColor Property. The items in this step are pretty standard for testing Design mode of an ActiveX control.

4. Next, we need to test it in run mode, which is the mode that the end user of the client will see. Design a few interface features around the SignatureBox control that you added to the form in the test project that make use of each of the properties and methods of the control. Figure 3-2 shows how a test client application might look.

A test run of our new ActiveX control and a good demonstration of the fact that a pencil is a much better signing tool than a computer mouse.

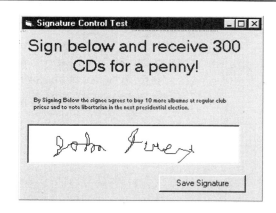

5. Once you are satisfied that the bugs have been worked out, compile the code and rerun the tests by using the compiled version of the control in the test client.

If you bought Visual Basic as part of Visual Studio 6.0 and installed the extra tools that come with it, there is another very effective way to test ActiveX controls without the need for a test project — "ActiveX Tool Test Container." If you do a lot of ActiveX control development, it is definitely worth a look.

CERTIFICATION OBJECTIVE 3.04

Creating an ActiveX Document

Okay, now before the process of building an ActiveX control gets filed away into long-term memory let's discuss ActiveX documents. Creating them is strikingly similar to creating ActiveX controls. The big difference in building them is that you use a UserDocument object instead of a UserControl Object that gives you access to some extra events, properties and methods that relate to the fact that it is running in an OLE Container Application. In Exercise 3-4 we are going to build an ActiveX document that functions as a mortgage payment calculator.

EXERCISE 3-4

Building an ActiveX Document that Functions as a Mortgage Payment Calculator

1. Open Visual Basic and Select the ActiveX document DLL project type. This will create a new project group containing a single UserDocument object. For the most part, you can treat these objects just like forms or UserControl objects.

2. Open the Project Properties dialog and set the project name to **Rcalc** and close the dialog to save the change.

3. Open the UserDocument1 object in Design mode and change its name property in the property sheet to **udRateCalc**.

4. Add the controls as shown in Figure 3-3 to the UserDocument object in the same way you would add them to a standard Visual Basic form. The text box control names are exactly as shown in the figure. The command buttons should be named **cmdCalculate** and **CmdGoHome.** The Loan Payment Calculator text label should be named **lblTitle.**

FIGURE 3-3

Your UserDocument should look like this when you have completed step 4 of Exercise 3-4.

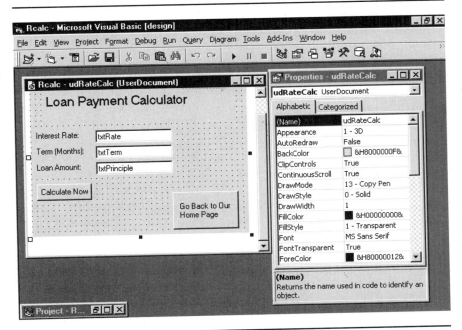

5. Add the following code to the click event of the Calculate Now button.

```
Private Sub cmdCalculate_Click()
    Dim Payment As Currency
    Dim Term as double
    Dim MonthlyRate as double
    Dim Principle as Currency

    'Divide the Rate by 12 to get the monthly rate
    Let MonthlyRate = cDbl(txtRate/100)/ 12

    'Convert the Term and Principle values to doubles
    Let Term = cDbl(txtTerm)
    Let Principle = cDbl(txtTerm)

    'Don't forget those seldom used VBA functions like PMT
    Let Payment = Pmt(MonthlyRate, Term, Principle)

    'Tell the user the damage
    MsgBox "The monthly payment would be " &
CCur(Abs(Payment))
End Sub
```

6. The UserDocument in an ActiveX document project exposes a Hyperlink property that allows you to force the container application to navigate to another document, replacing itself in the container. Add the following code to the click event of the "Go Back to Our Home Page" button to allow the user to navigate to a different page:

```
Private Sub cmdGoHome_Click()

    'Send the user off to whatever Website you designate
    UserDocument.Hyperlink.NavigateTo
"http://www.microsoft.com"

End Sub
```

7. To finish off our design, let's insure that the "Loan Payment Calculator" label is right justified in the area provided by the container application for the ActiveX document. This area is referred to as the Viewport. The following code shows how we can access the Viewport properties to find out how big it is:

```
Private Sub UserDocument_Resize()
    lblTitle.left = UserDocument.ViewPortWidth - lblTitle.Width
End Sub
```

8. Now that we have our form designed, compile it using the Make... option from the File menu. When prompted, the name of the compiled DLL will be **RCALC.DLL**

   Unlike compiling other project types, compiling an ActiveX document will produce several files. In this Case an RCALC.DLL and a udRateCalc.vbd file will be created. If we had added additional UserDocument Objects to the project, there would be VBD (Visual Basic Document) files for each UserDocument. The VBD file is the one that is opened from the OLE container application and which links to the functionality of the ActiveX document DLL or EXE. Also created is a Rcalc.lib library and a Rcalc.exp file, these files are a library and export files that are used by C++ to link a program that uses the interfaces exposed by the DLL in applications that host this ActiveX document. Since you cannot create this type of Host applications in Visual Basic, they are not very useful unless you plan to create a container in a language such as Visual C++.

9. Let's open our new Visual Basic Document. A quick way to do this is to open Internet Explorer and drag-and-drop the VBD file onto it. You can also open the ActiveX document by typing the path or URL to it in the address bar or even through a hyperlink on a Web page pointing to the VBD file. Open the VBD file in Internet Explorer using one of these methods.

10. Fill in values for the fields and hit the calculate button to see what the car payments would be on that new Ferrari.

11. Now click the "Go back to Our HomePage" button to jump to Microsoft's Web site to look up dates for taking your next Visual Basic Exam.

Testing and Debugging ActiveX Documents

An ActiveX document component is yet another special case for debugging components. Because these projects run only in OLE container applications that support ActiveX documents such as Microsoft Word or Internet Explorer, they cannot normally be embedded in a Visual Basic client application. This means that you will not be able to use either the standard in-process/out-of-process debugging method (described shortly) with this type of component. Don't let me discourage you here, you can still use all the tools available in Visual Basic such as setting breakpoints and watches, using debug statements, and so on when debugging ActiveX documents, but you will need to use Internet Explorer as the test client. Set the project so that it starts in Internet Explorer for debugging by selecting the Start Component radio button on the debugging tab of the project Properties dialog box, as shown in Figure 3-4.

At this point, you should be able to debug the ActiveX document using Internet Explorer by pressing the Run button on the tool bar. If you need to put an ActiveX document in break mode while it is running in Internet Explorer, press CTRL-BREAK or use the pause key in Visual Basic. Also, because the container that hosts the ActiveX document is using the objects that the ActiveX document provides, Internet Explorer will throw in a bunch of errors if you stop the project while the document is being displayed. To avoid this, close Internet Explorer before pressing the stop button in Visual Basic.

FIGURE 3-4

If you have more that one UserDocument in your component, you can specify which one you want to debug on the Debugging tab of the Project Properties dialog box.

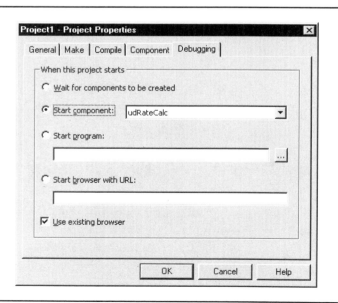

Creating ActiveX Code Components

ActiveX code components are built by encapsulating the functionality of the components into class modules, setting the instancing for each of the classes. Aside from compiling them into ActiveX DLL or EXE files, this process is exactly like creating class modules in standard EXE projects in Visual Basic. Rather than rehashing the steps involved in building a standard class module, I am going to focus on the issues involved in setting instancing options for classes, procedures for designing an effective object model, and procedures for debugging ActiveX code components.

Setting Class Instancing Options

The instancing property is used to designate classes as available to the client (Public) or for internal use only (Private). For public classes, the instancing property is also used to control the way objects are created when requested by a client. The instancing options for a class are set on the property sheet when the class is selected in the project Explorer window, as shown in Figure 3-5. The instancing options available to an ActiveX project vary by project type (see Table 3-2 for the instancing options available for each component type).

Private Instancing

The private instancing option is used to designate a class for internal use in the component only. These classes are not made available to the client.

PublicNotCreatable Instancing

Classes defined this way cannot be created from the client application, but can be used by the client if they are created from within the component and then passed to the client. Objects created from this type of class are called *dependent objects*. A common way to give references to these types of objects back to the client is to provide an externally creatable collection class, which

FIGURE 3-5

Instancing options for
classes are set in the
Properties dialog box.

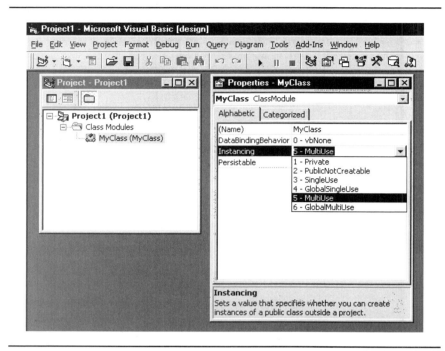

exposes an Add method that creates a new instance of the dependent object
and returns a reference to the object to the client.

MultiUse Instancing

This setting is used for *externally creatable classes*. Externally creatable classes
can be created from outside of the component using the CreateObject
method or the New Keyword. The "Multi" in MultiUse refers to the fact
that a single instance of your component can create multiple instances of
classes defined with this instancing option. This type of instancing makes
much more efficient use of memory than the SingleUse method because it
only needs one instance of the component for all of the objects created from
its classes.

SingleUse Instancing

This setting also allows for the creation of externally creatable classes. The
only difference between this option and the MultiUse setting is that each
instance of the component can create only one instance of the class. Each

additional instance of the class that is requested by the client will automatically create another instance of the component. A major benefit of this behavior is that each instance of the class runs on a separate thread of execution that can be independently, preemptively multitasked. This behavior also allows objects containing high-risk code to run in an isolated state that will not affect other objects created from the class if it happens to bomb. The downside of using this method is that this type of instancing uses a lot more overhead because it must start a separate instance of the component and all of the resources associated with that component for each object that the client requests. This setting is available for out-of-process (EXE) components only and is disabled in other project types.

GlobalMultiUse/GlobalSingleUse Instancing

The settings outlined in Table 3-2 work just like the MultiUse and SingleUse settings except that you can call the properties and methods of the class as if they were simply global functions in the client. The client does not need to explicitly create an instance of these classes first, because one will automatically be created.

Designing an Object Model

The object model of a component is the blueprint for how clients will access the objects exposed by your component. The best implementation of an object model is also usually the simplest. Navigating complex object models

	TABLE 3-2			
	Instancing Setting	**ActiveX Control**	**ActiveX DLL**	**ActiveX EXE**
	Private	✓	✓	✓
	PublicNotCreatable	✓	✓	✓
	MultiUse	✓	✓	✓
	GlobalMultiUse	✓	✓	✓
	SingleUse			✓
	GlobalSingleUse			✓

Instancing Options Available Vary Depending on the Type of Project.

can not only be confusing, but it also can take a lot of unnecessary time to de-reference all of the objects in the path of the object you are working with. This section will provide you with some pointers on designing a good object model.

Root Objects

The name of the root object varies, depending on the type of component. For example, application servers usually use the name "Application" for the root object; in-process components usually use a name that is more indicative of the functionality of the component and it usually has a name very similar to the name of the type library.

The root object's function is two-fold. Its first job is to create and hand out dependent objects (instanced as PublicNotCreatable) to the client application as they are requested through properties of the root object. Because the root object is usually the gatekeeper for all of the objects lower in the object model hierarchy, you almost always want to instance root objects as externally creatable, by using any of the options except Private or PublicNotCreatable for instance.

The second job of a root object is to expose the properties and methods that affect the entire component. For example, if you want the to allow the client to run the component in silence, you can implement a SilentMode property of the root object that is used component-wide to suppress the display of user interface elements.

Getting References to Dependent Objects

Dependent objects are normally instanced as PublicNotCreatable. This means that they cannot be created directly from the client, but instead must be created through calls to the methods or properties of an externally creatable object, and then passed back to the client from that object. The most common way that root objects expose dependent objects to the client is through an Add method. When the relationship between an object and a dependent object can be expressed as one-to-many, the dependent objects are normally stored in a property of the parent object declared as a collection. If the client application wants an instance of the dependent object, it can either retrieve an object from the collection property of the parent object or invoke the parent's Add method. The Add method is designed to allow the client to request a new instance of a dependent object. Upon receiving such a request, the parent object creates a new instance of the dependent object, adds it to the collection property, and returns a reference for the newly created object to the caller. Here is an example of how this could be coded in a Book object containing a Pages property that is a collection of Page objects:

```
'*** This code is contained in the Book Class

'****Local storage of property value
Private mPageas as Pages

Public Property Get Pages as Pages
    Pages = mPages
End Property

'*** This code is exposed in the Pages class

'****Local storage of property value
Private mPagesCol as Collection

Public Function Add(PageNumber as integer, PageText as string )
as Page
    Dim NewPage as Page

    NewPage.PageNumber = PageNumber
    NewPage.PageText = PageText
    mPagesCol.Add NewPage
    Set Add = NewPage
End Function

'This is code in the client used to get a page object
Public Sub DoBookThing
    Dim MobyDick as New Book
    Dim NewPage as Page
    Set NewPage = MobyDick.Pages.Add(1,"Call me Ishmael…")
End Sub
```

Dealing with Circular References

Containment relationships, like the one shown in the previous example, allow you to navigate through a hierarchy from a high-level object through the dependent objects that it contains. A *containment relationship* exists wherever a property of an object references one or more other objects. Normally, these containment relationships flow down the chain, with each object referencing only the objects below it. However, this model also allows for objects to be linked to objects higher in the chain.

The most common form of references pointing back up the object hierarchy is a *parent property*, which is a property used by an object to reference the object that contains it. When the object pointers in an object hierarchy form a circle like this, it is called a *circular reference*. In most cases, it is a good idea to avoid structures like this because they often violate the rules of encapsulation and can cause problems when tearing down the object hierarchy.

I will use the book component to illustrate this point. Let's say we have created a book object that contains a Pages property that holds a Pages collection object containing references to several pages objects. This structure is filled out in our library application as books are created and pages are added to them. When we are done with a particular book object, we destroy it by setting the object reference in the client application to nothing. This will trigger the following sequence of events:

1. The book object in the client is set to nothing. The reference counter drops to zero for the book object and all of the local variables are released.

2. One of the local variables is the member variable that points to the Pages collection. When this variable is released it lets the pages object's reference counter hit zero. The pages object is unloaded along with its local variables.

3. As each of the references in the pages object to the individual pages is wiped out, its reference counters hit zero and all are released until the entire object structure is unloaded from memory.

1. The book object in the client is set to nothing. The reference counter drops to 1 (remember that the Pages collection is still pointing at it). The book object remains in memory because it still has a reference pointing to it.

2. You now have no way to get back to the object hierarchy because you no longer have a reference to any object in it from the client.

3. The objects remain inaccessible in memory until you shut down Visual Basic and the inevitable GPF occurs when one of those objects tries to reference memory in the process space that is now gone.

4. Oops!

If you must set up parent properties, the best way to avoid this problem is by explicitly setting the parent property to nothing before destroying the parent object. Here is an example:

```
'**** Clear the parental reference
Set MyBook.Pages.Parent  = Nothing

'****Now it is safe to destroy the parent reference.
Set MyBook = Nothing
```

Debugging Code Components

Unlike ActiveX documents, ActiveX code components are debugged according to whether they are compiled as in-process (DLL) or out-of-process (EXE)-type components. The next two sections describe how to debug these types of ActiveX code component projects.

Debugging In-Process Components

To debug an in-process component you will need to create a client to test the component because a component cannot run on its own. Exercise 3-5 outlines the process to set up a client to test your application.

Setting up a Client to Test an Application

1. With your component project open, select the Add Project item from the File menu and add a new Standard EXE-type project to the development environment.

2. Make sure the new EXE project is selected in the Project Explorer window and add a reference to the component using the References dialog box. Note: Visual Basic sets up a temporary registration for the component when it is loaded into the current project. Any projects you add to this project group can use the component for testing purposes without the bother of registering the component first.

3. Add code to the EXE project to instantiate each of the objects in your component and to use their functionality.

4. Set breakpoints in either the client or component code as necessary, and then run the project group by selecting Start With Full Compile from the run menu. You will be able to step through code and stop on breakpoints in both the client and the component just as you would in a single standard EXE project.

Debugging Out-of-Process Components

Out-of- process means the component is running in a separate process from the client application. Therefore, you need to run your test program in a separate process, which means starting a separate instance Visual Basic.

To test an out-of-process component, follow the steps outlined in Exercise 3-6.

Testing an Out-of-Process Component

1. Compile your component into an ActiveX EXE project. The executable is only used to allow the test project to keep its reference; it is not used for debugging the component.

2. If your component is an application server, set the Component mode in the Start Mode box on the Components tab of the Project Properties dialog box.

3. Start your component by selecting the Start option from the Run pull down menu or by pressing CTRL-F5. Running your component makes Visual Basic switch the Registry entries for the component

from the compiled version, to a temporary reference, to the one running in the Visual Basic IDE. This allows you to use breakpoints, watches, and all of the other debugging features of Visual Basic with your component.

4. Open a second copy of Visual Basic and start a new standard EXE-type project.

5. Add a reference to the ActiveX EXE project you are testing in the References dialog box. If it does not appear in the References dialog box, check that it is still running in the other copy of Visual Basic. If your project is running and you still don't see it in the References dialog box, make sure that the component has at least one externally creatable class in the project.

6. Create the test project that calls the methods and properties of each public class provided by the component you are testing.

7. If testing reveals that changes need to be made to the component (and there will be changes), make sure to recompile the component with the Project Compatibility or Binary Compatibility option set after you make the changes and before you restart the test application.

CERTIFICATION OBJECTIVE 3.06

Asynchronous Processing in Visual Basic Using Components

Normally, only one line of code in a Visual Basic program can be executing at a time. This behavior extends to COM objects as well. For example, when you call a method of a COM object, Visual Basic waits patiently for the method to finish executing before resuming on the next line of code in the client application. When a component is called so that the component code must run its course before returning control to the client, the component code is said to be to *blocking* or running *synchronously*.

In most cases, this is exactly how you want your program to act. You generally want whatever that method was doing to finish before giving control back to the client because it probably sets the stage for whatever comes after that call in the application. Blocking is caused by the fact that each process can have only one piece of code executing at one time. When you run an in-process (DLL) component, it is loaded in the process space of the client, thus, the component and the client must share the virtual machine created for the process, and only one piece of code between them can execute at one time.

By using out-of-process components, you can get around this. As you may recall, out-of-process components get their own virtual machine (process) to execute code on; the component and the client can each receive their own time slices and can effectively run *asynchronously*. This property of out-of-process components allows the client to make a call to the functionality in a component and go about its business while the component continues to process the request. The component will then notify the client whenever it is done with the task or when a certain state is reached.

This asynchronous processing method can be accomplished by one of two methods: the *call-back* method and the *event notification* method. Both of these methods require some coding on both the client and server side of the relationship. In this section, I will discuss how to take advantage of this benefit of out-of-process components.

Using Call-Backs

A call-back is just what its name implies: the application makes a call to a function, method, etc. and goes about its business. When the external function has completed the task, it calls the application back by calling a function in the client designated to answer it. Although Windows programmers have done this for years, this technique is fairly new to Visual Basic.

On the component side of the component, you must:

1. Create a new ActiveX EXE-type project.

2. Define an externally-creatable class to manage each task or notification that will be handled by the component.

3. Create a type library containing the interface (or interfaces) that clients must implement in order to receive notifications. This interface must include all methods the component will use to notify

the client. To create an interface, open a new ActiveX EXE or DLL project and add the properties and methods to a class module, but don't add any code to them. This class will serve as a template of the class that will be called back in the client application. Name the class with the interface name you want to assign to the component. The standard method for interface names is a capital I followed by the class name, for example, IFileIONotify. Last, compile this component template into a DLL or EXE file. This compiled DLL or EXE file now contains a type library that can be used by an Implements statement in the component so that the component knows the calling conventions for the objects in the client that it has to call back.

4. Add the DLL or EXE to the project of the component by adding a reference in the References dialog box.

5. Add methods to the externally creatable class(es) that activates the code that will call back the client. It should take at least one parameter that is declared as the interface type we created in steps 2 and 3. This parameter is used to pass a reference to an object in the client's process that the external component can use to make the call-back, as shown in this example:

```
Public Sub OpenFileAsynch(Byval iCall-backObject as
IFileIONotify)
```

6. Add the code to the component's classes to do whatever it is that the component does when called. At the point that the component is supposed to call back the client, call the appropriate call-back method of the interface passed into the component, as shown in this example:

```
ICall BackObject.IFileIONotify_FileOpenComplete
```

on the **job**

You can also use the MKTYPLIB utility included in the Tools directory of Visual Studio to create a type library if you are feeling adventurous.

On the client side of the component, you must:

1. Add a reference to the type library created in steps 2 and 3.

2. Create a class with instancing set to PublicNotCreatable that implements the interface using the Implements keyword as shown in this example:

    ```
    Implements IFileIONotify
    ```

3. In this new class, re-create all the properties and methods exactly as defined when creating the type library. This time, however, you actually want to add the code to the method. These methods and properties will be the ones called when the component "calls back," so put code into these routines to do whatever you plan to do when the call-back occurs. Note: You must exactly reproduce all of the members that you put into the interface as defined previously. If you don't need one of the members in this particular application, you can always add the sub or function header with just comments inside for the code. Here is an example method that would be called by the call-back defined in step 6:

    ```
    Private Sub IFileIONotify_FileOpenComplete()
        MsgBox "File Opened Successfully."
    End Sub
    ```

4. Add a reference to the EXE component you created (not the type library, but the component that you expect to call your client back), and call the method to initiate the code that will call you back. Make sure that you have an instance of the class that receives the call-back available when the call-back happens. See Figure 3-6 for an example of the previous steps.

Using Events

You can also use events in Visual Basic to provide notification to the client after the component has completed its task. The benefit of this approach is that events call back the client anonymously. The object just throws the event notification to whichever clients are listening for them. This approach is also much easier to implement.

First, we set up the component to notify the client of when the requested task is complete or a specific condition arises.

1. Create a new ActiveX EXE-type project.

FIGURE 3-6

The component uses the
type library from the
template DLL to
determine the calling
interface for the call-back
to the client application.

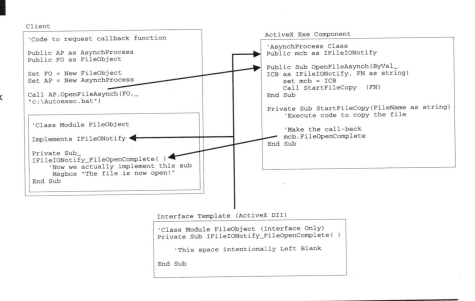

2. Define an externally creatable class that can be called by the client to initiate the notification process in the component.

3. Declare one or more events that will be raised when it is time to notify the client of a condition or that a task is complete.

4. Create a separate function or subprocedure that will raise the event(s) to notify the client when a task is complete or something has happened in the component.

Here is a sample component class module that will start a file copy and return control to the caller, and then notify the client via an event when the copy is done:

```
Public Event FileCopyComplete()

Public Sub CopyFile(FileName as string, NewFileName as string)
    'Start File Copy process running asynchronously
```

```
      StartCopy(FileName, NewFileName)
End Sub

Private Sub StartCopy(FileName as String, NewFileName as string)
     'Put code here to actually copy the file

     'Notify the client when copy is complete
     RaiseEvent FileCopyComplete()
End Sub
```

Next, we will set up the client to tell the component to respond to the events generated by the component:

1. Add a reference to the ActiveX EXE component in the client project using the References dialog box.

2. Declare an object reference to the class defined in the previous component above using the WithEvents keyword.

3. Write an event handler for the event(s) raised by the component.

4. Write code to request an instance of the component's class and point the object reference declared in step 2 to the new instance.

5. Write code to call the methods of the object in the component that initiates the notification.

Here is some sample code to call the component described in the previous example:

```
Public WithEvents FileCopierObject as clsFileCopy

Public Sub DoFileCopy
    'Start File Copy process running asynchronously
    Set FileCopierObject = new clsFileCopy
    FileCopierObject.CopyFile(FileName,NewFileName)
End Sub

Public Sub FileCopierObject_FileCopyComplete()
    MsgBox "Notification: File Copy has been
completed."
End Sub
```

on the **job**

Events cannot have named arguments, optional arguments, or ParamArray arguments. If you must use one of these constructs, you will have to use the call-back method.

CERTIFICATION OBJECTIVE 3.07

Setting Threading Options for a Component

Earlier in our discussion of the differences between in and out of process servers, I talked about how Windows distributes the functionality of the machine it is running on to each of the separate client processes. If we dig a little deeper into this interaction between applications and the operating system, we find threads.

If you recall, a process is only a "space" for an application to run in. A *thread* (or thread of execution) is the actual code executing in that space. In a simple world, applications run on a single thread inside of their own process. Windows prioritizes threads based on several factors, including the internal priority of the thread, and whether or not the thread is waiting on something. Based on this priority, it passes out time slices on the processor. When the allotted time for a thread is up, Windows preempts that thread and gives the next highest-priority thread to the processor. The applications get their code executed in small chunks until they are finished and the last executing thread dies, which kills the process.

So goes the life of an application in Windows. In practice, applications can have several threads going at one time in a process space. Although a single process can have multiple threads running simultaneously, only one of them at a time can have those coveted time slices that Windows allocates to the process.

In much the same way that processes are competing with each other for the processor's attention, threads within a process also compete with each other. Why then, would you care about splitting a task into multiple threads of execution if they all have to wait on the processor, anyway? Two reasons.

Number one, if you are running on Windows NT, the system can potentially have two processors, effectively giving Windows the capability to hand out two slices at a time and enabling real multitasking. Splitting an application across two processors should drastically improve the overall performance. Multiple processors? Okay, I'll admit that I don't write very many applications that run on power machines like this, which leads us to reason number two. Most applications spend a lot of time sitting around waiting for the slow physical devices to catch up, or (even worse) for the user who seems to move in geological time compared to a microprocessor that thinks in terms of nanoseconds. Why can't the computer do something else while you scratch your head over "Abort, Retry, Fail?" or while that 2x CD-ROM you are STILL using spins up? The answer: It can, as long as it is on its own thread competing against that thread that is sitting around waiting.

If you look back at the bottom right corner of the dialog box in Figure 3-1, you will see where you can set the threading options for Visual Basic. There are two basic threading options in Visual Basic: single and apartment.

Apartment Threaded

In the apartment-threading model, all objects created on a thread run in a separate space called an apartment. Objects in one apartment go about their business executing code, unaware of the objects in other apartments. The apartment-threading model provides thread safety by eliminating conflicts in accessing global data from multiple threads by giving each apartment its own copy of global data. This separation of global data means that you cannot use global data to communicate between threads using this threading model. Also, because each apartment has its own copy of global data that needs to be initialized, the Sub Main procedure will execute for each new apartment as it is created.

Unlike previous versions of Visual Basic, Visual Basic version 6.0 does not require you to suppress the user interface elements of a component to allow apartment threading. So if you are used to setting the unattended execution mode to enable apartment threading from Visual Basic 5.0, you don't need to worry about doing this anymore.

If you need to use ActiveX controls compiled as single threaded and can't update these controls, you will need to stick with the single-threaded mode because Visual Basic will not let you use a single-threaded control in an apartment-threaded project.

To set the project to the apartment-threaded model for in-process components, select the Apartment Threaded option on the General tab of the Project Properties dialog box. For out-of-process components, select either Thread per Object or Thread Pool, and allocate more than one thread to the pool.

Thread Pooling

The Thread Pool and Thread per Object options are not available to in-process components because in-process components cannot create their own threads; they must hook onto threads created by the client application. Out-of-process components, on the other hand, do create their own threads, and Visual Basic gives you some options about how many are created and how objects are assigned to them.

If you select the Thread per Object option, each object gets its own thread of execution as it is created. The downside to this approach is that the component does not control how many threads are created. Creating too many threads can really hurt performance. More threads only speed things up when each of the threads is idling a good portion of the time. If you flood the operating system with a lot of very busy threads, the overhead involved with managing all of the threads can more than negate the benefits of splitting the task up. As a general rule, you only want about one active thread going at a time for every processor in the machine.

Specifying a Thread Pool with a fixed number of objects can give the component control over the propagation of new threads being created. With this model, as each client requests an object, Visual Basic creates the object and associates it with the next thread in the pool. This process loops around to the first thread again once it reaches the last thread in the pool. This method for allocating objects to threads is called *non-deterministic* because there is no way to tell which object will be on which thread. Because only objects on the same thread can share data and you don't know what other objects, if any, are operating on the same thread, this model effectively takes away any practical use for global data in the component. Another problem with this threading model is the fact that objects have different lifetimes, depending on the client application that requested them. For this reason, the threads quickly get unbalanced. One thread can be burdened with handling five or six objects, while two or three others might only be handling one or even no objects. This can be troublesome because the likelihood of a single object blocking and causing the whole thread to wait for it is much more likely when there are more objects being serviced on the same thread.

Single Threaded

Okay, I lied. There is only one threading model. Single-threaded components are just apartment-threaded components that are limited to only one apartment containing all of the objects that the component provides. This allows a single-threaded component created with Visual Basic 6.0 to run safely with multithreaded clients. The Single Threading option is retained mainly for compiling components created in earlier versions of Visual Basic without having to rework them to take threading into account.

To use the single-threading model on in-process servers, select Single Threaded on the General tab of the Project Properties dialog box. For out-of-process components, you must select the Thread Pool setting and give it only a single thread in the pool.

on the job
If you need to know the Win32 ThreadID for Windows API calls, you can call the App.ThreadID property to retrieve this value for the thread calling the method.

CERTIFICATION OBJECTIVE 3.08

Setting Versioning Options

The capability of the functionality of a component to evolve without the need to modify the clients that use the component is a fundamental strength of the Component Object Model. The versioning capabilities of

COM fill this need. *Versioning* is the capability of a COM component to remain compatible with clients using older versions of the component while allowing the developer of the component to further enhance the component. This works because the only link between a client and the component itself is its *ClassID*, which is a unique, 128-bit number used by the Windows Registry to look up the component. As long as the new component still supports the same interfaces as the old version of the component and registers itself under the same ClassId, the client will always get the newest version of the component.

Setting Version Compatibility Options

When you are ready to update a component that you have already compiled, it is important to first set the compatibility options so that your component will work successfully with clients using the versions you have previously released. To set the compatibility level for your component, use the Version Compatibility box, located on the Component tab of the Project Properties dialog box, as shown in Figure 3-7.

There are three compatibility options available:

- **No Compatibility**   This is the default setting. When you compile a component with No Compatibility, set new class IDs and new interface IDs are then generated for the component. This effectively creates a new component with no relation to the old version and will require that all clients wanting to use the new version of the component to be updated. The first time you compile a new component, you must select this option because there is no earlier version of the component with which to maintain backward-compatibility.

- **Project Compatibility**   This option keeps the class IDs the same for each compile of the project, but will allow interface IDs to be changed for classes that are no longer binary-compatible with earlier versions of those classes. This is an improvement over Visual Basic 5.0, in which changing the interface of a single class in the project would cause all of the class IDs and Interface IDs to be changed if

FIGURE 3-7

The Component tab of the
Properties dialog box is
used to set compatibility
options for the project.

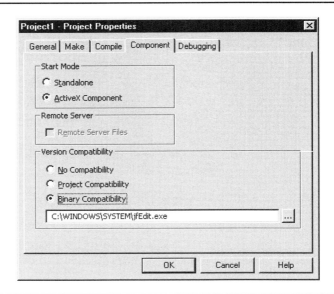

any of the classes was not binary-compatible with previous versions. This option is included for debugging purposes only. This setting is the same as No Compatibility with regard to releasing version-compatible versions of the component. It is included to make debugging easier by keeping compatibility with test projects during development of the component.

■ **Binary Compatibility** When programmers talk about version compatibility, this is what they mean. Binary compatibility ensures that when you compile an updated version of a component, it will work with clients that used previous versions of that component. If you select this option, you will also need to point Visual Basic at an earlier version of the component with which you want to maintain compatibility. When you compile a project with this option set, Visual Basic will check the compatibility with the selected component.

In order to maintain binary compatibility with previous versions of the component, you must not remove or change any of the existing interfaces in the component's classes. The single exception to this rule is that you are allowed to add optional parameters to an existing interface while still maintaining compatibility. If the compiler detects an incompatibility while compiling with this option set, it will alert you with a warning dialog box that gives you the option to break or preserve compatibility for the class interfaces that have not changed. Selecting the Break Compatibility option will cause the project to be compiled as a brand-new component with a new ClassID. This new component version will no longer support clients using previous versions of that component. If you must break compatibility, it is recommended that you change the name of the project so that the new component will not overwrite previous versions of the component already on the user's hard drive.

When to Use Version-Compatibility Options

Here are some sample scenarios that show when to use each of the compatibility that show options.

QUESTIONS AND ANSWERS

"While working on a new version I need to make interface changes that will break backward-compatibility."	Use No Compatibility. Remember to change the filename of your component so that the incompatible version won't overwrite earlier versions on the users' hard disks.
"I am compiling the first version of my component. Consequently, I do not have previous versions of the component to maintain compatibility with."	Use Project Compatibility. However, as soon as you have compiled the component, go back and set the compatibility option so you don't mistakenly compile an incompatible version of the component the next time you update it.
"I am updating a component and I want the new version of the component to work seamlessly with the other clients that use an older version of the same component already on the user's machines."	Use Binary Compatibility.

Registering and Unregistering Components

Before a component can be used in your application, it will need to be registered. *Registering* a component refers to the process of making entries into the Windows Registry that specify where a COM component is and index it with a unique identifier called a ClassID. When an ActiveX component is compiled, it is assigned a Globally Unique Identifier (GUID). A GUID used to identify a specific class is called a ClassID. This GUID or ClassID is a 128-bit number that is guaranteed to be unique, no matter how many you or everyone else generates.

The important point here is that no matter how many components mankind creates, we can be assured that each one of them has a unique ClassID identifying that component. If you want to see for yourself, open up Regedit.EXE and look at the entries under the "KEY_CLASSES_ROOT\CLSID" key. Here, you will see a lot of really long HEX numbers that refer to all the COM components registered on your system.

Why is it so important for this number to be unique? Well it's all in the way it is used. The client applications themselves don't know anything about the component except its ClassID. When they need to know more about the component, they look up the ClassID in the Windows Registry to get the location of the compiled version of the component. The client can then give the component the third degree about what interfaces it supports using an interface called the IUnknown interface.

In order to provide a friendly name for the component, the registration program also creates another key under the CLSID key in the Registry to store the AppId for each of the component's root level objects. The AppId is the same string used in the GetObject and CreateObject calls to get a reference to an object in a component (for example, the AppId for the Excel Application object is EXCEL.APPLICATION). Under the AppId Registry key the ClassId for the component is stored. These entries in the Registry are used to translate calls made by the application using the friendly name for a component into the ClassId that is actually used to find the component. Because you name the ClassId by specifying the Project Name property of your component in the Project Properties dialog box, combined with the name of your root objects, it is important to try to be a little creative with naming components and root objects to keep the AppIds unique.

So how do you register your new component? Well, once again that depends: What kind of component is it?

Registering In-Process (DLL/OCX) Components

In-process components are registered using the Regsvr32.EXE file that is located in the \Windows\System directory. In truth, all ActiveX components must provide an interface by which they can register and unregister themselves. The only thing the Regsvr32.EXE utility does is call that interface of the component.

To register ActiveX Components Component.DLL and Control.OCX, the syntax is:

```
Regsvr32  Component.DLL
Regsvr32 Control.OCX
```

To unregister the same components, the syntax is:

```
Regsvr32 /u Component.DLL
Regsvr32 /u Control.OCX
```

Registering Out-of-Process (EXE) Components

Registering EXE-type ActiveX components is even simpler. All you need to do is run the EXE file and the component will register itself automatically. When registering these components, you will normally only be notified if the component fails to register. That is, if you receive no message, it means that it registered normally.

Registering MyComponent.exe:

```
MyComponent.exe
```

CERTIFICATION OBJECTIVE 3.10

Using Visual Component Manager to Manage Components

Microsoft has been pushing the idea for some time that we should all be developing in components. With the introduction of the *Visual Component Manager* in Visual Basic version 6.0, they have finally given us a tool for keeping track of all these components that are beginning to pile up on our development machines. The Visual Component Manager, pictured in Figure 3-8, was added to tackle the problem of managing a large number of separate components in an application, and to give us a way to find the components we need when the time comes to reuse them in our applications.

Built on the Microsoft Repository technology, the Visual Component Manager allows you to publish components to a repository-based catalog, where they can easily be located, inspected, retrieved, and reused. In essence, it is a database of programming stuff. It is also quite useful for

FIGURE 3-8

The Visual Component Manager is a new feature in Visual Basic 6.0.

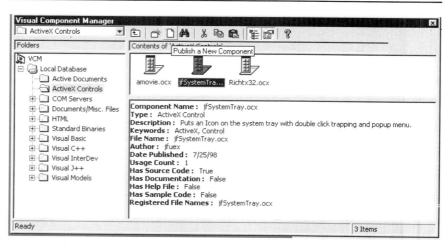

storing standard code modules that you reuse, but here I am going to limit the discussion to how it can help you manage your ever-growing list of components.

Publishing Components

Publishing a component to the Visual Component Manager stores it, along with some basic fielded information and keywords, into a Microsoft Repository database. The database can be stored locally in a Jet database or on the server in a Microsoft SQL Server Database. Here the components can be searched and retrieved for use in other projects by any developer with access to the Repository database. Exercise 3-7 outlines the process for publishing a component to the Repository.

EXERCISE 3-7

To Publish a Component to the Repository

1. Open the Visual Component Manager by selecting the Visual Component Manager option from the View menu.

2. Open the Local Database folder and select the subfolder that applies to the component you are adding to the Repository.

3. Press the Publish a New Component button (appears as a dog-eared sheet of paper on the Component Manager tool bar) to bring up the Visual Component Manager Publish Wizard, as pictured in Figure 3-9.

4. Select the primary component file and follow the wizard prompts to catalog the component.

Finding Components

Using the Visual Component Manager, you can search for a particular component by component name, type, description, keywords, or annotations. With full text search capability, you can find components even if you don't know the exact component name. Exercise 3-8 outlines the process.

FIGURE 3-9

Publishing a component
adds it to the Microsoft
Repository database.

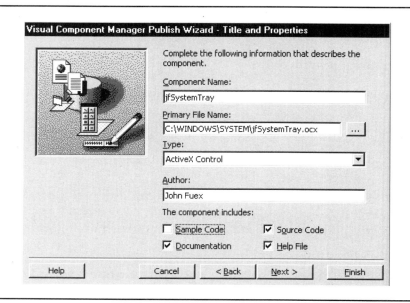

EXERCISE 3-8

To Search for a Component

1. Open the Visual Component Manager by selecting the Visual
   Component Manager option from the View menu.

2. Press the Find button (appears as binoculars on the Component
   Manager tool bar) to bring up the Find Items in Visual Component
   Manager dialog box, as shown in Figure 3-10.

3. Fill in your search criteria and click the Find Now button.

Reusing Components

Once you have found the component that you want to use in your project,
you can register it on your machine and add it to the project by simply
clicking Add to my project on the component's shortcut menu in the Visual
Component Manager. If a component has multiple files associated with it,
they are added to the project along with the primary component file. For
components stored in the Repository, you can use this process instead of
using the Components and References dialog boxes for adding ActiveX
controls or components to a Visual Basic Project.

Use the Find Items in Visual Component Manager dialog box to locate a specific component

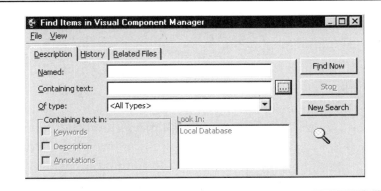

CERTIFICATION OBJECTIVE 3.11

Implementing Business Rules and Logic in COM

So where does all this COM stuff fit into the big picture? The modular nature of COM components and the capability to use DCOM to seamlessly run components on separate machines makes them a good choice for implementing multi-tiered applications. A *multitiered application* is simply an application that has its functionality broken out into components that are each tasked with a particular aspect of using the application. In this section, I will talk about the models associated with multitier, enterprise-level applications with a specific focus on the business logic layer.

The One-Tier Model

This is where it all started: a single PC running an application, storing the data, and implementing any business rules associated with the data all on one machine. This model is really the optimal model when it comes to speed because the data never has to travel over low-bandwidth network connections. The downside was obvious: to share data, you had to share a computer.

The Two-Tier Model

As networks became more prevalent, so did the two-tier moc
as client/server. The idea here was that all that the individual
on his machine was a client application to send a request to ;
database that everyone shared. The server side database woul
request, root through its database files and send just the answ
the wire to the client, who would format the data and show i
The administrator of the system had a choice about where to
business logic in this system. He could either put it on the cli
creating a distribution nightmare whenever the business rules
put it on the server and ensure downtime and complicated se
database programming when the rules changed.

The Three-Tier Model

Well, adding a tier helped before, why not try it again? This t
Internet was the real catalyst in adding a layer to this structure
realized that Web servers were a great way to distribute data, ;
inserted between the client and the server. This new middle l;
Web server, it read data from the database server, formatted it
and passed the information on client application (in this case
browser). At some point, a light turned on in someone's head
this middle layer that is pre-processing the data for consumpt
client, and accepting data and validating it before sending it k
server. I smell a new tier! The Business Services or Middle Tie

At this point I want to make it clear that an n-tier architec
imply that there are separate physical machines. It is perfectly
this model for the middle tier to run on the same machine as
server, or on a machine of its own in more data-intensive app
middle-tier, unlike the previous models was not built on the i
Although some performance gains can be realized by distribu
computing load in this fashion, the idea is that this middle la
modified and swapped out as business rules and logic change
that we need is an architecture that lets us update our rules ar
swap in the new version of the middle layer. Hey wait, COM

versioning and DCOM lets it run across separate machines! Admit it, you knew I was working my way back to this. One side affect of using a layer built on Object Oriented Programming architecture like COM is that the data logically should be modeled as objects.

Data Binding in COM Components

Up until this point, we have talked about how to use classes to encapsulate data and code into reusable components. This idea is exactly what is behind developing middle tier applications. However, when we talked about storing and returning data, we have been talking about *transient* data, which is information that is created and consumed at run time. For most classes, this is exactly what you need, but it doesn't do much in terms of using and storing data outside of your objects. If this middle tier is simply a filter for data, we need to be able to build classes that can retrieve and pass on data from and to other sources. Did I mention there are new properties of class modules in ActiveX components? I did? Well, there are two more, as shown in the following illustration.

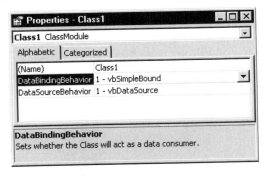

Creating a Data Source

You have two options for creating classes or controls that act as data providers. The simplest method is to build a class on the vbDataSource setting in the DataSourceBehavior property. This setting is used to create classes that expose one or more ADO Recordset objects. Exercise 3-9 is an example of creating a vbDataSource type class to expose two ADO record sets to the client.

Creating a vbDataSource Type Class

1. Bring up the property sheet for the class module that you want to act as the data source and set the DataSourceBehavior property of the class module to **1-vbDataSource**. Behind the scenes this adds a reference to Microsoft Data Source Interfaces to the project. You can verify this by looking in the References dialog box.

2. Add a reference to Microsoft ActiveX Data Objects 2.0 Library so that we can use ADO record sets.

3. Open the class module. There should be an event handler subroutine called Class_GetDataMember in the class module that was created when we set the property setting in step 1. We will fill in some code to allow the class to answer the client's requests for a data object:

```
'***** Class MySource *****
Private mRS_HR as ADODB.RECORDSET
Private mRS_CUSTOMERS as ADODB.RECORDSET

Private Sub Class_GetDataMember(DataMember as String, Data as
Object)
    '* Return the appropriate recordset object
    '* Based on the DataMember parameter.

    Select Case DataMember
        Case "HR" : Set Data = mRS_HR
        Case "Customers" : Set Data = mRS_CUSTOMERS
        Case Else : Set Data = mRS_HR
    End Select
```

4. Now before the client can use the record sets we exposed, the record sets need to be initialized and connected to actual data. In this example, let's do this in the class initialize event:

```
Private Sub Class_Initialize
    'Note HR_DATABASE refers to a data source set up in
    'the 32-Bit ODBC Section of Control Panel
    mRS_HR.Open "Employees" , "NWIND"
    mRS_CUSTOMERS.Open "Customers" , "NWIND"
End Sub
```

We could also have used the GetDataMember routine above to expose OLE DB objects instead of ADO record sets if we had set the DataSourceBehavior to **2-VBOLEDBProvider** and returned references to OLE DB objects in the data parameter.

on the **job**   *OleDBProvider classes cannot be instanced as private in your component projects.*

Creating a Data Consumer

On the other end of the equation, you can create data consumer classes and controls to connect to data providers in order to use the data that they expose. There are two options for classes that act as a consumer of the data provided by classes or controls set up as data providers in the previous section. Those options are set in the DataBindingBehavior property of the class module; your choices are 1-vbSimpleBound and 2-vbComplexBound.

- **SimpleBound**   When this option is set, an object created from the class will be bound to a single data field in an external data source.

- **ComplexBound**   This setting allows a class to be bound to a whole row of data in the external data source.

Exercise 3-10 shows the steps to create a consumer class to connect to the provider class defined in Exercise 3-9.

EXERCISE 3-10

Creating a Consumer Class

1. Create a new class and set the DataBindingBehavior to **1- vbSimpleBound.**

2. Add the following property definitions to the new class:

```
'***** Class MyConsumer ******
'*** Declarations Section
Private mEmployeeLastName as string

Public Property Get EmpLastName as string
     EmpLastName = mEmployeeLastName
End Property
Public Property Let EmpLastName(EN as string)
    mEmployeeLastName = EN
End Property
```

3. Add a reference in the References dialog box to **Microsoft Data Binding Collection.** The Data Binding collection is the glue between the data provider class and the data consumer class. Let's use it to connect the EmployeeName field in the MySource class' record set to the EmpLastName property of the MyConsumer class:

```
'*** In Class MyConsumer
'Declarations
Private DataSource as New MySource
Private Glue as New BindingCollection

Private Sub Class_Initialize
    '*** Set Data source for binding
    Set Glue.DataSource = DataSource

    '*** Bind EmployeeName field in the datasource to the
EmpLastName
    '*** property in the data consumer
    Glue.Add Me , "EmpLastName" , "EmployeeLastName"
End Sub
```

4. The MyConsumer class will now connect its EmpLastName property to the EmployeeName field of the record set exposed by the MyData class. You can test this by creating an instance of the class and testing the property. Note: This code will only work if you create a DSN for the NorthWind Traders database named NWIND.

```
'*** Some other module
Dim Employees as MyConsumer
Set Employees  = New MyConsumer
MsgBox Employees.EmpLastName
```

Creating an OLE DB Object

In the section on creating a data source, I mentioned that you could expose an OLE DB-type object. An OLE DB object has a lot of potential applications. An OLE DB class allows you to expose data from whatever persistent data storage mechanism you define, yet still be exposed as if it were a standard record set object. For example, you could create an OLE DB object that retrieves stock quotes from the Internet and presents them to the data consumers through a data provider class that can treat the data as if it just came out of a database stored on your local hard drive.

In Exercise 3-11, I describe the steps required to build your own OLE DB classes in Visual Basic. Creating this type of class centers around a pre-defined interface that, once you add it to your project, is simply a matter of filling in the blanks to create your new class.

Building OLE DB Classes

1. Add a reference to the standard OLE DB interface type library to your project. This is accomplished by adding a reference in the References dialog box to **Microsoft OLE DB Simple Provider 1.5 Library**.

2. Next, create a new class module. The DataSourceBehavior should be set to **none**. This may seem a little confusing, but this class will not expose itself to a data consumer directly, but instead will be exposed through another class with a DataSourceBehavior set to "OLEDBProvider."

   Open the new class and use the Implements statement as follows. This will add a template for the interface that the class needs to support to be an OLE DB Class. A class defined in this way with only headers and no actual code is called an *abstract class*.

   ```
   `Declarations Section of MyOLEDBClass
   Implements OLEDBSimpleProvider
   ```

3. In the Objects pull-down menu, you see that the OLEDBSimpleProvider Object has been added to the class module with its own set of methods and functions, as shown in Figure 3-11.

Implementing an interface is a contract that requires you to at least add a header to your class for every member exposed by the interface. You do not have to put code in all of these modules; you can just add a comment to them if you do not wish to actually implement one of these routines. Once you have implemented these properties, you have an OLE DB Class.

Building Components for Use with Microsoft Transaction Server

To further support the creation of middle-tier components in Visual Basic, Microsoft has added support for their Microsoft Transaction Server (MTS) to Visual Basic classes in ActiveX components. MTS is a system for developing server applications with a high requirement for robustness and

FIGURE 3-11

Implementing the
OLEDBSimpleProvider
interface adds the
OLEDBSimpleProvider
object to the class, along
with a host of methods and
functions that you must at
least stub up in your class.

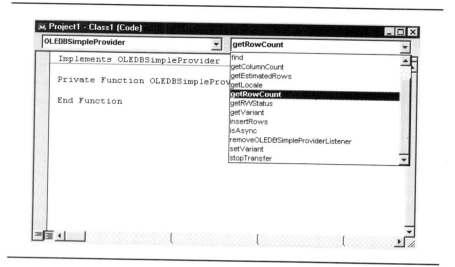

scalability. For more information on using MTS with Visual Basic, see Chapters 4 and 5 of this book.

Another property of a class module that is new to visual basic is the MTSTransactionMode property. This property setting tells Microsoft Transaction Server whether to create objects from this class to execute within a transaction, and whether the transaction is required or optional. When the component is not running in an MTS environment, this property is ignored.

The Settings for the MTSTransactionMode Property are outlined in Table 3-3.

TABLE 3-3

Settings for
MTSTransactionMode

MTSTransactionMode	Description
NotAnMTSObject	The component doesn't support Microsoft Transaction Server. This is the default setting.

TABLE 3-3	MTSTransactionMode	Description
Settings for MTSTransactionMode (*continued*)	NoTransactions	The component does not support transactions. The component's objects will not run within the scope of transactions. When a new object is created, its object context is created without a transaction, regardless of whether the client has a transaction.
	RequiresTransaction	The component's objects must execute within the scope of a transaction. When a new object is created, its object context inherits the transaction from the context of the client. If the client does not have a transaction, a new transaction is created for the object by MTS.
	UsesTransaction	The component's objects can execute within the scope of their client's transactions. When a new object is created, its object context inherits the transaction from the context of the client. If the client does not have a transaction, the new context is also created without one.
	RequiresNewTransaction	The component's objects must execute within their own transactions. When a new object is created, MTS automatically creates a new transaction for the object, regardless of whether its client has a transaction.

FROM THE CLASSROOM

Completely Clear...

Microsoft touts its vision of the object-oriented future of development in three letters: COM. Standing for Component Object Model, COM is the glue, the standards, and the interface model for interaction and communication between different objects written in any number of languages.

COM objects come in many forms, including ActiveX controls, ActiveX documents, or COM code components. Each of these categories has many uses, as well as competing and/or complementary technologies in the real world of development, especially concerning Web-based thin client development. ActiveX controls are often compared to Java applets when discussing encapsulated UI and logic functions. ActiveD documents are, to be honest, the black sheep of the family of ActiveX world. Similar functionality can be achieved through the use of DHTML. DHTML, for the time being, while not limited to just Internet Explorer, does suffer from some cross-platform issues. ActiveX documents are for use only by Internet Explorer while incurring far more

overhead, hence the weak adoption rate by the development world.

COM-based development offers many choices. Many of these choices deal with deciding within what process the component runs. For the exam, be aware of the differences of in-process versus out-of-process. Also, threads, which are a subset of a process in a manner of speaking, require choices. Single-threaded ActiveX controls cannot be used in projects set to apartment threading. Visual Basic 6.0, in particular, has added some new issues, such as the fact that apartment threading no longer requires suppression of UI elements or setting of unattended execution mode. Finally, be aware of performance issues relating to the different choices of threading and process type.

COM is certainly an area that can pose some potentially difficult question on the exam, so be familiar with all technical aspects of its implementation within Visual Basic development.

— *By Michael Lane Thomas, MCSE+I,*
MCSD, MCT, A+

CERTIFICATION SUMMARY

In this chapter, we have covered the types of COM components available to the Visual Basic developer and how they can be used to implement business services in an enterprise solution. At this point you should be familiar with creating externally creatable root and privately creatable/publicly accessible dependent classes to build a sound object model. You should also be able to combine these classes into version-compatible components, register and unregister them, and manage them using the Virtual Component manager.

 # TWO-MINUTE DRILL

- ❏ COM is a set of standard binary interfaces that define the way components should expose their functionality to other components.

- ❏ If you want a component that provides a user interface element that can be dropped into an application or Web page, an ActiveX control is the best fit.

- ❏ If you want a component that runs behind the scenes through programmatic calls to methods and properties instead of user interaction with a visual element, an ActiveX code component is usually the way to go.

- ❏ ActiveX code components come in two subtypes: DLL and EXE.

- ❏ Unlike ActiveX controls that can also be used in Internet Explorer, an ActiveX document is not embedded in a Web page; it appears as the entire page.
  The advantage of using an ActiveX document instead of HTML for a Web page is that it is much easier to lay out a Visual Basic form.

- ❏ *Marshalling* is where the operating system acts as a translator; it translates communication between applications and/or components that need to talk across process boundaries.

- ❏ Through *remote procedure calls* and *Distributed COM* (DCOM), Windows can access the process of a component running on another machine and represent it to the client as if it were running locally.

❑ The instancing property is used to designate classes as available to the client (Public) or for internal use only (Private).

❑ Containment relationships allow you to navigate through a hierarchy from a high-level object through the dependent objects that it contains. A containment relationship exists wherever a property of an object references one or more other objects.

❑ An out-of- process component is a component is running in a separate process from the client application.

❑ In the apartment-threading model, all objects created on a thread run in a separate space called an apartment.

❑ The apartment-threading model provides thread safety by eliminating conflicts in accessing global data from multiple threads by giving each apartment its own copy of global data.

❑ Single-threaded components are just apartment-threaded components that are limited to only one apartment containing all of the objects that the component provides. This allows a single-threaded component created with Visual Basic 6.0 to run safely with multithreaded clients.

❑ *Registering* a component refers to the process of making entries into the Windows Registry that specify where a COM component is and index it with a unique identifier called a ClassID.

❑ The Visual Component Manager was added to VB to tackle the problem of managing a large number of separate components in an application, and to give us a way to find the components we need when the time comes to reuse them.

SELF TEST

The following Self-Test questions will help you measure your understanding of the material presented in this chapter. Read all the choices carefully, as there may be more than one correct answer. Choose all correct answers for each question.

1. What property of COM objects gives them the capability to be reused in any other COM-compatible development environment?

   A. Encapsulation of Source Code

   B. A standard set of binary interfaces

   C. Versioning

   D. Object Manager

2. What type of component would be best suited for implementing a special text box that could be dropped on a Web page to display images stored in a proprietary format?

   A. ActiveX EXE Document

   B. ActiveX DLL code component

   C. ActiveX EXE code component

   D. ActiveX control.

3. You are developing a component that will be used to provide spell-checking services to the client through calls to methods and properties of the component. The specification requires that your component work with both 16- and 32-bit clients. Which type of component would be best?

   A. ActiveX DLL Document

   B. ActiveX DLL code component

   C. ActiveX EXE code component

   D. ActiveX control.

4. Which of the following project types will run inside Microsoft Binder?

   A. ActiveX EXE Document

   B. ActiveX DLL code component

   C. ActiveX EXE code component

   D. ActiveX control

5. Which of the following is a benefit of a component running in the process space of the client?

   A. Speed

   B. Safety

   C. Freedom from bitness considerations

   D. Security

6. How is the Project Description field on the Project Properties dialog box used by Visual Basic?

   A. It is used as the default name for instances of that object in the client project

   B. It is used in the Components or References dialog box to identify an ActiveX Component.

   C. It is returned by the ProductName property of the App object provided by Visual Basic.

7. If you were designing a text-editing ActiveX control that exposed a font property, where should the font property be stored when the component is unloaded?

   A. In the Registry

   B. In an INI file

   C. In the PropertyBag object of the client

   D. In the PropertyBag object of the ActiveX control

8. Which event should you use to set the default values to the properties of an ActiveX control?

   A. InitProperties

   B. ReadProperties

   C. InitializeProperties

   D. GetDataMember

9. How can you make Visual Basic fire the InitProperties, ReadProperties, and WriteProperties for the objects created from a standard class module in a component?

   A. Class modules cannot use these events

   B. Set the PersistData property to **Persistable**

   C. Set the DataBindingBehavior property to **SimpleBound** or **ComplexBound**

   D. Set the persistable property to **Persistable**

   E. Both B and C.

10. While testing an ActiveX control, you create a test project in the same project group as your control. The control appears in the toolbox of the test project, but it is disabled. What is wrong?

    A. The control is not registered

    B. The control is open in Design view in another window

    C. The control does not expose any public properties

    D. ActiveX controls cannot be debugged from within the same project group

11. When does the Initialize event fire for an ActiveX control?

    A. When the control is added to the host form from the toolbox

    B. When the hose form containing the control is opened

    C. When the host form sets a property of the control

12. Which type is the central type of object in an ActiveX document project?

    A. Class module

    B. Form

    C. UserControl

    D. UserDocument

13. What is the proper syntax in an ActiveX document named to cause the container application to replace the current with another document?

    A. UserDocument.Hyperlink.Navigate "c:\fullpath\Otherdocument.doc"

    B. UserDocument.URL = "c:\fullpath\Otherdocument.doc"

C. UserDocument.Navigate
   "c:\fullpath\Otherdocument.doc"

D. UserDocument.Document =
   "c:\fullpath\Otherdocument.doc"

14. An in-process ActiveX document project named "MyAXDoc," containing one UserDocument object named "UDoc1," is compiled. What is the name of the file that is opened in the container application to view the object?

   A. MyAXDoc.DLL

   B. UDoc1.EXE

   C. MyAXDoc.OCX

   D. MyAXDoc.vbd

15. How do you stop pause execution while testing an ActiveX document project?

   A. Press the Pause button in Visual Basic

   B. Press CTRL-BREAK

   C. Press the stop button in the browser window

   D. Press the stop button in Visual Basic

   E. Any of the above

   F. Both A and B

16. How are dependent objects instantiated by the client application?

   A. Through calls to CreateObject

   B. Through calls to GetObject

   C. Using the New Keyword

   D. They must be accessed through the properties and methods of a root level object in the component that creates them

E. Both A and B

17. Which of the following instancing options is appropriate for a root object in an ActiveX DLL project?

   A. Private

   B. PublicNotCreatable

   C. MultiUse.

   D. SingleUse

18. Which instancing type allows the client to create multiple objects from a single instance of the component?

   A. MultiUse

   B. SingleUse

   C. Private

   D. PublicNotCreatable

19. How are one-to-many relationships modeled in an object hierarchy?

   A. Using properties that expose arrays

   B. Using properties that expose collection objects

   C. Using multiple root objects.

   D. Using multiple inheritance

20. What problems can circular references in an object model cause?

   A. Recursive function calls

   B. Compile errors

   C. Runtime errors

   D. Objects that cannot be destroyed

21. What is the term used to describe a function call that requires the caller to

wait for the execution of that function to complete before returning control to the caller?

A. Blocking

B. Asynchronous execution

C. Call-backs

D. Freezing

22. Which of the following statements about a process is untrue?

A. A process is an executing piece of code

B. A process can be either 16- or 32-bit, but not both

C. A process can contain multiple threads

D. Only one process per processor can execute a command at a time

23. In a data consumer, how do you map the local properties to the data provided by the data provider?

A. Using the glue method of the DataConnector object

B. Using the Add method of the DataBindings collection

C. By naming the properties to the field names exposed by the data provider

D. By referencing the properties of the data provider class from within the properties of the data consumer and copying the values over to local storage

24. What does the data parameter return from the GetDatamember routine in a class built as a data source that has its datasource set to 1-vbDataProvider?

A. A DAO record set object

B. An OLEDB data source object

C. A two-dimensional variant array

D. An ADO record set object

25. Which of the following instancing options, when used for a class in an ActiveX DLL project, allows methods and properties of a class to be accessed without first creating an instance of that object?

A. MultiUse

B. GlobalMultiUse

C. PublicNotCreatable

D. GlobalSingleUse

26. How would you limit the number of threads used for objects in an ActiveX EXE project?

A. Mark the process to run with "Unattended Execution"

B. Use the Thread Per Object setting

C. Use the Thread Pool setting.

D. Check the App.ThreadId property in the object code

27. When VB executes the statement CreateObject ("EXCEL.APPLICATION"), how does VB know what interfaces are supported by the application object of Excel?

A. It looks up the ClassID that is stored in the Visual Basic Project File, looks up the ClassID in the Registry to find the location of EXCEL.EXE, and asks

EXCEL.EXE about its interfaces using the Iunknown interface

B. It looks up the AppID in the Registry to find the ClassID of EXEL.APPLICATION, uses the ClassID to find EXCEL.EXE, and finally asks EXCEL.EXE about its interfaces using the Idispatch interface

C. It uses the ClassID to get the AppID from the Registry to look up the interfaces that are also stored in the Registry

D. A. It looks up the AppID in the Registry to find the ClassID of EXEL.APPLICATION, then uses the ClassID to find EXCEL.EXE, and finally asks EXCEL.EXE about its interfaces using the IUnknown interface

28. Which of the following commands can be used to register COMPONENT.EXE (an out-of-process server)?

A. Regsvr32 COMPONENT.EXE

B. Regsvr32 /U COMPONENT.EXE

C. COMPONENT.EXE

D. Regsvr COMPONENT.EXE

29. What model does a Web published database fit?

A. One-tier

B. Two-tier

C. Three-tier

D. None of the above

4

Introduction to Microsoft Transaction Server (MTS)

CERTIFICATION OBJECTIVES

Microsoft Transaction Server, or MTS, has become a major factor in Microsoft's set of solutions for building distributed applications. In this chapter, you will gain an overview of MTS and its architecture, and you'll learn how to perform many administrative functions using the MTS Explorer.

Overview of MTS

MTS is essentially a component manager that provides transaction-processing capabilities. It is a technology that extends COM, the Component Object Model. ActiveX DLL components can be built by using Visual Basic or any other ActiveX tool. The MTS Explorer is used to configure these components to run under the control of MTS. MTS defines the application programming model for developing these components, and it also provides a runtime infrastructure for deploying and managing the distributed application.

A large part of the learning curve for MTS lies in its administration aspects because MTS removes most of the burden from the programmer when it comes to building robust, scalable, distributed transaction-based applications. MTS provides the runtime infrastructure, which is configured through the MTS Explorer. Throughout this chapter, you will encounter references to the MTS Explorer, as well as to the many aspects of configuring MTS packages.

Installing MTS

MTS is installed from the Windows NT Options Pack, which has directories for Windows NT Server and Windows NT Workstation. The setup of MTS requires that both the NT Service Pack 3 and Internet Explorer 4 are installed (these can both be installed from the same

CD-ROM). I recommend that when preparing for the exam, you select the options to install the samples and the documentation.

MTS in a Distributed Application

The first step in obtaining an overview of MTS is to understand where MTS fits in to the runtime operation of a distributed application. Figure 4-1 shows where the MTS runtime environment fits into the scheme of things. You will notice that the diagram displays three tiers, as follows:

Tier 1	Tier 1 comprises the client applications: these applications are likely to be running on many different machines, possibly at multiple locations. The client applications may be executables written in Visual Basic, Visual C++, or another COM-enabled development environment. Client applications may even be Web browser-based applications communicating with Internet Information Server (IIS). The one thing that these client applications have in common is that they provide the user interface. The client applications may run on any computer that is running DCOM, which is included in Windows NT version 4.0 (and in the version to come, version 5.0) and Windows 98. DCOM is available as a free download for Windows 95.
Tier 2	Tier 2 contains components that implement the business logic, which may run on one or more machines. Although they do not have any user interface functionality or complex data storage capabilities, the components in this tier have several important requirements. They: ■ will be accessed by many client applications simultaneously, so they must be thread-safe. ■ must be scalable, so that many clients can access them without overflowing any resource restrictions. ■ must be robust because any instability could affect huge numbers of clients simultaneously. ■ must participate in transactions spanning multiple databases or other Resource Managers.
Tier 3	Tier 3 includes databases, as well as other back-ends such as mainframes: there may be many databases or other Resource Managers located on many platforms.

Middle-tier components deployed within the Microsoft Transaction Server (MTS) runtime environment

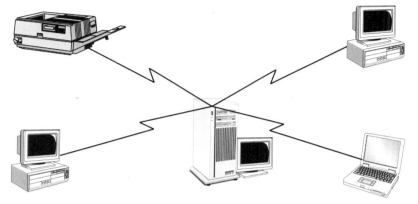

Network printing enables multiple users to share a single printer.

You can see that it is the middle-tier components that run within the bounds of Microsoft Transaction Server. There may be multiple installations of MTS on various computers, and components may be configured to run under any of these instances of MTS. Both the client applications and the databases (and even the components themselves) need to be only barely aware that MTS actually exists.

CERTIFICATION OBJECTIVE 4.02

MTS Architecture

MTS is really quite a different "beast" from anything you are likely to have encountered before, and it is important to obtain a strong grasp of its architecture prior to diving into any implementation details. There are five major elements of the MTS architecture covered in this section:

- The Transaction Server Executive (TSE)
- ActiveX components
- Server processes
- Resource Managers and Resource Dispensers
- The Microsoft Distributed Transaction Coordinator

The Transaction Server Executive

Implemented as a DLL, the Executive provides such runtime services as thread and context management for components. The Transaction Server Executive (TSE) will execute in the same processes as the ActiveX components that use its services. The use of the TSE will be covered in more detail in Chapter 5.

ActiveX Components

As mentioned previously, MTS is essentially a manager of components, and it is these components that implement the business rules in a distributed application. If the state of the application is represented by records in third-tier databases, and the user interface is implemented by the client applications, the "go-between" code in the middle tier consists of ActiveX components residing in the MTS environment. The components may be developed by any development tool that is ActiveX-compatible.

If you think of an example of a banking application, the role of these components is easily visualized. The customer, via a client application, makes a request to transfer $1000.00 from account A to account B. It is then up to the components, in conjunction with the services offered by MTS, to perform the following operations:

- Ensure that the customer is authorized to withdraw money from account A.
- Perform a database query to ensure that there are enough funds in account B.

- Assuming that there are enough funds, reduce the balance of account A by $1000.00, and increase the balance of account B by $1000.00.

- If either of these database updates fails, it is imperative that both operations are "rolled back," or else the bank or the customer are going to be heavily out of pocket!

- The results of the transaction and the new account balances must be returned to the client application.

- Finally, it is necessary for these components to service several hundred (or more) such transaction requests simultaneously.

Most of this functionality must clearly be built into the components themselves; this functionality is the implementation of the business rules, such as "In order for funds to be transferred between accounts, there must be sufficient funds in the source account." Other functionality (in this case, the transactional rollback and the concurrency issues) is largely due to MTS.

Server Processes

Although the components are implemented as in-process servers (DLLs), unlike the traditional COM model in which an in-process component is loaded into the client process, Microsoft Transaction Server actually controls the process in which the server component runs.

The net effect is that the server DLL actually runs out-of-process with respect to the client application, but in-process within the surrogate Server Process.

An MTS Server Process may host a number of components, and each can serve an enormous number of clients. It is possible to configure components to be loaded directly into client processes or into other processes such as Internet Information Server (IIS).

Resource Managers and Resource Dispensers

MTS provides Resource Managers and Resource Dispensers to manage data. The distinction is made with regard to the volatility of that data: Resource Managers manage durable data, such as account balances stored on a database, whereas Resource Dispensers manage non-durable data that is shared between the components in a process.

Resource Managers work in conjunction with the Distributed Transaction Coordinator, and as long as they support either the OLE Transactions protocol or the X/Open XA protocol, MTS can guarantee that transactions either succeed or fail as a unit. Examples of Resource Managers include Microsoft SQL Server (versions 6.5 and above) and Microsoft Message Queue Server (MSMQ).

The data that is managed by Resource Managers is known as *durable* data because it is non-volatile, and will survive such events as program termination or even a complete server crash. You can understand the importance of this by considering that you would want your bank account balance to remain intact if the bank's computers were restarted!

MTS provides two Resource Dispensers:

ODBC Resource Dispenser	The ODBC Resource Dispenser manages a pool of ODBC database connections that can be dispensed to components as they are needed. They are reclaimed and reused, thus saving components from having to either regularly open connections (which takes time) or hold connections open (which are a limited resource).
Shared Property Manager	The Shared Property Manager, as its name implies, provides access to variables that are shared within a process. These variables, or properties, are non-durable and therefore will not outlast the life span of the process.

The Microsoft Distributed Transaction Coordinator

The Distributed Transaction Coordinator, or DTC, was originally released as a part of Microsoft SQL Server, and is used extensively by MTS. The DTC allows transactions to span a number of Resource Managers. This means that an operation that can perform updates to a number of databases (residing on various computers) and send messages via MSMQ can be treated as a single transaction, and can pass or fail as an atomic unit.

Using the MTS Explorer

The MTS Explorer is the administrative GUI tool that enables you to perform tasks such as placing components into the MTS environment, and configuring who can and who cannot access them. The MTS Explorer is shown in Figure 4-2.

The MTS Explorer is actually an extension, or *plug-in*, to the *Microsoft Management Console (MMC)*. The MMC is an administrative console that is used to manage various Microsoft products, including Internet Information Server (IIS).

FIGURE 4-2

Becoming familiar with the MTS Explorer

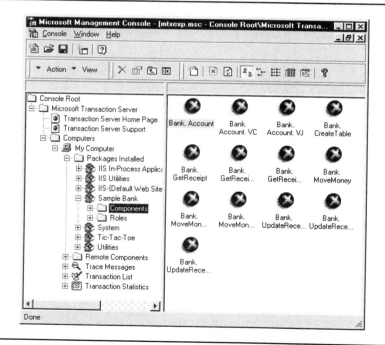

The MTS Explorer Hierarchy

You will immediately notice that the format of the MTS Explorer is very similar to that of the Windows Explorer. There are two main panes: the left pane contains a hierarchical tree of objects, and the right hand pane displays a list view of the contents of the node currently selected in the tree (this list view may be displayed in various formats). There are a number of different kinds of folders and objects displayed in the left pane: The "hierarchy" of the MTS Explorer is a design factor completely controlled by the MTS Explorer being implemented as an MMC plug-in.

Console Root

This is the top of the hierarchy within the Microsoft Management Console.

Microsoft Transaction Server

This is the root folder for all of the objects within MTS.

Hyperlinks (Transaction Server Home Page / Transaction Server Support)

These are links to Microsoft sites on the World Wide Web, and require an active Internet connection.

Computers

This folder contains all of the computers that have been added to this folder. By default, the local computer appears as "My Computer." Other computers on a network can be added to this folder.

Packages Installed

Packages are a basic grouping of components within MTS. All of the packages that are installed on a certain computer will appear in this folder. Each installed package contains a Components folder, which contains all of the components belonging to the package. This hierarchy continues with folders for the Interfaces belonging to a component and the Methods of each interface.

There are also Roles folders belonging to each package, and Role Membership folders belonging to components and component interfaces. These folders are used for declarative security, which you will learn about later in this chapter.

Remote Components

These are components that have been configured locally on a computer to run remotely on another computer. The remote computer must have been added to the Computers folder.

Trace Messages

These are messages that are logged by the Distributed Transaction Coordinator (DTC). Tracing has an effect on performance, and it can be configured with five levels that range from "Send no traces" to "Send all traces."

Transaction List

This list displays current transactions in which this computer is participating.

Transaction Statistics

Statistics are divided into two categories: statistics on current transactions in which this computer is involved, and cumulative or aggregate statistics maintained over time.

Using the Package and Deployment Wizard to Create a Package

The Package and Deployment Wizard mentioned in the exam objectives is merely the package import and export capabilities that MTS provides via wizards. You could consider them to be separate wizards, but that is more of a UI design decision made by Microsoft. Effectively, it is an arbitrary distinction because the processes are conceptually closely related. The "Package" portion of the wizard title refers to the creation or import of a new package into a given MTS installation; the "Deployment" portion refers to the exporting of a package, resulting in the client executable, required COM DLLs, and PAK file.

A package is a fundamental object within MTS. In this section, you will learn more about what constitutes a package, and then you will find out how to either create a new package or import a previously created package into an installation of MTS.

What is a Package?

When components are integrated into MTS, they are grouped into a unit called a *package*. The package is given a name, and should contain a set of functionally related components. As you can see in Figure 4-2, the Sample Bank package (one of the samples that ships with MTS) contains a number of components, such as Bank.Account, which have an obvious functional relationship.

The grouping of a package goes further than just administrative convenience. All of the components within a package will be executed at runtime within the same MTS server process, and the package boundary also defines when security credentials will be verified. Security will be discussed in a later section.

There are two types of packages in MTS:

Library Packages	Library packages run in the process of the client that creates them. This means that the components will run in-process, but it limits the MTS features that are available to the package. Most notably, role-based security is not supported for library packages.
Server Packages	These are the packages you will create in order to take advantage of role-based security, process isolation (a component crash will not crash the client application), and many other features of MTS. Server packages run within isolated processes on the computer on which they are installed.

Invoking the Package Wizard

Packages are created with the MTS Package Wizard. In the MTS Explorer's left pane, select the computer (probably MyComputer) on which you want to create the package, and then select the Packages Installed folder. At this point there are three ways of invoking the wizard:

■ From the Action menu, select New | Package

■ Right-click on the folder and select New | Package

■ Select the Create a new object button on the toolbar

Figure 4-3 shows the first screen that you will see when you invoke the Package Wizard.

As you see in Figure 4-3, there are two ways of creating a package:

Install pre-built packages	This option is an import operation. It creates a new package from a *package file* that was previously exported by an installation of MTS.
Create an empty package	This is the option you will use to create a brand new package.

The initial screen of the Package Wizard

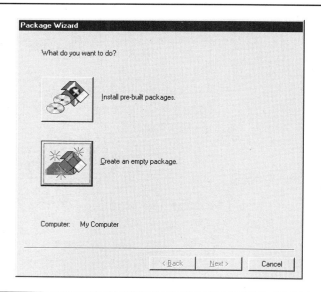

Once you click on the Create an empty package button, you will see the Create Empty Package dialog box, which is shown in the following illustration. This screen prompts you for a name for the package (the name can be changed later on).

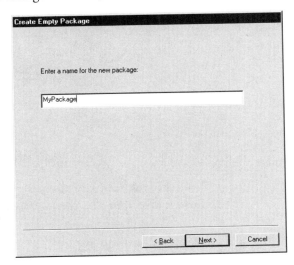

Once the package name has been allocated, the *Package Identity* must be set. The identity of a package is a Windows NT user account under which the components in the package will run. The options are:

Interactive user: the current logged-on user	This option selects the user who is currently logged on to the local machine where the MTS Explorer is running.
This user	Selecting this option allows you to browse the available list of user accounts and select one.

The following illustration shows the Set Package Identity dialog box. In this case, a user called "timc" has been selected as the package identity. "SERVER" is the name of the computer on which the package is being created.

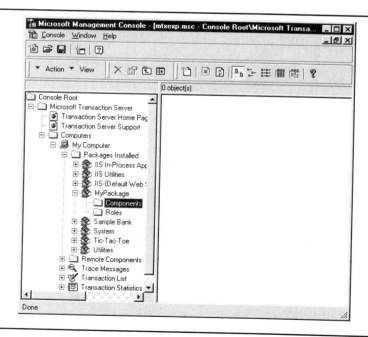

Once the new package has been created, it will appear in the Packages Installed folder in the left pane of the MTS Explorer. As can be seen in Figure 4-4, the new package is completely empty when it is created; it does not contain any components.

The new package appears in the left-hand pane

Importing Existing Packages

The other Package Wizard alternative is to import existing packages (that is, packages that have been exported from another installation of Microsoft Transaction Server). When a package is exported, a .PAK file is created. Also, all of the files that contain or are associated with the components from the package are copied into the same directory. You will learn about exporting packages in the section titled "Deploying an MTS Component."

When you select the Install pre-built packages option from the Package Wizard, the Select Package Files dialog box is displayed in a similar fashion to the following illustration. This allows you to select one or more .PAK files, and will import the selected package or packages along with all component-related files.

Once the packages have been selected, the Installation Options dialog box is displayed, as shown in the following illustration. This dialog box allows for a selection of the directory (or folder) where the component files will be installed. Use the Browse button to navigate through the directory structure.

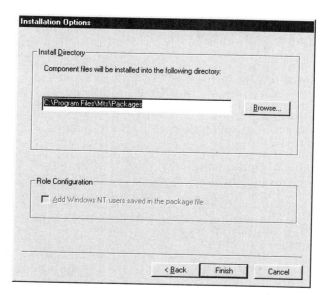

The Role Configuration section contains a single option: Add Windows NT users saved in the package file. A .PAK file may have been exported with Windows NT users included within it. If these users are relevant to the local computer and you wish to include them in role-based security, then this box should be checked.

Modifying Package Properties

Once you create or import a package, you can set or modify many of the properties associated with it. In the following sections, you will become familiar with the Properties settings for packages, including setting the name and the security options.

By selecting a package and then selecting Properties from either the Actions menu or the right-click context menu, the tabbed property sheet for the package is displayed, as shown in Figure 4-5. The properties are logically grouped under five different tabs. The two that are relevant to the exam are:

- General: Contains settings for the package name and description, and a read-only display of the package name.

- Security: Allows you to enable security on the package and to set the COM authentication level for the components.

Using the General tab of
the package properties to
set the name

Assigning Names to Packages

The first tab is the General tab, illustrated in Figure 4-5, which allows you
to modify the package's name, add or change its description, and view its
Package ID. The ID is a unique identifier by which the computer knows it.
To you and me, it is much better known by its name and description!

Assigning Security to Packages

You can assign security properties of a package through the security tab of
the Properties dialog box, as shown in the following illustration. There are
two settings here: Enable authorization checking, and Authentication level
for calls. The latter of these sets the standard COM authentication levels for
the components in the package. If you don't understand these options, it is
wise to retain the default setting of Packet level authentication.

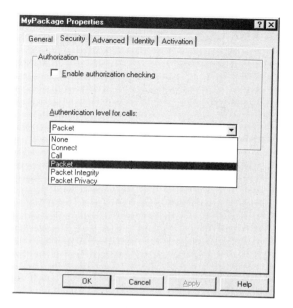

In order to activate declarative security, the Enable authorization checking box must be selected. Declarative security, which is based on roles, is an administrative level (as opposed to programmatic level) security paradigm that we will look at shortly.

exam
ⓦatch

Unless the Enable authorization checking option is checked, role-based security will not be enabled on the package, regardless of whether roles have been configured. (The section titled "Using Role-Based Security to Limit Use of an MTS Package to Specific Users" will cover security in more detail.)

CERTIFICATION OBJECTIVE 4.04

Adding Components to an MTS Package

As you now know, packages are logical groupings of components. Once a brand new package has been created and its properties configured, it needs to be populated with components. There are a couple of ways of going about this process. In this section, I will cover these alternatives and then go on to show how to set some of the properties of the components you have added.

Options for Adding Components

The possibilities are that you can move an existing component from one package to another or simply add a new component to a package. If you are adding a new component you need to know whether the COM component is already registered on this computer or if it requires registration.

Moving a Component from One Package to Another

This is achieved within the MTS Explorer: you can drag and then drop components between packages in the same way that you move files between folders in Windows Explorer.

Using Component Wizard to Install a New Component

Installing a new component involves adding the component to an MTS package and also registering it with the operating system. The *Component Wizard* will accomplish both of these tasks when the Install new component(s) option is selected. Select the Components folder of the package to which you want to add the component, select New | Component from either the Actions menu or the right-click context menu, and the Component Wizard will be displayed, as shown in Figure 4-6.

Select the option to Install new component(s), and the Select files to install dialog box, shown in the following illustration, appears. Browse for the file or files that contain the component or components you want to install, and click on the Open button. Remember that if there are additional files associated with the component (type library or proxy/stub DLLs), you should also select these files.

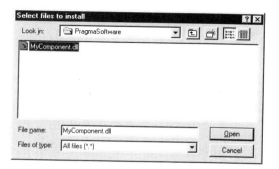

Once you have selected the files and pressed Open, the component or components should have been registered and will appear in the MTS Explorer in the Components folder of the desired package. (MTS will modify component registry entries on the server appropriately to allow proper interaction of the component within the MTS package.) After adding the component, you will also see that you can browse the component's interfaces and their methods within the MTS Explorer.

Importing a Component that Is Already Registered

If a component has already been registered on the local computer, you can still add it to a MTS package. Although the Component Wizard does not

Using the Component Wizard to add or import components

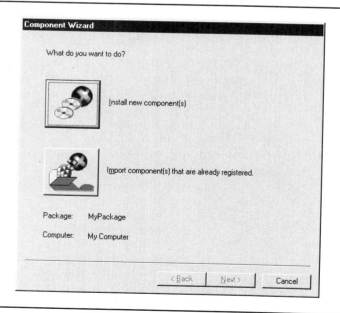

need to register the component with the operating system, it may have to modify some registry settings. Initiate the Component Wizard via the New | Component menu selection as described previously, and then select the Import component(s) that are already registered options. You should then see the Choose Components To Import dialog box, as shown below.

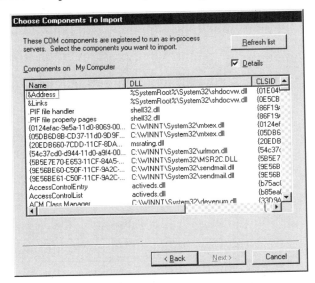

It is generally a good idea to select the Details checkbox; otherwise, only the Name column will be shown. Because some names default to the CLSID (which is highly meaningful to the computer, but absolutely meaningless to you or me) the DLL column can be very useful. Notice in this situation that you are not directly selecting files; you are selecting from the list of in-process servers (DLLs) that were previously registered on this computer. Once you have selected one or more components, click on the Finish button; the components will be added to the selected package. Note, however, that in this situation the interfaces and their methods for the imported components are not displayed within MTS.

Setting Transactional Properties of Components

MTS provides a feature known as Automatic Transactions. Instead of having server components' objects calling BeginTransaction and EndTransaction, MTS will automatically start and end transactions. It even allows multiple objects to participate in the same transaction or certain objects to participate in a transaction, while other objects are independent of the transaction. You decide about the way MTS will behave in this regard on a component-by-component basis through settings in the component's *Transaction Tab*, illustrated below.

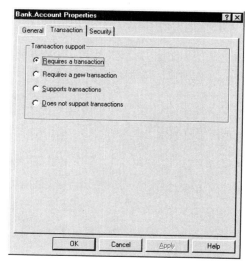

There are four transactional settings that a component may have:

- Requires a transaction
- Requires a new transaction
- Supports transactions
- Does not support transactions

These options are discussed in the following sections.

Requires a Transaction

If a component is configured as requiring a transaction, any of its objects will be created within the scope of a transaction. Whether this will be a new transaction or not depends upon the context of the client. If the object that created this object was part of a transaction, this object will inherit, or participate in, the same transaction. However, if the object was created from a context that did not have a transaction, MTS will automatically create a new transaction for this object.

Requires a New Transaction

This option is similar to the previous setting, except that it will always exist in a new transaction, regardless of the context in which the object is created. Thus an object from such components will always be the *root object* of a transaction. It can enlist other objects into the same transaction by creating objects from components configured as "Requires a transaction" or Supports transactions.

Supports Transactions

This indicates that the component's objects can execute within the scope of a transaction if they are created from a context that has one. If an object is not created by another object that is part of a transaction, the object will not exist within the scope of a transaction.

Does Not Support Transactions

If a component is configured as Does not support transactions, its objects will never exist within the scope of a transaction. Regardless of the context it is created from, such an object will not participate in a transaction.

Now that you have seen the four possible transaction settings for components, here are some typical scenarios relating to them:

QUESTIONS AND ANSWERS

Component A contains a class clsAcctSec that performs programmatic security checking for bank accounts, and Component B contains a class clsAcctDebit, which deducts money from an account. A clsAcctSec object is required to create an instance of clsAsstDebit, and both objects must participate in the same transaction.	Component A could be configured as Requires a transaction or Requires a new transaction; Component B could be configured as Requires a transaction or Supports transactions.
You are using a component that does some mathematical calculations and does not access a database	The component should be configured as Supports transactions.
You are configuring a component that is writing non-critical logging data to a database.	The component should be set to Requires a new transaction so that if it fails, it will not cause a parent transaction to fail.

Setting Security Properties of Components

Because role-based security is not available to library packages, you must ensure that the package in which a component resides is configured as a server package if you want to configure security for the component. The Security tab on a component's Properties dialog box (see below) contains a single option: Enable authorization checking. By setting this option, you tell MTS to check the credentials of any client that attempts to access this component. You will learn all about role-based security in the next section.

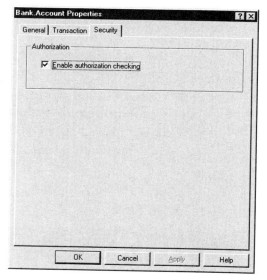

Using Role-Based Security to Limit Use of an MTS Package to Specific Users

In this section, you will become familiar with the use of role-based security and its use in restricting the use of packages to specific users. These users are grouped into one or more roles, which are added to the package.

Declarative Security

Declarative Security under MTS is an administrative-level security paradigm, which allows you to configure the security of an entity by using the MTS Explorer. Declarative security can be applied to the following items:

- Packages: Once roles are created for a package, users or groups are added to the role, authentication checking is enabled on the package, and the use of the package is limited to the users or groups contained within the roles.

- Components: A component may be provided with a subset of its package's roles. As long as authentication checking is enabled on the component, the use of the component is further limited to the users contained within those roles.

- Component Interfaces: Likewise, a single interface within a component may have access limited to the users contained within a subset of a package's role. This is the lowest-level item that may be protected by declarative security: the individual methods within an interface will all be accessible to the users who have access to the interface.

For any package installed in MTS, *roles* can be created. A role is simply a collection of Windows NT user accounts: Roles are created first, and then users are mapped to those roles. The roles are given a name that is unique within the package. Once the roles have been created and users have been added to them, it is simply a matter of assigning the roles to components or interfaces.

Role-Based Security

Role-based security is only enforced on a package when the Enable authorization checking option is selected for the package.

Creating Roles

Because roles belong to packages, the first step is to select a package from the left pane of the MTS Explorer. Once this is done, the New Role dialog box can be invoked by either selecting Action | New | Role or by clicking the Create new object button in the Roles folder. The New Role dialog box is shown below.

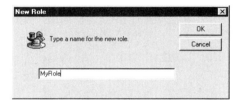

In the dialog box, type the name of the new role and click **OK**. At this point, you have created a role but no users are mapped to it.

Adding Users to Roles

Your newly created role is quite meaningless until you add users to it. In fact, until at least one user is added to the role, nobody at all can access any components within the package!

Any Windows NT users or groups can be added to roles because a role is just a named collection of those users. To add users to a role, expand the node for the appropriate role in the left pane of the MTS Explorer and select the Users folder. Select New | User from either the Actions menu or the right-click context menu, and the Add Users and Groups to Role dialog box will appear, as shown in the following illustration.

The Search button can be used to locate a remote user. In the example shown below, the name of the local computer is SERVER, which is displayed in the List Names From drop-down list. Once the appropriate names have been added and OK is pressed, the user names will appear in the Users folder under the role to which they have been bound.

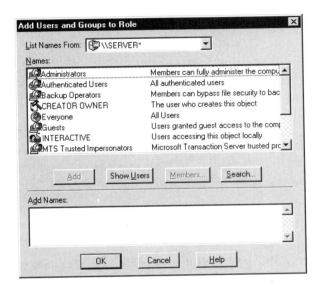

If you want to move a user from one role to another, you must delete that user from the first role and add it to the second. A user can be deleted from a role by selecting the user from the Users folder under the appropriate role, and then selecting Delete from either the right-click context menu or the Actions menu.

Assigning Roles to Components or Component Interfaces

Both components and component interfaces contain *Role Membership* folders. A Role Membership folder contains the set of roles that may access the object. Any role belonging to the package containing the component may be added to the Role Membership folder.

To assign one or more roles to a component or a component interface, select the appropriate Role Membership folder, and then select New | Role from either the right-click context menu or from the Actions menu. The Select Roles dialog box will appear, as shown below. All of the roles belonging to the appropriate package will be displayed, and one or more may be selected. Once OK is pressed, the selected roles will appear in the Role Membership folder.

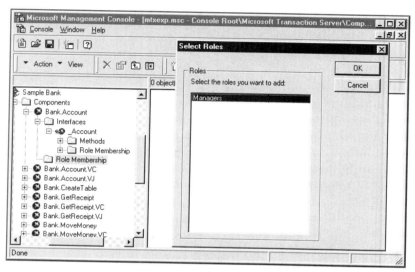

CERTIFICATION OBJECTIVE 4.06

Deploying an MTS Component

If a client application is to make use of an MTS component, a package containing the component must be registered on the client computer. A client computer does not need to be running MTS; it can run any Windows operating system with DCOM support. Microsoft Transaction Server has the capability to create an executable setup program for a package, which can then be used to automatically register that package's components on the client machines.

The first step in exporting is to select the required package in the left-hand pane of the MTS explorer. Then either right-click the package, or drop down the Actions menu and select Export. I attempted to export the Sample Bank package, and the following screen was displayed. The Browse button allows you to select the folder and the base filename of the exported package file. The option to Save Windows NT user IDs associated with roles allows for the cases in which you would not want any NT user names to travel with the exported package.

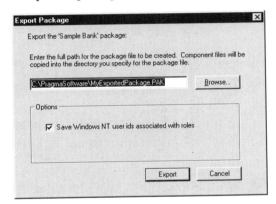

After clicking Export to initiate the exporting of the package, the export utility performs the following actions:

- It creates a .PAK file in the specified folder.

- It copies all of the components from that package into the same folder as the .PAK file.

- It also creates a folder directly below the specified folder, called "clients."

- It places a .EXE file with the same base filename as the .PAK file into the clients folder.

The .PAK file can be imported into another installation of MTS, per the previous section titled "Importing Existing Packages."

The .EXE file is the application that is used for deploying the components on the client computer. A big word of caution, however: DO NOT run this on the local machine (the machine on which it was created). It is a setup application, which is intended to run on the client computer in order to register the components on that computer.

When it runs on a DCOM-capable client computer, this setup file will do the following:

- If the components do not already exist on the client computer, it will install them.

- If the components existed on the client computer, it will update them.

- It will create an uninstall item in the Add/Remove Programs control panel application.

EXERCISE 4-1

Adding a Component to a Package

In this exercise, you will create a component (covered in Chapter 3), create an empty package, and add the component to the package. To create an in-process component:

1. Start Microsoft Visual Basic 6, and select a new ActiveX DLL project.

2. Set the project name to "Chapter4."

3. VB will create a default class called "Class1." Set this class name to "Adder."

4. In the code window for the Adder class, add the following function:

```
Function Add(x As Integer, y As Integer)
Add = x + y
End Function
```

5. Save the project in a folder called "Chapter4."

6. Select File | Make Chapter4.dll.

7. A file named "Chapter4.DLL" should now have been created in the Chapter4 folder

8. Exit Visual Basic.

The next step is to create an empty package:

9. Start the MTS Explorer.

10. Expand the tree in the left-hand pane down to the level of Console Root | Microsoft Transaction Server | Computers | My Computer | Packages Installed.

11. Right-click on Packages Installed and select New | Package.

12. On the Package Wizard dialog box, select Create an empty package.

13. Enter the package name as "Ch4 Package."

14. Leave the Account option as Interactive user - the current logged on user and select Finish.

15. A new package called "Ch4 Package" should appear in the tree in the left-hand pane of the Explorer.

Finally, add a component to the package:

16. Select the Ch4 Package in the left-hand pane and drill down to the Components folder (which should currently be empty).

17. Right-click on the Components folder and select New | Component.

18. On the Component Wizard dialog box, select Install new component(s).

19. Click the *Add Files* button and browse for the file Chapter4.DLL.

20. Click OK and the Adder component will be added to Ch4 Package as Chapter4.Adder.

21. Drill down on the Adder component and observe that it contains an interface named Adder and a number of methods including Add, as shown in Figure 4-7.

FIGURE 4-7

The Adder component, with its Add method to the package

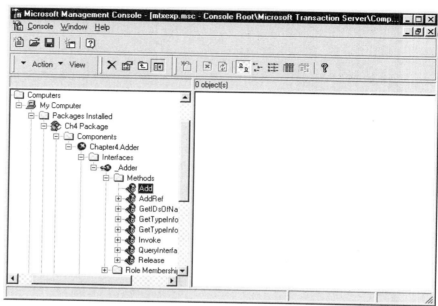

CERTIFICATION SUMMARY

The Microsoft Transaction Server (MTS) architecture consists of the Transaction Server Executive (TSE), ActiveX components, server processes, Resource Managers and Dispensers, and the Microsoft Distributed Transaction Coordinator.

The MTS Explorer, a GUI tool, enables you to place components into the MTS environment and determine user access.

MTS uses its Package Wizard to create packages. After a package is created and configured, it needs to have components added to it. You can move a component from one package to another, install a new component, or import a component that is already registered.

MTS automatically starts and ends transactions via its Automatic Transactions feature. It enables exporting by creating an executable setup program for a package, which then automatically registers the package's components on the client machines.

✓ TWO-MINUTE DRILL

❑ MTS is essentially a component manager that provides transaction-processing capabilities. It is a technology that extends COM, the Component Object Model.

❑ MTS is installed from the Windows NT Options Pack, which has directories for Windows NT Server and Windows NT Workstation.

❑ MTS provides Resource Managers and Resource Dispensers to manage data.

❑ The ODBC Resource Dispenser manages a pool of ODBC database connections that can be dispensed to components as they are needed.

❑ The Shared Property Manager provides access to variables that are shared within a process.

❑ The MTS Explorer is actually an extension, or *plug-in,* to the *Microsoft Management Console* or *MMC.*

❑ When components are integrated into MTS, they are grouped into a unit called a *package.*

❑ Once a package name has been allocated, the *Package Identity* must be set. The identity of a package is a Windows NT user account, under which the components in the package will run.

❑ When a package is exported, a .PAK file is created. Also, all of the files that contain or are associated with the components from the package are copied into the same directory.

❑ You can assign security properties of a package through the security tab of the Properties dialog box.

❑ There are four transactional settings that a component may have: Requires a transaction, Requires a new transaction, Supports transactions, and Does not support transactions.

❑ *Declarative Security* under MTS is an administrative-level security paradigm, allowing you to configure the security of an entity by using the MTS Explorer.

SELF TEST

The following Self-Test questions will help you measure your understanding of the material presented in this chapter. Read all the choices carefully, as there may be more than one correct answer. Choose all correct answers for each question.

1. What are three benefits of Microsoft Transaction server? (Choose all that apply.)

   A. Scalability

   B. Ease of programming

   C. Reduced method invocation overhead

   D. Robustness

2. Durable data is managed by:

   A. Shared Property Manager

   B. Resource Managers

   C. Distributed Transaction Coordinator

   D. ODBC Resource Dispenser

3. Which two protocols for Resource Managers allow MTS to manage transactions?

   A. ODBC Compliance protocol

   B. OLE Transactions protocol

   C. Distributed Transactions protocol

   D. X/Open XA protocol

4. A customer's address is durable data. True or false?

   A. True

   B. False

5. Packages contain which of the following objects? (Choose all that apply.)

   A. Roles

   B. Hyperlinks

   C. Components

   D. Interfaces

6. What kinds of packages run within the client process?

   A. Library packages

   B. Server packages

   C. No packages run within the client process under MTS

   D. All packages run within the client process under MTS

7. Role-based security is available for which kind of packages?

   A. Library packages

   B. Server packages

   C. No packages

   D. All packages

8. A role serves what purpose?

   A. Determines who can access a package or its component

   B. Determines in which user context the components in a package will be run

   C. Determines under which process a component will run

   D. Roles serve no necessary function in MTS

9. Roles can contain which of the following? (Choose all that apply.)

   A. Windows NT permissions

   B. Windows NT groups

   C. Windows 95/98 users

   D. Windows NT users

10. Which entities can be protected by role-based security? (Choose all that apply.)

    A. Files in NTFS partitions

    B. Packages

    C. Components

    D. Interfaces

    E. Methods

11. What kinds of machines can run client applications that access MTS?

    A. Any platform with a Java Virtual Machine

    B. Any platform with DCOM support

    C. Windows for Workgroups and above

    D. Only Microsoft Windows NT

12. Exporting a package generates which files? (Choose all that apply.)

    A. A file named <PACKAGE NAME>.PAK

    B. A copy of all of the files associated with the components in the package

    C. A self-installing setup file called SETUP.EXE

    D. A self-installing setup file in the "Clients" folder called <PACKAGE NAME>.EXE

13. From where is MTS installed?

    A. Windows NT Workstation CD-ROM

    B. Windows NT Server CD-ROM

    C. Microsoft Management Console CD-ROM

    D. Windows NT Options Pack

14. Which of the following are components of MTS? (Choose all that apply.)

    A. Microsoft Distributed Transaction Coordinator

    B. Microsoft SQL Server

    C. Microsoft Message Queue Server

    D. Transaction Server Executive

15. In an MTS application, business rules are implemented by:

    A. SQL Server stored procedures

    B. Resource Managers

    C. Resource Dispensers

    D. Client applications

    E. ActiveX components

16. An MTS server process may host how many components?

    A. MTS server processes do not host components

    B. One

    C. Thirty-two

    D. Any number

    E. It depends on the platform running MTS

17. Resource Managers work in conjunction with which elements of MTS?

    A. MTS Explorer

    B. Distributed Transaction Coordinator

    C. Resource Dispensers

    D. OLE Transaction Manager

18. Which of the following are MTS Resource Dispensers? (Choose all that apply.)

    A. Shared Property Manager

    B. X/Open XA

    C. OLE Resource Dispenser

    D. ODBC Resource Dispenser

19. MTS provides rollback facilities in which circumstances?

    A. Only transactions involving a single database

    B. Transactions involving multiple databases, only if the code handles the commit or rollback after each database access

    C. Transactions involving multiple databases, only if the databases support certain transaction protocols

    D. Explicit rollback support is only provided for MSMQ transactions

20. In what circumstances do you access variables through the Shared Property Manager?

    A. To provide access to properties with lower security levels

    B. To retain properties after the machine is shut down

    C. To share properties with in-process COM servers

    D. To access common non-durable variables

21. The Microsoft Management Console is also used to manage which application?

    A. Windows Explorer

    B. Internet Explorer

    C. Internet Information Server

    D. Windows NT Control Panel

22. MTS Explorer can display packages from which computers?

    A. Any computer on the network running MTS

    B. Any computer on the network with DCOM support

    C. Any computer on the network running Windows for Workgroups or above

    D. Only the local computer

23. If you add a role to a package, but all users can still access its components, what is the most likely cause?

    A. Authorization checking has not been enabled on the package

    B. No users have been added to the role

    C. You do not have permissions to administer declarative security

    D. The users all have administrative privileges

24. If you add a role to a package and no users can access its components, what is the most likely cause?

    A. Authorization checking has not been enabled on the package

    B. No users have been added to the role

    C. You do not have permissions to administer declarative security

    D. The users all have administrative privileges

25. Role-based security which is administered through the MTS Explorer is known as:

    A. Programmatic security

    B. Administrative security

    C. Declarative security

    D. Server-level security

26. Trace messages can hinder runtime performance. True or false?

    A. True

    B. False

27. To restrict access to an interface to certain users, a role should be added to the following:

    A. The Roles folder of an interface

    B. The Roles folder of a method

    C. The Role Membership folder of a component

    D. The Role Membership folder of an interface

28. You are required to configure a component that must write data to a log table in the database. These database writes must exist within a transaction, but if they fail, they should not affect any transactions that other components are involved in. What level of transaction support should you configure for the component?

    A. Requires a transaction

    B. Requires a new transaction

    C. Supports transactions

    D. Does not support transactions

29. Components may be imported from the following:

    A. A list of in-process servers installed on the local machine

    B. A list of ActiveX controls installed on the local machine

    C. A list of all COM components on any computer on the network

    D. Components cannot be imported into MTS

30. The interfaces and methods can be browsed in the MTS Explorer for the following:

    A. All components

    B. No components

    C. Components that were installed with Component Wizard

    D. Components that were imported with Component Wizard

31. Components can be dragged and dropped between packages within MTS Explorer. True or false?

   A. True

   B. False

32. What is the default authentication level for package security?

   A. None

   B. Administrator

   C. Packet

   D. Packet integrity

33. When importing an existing package, you have the option of also importing the following:

   A. Components belonging to the package

   B. Roles belonging to the package

   C. NT users saved within the package

   D. Transaction statistics belonging to the package

34. When a new package is created it contains the following:

   A. The default MTS component

   B. An empty component

   C. Components inherited from its parent

   D. No components

35. The package identity determines the following:

   A. The NT user account under which the components will run

   B. The name of the package

   C. The text that comes before the dot in component names for that package

   D. The CLSID of the package

36. Process isolation is provided by library packages. True or false?

   A. True

   B. False

37. MTS trace messages are logged by the following:

   A. The DTC

   B. The SDLC

   C. The MTS Executive

   D. Resource Managers

MICROSOFT CERTIFIED SOLUTION DEVELOPER

5

Using Microsoft Transaction Server Services

CERTIFICATION OBJECTIVES

T his chapter provides all the necessary information to build MTS components using Visual Basic. It helps you to know the importance of Object State and managing it for efficient transactions. It also provides knowledge about how just-in-time activation changes the way objects behave in the MTS environment. After reading this chapter, you will be able to build efficient MTS components, trap errors, and debug the components using the tools provided by Visual Basic.

Microsoft Transaction Server Overview

In this chapter, you will learn how to build MTS components that participate in transactions. First, you will learn how to get a reference to an ObjectContext object, which enables you to obtain information about your object and controls the way MTS processes the transaction. Then, you will learn how to list other objects in your transaction by calling the CreateInstance method. You will also learn how to use the SetAbort, SetComplete, EnableCommit, and DisableCommit methods of the ObjectContext object to notify MTS of the completion status of your object's work.

Next, you will learn how to determine the outcome of a transaction that involves multiple objects, you will learn about the importance of object state in the MTS programming model, and how just-in-time activation changes the way objects behave in the MTS environment. You will also learn when it is appropriate to store object state for an MTS component and the different methods you can use.

You also will learn how to use the Shared Property Manager, a Resource Dispenser that runs in the MTS environment, and you will study connection-pooling. You will learn about the types of errors that can occur in MTS. You will learn how to debug your MTS components by using the tools provided by Visual Basic. You will also learn how to use other tools to debug your MTS components and monitor how they run under MTS. Finally, you will learn the best ways of MTS programming.

Building MTS Components

In this section, you will learn how to build MTS components. You will learn how to get the context objects CreateInstance, SetComplete, SetAbort, EnableCommit, and DisableCommit. Finally, you will study the transaction life and its outcome.

Basics of MTS Components

To get a reference to a context object, call the GetObjectContext function; this function then returns a reference to the ObjectContext instance for the object. To call the GetObjectContext function in Visual Basic, you must first set a reference to Microsoft Transaction Server Type Library (MTXAS.DLL) by choosing Project/References. The following example shows how to call GetObjectContext to return an ObjectContext object:

```
Dim ctxtObject As ObjectContext
Set ctxtObject = GetObjectContext()
```

The following code snippet shows how you can use GetObjectContext to call methods on the ObjectContext object without maintaining a separate object variable:

```
GetObjectContext.SetAbort 'This aborts the current
transaction
```

The uses of ObjectContext object are as follows:

- Declare that the object's work is complete.
- Prevent a transaction from being committed, either temporarily or permanently.
- Instantiate other MTS objects and include their work within the scope of the object's transaction.
- Find out if a caller is in a particular role.

■ Find out if security is enabled.

■ Find out if the object is executing within a transaction.

■ Retrieve Microsoft Internet Information Server (IIS) built-in objects.

Calling CreateInstance

Most of the time, your object creates and uses other objects to complete the task/transaction. If the new object must participate in the same, it must inherit its context from the creating object. To achieve this, you must use the CreateInstance method on the ObjectContext object to create a new MTS object and pass context information to that new object. Please note that the object being created must have its transaction attribute set to Requires a transaction or Supports transactions. Any other transaction attribute does not include the object in the existing transaction.

If you have created an MTS object by calling CreateInstance, a new context object is created for it because all MTS objects always have an associated context object. So the context object inherits information such as the current activity, security information, and the current transaction. And so your new object participates in the same transaction as the calling object.

If a call to CreateInstance is used to create a non-MTS object, a new object will be created that does not have a context object, so it does not participate in the existing transaction.

The CreateInstance method takes one parameter: the progID of the object being created. Look at the following lines of code:

```
Dim ctxtObject As ObjectContext
Dim objAccount As Bank.Account

' Get the object's ObjectContext.
Set ctxtObject = GetObjectContext()

' Use it to instantiate another object.
Set objAccount =
ctxtObject.CreateInstance("Bank.Account")
```

CreateObject, New, and CreateInstance

You can create an object in Visual Basic using CreateObject, New, and CreateInstance. You may wonder why you should use CreateInstance for the ObjectContext object when you can call CreateObject or use New keyword to create objects.

Although using New keyword to create an object is better than calling CreateObject, New keyword creates the object internally instead of using COM services to create it. If the object created is an MTS object, this yields undesirable effects because MTS uses COM services to host its objects. Thus, if COM is not used to create the object, MTS cannot host the object. So you have to use CreateObject call to create the object, which uses COM services to create it.

Even though you have created the MTS object by using either New or CreateObject, the object does not inherit its context from the caller. Which means that it cannot participate in the existing transaction, even if its transaction attribute is set to Requires a transaction or Supports transactions. Because it is not part of the same activity, it does not have access to security information.

If CreateInstance is used to create an MTS object, that object can participate in the existing transaction, and it inherits its context from the caller (this includes the current activity, security information, and current transaction).

Calling SetComplete and SetAbort

ObjectContext provides two methods, SetComplete and SetAbort, to notify MTS of the completion status of the work performed by your object, which should have a reference to the context object.

SetComplete Method

This method declares that the current object has completed its work successfully and should be deactivated when the currently executing method returns to the client. For objects that are executing within the scope of a transaction, it also indicates that the object's transactional updates can be committed. The SetComplete method informs the context object that it can commit transaction updates and can release the state of the object, along with any resources that are being held. If all other objects involved in the transaction also call SetComplete, MTS commits the transaction updates of all objects.

SetAbort Method

This method declares that the transaction in which the object is executing must be aborted, and that the object should be deactivated on returning from the currently executing method call. If an MTS object's method that completes a transaction is unsuccessful, it must call the SetAbort method of the ObjectContext object before returning. SetAbort informs the context object that the transaction updates of this object and all other objects in the transaction must be rolled back to their original state. If an object involved in a transaction calls SetAbort, the updates roll back, even if other objects have called the SetComplete method.

The following code exemplifies SetComplete and Set Abort methods.

```
Dim ctxtObject As ObjectContext
Set ctxtObject = GetObjectContext()
On Error GoTo ErrorHandler

' Do some business here. If the business was successful,
' call SetComplete.
ctxtObject.SetComplete
Set ctxtObject = Nothing
Exit Function

' If an error occurred, call SetAbort in the error
' handler.
ErrorHandler:
    ctxtObject.SetAbort
    Set ctxtObject = Nothing
    Exit Function
```

Calling EnableCommit and DisableCommit

ObjectContext provides two methods, EnableCommit and
DisableCommit, to enable an object to remain active in a transaction while
performing work over multiple method calls. This helps to handle cases in
which an object requires several method calls to it before its work is finished
in the transaction.

EnableCommit Method

EnableCommit declares that the current object's work is not necessarily
finished, but that its transactional updates are consistent and could be
committed in their present form. When an object calls EnableCommit, it
allows the transaction in which it's participating to be committed, but it
maintains its internal state across calls from its clients until it calls
SetComplete or SetAbort, or until the transaction completes.
EnableCommit is the default state when an object is activated. This is why
an object should always call SetComplete or SetAbort before returning from
a method, unless you want the object to maintain its internal state for the
next call from a client. EnableCommit takes no parameters.

```
Dim objCtxt As ObjectContext

Set objCtxt = GetObjectContext()
objCtxt.EnableCommit
```

DisableCommit Method

DisableCommit declares that the object's transactional updates are
inconsistent and can't be committed in their present state. You can use the
DisableCommit method to prevent a transaction from committing
prematurely between method calls in a stateful object. When an object
invokes DisableCommit, it indicates that its work is inconsistent and that it
can't complete its work until it receives further method invocations from
the client. It also indicates that it needs to maintain its state to perform that
work. This prevents the MTS run-time environment from deactivating the
object and reclaiming its resources on return from a method call. Once an
object has called DisableCommit, if a client attempts to commit the

transaction before the object has called EnableCommit or SetComplete, the transaction will abort. DisableCommit takes no parameters.

```
Dim objCtxt As ObjectContext

Set objCtxt = GetObjectContext()
objCtxt.DisableCommit
```

Transaction Life

You know that each transaction involves many objects in a critical transaction. So MTS should be aware about when the transaction ends. And also it is its responsibility to determine the transaction outcome.

If any of the objects in a transaction call SetAbort or DisableCommit, MTS aborts the transaction; if all of them call SetComplete, it commits the transaction. A transaction begins when a client calls an MTS object with its transaction attribute set to Requires a transaction or Requires a new transaction. This object is the root of the transaction because it was the first object created in the transaction and MTS determines the outcome of transaction at the end of the transaction, and either commits or aborts the transaction. Any transaction can be brought to an end when:

1. The root object calls SetComplete or SetAbort
2. The transaction times out
3. The client releases the root object

The transaction ends whenever the root object calls either the SetComplete or SetAbort method. Remember that that the objects, which are created as part of the same transaction, will not have any effect on the transaction lifetime, even if they call SetComplete or SetAbort. The transaction does not end, even if the root object calls EnableCommit or DisableCommit. In order to retrieve the information needed from the client, you can keep the transaction alive by using the EnableCommit or DisableCommit methods.

A transaction also gets killed if it times out. The default time for a transaction is set to 60 seconds. You can change this to another value. In order to change the timeout value, right-click on the computer icon in the MTS Explorer and then click the Properties option. Click on the Options tab and change the Transaction Timeout property's value.

If the client releases the root object, it can bring the transaction to an end. This happens whenever the root object calls EnableCommit or DisableCommit and returns to the client. The client then releases the object.

Transaction Outcome

At the end of the transaction, MTS must determine the transaction outcome. This is something similar to group decision-making, in which the group must reach a unanimous decision to commit the transaction. Each object casts its vote by calling SetComplete, SetAbort, EnableCommit, or DisableCommit. MTS tallies each object's vote and determines the outcome. If all objects called SetComplete or EnableCommit, the transaction commits. If any object called SetAbort or DisableCommit, the transaction aborts.

If an object does not call SetComplete, SetAbort, EnableCommit, or DisableCommit, MTS treats the object as if it called EnableCommit. EnableCommit is the default status for an object.

CERTIFICATION OBJECTIVE 5.03

Managing Object State

This section discusses just-in-time activation, shows how to store the object state, and covers the Shared Property Manager (SPM).

One of the most important factors to consider while designing MTS components is state management, which directly affects the scalability of the MTS components. State, simply speaking, is object data that is kept over more than one method call to the object. It can be stored in any of the three tiers: the client, MTS objects, or the database. Here you study how state is managed in the middle tier (in MTS objects) and how that affects MTS and the design of your objects.

State stored in MTS objects is also called local state; properties are good examples of it. An object can have properties that store the information and also can have methods, which retrieve or update these properties. The object exists and keeps this information until the client releases it. An object that maintains state internally over multiple method calls like this is called a stateful object.

If the object doesn't expose properties, however, and the values of the properties (state) are passed each time a method call is made instead, it is a stateless object. Stateless objects do not remember anything from previous method calls.

Stateful objects often require server resources such as memory, disk space, and database connections, which impact the scalability of the application. These resources are normally held until the client releases the object because state is often client-specific. The decision to hold resources, either locally in a stateful object or not, has to be balanced against other application requirements. Because the stateful objects drastically reduce the scalability, official Microsoft documentation advises that if COM components are written to run within MTS, they should be stateless.

You have to remember which states consume more scarce or expensive resources and which do not before designing the component. For example, storing database connection consumes scarce resources, which reduce the scalability because there are a limited number of database connections that can be allocated, and used connections cannot be pooled.

Sometimes, storing some states can increase application scalability. Consider a banking transaction. Storing an account holder's information, such as name and address, consumes relatively less memory, but reduces the amount of data being passed over the network on each method call to the object. You have to analyze extensively to determine if a solution is scalable under normal use of the application.

One way of reducing consumption of system resources is just-in-time activation, which recycles objects when they finish with their work. This also helps ensure the isolation of the transaction, so that information from one transaction is not carried into the next transaction. MTS helps conserve server memory by keeping an instance of an object alive only when a client is calling the object, which is known as just-in-time activation. Just-in-time activation allows the server to handle more clients than the actual number possible when the objects remain active.

When a client calls a method on an object, MTS activates the object by creating it and allowing the method to go through to the object. When the object is finished and it calls SetComplete or SetAbort, it returns from the method call, and MTS deactivates the object to free its resources for use by other objects. Later, when the client calls another method, the object is activated again. MTS deactivates an object by releasing all references to it, which in turn destroys the object.

Because the object is destroyed, it loses all of its local state, such as local variables and properties. However, MTS manages the client pointer so that the object remains valid. When the client calls a method on the deactivated object, MTS activates it by re-creating it and allowing the method to go through with one exception: the object's local state is reset and it does not remember anything from the previous activation. MTS manages the client's pointer so that the client is unaware that the object has been destroyed and re-created. An object is only deactivated when it calls SetComplete or SetAbort and returns from the method call. It will not get deactivated even if it calls EnableCommit or DisableCommit. It's not deactivated when the transaction ends; for example, if the transaction times out. When an object calls SetComplete or SetAbort, it loses its local state as soon as the method returns. Therefore, objects that participate in transactions must be stateless because any instance data is lost whenever they are deactivated. This doesn't mean that you should always design towards a stateless programming model. You can store state outside the object. So just-in-time activation has a potential effect on object state.

Just-in-time activation forces objects to be stateless, and so loses the entire local variables and properties. Most of the time, you need to store state for MTS objects. For example, consider a transaction in which you need to search a city depending on the ZIP code entered (like searching for a store nearest to a customer). If you do not store this kind of static data, repeatedly looking up the information is inefficient. You can store the state on the client side, which is useful for tasks in which a variety of information must be gathered from the user (storing items in a virtual shopping cart until the user decides to place an order, for example). Users are allowed to delete items from the cart and update quantities until they get to the virtual counter. If you store this kind of data on the client side, the server resources are conserved while multiple users are shopping.

A state can also be stored in a database if your object state needs the protection of transactions and is likely to be accessed by other applications. The main task is storing state for the middle tier because an object's data is only active until its transaction completes. When the object is again brought back (activated), it does not have any instance data from its previous transaction. It is possible to store instance data within a transaction; an object does not have to call SetComplete or SetAbort when it returns from a method call. When the transaction gets complicated, it requires several calls from the client, each performing a part of the work until the last method calls SetComplete or SetAbort. Here, state can be maintained as instance data in local variables over each call. When the final method calls SetComplete or SetAbort, the object is finally deactivated, releasing the instance data.

Another alternative is storing state in a file on the same computer that the objects reside, avoiding network trips. The advantage is that they protect from concurrent access and keep state across multiple transactions; the disadvantage that is you can lock the entire file not at the record level can be locked. Because the states are stored as records, unlike plain data, you have to lock the entire file to get a particular state stored in the file. Therefore, storing state in files is not useful for storing state shared with many objects because any one object can effectively prevent all other objects to use a state stored in a file by locking the entire file, which could harass the transactions.

State can be stored in a Windows NT service, which can give faster access to state. You can create a Windows NT service that exposes COM services to store and retrieve data, and all the objects that access state should do so through this COM object. Here, the state is available to all packages on the same computer. The only disadvantage is you have to write these services and implement the locking mechanisms to ensure that multiple objects can access the state.

MTS provides a Resource Dispenser, Shared Property Manager (SPM), to store state. SPM allows you to store properties programmatically and share that data with all objects in the same package. The SPM is fast because access to its properties is in the same process as the package, and it provides locking mechanisms to guard against concurrent access.

The SPM object hierarchy consists of the following three objects:

Object	Usage
SharedPropertyGroupManager	Used to create shared property groups and obtain access to existing shared property groups.
SharedPropertyGroup	Used to create and access the shared properties in a shared property group.
SharedProperty	Used to set or retrieve the value of a shared property.

In order to organize and access data that is shared between objects and object instances within the same server process, you use the objects provided by the SPM. Groups within the process organize shared properties. You can create a shared property group by using the SharedPropertyGroupManager object. You must first set a reference to Shared Property Manager Type Library (MTXSPM.DLL) from Project/References in Visual Basic to use the SharedPropertyGroupManager object. Once this library is referred, you can create the object by using CreateObject function.

```
Dim spmManager As SharedPropertyGroupManager
Set spmManager = New SharedPropertyGroupManager
```

You can also use the CreateInstance method of the ObjectContext. MTS always ensures that only one instance of the SharedPropertyGroupManager object exists per server process. If the SharedPropertyGroupManager object already exists, MTS creates a reference to the existing instance. The SharedPropertyGroupManager object provides the following two methods:

- The CreatePropertyGroup method creates and returns a reference to a new shared property group. If a property group with the specified name already exists, CreatePropertyGroup returns a reference to the existing group.

- The Group method returns a reference to an existing shared property group, given a string name by which it can be identified.

The CreatePropertyGroup method takes four parameters: the name of the new property group; the isolation mode; the release mode; and an out parameter that returns, whether or not the group already exists.

The name parameter defines the name of the shared property group. Other objects can call the Group method and pass this name to get a reference to the shared property group.

The isolation-mode parameter controls the way locking works for the group. Because the properties in the group are shared, multiple objects can access and update properties at the same time. The Shared Property Manager provides locking to protect against simultaneous access to shared properties. There are two values you can specify for locking:

- **LockSetGet** This is the default lock constant, and it's physical value is 0. This constant locks a property during a Value call, assuring that every get or set operation on a shared property is atomic. It ensures that two clients can't read or write to the same property at the same time, but it doesn't prevent other clients from concurrently accessing other properties in the same group.

- **LockMethod** The physical value of this constant is 1. This constant locks all of the properties in the shared property group for exclusive use by the caller as long as the caller's current method is executing. This is the appropriate mode to use when there are interdependencies among properties, or in cases in which a client may have to update a property immediately after reading it before it can be accessed again.

The release-mode parameter controls how the shared property group is deleted. There are two values you can specify for release, as follows:

- **Standard**   The physical value of this constant is 0. The release mode parameter is set to Standard, which means that when all clients have released their references on the property group, the property group is automatically destroyed.

- **Process**   The physical value is 1. The release mode parameter is set to Process, which means that a property group isn't destroyed until the process in which it was created has terminated. You must still release all SharedPropertyGroup objects by setting them to Nothing.

The last parameter is a Boolean value that returns whether or not the group already exists. If it does exist, CreatePropertyGroup returns a reference to the existing group.

The following example code uses the CreatePropertyGroup method to create a new property group called MsgSystem:

```
Dim spmGroup As SharedPropertyGroup
Dim bExists As Boolean
Set spmGroup =
spmManager.CreatePropertyGroup("MsgSystem", _
    LockMethod, Process, bExists)
```

An object should never attempt to pass a shared property group reference to another object. If the reference is passed outside of the object that acquired it, it's no longer a valid reference. Property groups must be created and initialized. The best time to do this is when the server creates the process. There is no way for the MTS objects in a process to detect process creation, however. Therefore, the first MTS object to access the property group must be the one to initialize it. If several MTS objects can potentially access the property group first, they must each be prepared to initialize it. Use the last parameter of CreatePropertyGroup to determine whether the properties must be initialized. If it returns False, you must create and initialize the properties.

Once you have created a new shared property group, you can use it to create a new property that is identified by either a numeric value or a string expression.

The SharedPropertyGroup object has the following methods and properties:

- **CreateProperty**   Creates a new shared property identified by a string expression that's unique within its property group.

- **CreatePropertyByPosition**   Creates a new shared property identified by a numeric index within its property group.

- **Property**   Returns a reference to a shared property, given the string name by which the property is identified.

- **PropertyByPosition**   Returns a reference to a shared property, given its numeric index in the shared property group.

The first MTS object that accesses a shared property group must initialize all of its properties. And it should call CreateProperty by passing the name of the property. CreateProperty returns a Boolean value, indicating whether the property already exists. If it doesn't, the MTS object should initialize it. The following code exemplifies this:

```
Dim spmPropMsgCount As SharedProperty

Set spmPropMsgCount = _
    spmGroup.CreateProperty("MsgCount", bExists)

' Set the initial value of MsgCount to
' 0 if MsgCount didn't already exist.
If bExists = False Then
    spmPropMsgCount.Value = 0
End If
```

After creating or obtaining a shared property, you can work with it through the SharedProperty object. It has one property, Value, which is used to set or return the value of the property. The following code increments the MsgCount shared property when a new message is received:

```
Set spmPropMsgCount = spmGroup.Property("MsgCount")
spmPropMsgCount.Value = spmPropMsgCount.Value + 1
```

FROM THE CLASSROOM

Transactional Frame of Mind

Microsoft's Transaction Server provides numerous benefits: database-connection pooling, thread pooling, object brokering, run-time transaction support, and just-in-time activation, to name just a few. With the expansive functionality provided by MTS, certain design issues should be kept in mind to assist or improve upon the performance benefits generated. Because stateful COM components, such as those using public properties, must maintain information between calls, avoiding coding for local state maintenance can drastically improve scalability. Creating database connections at the last possible moment and releasing them as soon as possible can greatly assist the database-connection pooling features of MTS. Because MTS manages just-in-time activation, coding components to avoid cross-component state dependencies should also be avoided.

Finally, process isolation is possible due to the MTS management of process space. To facilitate this feature, all COM components must be written as apartment threaded.

Before a developer can create an ObjectContext object, or use any of the Shared Property Manager objects, references to the appropriate DLLs must be made within your project. Before an instant of SharedProperty, SharedPropertyGroup, or SharedPropertyGroupManager objects may be made, the MTXSPM.DLL file must be referenced. Before the ObjectContext object can be created, the MTXAS.DLL file must be referenced. The latter file is inherently required to create COM components designed to work within an MTS environment.

— *By Michael Lane Thomas, MCSE+I, MCP+SB, MCSD, MCT, A+*

Connection Pooling

Because database connections are scarce and expensive resources, you have to keep this in mind whenever your codes access databases. Creating and destroying connections consumes precious time and network resources. If you create and destroy database connections, it can impact your MTS object's performance. You can handle this effectively by using the connection-pooling feature available in MTS. Connection-pooling enables an application to use a connection from a pool of connections that do not need to be re-established for each use. Once a connection has been created and placed in a pool, an application can reuse that connection without performing the complete connection process. Using a pooled connection can result in significant performance gains because applications can save the overhead involved in making a connection. This can be particularly significant for middle-tier applications that connect over a network, or for applications that repeatedly connect and disconnect, such as Internet applications.

CERTIFICATION OBJECTIVE 5.04

Debugging and Error Handling

In this section, you'll learn about error-handling in MTS—how to debug a component and the tools available for debugging and monitoring.

Handling Errors in MTS

All errors that occur within and outside the MTS object should be handled by the object itself. The object should also report errors to MTS and, optionally, to clients. The three types of errors that can be considered in an MTS application are business-rule errors, internal errors, and Windows exceptions.

Business-rule errors occur whenever an object violates business rules. One example of such an error is a client trying to reserve an already occupied seat on a flight in an airline reservation application. You'd have to write the MTS object, which detects this kind of error, and it should enforce the business rules by checking client actions against business rules.

When an object performs an operation that violates business rules, the object causes a business-rule error. An example of such an error is a client attempting to withdraw money from an empty account. You should write MTS objects that detect these types of errors. They enforce the business rules by checking client actions against business rules. Business rules can also be enforced in the database itself. In both cases, the object should abort the current transaction and report the error to the client. This gives the user a chance to modify his request or information accordingly. To abort a transaction, call SetAbort, and MTS rolls back the transaction. To report the error back to the client, raise the error using the Err.Raise method with a custom error definition.

Sometimes, you'll get unexpected errors while your objects are in a transaction. These types of errors are known as internal errors (network errors, database-connectivity errors, missing files or tables, and so on). You must write code to trap these kinds of errors and attempt to correct them, or abort the transaction, depending on the error. In Visual Basic, these errors are detected and raised by Visual Basic itself. In some scenarios, you are required to report these kinds of errors to the client, for example, file or table not found, and abort the transaction. You are also required to display the transaction status with the appropriate error definition to the user. To do this, use the Err.Raise method. If you do not report an error to a client whenever a transaction is aborted or an error condition exists, MTS forces an error to be raised.

Sometimes, an error in your object, such as a memory-allocation error, can cause the Windows system to crash. MTS shuts down the process that hosts the object and logs an error to the Windows NT event log. MTS checks extensively for internal integrity and consistency. If MTS encounters an unexpected internal error condition, it immediately kills the process and aborts all transactions associated with it. This kind of operation, known as failfast, facilitates fault containment and results in more reliable and robust systems.

In general, most business transactions involve more numbers of objects to be created to implement the transaction. Whenever you are required to report an error to a client that is several calls deep from the root object, you should use error-trapping code in each object that uses the On Error GoTo syntax. Some errors cannot be corrected, so you have to abort the transaction by using a SetAbort call and raising the same error by using the Err.Raise method. Each calling object should handle the error in the same way by calling SetAbort and raising the error by using the Err.Raise method. Finally, the root object returns the error to the client and the transaction is aborted.

Debugging a Component

Whenever errors occur, you are required to debug the component. Through VB 6.0 IDE, you can debug your components and rectify the errors. What you have to do is open the component project in Visual Basic. Next, set the MTSTransactionMode property to a value other than 0, NotAnMTSObject. From the Project menu, click Properties and enter the start program on the Debugging tab. The start program is the client application that calls this component. Press F5 to begin debugging the component. It is highly recommended that you set the binary compatibility for components that are debugged by using VB, so future builds do not change any CLSIDs or interface IDs. After pressing F5, VB launches the client application and runs the component in debug mode. You can place breakpoints in the component's code and set watches on the variables. You also can debug components which are not inside the MTS package. For these components, VB automatically attaches to MTS and requests a context object for the component. This allows you to test components before placing them in MTS.

While debugging MTS components in Visual Basic, note the following points:

- You should not add components to an MTS package while it is being debugged. Doing so can cause unexpected results.

- MTS components running in the debugger always run in process as a library package, even if they are inside a server package. As a result, the component icons in the MTS Explorer do not spin as the components are debugged, and component tracking and security are disabled.

- Multiple clients cannot access the component while the component is being debugged.

- Multithread issues are not supported in debugging.

- You should not export a package while one of the MTS components is being debugged. Doing so causes unexpected results in the exported files.

- To debug components with security enabled, or for multiple-client access, use Visual Studio IDE debugger instead of VB IDE debugger.

- If you want to debug your components after they are compiled, you cannot use the Visual Basic debugger, which only debugs at design time. To debug a compiled Visual Basic component, use the functionality of the Visual Studio debugger.

To facilitate application debugging using VB, a component that uses ObjectContext can be debugged by enabling a special version of the object context. This debug-only version is enabled by creating the following registry key:

```
HKEY_LOCAL_MACHINE\SOFTWARE\Microsoft\Transaction Server\Debug\RunWithoutContext
```

Note that when running in debug mode, none of the functionality of MTS is enabled. GetObjectContext will return the debug ObjectContext rather than returning Nothing.

When running in this debug mode, the ObjectContext operates as follows:

- **ObjectContext.CreateInstance** calls COM CoCreateInstance (no context flows, no transactions, and so on)
- **ObjectContext.SetComplete** no effect
- **ObjectContext.SetAbort** no effect
- **ObjectContext.EnableCommit** no effect
- **ObjectContext.DisableCommit** no effect
- **ObjectContext.IsInTransaction** returns FALSE
- **ObjectContext.IsSecurityEnabled** returns FALSE
- **ObjectContext.IsCallerInRole** returns TRUE (same as normal when IsSecurityEnabled is FALSE)

Debugging and Monitoring Tools

Additional tools are available to debug MTS components, as described in the following sections.

MTS Spy

The Microsoft Transaction Server Spy (MTS Spy) is a useful tool for diagnosing problems and monitoring components as they work. It attaches to MTS processes and captures information such as transaction events, thread events, resource events, objects, methods, and user events.

Windows NT Event Log

All internal errors are eventually recorded in the Windows event log, which contains information about the problem. Check the Windows NT Event viewer to find errors logged by MTS. The error information, which shows the component that caused the error, can help diagnose the problem. To read the log, open Windows NT Event Viewer and go to Log menu select application. In the View menu, choose Filter, set the Source to Transaction Server, and click OK.

DTC Monitoring

MTS uses the Microsoft Distributed Transaction Coordinator (DTC) to manage transactions. You can use MTS Explorer to monitor DTC actions. You can view trace messages, the transaction list, and transaction statistics that are all generated by the DTC. These views are available under the Computer folder in MTS Explorer.

Trace Messages

The Trace Messages window lists current trace messages issued by the DTC. Tracing allows you to view the current status of various DTC activities such as startup and shutdown, and to trace potential problems by viewing additional debugging information.

Transaction List

The Transaction List window is useful for viewing the current transaction in which the computer participates. This also displays any transactions whose status is doubtful.

Transaction Statistics

The Transaction Statistics window is useful for viewing information about all transactions that have occurred since the DTC was started. It provides detailed information about current transactions, such as how many were aborted, committed, and so on.

MTS Programming Best Practices

There are many ways to improve the efficiency of the objects managed using MTS, including the following:

- By minimizing the number of hits required to use your objects. Each property exposed in the object requires at least one round trip in the network to set or get the value. If there are several properties that the client should set, this increases network traffic by more hits. To avoid this, you could use a method that sets all or most of the properties at once, reducing the number of network trips. Keep in mind that Microsoft documentation says that COM objects running in MTS should be stateless, hence there would be no public properties, which automatically reduces the number of hits.

- By using the ADO Recordset object to return large amounts of data that frees up server resources. ADO provides a disconnected recordset that can be marshaled by value to the client. And the disconnected recordset moves state to the client, so it frees the server resources.

- By avoiding passing or returning objects. By default, objects are passed by reference. If you pass the objects by value or return objects, all method calls on remote instances of your objects are across the network, consuming network resources.

- By avoiding generating events. If you create a component that generates events that must remain alive and active on the server, monitoring for the conditions to trigger events. Mostly, this process involves consuming resources that may decrease the scalability of the server.

- By passing arguments by value (ByVal) whenever possible. By default, Visual Basic passes arguments by reference. If you pass arguments by value, it minimizes trips across networks because the data does not need to be returned to the client.

Remember that the following are the core requirements of the COM components running under the MTS environment:

- Your components should obtain resources late and release them early. If you keep the database connections and network connections alive, it maximizes the chances of preventing another client to use those resources by locking that client.

- Your components should be apartment-threaded, so they enable MTS to run simultaneous client requests through objects. In Visual Basic, you can select the Apartment Threaded option for project properties to make objects apartment-threaded.

- Your components should call SetComplete, even if you are participating in a transaction. SetComplete deactivates your object instance and frees server resources associated with this instance.

CERTIFICATION SUMMARY

In this chapter, you read about using MTS services effectively to develop COM components to run in MTS environments. Most of the time, your object creates and uses other objects to complete the task/transaction. If the new object must participate in the same, it must inherit its context from the creating object. To achieve this, you must use the CreateInstance method on the ObjectContext object to create a new MTS object and pass context information to that new object.

You can create an object in Visual Basic by using CreateObject, New, and CreateInstance. Even though you have created the MTS object by using either New or CreateObject, the object does not inherit its context from the caller. It cannot participate in the existing transaction, even if its transaction attribute is set to Requires a transaction or Supports transactions. It is not part of the same activity, and it does not have access to security information. In order to notify MTS about the completion status of the work performed by your object, you can use the methods provided by ObjectContext: SetComplete and SetAbort. ObjectContext provides two other methods, EnableCommit and DisableCommit, which enable an object to remain active in a transaction while performing work over multiple method calls. This is useful for handling cases in which an object requires several method calls to it before its work is finished in the transaction.

One of the most important factors to consider while designing MTS components is how to manage state, which directly affects the scalability of the MTS components. Microsoft strongly recommends that the COM components are used in MTS environments should be stateless.

To store state over across object method calls, MTS provides a Resource Dispenser that is also known as Shared Property Manager (SPM). SPM allows you to store properties programmatically and share that data with all objects in the same package. The SPM is fast because access to its properties is in the same process as the package, and it provides locking mechanisms to guard against concurrent access.

Database connections are scarce and expensive resources. Creating and destroying connections consumes precious time and network resources, which affects MTS performance. In order to handle this effectively, you can use connection-pooling features available in MTS. Connection-pooling enables an application to use a connection from a pool of connections that do not need to be re-established for each use.

The errors that occur within and outside of the MTS object should be handled by the object. The object is also required to report errors to MTS and, optionally, to clients. The three main errors that commonly occur in MTS objects are business-rule errors, internal errors, and windows exceptions. To debug the component, you can use VB 6.0 IDE debugger or Visual Studio IDE debugger. The limitation of VB debugger is that you can debug the component at the design time only, whereas you can debug a compiled component using VS debugger. You can also debug the components using MTS Spy, Windows Event Log, and DTC monitoring.

 # TWO-MINUTE DRILL

❑ To get a reference to a context object, call the GetObjectContext function; this function then returns a reference to the ObjectContext instance for the object.

❑ The ObjectContext object can be used to declare that the object's work is complete, to prevent a transaction from being committed (either temporarily or permanently), and to instantiate other MTS objects and include their work within the scope of the object's transaction.

❏ You can create an object in Visual Basic using CreateObject, New, and CreateInstance.

❏ ObjectContext provides two methods, EnableCommit and DisableCommit, to enable an object to remain active in a transaction while performing work over multiple method calls.

❏ One of the most important factors to consider while designing MTS components is state management, which directly affects the scalability of the MTS components.

❏ DisableCommit declares that the object's transactional updates are inconsistent and can't be committed in their present state.

❏ Stateful objects often require server resources such as memory, disk space, and database connections, which impact the scalability of the application.

❏ The CreatePropertyGroup method creates and returns a reference to a new shared property group. If a property group with the specified name already exists, CreatePropertyGroup returns a reference to the existing group.

❏ The Group method returns a reference to an existing shared property group, giving it a string name by which it can be identified.

❏ Once you have created a new shared property group, you can use it to create a new property that is identified by either a numeric value or a string expression.

❏ You should not add components to an MTS package while it is being debugged; doing so can cause unexpected results.

❏ Multiple clients cannot access the component while the component is being debugged.

❏ Multithread issues are not support in debugging.

❏ You should not export a package while one of the MTS components is being debugged; doing so causes unexpected results in the exported files.

❏ To debug components with security enabled, or for multiple-client access, use Visual Studio IDE debugger, not VB IDE debugger.

SELF TEST

The following Self Test questions will help you measure your understanding of the material presented in this chapter. Read all the choices carefully, as there may be more than one correct answer. Choose all correct answers for each question.

1. Which of the following are uses of ObjectContext object?

    A. Declares that the object's work is complete

    B. Prevents a transaction from being committed, either temporarily or permanently

    C. Instantiates other MTS objects and includes their work within the scope of the object's transaction

    D. All of the above

2. Which is best way to create an MTS object?

    A. Create the object using New word

    B. Create the object by calling CreateInstance method

    C. Create the object by using CreateObject method

    D. None of the above

3. Which of the following functions would notify MTS that the transaction is over?

    A. SetComplete, SetAbort

    B. EnableCommit, DisableCommit

    C. All of the above

    D. None of the above

4. Which of the following functions enable the object to be active throughout the transaction?

    A. SetComplete, SetAbort

    B. EnableCommit, DisableCommit

    C. All of the above

    D. None of the above

5. Which of the following is true?

    A. When the root object calls either SetComplete or SetAbort method the transaction ends

    B. Any object created in part of the transaction calls either SetComplete or SetAbort and the transaction ends

    C. If either EnableCommit or DisableCommit is called by the root object. the transaction ends

    D. None of the above

6. Which of the following is the default method called in transaction on an object?

    A. EnableCommit

    B. DisableCommit

    C. SetAbort

    D. SetComplete

7. Which of the following statements is true?

    A. A stateful object remembers state over multiple method calls

    B. A stateless object does not keep track of the state at all

C.   A stateful object impacts the scalability of the application

D.   All of the above

8.   The Shared Property Manager consists of which of the following objects?

A.   SharedPropertyGroupManager

B.   SharedPropertyGroup

C.   SharedProperty

D.   All of the above

9.   Which of the following methods creates and returns a reference to a new shared property group?

A.   CreateInstance

B.   CreatePropertyGroup

C.   Group

D.   All of the above

10.   SharedPropertyGroup consists of which of the following methods and properties?

A.   CreateProperty, CreatePropertyByPosition

B.   Property, PropertyByPosition

C.   All of the above

D.   None of the above

11.   Which of the following statements are correct?

A.   SharedProperty object consists of one property: Value

B.   After creating a shared property, you can work on it through the SharedProperty object

C.   All of the above

D.   None of the above

12.   Which of the following is the best way to handle errors?

A.   Terminate the transaction calling SetAbort on the root object

B.   Report the error back to the client in a well-defined manner by calling Err.Raise method.

C.   All of the above

D.   None of the above

13.   While debugging MTS components, what do you have to keep in mind?

A.   You should not add components to an MTS package while it is being debugged

B.   You should not export a package while one of the MTS components is being debugged

C.   All of the above

D.   None of the above

14.   Windows NT Event Log is useful for which of the following?

A.   To verify the internal errors that are recorded in the event log

B.   To trace messages issued by Distribution Transaction Coordinator

C.   All of the above

D.   None of the above

15.   Which of the following statements are true about improving efficiency of MTS objects?

A.   By minimizing the number of hits required to use objects

B.   By avoiding generation of events

C.   By making objects apartment-threaded

D.   All of the above

6

Accessing Data from the Middle Tier

M ost of today's organizations are meeting a challenge to access non-traditional data and use it in their applications, along with traditional client/server SQL-based relational databases. The modern information systems include data from email, directories, file systems, images, multimedia systems, and so on, as well as traditional ones.

In the first sections of this chapter, we'll discuss Microsoft's strategy for handling this scenario: Universal Data Access (UDA). In the later sections, we'll study UDA's main component, ActiveX Data Objects, also known as ADO. Next, we'll explore ways to implement ADO in applications' middle tier to access data intrinsic of ADO, including its objects, error handling, and the cursor types provided by its objects. In the final sections, we'll study how to use appropriate locking strategies to ensure data integrity, manage database transactions to ensure data consistency and recoverability, and advanced topics (disconnected recordsets).

CERTIFICATION OBJECTIVE 6.01

Universal Data Access (UDA) Overview

A modern database application requires the integration of a variety of data types apart from the traditional ones. The traditional database management systems wouldn't allow the user to access the information stored in non-standard data systems like file systems, indexed-sequential files, desktop databases, spreadsheets, project-management tools, electronic mail, directory services, multimedia data stores, and more. So, most large corporations hire consultants to extend the database engine of the traditional database management system by using its programming interface to support this kind of non-traditional/non-relational data (audio, video, text stored in files, information stored in electronic mail, spreadsheet content, and so on). Such application development requires moving all the data needed by the application, which can be diversified across a corporation, into the development systems (which means into a single data store). These processes are expensive and waste resources and time.

To handle this kind of scenario, Microsoft introduced a strategy known as *Universal Data Access (UDA)*. The key strategy of Universal Data Access is that it allows applications to efficiently access data where it resides without replication, transformation, or conversion. You can use UDA as an alternative to the extension of the database engine or to be complementary to it, thus utilizing the developed extensions to the database engine.

Universal Data Access eliminates the expensive and time-consuming movement of data into a single data store and the commitment to a single vendor's products. It is based on open industry specifications that extend support to all major established database platforms such as SQL Server, DB2, Oracle, Sybase, and Ingres.

Universal Data Access provides high performance by offering the capability to scale applications to support concurrent users without taking a performance hit. It also provides increased reliability by reducing the number of components that need support on the PC, which in turn reduces possible points of failure.

Universal Data Access Architecture

Universal Data Access can be achieved through Microsoft Data Access Components (MDAC). MDAC contains ActiveX Data Objects (ADO), Remote Data Services (RDS), OLE DB, and ODBC. Figure 6-1 shows the architecture of Universal Data Access.

Microsoft ActiveX Data Objects (ADO) is a language-neutral object model that is the basis of Microsoft's Universal Data Access strategy. ADO is the object-based interface to OLE DB. OLE DB, the low-level, object-based interface, is the core of UDA. It is created to provide access to almost any type of data, regardless of the data's format or storage method. OLE DB allows client applications to access and manipulate data in the data store through any OLE DB provider, making it a simple, high-speed, low-memory overhead solution to data access.

ADO is an application-level programming interface to data and information. It supports a wide range of development activities, including database front-ends and middle-tier business objects using applications, tools, languages, or browsers. ADO extensively supports business

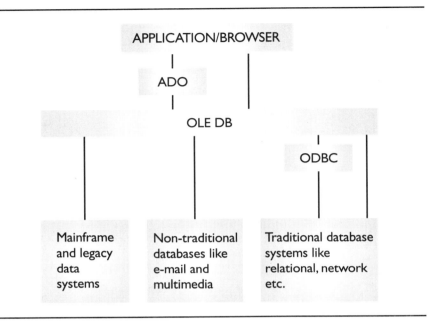

FIGURE 6-1

Universal Data Access
architecture

objects/clients developed by using Visual Basic, and it enhances Internet
Information Server 4.0 Active Server Page development. These
enhancements include a more-powerful and versatile client-side cursor
engine that is capable of working with data offline, thus reducing the
network traffic and load on the server. It fetches data asynchronously for
faster client response and has options for updating data on a remote client.
ADO also supports integrated remote capabilities, which are achieved by
Remote Data Services, the integrated interface of ADO. RDS, referred to
earlier as Active Data Connector, is a client-side component that interfaces
with ADO and provides key features such as cursors, remote-object
invocation, explicit recordset remoting, and implicit remote recordset
functionality such as fetch and update. RDS provides client-side and
middle-tier caching of recordsets, and thus improves overall performance by
minimizing the network traffic.

ADO provides only a thin and efficient layer to OLE DB. It eliminates
unnecessary objects and optimizes tasks. It exposes everything a data
provider can do and creates shortcuts for common operations.

ADO automatically adjusts itself, depending on the functionality of the data provider. Consider Microsoft Excel and SQL Server: Excel gives limited scope for database functionality, whereas SQL Server is pure database engine. ADO automatically adjusts itself to provide database functionality.

ADO contains seven objects: Command, Connection, Error, Field, Parameter, Property, and Recordset. These objects are discussed in the following sections.

- **Connection**   This object maintains the connection information with the data provider and represents the active connection to a database. You can use it to execute any command. If this command returns rows, a Recordset object is created automatically and returned. If your application requires more complex recordsets with cursors to handle data and its presentation, create a Recordset object explicitly, connect it to the Connection object, and then open the cursor.

- **Recordset**   This object contains the data returned by the query. This object's interface contains the most properties, functionality, and methods of all objects; and it maintains the cursor-management functionality. You can open a recordset without explicitly opening a connection. If your application requires opening multiple recordsets, opening a Connection object first is advisable. Recordset objects allow you to browse and manipulate the contents.

- **Field**   This object contains the information regarding a single column of data within a recordset. You can use it to read from or write to the data source. *Fields* is a collection of all Field objects, which are featured in the recordset.

Using these three objects, we can access the data from the data source for our applications.

The following are optional objects, which can be useful whenever our applications require a complex and enhanced manipulation of the data.

- **Command**   This object maintains information about a command, such as a query string, parameter definitions, stored procedures, etc.

We can execute a command string on a Connection object or query string as part of opening a Recordset object, without defining a Command object, which means that this is an optional object. We use the Command object when we expect output parameters while executing a stored procedure or when we want to define query parameters (make prepared query statements).

- **Parameter** This object is part of the *Parameters* collection, which is used to specify the input and output parameters for parameterized commands.

- **Error** Each single Error object found in the *Errors* collection represents extended error information raised by the provider. The *Errors* collection can contain more than one Error object at a time, all of which result from the same incident.

- **Property** This object represents provider-defined characteristics of an ADO object such as Recordset, Connection, and so on.

Dynamic Properties Collections

The Connection, Command, Recordset, and Field objects each contain a *Properties* collection to handle parameters of those objects.

The *Properties* collection contains any dynamic or "provider-specific" properties, exposed through ADO by the provider. We can use the Collection and Item method to reference the property by its name or by its ordinal position in the collection. Here is an example:

```
Command.Properties.Item (0)
Command.Properties.Item ("Name")
```

The Item method is a default method on an ADO collection; we can simply omit it.

```
Command.Properties (0)
Command.Properties ("Name")
```

Further, the *Properties* collection itself is the default collection for the Connection, Command, and Recordset objects, so we can omit it as well:

```
Command (0)
Command ("Name")
```

All of these syntax forms are identical. Figure 6-2 explains the ADO hierarchy.

From ADO2.0, event-based programming is introduced in ADO. Events are notifications that certain operations are about to occur or have already occurred. In general, they can be used to efficiently orchestrate an application that consists of several asynchronous tasks. Even though the

---

FIGURE 6-2   ADO hierarchy

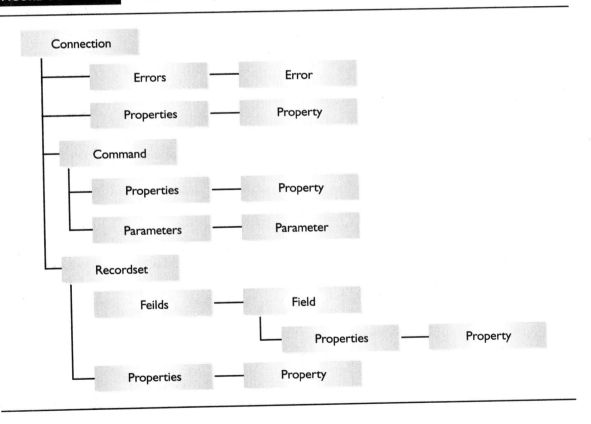

ADO object model does not explicitly embody events, it represents them as calls to event handler routines. Event handlers give us an opportunity to examine or modify an operation even before it starts, and then gives us a chance to either cancel or allow the operation to complete. ADO 2.0 introduces several operations that have been enhanced to optionally execute asynchronously. For example, an application that starts an asynchronous Recordset. Open operation is notified by an execution complete event when the operation concludes. ADO2.0 comes with two families of events:

- **ConnectionEvents** Events are issued when transactions on a connection begin, are committed, or rolled back; when commands execute; and when connections start or end.

- **RecordsetEvents** Events are issued to report the progress of data retrieval; when you navigate through the rows of a Recordset object; change a field in a row of a recordset, change a row in a recordset, or make any change in the entire recordset.

The Connection object issues ConnectionEvent events and the Recordset object issues RecordsetEvent events. Events are processed by event handler routines, which are called before certain operations start or after such operations conclude. Some events are paired. Events called before an operation starts have names of the form WillEvent (Will events) and events called after an operation concludes have names of the form EventComplete (Complete events). The remaining, unpaired events occur only after an operation concludes. (Their names are not formed in any particular pattern.) The event handlers are controlled by the status parameter. Additional information is provided by the error and object parameters. We can request that an event handler not receive any notifications after the first notification. For example, we can choose to receive only Will events or Complete events. In certain programming languages, one event handler can process events from multiple ADO objects. And, although less common, one event can be processed by multiple event handlers.

Microsoft specifies the following as general characteristics of ADO in its documentation:

- Ease of use

- High performance

- Programmatic control of cursors

- Complex cursor types, including batch, server-side, and client-side cursors.

- Capability to return multiple result sets from a single query

- Synchronous, asynchronous, or event-driven query execution

- Reusable, property-changeable objects

- Advanced recordset-cache management

- Flexibility; it works with existing database technologies and all OLE DB providers

- Excellent error-trapping

We can use ADO as the interface for all our client/server and Web-based data access solutions. ADO is a totally flexible and adaptable solution for all applications that require data access.

CERTIFICATION OBJECTIVE 6.02

Retrieving and Modifying Records Using ActiveX Data Objects (ADO)

The functionality flow of ADO-based applications to access the data sources are as follows:

- **Open the data source by creating the Connection object**   This specifies the connection string as its first part with information such as data source name, user identification, password, connection time-out, default database, and cursor location. A Connection object represents a unique session with a data source. We can even control the transactions through the Connection object by using the BeginTrans, CommitTrans, and RollbackTrans methods. The second part of this process is opening the ADO connection to the data source mentioned previously.

- **Execute a SQL statement**   Once the connection is open, we can run a query on the data source. We can run this query asynchronously and also choose to process the query's result set asynchronously. By choosing this option, we are giving permission to ADO to let the cursor driver populate the result set in the background, which in turn lets the application perform other process without waiting for the result set. Once the result set is available (depending on the cursor type), we can browse, and change the row data at either the server or client side.

- **Close the connection**   Once the task with the data source is done, we can drop the connection by close string.

The following Visual Basic code snippet demonstrates how to access data from a data source without opening a Connection to it by using only Recordset object.

We know that the main interface to data is the Recordset object in ADO. Although the rest of the objects in ADO are useful for managing connections, collecting error information, persisting queries, and so on. Most of our code's interaction with ADO will definitely involve one or more Recordset objects.

```
Set RS = CreateObject ("ADODB.Recordset")
RS.Open "Select * FROM SalesReport", "DATABASE=SQLProd1; UID=prod1; PWD=;" _
            & "DSN=SalesData"
' Use this recordset to manipulate with the data
'Close it
RS.Close
```

This code generates a forward-only, read-only Recordset object. With a few modifications, we can obtain a more functional Recordset (one that is fully scrollable and batch updateable). The following modifications to the code snippet exemplify that:

```
Set RS = CreateObject ("ADODB.Recordset")
RS.Open "Select * FROM SalesReport", "DATABASE=SQLProd1;
UID=prod1; PWD=;" _ DSN=SalesData", adOpenKeyset,
adLockBatchOptimistic
```

Once we retrieve the complete data, we can browse through it, modify it, or process it for our application's needs.

The following code is a fully functional program that retrieves data fields from a table and fills a list box using ADODB connection and Recordset objects that use VB6.0. This example assumes that you have a data table (any relational database system such as SQL Server, Oracle, or MS Access) and that you have created an ODBC data source using the ODBC Data Source Administrator utility. (Creating an ODBC Data Source and database tables is beyond the scope of this book.)

1. Create a new project and add a form to your project. Name your form as frmADOList.

2. Add a list box and a command button to the form.

3. Add ActiveX Data Objects 2.0 Library to your project by selecting Project/References.

Add the following code to the command button's click event:

```
Dim frmConnection As ADODB.Connection
Dim frmRecordset As ADODB.Recordset
 'Create a new Connection
Set frmConnection = New ADODB.Connection
 'Create a new Recordset
Set frmRecordset = New ADODB.Recordset
```

The following string is used to open the connection for a DSN-based connection. Just replace this with another statement that is in the body text for a DSN-less connection.

```
frmConnection.Open
"LoginDatabase","UserTable","computer"
frmRecordset.Open "Select * from Login", frmConnection
Do While Not frmRecordset.EOF
    List1.AddItem frmRecordset!UserID
```

```
      frmRecordset.MoveNext
Loop
frmRecordset.Close
frmConnection.Close
Set frmRecordset = Nothing
Set frmConnection = Nothing
```

Here, we opened two ADO objects, Connection and Recordset, to retrieve the information. To retrieve a particular field value from a row of the recordset, we can use the "!" operator. To retrieve the next row in the recordset, we have to move the cursor location to the next row by using the frmRecordset.MoveNext method.

Suppose we want to use a DSN-less connection. We can replace the previous frmConnection.Open statement with the following:

```
frmConnection.Open "Provider=Microsoft.Jet.OLEDB.3.51;" _
        & "Data Source=C:\Mydocuments\db1.mdb"
```

Obviously, we understand that this statement is using the Microsoft Jet OLE DB data source. Just refer to your database management system documentation for the OLE DB provider string and pass it as an argument to frmConnection.Open.

The documentation for the ADO Error object states that the Error Collection will be populated if any error occurs within ADO or its underlying provider. This is incomplete. Sometimes, with an error in the provider (OLE DB) or ADO, the *Errors* collection may not be populated. We have to check both the VB Error object as well as the ADO *Errors* collection.

Because the *Errors* collection is only available from the Connection object, we need to initialize ADO off a Connection object. Following is an example that demonstrates the errors encountered:

```
Private Sub Command1_Click()
    Dim frmConnection As ADODB.Connection
    Dim frmErrors As Errors
    Dim i As Integer
    Dim StrTmp
    On Error GoTo AdoError
```

```
      Set frmConnection =  New ADODB.Connection
      ' Open connection to some ODBC Data Source db1.mdb
      FrmConnection.ConnectionString = "DBQ=db1.mdb;" & _
                  "DRIVER={Microsoft Access Driver (*.mdb)};" & _
                  "DefaultDir=C:\mydocuments\;" & _
                  "UID=LoginTable;PWD=computer;"
      FrmConnection.Open
      ' The business logic to work on data goes here
   Done:
      ' Close all open objects
      frmConnection.Close
      ' Destroy frmConnection object
      Set frmConnection = Nothing
 ' Better quit
 Exit Sub
   AdoError:
      Dim errLoop As Error
      Dim strError As String
      ' In case frmConnection isn't set or other initialization problems
      On Error Resume Next
      i = 1
      ' Process
      StrTmp = StrTmp & vbCrLf & "Visual Basic Error # " & Str(Err.Number)
      StrTmp = StrTmp & vbCrLf & " and is generated by "& Err.Source
      StrTmp = StrTmp & vbCrLf & " and it is " & Err.Description
      ' Enumerate Errors collection and display properties of
      ' each Error object.
      Set frmErrors = frmConnection.Errors
      For Each errLoop In frmErrors
          With errLoop
              StrTmp = StrTmp & vbCrLf & "Error #" & i & ":"
              StrTmp = StrTmp & vbCrLf & " The ADO Error  #" & .Number
              StrTmp = StrTmp & vbCrLf & " And it's description is: " & _
                                          .Description
              StrTmp = StrTmp & vbCrLf & " The source is: " & .Source
              i = i + 1
          End With
      Next
      MsgBox StrTmp
      ' Clean that
      On Error Resume Next
      GoTo Done
   End Sub
```

CERTIFICATION OBJECTIVE 6.03

Using ADO from the Middle Tier

We know that the middle tier consists of the functional modules that actually process data. This middle tier runs on a server and is often called the application server (for example, Microsoft IIS4.0 with ASP and ADO2.0).

The other two tiers are user interface, which runs on the user's computer (the client) and a database management system (DBMS) that stores the data required by the middle tier. This tier runs on a second server, often called the database server.

The three-tier design has many advantages over traditional two-tier or single-tier designs:

- The added modularity makes it easier to modify or replace one tier without affecting the other tiers.

- Separating the application functions from the database functions makes it easier to implement load balancing.

A good example of a three-tier system is a Web browser (the client), IIS with ASP and ADO (the application server), and a database system (Access, SQL Server, Oracle, etc.).

We could use ADO in the middle tier directly (calling ADO from ASP in the case of IIS) or use it to create business objects. After creating business objects, we could call it in ASP or use it in our database applications.

Let us see how we could use ADO in the middle tier in ASP after creating a business object that can be used to read and write data into a table.

CERTIFICATION OBJECTIVE 6.04

Accessing and Manipulating Data

We can access and manipulate data through ADO by using the Connection, Recordset, and Command objects. It is possible to open a Recordset without opening a connection to the database first. This is done automatically when a Recordset is opened. Similarly, there is no need to create a connection before we open a Recordset. For example, with this flexibility we can attach a Command object to Connection A, and attach it to Connection B at a later stage without having to rewrite the query string or change parameters. We can simply rerun the command to create a recordset. To access and manipulate data, we open a Recordset object (either by using a stand-alone Connection object; or by creating a recordset and attaching it to a connection, and executing a query or stored procedure).

To open a recordset, we use the Execute method on either the Connection or Command object, or we can use the Open method on the Recordset object.

The following example shows the Execute method for opening a recordset to access and manipulate data:

```
Dim conn As ADODB.Connection
Dim rs As ADODB.Recordset
Set conn = New ADODB.Connection
' Establish a connection
With connBookstore
     .Provider = "SQLOLEDB"
     .ConnectionString = "User
ID=computer;Password=win98;" & _
                        "Data Source=SalesHawk;"

     .Open
End With
 ' Build the recordset
Set rs = conn ("Select * from SalesReport")
' code for manipulation on the data  goes here
'close the recordset and connection
 rs.Close
conn.Close
```

CERTIFICATION OBJECTIVE 6.05

Executing Stored Procedures from the Command Object

Whenever our application needs to update data in an external data source, we can either execute SQL statements directly or use a Recordset object and its various methods for modifying data. If we do not need to create a recordset, we can use a Command object and execute an SQL Insert, Update, or Delete statement to add or modify records. Recordsets utilize cursors, which consume resources. Using an SQL statement such as Insert is more efficient than creating a recordset and using the AddNew method of the Recordset object in enterprise systems. We can use either a Connection object or a Command object to execute SQL statements directly. To use the SQL command only once, use a Connection object. To execute stored procedures or parameterized SQL statements, use a Command object. Both Command and Connection objects use the Execute method to send the SQL statement to the data source. The following example shows this:

```
Dim conn As ADODB.Connection
Dim strSQL As String
Set conn = New ADODB.Connection
With conn
      .Provider = "SQLOLEDB"
      .ConnectionString = "User ID=Computer; Password=Win98;" & _
                          "Data Source=SalesHawk;"
      .Open
End With
' Build the SQL command
strSQL = "UPDATE SalesReps SET RepID = 101 WHERE RepName = 'John Hawk'"
" Execute the SQL command
conn.Execute strSQL
conn.Close
```

If our application has already opened a recordset, we can modify data by using the recordset's methods. We can modify records with a Recordset object only one at a time.

For multiple updates at once, we can use the Connection object's Execute method for better performance. The following example uses the Recordset object to modify data that is already opened:

```
Dim rs as Recordset
Set rs = New Recordset
'Use existing connection
Set rs.ActiveConnection = conn
'The cursors are discussed later in this chapter.
rs.CursorType = adOpenKeyset
rs.LockMode = adLockPessimistic
```

```
'Open recordset and change last representative's title since he got promoted to
'senior position
rs.Open "Select * from SalesReps"
rs.MoveLast
rs!Title = "Sales Manager"
rs.Update
rs.Close
```

Accessing and Manipulating Data by Using the Prepare/Execute Model

Prepare/Execute actually consists of preparing a SQL statement on-the-fly, depending on the user choice, and executing it for accessing and data manipulating. Normally, we see this kind of strategy in Internet search wizards.

Consider the following example, which prepares the query on the user selection and executes on the database for accessing the data:

```
Public Function BuildQuery (ByVal RepId As String, ByVal LastName As String, ByVal
FirstName As String, ByVal Title As String) As String
Dim strSql As String
strSql = "Select * From "
If Title="Rep" Then
  strSql= strSql & "SalesRep where
Else If Title="Mgr" Then
             strSql= strSql & "SalesMgr where "
                   End If
          End If


  If  LastName<>"" Then
       strSql = strSql & "LastName Like '" & LastName & "'"
  End If
If  FirstName<>"" Then
      strSql = strSql & "FirstName Like '" & FirstName & "'"
End If
If RepID<>"" Then
    strSql = strSql & "RepID Like '" & RepID & "'"
End If
End Function
```

Now we can use this function to access and manipulate the data in our data access module:

```
Dim rs as Recordset
sqlStr As String
Set rs = New Recordset
'Use existing connection
Set rs.ActiveConnection = conn
'The cursors are discussed later in this chapter.
rs.CursorType = adOpenKeyset
rs.LockMode = adLockPessimistic
'Open recordset and change the selected Manager's Position since he got promoted
'to VP Technology since from a Director position
sqlString = BuildQuery "1","Hawk", "John","Mgr"
rs.Open BuildQuery
rs!Position = "VP Technology"
rs.Update
rs.Close
```

Accessing and Manipulating Data by Using the Stored Procedures Model

We can improve the robustness of our application by using stored procedures. By using stored procedures to execute a query on a database, we allow the RDBMS to cache those SQL queries; subsequent requests can retrieve this information from cache, resulting in performance enhancement. Stored procedures is the added level of indirection between application and database, so even if our database structure changes often, we are not required to rewrite the client apps (assuming that the same result set is returned from our stored procedure). By encapsulating batch SQL statements, stored procedures reduce the network traffic. Instead of sending multiple requests from the client, we can send the requests in batches efficiently by using stored procedures and communicating whenever necessary. Stored procedures are compiled collections of SQL statements that execute quickly.

Using a Stored Procedure to Execute a Statement on a Database

Although executing stored procedures is similar to executing SQL statements, stored procedures exist in the database and remain there, even after execution has finished. The stored procedures hide potentially complex SQL statements from the components, which call them to retrieve data from the database. Because stored procedures are syntax-checked and compiled, they run much faster than SQL statements, which run as separate SQL queries.

```
Dim Conn As ADODB.Connection
Dim RS As ADODB.Recordset
Set Conn = New ADODB.Connection
Set RS = New ADODB.Recordset
Conn.Open "UserData", "User", "PassMe"
    'Say UserData is DSN, User is UserID and  'PassMe is
Password to it
RS = Conn.Execute "call spUserCount", numRecs,
adCmdStoredProc
    'spUserCount is Stored procedure to  count number of
Users in the login table
```

Here, stored procedure spUserCount is executed on the Connection object. The Execute method on the Connection object takes three parameters: CommandText, Number of records, affected and options (options can be adCmdText, adCmdTable, adCmdStoredProc, or adCmdUnknown, which is the default). The CommandText can be a simple SQL statement or a call to a stored procedure. But to execute a stored procedure, the options argument should be set to adCmdStoredProc constant.

The stored procedure spUserCount for a SQL Server database is as follows:

```
CREATE PROCEDURE spUserCount AS
    declare @usrcount as int
    select @usrcount = count(*) from LoginData
    return @usrcount
GO
```

Using a Stored Procedure to Return Records to a Visual Basic Application

The stored procedures on Microsoft SQL Server have the following capabilities for returning the data:

- One or more result sets
- Explicit return value
- Output parameters

Likewise, SQL Server handles the input parameters just like input parameters. The simplest way to return data is return values, which always returns the integer values (as shown in the example in the previous sections). Most of the time, it is required to return more than one value and it also requires returning data types other than integers (output parameters can be used for that). The following examples show how to return an output parameter instead of returning it as a value:

```
CREATE PROCEDURE spUserCount
    @count int output
AS
    select @count=count(*) from LoginData
GO
```

The following code shows how to use input and output parameters to return the password for the given user:

```
CREATE PROCEDURE spUserData
    @username varchar(255)
    @passwd varchar(255) output
AS
    select @passwd = passwd from LoginData where UserID Like @username
GO
```

We can return the recordsets to our application by using the Connection object and creating the recordsets on-the-fly, as in this example:

```
Dim conn As ADODB.Connection
Dim rs As ADODB.Recordset
Set conn = New ADODB.Connection
With conn
     .Provider = "SQLOLEDB"
     .ConnectionString = "User ID=Computer;Password=Win98; Data Source=LoginData"
     .Open
End With
' Build the recordset
Set rs = Conn.Execute "call spUserCount", numRecs, adCmdStoredProc
```

Setting the CommandType property of the Command object to the constant adCmdStoredProc and setting CommandText to the name of the stored procedure allows us to execute the stored procedure instead of a SQL query. The following example shows this:

```
Dim cmd As ADODB.Command
Dim rs As ADODB.Recordset
Set cmd = New ADODB.Command
'Use a previously created connection
Set cmd.ActiveConnection = conn
cmd.CommandType = adCmdStoredProc
cmd.CommandText = "spUserData"
Set rs = cmd.Execute
```

Most of the time, stored procedures require that one or more parameters be passed to them. For each required parameter, a Parameter object should be created and appended to the Parameters collection of the Command object. There are two approaches to populating the Parameters collection. For situations in which access to the data source is fast, or for rapid development purposes, we can have the data source automatically populate the parameters by calling the Refresh method of the collection. But the command must have an active connection for this to succeed. Once completed, we can assign values to the parameters and then run the stored procedure.

```
Dim conn As ADODB.Connection
Dim cmd As ADODB.Command
Dim rs As ADODB.Recordset
Set conn = New ADODB.Connection
Set cmd = New ADODB.Command
conn.ConnectionString = "DSN=SalesHawk;UID=Computer;PWD=Win98"
conn.Open
Set cmd.ActiveConnection = conn
cmd.CommandType = adCmdStoredProc
cmd.CommandText = "spSalesProspects"
cmd.Parameters.Refresh
'To retrieve the Sales Prospects in Chicago area using stored procedure to get
'that information
cmd.Parameters(1) = "Chicago"
Set rs = cmd.Execute
```

If we use the Refresh method, it causes ADO to make an extra trip to SQL Server to collect the parameter information. By creating parameters in the collection in our components, we can increase the performance and avoid the extra network trip. To do so we create the separate Parameter objects to fill the Parameter collection, fill in the correct parameter information for the stored procedure call, and then append them to the collection by using the Append method. For multiple parameters, we must append the parameters in the order that they are defined in the stored procedure. The following example shows how to create the parameters:

```
Dim conn As ADODB.Connection
Dim cmd As ADODB.Command
Dim rs As ADODB.Recordset
Dim prm As ADODB.Parameter
Set conn = New ADODB.Connection
Set cmd = New ADODB.Command
conn.ConnectionString = "DSN=SalesHawk;UID=Computer;PWD=Win98"
conn.Open
Set cmd.ActiveConnection = conn
cmd.CommandType = adCmdStoredProc
cmd.CommandText = "spSalesProspects"
Set prm = cmd.CreateParameter("varCity", adVarChar, adParamInput, 25, "Chicago")
cmd.Parameters.Append prm
Set rs = cmd.Execute
```

Retrieving and Manipulating Data by Using Different Cursor Locations

Every cursor requires system resources to hold data. These resources can be RAM, disk paging, temporary files on the hard disk, or even a temporary storage in the database itself. If the cursor uses client-side resources, it's called a client-side cursor; if it uses server-side resources, it's called a server-side cursor.

The CursorLocation property in a Recordset object sets or returns a long value that can be any of the three constant values (adUseNone, adUseClient, and adUseServer), that represent the location of the cursor. To set the CursorLocation property or to get the cursor location, we can use it as follows:

```
    recordset.CursorLocation = adUseClient 'to set the cursor on client side.
Dim adCurLoc
adCurLoc = recordset.CursorLocation 'to get the cursor location
```

The constant adUseNone can be used to tell that no cursor services are used. However, it is now obsolete and kept only for backward compatibility.

The constant adUseClient can be used to create a client-side cursor supplied by the local cursor library of the client. For backward compatibility, the synonym adUseCompatibility is still supported.

The constant adUseServer can be used to create the default server-side cursor. It uses data-provider or driver supplied cursors. These are sometimes flexible and allow for additional sensitivity to the changes made to the data source by others. Some features provided by the client-side cursor, such as disassociated recordsets, are not available on server-side cursors.

The setting of this property does not affect existing connections. This is a read/write property on either a connection or a closed recordset; it is only a read property on an open recordset. Connection.Exeute cursor will inherit this setting and recordsets will automatically inherit this setting from their associated connections.

The following example sets the location of the cursor to the client side:

```
Dim rs As ADODB.Recordset
Set rs = New ADODB.Recordset
rs.CursorLocation = adUseClient
rs.CursorType = adOpenKeyStatic
rs.Open "Select * from SalesReport", "DSN=SalesRep;UID=Computer;PWD=Win98;"
```

Client Side

If we chose to use a non-keyset client-side cursor, the server sends the entire result set across the network to the client machine. It allows the client-side application to browse through the entire result set to determine which rows it requires. Static and keyset-driven client-side cursors may place a significant load on the workstations if they include too many rows. Fetching such large row sets may affect the performance of the application, with some exceptions. For some applications, a large client-side cursor may be perfectly appropriate. The client-side cursor responds quickly and allows us to browse through the rows very fast. Applications are more scalable with client-side cursors because the cursor's requirements are placed on each separate client and not on the server.

Server Side

The server-side cursor returns only the requested data instead of entire rows over the network. This could be an obvious solution wherever excessive network traffic is present. Server-side cursors also permit more than one operation on the connection. That is, once we create the cursor, we can use the same connection to make changes to the rows without having to establish an additional connection to handle the underlying update queries. But it consumes, at least temporarily, server-side resources for every active client. Because there is no batch cursor available on the server side, it provides only single-row access, which in turn can be slow in operation. Server-side cursors are useful when inserting, updating. or deleting records. With server-side cursors, we can have multiple active statements on the same connection. Server-side cursors do not support the execution of queries that return more than one result set, which avoids the scrolling overhead associated with cursors and enables the cursor driver to manage each result set individually.

Retrieving and Manipulating Data by Using Different Cursor Types

There are four different types of cursors defined in ADO: forward-only, static, dynamic, and keyset. The CursorType property sets the type of cursor used in a Recordset object. Set the CursorType property prior to opening the Recordset object or pass a *CursorType* argument with the Open method. Some data providers do not support all cursor types. The default cursor type is a forward-only cursor, which sets or returns one of these CursorTypeEnum values: adOpenForwardOnly, adOpenStatic, adOpenDynamic, and adOpenKeyset.

The constant adOpenForwardOnly sets or returns the default forward-only cursor. It is useful for any application that requires a single pass through the data (sales reports, for example). This allows the application to scroll in the forward direction only.

The constant adOpenStatic sets or returns a static cursor. Although it can be used just like the forward-only cursor, we can scroll in both directions; and additions, deletions and other changes made by other users are not visible.

The constant adOpenDynamic sets or returns a dynamic cursor. Here, we are allowed to modify, add, or delete the data. Additions, changes, and deletions by other users are visible and all types of movement through the recordset are allowed, except for bookmarks if the provider doesn't support them.

The constant adOpenKeyset sets or returns a keyset cursor. This is similar to the dynamic cursor (except that the additions and deletions made by other users are inaccessible), but we can see the changes made by other users.

The CursorType property is read/write when the recordset is closed, and read-only when it is open. If we are using a client-side cursor by setting the CursorLocation property to adUseClient, only the static cursor is supported. If, by mistake, we set the CursorType property to an unsupported cursor type, the closest supported value will be used instead of returning an error. If a provider does not support the requested cursor type, the provider may return another cursor type. By using the supports method, we can verify the functionality of a cursor. Once we close the Recordset object, the CursorType property is set back to its original value.

Forward-Only

We can create a forward-only cursor by setting the CursorType Property to adOpenForwardOnly. This creates a cursor with which we can retrieve a static copy of a set of records; and the changes, including additions and deletions made by others, will not be seen. Because this is a forward only cursor, we scroll in the forward direction. This is the default cursor.

Static

We can create a static cursor by setting the CursorType Property to adOpenStatic. This creates a cursor with which we can retrieve a static copy of a set of records; and the changes, including additions and deletions made by others, will not be seen.

Dynamic

We can create a dynamic cursor by setting the CursorType Property to adOpenDynamic. Changes, including additions and deletions made by others, are visible and we can scroll in both directions in the result set. Bookmarks are available, provided that the data provider supports them.

Keyset

You can create a keyset cursor by setting the CursorType Property to adOpenKeyset. Though you can see changes in data, as when using a dynamic cursor, you cannot view any additions or deletions made by other users.

CERTIFICATION OBJECTIVE 6.08

Using Appropriate Locking Strategies to Ensure Data Integrity

Most of the time, concurrency problems in a multiuser database application evolve when several users try to access or update the same information at the same time. This is a big issue to be managed. Cursor locking is a strategy to separate applications by having them not interfering with one another.

With pessimistic cursor locks we can temporarily prohibit read access or changes by other applications. With optimistic cursor locks, we expect no concurrent changes and do not prohibit access or changes by other applications. The temporary updates, which are due to the uncommitted updates of one transaction that is read by another, cause the concurrency problem. If the first transaction does a rollback, the second transaction has misleading data. The solution is to prevent access to uncommitted updates. The lost updates, which are due to the update of the same data by more than one transaction at one time, can cause the concurrency problem. Here, the first update might be lost because the second update, arriving moments later, is based on the original value. Using a lock with the intent to update prevents this problem. The incorrect summaries, which occur when a single transaction updates two items, can also cause a concurrency problem. The database is in an inconsistent state until both updates have completed. If a summarization query reads the two items while the update is in progress, the summary can be erroneous. A read-lock on the result set eliminates the problem.

Our application can handle concurrency issues by using locks. Locking can prevent one process from reading data that is being changed by another process, and it can prevent a process from changing data that is about to be changed by another concurrent process. Locking provides the benefit of ensuring correct data, but it also makes the other concurrent applications wait to apply their changes. We can set or return the lock type by using Recordset object's LockType property. This property sets or returns by taking one of these four LockTypeEnum values: adLockReadOnly, adLockPessimistic, adLockOptimistic, or adLockBatchOptimistic.

The constant adLockReadOnly, which is the default, ensures that the cursor is a read-only one: we cannot alter the data.

The constant adLockPessimistic locks record by record.

The constant adLockOptimistic locks record by record only when we call the Update method.

The constant adLockBatchOptimistic also locks record by record, which is required for batch update mode (as opposed to immediate update mode).

The LockType property is read/write when the Recordset is closed and it is read-only when it is open. To determine the actual locking functionality available in a Recordset object, we can use the Supports method with adUpdate and adUpdateBatch. For a client-side cursor, the pessimistic locking is not supported. If we use an unsupported value instead of returning an error, it will set the closest value to it.

The following example opens a read-only, dynamic cursor recordset:

```
Dim Rs As ADODB.Recordset
Set Rs = New ADODB.Recordset
rs.LockType = adLockReadOnly
rs.CursorType = adOpenDynamic
rs.Open "Select * from SalesProspects", "DSN=Salesproc;UID=Computer;PWD=WinIt;"
```

Read-Only

Setting the LockType property to adLockReadOnly creates the Read-only lock on the Recordset object, which is the default lock type. It prevents us from altering the data by chance, which is useful for generating reports that do not require any data changes.

Pessimistic

Setting the LockType property to adLockPessimistic creates the Pessimistic lock on Recordset object, which allows us to lock the recordset record by record. The provider should ensure successful editing on the records and lock them immediately at the data source after editing.

Optimistic

Setting LockType property to adLockOptimistic creates the Optimistic lock on the Recordset object, allowing us to lock the recordset record by record, but the provider locks the records only after calling Update method on them.

Batch Optimistic

Setting the LockType property to adLockBatchOptimistic creates the Batch Optimistic lock on the Recordset object. Although it is similar to the Optimistic lock, it requires Batch Update mode instead of immediate Update mode, so the provider locks the records only after calling UpdateBatch method on them.

CERTIFICATION OBJECTIVE 6.09

Managing Database Transactions to Ensure Data Consistency and Recoverability

Transactions are useful and sometimes necessary to make a lot of changes at once. We can imagine a transaction as a logical unit of work; if something fails, the whole thing should get rolled back. Transactions are used to group together code statements that must either all be executed successfully or have no action performed at all. The Connection object has three methods that take care of transactions: BeginTrans, RollbackTrans, and CommitTrans. Normally, successful transactions begin with BeginTrans and end with CommitTrans; if an error occurs, we have to call RollbackTrans to withdraw all the changes made since BeginTrans.

The following example depicts the transactions on a database. If the input to the city is Buffalo, it rolls back to the original. Otherwise, it adds new data to the table. This is an ASP example:

```
On Error Resume Next
Set Conn = Server.CreateObject("ADODB.Connection")
Set RS = Server.CreateObject("ADODB.Recordset")
Conn.Open "SalesData","Computer","Win98"
Conn.BeginTrans
Rs.Open "SalesLocations", Conn, adOpenKeyset, adLockOptimistic
RS.AddNew
RS("RepName") =Request("RepName")
RS("RepID") = Request("RepID")
RS("Location")=Request("Location")
If Location="Buffalo" Then Conn.RollbackTrans
RS.Update
Conn.CommitTrans
RS.Close
Conn.Close
```

Transactions are necessary whenever our application performs longer database insertions and changes because the user may lose network connectivity or abort the applications; we can roll back to the original status and hence will not lose any data.

CERTIFICATION OBJECTIVE 6.10

Advanced Topics

ADO introduced another advanced feature: the disconnected recordset. A disconnected recordset contains a recordset that can be viewed and updated, but it does not carry with it the overhead of a live connection to the database. This is a useful way to return data to the client that will be used for a long time without tying up the MTS server and database server with open connections. The client can make changes to the disconnected recordset by editing the records directly, or by adding or deleting them using ADO methods such as AddNew and Delete. All of the changes are stored in the disconnected recordset until it is reconnected to the database. In a three-tier situation, the disconnected recordsets are created on the middle tier and it returns them to the client. For example, a client may request a list of all sales representatives for a specific region or state. The user on the client computer may wish to compare the list of sales representatives with another list, in order to make corrections or other changes. This process may take a substantial amount of time. Here, the disconnected recordset is ideal. Have the middle tier create the disconnected recordset and return it to the client. Once the recordset is created and returned to the client, it is disconnected from the database and the client can work on it as long as necessary without tying up the open connection to the database. Once the user is ready to submit changes, the client calls a SubmitChanges method. The disconnected recordset is passed in as a parameter and the SubmitChanges method reconnects the recordset to the database. SubmitChanges calls the UpdateBatch method; if there are any conflicts, SubmitChanges uses the existing business rules to determine the proper action. Optionally, SubmitChanges can return the conflicting records to the client to let the user decide how to handle the conflicts. To accomplish this, a separate recordset, which contains the conflicting values from the database, must be created and returned to the client,.

To create a disconnected recordset, we must create a Recordset object that uses a client-side, static cursor with a lock type of adLockBatchOptimistic. The ActiveConnection property determines whether the recordset is disconnected. If we explicitly set it to Nothing, we disconnect the recordset. We can still access the data in the recordset, but there is no live connection to the database. After the all the changes are done, we can explicitly set ActiveConnection to a valid Connection object to reconnect the recordset to the database.

The following example shows how to create a disconnected recordset:

```
Dim rs As ADODB.Recordset
Set rs = New ADODB.Recordset
rs.CursorLocation = adUseClient
rs.CursorType = adOpenStatic
rs.LockType = adLockBatchOptimistic
rs.Open "Select * From SalesReps", "DSN=SalesHawk; uid=Computer; pwd=Win98"
Set rs.ActiveConnection = Nothing
```

If we return the disconnected recordset from a function, either as the return value or as an out parameter, the recordset copies its data to the caller. If the caller is a client in a separate process or on another computer, the recordset marshals its data to the client's process. When the recordset marshals itself across the network, it compresses the data to use less network bandwidth. This makes the disconnected recordset ideal for returning large amounts of data to a client.

While a recordset is disconnected, we can make changes to it by editing, adding, or deleting records. Since the recordset stores these changes, we can eventually update the database. When we are ready to submit the changes to the database, we reconnect the recordset with a live connection to the database and call UpdateBatch. UpdateBatch updates the database to reflect the changes made in the disconnected recordset. Remember that if the recordset is generated from a stored procedure, we cannot call UpdateBatch because UpdateBatch only works on recordsets created from the SQL statements.

The following example code shows how to reconnect a disconnected recordset to the database and update it with the changes:

```
Dim conn As ADODB.Connection
Set conn = New ADODB.Connection
conn.Open "DSN=Pubs"
Set rs.ActiveConnection = conn
rs.UpdateBatch
```

When we call UpdateBatch, other users may have already changed records in the database, and there is a danger of overwriting these changes in the database with changes in the disconnected recordset. To prevent those situations, the disconnected recordset contains three views of the data: original value, value, and underlying value.

The constant Original allows us to access the original values in the recordset. The constant Value allows us to access the current values in the recordset. These values also reflect any changes that we have to make to the recordset.

The constant Underlying allows us to access the underlying values in the recordset. These values reflect the values stored in the database. These are the same as the original values of the recordset and are only updated to match the value when we call the ReSync method.

The UpdateBatch method creates a separate SQL query for each changed record to modify in the database while it is being called. This SQL query compares the underlying value against the database value to check whether the record has been changed since the recordset was first created. If they are same, the database has not changed and an update can proceed, or else somebody has updated the database and our update call fails. Whenever a failure occurs, the UpdateBatch flags it by changing its Status property. We can check to see if there are any conflicts by setting the Filter property of the recordset to adFilterConflictingRecords. This forces the recordset to navigate only through the conflicting records; if there are any, we can check the Status property to determine why the update failed and perform the relevant action on it. To make a decision about the conflicting records, we can update the underlying values in the disconnected recordset to examine the conflicting values in the database. To update the underlying values, we have to call the Resync method, with the adAffectGroup and adResyncUnderlyingValues parameters. The following example code shows how to resynchronize the underlying values in a recordset:

```
rs.Filter = adFilterConflictingRecords
rs.Resync adAffectGroup, adResyncUnderlyingValues
```

After the synchronization of the underlying values with the database values, we can see the changes made by others through the Underlying property and decide whether to overwrite them or not. To override them, we simply call the UpdateBatch again; because the underlying values match with the database and no conflicts exist, the update occurs. Remember that when the disconnected recordset is passed from one process to another, it does not marshal the underlying values. So if we want to return a disconnected recordset to a client for conflict resolution, we must pass the underlying values via mechanisms such as separate disconnected recordsets that contain only the underlying values.

CERTIFICATION SUMMARY

Universal Data Access (UDA) is a platform for developing multi-tier enterprise applications that require access to diverse relational or nonrelational data sources across intranets or the Internet. Nonrelational data sources are document containers such as Internet Explorer, e-mail, and file systems. UDA uses OLEDB as its core to access data from variety of sources. The UDA strategy is based on COM. As a result, the UDA architecture is open and works with tools or programming languages that support COM. Thus, we do not need to use new tools to work with UDA.

The main underlying component of UDA is ActiveX Data Objects. ADO enables us to write applications or components to access and manipulate data from a variety of data sources including traditional and nontraditional data sources. ADO is a high-level, language-independent data access interface.

By opening a Connection object we can establish a connection with a data source. The Errors collection contains Error objects and each Error represents the OLEDB errors, ADO Errors, and other errors generated while working an ADO connection. The Command object contains the definition of a command that we run against a data source to access data. The Recordset object enables our application to access data returned by executing a command on Recordset, Command, or Connection object. We can open a Recordset without explicitly opening a Connection. Similarly we can open a Recordset just by executing a command on Connection object without explicitly opening a Recordset.

Stored procedures are compiled collections of SQL statements and control-of-flow language that execute quickly. Executing a stored procedure is similar to executing a SQL command, except that the stored procedure exists in the database as an object, even after execution has finished. Stored procedures hide potentially complex SQL statements from the components that use them. SQL Server compiles and stores stored procedures, which makes them run much faster than submitting the SQL statements as separate SQL queries.

The values of the CursorLocation and CursorType properties determine the functionality of the recordset we create. By default, server-side cursors are created. To create a client-side cursor we have to set the CursorLocation property to adUseClient. To create a server-side cursor, we explicitly set CursorLocation property to adUseServer.

To select the cursor type for a Recordset object, we set the CursorType property to adOpenForwardOnly, adOpenStatic, adOpenKeyset, or adOpenDynamic.

With the LockType property of the Recordset object we could determine the type of lock placed on the data of the underlying database during editing. By default the recordset is set to a read-only lock. So we could not modify the data. We'd set the LockType property to adLockReadOnly, adLockPessimistic, adLockOptimistic or adLockBatchOptimistic depending upon the requirement.

One of the advanced features of ADO is disconnected recordset. A disconnected recordset contains a recordset, which can be viewed and modified, but which does not have a live connection to the database.

TWO-MINUTE DRILL

- ❑ The key strategy of Universal Data Access is that it allows applications to efficiently access data where it resides without replication, transformation, or conversion.

- ❑ ADO contains seven objects: Command, Connection, Error, Field, Parameter, Property, and Recordset.

- ❑ The *Properties* collection contains any dynamic or "provider-specific" properties, exposed through ADO by the provider.

- ❑ Events are issued when transactions on a connection begin, are committed, or rolled back; when commands execute; and when connections start or end.

❑ We know that the middle tier consists of the functional modules that actually process data. This middle tier runs on a server and is often called the application server.

❑ To open a recordset, we use the Execute method on either the Connection or Command object, or we can use the Open method on the Recordset object.

❑ Whenever our application needs to update data in an external data source, we can either execute SQL statements directly or use a Recordset object and its various methods for modifying data.

❑ The stored procedures on Microsoft SQL Server have the following capabilities for returning the data: one or more result sets, explicit return value, and output parameters.

❑ Most of the time, stored procedures require that one or more parameters be passed to them.

❑ If we chose to use a non-keyset client-side cursor, the server sends the entire result set across the network to the client machine.

❑ Every cursor requires system resources to hold data. These resources can be RAM, disk paging, temporary files on the hard disk, or even a temporary storage in the database itself.

❑ The constant adLockPessimistic locks record by record.

❑ The constant adLockOptimistic locks record by record only when we call the Update method.

❑ The constant adLockBatchOptimistic also locks record by record, which is required for batch update mode (as opposed to immediate update mode).

❑ We can create a static cursor by setting the CursorType Property to adOpenStatic.

❑ We can create a dynamic cursor by setting the CursorType Property to adOpenDynamic.

❑ A disconnected recordset contains a recordset, which can be viewed and modified, but which does not have a live connection to the database.

SELF TEST

The following Self Test questions will help you measure your understanding of the material presented in this chapter. Read all the choices carefully, as there may be more than one correct answer. Choose all correct answers for each question.

1. Universal Data Access eliminates

    A. The commitment to a single vendor's products

    B. An expensive and time-consuming movement of data into a single data store

    C. Both of the above statements are correct.

    D. None of the above.

2. ADO automatically adjusts itself to the functionality of the data provider.

    A. True

    B. False

3. What is required to access a database through ADO?

    A. Recordset Object

    B. Connection Object

    C. Either Connection or Recordset object

    D. None of the above

4. Which of the following are true statements?

    A. Using Connection, Recordset, and Field objects, we can access a data source.

    B. Without explicitly opening a Connection object, it is possible to access a data source with a Recordset object.

    C. Both of the statements are correct.

    D. Neither statement is correct.

5. Properties is a collection to handle the collection of parameters of Connection, Command, Recordset, and Field objects. Which of the following methods is useful to extract the Property of that particular object?

    A. Item

    B. Value

    C. Both of the above.

    D. None of the above

6. Which of the following is true? (Choose all that apply.)

    A. Connection Events are issued when transactions on a connection begin, are committed, or are rolled back; when Commands execute; and when Connections start or end.

    B. Recordset Events are issued to report the progress of data retrieval; when you navigate through the rows of a Recordset object; when we change a field in a row of a recordset, change a row in a recordset, or make any change in the entire recordset.

    C. Only A is correct.

    D. Both A and B are correct.

7. What is ADO known for?

    A. Ease of use

    B. Programmable cursor sets

    C. Capability to return multiple resultsets from a single query

    D. All of the above.

8. We can control the transaction by using which of the following?

   A. BeginTrans

   B. CommitTrans

   C. RollbackTrans

   D. All of the above methods through the Connection object

9. What is used to retrieve a particular field value in a row? (Choose all that apply.)

   A. ! operator

   B. ~ operator

   C. Field object

   D. A and C

10. We can open a DSN-less Connection, too.

    A. True

    B. False

11. Because the Errors collection is only available from the Connection object, we need to initialize ADO off of a connection object.

    A. True

    B. False

12. What are the advantages of the three-tier design over traditional two-tier or single-tier designs? (Choose all that apply.)

    A. The added modularity makes it easier to modify or replace one tier without affecting the other tiers.

    B. Separating the application functions from the database functions makes it easier to implement load balancing.

    C. None of the above.

    D. Both A and B are correct.

13. To open a recordset we can use which of the following? (Choose all that apply.)

    A. Execute method on either Connection or Command object

    B. Open method on Recordset object

    C. None of the above

    D. Both A and B are true

14. With the Execute Direct method, we execute already prepared SQL statements to access data. With the Prepare Execute method, we create SQL statements on the fly by using user input and execute these statements to access data.

    A. True

    B. False

15. By using stored procedures to execute a query on a database, we are allowing the RDBMS to cache those SQL queries.

    A. True

    B. False

16. The stored procedures on Microsoft SQL Server have the following capabilities in returning the data:

    A. One or more result sets

    B. Explicit return value

    C. Output parameters

    D. All of the above.

17. How do we execute a stored procedure from the Command object? (Choose all that apply.)

A. Simply set the CommandType property to adCmdStoredProc

B. Simply set CommandText to the name of the stored procedure

C. None of the above

D. Both A and B are correct

18. If we use the Refresh method, it causes ADO to make an extra trip to SQL Server to collect the parameter information.

A. True

B. False

19. By setting CursorLocation property of Recordset object to this value, we can create a client-side cursor.

A. adUseNone

B. adUseClient

C. adUseServer

D. None of the above

20. Server-side cursors do not support the execution of queries that return more than one result set.

A. True

B. False

21. To open a dynamic cursor, set the CursorType property of Recordset object to this:

A. adOpenDynamic

B. adOpenStatic

C. adOpenReadOnly

D. adOpenKeyset

22. What is the difference between a dynamic cursor and a keyset cursor? (Choose all that apply.)

A. By using a dynamic cursor, we could see all the changes, including additions and deletions made by other users.

B. By using a keyset cursor, we could see all the changes, including additions and deletions made by other users.

C. None of the above.

D. Both A and B are correct.

23. By setting LockType property of a Recordset object we can create a read-only locked cursor:

A. adLockReadOnly

B. adLockPessimistic

C. adLockOptimistic

D. adLockBatchOptimistic

24. Transactions are necessary whenever our application performs longer database insertions or changes because the user may lose network connectivity or abort the applications. We can roll back to the original status and hence will not lose any data.

A. True

B. False

25. A disconnected recordset is a useful way to return data to a client that will be used for a long time, without tying up the MTS server and database server with open connections.

A. True

B. False

A. True

B. False

26. The UpdateBatch method creates a separate SQL query for each changed record to modify in the database while it is being called.

A. True

B. False

MICROSOFT CERTIFIED SOLUTION DEVELOPER

7

Building Stored Procedures with SQL

A fter completing this chapter you will be able to: understand the function of SQL Server; write SQL statements to retrieve and modify data; use joins that will combine data from multiple tables; program with Transact-SQL, and create stored procedures.

CERTIFICATION OBJECTIVE 7.01

Introduction to Microsoft SQL Server

What is Microsoft SQL Server? SQL Server is a relational database management system (RDMS or RDBMS) that can handle large amounts of data and which allows a number of users to concurrently access this data. SQL Server allows you to "house" your data on a separate server, thus reducing network traffic on your network server because requests for the data are sent to the SQL Server instead of the main file server. SQL Server provides for data integrity by assuring that two users are not trying to update the same data simultaneously. It provides security and can even restrict the viewing of tables to only those who are authorized to see them. Additionally, SQL Server provides support for Web-based applications, allowing you to access data from an SQL Server through the Internet or an intranet. It even gives the Webmaster or database administrator the ability to automate the publishing of database information directly to HTML documents. SQL Server also allows for the replication of information to non-SQL Server databases including Microsoft Access, ORACLE, Sybase, and DB2. The Enterprise edition of Visual Basic 6.0 is designed so that you can incorporate SQL Server 6.5 database functions into your applications.

CERTIFICATION OBJECTIVE 7.02

Implementing Business and Data Services with SQL Server

Microsoft has developed a series of models that are designed to assist an organization in determining what resources (personnel and equipment) it needs so that its technology will allow it to attain its business objectives. This is called the Microsoft Solutions Framework (MSF). This framework helps guide a business through the software development and deployment processes. The model that concerns the actual development of the software is called the *Application Model.*

As defined in the Microsoft *Windows Architecture for Developers Training Manual,* the Application Model "describes the development of multitier applications built on user, business, and data services. It establishes definitions, rules, and relationships that form the structure of an application. It also offers guidelines on splitting an application into a network of services so that features and functionality can be packaged for reuse across functional boundaries."

The Application Model consists of three categories of services: user services, business services, and data services. The *Microsoft Windows Architecture for Developers Training Manual* defines a service as "a unit of application logic that implements an operation, function, or transformation that is applied to an object." These services can be used to enter data, manipulate data, and enforce policies that can ensure the protection of this data. An application consists of these three services.

In their most basic of definitions, user services provide the user with the application's interface, business services control the business rules for the application, and data services provide for the manipulation of data. These services play a key role in the development of applications, especially in the context of the World Wide Web. They allow you to develop software that will work across different platforms, provide consistency within your applications, and simplify these applications.

Writing SQL Statements that Retrieve and Modify Data

Before we begin talking about SQL statements, let's look at what SQL is. In the mid-70s, IBM developed SQL as a uniform means of accessing information in a relational database. In 1989, the American National

FROM THE CLASSROOM

Simply SQL

Microsoft touts heavily the practical importance of developing distributed applications along the lines of a three-tier architecture. A distributed application built along this methodology is split into three distinct tiers: presentation, business, data services. The data services tier centers on the process of actual data retrieval, which often necessitates extensive use of the Structured Query Language, or SQL. With Microsoft SQL Server, Transact-SQL (T-SQL) is the variation of SQL that should be focused on being used.

T-SQL provides a great flexibility in writing queries to return information. Being aware of the numerous SQL command keywords is instrumental in building efficient database queries to supply your COM components, and ultimately your application, with data.

Table and general rules for database design should be followed. Whenever converting your conceptual database design into a physical and ultimately logical design, this process should not be taken lightly. Certainly, this process should not be viewed as a second-hand step that is to be taken. Poor table design, combined with inefficient query design, can result in delays in data retrieval that far exceed any delays in processing that component congestion, network congestion, or inefficient application logic may induce.

Use of the Data Designer within Visual Basic 6.0 should be used to create straightforward, stored procedures and queries. For more complex commands requiring extensive testing, it is highly recommended to become familiar with T-SQL as much as possible, and utilize the I-SQL/w utility that comes with the client tools for SQL Server.

— *By Michael Lane Thomas,*
MCSE+I, MCSD, MCT, A+

Standards Institute (ANSI) published a standard form of SQL, SQL-89. In 1992, it published a more recent "dialect" of SQL and named it, appropriately, SQL-92. Though there are more dialects of SQL, the 1989 and 1992 versions are most relevant. By standardizing SQL, it became much easier to learn one language and then utilize it to retrieve and manipulate data from such products as Access, Oracle, SQL Server, and dBase. ANSI-SQL includes the following components: Data Definition Language (DDL), which can be used to create and drop data structures and for managing object-level security; Data Manipulation Language (DML), which can be used to add, modify, and remove data in tables; and Data Control Language (DCL), which is used to control access to data and actions.

SQL allows you to write statements, or "queries," that retrieve and modify data from existing databases. These queries can range from the most basic to the extremely complex. In the following lines we give some examples of what can be accomplished through the use of queries. In this chapter, we will be working with the Pubs database, which it installed by default. Although this database contains many tables, we will only be using Authors, Pub_info, Publishers, Titleauthors, and Titles. Before we begin to work with queries, let's look at how Visual Basic 6.0 can help you develop database applications, and how it can make it easy for you to write and test your SQL queries. Visual Basic 6.0 offers an excellent way to develop databases using the Visual Data Manager add-in. Visual Data Manager lets you create new databases or work with existing Microsoft Access, Dbase, FoxPro, and Paradox databases. Additionally, the Visual Data Manager contains a utility that you can use to write your queries. This utility is called Query Builder. Let's take a quick glance at this tool by following the steps in Exercise 1.

Opening the Visual Data Manager

1. Launch Visual Basic.

2. Choose Add-Ins from the menu bar and select Visual Data Manager as shown in Figure 7-1.

3. Now open the Biblio database by selecting File from the menu bar, select Open, then select Access, as shown in Figure 7-2.

4. Now examine the Visual Data Manager. Notice there is a database window which displays the properties of the database and any tables that belong to that database. There is also an SQL statement

Accessing the Visual Data Manager add-in

FIGURE 7-2

Opening a database in
Visual Data Manager

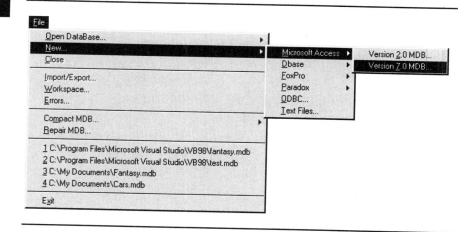

window that allows you to write and execute queries. You may even
save your queries, which will then be added to the database. This
can come in handy should you wish to save any of your queries and
even use these queries as a basis for creating others in another
database.

5. Click on Utility on the menu bar and select Query Builder, as shown
   in Figure 7-3.

6. Now take a quick glance at the Query Builder window, as shown in
   Figure 7-4. This will be a great tool to assist you in building your
   queries for Visual Basic applications. The Query Builder window will
   display the tables of the open database and will also display the fields
   of any highlighted tables.

FIGURE 7-3

Accessing the Query
Builder window

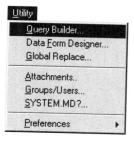

FIGURE 7-4

The Query Builder window

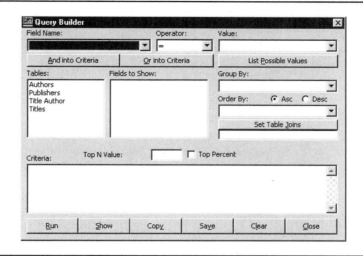

Building a Basic Query

Now let's begin to build some basic queries. A query contains several pieces of information that you must supply. In order to get information, a query needs to know where this information can be found. Therefore a table must be stated, along with a particular row or group of rows from that table. The keyword SELECT is the first building block of any data retrieval statement. SELECT is the way SQL determines which row or group of rows is to be retrieved. The keyword FROM designates the table from which the data is to be retrieved. While creating a query, you may insert comments, just like in VB 6.0, and this may be beneficial for a variety of reasons. Also, it's a good idea to place each clause on its own line. You may make the parts of the queries even more distinguishable by tabbing from the keyword to the lists. For example:

```
SELECT      *
FROM        Tablename
```

For this section, we will be accessing the Authors table, which contains the rows AU_ID, AU_LNAME, AU_FNAME; and address information. If you wanted to write a query to retrieve the entire contents of the table AUTHORS, you would write something like this:

```
SELECT      *
FROM        Authors
```

Because the wildcard * follows the keyword SELECT, this query returns the contents of all the rows in the table. If you only wanted to return a single column from the table, that row would be distinguished. For example:

```
SELECT      au_id
FROM        Authors
```

This query would return the columns containing the AU_ID, AU_LNAME, and AU_FNAME of the authors that are in the AUTHORS table. To return multiple rows, the following query would work:

```
SELECT      au_id, au_lname, au_fname
FROM        Authors
```

This query would return the rows AUTHOR, AU_LNAME, and AU_FNAME.

Using Expressions, Conditions, and Operators to Refine Your Query

The most basic definition of an *expression* is something that returns a value. In fact, just about any SQL query qualifies as an expression. You use a *condition* when you want to search for a particular value from within the data. For example, if you wanted to search the list of rushers to see if there were any from a specific team, you could do that by using a condition. *Operators* are the means by which conditions are met. Operators consist of six types: arithmetic, comparison, character, logical, set, and miscellaneous.

The condition WHERE further defines the results of a query by allowing you to determine what you would actually like to find. Let's say you wanted to write a query to search for a particular author and you knew the author's ID (AU_ID) but not the author's actual name. You could build a query like this:

```
SELECT      *
FROM        Authors
WHERE       AU_ID = '527-72-3246'
```

Comparison Operators

Comparison operators consist of equal (=), greater than (>), greater than or equal to (>=), less than (<), and less than or equal to (<=). In addition, there is an operator for inequalities (<> or !=), which functions similar to the NOT keyword.

Notice that these operators are available in the operator drop-down box in the Query Builder window. An example would be if you wanted to create a result set of titles that cost more than $20.

```
SELECT      *
FROM        Titles
WHERE       price > 20
```

Character Operators

Character operators consist of LIKE in combination with the percent sign (%), underscore (_), and concatenation (&). The LIKE operator allows you to search your tables for similar entries. For example, if you wanted to find all the players whose names began with the letter "S," you would type the following.

```
SELECT      *
FROM        Authors
WHERE       au_lname LIKE      'D%'
```

The "_" operator functions as a single-digit wildcard. For example, if you had a table with state abbreviations and you wished to return all values that began with the letter "M," you would build the following query:

```
SELECT      *
FROM        Authors
WHERE       state LIKE      'm_'
```

The concatenation character ("&") allows you to create a result set from two different fields and combine them into one. For example, if you wanted to create a result set with one column that would contain the author's last name (AU_LNAME) and first name (AU_FNAME), you could return one row with the names combined by using the concatenation operator.

```
SELECT      au_lname + au_fname
FROM        Authors
```

Arithmetic Operators

Arithmetic operators consist of plus (+), minus (-), divide (/), and multiply (*). These operators can come in handy if you want to manipulate some of your data. You can use these operators to automatically add or subtract from your inventory, add or subtract prices from books, calculate a discount or markup, or calculate an average cost for a number of books. For example, this query would add $2.00 to all the titles in the table:

```
SELECT      Title, price + 2
FROM        Titles
```

This query would subtract $2.00 from all titles in the table.

```
SELECT      Title, price - 2
FROM        Titles
```

This query would return the cost of a book during a half-price sale.

```
SELECT      Title, price /2
FROM        Titles
```

This query would return a result set of how much the books would cost with a 20% markup.

```
SELECT      Title, price * 1.2
FROM        Titles
```

Logical Operators

Logical operators consist of AND, OR, and NOT. These operators allow you to combine other operators in one statement. For example, if you wanted to see all the titles of books that were more than $10 and were in the BUSINESS genre, you could run the following query:

```
SELECT      *
FROM        Titles
WHERE       price > 10
AND         type = 'business'
```

Or you could find out which books were more than $10 or were in the BUSINESS genre:

```
SELECT      *
FROM        Titles
WHERE       price > 10
OR          type = 'business'
```

You can use the NOT operator to see which books were not published in any given year. Note that if you run a query on a row with a space in the name, the name of that row needs to be offset in brackets:

```
SELECT      *
FROM        Titles
WHERE       NOT type = 'business
```

Set Operators

Set operators consist of UNION, UNION ALL, INTERSECT, and MINUS (Difference). UNION returns the results of two queries without giving the duplicate values. For example, both the Publishers and the Titles tables contain a field for the pub_id. Running the following query will return the number of unique values in the pub_id field (it will not contain any duplicate values). This database does not serve as a perfect example for these operators since all the pub_id's are utilized in the Titles table. A normal database would not necessarily have all values being utilized in both tables.

```
SELECT      pub_id
FROM        Publishers
UNION
SELECT      pub_id
FROM        Titles
```

If you wanted to see which pub_id's were in either of two tables, you could extract this information by using the UNION ALL operator, which shows all entries from both tables and does not eliminate duplicates. Notice the number of records returned. This basically gives you all records that contain a pub_id value from both tables and adds them together.

```
SELECT      pub_id
FROM        Publishers
UNION ALL
SELECT      pub_id
FROM        Titles
```

Miscellaneous Operators

The miscellaneous operators IN and BETWEEN are basically shortcuts to other functions.

The operator IN can be used instead of multiple OR expressions. For example, if you wanted to design a query that would tell you which books were in the business or psychology genre, you could write this query:

```
SELECT      Title
FROM        Titles
WHERE       type = 'business'
OR          type = 'psychology'
```

Or you could write this query:

```
SELECT      Title
FROM        Titles
WHERE       type IN ('business', 'psychology')
```

The operator BETWEEN allows you to extract a result set if you want to return records that contain values from within a certain range. For example, if you wanted to search to see which books cost between $10 and $20, you could use the BETWEEN operator. For example:

```
SELECT      *
FROM        Titles
WHERE       price BETWEEN 10 and 20
```

Using Functions in Queries

Functions in SQL allow you to perform a variety of calculations including arithmetic, date and time functions, character functions, conversion, and aggregate functions. However, not all of these will be applicable or useful to us in manipulating the Pubs database.

Arithmetic Functions

You can use arithmetic functions to perform mathematical calculations on your data. You can use the ABS function to return the absolute value of a number, use CEIL and FLOOR to return the smallest integer or whole number equal to or greater than the value in the argument (CEIL), or return the largest integer or whole number equal to or less than the value in the argument (FLOOR). You can also perform trigonometric calculations using COSH, SIN, SINH, TAN, and TANH; perform logarithmic calculations using LN and LOG; return a value based on the value of a field (SIGN); and determine the square root of a number (SQRT).

Date and Time Functions

You may also write queries that perform such date and time functions as adding months to a date (ADD_MONTHS), determining the last day of a specified month (LAST_DAY), determining how many months are between two dates (MONTHS_BETWEEN), adjusting a time for a different time zone (NEW_TIME), finding the first day of the week that is equal to or later than a specific date (NEXT_DAY), and returning a system date (SYSDATE). Though our database does not contain dates, such functions might be useful in automatically determining dates for sales, and so on. A sample query would look something like this:

```
SELECT      *
Add_Months  RowName, 6)
FROM        TableName
```

This query would add six months to the specified row. Creating queries using the remaining date and time functions would be similar to the above example.

You can also write queries that perform date parsing and date arithmetic. Date functions include GETDATE( ), DATENAME, DATEPART, DATEDIFF, and DATEADD.

In conjunction with the date functions are *date parts*. These are year (abbreviation = YY), quarter (QQ), month (MM), day of year (DY), day (DD), week (WK), weekday (DW), hour (HR) minute (MI), second (SS), and millisecond (MS). Now, let's look at some examples.

GETDATE( ) returns the current system date and time.

```
Select getdate()
```

DATEADD(*DATEPART, NUMBER, DATE_EXPR*) allows you to add the specified NUMBER to the specified DATEPART. For example, this query would add six months to the current date.

```
Select dateadd(mm, 6, getdate())
```

DATEDIFF(*DATEPART, DATE_EXPR1, DATE_EXPR2*) allows you to calculate the difference between two dates by the specified DATEPART. For example, if you wanted to know how many days until the millenium you could write this query:

```
Select datediff(dd, getdate(), "1/1/00") "Days to the Millenium"
```

If you just wanted to return part of the date, you could use DATEPART(*DATEPART, DATE_EXPR*), which returns the part of *DATE_EXPR* as an integer

```
Select datepart(mm, getdate()
```

Finally, if you wanted to return the current day, you could use DATENAME. DATENAME (*DATEPART, DATE_EXPR*) returns the specified part of *DATE_EXPR* as a string and converts it to a name. For example, if you wanted to write a query to tell you what day it is, you could write something like this:

```
Select "Today is " + datename(dw, getdate())
```

This will return the day of the week (DW = day of week). If you wanted to return the month, you could use MM.

Character Functions

Character functions allow you to manipulate characters and character strings. You can capitalize the first letter of a word (INITCAP), change characters into either upper -or lower case (UPPER and LOWER), combine two rows into one (CONCAT), replace some characters for others (REPLACE), extract part of a string (SUBSTR), determine where a particular character occurs in a string (INSTR), determine the length of a string (LENGTH), translate some characters to something else (TRANSLATE), pad a field (LPAD and RPAD), or trim a field (LTRIM and RTRIM). Although these may not seem too useful, you never know when they might come in handy.

Conversion Functions

Conversion functions include: one to convert a number into a character (TO_CHAR), one to convert a character to a number (TO_NUMBER), and one to determine the length of a string (LENGTH).

Aggregate Functions

The COUNT function can be useful if you wished to determine how many books cost less than a certain amount. For example, if you wished to display all the books under $20, you could do that by entering the following query:

```
SELECT     *
FROM       Titles
WHERE      price < 20
```

This will display all titles that are under $20. But, let's say you were only interested in a count rather than a list. You could then use the COUNT function.

```
SELECT     Count (*)
FROM       Titles
WHERE      price < 20
```

Now all that your result set will consist of is one record with the number of books that cost less than $20. You can further enhance the COUNT function by giving the row a name. Notice that when you run the query, the row probably has the same generic name as the label. You can give the resultant row a name with the COUNT function. Here's how:

```
SELECT     Count (*)
AS         "Books under $20"
```

```
FROM        Titles
WHERE       price < 20
```

Notice that the word AS is added and the table name is surrounded by brackets. This is what will give the row a name in the result set.

The SUM function allows you calculate the total value of a row. If someone came to your bookstore and asked for one of every book in the business genre and asked how much each cost, you could tell by running a query similar to the following.

```
SELECT      SUM (price)
AS          "Total cost of business books
FROM        Titles
WHERE       type = 'business'
```

You may also wish to determine the average price of your books. You can use a query to do this.

```
SELECT      AVG (price)
AS          "Average book cost"
FROM        Titles
```

You can also use a query to return the minimum (MIN) or maximum (MAX) values in a particular row. For example, to determine the least expensive book in your inventory, you could use the following query:

```
SELECT      MIN (price)
AS          "Least expensive book"
FROM        Titles
```

If you wished to return the most expensive book in your inventory, you could basically use the same query, except to change the MIN to MAX.

```
SELECT      MAX (price)
AS          "Most expensive book"
FROM        Titles
```

You can also perform VARIANCE or standard deviation (STDDEV) calculations on your table. Since these functions are not useful for our purposes, the syntax is virtually the same as the above examples.

Using Clauses in Queries

Clauses allow you to further enhance your queries by defining your searches even more.

We have already worked with the WHERE clause and saw how it can assist in retrieving records that meet specific criteria. Now, let's see what else we can do with clauses.

The GROUP BY Clause

The GROUP BY clause can be used only in conjunction with an aggregate function. For example, let's say you want to see which books in your inventory have a particular publisher. You could determine this by writing the following query:

```
SELECT      pub_id, count(pub_id)
FROM        Titles
GROUP       by pub_id
```

This query returns a count of how many instances of the publishers appear.

You can further enhance this query by giving the expression field a name. Since the value that will be returned in this field is a count of how many instances of the publisher exist in the database, you can give this field another name. Now, try this query:

```
SELECT      pub_id, count(pub_id)
AS          Instances
FROM        Titles
GROUP BY    pub_id
```

Now your field has a name and may have a little more meaning.

The ORDER BY Clause

The ORDER BY clause allows you to create your query so that you can have the result set be sorted by whatever field you determine in either ascending order (ASC keyword) or descending order (DESC keyword). For example, let's say you want to get an alphabetical listing of all the books in the Titles table. You could write a query like this:

```
SELECT      title
FROM        Titles
ORDER BY    title
```

You can use the ORDER BY clause to sort by any field. You could also write a query to return a result set that is sorted by any other column in the table. Let's say however, that you wish to retrieve the titles in reverse alphabetical order. You can do so by using the keyword DESC. Try this:

```
SELECT      title
FROM        Titles
ORDER BY    Title DESC
```

Notice that you now have a result set that is in reverse alphabetical order. By default, the ORDER BY clause uses the ASC keyword.

One more thing about the ORDER BY clause: You can use this clause and sort by a row even if you do not have it named in your query. For example:

```
SELECT      title
FROM        Titles
ORDER BY    type
```

This returns a result set that contains only the title row, yet is sorted by the year it was published.

Subqueries

You can tie the result set of one query to the result set of another query. This is called a *subquery.* The subquery is contained within the query and is surrounded by parentheses, which is called *nesting.* You may nest up to sixteen subqueries within a query. A subquery can also function as a join, with the exception that a subquery will not return rows from two different tables.

Writing SQL Statements that Use Joins to Combine Data from Multiple Tables

Joins are invaluable as a means to collect data from different tables. By being able to use joins to collect data from different tables, you can create separate tables with pertinent data, instead of one large table. This keeps the size of tables to a minimum and makes managing your database exponentially easier. For an example, all you need to do is try to join the Authors and Publishers tables by creating and running the following query. However, this query will take some time to process, and you may elect not to do it. The reason is that this query will add each row from the Publishers table to each row in the Authors table, thus creating a result set which is not very useful. This is called a cross-join.

```
SELECT      *
FROM        Authors, Publishers
```

Performing an Inner Join

Not all joins are as inclusive as the cross-join. An inner join (also called an equi-join) can create a result set that contains only those records that have an exact match in both tables. For example, the Titles table contains a row called PUB_ID, as does the Publishers table. If you wanted to create a table that would return all the TITLES of a particular publisher, you would create an inner join. The following statement will return a result set that will show the PUB_ID and TITLE from the two tables.

```
SELECT      titles.pub_id, titles.title,
        publishers.pub_id
FROM        Titles, Publishers
WHERE       titles.pub_id = publishers.pub_id
```

The result set will contain the same number of records as the Titles table (one record per title), and will include the corresponding publisher's

PUB_ID. Basically, what the query did was to display the title from the Titles table and the PUB_ID, where the PUB_ID field was the same in both the Publishers and Titles tables. Also, notice that the specified result set should contain only the PUB_ID and TITLE. If you do not specify certain rows, and instead have all returned, it would return a table with all fields from both tables, and the PUB_ID would be duplicated. Now, modify the query a little and you can see what we mean.

```
SELECT      Titles.*, Publishers.*
FROM        Titles, Publishers
WHERE       titles.pub_id = publishers.pub_id
```

Now, let's say you want a similar result set, but only want to find the works of one author. You could write something like this:

```
SELECT      titles.pub_id, titles.title, publishers.pub_id
FROM        Titles, Publishers
WHERE       titles.pub_id = '1389' and titles.pub_id = publishers.pub_id
```

This query only returns the works of pub_id 1389 and Algodata Infosystems, and should only contain six records.

As we can see from these examples, inner joins can be particularly helpful when there is a common row in both tables and you wish to create one table that will display those rows. The inner join will also allow you retrieve information from either table and display it in the same result set, as seen in the previous examples.

Performing Outer Joins

The left join (along with the right join) is one of two outer joins that can be executed within SQL. Whereas the inner join only returned records that had corresponding values in both tables, the left join will return all records from the first table (or the table on the left, hence the name "left join"), whether there are corresponding values in the second table or not. In other words, as long as there is an entry in the first table, there will be a record displayed, even if there is no corresponding match in the second table. To see what I'm talking about, run the following query:

```
SELECT      titles.title, publishers.pub_name
FROM        Titles
LEFT JOIN   Publishers
ON          titles.pub_id = publishers.pub_id
```

Notice that instead of using the WHERE operator, ON is used.

A right join is similar, except the result set is based on the second table (or right table) in the join statement. Now run the same query, except this time make it a right join.

```
SELECT      titles.title, publishers.pub_name
FROM        Titles
RIGHT JOIN  Publishers
ON          titles.pub_id = publishers.pub_id
```

There is a possibility that the result set could contain a different number of records than the result set from the Left Join; if a publisher doesn't exist in the Titles table it won't even be listed in this result set.

Performing Joins with Multiple Tables

You can also join two tables that may not have a common row in each other, but may have a common row in a third table. This could be particularly helpful in the Pubs database. For example, the Titles table contains the title of the book. There is no indication as to who the author of the book is, but we know that the Authors table has something in common with the Title Author table—the AU_ID row. Looking further at the Title Author table, it has the TITLE_ID row in common with the Titles table. So, by joining these three tables together, we can create a result set that will display the Author along with the Title of the book. For example:

```
SELECT      authors.au_id, titles.title
FROM        Authors, Titles, Titleauthor
WHERE       titleauthor.title_id = titles.title_id
AND         titleauthor.au_id = authors.au_id
```

As you can see, this query returns a result set that will only contain the Author and Title of each book.

Let's take this one step further and also include the Publisher. In order to add the Publisher name, we need to determine what row we can use to accomplish this. If you look at the Titles table, there is a row called PUB_ID, which also exists in the Publishers table. So, let's write our query.

```
SELECT      authors.au_id, titles.title
FROM        Authors, Titles, Titleauthor, Publishers
WHERE       titleauthor.title_id = titles.title_id
AND         titleauthor.au_id = authors.au_id
AND         titles.PubID = publishers.PubID
```

The result set now includes the publisher name. One thing to remember while retrieving data from multiple tables is that it's a good idea to limit the rows so you only get the pertinent data and not every row from every field. Had we not specified which rows to return on the last query, we'd have had a result set that had 23 rows.

CERTIFICATION OBJECTIVE 7.06

Programming with Transact-SQL

Transact-SQL (subsequently known as T-SQL) differs from ANSI-SQL syntax in some instances, so you will need to make sure your syntax will work. T-SQL extends SQL by adding three flow control statements (if, while, and return), variables (local and global), and some other capabilities that allow you to create more complex queries.

You can also create a batch that is nothing more than one or more SQL statements that are sent to the SQL Server to be compiled and executed. In addition, T-SQL allows you to create stored procedures and triggers (not covered here), which reside on the server. Just like ANSI-SQL, you can include descriptive comments in stored procedures.

Much of what has already been covered is applicable in T-SQL. You can write queries similar to those presented previously. However, some of the syntax may need to be changed, though for the most part, it's very similar. For the following examples, I will be using SQL Server 6.5's ISQL/w utility.

If it is not already installed, now would be a good time to install it. The Pubs database, which is installed by default during the installation of SQL Server 6.5, will be used in the following examples.

Batches

Batches allow you to place multiple queries into one group, which can be sent to the server to be compiled and executed as if it were only one query (stored procedures, which will be covered later, can also consist of multiple queries). This batch then goes through a five-step process in which the syntax is parsed, the referenced objects are parsed, the batch is optimized and compiled, and then it is executed. For example, you can group two select statements together and run it as a batch. The server will process both and return two separate result sets, one for each of the select statements. However, if there is an error at any point in the process the process will be aborted.

You can also take the same batch and split it up simply by inserting the word GO. However, the word GO must appear on its own line.

Batches can be helpful because if you wish to execute a number of statements or queries, it is more efficient for the server to compile and execute a single batch that contains all these statements or queries than it would be to process each one individually. This is not without its risks, however. If the batch fails at any point in the process, the entire process will fail.

Using Local Variables

Local variables can be used in a batch, a stored procedure, or a trigger. You can create a local variable by using a DECLARE statement. A DECLARE statement consists of the DECLARE keyword followed by the "@" sign, followed by the name of the variable, and finishing with the data type of the variable. For example:

```
DECLARE @var int
```

Table 7-1 shows some of the more common data types.

You may declare multiple variables from within the same DECLARE statement. In fact, it is a good idea to so. Simply insert a comma between variables. For example:

```
DECLARE @var1 int, var2 char(20), var3 text
```

You can also assign values to a variable. This can be done in one of two ways, both of which use a SELECT statement. First, you can assign the variable a predetermined value. For example, let's say you want to declare a variable, then assign a numerical value for that variable. You could do something like this:

```
DECLARE @var int
SELECT @var = 1
```

This would assign your variable a value of 1. One possible use for something like this would be if you were creating a database to track students' grades. You could create a group of variables, one for each grade, assign each grade variable a number, and then write a query which could calculate a student's grade point average.

TABLE 7-1

Commonly used data field types

Name	Name used in code	Description
character	char(*value*)	Is good for those fields whose length is uniform or almost uniform
integer	int	Can be any value between +/- two billion
datetime	datetime	Can display up to a millisecond. Dates can range from January 1, 1753 to December 31, 9999
money	money	Can be any value between +/- 922 trillion
variable character	varchar(*value*)	Is best suited for fields whose length can vary considerably

The other way to assign a value of a variable is to assign it a value from a table. For example:

```
DECLARE      @var int
SELECT       @var = RowName1
FROM         TableName
WHERE        RowName2 = desired value
```

This query assigns the variable a value by looking to the desired row, and then searching for a particular record that matches the criteria you determine. For instance, if you already had a table showing how many points a grade is worth, you could simply point the variable to the corresponding row in the grade table.

You may be asking yourself whether you ever need to use local variables. Well, they can perform a variety of helpful tasks. First of all, you can use them as counters, which will let you perform a certain task a predetermined number of times. For example, if you wanted to insert data into a table a prescribed amount of times, you could accomplish this with a local variable. You can also use a local variable to retrieve a value and have a procedure executed, based on the returned value. Local variables also allow you to do some things in conjunction with global variables and from within stored procedures.

A variable may also be changed by an UPDATE statement. The UPDATE statement allows you to update the value of a field in a table and update the variable at the same time. A good example would be updating your inventory after a sale or after you have received some inventory. You could do this with the following example:

```
DECLARE      @var int
UPDATE       TableName
SET          RowName = RowName + 10,
@var =       RowName
WHERE        ProductCode = x
```

One more thing about local variables: As soon as that batch has been completed, the variable is removed from memory. Subsequent batches will not be affected by local variables from a previous batch because there will be no trace of that local variable.

Using Global Variables

Global variables are used to provide information to the client and are read-only. They are not set by the client, but are automatically set by the server. The process of declaring global variables is similar to the process of declaring local variables except that you need to place two "@" signs in front of the variable rather than one. Global variables can be used to provide information inside triggers and stored procedures.

There are two types of global variables: server-specific and connection-specific. Server-specific global variables deal mostly with statistics, which can be seen in Table 7-2.

Connection-specific variables are variables that provide information about your current connection or session. Table 7-3 contains some of the more common connection-specific global variables.

TABLE 7-2	Variable	Description
Server-specific global variables	@@connections	Total number of logins, both successful and unsuccessful
	@@cpu_busy	Returns the amount of time the server is spent doing work
	@@idle	Amount of time server is idle
	@@io_busy	Amount of time spent reading and writing information to disk
	@@pack_received	Number of packets received
	@@pack_sent	Number of packets sent
	@@packet_errors	Number of errors encountered while sending or receiving packets
	@@total_read	Number of disk reads
	@@total_write	Number of disk writes

TABLE 7-3	Variable	Description
Connection-specific global variables	@@error	Returns an error number
	@@identity	Displays the value inserted in a table by the server
	@@nestlevel	Displays a number which represents the level of nesting in a stored procedure or trigger
	@@rowcount	Displays the number of rows processed by the previous command
	@@servername	Returns the name of the local SQL Server
	@@spid	Returns the server process ID (SPID) for the current process
	@@transtate	Displays the current state of a transaction
	@@version	Displays the version of the SQL Server

Now that you know more than perhaps you wanted to know about global variables, I'm sure you're curious about how we can use a global variable. Simple. You can use a global variable to keep track of the last error that occurred. This can be helpful in diagnosing problems that may occur in a batch. As mentioned previously, when the server encounters a problem during the execution of a batch, the batch is halted and nothing is returned. Setting a global variable would return an error that may point where you need to go to alleviate the problem.

Using Flow Control Statements

Now let's look at the three flow control statements. Basically there are three flow control statements that you can use while creating queries: IF, WHILE, and RETURN.

Using IF in statements

The IF keyword can be used in queries, just as it would be used in writing code in VB. If the statement fulfills the IF expression, it will be executed. If the statement does not fulfill the IF expression, it will not be executed.

Using WHILE in Statements

The WHILE command allows you to create loops. For example, if you wish for a procedure to run a predetermined number of times, you could use the WHILE command to set the limit on how many times you wish it to run. Once the procedure has run the predetermined number of times, you can have the procedure end.

Using RETURN in Statements

You can use the RETURN command to immediately end a batch. For example, if you have an IF statement and you want for a batch to end, depending on the results of that statement, you could insert the RETURN command and the batch would end.

CERTIFICATION OBJECTIVE 7.07

Creating Stored Procedures

A stored procedure is a batch that is stored on the server and executed from the server. A stored procedure, when executed, is located and loaded into cache, parameter values are substituted, and the procedure is optimized; it is then compiled and executed. Once the procedure has been executed for the first time, the optimizing and compiling is no longer necessary.

Stored procedures make administering a database easier. Because the batch resides on the server instead of the client machines, whenever a change is necessary, you can simply change the stored procedure instead of changing the batch on all the client machines. Creating a stored procedure is a simple process. You can turn any query, from the most simple to the extremely complex, into a stored procedure. For example, the following uses a stored procedure to run a simple query:

```
CREATE proc pr_name
AS
SELECT      rowname
FROM        tablename
WHERE       value = xxx
```

The procedure can then be executed by entering the procedure name. Using the EXEC keyword (the EXEC keyword tells the server that what follows is a stored procedure) before the procedure name to execute the procedure is a good habit to develop. Though this is not necessary to execute a stored procedure, it is needed if you ever decide to call a stored procedure from within another query. The exception is when that stored procedure is in the first line. For example, suppose you have a stored procedure that calls another stored procedure. In order for the server to execute the query, you would need to place the EXEC keyword before the stored procedure name, or else the server will return an error and the query will not run. By getting in the habit of using the EXEC keyword whenever you reference a stored procedure, you can avoid any headaches if you create a query and forget to add the EXEC keyword.

SQL Server contains some stored procedures that may be useful to you. Among these are SP_HELP (which returns a list of all objects in the database), SP_HELPDB (which returns a list of available databases), and SP_HELPTEXT (which, when the procedure is stated afterward, returns the code of that procedure).

You can also create a stored procedure that can be used with a parameter. Instead of providing the stored procedure the value, you can create the procedure with a local variable as the value. Then, when you run the procedure, you supply the variable after the procedure name; the procedure then fills the parameter into the local variable. This saves you from creating multiple queries for different values!

Stored procedures are very efficient because they reside on the server (as opposed to on the individual machines), which allows for central administration of the procedures. The server also is responsible for executing the procedure that is done by parsing and optimizing the procedure. If there is an error at any point in the procedure, the procedure is ended.

CERTIFICATION SUMMARY

In this chapter, you have been introduced to the function of SQL Server; learned how to write SQL statements that retrieve and modify data; used joins that combine data from multiple tables; programmed with Transact-SQL, and created stored procedures.

TWO-MINUTE DRILL

❑ SQL Server is a relational database management system (RDMS or RDBMS) that can handle large amounts of data and allows a number of users to concurrently access this data.

❑ Microsoft has developed a series of models, called the Microsoft Solutions Framework (MSF), that are designed to assist an organization in determining what resources (personnel and equipment) it needs so that its technology will allow it to attain its business objectives.

❑ A query contains several pieces of information that you must supply. In order to get information, a query needs to know where this information can be found. Therefore a table must be stated, along with a particular row or group of rows from that table.

❑ The keyword SELECT is the first building block of any data retrieval statement. SELECT is the way SQL determines which row or group of rows is to be retrieved.

❑ The most basic definition of an *expression* is something that returns a value. In fact, just about any SQL query qualifies as an expression.

❑ You use a *condition* when you want to search for a particular value from within the data.

❑ Set operators consist of UNION, UNION ALL, INTERSECT, and MINUS (Difference).

❑ Arithmetic operators consist of plus (+), minus (-), divide (/) and multiply (*). These operators can come in handy if you want to manipulate some of your data.

❑ Character functions allow you to manipulate characters and character strings.

❑ You can tie the result set of one query to the result set of another query. This is called a *subquery*.

❑ T-SQL extends SQL by adding three flow control statements (if, while, and return), variables (local and global), and some other capabilities that allow you to create more complex queries.

❑ *Batches* allow you to place multiple queries into one group, and then sent to the server to be compiled and executed as if it were only one query.

SELF TEST

The following Self-Test questions will help you measure your understanding of the material presented in this chapter. Read all the choices carefully, as there may be more than one correct answer. Choose all correct answers for each question.

1. How do you define a local variable while programming in Transact-SQL?

    A. DECLARE #*VAR INT*

    B. DECLARE ##*VAR INT*

    C. DECLARE @*VAR INT*

    D. DECLARE @@*VAR INT*

2. What kind of join would you employ if you wanted to display data from two different tables where there are entries in the first table but not in the second table? (Choose all that apply.)

    A. Inner join

    B. Left join

    C. Right join

    D. Cross join

3. What happens if, in the process of execution, there is an error within a stored procedure?

    A. The procedure will finish but return an incomplete result set

    B. The procedure will finish but nothing will be returned

    C. The procedure will be halted and return an incomplete result set

D. The procedure will be halted and nothing will be returned

4. How can you write a simple query that will look for a condition?

    A. By using the WHERE CLAUSE

    B. By using the IN KEYWORD

    C. By using the HAVING CLAUSE

    D. By using the IF STATEMENT

5. Which of the following is true of a query? (Choose all that apply.)

    A. A query can retrieve data from different databases

    B. A query can retrieve data from different tables

    C. A query can retrieve data from different rows

    D. A query can retrieve data from different fields

6. Which kind of join would you employ to retrieve data from two tables which do not have any rows in common?

    A. Inner join

    B. Left join

    C. Right join

    D. Cross join

7. Which of the following are global variables that are connection-specific? (Choose all that apply.)

    A. @@idle

    B. @@error

C. @@connections

D. @@spid

8. In what manner may a local variable be used? (Choose all that apply.)

A. Within a stored procedure

B. Within a WHERE STATEMENT

C. Within a subquery

D. Within a JOIN STATEMENT

9. What is a parameter used for when running a stored procedure? (Choose all that apply.)

A. To guide the procedure to look for a certain row

B. To guide the procedure to look for a certain table

C. To guide the procedure in filling in a global variable

D. To guide the procedure in filling in a local variable

10. Which is true of a global variable? (Choose all that apply.)

A. They can be used within stored procedures

B. They can be changed by running a stored procedure

C. They can be used by local variables

D. You create one by preceding the variable by "@"

11. How many subqueries can you nest in a query?

A. four

B. eight

C. sixteen

D. thirty-two

12. Which of the following are characteristics of SQL Server? (Choose all that apply.)

A. Provides centralized administration of databases

B. Provides data security

C. Provides data integrity

D. Provides data storage

13. How can you run a group of queries? (Choose all that apply.)

A. Through a batch

B. Through a join

C. Through a stored procedure

D. Through a query

14. Which global variable would you use to display an error number?

A. @error

B. @@error

C. @error_number

D. @@error_number

15. Which of the following are valid methods of declaring multiple local variables?

A. DECLARE @VAR1 INT @VAR2 CHAR(20)

B. DECLARE @VAR1 INT, @VAR2 CHAR(20)

C. DECLARE @VAR1 INT DECLARE @VAR2 CHAR(20)

D. DECLARE @VAR1 INT, DECLARE @VAR2 CHAR(20)

16. Which of the following data types can be used in declaring a local variable? (Choose all that apply.)

    A. char(20)

    B. varchar(20)

    C. integer

    D. money

17. Which of the following services are part of the Application Model in the Microsoft Solution Framework? (Choose all that apply.)

    A. Business services

    B. Data services

    C. Network services

    D. User services

18. Which of the following are valid groups of operators? (Choose all that apply.)

    A. arithmetic operators

    B. comparison operators

    C. conversion operators

    D. logical operators

19. Which of the following support SQL? (Choose all that apply.)

    A. Access

    B. dBase

    C. Oracle

    D. SQL Server

20. Which of the following are global variables?

    A. @error

    B. @idle

    C. @spid

    D. @version

8

Implementing Security

I n this chapter, you will learn to use the security options of SQL Server and Microsoft Transaction Server (MTS) to provide appropriate security for your Visual Basic 6 distributed application. Both MTS and the preferred implementation of SQL security are built on top of standard Windows NT system security, so a general understanding of the concepts of NT users and groups is a prerequisite to discussing application security.

CERTIFICATION OBJECTIVE 8.01

Introduction to Security

All Windows NT security is built upon the individual user ID, which uniquely identifies a user within a particular NT domain and assigns particular rights or authorizations to that ID. Individual user IDs in turn can be assigned to groups, which are named sets of user IDs that have identical rights and can be used in both SQL Server and MTS security operations in place of individual user IDs. Although the details of setting up SQL and MTS security differ slightly, in general they both extend NT security through the assignment of NT users and/or groups to particular security privilege levels. These security levels determine the kinds of operations allowed for a particular user or group of users.

Two-tier Versus Three-tier Security

Traditionally, in two-tier client-server systems, the individual user must be granted access to the database, either through a login with his or her own user ID or perhaps as a member of a larger group login. However, there are a limited number of connections available to a particular database, and each unique login uses up a connection, thus limiting scalability. The technology exists for pooling database connections, but only for a particular login/rights combination.

Also, in a two-tier implementation, it is often problematic to have one application call another; either the user must be known to both applications (requiring administrative coordination), or the user must logon separately to each application.

In a three-tier approach, business rules are implemented in a middle tier between the database access and the user interface. Users no longer have a direct connection to the database; instead they access the business tier components running under MTS, which validate the users' authority and then access the database on their behalf. The business tier components all run under a single identity (or at least a very few identities), which allows for efficient connection pooling at the database.

FROM THE CLASSROOM

Three-tier Security

In a three-tier distributed application, database security is usually encapsulated in the appropriate data access COM component running within MTS, functioning as a data component element that operates within the middle business tier. Because the database access is coded into an MTS COM component, the effective security mechanism rests in the combination of the package identity and the appropriate SQL Server logins and database user name. Owing to this combination of security concepts, it is important to guarantee that the developer understands the ramifications of incorrectly setting MTS package identities.

MTS and SQL Server provide a secure and robust combined security mechanism through the use of roles, logins, and database user names. With this in mind, the developer should be absolutely sure that the idiosyncrasies of implementing programmatic security are not only understood, but the need for using such a complex security mechanism

is justified. Because taking the security of MTS component behavior into your own hands can pose complex difficulties, doing so should be fully justified.

Using role-based security at the package or component level should be clearly understood for the exam. In a nutshell, package level role-based security overrides the existence of underlying component level security. If package level role-based security is enabled, the security set at the individual component level is checked.

When attempting to simplify database access, separating database into separate data components within the business tier can greatly simplify security. Using ADO with explicit DSN strings can allow the account used to access a given application's database to not only simplify but tightly secure access to that database data.

— By Michael Lane Thomas, MCSE+I, MCSD, MCT, A+

Implementing a three-tier security scheme involves a combination of application and database security. Application security is applied through MTS package security, and database security through SQL Server. To summarize, the five advantages of three-tier security are as follows:

1. Database access is controlled by limiting user access to that which is obtained through middle-tier components, which contributes to database integrity.

2. Multiple users accessing a database through a single user identity allows the use of connection pooling for scalable and efficient database usage.

3. Administration is reduced because each user does not need an individual security identity at the database.

4. The developer can consider user authorization in terms of the roles the end user has in the organization, rather than in terms of databases and tables.

5. When one application calls another, you don't need a separate client identification or login. MTS can be configured to handle application-to-application calls.

on the
job

One disadvantage of three-tier security is that you cannot perform user auditing at the database level (because all access occurs under the same middle-tier user ID). However, there are ways to audit use in the middle-tier to get the same effect, if required.

CERTIFICATION OBJECTIVE 8.02

Implementing Security in Microsoft Transaction Server Applications

There are two types of MTS security available, *declarative* and *programmatic*. MTS security is managed at the package, component, or individual interface level through the use of *roles*. Roles are symbolic names for groups of users and are similar to the concept of user groups in Windows NT. In fact, both NT users and groups may be used to populate MTS roles. Declarative security is "defined" security: that is, the roles allowed to access a particular component or interface are pre-defined using the MTS Explorer application. Programmatic security, on the other hand, is dynamic and is enforced "in-code" at runtime through use of the IsCallerInRole method, which we will discuss later.

exam

ⓦatch

Declarative security requires the use of NT users and groups. Therefore, it cannot be used on computers running Windows 95 or Windows 98.

Package Identity

Before discussing MTS security in detail, the concept of package *identity* must be understood. An MTS package identity is the NT user identification that is assumed by the components in the package while they are running. This is the identity that provides database security (and allows pooling of connections). Assigning an identity to a package, along with other MTS configuration operations, is performed in the MTS Explorer, which runs as a snap-in component of the Microsoft Management Console (MMC). In Exercise 8-1, we will assign an identity to a package (you may choose one of the sample packages distributed with MTS or another package of your choice).

| EXERCISE 8-1 |

Adding an identity to an MTS package

1. Open the MTS Explorer in the Microsoft Management Console application.
2. In the left pane, open the Computers folder and select My Computer (or another computer, if appropriate).
3. Open the Packages Installed folder.
4. Select and right-click on the package for which you wish to set the identity.

5. Select Properties from the pop-up menu.

6. Select the Identity tab from the Properties dialog box (see Figure 8-1).

7. By default, Interactive User is selected. This is usually not appropriate for a server-based application because there is usually no interactive user logged on. Select this user and press the Browse button. This will bring up a selection box of available NT users that you may select from.

8. After adding the user ID to be used as the identity, type the password associated with this user ID (twice) in the boxes, and then press OK.

The identity (user ID) selected here should map to a valid SQL Server login for those applications utilizing database services. All client interactive users who access a component in this MTS package will appear as this user to the database, simplifying database security administration and improving application performance and scalability. Likewise, access may be restricted for

FIGURE 8-1

Providing an MTS package identity

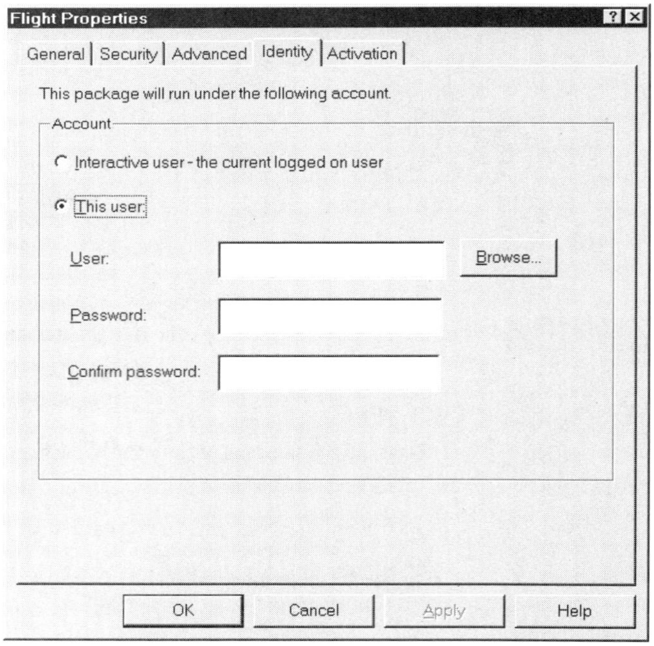

particular users if the "Identity" user ID for a package has read-only or other restricted database rights. Note that the Identity is a package-level property and thus implies that security considerations may have an impact on the way you choose to package your MTS components. Also, do not confuse the package identity with the MTS concept of the OriginalCaller, which is usually the client user ID who started the transaction process. See Figure 8-2 for a graphic look at the concept of OriginalCaller and package identities.

FIGURE 8-2 Original caller and identity: one client, one server, two MTS packages

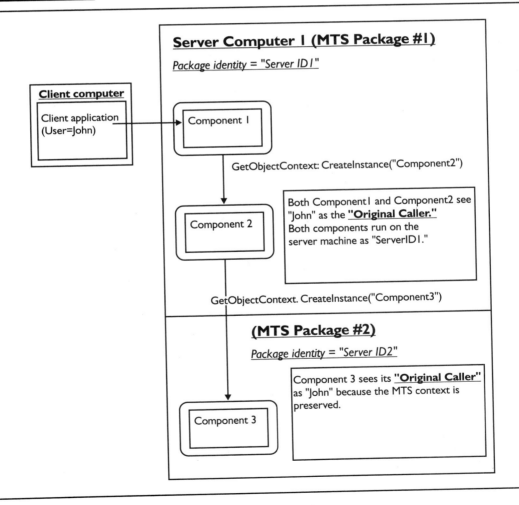

Declarative Security

Declarative security is activated through the process of applying *roles* to components and interfaces to allow users (or groups of users) to access and use the components in a particular MTS package. Think of roles as another layer of abstraction over the NT security model—they really operate in much the same manner. It is highly unlikely that a developer will know which user IDs are to be granted which rights in an application at development time. However, by utilizing role names, it is possible to develop a secure application, granting access to those portions of the application requiring security checking only to those particular named roles. At deployment time, it becomes an administrative task to assign users at a particular installation to the appropriate roles.

Selecting the level at which to apply roles in MTS affects the granularity of the security scheme, with package security offering the least (or "blanket") security to all components, while interface security is the most restrictive level of declarative security.

An important point to remember is that declarative security only applies between packages, not between components within a particular package. Another way of stating this is that all components within a package implicitly "trust" one another. Once a particular user has been granted the right (through a role) to access a component in the package, that component may call (instantiate) any other component within the same MTS package without further security checking. If a component calls across a package boundary (calls a component defined in a different MTS package) however, security authorization checking will be performed. Note that once security authorization checking is enabled for a package, the components in that package cannot be called if there are no valid users in any role associated with the package.

In Exercises 8-2 and 8-3, we will enable MTS package security. All operations are again conducted in the MTS Explorer application in the MMC.

EXERCISE 8-2

Defining roles in MTS

To define a new MTS Role, open the MTS Explorer:

1. In the left pane, select the package that you want to work with.

2. Open the Roles folder under this package.

3. Do one of the following:

   - Open the Action menu at the top of the MTS Explorer window and select New, or

   - Select the Roles folder and click the Create new Object icon in the Explorer toolbar, or

   - Right-click the Roles folder and select New, and then choose Role.

4. In the New Role dialog box, type the name of the new role you are creating, and then press OK.

Mapping users and groups to roles

To map existing NT users and groups to an MTS role (see Figure 8-3):

1. In the left pane, select the package whose roles you want to work with.

2. Open the Roles folder under that package.

3. Double-click (open) the role to which you want to assign users or groups.

4. Open the Users folder.

5. Do one of the following:

   - Open the Action menu at the top of the MTS Explorer window and select New, or

   - Select the Users folder and click the Create new Object icon in the Explorer toolbar, or

   - Right-click the Users folder and select New, and then choose Users.

6. In the dialog box that appears, select groups and users (use the Show Users button) to be added to the role.

7. Click OK.

It is possible to restrict access through declarative security at the component or interface level, giving you two more levels of security granularity beyond that afforded by the MTS package. In Exercise 8-4, security will be added to a component or an interface.

Restricting access to components or interfaces

1. Find and select the Role Membership folder for either a component or an interface item in the left pane in the same package to which you added users and roles.

2. Either use the Action menu and select New/Role, the Create New Object icon, or right-click on the Role Membership folder and select New/Role.

3. From the resulting dialog box (which lists all roles in the package's Roles folder), select the roles you wish to allow access to this component or interface.

4. Press OK.

Table 8-1 outlines the effects of various combinations of authorization checking at the package and/or component level.

Defining roles alone will not implement MTS declarative security. If you do not activate it at the appropriate levels, MTS will perform no security

TABLE 8-1

Effects of various declarative security settings

Package Security	Component Security	Result
Enabled	Enabled	Component security checking is enabled.
Enabled	Disabled	Disables security for this particular component, but security is enabled for other components in the package with component security enabled.
Disabled	Enabled	Disables security for *all* components in the package. (The component security setting has no meaning.)
Disabled	Disabled	Disables security for *all* components in the package.

FIGURE 8-3

Adding users to MTS roles

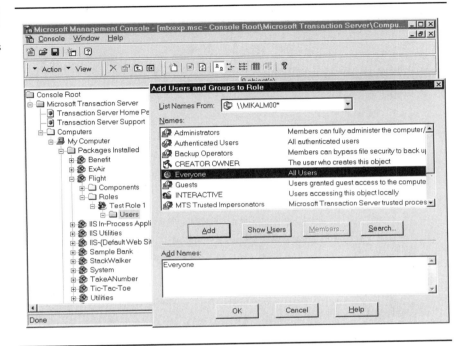

checking at all. In Exercise 8-5, we will activate MTS authorization checking, which will cause all of the declarative security settings we have just made to take effect. Remember that before activating security authorization checking, you must have placed at least one valid user in a role associated with this package (see the two previous steps).

EXERCISE 8-5

Activating MTS authorization checking

1. Access the property sheets of the package you have been working with, either through the Properties selection on the Action menu, the properties icon on the toolbar, or by right-clicking on the package name and selecting Properties.

2. Select the Security tab of the Package property sheets.

3. Check the Enable authorization checking checkbox.

4. Press OK.

5. You must shut down any running package processes in the MTS Explorer before the security changes will take effect:

- In the left pane, right-click on the package name that you are configuring security for.
- Click on Shut Down in the pop-up menu.

See Figure 8-4 to see what the sample MTS Flight component with a single role containing a single NT group of users ("Everyone") defined looks like in the MTS Explorer. Note that we have decided to implement roles at the component level and not at the interface (if the Role Membership folder under the Interfaces folder is empty).

exam
ⓦatch

The activation of declarative security through the Enable authorization checking setting has no effect on programmatic security, which is active at all times in the MTS environment.

FIGURE 8-4

MTS sample "Flight" component with roles assigned

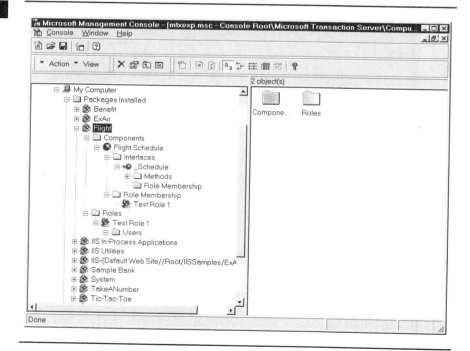

The System Package

There is a special package in MTS called *System*. It comes with two predefined roles, *Administrator* and *Reader*. Administrator is, as its name implies, the role that can alter package and component settings within the MTS Explorer. Readers can view settings but cannot alter them. It is vitally important that when activating MTS security for the first time, you assign a valid NT user ID (or group) to the Administrator role. By default, no one is assigned to these roles and security on the system package is disabled (and therefore, anyone can alter the MTS settings). For this reason, it is recommended that you assign someone at least to the Administrator role, but if you do not and activate system package security, the MTS Explorer will become unusable.

Furthermore, the system package contains components that implement internal functionality for the MTS Explorer. If you want to administer MTS from a remote MTS computer, you must give the system package a specific *identity*. (See "Assigning MTS Package Identities for how to do this.") Assigning the appropriate identity will allow you to update packages and components from a remote MTS Explorer session.

on the **Job**

Always assign someone to the Administrator role in the system package before doing anything else with MTS security.

Programmatic Security

MTS programmatic security places control completely in the hands of the developer, who through the use of the IsCallerInRole method on the MTS Object Context can query if the *direct caller* (usually the client user who started the process) is a member of a particular role, and thus eligible to perform certain operations. Programmatic security is not available to components installed in a library package, only to server packages. This offers a great deal of flexibility because the calls can be placed anywhere in your code and can query against any defined role in the MTS package.

A crucial element to programmatic security is that when creating an MTS object programmatically, you must use the CreateInstance method of the ObjectContext object. Use of either the Visual Basic CreateObject function or the VB New operator to set an object pointer to an MTS object will prevent the Object Context from being inherited from the caller, and the security information (and the current transaction state) will be unavailable to the new object.

on the

Always use the CreateInstance method of the MTS ObjectContext object to create an MTS object in a VB program.

Using Programmatic Security

To use programmatic security, first set up the desired roles and populate them with NT user IDs or groups, as described earlier. It is then necessary to set a reference in the VB project you are working on for the MTS type library to gain access to the methods provided. Exercise 8-6 will accomplish this (also see Figure 8-5).

FIGURE 8-5

Setting a reference to the MTS type library in Visual Basic 6.0

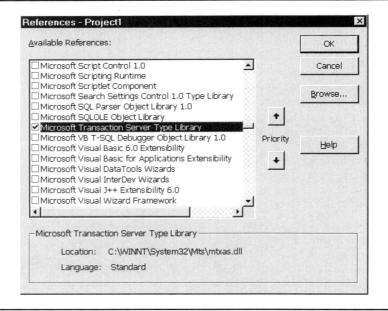

Setting a reference in a VB project for the MTS type

1. Open the desired ActiveX DLL project (or create a new one) in Visual Basic 6.0.
2. On the Project menu, select References.
3. In the References dialog box, scroll down until you find the Microsoft Transaction Server Type Library and check the box at the left (see Figure 8-5).
4. Press OK.

You can easily check for this by calling the IsSecurityEnabled method on the MTS ObjectContext object. If your component is running in a non-MTS environment but the MTS DLL (mtsax.dll) is available, this method will return False. If it runs in a non-MTS environment with the MTS DLL unavailable, a runtime error will occur. Either way, you will know that something is wrong.

The following simplified code sample demonstrates the use of programmatic security. In a real application, you would probably choose to use more robust error handling if you discover that MTS is not available or security is not enabled for your component.

```
Public Function SecuredProcess()
    ' Preset false in case of failure
    SecuredProcess = False

    ' Define an object variable for the context
    Dim oMTSCtx as mtxas.ObjectContext

    ' Get the object context from MTS
    Set oMTSCtx = mtxas.GetObjectContext

    ' If we are not running in MTS, exit
    If (oMTSCtx Is Nothing) Then Exit Function    ' Or raise error etc.

    ' We are in an MTS environment, so see if programmatic security is available
    If (Not oMTSCtx.IsSecurityEnabled) Then Exit Sub ' Or raise error etc.
```

```
' We know programmatic security is available, so see if this caller
' is a member of the role Supervisors
If oMTSCtx.IsCallerInRole("Supervisors") Then
     SecuredProcess = True               ' Indicate caller is authorized
     Exit Function
Else
     SecuredProcess = False              ' Indicate caller is not authorized
     Exit Function
End If
End Function
```

CERTIFICATION OBJECTIVE 8.03

Overview of SQL Server Security

In this section, we will discuss the basic elements of SQL Server security and how they affect the developer of three-tier applications. Note that this section deals only with SQL Server version 6.5. SQL Server 7.0 will bring significant changes to SQL Server security, primarily in the administration tools. Most of the basic concepts of SQL security will remain as they are in SQL 6.5. To begin to understand SQL security, we must first discuss the three mutually exclusive modes of SQL security. It is important to understand that user authentication (granting the right to access SQL Server) does not in itself grant access to an application's database. These rights are granted through the assignment of specific database access rights to logins, which we will discuss later.

- **Standard** All connections are validated using SQL Server's own login-validaion processes. This type of connection is known as a *non-trusted* connection. To log on to a SQL Server, each user must provide a valid SQL Server login ID and password. Standard security is useful in network environments with a variety of clients, some of which may not support other connection types.

- **Integrated** SQL Server uses Windows NT's user authentication mechanisms to validate SQL Server connections. These connections are known as *trusted* connections, and cannot be mixed with *non-trusted* connections in the same SQL Server environment. This allows one user login to be used for both NT security and SQL security. When MTS components are used, their identity is used in integrated security to gain access to a SQL database. This is the preferred mode of SQL Server security operation because it is the easiest to administer and the most convenient for the user.

■ **Mixed**   Both integrated and standard connections are allowed in this mode. Trusted and non-trusted connections can coexist in this mode. Usually, this mode is used in environments with a diverse client base, some of which must use standard security.

An MTS component is authenticated for connection in slightly different ways, depending on the security mode in use for the SQL Server. Note that access to individual SQL database tables is controlled through permissions granted to SQL logins internally to SQL Server. These permissions may grant a particular login id the right to perform certain functions (Select, Update) against particular database tables. The authentication process we are discussing here is at initial connection time.

Standard Mode Authentication

When standard mode is in effect, the following steps are used to authenticate an MTS component:

1. SQL Server looks in the syslogins database table for the user ID and password supplied by the component through the ConnectionString property of the ADO Connection object.

2. If the user ID and password are valid, the component is connected to SQL Server.

3. If the user ID and password are not valid, the component will not be granted access to SQL Server, even though the component's package identity may logged in to NT Server. The NT Server user ID and password have no effect in standard security.

Integrated Mode Authentication

To use integrated SQL security mode, an MTS component must first have a valid NT user ID and password assigned to its Identity property (see the "Package Identity" section). The user ID and password for the component are authenticated during the startup of the MTS package's server process in the same manner as an interactive NT account. It depends on whether the user ID is defined as part of an NT Domain, as a member, or as a local NT Workgroup.

When the MTS component attempts to connect to SQL Server, the server looks in the syslogins database table for a mapping to an SQL Server login id. If one is found, the connection is made by using the privileges associated with that login id. If a mapping is not found, the component may be connected to a default account (usually Guest), which may have limited privileges. If the MTS identity of the component has NT Administrator rights, it may be connected as SA (the SQL Administration account).

If no mapping exists and the SQL Administrator has not defined any default accounts, the connection will be denied.

Mixed Mode Authentication

When you set a SQL Server's login security mode to Mixed, a component's connection attempt may come in over either a trusted (integrated) or non-trusted (standard) connection. The following sequence is used to authenticate it:

1. When using a trusted connection, SQL Server compares the component's SQL login name to the component's network user name. If they match, or if the supplied login name is blank or comprised of spaces, SQL Server uses the Windows NT integrated login rules (integrated security).

2. If the requested login name is any other value, the component must also supply the correct SQL Server password (through the ConnectionString property) and SQL Server internally validates it (standard security).

3. If the login attempt is over a non-trusted connection, the component must supply the correct login ID and password, and then standard security authentication applies.

on the job

Mixed mode authentication will not be available starting with SQL version 7.0, so it would be inadvisable to design any new security schemes that rely on it.

CERTIFICATION OBJECTIVE 8.04

Using SQL Server Integrated Security

To set up three-tier applications to use SQL Server integrated security, you must first set up the NT user account (user ID) to use as the MTS package identity. In Exercise 8-7, we will use the NT User Manager for Domains to create a new NT User account.

EXERCISE 8-7

Creating a new NT user account

1. Start the User Manager for Domains. The User Manager is launched from the Start menu under Programs/Administrative Tools on a Windows NT Server.

2. On the User menu, click New User.

3. In the dialog box that appears, enter the user name (see Figure 8-6). You may want to have the user name start with "MTS" or something else meaningful to readily identify the account's purpose. Because of SQL limitations, the length of the account name must be fewer than 30 characters and contain no SQL-prohibited characters such as underscores.

4. Choose the following account options:
   - User cannot change password.
   - Password never expires.

5. Set and remember the password for this user.

6. Click the Add button.

A completed dialog box for a new NT user ID

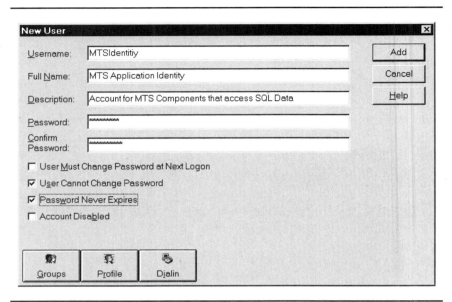

Although not required, adding your MTS package NT accounts to SQL Server will be easier if you put all of them in an NT Local Group. Exercise 8-8 will lead you through the steps to do this.

Creating and populating an NT user group for MTS components

1. Start the User Manager for Domains (Start | Programs | Administrative Tools).

2. On the User menu, click New Local Group.

3. Set the Group Name to **MTS Packages** or another recognizable name.

4. Click the Add button and select the existing package-user accounts you just created from the pop-up dialog box.

5. If necessary, click the Remove button to remove any non-package-user accounts you do not want in the group.

6. Click OK to create the new group account (see Figure 8-7).

FIGURE 8-7

Creating and populating a
new NT Local Group

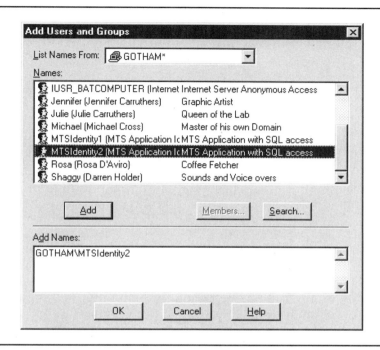

The next step in setting up integrated SQL security for the MTS
components is to associate the NT user accounts just created with SQL Server
logins using the SQL Security Manager. Exercise 8-9 will create these logins.

EXERCISE 8-9

Creating SQL logins for NT user accounts

1. Start the SQL Security Manager and connect to SQL Server as the
   system administrator (SA) or other account granted administrative
   authority.

2. From the View menu, click User Privilege. You will want to grant
   almost all MTS packages at least user privileges.

3. From the Security menu, click Grant New. This displays the Grant
   User Privilege dialog box (see the following illustration).

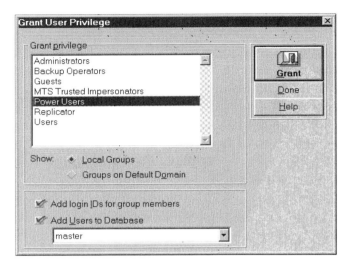

4. Choose the Windows NT group to which you want to grant privileges. This is MTS Packages or whatever name you chose when creating the package group.

5. Choose to add login IDs for group members. This creates the logins for each member of the MTS Packages group.

6. Click Add Users to Database, and choose which database to add the users to. If you do not select a database, the Master database is the default.

7. Click Grant, and logins are generated for the users on the selected database.

The final configuration step is to set specific permissions for the new SQL logins, granting each of them a particular permission, according to the application's business and security requirements. Note that a particularly attractive option, both from a security standpoint and a performance standpoint, is to use SQL *stored procedures,* which can perform functions for which a particular component may not be specifically authorized. This allows you to just grant a component execute permissions for particular stored procedures, and not have to be concerned with the myriad combinations of specific permissions required on a particular database table. These procedures can also be maintained centrally by a database administration team and provided as needed to developers. Exercise 8-10 will lead you through setting SQL permissions.

EXERCISE 8-10

Setting SQL Permissions on logins

1. Start SQL Enterprise Manager and connect to SQL Server as the system administrator (SA) or other login with administrative permissions.
2. Select the database table on which you want to set permissions.
3. From the Object menu, click Permissions.
4. You will see the logins that were added by the SQL Security Manager. Select the permissions you want for each login on the table, and click Set.
5. Repeat steps 2 through 4 for other tables that may need to be accessed by the new logins.

CERTIFICATION OBJECTIVE 8.05

Security Best Practices

Security can be challenging to implement—in many organizations specialists manage security. However, frequently the developer is in a unique position to understand the ramifications of security, as well as the requirements of a particular application. Listed here are some best practices to help you implement security in your applications.

- Set up SQL Server for integrated security whenever possible. If necessary, use mixed security. Using integrated or mixed security, you avoid coding login IDs and passwords directly into MTS components or ODBC DSNs. Security can be changed by modifying a package's NT user account rather than recompiling the components in the package.

- Use stored procedures for all data access, which allows you to secure the stored procedures for package access rather than try to determine all the specific types of permissions each package should have. Also, stored procedures run much faster than individual SQL statements submitted by the components.

■ Run applications in a test environment before moving them to production. The test server should have the same security settings as the production server on which the application will ultimately run. These security settings should include NT File System (NTFS) permissions, MTS roles, and SQL Server logins. The danger in not doing this is that an application that runs on a developer's machine will have security problems (it will either not run at all or it will allow inappropriate access) when put into a production environment.

■ Grant users access to resources through group accounts rather than individual accounts. The end users of an application should receive all security permissions through membership in an NT group, rather than through direct individual permissions. This makes managing security much simpler because security is handled at one point (the NT groups) rather than on a number of individual users tied to a large number of resources.

■ Create at least one Windows NT group account for each application. Differing business functions might require different levels of access to resources, and therefore multiple NT groups such as Bank Tellers and Bank Managers.

■ Create at least one role for every MTS package. The same comment as for NT groups applies here. It is not surprising that there is nearly a one-to-one relationship between NT groups and MTS roles.

■ Design audit requirements into your business and database components. Auditing database access does not work the same way under the three-tier security model as it does under two-tier security. This is because all end users access the database through the same user ID (the MTS package's account). To implement logging on your MTS component, use the GetOriginalCallerName method on the MTS Security object. This returns the NT user ID (name) of the end user, even if the MTS component was called directly by another component.

CERTIFICATION SUMMARY

MTS and SQL security work hand-in-hand over NT security to provide a robust, flexible method of securing three-tier applications. Three-tier applications offer significant advantages in the areas of data integrity, application scalability, administration effort, security design, security management, and application integration. The approach to security in the three-tier model is somewhat different from past architectures. The general concept is to authenticate "at the front door" and perform auditing in the business tier (middle tier) components.

MTS declarative and programmatic security are both based on the concept of roles: business functions that must be performed by the individuals in an organization. Roles share many similarities with NT groups, but are somewhat more flexible and easy to use (particularly in programmatic security). Programmatic security allows the developer to provide as much or as little security as needed for the application.

SQL security provides the database-level security in the three-tier model by controlling component access to database tables (generally through granting them execution access to SQL stored procedures). This is in contrast to prior architectures, in which individual end-users needed to be managed at the database table level, and generally each user had a separate, non-poolable connection to the database.

TWO-MINUTE DRILL

- ❑ All Windows NT security is built upon the individual user ID, which uniquely identifies a user within a particular NT domain and assigns particular rights or authorizations to that ID.

- ❑ In a two-tier implementation, it is often problematic to have one application call another; either the user must be known to both applications (requiring administrative coordination), or the user must logon separately to each application.

- ❑ One disadvantage of three-tier security is that you cannot perform user auditing at the database level (because all accesses occur under the same middle-tier user ID).

❏ An MTS package identity is the NT user identification that is assumed by the components in the package while they are running.

❏ Declarative security is activated through the process of applying *roles* to components and interfaces to allow users (or groups of users) to access and use the components in a particular MTS package.

❏ Programmatic security is not available to components installed in a library package, only to server packages.

❏ It is possible to restrict access through declarative security at the component or interface level, giving you two more levels of security granularity beyond that afforded by the MTS package.

❏ If you want to administer MTS from a remote MTS computer, you must give the system package a specific *identity*.

❏ To use integrated SQL security mode, an MTS component must first have a valid NT user ID and password assigned to its Identity property.

❏ SQL security provides the database-level security in the three-tier model by controlling component access to database tables.

SELF TEST

The following Self-Test questions will help you measure your understanding of the material presented in this chapter. Read all the choices carefully, as there may be more than one correct answer. Choose all correct answers for each question.

1. Which of the following is not an advantage of the three-tier architecture?

   A. Application scalability

   B. Reduced reliance on SQL Server security

   C. Application security designed around business roles

   D. Increased usage of database connection pooling

2. Which of the following are the two types of security under MTS?

   A. Users and groups

   B. Users and roles

   C. Declarative and programmatic

   D. Component and objects

3. Which of the following statements are true about declarative security under MTS?

   A. It cannot be used under Windows 95

   B. It cannot be enabled or disabled

   C. Developers use the IsCallerInRole method to implement it

   D. It is defined through the NT User Manager for Domains

4. Which of the following statements are true about programmatic security under MTS?

   A. It relies on SQL security

   B. It can be enabled or disabled

   C. Developers use the IsCallerInRole method to implement it

   D. It is defined through the NT User Manager for Domains

5. To use MTS security in your VB application you must set a reference to what resource?

   A. None, VB will take care of it automatically at runtime

   B. The Microsoft Transaction Server Security Library

   C. The VB Common Controls Type Library

   D. The Microsoft Transaction Server Type Library

6. Which of the following errors will cause the caller's identity to be lost to MTS security, thereby making IsCallerInRole useless?

   A. Forgetting to set the package's identity in MTS Explorer

   B. Using the VB CreateObject function to instantiate another component

   C. Forgetting to call IsSecurityEnabled first thing in the program

   D. Calling a utility function in a common .bas file

7. Which of the following is not a place where roles may be applied to enforce security?

   A. Components

   B. Interfaces

   C. Database tables

   D. Any point in the code of a component

8. Component A in Package 1 is calling Component B in the same package. Which of the following describes how the roles must be set up to allow this to happen?

   A. The same roles must be assigned to both components Role Membership folder

   B. The Interface being called in Component B must have the same role assigned as the calling Interface in Component A

   C. The identity of Package 1 must be in the same role as Component A

   D. Nothing

9. Which of these best describes the MTS term OriginalCaller?

   A. The NT end user who initiated the transaction or process that is running in MTS

   B. The identity of the MTS package that the caller is executing in

   C. The identity of the MTS component that created (instantiated) the current one

   D. The user in the Administrator role of the system package

10. If authorization checking is disabled at the package level, and enabled at the level of Component A, which of the following statements is true?

    A. Callers of Component A must be present in the Role Membership folder under the component

    B. Programmatic security is disabled for the package

    C. Any other component in the Package calling A will fail

    D. Declarative security is disabled for all components in the package, including Component A

11. After all the roles for a particular MTS package have been defined and authorization checking enabled, what else must be done to complete the configuration of MTS security?

    A. Assign an identity to SQL Server so the components can access it

    B. Assign NT users and/or groups to the various roles

    C. Make the user ID assigned as the package identity part of the Domain Administrators group

D. Be certain the MTS role names appear in at least one NT group

12. Which of the following is the preferred mode for SQL Server security?

A. Roles

B. Mixed

C. Integrated

D. Standard

13. The right to perform operations on SQL tables is granted to which of the following?

A. MTS roles

B. SQL Server logins

C. Any NT user ID in the SQL Users group

D. Any domain user

14. Which of the following is not an advantage of SQL stored procedures?

A. Centralized administration of SQL queries

B. Simplified SQL security management

C. Better performance

D. Support for more types of clients

15. For SQL Standard security mode authentication, which property does the developer need to set in order to provide the login info to SQL?

A. ConnectionString on the ADO Connection object

B. IsCallerInRole property

C. IsSecurityEnabled property

D. DSN parameter

16. In the three-tier architecture, where is user database auditing is best performed? (Choose all that apply.)

A. In the Data Access (lowest) tier

B. In the Business (middle) tier

C. In the (top) tier

D. A and B

17. In SQL Server mixed-mode security and a trusted connection, which of the following describes the order of authentication attempts?

A. Integrated, then standard

B. Standard only

C. MTS Roles, then integrated

D. Integrated only

18. Which method can be used in your code to return the ID of the caller that initiated a particular application process independently of the running component's identity?

A. GetOriginalCallerName on the application context object.

B. GetOriginalCallerName on the security object.

C. IsCallerInRole

D. GetUserID

19. What kinds of components can take advantage of MTS programmatic security?

    A. Any component with a pointer to the MTS application context object.

    B. Any MTS component

    C. Any MTS component installed in a server package

    D. Any MTS component installed in a library package

20. What should you remember about the system package in MTS?

    A. It is necessary to assign a valid NT user to the Administrator role before doing anything else with security

    B. The system package is only necessary at MTS installation, and can be deleted after it is complete

    C. The NT user Administrator is the only one that can open this package

    D. User components requiring a high degree of security should be placed in the system package

9

Advanced Client/Server Technologies

Designing and building distributed applications takes more than knowledge of Visual Basic and the VB language. It requires an understanding of client/server technologies; what they are and how they relate to a VB application. As we saw in the Microsoft Transaction Server section of Chapter 1, distributed applications may need to interact with specialized services on a network server. Because of this, it's important to know what's available and what you may be dealing with before designing and building a distributed application. In this chapter, we will discuss several of the advanced technologies that run under the Windows NT Server 4.0 operating system.

There are still a lot of old systems out there. These older systems contain data that is still used in the enterprise, but require special programming in applications to access the data. This chapter will introduce you to the ways in which Visual Basic can be used to access data in such legacy systems.

Overview of Advanced Client/Server Technologies

In Chapter 1, you were introduced to the way distributed applications may be integrated with other software like Microsoft Transaction Server (MTS). You saw how MTS could work with programs to enhance the functionality of an application. In this chapter, you'll see how other Microsoft technologies can work with MTS, and how to enable applications to work with legacy systems, send messages to queues, and work with clusters of servers.

Server clusters are made up of several NT Server computers that are grouped together using Microsoft Cluster Server (MSCS). MSCS is a built-in feature of Windows NT, that allows NT Servers to be accessed and managed as a single system. From the point of view of the network, the cluster appears as a single system. When one server in the cluster fails, another cluster server picks up where the other left off. If a client were using a server application during the failure, another cluster server would start up the failed application. If the user notices any disruption of service, it would be momentary and negligible.

Clusters have the attribute of being highly scalable, which can enhance the performance of a distributed application. "Scalability" means that it can be expanded to meet future needs. Server clustering allows CPU, I/O, storage, and application resources to be added. Rather than having to add enormous systems to the network, small standard systems can be added to meet the resource requirements of distributed applications. This means that clustering technology will allow the server cluster to meet the overall processing power requirements, and thereby enhance the performance of distributed applications using the cluster.

Microsoft Message Queue Server (MSMQ) is another advanced client/server technology that we will explore in this chapter. By building distributed applications that use MSMQ, you can create applications that have an easy-to-use, fault-tolerant method of transporting information. Rather than needing a connection to a computer, messages are sent to a message store, and then passed on to the receiving computer. This means that even if the receiver isn't online, it will still receive the message.

MSMQ can also be integrated with Microsoft Transaction Server, allowing certain conditions to be met before a message is delivered. If messages are made part of MTS transactions, their delivery depends on the success or failure of a transaction.

Another advanced client/server technology we'll explore in this chapter is SNA Server. SNA server enables distributed applications to access data on mainframes. Before client/server technologies made it possible to distribute work among computers, mainframes and dumb terminals were used. Dumb terminals accessed data on enormous machines that stored information and ran programs. SNA Server allows these disparate systems to communicate with one another, so that data can be accessed from mainframes.

Mainframes are what are described as being "legacy" systems. While mainframes were popular 20-30 years ago, client/server technologies have superceded them. As is the way with new technologies, there must be a way to translate the old data stored on mainframe computers so that new systems like NT Server, NT Workstation, and Windows 9x can use the information. For example, IBM mainframes often store data in VSAM or DB2 databases, which the Microsoft systems on an enterprise network don't use.

So why not simply stop using mainframes? It would seem to make sense to replace the old beasts, migrate the data to NT Servers, and create new applications that perform the same functions as the existing mainframe programs. The reason why this hasn't happened is mainly its cost. Most of the data on enterprise networks throughout the world is stored as VSAM files. It can be incredibly expensive, complex, and time-consuming to move this data to newer systems. For example, in the case of non-relational databases, you would have to create relational databases, and then transfer the data to the new DBMS. Also, number-crunchers are hesitant to fork out such large amounts of cash to do this because the old mainframes are still functional and providing data to the end user. Basically, because the legacy systems are still working, there is an understandable hesitation to pay to have them "updated."

on the
()ob

Most of the world's data is stored as VSAM files on mainframes. When the programs for these systems were written, programmers felt that technology would advance to the point that the mainframes would no longer be needed. So they entered a two-digit date for the year rather than 1998, 1999, 2000, (they entered 98, 99, 00). Because of this, on January 1st of the new millennium, the date (on mainframes that don't have the two-digit problem fixed) will enter the year 1900. This is what the Y2K problem entails. Some software developers are creating solutions that implement SNA Server to access these mainframes, so that the software can analyze and fix the lines of code that need repair. While the solution does the work of fixing the Y2K bug, it is SNA Server that enables access to the affected files.

CERTIFICATION OBJECTIVE 9.02

Message Queuing

"Please leave a message at the tone."

We've all heard that when we've phoned a person and reached an answering machine instead. Communication between the two people couldn't be established, so the message was "queued" in the answering machine. When the other person checks their messages, they can then play telephone tag and leave a message on your machine. In a nutshell, that's the basic principle of message queuing.

Just as you can communicate by talking directly to someone or leaving a message, a computer can send messages directly to another computer or have them queued. When one computer communicates directly with another, synchronous communication or message passing occurs. This can be a problem if both devices aren't online and messages can't be sent or received. Message queuing sidesteps this problem because any data sent from one computer to another goes directly into a message queue first.

Message queuing is also known as asynchronous communication. When a message is sent from a computer, it goes to a message queue. This message store is located on a server, where the message resides until the computer is ready to receive this data. Since the communication is indirect, the receiving computer doesn't have to be online or connected to the network when the message is sent. If the receiving computer is online when the message is sent, the sending computer's message still goes into the message store, but it is automatically sent from there to the receiving computer.

exam
watch

It is important to remember that asynchronous communication is message queuing and synchronous communication is message passing, and also to know what each of them does. The terms can be used interchangeably, and may appear as such in some questions of the exam.

When you create applications that communicate with one another through message queues, you are working with something called "Message Orientated Middleware," or MOM. Microsoft Message Queue Servers (MSMQ) is an example of this type of middleware. MSMQ provides guaranteed delivery, ensuring that all messages will eventually make it to their proper destination. It allows applications to communicate across heterogeneous networks, provides efficient routing, security, and priority-based, reliable messaging. Best of all, it is connectionless, meaning that applications don't need to maintain sessions to communicate. Messages from sending computers are stored until the receiving computer is ready to read the message from the queue.

One of the biggest reasons for developers to use asynchronous communication over synchronous is that the receiver isn't required to be online. For developers, asynchronous communication (or message queuing) is effective for distributed applications for a number of reasons. Since messages are stored in a queue rather than directly sent to another application, the sending application doesn't need to wait for a response. When a message is sent using synchronous communication, an application sends the message and must then wait for a response from the receiving computer. This response lets the sender know that the message was received properly. With asynchronous communication, the sender can perform other work while waiting for a response to a request. This type of communication is also useful when responses aren't required, and it is unnecessary to wait for the receiving computer to process a request. Since synchronous communication requires a connection, communication will fail if a receiving computer isn't available on the network.

Installing MSMQ

Installing MSMQ is a two-part process. First, you must install an MSMQ server on your network. If you don't have an MSMQ server installed, you won't be able to install the client portion. The MSMQ server can only be installed on Windows NT Server, and it is included with NT Server 4.0 and higher.

The client portion of MSMQ is available as part of the NT Option Pack on the Visual Studio 6.0 installation CD or through Microsoft's Web site (as explained in Chapter 1). The "Microsoft Transaction Server 2.0, Developer Edition" is also available on the Visual Basic 6.0 installation CD. As is common with modern Microsoft products, an Installation Wizard steps you through the process of setting up your MSMQ Client. When you install the client portion, you're offered a choice of client types: Independent and Dependent, as shown in Figure 9-1.

Independent Clients have a message store located on their local hard drive. This allows the client to send and receive messages at any time because it doesn't depend on a connection to the message store located on a MSMQ Server. When installing an Independent Client, you're required to enter the name of an MSMQ Site Controller, as shown in Figure 9-2. An

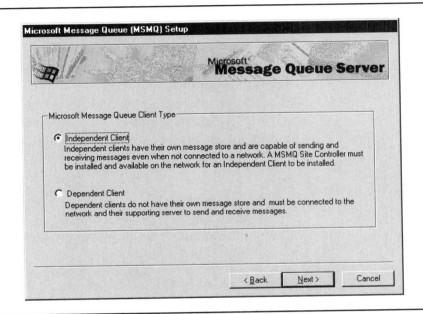

MSMQ Site Controller is one of the modes you can choose when installing MSMQ Server on an NT Server computer. The Site Controller must be available on the network, so information can be registered in the MSMQ Information Store database. The client portion cannot be installed if the server is unavailable.

Dependent Clients use the message store of an MSMQ Server or Site Controller. Since messages are stored on the MSMQ server, the client must have a connection to the server in order to send and receive messages.

EXERCISE 9-1

Installing a Microsoft Message Queue Client from NT Option Pack

Note: An MSMQ Server or Site Controller must be installed and available on your network in order to complete the following exercise. Confirm with your Network Administrator that these requirements are met before proceeding. If they are not, you will only be able to continue up to step 6; when the installation will fail.

1. Start the Setup program on your Visual Studio installation disk. When the Installation Wizard starts, select Server Applications and Tools (Add Only), and then click Next. From the list of server components, select NT Option Pack (for Windows 9x); then click Install.

2. A welcome screen for Personal Web Server will appear. Click the Next button.

3. In Chapter 1, we installed part of the NT Option Pack (Microsoft Transaction Server). As such, the screen that appears displays two buttons: Remove All and Add/Remove. Click the Add/Remove button to display a list of components that we can add to our previous installation.

4. From the listing of components, select Microsoft Message Queue; and click Next.

5. The Microsoft Message Queue Client Type screen allows you to choose between installing as an Independent Client or as a Dependent Client. The type of client you select here determines how the remainder of the setup will proceed. Independent Clients have their own message store, allowing them to send and receive messages at any time. Dependent Clients use the message store of an MSMQ Server, and must have a connection to it in order to send and receive messages. Select one of the two options; click Next.

6. If you selected Independent Client, you are required to enter the name of an MSMQ Site Controller, so you can be registered in the MSMQ Information Store database on that computer. If you selected Dependent Client, you must enter the name of a MSMQ Server or Site Controller. Enter the appropriate data; then click Next. The setup program will search for the server, and then continue with the installation.

7. You must enter the path of the folder that will store administration tools and SDK (Solution Developer Kit) files into. If you're unsure of the directory you'd like to use, click the Browse button to look through your hard disk for an appropriate folder. Click Next, and the setup program will begin transferring files to the folder you selected.

MSMQ and ActiveX

MSMQ provides ActiveX components that allow developers to manage messages and queues. These components also support queue lookup, queue administration, and transaction support. The components also allow access to MSMQ from Microsoft Transaction Server (MTS), Internet Information Server (IIS), Active Server Pages (ASPs), Visual Basic 6.0, NT Server's built-in Web server, and Microsoft applications (like Excel). These components implement an application-programming interface to the features in MSMQ.

As shown in Table 9-1, MSMQ has a number of ActiveX objects that can be used in developing applications. Using these objects, you can access MSMQ programmatically through Visual Basic 6.0.

MSMQApplication is used to obtain the machine identifier of a computer. When a computer is added to the connected network of MSMQ, Microsoft Message Queue Server generates a computer identifier, which is a unique number that identifies the computer. MSMQApplication is used with the MachineIdOfMachineName method. This method returns the machine identifier of a specific computer. MSMQApplication works as a parent object, and like any application object, you don't have to explicitly reference it when calling this method. For example, each of the following examples of syntax will obtain a machine identifier:

```
MSMQApplication.MachineIdOfMachineName("machinename")
MachineIdOfMachineName("machinename")
```

TABLE 9-1

MSMQ ActiveX
Component Reference

MSMQApplication	Used to obtain the machine identifier of a computer.
MSMQCoordinatedTransactionDispenser	Used to obtain MS DTC transaction objects.
MSMQEvent	Used for the notification of message arrivals and for describing outgoing MSMQ events.
MSMQMessage	Used to define a message and send it to a specific queue.
MSMQQueue	Used to represent an MSMQ message queue.
MSMQQueueInfo	Used for queue management, this object is used to create, open, and delete queues. It is also used to change a queue's properties.
MSMQQueueInfos	Used to select a specific queue from a collection of MSMQ message queue objects.
MSMQQuery	Provides MSMQ lookup facilities.
MSMQTransaction	Transaction object that's obtained internally using MSMQTransactionDispenser or externally using MSMQCoordinatedTransaction-Dispenser.
MSMQTransactionDispenser	Used to create an MSMQ internal transaction object.

By using this syntax, you could place the machine identifier into a variable to later reference a specific computer in your code.

MSMQMessage is used to define MSMQ messages and send them to their destinations. This object has a number of properties that define a message. For example, the Label property can be used to provide a brief description of a message, while the Body property is used to specify the contents of a message. This is shown in the following example, in which a new MSMQMessage is created, and string data is applied to the Label and Body:

```
Dim MyMsg as New MSMQMessage
MyMsg.Label = "This is my Message"
MyMsg.Body = "A body has a Variant data type."
```

Once this has been done, the Send method of the MSMQMessage can be used to send the message to a specific queue. This method can be used for both transaction and non-transaction messages. In the following example of code, we use the Send method to send the message "MyMsg" to a queue named "MyQueue."

```
MyMsg.Send MyQueue
```

MSMQQueueInfo is used for managing queues. Its Create and Open methods allow you to create new queues and open existing queues, respectively. This object also allows you to change a queue's properties or delete a queue. An MSMQQueue object is used to represent an instance of an MSMQ queue. When using an MSMQQueue object, the properties of the queue are based on the current properties of the MSMQQueueInfo object.

When a collection of queues exists, and you need to select a specific queue from the collection, the MSMQQueueInfos object is used. This object is used after MSMQQuery, which provides MSMQ lookup facilities. When the LookupQueue method of MSMQQuery is used, it returns a collection of queues. To select one queue from this collection, you use MSMQQueueInfos.

MSMQCoordinatedTransactionDispenser is used to obtain a Microsoft Distributed Transaction Coordinator (MS DTC) transaction object. You'll remember from Chapter 1 (when we discussed Microsoft Transaction Server) that a transaction is a set of instructions that are processed as a single unit of work. When transactions are used and one (or more) Resource Manager is required, a transaction object is created externally by MS DTC, along with an explicit reference for that object. If only one Resource Manager is required, an MSMQTransactionDispenser is used to internally create a transaction object. The MSMQTransaction object is returned to MSMQ so that it can send and retrieve messages of this type.

MSMQEvent is used for creating event handles that support multiple queues. It deals with events that include such things as the notification of a message's arrival and errors that occur when a message is being delivered. When messages are read from a queue, MSMQEvent is used for such events as messages not arriving at the queue before its receive timeout timer expires. Rather than having a different event handler for each MSMQ queue, a single event handler can be used to deal with errors and tasks in the same way.

Creating a Simple MSMQ Application

1. Start Visual Basic 6.0, and select Standard EXE from the New Project dialog box.

2. From the Project menu, select References. When the References dialog box appears, check the checkbox beside Microsoft Message Queue Object Library in the Available References list, and then click OK. This will allow us to use MSMQ ActiveX objects in our application.

3. Open the Code Window for the Form by clicking the View Code button of the Project Window or by selecting Code from the View menu. When the Code Window opens, it should open to the General Declarations section.

4. We will now declare three variables as objects. In General Declarations, enter the following code:

```
Dim MyQInfo As MSMQQueueInfo
Dim MyQueue As MSMQQueue
Dim MyMsg As New MSMQMessage
```

5. On the Form, add a new command button. In the Name property of the button, change the value to "Start."

6. Double-click on the newly added command button to bring up the Code Window. In the command button's Click event, add the following code to create a queue. The first line of this code sets MyQInfo as a new queue. By using a period in the pathname, the second line specifies the pathname of "MyFirstQueue" as being on the local computer. The third line labels the queue as "My First Queue;" the final line of code creates the queue.

```
Set MyQInfo = New MSMQQueueInfo
MyQInfo.PathName = ".\MyFirstQueue"
MyQInfo.Label = "My First Queue"
MyQInfo.Create
```

7. Below the code you entered in step six, enter the following line of code to open your queue:

```
Set MyQueue = MyQInfo.Open(MQ_SEND_ACCESS,
MQ_DENY_NONE)
```

8. Below the code you entered in step 7, enter the following lines of code to send a message, and then close the queue. The first line of code assigns a string as the message's label, while the second line assigns a string as the text body of the message. In the third line of text, we send the message to the queue we created and opened. Finally, we close the queue.

```
MyMsg.Label = "My message description"
MyMsg.Body = "This space for rent."
MyMsg.Send MyQueue
MyQueue.Close
```

CERTIFICATION OBJECTIVE 9.03

Server Clustering

Server clustering occurs when two or more NT Server machines are accessed and managed as a single system. Clustering can be used to increase performance and availability of distributed applications on a network. When servers are set up as a cluster, they appear as a single system on the network. If one of the servers in the cluster fails, the other servers can continue to provide service, allowing server applications to continue to be available to clients.

Microsoft Cluster Server (MSCS) is a built-in feature of the Enterprise Edition of NT Server 4.0 (with enhancements planned for the next version of NT, Windows 2000). It allows a minimum of two independent servers to be managed as a single system. This allows for higher availability, increased scalability, and easier manageability. When an application or server fails, MSCS detects the failure and starts the application on another server in the cluster. Future requests are redirected to this server, shielding end users from realizing that a problem has occurred. Administrators are able to move the workload performed on servers to other servers, allowing them to perform manual load balancing and to increase performance. Dynamic load balancing can also be programmed into applications through MSCS's Application Programming Interface (API).

on the
Job

Microsoft commonly conducts customer surveys to determine where and how its products are being used. Through these surveys, Microsoft has found that server clustering with MSCS is used for general business applications, mission-critical database management, intranet data sharing, file data sharing, and messaging. These are the types of applications you can expect to encounter when using MSCS in the real world.

Most of the APIs available for MSCS are for the development of applications written in the C++ language. At present, Visual Basic developers are limited to the Cluster Automation Server API, which gives an application the ability to administer clusters.

The Cluster Automation Server API doesn't come with Visual Basic 6.0 or Visual Studio 6.0; it must be installed through the Microsoft Cluster Server Software Development Kit (SDK). This SDK, and others, is available free from the Microsoft's Developer Network (MSDN) Web site at http://msdn.microsoft.com/developer/sdk. Installing this SDK will install and register the dynamic link library MSCLUS.DLL. This DLL contains the Cluster Automation Server API.

To use the API in Visual Basic 6.0, you must first use References from the Project menu. When the References dialog box appears, look in the Available References listing for MS Cluster 1.0 Type Library. Check the checkbox beside this name; then click OK to add the reference.

If the MS Cluster Type Library does not appear in the Available References listing, the SDK hasn't properly registered MSCLUS.DLL with your system registry. Usually (during installation of the SDK) the SDK will properly register the DLL. If you are victim to the SDK not registering it, use the system registry program REGSVR32 to register this file.

Once you've added the reference, you can use the Object Browser in Visual Basic 6.0 to view the objects that can be used in creating cluster-management applications. Once these cluster objects are added to an application, you can call their methods and set their properties as you would with any other object.

CERTIFICATION OBJECTIVE 9.04

Accessing Mainframe Data

In modern lingo, people have come to refer to a "mainframe" as any large computer that services large amounts of users. Before personal computers came on the scene, this mainframe referred to enormous cabinets containing the central processor unit (CPU) that generally stored data on huge tape reels. Mainframes were once the center of the networking universe. Programmers used archaic languages like FORTRAN and COBOL to create programs for them, and end users worked on computers called "dumb terminals" to access data. While they're generally considered dinosaurs today, they still contain reams of information that companies and governments still use.

In the enterprise, it is not uncommon to deal with mainframes. While client/server technologies have superceded mainframes, many modern networks grew from old networks that used mainframe technologies. As such, NT Servers will reside on the same network as these old servers. In addition to NT Servers, you may also deal with operating systems like Multiple Virtual Storage (MVS/ESA), OS/390, Virtual Storage Extended (VSE), Virtual Machine (VM), and AS/400. For developers, this means that applications must be able to deal with diverse storage technologies and operating systems.

Some of the storage technologies you may encounter are Information Management System (IMS), DB2, and Virtual Sequential Access Method (VSAM). DB2 is a relational database management system developed by IBM. IMS is also from IBM, and provides hierarchical database management, transaction management services, and data communication services. VSAM is one of the most common mainframe storage technologies. In fact, most of the world's data is still in VSAM files! This is because most of the data in enterprises reside on mainframes, and most of the files on these mainframes are in VSAM format. To connect to VSAM, DB2, and ISM databases, you can utilize the abilities of SNA Server.

SNA Server

Microsoft SNA Server enables client workstations to access the data and applications that reside on mainframes. SNA is an acronym for "Systems Network Architecture," which is a complex and proprietary network architecture developed by IBM. SNA Server acts as an SNA gateway, allowing NT Servers to integrate with IBM mainframes and AS/400 mainframes using the following connections:

- Client to server
- Server to mainframe

The client-to-server connection provides the network connection for workstations and server applications. SNA Server then uses the server-to-mainframe connection to provide the physical and logical connections between SNA Server and the mainframe. This is what a gateway does: it provides translation of protocols and data between computers, allowing one computer to interact with the other.

SNA Server is actually a suite of services, made up of three components:

- OLEDB/DDM Provider
- Component Object Model Transaction Integrator (COMTI)
- Host Data Replicator (HDR)

The OLEDB/DDM (Object Linking and Embedding Database/Distributed Data Management) Provider is used to access VSAM and AS/400 files. The second component, COMTI, allows access to Customer Information Control System (CICS) and Information Management Systems (IMS) programs running on the Multiple Virtual

Storage (MVS) operating system. Finally, the Host Data Replicator allows access to relational databases on IBM mainframes by copying the data from the mainframe database to SQL Server databases.

COMTI allows you to integrate applications with data, transactions, and applications that run on mainframes. Your applications can be integrated with CICS and IMS programs running on the Multiple Virtual Storage (MVS) operating system. Since you are able to access programs in addition to data, you can extend your distributed application through CICS to work with any other program on an MVS mainframe. COMTI intercepts the method calls of objects and redirects them to mainframe programs, thereby acting as a proxy for the mainframe. In addition, it handles any parameters and values returned by the program on the mainframe. For example, your application could make a request to a program on the mainframe. Depending on what information is returned by the mainframe program, another program on the mainframe or an application on the server could start up or be controlled. When parameters and values are returned by a mainframe program or method calls are intercepted and sent to the mainframe, COMTI is responsible for converting and formatting it so the receiver can understand it. This gives great flexibility in what can be done with applications and what can be accessed on the mainframe.

Another benefit of COMTI is that all processing is done on NT Server, meaning that you won't have to rewrite most (if any) code for programs on the mainframe, and no COMTI code needs to run on the mainframe. This shields the developer from having to learn how to code in such languages as Cobol.

COMTI can extend transactions from NT Server to mainframe environments using Microsoft Transaction Server (MTS). COMTI functions as a component of MTS. Together, they make IMS and CICS programs appear as MTS components, which can be packaged with other components. In addition, it allows drag-and-drop registration of type libraries, and it takes advantage of MTS features like multithread processing and object caching.

The OLEDB/DDM Provider component of SNA Server enables applications to access mainframe data in VSAM and AS/400 file systems. This component is an OLE DB data provider for the Distributed Data

Management (DDM) architecture developed by IBM, and offers record level I/O access.

The Host Data Replicator allows access to relational databases located on mainframes. It is used to copy such relational data between mainframes and SQL Server databases. When compared to using an ODBC (Open Database Connectivity) driver, the Host Data Replicator is considerably fast. The downside of this component is that it takes more to set up because SQL Server is used. In using the Host Data Replicator, data can be moved from the mainframe to the server or from the server to the mainframe. Data can be copied on demand or scheduled to be copied at regular intervals.

In addition to the three components covered so far, you can also access relational databases on mainframes using the ODBC driver. This driver is built into SNA Server and provides direct access to a mainframe's relational database. Using this driver, you can view, modify, and delete data. The ODBC driver provides the following features:

- Scrollable cursors
- Full transaction support
- Use of stored procedures
- Asynchronous calling
- Array fetch and update

ODBC provides a flexible connection model and preserves the integrity, storage, management, backup, and security provided by the mainframe system.

For databases that use the Distributed Relational Database Architecture (DRDA) protocol, the ODBC/DRDA driver can be used. This driver accesses databases such as DB2 for OS/390, DB2 for VM, and DB2/400 for AS/400. This driver should only be used in cases where the DRDA protocol is used.

DCOM (Distributed Component Object Model) is also of great use for creating distributed applications that access data from mainframes. DCOM allows you to create user-defined data types, which make object calls to a user interface more accessible. Data types created by a developer can be of any complexity. DCOM also supports embedded structures and

Automation data types, and allows you to marshal the interface of a server object to a different server. This allows you to create an object broker on the mainframe to take client requests, find and instantiate an object, and then pass the interface back to a client.

QUESTIONS AND ANSWERS

I want to have my application send messages depending on the result of a transaction. How is this possible?	Microsoft Message Queue Server can be integrated with Microsoft Transaction Server, so that messages are only sent depending on the result of a transaction.
After selecting References in Visual Basic, I can't find the Cluster Automation Server API in the Available References listing. Why?	You need to install the Microsoft Cluster Server SDK. This will install Cluster Automation Server API on your system.
I need to copy relational data from a database located on the mainframe to a SQL Server database. Which component of SNA Server should I use?	Host Data Replicator enables data to be copied from relational databases on mainframes to SQL Server databases. This data can be copied on demand, or at regular scheduled intervals.
I want to extend transactions from an NT Server to a mainframe. Which SNA component should I use?	Use COMTI to extend transactions from NT Server to mainframe environments using Microsoft Transaction Server (MTS).
I am creating an application to access a mainframe database that uses the Distributed Relational Database Architecture (DRDA) protocol. Which driver should I utilize to access the database?	Use the ODBC/DRDA driver. This driver is used to access databases that use the DRDA protocol.

CERTIFICATION SUMMARY

Microsoft Message Queue is an example of Message Orientated Middleware, which uses message queues. Message queues are known as asynchronous communication and have messages placed into a queue, rather than sent directly to another application. This allows applications to communicate, even if one is offline.

Server clustering is when two or more NT Server computers are accessed and administered as a single system. When clustering is used, these computers appear as a single system on the network. If one of the computers in the cluster fails, the other systems continue providing service. This enhances the availability of server applications because requests can be redirected to another server in the cluster that also carries the application.

SNA Server is a suite of components that allows integration of your NT Server network with IBM mainframe environments. Using SNA Server allows you to access programs and data located on an IBM mainframe.

TWO-MINUTE DRILL

- ❏ Server clusters are several NT Server computers that are grouped together using Microsoft Cluster Server (MSCS). MSCS is a built-in feature of Windows NT, and allows NT Servers to be accessed and managed as a single system.

- ❏ Clusters have the attribute of being highly scalable, which can enhance the performance of a distributed application.

- ❏ "Scalability" means that it can be expanded to meet future or growing needs.

- ❏ Server clustering allows CPU, I/O, storage, and application resources to be added.

- ❏ It is important to remember that asynchronous communication is message queuing and synchronous communication is message passing.

- ❏ When you create applications that communicate with one another through message queues, you are working with something called "Message Orientated Middleware," or MOM.

- ❏ MSMQ provides ActiveX components that allow developers to manage messages and queues. These components also support queue lookup, queue administration, and transaction support.

❑ Server clustering can be used to increase performance and availability of distributed applications on a network. Clustering is when two or more NT Server machines are accessed and managed as a single system.

❑ Microsoft Cluster Server (MSCS) is a built-in feature of the Enterprise Edition of NT Server 4.0 (with enhancements planned for the next version of NT, Windows 2000). It allows a minimum of two independent servers to be managed as a single system.

❑ Microsoft SNA Server enables client workstations to access the data and applications that reside on mainframes. SNA is an acronym for "Systems Network Architecture," which is a complex and proprietary network architecture developed by IBM.

❑ SNA Server is actually a suite of services, made up of three components: OLEDB/DDM Provider, Component Object Model Transaction Integrator (COMTI), and Host Data Replicator (HDR).

❑ DCOM (Distributed Component Object Model) is also of great use for creating distributed applications that access data from mainframes. DCOM allows you to create user-defined data types, which make object calls to a user interface more accessible.

SELF TEST

The following Self-Test questions will help you measure your understanding of the material presented in this chapter. Read all the choices carefully, as there may be more than one correct answer. Choose all correct answers for each question.

1. Which of the following occurs when one application communicates directly with another?

   A. Asynchronous communication

   B. Message queuing

   C. Message passing

   D. Clustering

2. Which of the following is a hierarchical database management system?

   A. DB2

   B. AS/400

   C. IMS

   D. SQL

3. You need to access data located on an IBM database. Which of the following will you have your applications interact with to achieve this?

   A. SQL Server

   B. SNA Server

   C. Cluster Server

   D. IBM Server

4. Which of the following would you use to copy relational data between mainframe databases and SQL Server databases?

   A. COMTI

   B. OLEDB/DDM

   C. ODBC

   D. Host Data Replicator

5. Which of the following is an example of MOM (Message Orientated Middleware)?

   A. Cluster Server

   B. Microsoft Transaction Server

   C. NT Server

   D. Microsoft Message Queue Server

6. You are creating an application that accesses data from the mainframe. You require user defined data types in this application. Which of the following will you use to access the mainframe data?

   A. ODBC

   B. ODBC/DRDA

   C. DCOM

   D. Host Data Replicator

7. Which of the following is used to obtain the machine identifier of a computer?

   A. MSMQQuery

   B. MSMQQueue

   C. MSMQIdentity

   D. MSMQApplication

8. Which of the following objects would you use to create, open, and delete queues?

   A. MSMQQueue

   B. MSMQQueueInfo

   C. MSMQCreate

   D. MQMQQueueProp

9. Which of the following can be used to extend transactions from NT Server to mainframe environments using Microsoft Transaction Server (MTS)?

   A. COMTI

   B. DB2

   C. SNA Transaction Component

   D. OLEDB/DDM

10. Which of the following is also known as asynchronous communication?

    A. Message passing

    B. Message queuing

    C. Message clustering

    D. Message quelling

11. Which of the following is a relational database management system developed by IBM?

    A. DB2

    B. IMS

    C. SQL Server

    D. Access

12. What do the letters "SNA" stand for?

    A. Simple Network Application

    B. Systems Network Architecture

    C. Simple Network Architecture

    D. Super Network Application

13. You are creating an application that accesses data from the mainframe. You require support for Automation data types and embedded structures. Which of the following will you use to access the mainframe data?

    A. ODBC

    B. DCOM

    C. Automation Data Replicator

    D. Host Data Replicator

14. Which of the following would you manipulate the properties of to define the label and body of a message?

    A. MSMQLabel

    B. MSMQBody

    C. MSMQQueue

    D. MSMQMessage

15. Which of the following would be used to determine if messages are delivered, depending on whether certain conditions are met? (Choose all that apply.)

    A. SNA Server

    B. Microsoft Cluster Server

    C. Microsoft Message Queue Server

    D. Microsoft Transaction Server

16. Which of the following are features of using the ODBC driver to access data from a mainframe? (Choose all that apply.)

    A. Scrollable cursors

    B. Synchronous calling

    C. No transaction support

    D. Use of stored procedures

17. You are installing Microsoft Message Queue Client on your computer and choose Independent Client as the mode of installation. Where will the message store reside with this installation?

    A. Local hard drive

    B. MSMQ Server hard drive

    C. A mainframe

    D. Site Controller

18. Which of the following best defines a server cluster?

    A. An NT Server that is accessed and managed as a single system

    B. Two or more NT Servers that are accessed and managed as a single system

    C. Three or more NT Servers that are accessed and managed as a single system

    D. A network segment that is accessed and managed as a single system

19. You want to create a program that manages a Microsoft Cluster Server. When you attempt to make a reference to the appropriate API, you notice that the API isn't included with Visual Basic 6.0. Why not, and how can you remedy this?

    A. Cluster API doesn't come with Visual Basic 6.0 or Visual Studio 6.0. It must be installed through the Microsoft Cluster Server SDK.

    B. Cluster Automation Server API doesn't come with Visual Basic 6.0 or Visual Studio 6.0. It must be installed through the Microsoft Cluster Server SDK.

    C. The NT Option Pack needs to be installed for the API to appear.

    D. Visual Basic 6.0 hasn't had all Data Access Objects installed. Install the DAO objects from the installation disk.

20. Which of the following is used for notification of message arrivals?

    A. MSMQApplication

    B. MSMQMessage

    C. MSMQEvent

    D. MSMQQueue

21. A user plans to send a message with your application, which uses Microsoft Transaction Server. The receiver of the message has turned off her computer and gone home for the day. What will happen when the user sends the message?

A. The message will be returned to the sending user

B. An error message, stating the message is undeliverable, will appear to the sending user

C. The message will be stored on a mainframe's database until the receiver reads the message from the database

D. The message will be stored in a queue, until the receiver reads the message from the queue

22. Which of the following APIs can you use for cluster server programming with Visual Basic 6.0?

A. Cluster API, for enabling a resource DLL or application to communicate with the Cluster Service and cluster database

B. Resource API, for enabling Cluster Service to communicate through Resource Monitor with a resource

C. Cluster Automation Server API, which gives an application the capability to manage clusters

D. Cluster Administrator Extension API, which allows context menus and Property Pages to be integrated into Cluster Administrator

23. Which components are parts of SNA Server? (Choose all that apply.)

A. OLEDB/DDM Provider

B. Component Object Model Transaction Integrator (COMTI)

C. OLE Provider

D. Host Data Replicator (HDR)

E. Component Object Model Integrator (COMI)

24. You are installing Microsoft Message Queue Client on your computer and choose Dependent Client as the mode of installation. Where will the message store reside with this installation? (Choose all that apply.)

A. Local hard drive

B. MSMQ Server

C. Site Controller

D. On a mainframe

25. Which of the following objects is used to send a message to a specific queue?

A. MSMQMessage

B. MSMQEvent

C. MSMQQueue

D. MSMQQueueInfo

26. You have installed the Microsoft Cluster Server SDK on your computer. When you open references from the Project menu in Visual Basic 6.0, you notice that the MS Cluster Type Library doesn't appear in the listing of Available References. Why not, and how will you fix this?

A. The SDK hasn't registered MSCLUS.DLL with the system registry. Use REGSVR32 to register this file.

B. Visual Basic hasn't registered the SDK. Reinstall Visual Basic.

C. Visual Basic hasn't registered the SDK with the system registry. Use REGSVR32 to register the SDK.

D. The MS Cluster Type Library isn't included in the Microsoft Cluster Server SDK.

10

Testing the
Solution

T esting and debugging are not only important issues to master for the real world, but you'll also find that these topics get plenty of attention on the exam. In fact, I would go so far as to say that this is an easy area to stockpile some points because it's not really very big or complicated and it has a disproportionately large number of test questions. In this chapter, we will probe into testing and debugging.

Selecting Appropriate Compiler Options

They say that there is more than one way to skin a cat. Well, fortunately, I've never had to skin a cat, but I do get the opportunity to compile a VB program every now and then, and there's definitely more than one way to do that. In fact, there are lots of compiler options that enable programmers to customize their executables to a variety of specific needs.

Compiler options enable you to change specific attributes of the executable or DLL that Visual Basic will generate when you compile your project. These options reside under the Compile tab in the Project Properties dialog box, which you access by selecting <Project Name> Properties under Project on the main menu bar (see Figure 10-1).

Probably the most important concept in this section is the distinction between *p-code* and *native code*.

P-Code

P-code is short for pseudo-code. The definition of pseudo-code here is different from the one you're probably used to. Most people think of pseudo-code as a way of generically constructing program logic or algorithms. This kind of pseudo-code is for human eyes only and useless to a machine. P-code, however, is a special kind of executable code that will run on a variety of processors such as the Motorola 68000, the Dec Alpha, and the Intel x86 families, provided a VB translator is present. This, of course, does not come without strings attached. Any time you run a p-code

Compile tab of the Project
Properties dialog box

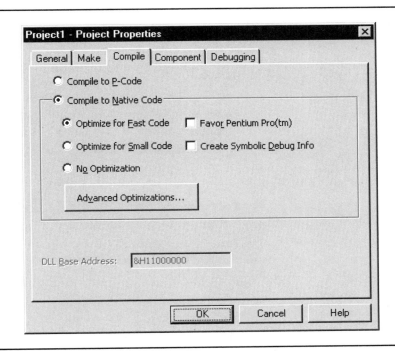

application, there is an intermediate step involved, in which the operating
system translates the p-code into code that will run on the processor being
used. This extra step will have a slight impact on performance, especially in
looping constructs and mathematical calculations. Contrary to intuition,
p-code executables will usually be smaller than executables compiled as
native code.

Native Code

Native code is real machine code—the native instructions of the processor
chip. This is the kind of code that Visual C++ generates. Native code is
what you use for that extra little performance boost, but only when you're
sure that computers using different families of processors will never need to
run your application. The performance boost will be most noticeable in

calculation intensive applications. The optimization options offered by Visual Basic pertain to native code only.

Optimize for Fast Code

When you build a Visual Basic application, you can either optimize for speed or optimize for size, but not both. The speed optimization can reorganize portions of your code and substitute faster function sequences at compile time to take advantage of the way the computer processes machine code.

Optimize for Small Code

In many cases, the Visual Basic compiler can decrease the size of your application by substituting code that is smaller but equal in functionality. Your program will take up less disk space but may sacrifice some performance.

No Optimization

This option will not optimize for speed or size.

Favor Pentium Pro

If you intend your program to be primarily used on Pentium Pro machines, you should compile with this option. It will modify your executable to take advantage of the custom capabilities in the Pentium Pro architecture. Programs compiled with this option will still run on other chip families, but not nearly as efficiently as if you had not used this option.

Create Symbolic Debug Info

This option embeds symbolic debug information in your application and creates a .pdb (program database) file that will house information used by your program during execution. Selecting this option will increase the size of your application but allow you to debug your executable using Visual C++ or any other CodeView style debugger.

DLL Base Address

By default, DLLs will attempt to load at 0X10000000 in memory. When this memory space fills, the operating system is forced to relocate the DLL to avoid collisions with other DLLs. Relocation will increase the load time for the DLL. To avoid this, change the DLL Base Address. Visual Basic will only let you enter values between &H1000000 (16,777,216 in decimal) and &H80000000 (2,147,483,648 in decimal) and will round the specified address up to the nearest multiple of 64K.

Advanced Options

You probably will only need to use these options if you are really pressed for performance, but make sure you know what you're doing first. By default, all the advanced options (see Figure 10-2) are unselected and selecting them may cause strange side effects if you're not sure what you're doing. So let's make sure you know what you're doing.

Assume No Aliasing

An *alias* is a special code that a compiler gives to all variables referencing identical memory locations. By default, the compiler will assume that a variable can be changed by some unseen force, like a pointer, even if it's not actually changed. If you use the Assume No Aliasing option, the compiler can assume that any variable not directly modified by an assignment operation within the local scope will remain static. By ignoring aliasing precautions, you will enable the compiler to optimize your application in certain areas, such as storing variables in registers and optimizing looping constructs. However, if two variables modify the same memory location (for example, a global and the local version of that global), the resulting value could differ from what you expected. A *register* is a high-speed memory location within the CPU that is used for variables that a program will reference excessively.

Remove Array Bounds Checks

By default, a program generated by Visual Basic will verify that an index is within the array's range whenever accessing it. If the index isn't in range,

FIGURE 10-2

Advanced Optimizations
dialog box

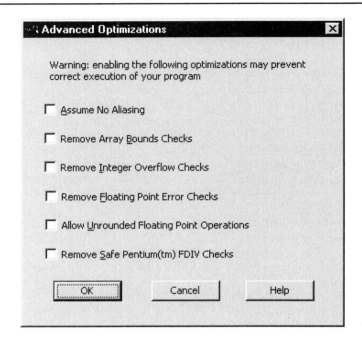

the application will generate a trappable error. For instance, selecting this
option would be considered safe in a program in which all array indices are
hard-coded. A minute performance increase will be realized when accessing
arrays in a program compiled with this option selected, but because this
option is somewhat dangerous and could potentially result in undesired
errors, caution is advised.

Remove Integer Overflow Checks

Integer-style variables (bytes, integers, and longs) lay claim to a finite
amount of space in memory. Normally, Visual Basic applications screen all
integer-style assignments to catch values that require more space than
allotted. When a culprit is detected, a trappable error is generated. For
example, a Visual Basic integer is two bytes, and thus ranges from –32,768

to 32,767. If we try to assign 60,000 to an integer, normally the application will trigger a trappable error and abort the assignment operation. With no overflow checking, however, 60,000 would be stored as −5536 and the computer would not realize this was incorrect. You can gain a small performance increase by selecting this option, but because this option is somewhat dangerous and could potentially result in undesired side effects, caution is advised.

Remove Floating-Point Error Checks

This is similar to the Remove Integer Overflow Checks option, except that it pertains to floating-point data types (singles and doubles), and also includes additional data verifications such as checking for division by zero. You can gain a small performance increase, but this option can be somewhat dangerous and can potentially result in errors.

Allow Unrounded Floating-Point Operations

Normally, Visual Basic applications will round floating-point-style values to their correct precision during comparison operations. By allowing unrounded operations, you will actually have higher precision, resulting in the possible side effects from left-over bits in memory. This may result in incorrect comparisons of values that should be equal. By using the Allow Unrounded Floating-Point Operations option, the compiler will be able to make better use of floating-point registers and make faster floating-point comparisons but it is somewhat dangerous and can potentially result in incorrect floating-point comparisons.

Remove Safe Pentium FDIV Checks

Early versions of Intel's P-60, P-66, and P-90 Pentium processors were shipped with a bug that caused some complex floating-point division calculations to generate slightly inaccurate results, varying no more than .0000001 from the correct result. Applications compiled with Visual Basic normally check for this error. By removing this check, you'll gain a tiny performance boost when using the division operation on floating-point style numbers. Processors with this error today are rare, so it's probably okay to check this option most of the time.

Controlling an Application Using Conditional Compilation

Conditional compilation directives allow programmers to tell the compiler to include or exclude fragments of code, based on the evaluation of condition expressions. This enables programmers to include multiple versions of a program in a single project. It is common to use conditional compilation directives to incorporate debugging information into a project that can be excluded from the release version, in order to create a project that can be compiled for different operating systems, or to create a project that can be compiled for different languages (English, French, and so on).

It's also common practice to use conditional compilation directives to comment out large blocks of code.

on the
ﾒﾞob

Even though conditional compilation directives are used to compile executables into different languages (English, German), it is generally considered better practice to use a resource file to store all strings. This will enable you to switch or even add new languages without having to recompile the executable. It also allows anyone to fix typos.

The following listing demonstrates the syntax of conditional compilation directives.

```
#If <expression> Then
  code
#ElseIf <expression> Then
  code
#Else
  code
#End If
```

The #ElseIf and #Else clauses are optional.

The expression can be a constant or any mathematical equation. If it evaluates to zero, it is false; anything else yields true. When an expression includes a constant that has not been defined, the constant will evaluate to zero.

Conditional compilation constants can be declared three ways in Visual Basic. You can embed a constant declaration in your code by using the #Const directive. You can use the Conditional Compilation Arguments field on the Make tab of the Project Properties dialog box. You can use the /d or /D flag when compiling a project from the command line.

Unlike C++, constants in Visual Basic must be given a value.

Embedding constant declarations in your source code using the #Const directive has the highest precedence, meaning it will override constants defined on the command line or in the Project Properties dialog box. An example of the syntax follows:

```
#Const DEBUG = 1
#Const WIN98 = 1
```

A #Const declaration must be positioned in your code so that the compiler will evaluate it prior to any #If statements that reference the constant. If the constant is not defined, it will be unrecognized and thus be evaluated as false (or zero).

The Make tab in the Project Properties dialog box, as shown in Figure 10-3, has the lowest precedence, meaning either an embedded directive or a command line declaration will override any value assigned here. When declaring multiple constants, separate them by using ":" as a delimiter.

VB programs can be compiled from the MS-DOS prompt or the Start menu by running Visual Basic using the /make flag. Additionally, compilation constants can be specified here by using a /d or /D flag, followed by the constant declarations. Constants declared here will override constants declared in the Project Properties dialog box, but not the constants embedded in code using #Const. An example of the usage follows:

```
vb6.exe /make Project1.vbp /d DEBUG=1:WIN98=1
```

FIGURE 10-3

Make tab of the Project
Properties dialog box

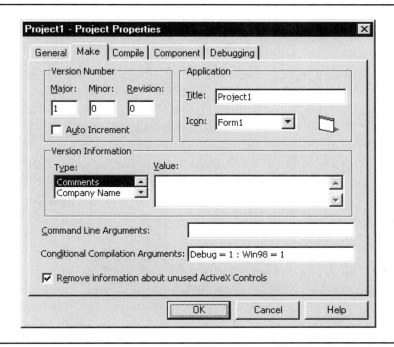

EXERCISE 10-1

Using Conditional Compilation

1. Create a new project in Visual Basic.

2. Create a label on Form1.

3. Double-click on the form to get to Form_Load().

4. Add the following code in the Form_Load() subroutine:

```
#Const Win98 = 1

#If Win98 Then
    Label1.Caption = "Windows 98"

#ElseIf WinNT Then

    Label1.Caption = "Windows NT"
#Else
    Label1.Caption = "Unknown Operation System"
#End If
```

5. Run the program by selecting start on the Visual Basic's Run menu.

6. Observe that "Windows 98" appears in the label and hit the End button.

7. Remove the line containing the #Const declaration in the Form_Load() subroutine.

8. Run it again, verify the "Unknown Operation System" message in the label field and quit the program.

9. Now, open the Project Properties dialog box. Select the Make tab and enter **WinNT=1** in the Conditional Compilation Arguments field.

10. Run the program again and observe that the label reads "Windows NT" this time.

Break Mode and Setting Breakpoints

Visual Basic provides programmers with a method to pause an executing program when it is running within the Visual Basic development environment. This special suspended state is called Break mode. While in Break mode, you can view variable values, change variable values, execute the program line-by-line, execute arbitrary procedures that will affect the current program state, move the Current Statement Indicator, edit the code, revise the watch set, and resume normal execution of our program. We will look at these in greater depth throughout the rest of this chapter.

There are several ways to trigger Break mode: setting a breakpoint, pressing CTRL-BREAK or the VB pause button, using a watch expression, using Debug.Assert, embedding the Stop keyword, running to cursor, and breaking on errors. These methods will also be covered throughout this chapter.

Entering Break Mode by Setting Breakpoints

The most straightforward method used to enter Break mode is to set a breakpoint.

A breakpoint marks a single line of code within the Visual Basic environment. Whenever this line is about to execute, the program will pause and enter Break mode before it executes the line. Notice that there is a vertical gray bar on the left of the code window in Figure 10-4. This is the *margin indicator bar*. To set a breakpoint, open up a code window in the Visual Basic development environment and single-click on the margin indicator bar next to the line you wish to break on. When a breakpoint is set, the line corresponding to the breakpoint will be highlighted in red and a red dot will be fixed to it in the margin indicator bar. To clear the breakpoint, click on it again.

You may also set and remove breakpoints by positioning your cursor on the line where you wish to place a breakpoint and pressing F9, or selecting Toggle Breakpoint from the Debug tool bar, the Edit tool bar, the Debug menu, or the code window's pop-up menu. To remove all breakpoints select Clear All Breakpoints from the Debug menu (or press CTRL-SHIFT-F9).

FIGURE 10-4

Setting a breakpoint

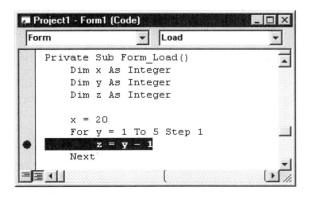

Two other ways to enter Break mode that are similar to breakpoints and deserve a brief mention are the *Run to Cursor* command and the *Stop* keyword.

Run to Cursor treats the line your cursor is positioned on as a breakpoint. The program will run until this line is encountered and then enter Break mode.

When you close the Visual Basic development environment session, all your breakpoints will be lost. The Stop keyword is a more permanent way to set a breakpoint because it is embedded in the source code just as any other VB keyword would be. One thing to keep in mind with Stop is that if you include it in an EXE, it will mimic End. I recommend that you do not use Stop.

The Debug Tool Bar

Visual Basic provides many tools for debugging in Break mode. These are available on the Debug, View and Start menus. Microsoft also provides us with a Debug tool bar, containing a subset of frequently used debugging functions. The tool bar is shown in Figure 10-5.

The Debug tool bar can be activated by selecting Debug from the cascading Tool bars button on the View menu. It can also be brought forth by right-clicking on any tool bar or menu bar, and selecting Debug from the pop-up menu.

The Start button on the Debug tool bar (or F5) will run your program in Debug mode. At any time during the execution of your program, you can hit the Pause Button (or CTRL-BREAK) to enter Break mode. The End button terminates the program. The remaining options on the Debug tool bar will be presented throughout the rest of the chapter.

FIGURE 10-5

The Debug tool bar

In some cases, such as endless loops, the Pause button will not work properly. Make sure to try CTRL-BREAK a couple of times before you kill VB with the Task Manager (CTRL-ALT-DEL).

Stepping through a Visual Basic Program

While in Break mode, you can execute code one line at a time. This capability is called *stepping*. On the Debug tool bar and in the Debug menu, you will notice several stepping functions. Step Over (or SHIFT-F8) enables you to execute the next line of code in the function that is currently running. Step Into (or F8) will jump into a function that is called on the line that is currently being executed, enabling you to dissect sub-functions. If no function call is made on the current line, Step Into will mimic Step Over. Step Out (or CTRL-SHIFT-F8) will run a program until the current function completes, and then re-enter Break mode at the line of code that called the function you stepped out of. If the current function was not called by another function, Step Out will act just like continue.

If you find yourself hitting the Step Over key over and over and over, especially within looping constructs, explore other ways to move through your program, such as watch expressions, breakpoints, and running to cursor.

Moving the Current Statement Indicator

The Visual Basic development environment provides programmers with the capability to change the next statement in the execution flow by repositioning the Current Statement Indicator. The Current Statement Indicator is a yellow arrow that appears in the Margin Indicator Bar while in Break mode. It signifies the next line of code that is to be executed during the normal program progression. To move the Current Statement Indicator, left-click on the yellow arrow and drag it up or down to any other executable line of code within the currently executing function. This can come in handy for skipping code segments, rerunning fragments of code, and testing alternative outcomes to conditional statements.

Visual Basic also provides us with the Set Next Statement command to move the Current Statement Indicator. The Set Next Statement command moves the Current Statement Indicator to the line of code where your cursor is positioned. The same rules apply; it must be an executable line within the currently executing function. Set Next Statement's counterpart, Show Next Statement, does just the opposite. It moves your cursor to the Current Statement Indicator. You will find both the Set Next Statement and the Show Next Statement commands in the Debug menu or on the pop-up menu, generated by right-clicking over the code window in Break mode.

CERTIFICATION OBJECTIVE 10.04

Setting Watch Expressions During Program Execution

The Visual Basic development environment enables programmers to track the values of variables or expressions during the debugging process by adding watches to the Add Watch window (shown in Figure 10-6). There are three kinds of watches available for programmers to use: a watch expression, a break when a value is true expression, and a break when a value changes expression.

Watch Expressions

Watch expressions are used to display the current value of a variable or an expression in the Watch window while executing an application from within the Visual Basic development environment.

Break When Value Is True

Break When Value Is True is used to suspend execution immediately after the value of an expression in the Watch window becomes true. When

FIGURE 10-6

Add Watch dialog box

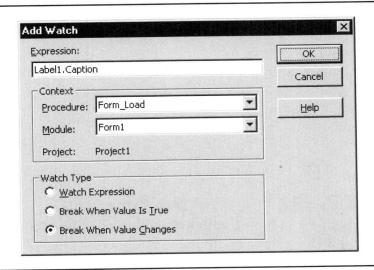

program execution is suspended, the application will be put into Break mode. You might stop to think to yourself, how do I break when the value is false? Keep in mind that it's the expression that is evaluated, not the variable, so if you want to know when an x becomes false, use (x = False) as your expression.

Break When Value Changes

Break When Value Changes is used to enter Break mode immediately after the value of a variable changes. Thus, a good time to use it might be to determine why that variable you specifically assigned zero suddenly equals 99999999. Note that in order to enter Break mode, the value must actually change, not merely be assigned. For example, assigning "True" to x when x already equals "True" will not break.

Using the Watch Window to Evaluate Expressions

There are several ways to set a watch. The easiest is to highlight a variable or an expression in the source code and right-click on it, and then select the

Add Watch option on the pop-up menu. The advantage of this method is that many of the fields on the Add Watch dialog box will be completed for you by VB. You can also find Add Watch in the Debug menu or by right-clicking over the Watch window, which is shown in Figure 10-7.

While in Break mode, the values of the variables that you are monitoring in the Watch window can be changed by clicking on the value in the value column. The new value will be the one your program uses upon resuming execution. This, of course, is not possible if you are monitoring an expression instead of a variable.

EXERCISE 10-2

Adding Watch Expressions

1. Create a new project in Visual Basic.

2. Double-click on the form to get to Form_Load().

3. Add the following code in the Form_Load() subroutine:

```
Dim x As Integer
Dim y As Integer
Dim z As Integer

x = 20
For y = 1 To 5 Step 1
    z = y - 1
Next
```

4. Right click over any occurrence of x in the code window, and select Add Watch from the pop-up menu.

5. Verify that the expression is set to x and select OK. (If the Watch window wasn't visible on your screen, it should be now. (You can always get to the Watch window from the Debug tool bar or the View menu if not.)

6. Right-click on the Watch window and select Add Watch from the pop-up menu. This time, change the expression to z = 2 and select *Break When Value Is True.*

7. Run your program using the Start option on VB's Run menu or the Start button on the Debug tool bar. The program will break when the value of z becomes 2. (If your Debug tool bar is not visible, select View | Toolbars | Debug from the main menu.)

8. Notice in the Watch window that x is 20 and that z = 2 is true.

9. Place your pointer over any occurrence of z in the code window and notice that z's value appears in a ToolTip-like window. Now highlight the expression y − 1 and place your pointer over it. Notice that VB evaluates the whole expression.

10. Press the Step Over button on the Debug tool bar twice and note that z = 2 now equates to false in the Watch window.

11. Press the End button on the Debug tool bar to terminate the application.

Defining the Scope of a Watch Variable

On many occasions, you will have variables using the same names scattered throughout your program in different routines. When setting a watch expression, you might want to let Visual Basic know which variable you mean to monitor. In the Add Watch dialog box, there is a context section that enables you to define an expression's scope by setting the module and the procedure of the variable you need to keep tabs on. You may also find it helpful, when monitoring global or member variables, to set *Break When Value Is True* and *Break When Value Changes* expression only on trouble-spots, as opposed to the entire application. Keep in mind that after specifying a watch's context, Break mode will be entered from only the function specified in the context section or any subsequent sub-function

FIGURE 10-7

The Watch window

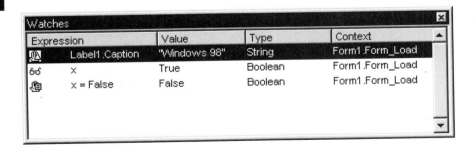

called from within that function. Setting a watch's scope will also provide a slight boost in performance because evaluations are only performed inside the specified context and not universally throughout the whole application.

Monitoring Expressions and Variable Values Using the Debug Window

Visual Basic provides some powerful tools to help programmers debug their programs. Among them are the Watch window, the Immediate window, the Locals window, and the Call Stack window. We've already taken a look at the Watch window. Let's examine the others.

Using the Immediate Window to Check or Change Values

The Immediate window, shown in Figure 10-8, lets programmers directly interact with a program in Break mode by entering executable code. Common uses include calling functions, setting variables, printing current values of variables, and the elaboration of error codes.

You enter code into the Immediate window just as you would enter it into your program. Upon pressing the ENTER key, the code will be executed just as if it were embedded in your program. You can assign values to variables and execute functions. If you execute a function that changes the value of a variable within the local scope of the currently paused function, the variable is changed. You cannot declare a variable or a function in the Immediate window. One shortcut to keep in mind is that you can use the question mark in place of the print keyword. Many programmers find it useful to be able to use the Immediate window to determine the meaning of error code. This can be done by entering the error keyword, followed by the error code to be resolved (for example, **error 58**).

Using the Locals Window to Check or Change Values

The Locals window, shown in Figure 10-9, allows you quick access to all the local variables and their values. This is not to be confused with

FIGURE 10-8

The Immediate window

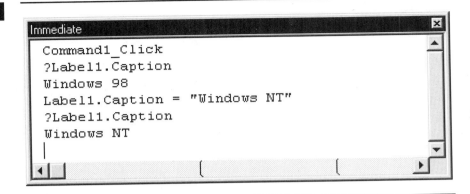

```
Command1_Click
?Label1.Caption
Windows 98
Label1.Caption = "Windows NT"
?Label1.Caption
Windows NT
```

displaying all the variables within the current scope. The Locals window includes only variables declared within the procedure currently executing, not global or member variables. The Locals window is only updated in Break mode.

Because programs can instantiate several instances of a class at the same time, the Locals window always provides a reference to Me when inside a class module. Me is a special structure that contains the vital information pertaining to the specific instance of code that is executing. You may change the values of the variables in the Locals window by clicking on the value to be changed in the Values column and entering the new value. This includes the members of structures and classes like Me.

Using the Call Stack Window

The Call Stack window, shown in Figure 10-10, displays the current functional call stack of an executing program when the program is in Break mode. A call stack is a list of every function and procedure that has not yet finished because it has been interrupted by a function call leading to the function that is currently executing. The topmost call in the call stack window is the function or procedure that is actively executing. This window provides static information that cannot be changed. When you double-click on a function displayed in the Call Stack window or highlight a function and press the Show button, VB will take you to its *call stack pointer* in a code window. The call stack pointer is a green arrow in the margin indicator bar that defines where a particular function call was made.

FIGURE 10-9

The Locals window

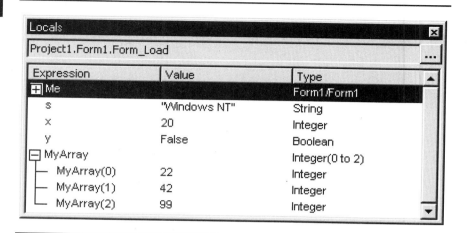

a t c h

It is very important to know the differences between the Local, Immediate, Watch, and Call Stack windows. Also, keep in mind that the exam asks for the best answer, not necessarily the right answer. Therefore, if a question requests that you pick the Debug window that enables you to enter Break mode, the answer will be the Watch window (although technically, watches trigger breaks and not the Watch window itself).

CERTIFICATION OBJECTIVE 10.06

Implementing Project Groups to Support the Development and Debugging Process

Sometimes, programmers will find it advantageous to be able to work with many projects in the same Visual Basic session. For instance, when testing and debugging user-built VB libraries, ActiveX controls and components. *Project groups* are collections of projects saved in a .VBG file. To create a project group, select Add Project from the File menu or select the Add <project type> File from the Standard tool bar. When you've set up a project group, you have to let Visual Basic know which project to execute

The Call Stack window

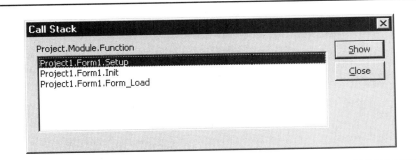

when you hit the Start button. You can set any project to be the start-up module by right-clicking on the project name in the Project Explorer window and selecting Set As Start Up on the pop-up menu. The current startup project name is always displayed in a bold face font.

Debugging DLLs in Process

DLLs (dynamically linked libraries) are libraries of executable code that do not run as stand-alone programs, but instead rely on other programs to call them and run their routines. This is referred to as in-process because the DLL runs in the same process space as the application that uses the DLL. This leads us to pose the question, how can we debug a program that we can't directly run?

When we include a DLL project in the same project group as the application that uses it, we can make use of all the Visual Basic debugging tools as if the DLL and the executable are one and the same. Thus, to thoroughly test a DLL, we can include a standard EXE testing shell in a project group containing the DLL it uses.

Testing and Debugging a Control in Process

ActiveX controls (discussed in Chapters 2 and 3) allow programmers to add custom controls to the existing set provided by Microsoft. Like DLLs, ActiveX controls cannot be run by themselves and thus require other applications, called containers, to act as their hosts. The Microsoft Internet Explorer is one such container that can be used to test ActiveX controls. Another way to test ActiveX controls is to create a project group and include both the ActiveX control and a standard EXE in one neat package. As we saw with DLLs, when we include these projects together in a project group, we can run and debug them just as if they were part of the same program.

Debugging an ActiveX Control Using a Project Group

1. Load Visual Basic and create an ActiveX control project.

2. Add two buttons named cmdTrue and cmdFalse to Form1 and change the captions accordingly.

3. Double-click on your true button and enter the following code in the cmdTrue_Click() subroutine:

   ```
   MsgBox "True has been selected"
   ```

4. Double-click on your false button and enter the following code in the cmdFalse_Click() subroutine:

   ```
   MsgBox "False has been selected"
   ```

5. Close the UserControl 1 code and object windows.

6. Add a standard EXE to the project group by selecting the Add Standard EXE on the submenu of the Add <project type> File on the Standard tool bar. Notice that the title of the Project Explorer window now reads "Project Group" and there are two projects in the window.

7. Add your new control to Form1 of the standard EXE by opening the Form1 window of Project 2 and double-clicking on the control icon in the Toolbox window.

e x a m
Ⓦa t c h

If the control is grayed-out, you have not closed all the windows in the control project. These windows must be closed because the code implementing the control actually runs when you place the control on a form.

8. Set a breakpoint on the line containing the MsgBox in the cmdFalse_Click() subroutine in UserControl 1.

9. Hit the Start button on the Debug tool bar and press OK on the window that asks if you want to start component: UserControl 1.

10. Microsoft Internet Explorer will pop up and proudly display your True/False control. Try out the buttons and observe as VB jumps into Break mode after you click on False. Hit the End button on the Debug tool bar to kill the program.

11. The reason IE ran when you executed your program is that UserControl I was set as your start-up module and ActiveX controls use IE as their default container. Right-click on Project2 in the Project Explorer window and select Set as Start Up. Notice that it turns bold.

12. Hit the Start button on the Debug tool bar again. This time Project2 boots up, proudly sporting your magnificent True/False control. Press the True and False buttons again and VB will enter Break mode again upon encountering the breakpoint.

CERTIFICATION OBJECTIVE 10.07

Using the Debug Object

Visual Basic provides a special object that you can use in your source code just for debugging. The Debug object will only affect a program executing within the Visual Basic development environment. The Debug object has only two methods: Print and Assert. The Print method enables programmers to send output to the Immediate window. The Assert method allows programmers to enter Break mode when the condition provide is evaluated as false. Keep in mind that the Boolean logic used in the Visual Basic assert statement is the opposite of its C++ counterpart.

The following Q & A section pertains to this small fragment of code. This code is supposed to call the DoSomething function 100 times:

```
Dim x As Integer
Dim b As Boolean
while x <> 100 Or b = False
    DoSomething
Wend
Debug.Print x
```

QUESTIONS AND ANSWERS

"When I run my program it gets stuck. What should I do?"	Hit CTRL-BREAK to send the program into Break mode.
"My program appears to have been stuck in the while loop. Why?"	Open the Locals window and check the values of x and b.
"x is 0 and b is False."	There's no code to increment the counter. Add x = x + 1 directly below "DoSomething." Then hit Continue on the Debug tool bar.
"Now my program dies with "Run-time error 6: Overflow." What now?	Click the Debug button in the Error dialog box and open the Locals window. Now, check the values of x and b again.
"b is still False, but x equals **32767** and it should never exceed 100. What happened?	Test the while condition. Click on the value of x in the Locals window and set it to 100. Drag the current statement indicator back to the line containing the while statement and hit the Step Over button on the Debug tool bar.
"The while condition isn't stopping when x = 100. Why not?"	Evidently, the while condition is phrased incorrectly. The key is that b still equals False and you are checking the two conditions with an "Or" statement. Change Or to And and it will work.

CERTIFICATION SUMMARY

Visual Basic allows for the compilation of both native code and p-code. When compiling native code, there are many compiler options offered by Visual Basic to enable programmers to optimize their programs.

Visual Basic provides a set of conditional compilation directives that allow programmers to include or exclude fragments of code from the executable. This can be used to create a project that is compilable into code that will run on multiple operation systems, or for different languages, or that contains embedded debugging information.

Visual Basic offers programmers many ways to suspend the execution of a program so that it may be debugged. This suspended state is called Break mode. While in Break mode, programmers can step through the program one line at a time, monitor and change the values of variables, execute code that does not follow the normal execution order, check the call stack, modify the code, reposition the Current Statement Indicator, revise the watch set, or continue execution from the Current Statement Indicator position. There are four debugging windows that provide programmers with information while in Break mode: the Watch window, the Immediate window, the Locals window, and the Call Stack window.

Visual Basic provides the capability to assemble project groups. These groups enable programmers to work with multiple projects using only a single instance of the Visual Basic development environment. All the projects in a project group will act as a single entity when running and debugging your program from within the Visual Basic development environment.

Last but not least, Visual Basic includes a Debug object that enables programmers to log status messages to the Immediate window by using its Print method or conditionally entering Break mode using its Assert method.

 # TWO-MINUTE DRILL

❑ *P-code* compiles into a portable application.

❑ *Native code* compiles into machine code that will be fast for loops and intense math.

❑ *Optimization techniques* can only be employed on native code.

❑ *Advanced optimizations* disable safe modes or eliminate certain error-checking.

❑ *Conditional compilation directives* enable you to conditionally exclude fragments of code bases on user-defined compiler constants.

❑ *Conditional compilation constants* can be defined using the #Const directive, the /d (or /D) argument when compiling from the command line, or the Conditional Compilation Arguments field on the Make tab of the Project Properties dialog box.

❑ *Break mode* pauses the execution of a program so that you may test or change the current state of the program.

❑ You can enter Break mode by setting a breakpoint, hitting CTRL-BREAK or the VB Pause button, using a watch expression, using Debug.Assert, embedding the *Stop* keyword, running to cursor, and/or encountering an error when *Breaking On Errors* is set.

❑ *Breakpoints* are user-defined markers that instruct VB to enter Break mode whenever that line of code is to be executed.

❑ The *current statement indicator* is a yellow arrow that marks the next line of code to be executed when in Break mode.

❑ The *current statement indicator* can be moved to another executable line within the same function.

❑ *Step Into* enables you to move into the function that will be called on the current line of execution while in Break mode.

❑ *Step Over* enables you to execute the current line of code and move to the next executable line within the current function.

❑ *Step Out* enables you to complete the currently executing function and re-enter Break mode at the point where the function you stepped out of was called.

❑ *Run to Cursor* executes your program until it is about to execute the line of code where your cursor is positioned. VB then enters Break mode.

❑ The *Stop* keyword is a way to hard code a breakpoint into source code. It is equated to End when compiled into an executable.

❑ *Watch Expressions* monitor user-defined expressions in the Watch windowWatch window. They are set in the Add Watch dialog box.

❑ *Break When Value Is True* is a watch that enters Break mode when the expression you are monitoring becomes true.

❑ *Break When Value Changes* is a watch that enters Break mode when the value of the expression you are monitoring changes in any way.

❑ The scope of a watch expression can be specified in the context section of the Add Watch dialog box.

❑ There are four debugging windows in Visual Basic: the Watch window, the Immediate window, the Locals window, and the Call Stack window.

❑ *The Watch window* enables you to monitor a user-defined set of expressions, and change values of variables or values in structures.

❑ *The Immediate window* enables you to print values, change variable values, and call functions.

❑ *The Locals window* displays all variables declared in the current function and the special Me structure when appropriate.

❑ *The Call Stack* window displays all functions started but not finished because of a function call leading to the currently active function.

❑ *Project groups* allow programmers to include multiple projects into a single Visual Basic workspace.

❑ In-process components, such as DLL and ActiveX controls, can be debugged by creating a project group containing the in-process component and a Standard EXE testing shell.

❑ The *Debug object* provides two methods that can only be used in the VB development environment: Print and Assert.

❑ *Debug.Print* sends output to the Immediate window.

❑ *Debug.Assert* breaks when its condition is NOT true.

SELF TEST

1. You need to compile an executable that will run on computers housing either an Intel 80x86 or a Motorola 68000 processor. Which compiler option should you select to ensure that your application will run?

   A. Select the Compile to Native Code option in the Compile tab of the Project Properties dialog box

   B. Select the Compile to P-Code option in the Compile tab of the Project Properties dialog box

   C. Select the Platform Portability option in the Link tab of the Project Properties dialog box

   D. Select Intel 80x86 and Motorola 68000 from the Portability list in the Link tab of the Project Properties dialog box

2. When a *Break When Value Changes* condition triggers the program to transition to Break mode, where will the program break?

   A. The line before the value is changed

   B. The line where the value is changed

   C. The line after the value is changed

   D. Assembly code does not correspond to VB code line by line

3. Which of the following allows programmers to dynamically change the value of a variable while an executing program is in Break mode? (Choose all that apply.)

   A. The Immediate window

   B. The Locals window

   C. The Watch window

   D. The Call Stack window

4. The Immediate window can be used for which of the following? (Choose all that apply.)

   A. Calling procedures

   B. Displaying values of local variables

   C. Moving the *current statement indicator*

   D. Setting variable values

5. Which functionally does the Watch window provide that the Immediate window does not?

   A. The capability to display the values of global variables

   B. The capability to change the value of a variable

   C. The capability to execute a procedure

   D. The capability to trigger breaks

6. The Debug object can be used to do which of the following? (Choose all that apply.)

   A. Determine the level of the executing function in the call tree

   B. Send output to the Immediate window

C. Dynamically set watch expressions

D. Suspend execution of the program where it resides

7. Which of the following will appear in the Locals window? (Choose all that apply.)

A. All variables within the current scope of the function that is executing

B. All variables within the current class of the executing function

C. Me

D. Variables declared in the current functions

8. Which of the following CANNOT be performed in Break mode?

A. Moving the *current statement indicator* to a different function

B. Executing procedures in an order other than that of the normal execution flow

C. Changing a variable's values

D. Toggling breakpoints

9. On the following fragment of code, which error will eventually occur?

```
Dim x As Integer
While 1
  x = x + 1
Wend
```

A. Stack overflow

B. Segmentation fault

C. Subscript out of range

D. Overflow

10. The #If conditional compilation directive can be used for which of the following?

A. Including specific fragments of code in an executable and excluding others

B. Triggering breaks

C. Printing information into the Immediate window

D. Checking for stack violations

11. While in Break mode, which of the following CANNOT be performed?

A. Adding another watch expression

B. Undoing the last line of code that was executed

C. Moving the *current statement indicator*

D. Editing the source code

12. What are some of the effects of defining the context in which a watch expression is to be evaluated? (Choose all that apply.)

A. Increased speed at which your program executes

B. Eliminating breaks that occur in functions that you're not interested in working with

C. Decreased speed at which your program executes

D. Alleviating ambiguity if more than one variable in your code has the same name

13. When the Debug object generates output using the print method, where is the output sent?

A. stderr

B. The console window

C. The Immediate window

D. The Watch window

14. What advantages does p-code hold over native code? (Choose all that apply.)

    A. P-code is usually smaller than native code

    B. P-code can run on different platforms, provided that a VB interpreter is present

    C. P-code provides better performance than native code

    D. P-code is easier to read than native code

15. What effect will *step into* have if it is used when the program is in Break mode at the following line of code? (Choose all that apply.)

    `x = MyFunction`

    A. The program will resume execution until another breakpoint is encountered

    B. The Call Stack window will have another function on top and the Locals window will have a new set of variables

    C. A dialog box will prompt you for a return value for MyFunction and assign it to x

    D. Execution will resume and pause again on the first executable line in MyFunction

16. What attributes are NOT possessed by the *Break When Value Is True* expression?

    A. It allows you to break when the value of a variable becomes false

    B. It only breaks when expressions are true within the current scope of the context specified in the watch expression

    C. You must remove the expressions before you distribute the program

    D. It allows you to break when the value of a variable becomes true

17. When CONST_VAL = 1 is specified on the Make tab of the Project Properties window, CONST_VAL = 2 is specified on the command line used to compile the application, and #Const CONST_VAL = 3 appears in the source code of your program before any #If statements, what will the value of CONST_VAL be when it is evaluated by an #If statement?

    A. 1

    B. 2

    C. 3

    D. 6

18. What is the relationship between the Watch window and the Locals window?

    A. The Watch window is capable of displaying anything that the Locals window can display

    B. The Locals window is capable of displaying anything that the Watch window can display

C. Only the Watch window can change the value of a variable

D. Only the Locals window can change the value of a variable

19. Which Visual Basic debugging tool can be used to trigger a break?

   A. The Immediate window

   B. The Watch window

   C. The Locals window

   D. The Call Stack window

20. Before you enable the *Assume no Aliasing* compiler option, which of the following should you verify?

   A. No variable will over extend its allotted memory space

   B. Your program does not spawn multiple threads

   C. Your computer does not provide common registers

   D. No more than one variable name references a single value in memory

21. You are sure your program performs no floating-point comparisons. Which of the following can you enable?

   A. Remove Safe Pentium FDIV Checks

   B. Allow Unrounded Floating Point Operations

   C. Remove Floating Point Error Checks

   D. A and C

22. What will happen when you *step over* the following line of code when your program is in Break mode?

```
x = MyFunction
```

   A. The line will be skipped and no assignment will be made to x

   B. The line will be skipped and a marker in the Locals window will indicate that x possibly has an incorrect value

   C. The line will be executed normally and pause at the first executable line directly below it

   D. The line will execute but no assign will be made to x

23. When you enable the *Remove Referential Integrity Checking* compiler option, you must first ensure which of the following?

   A. All variable names correspond to an existing and accessible location in memory

   B. No variable values will exceed their allotted space in memory

   C. If you are using DAO, RDO, or ADO to access a database, no foreign keys can exist

   D. This option does not exist

24. When declaring multiple constants in the Make tab of the Project Properties dialog box, what character is used as a delimiter?

   A. A space

   B. A colon

   C. A semicolon

D. A comma

25. Which of the following describes the Call Stack window?

A. It displays the call stack with the currently executing function at the top of the list

B. It displays the call stack with the currently executing function at the bottom of the list

C. It displays all functions started but not finished, with the exception of the currently executing function

D. It enables you to move the call stack pointer

26. Which of the following would be a good reason to create a project group?

A. Debugging multithreaded programs

B. Debugging ActiveX controls

C. Debugging Standard EXEs

D. Debugging code written in Visual C++ or Visual J++

27. Which of the following DLL Base address is valid?

A. &H100000 (in hexadecimal)

B. &H1004000 (in hexadecimal)

C. &H10040000 (in hexadecimal)

D. &H0128000 (in hexadecimal)

28. Not selecting the *Remove Safe Pentium FDIV Checks* compiler option does which of the following?

A. Prevents you from formatting a disk drive at the application level

B. Catches and corrects floating-point errors caused by a flaw in the Pentium chip

C. Allows your program to share the processor with other processes ,as long as they are on the Pentium Platform

D. Allows applications to check the processor it is running on to see whether it is a member of the Pentium family

29. While in Break mode, what is the most efficient way to return to the line that called the currently executing function?

A. Step Over

B. Step Up

C. Step Out

D. Set a watch expression on the return value of the calling function

30. Which of the following attributes describes the *current statement indicator*?

A. It cannot be moved

B. It can be moved to another executable line of code within the currently executing function

C. It can be moved to another executable line of code within the currently executing class module

D. It can be moved to another executable line of code within the currently executing program

31. Which of the following are correct statements about the #Const directive?

A. A #Const statement must be provided both a name and a value

B. You must declare a #Const statement in the Make Tab of the Project Properties dialog box

C. If an #If directive attempts to evaluate a constant that is assigned a value by a #Const directive positioned below it, a compilation error will occur

D. You must declare a #Const statement in the file that it is to be used

32. Which of the following will creating a project group enable you to do.

A. Bind two projects together

B. Work with different projects from the same development environment instance

C. Organize folders to make use of common libraries

D. Include multiple files in a single instance of the development environment

33. Which of the following would not increase the speed of numeric computations?

A. Selecting the *Assume No Aliasing* compiler option

B. Selecting the *Remove Integer Overflow Checks* compiler option

C. Selecting the *Allow Unrounded Floating Point Operations* compiler option.

D. Selecting the *Remove Array Bounds Checks* compiler option

34. Which of the following optimizations can we take advantage of when compiling a program into p-code?

A. Optimized for Fast Code.

B. Optimized for Small Code.

C. Either A or B.

D. P-code can not be optimized.

35. Which scenarios will produce the OpSys variable to equate to "Window 98" given the following code? (Choose all that apply.)

```
#If WinCE
  OpSys = "Windows CE"
#Else
  OpSys = "Windows 98"
#End If
```

A. If WinCE is not defined

B. If WinCE is equal to False

C. If WinCE is set to 1 in the Make tab in the Project Properties dialog box and set to 0 as an argument when compiling from the command line

D. If WinCE is set to −1

36. The *current statement indicator* marks the currently executing line of code. What are some of its characteristics? (Choose all that apply.)

A. It can be moved in a drag-and-drop fashion

B. It cannot be moved

C. It is represented by a yellow arrow

D. It is only visible when the call stack window is visible

37. What effect will selecting the *Remove Safe Pentium FDIV Checks* compiler option have?

    A. It will have no effect on machines that do not require it

    B. It will increase performance slightly on all machines

    C. It will cause a program to crash if it is run on a DEC Alpha machine

    D. It will cause major problems for programs running on Pentium platforms with this flaw

38. Which of the following CANNOT be used to trigger Break mode?

    A. Debug.Assert 0

    B. Ctrl-Break

    C. Using the Break keyword

    D. Creating a breakpoint by clicking in the margin indication bar

39. Which of the following can be used when testing an ActiveX control?

    A. Microsoft Internet Explorer 4.01

    B. A project group containing both the ActiveX control project and the standard EXE project

    C. A and B

    D. The only way to test an ActiveX control is by using the Active Test program

40. Which of the following is NOT an attribute of the #Const compiler directive in Visual Basic?

    A. A constant's value may be used as part of the conditional expression of a Visual Basic while loop

    B. Constant declarations must provide both a name and a value

    C. Constants will be evaluated as zero if they are referenced before they are declared

    D. Once a constant's value is defined it can not be changed or redefined

11

Deploying an Application

S o you've developed an application, and now want to get it to the user. This is one of the important phases of application development. It requires that you package your application into a setup program and deploy it to some sort of distribution media, such as floppy disks. This allows the users to buy or obtain your application and set it up on their computers.

There are a number of ways to deploy an application, which we'll cover in this chapter. Floppy disks have traditionally been the common method of deployment, but technologies over the last decade have brought CD-ROMs and network deployment to the forefront. In this section, we'll cover these and other deployment methods, as well as issues that deal with COM and DCOM.

CERTIFICATION OBJECTIVE 11.01

Using the Package and Deployment Wizard to Create a Setup Program

The Package and Deployment Wizard is an old tool with lots of new bells and whistles. Veterans of Visual Basic will remember the Setup Wizard that shipped with previous releases of VB. Visual Basic 6.0 is the first version of VB to include the Package and Deployment Wizard, which not only allows you to create a Setup program, but also to deploy your application to different media.

The Package and Deployment Wizard is a separate program that ships with Visual Basic 6.0. It resides in the Visual Basic folder, which is accessed by clicking the Windows Start menu, going into Programs, and choosing your Visual Basic or Visual Studio folder. Once you start it, the main screen of the Wizard, shown in Figure 11-1, will appear on your screen.

The Package and Deployment Wizard is made up of three portions that are accessed from the main screen. Two of these sections access wizards that step you through packaging and deploying your program, while the third is

FIGURE 11-1

Main screen of the Package
and Deployment Wizard

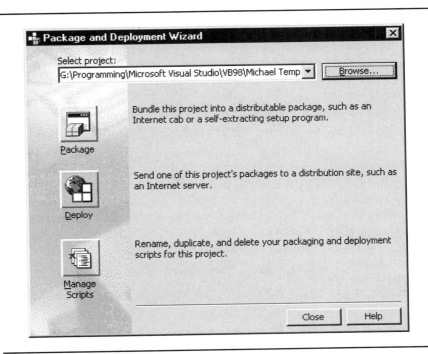

used for managing scripts created with the previous two portions. Clicking
the Package button starts a wizard that helps you package your application
into CAB files or a self-extracting executable. Clicking the Deploy button
also starts a wizard, but this one is used for copying your package to a
distribution site or media. Finally, clicking Manage Scripts opens a dialog
box that allows you to rename, delete, and duplicate a package and
deployment scripts created during package or deploy sessions.

Before using the Wizard to package an application, you should first
compile it. Compiling an application is extremely easy. To do so, start
Visual Basic, and open the project you wish to compile. Once this is done,
click on the File menu, where you will see a command that says, "Make,"
followed by your project name with an .EXE or .DLL extension. For
example, if your project is called Project1 and is a Standard EXE project,
this menu item would say "Make Project1.EXE." Selecting this option
makes Visual Basic compile your project into an executable file.

If you want to compile a project that's part of a project, you must first select which project in the group you want to compile. This is done through the Project window. Select the project you want to compile by clicking on it, and then select the Make command from the File menu. If you want to compile the entire project group, you don't need to select anything from the Project window. Simply select Make Project Group from the File menu. When a dialog box appears, click the Build button, and the group will be compiled.

If you use the Package and Deployment Wizard on a project that isn't compiled yet, the Wizard will inform you of this. Clicking the Package button will result in a message stating that the application isn't compiled, and give you the option of compiling it from here. This saves you from having to re-enter Visual Basic and compiling the project before using the Wizard. Clicking the Compile button on this message box causes the project to be compiled. When this is done, it will then move on to the Package portion of the Wizard.

Creating a Setup Program for Distributed Application Installation

Creating a setup program is done through the Package portion of the Wizard. Before clicking the Package button however, you must first tell the Wizard what it is you want bundled into a setup package. On the Package and Deployment Wizard's main screen, the Select Project list box contains a listing of projects that were previously used in the Wizard. If you're rebundling a project into a setup package, you can select it from this list. If you wish to bundle a new project, click the Browse button and select a saved project from the hard disk.

After choosing the project you want to use, click the Package button. The Package portion of the Wizard starts by analyzing your project for such things as runtime dependencies, determines which files are required for the application to run, loads project types, and so forth. After it finishes analyzing the project, the Package Wizard displays a screen asking you which script you want to use, which allows you to load a script of settings saved from a previous session in the Wizard. If you've never used the

FROM THE CLASSROOM

Instill Some Skill in Your Install...

Creating an installation program is equal to designing the initial impression your clients or customers will have of your application. When they install your new application, the look and feel of your installation program will provide the first impression they form. Knowing this, you should be aware of all the options you have for jazzing up that installation.

Visual Basic 6.0 continues to provide a setup toolkit that the developer can use to provide a customized installation. This allows the flexibility to alter the images, messages, and design of the setup program. The Visual Basic project file SETUP1.VBP, can be found in the \Wizards\PDWizard\Setup1 directory. This project includes pre-built forms for a welcome, copy, path, and assorted other screens for use in a basic setup program.

For the developer looking for an extremely polished installation application, the use of leading third-party products should be

considered. Although not provided with Visual Basic 6.0, InstallShield ships with another Visual Studio 6 component: Visual C++. InstallShield is an industry-recognized leader in the area of application installation/deinstallation development tools.

Regarding proper inclusion of all required files, any component references left in your application that involve ActiveX controls, type libraries, or assorted files that are actually unused in your application will still result in those files being listed in the included files list. Look at the list carefully and remove any files that are not actually needed. Also, if certain files are known to already be included on the client, those files can also be removed from the list of included files.

— By Michael Lane Thomas,
MCSE+I, MCSD, MCT, A+

Wizard before, only "Standard Setup Package 1" will appear in the list box. Accept this setting and click Next to continue.

The Packaging Type screen gives you different options for proceeding. These options determine the type of package the Wizard will create. The first option you have is to create a Standard Setup Package, which is used to create a package that is installed by a SETUP.EXE file. If your application is an Internet application, such as an IIS application, an option for Internet Package appears. This allows you to create a CAB-based installation that can be downloaded from a Web site or posted to a Web server, and only appears for Web applications. Another option is to create file-listing information about the runtime components required by your application to run. To create a setup program for your application, select Standard Setup Package and click Next.

The Package Folder screen allows you to set where the package will be bundled. You can specify whether you'd like the package assembled in an existing local folder or network folder, or to create a new folder for bundling (by using the New Folder button). Accepting the default location creates a new folder called "Package" in the directory that contains your project. If you accept this default location and click Next, a message box appears asking whether the Wizard should create the new folder. Clicking OK creates the Package folder and moves you to the next screen.

The DAO Drivers screen appears if your application uses Data Access Objects, and allows you to include drivers on your system to be packaged with the application. If your application accesses Access or ODBC databases, Excel or Lotus spreadsheets, and so forth, you may want to add certain drivers so your application functions properly. Drivers on your system are displayed in the left panel, while the right panel displays drivers to be included with the package. Arrow buttons between these two panes allow you to add and remove drivers from the package.

The Included Files screen, shown in Figure 11-2, lists files that the Wizard will include with your package. When you started the Package portion, this information was gathered when it analyzed your project. Generally, the files shown in the listing are correct and every file needed for your application to run is included. You should always review the listing for missing files, however. For example, let's say your application used an Access database to retrieve and store information, and it wasn't included in the listing. In such a case, you would have to click the Add button, which brings up a dialog box that allows you to search your hard disk for a file to include with the package. If you decide you don't need a certain file to be included with the package, uncheck the check box beside the file's name.

FIGURE 11-2

Include Files screen of the
Package and Deployment
Wizard

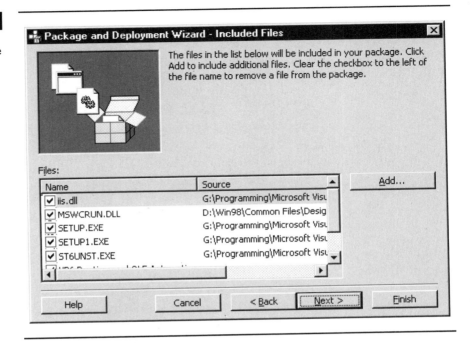

 on the job

Always review files that the Wizard has concluded are necessary for your package. If your application uses third-party controls (for example, ActiveX controls), the end user will experience real problems if the OCX file for the control isn't included with the package. Also, review the licensing for any third-party controls you want to include with a package. If you aren't permitted to include the control for distribution, you'll have to remove it from your program before packaging and deploying it.

The CAB Options screen follows this one, and it is used to determine if the package will have one huge CAB file, or multiple CAB files. A CAB file is a setup file that contains INF files, OCX files, and other files your application depends on to run. Generally, if you plan to deploy your application to CD-ROM, to a network or local folder, or over the Internet, you should have your files packaged to a single CAB. If you plan to deploy your package to floppy disk, you should choose multiple CABs.

When you select multiple CABs for a floppy-disk distribution, the CAB size list box becomes enabled, allowing you to specify whether the multiple CAB files created for packaging will be 1.44 MB, 2.88 MB, 1.2 MB, or 720 KB in size. What you choose as your CAB size will depend on the size of the floppy disks you're using. Because you can only choose one size for the CAB files, all of your floppy disks will have to be the same size (you can't mix and match different-sized floppies).

Once you've determined which CAB options to use, clicking Next will bring you to the Installation Title screen. This is where you'll set the title that will be displayed when your application is installed by the end user. The default name in the Installation Title TextBox of this screen is the project's name. If you'd like to have something else displayed during the installation, type it into this field. You are limited to 256 characters for the Installation Title, which also allows spaces between words. However, remember that brevity will often be appreciated by the end user, so try to keep your title short and sweet.

Figure 11-3 shows the Start Menu Items screen, which allows you to specify how your application will appear in the Start menu and what will appear in it. The screen has a Windows Explorer-style interface, showing a tree representing the folders and files of a Start menu. By using the command buttons on this screen, you can manipulate folders and items that will appear in the end user's menu.

When you first view this screen, your executable's name will appear as a menu item inside of a menu with the same name. You may want to modify the entries of the Start menu because many executable names don't fully reflect what the application is. For example, although Vb6.exe may be a nice name for an executable, it makes for a lousy menu item name. It is much easier to see an entry called "Microsoft Visual Basic 6.0."

By selecting a menu item and clicking the Properties button, a dialog box appears that allows you to change the name and properties of a menu group or item. The Name field of this dialog box displays the current name of the item or group. As shown in Figure 11-3, Start menu items can have names with spaces and special characters. If you are editing the properties of a menu group, you can set it to be either a Private or Common group. If you are editing a menu item, this dialog box will also allow you to change the

Start Menu Items screen
of Package and
Deployment Wizard

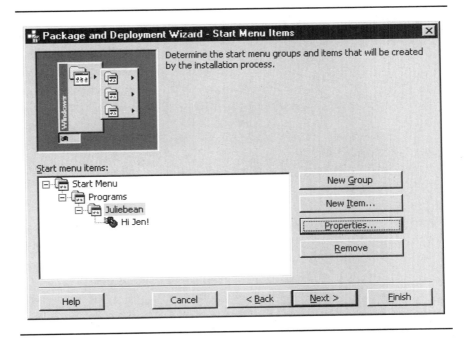

Target (the application that the item represents) and the location where the application will start (such as the system path, application path, and so on).

Other commands on the Start Menu Items screen include New Item, New Group, and Remove. If you want to add additional groups to the start menu, you can click the New Group button. New Item similarly allows you to add new items to the Start menu. Clicking this will open a dialog box identical to the one that appears when you click Properties for a menu item. The Remove button is used to remove groups and items as Start menu items.

Clicking Next will bring you to the Install Locations screen. From here, you can modify where certain files, such as your applications executable, will be installed. There are three columns of information on this screen: Name, Source, and Install Location. Entries in the Name column show the filenames of files included in your package, while the Source column shows the path to where they are located. The third column is Install Location, which allows you to determine where the files will be installed. Clicking an entry in this column displays a listbox box containing eight choices for locating the file. Choices here include the system path, application path, font folder, common files folder, and so on.

Clicking the Next button brings you to the Shared Files screen. Here, you will see a listing of files that can be shared by other applications. If nothing else, the name of your application's executable file is listed here. If you want the listed files to be shared by other applications, you must check the check box beside the file's name. Any files designated as shared will remain on the user's hard disk if they uninstall your application. The files will only be removed if every application using the file is removed from their system.

exam
Watch

Shared files are files that are used by other applications. Any files that are shared won't uninstall from the end user's computer if other programs still use the file. These files will only be removed during an uninstall operation if every application using the file is removed from the system.

When you click Next from here, you reach the final screen. The Finished! screen allows you to save the session settings by specifying the name of a script. This allows you to reuse settings from this session for other applications that you plan to package. After naming this script, you can later rename, delete, or duplicate it by clicking Manage Scripts on the Package and Deployment Wizard's main screen. Clicking the Finish button from this screen starts the bundling of your package, based on the settings chosen during this session.

Registering the COM Components in a Distributed Application

When an application containing COM components is deployed, all of the components used in the application must be included. This means that any ActiveX controls (OCX files), and ActiveX DLLs must be part of the package. Such files are listed on the Included Files screen of the Package portion of Package and Deployment Wizard. You should always confirm that such files are included, or an error will result when the program is installed and used.

When a user installs your application and a COM component can't be found, Visual Basic Run time Library produces a "File not found" message. All OCX files should be installed into the Windows/System directory. If an OCX doesn't have this path, it should be changed in the Install Location column of the Install Locations screen during Packaging.

There are some components, such as those included in Visual Basic 6.0, that you won't need to worry about registering with the Windows Registry. This is because such COM components register themselves automatically. However, if you want to use an ActiveX component you've created, dependency files can be used so the component can be added to the SETUP.1ST and then registered upon installation.

Dependency files have the extension .DEP, and contain information about an application or component's runtime requirements such as the files needed by your component or application, where the files should be installed, and how they should be registered with Windows Registry.

When you click the Package button on the main screen of Package and Deployment Wizard, it scans for dependency information. The Wizard reads the information, builds a list of required files, and then builds a listing of installation information. Dependency files are read and their information is added to the SETUP.1ST, which resides outside of a Standard Setup Package's SETUP.EXE file. If you're creating an Internet Package, the dependency file's information is written to an .INF file that's stored in the CAB.

You can create a .DEP file with the Package portion of the Package and Deployment Wizard. Here, you can choose to create a Standard Setup Package or a Dependency File. After selecting Dependency File and clicking Next, you will see a Package Folder screen, where you specify a location the Wizard can use for assembling its package. This acts as a work directory.

The next screen is the Included Files screen, where you can specify which files to include with a package. The list presented on this screen includes all the dependent files that the Wizard has determined necessary for your application to function. After reviewing the files to include, click Next.

The Include Files screen is only important if you are bundling the dependency file into a CAB file for dependency on the Internet. If so, you will need to enter the name for the CAB file, an URL it can be retrieved from, and the default file to execute when the file is downloaded. The file to execute can either be an executable or an .INF file. If you aren't packaging a dependency file for the Internet, accept the default information and choose Next.

The next screen is the Install Locations screen, used to specify where files are to be installed. As mentioned earlier, the location to install files can be modified through the Install Location column. To modify the install location, click an entry in this column and select where you want the file to be installed.

The final screen allows you to name the script for dependency settings from this session. If you wish to modify the script, click the Modify Script button on the main screen of the Package and Deployment Wizard.

In addition to using .DEP files, you can programmatically manipulate the Windows Registry. This is done with the GetSetting and SaveSetting functions, which are built-in procedures that access entries under the HKEY_CURRENT_USER\Software\VB and VBA Program Settings. By using the GetSetting function, you can read information from the Windows Registry. The SaveSetting function is used to write information to and from the Registry.

The GetSetting function has the following arguments: appname, section, and key. The first of these arguments, appname, is the application's name. The section argument specifies the name of the section in which a key setting is found, while the key argument is the name of the key to return.

The SaveSetting function has the same three arguments as GetSetting, but includes a fourth: value. The value argument specifies the contents to be stored in the Windows Registry. The following example shows how to save settings to the Registry:

```
SaveSetting app.exename, strUser, strID, txtUser.Text
```

In this example, the SaveSetting function takes the name of the currently running program and the values of the other variables, and saves them to the Registry. To retrieve this same information from the Registry, the GetSetting would be used as follows:

```
txtRegInfo.Text=GetSetting (app.exename, strUser, strID)
```

Unlike most of the other material in this chapter, the GetSetting and SaveSetting functions are used in code, not through the Package and Deployment Wizard. By using GetSetting and SaveSetting, you are able to access and manipulate data contained in the Registry.

Allowing for Uninstall

Like it or not, there will be times when a user will want or have to uninstall your application from their computer. To do this, they can use the Add/Remove Programs applet in Control Panel. In addition to this, the Package and Deployment Wizard adds a program to your package that works with the Add/Remove Programs so a user can uninstall your application. During the Package portion of the Wizard, a file called ST6UNST.EXE is added. This is the application-removal utility, and will install in the \Windows or \Winnt directory.

When the user installs your application, a file called St6unst.log is created in the application directory. It contains information about which directories were created during installation; Registry entries that were created and modified; and self-registered .DLL, .EXE, or .OCX files. In addition, this file contains information on the links and Start menu items that were created.

The log file also has information on the files that were installed and their locations. The listing of files is comprehensive: It lists all files in the setup program, including ones that weren't installed because newer or identical files existed. It also specifies whether files are shared files and (if shared) whether setup replaced the existing file.

ST6UNST.EXE reads the log file and determines which should be removed. When executed, it will remove all files, directories, and other items logged in the ST6UNST.LOG. It allows the user to fully remove your application from their system.

Registering a Component that Implements DCOM

Like COM components, components that implement DCOM must also be registered on a system. The SETUP.1ST file created during the Package portion of Package and Deployment Wizard can determine how such files are registered. The Registry key in SETUP.1ST can be edited to indicate that a file doesn't need to be registered, is self-registering, or contains information for the Registry.

Table 11-1 outlines the various entries that can appear in the Registry key of the SETUP.1ST file.

If your project references registration files (which have the extension .REG), the Package and Deployment Wizard will show an additional screen, which allows you to determine how the how Registry information will be handled. The choices available here are to copy the .REG files to the user's computer; or have the Registry files parsed (read), stored in the Registry, and automatically registered.

TABLE 11-1

Registry keys in SETUP.1ST

Registry Key	Description
(no key)	The file doesn't need to be registered.
$(DLLSelfRegister)	The file is a self-registering DLL, OCX, or other dynamic link library file.
$(EXESelfRegister)	The file is an ActiveX EXE component. It can also indicate that it is another kind of EXE file that supports /RegServer and /UnRegServer switches, and is self-registering.
$(TLBRegister)	The file is a type library, and is to be registered as such.
$(Remote)	The file is a remote support file (also referred to as remote server file). (Described in the next section.)
Filename.reg	The file contains Registry information that can be used to update the Windows Registry.

Remote Server Files

Remote server files (also called remote support files) have the file extension .VBR and contain information required by the Registry to run ActiveX servers on remote computers. They are used for registering information on components that implement DCOM or utilize remote code components (which were previously called OLE Servers). The .VBR file is used by the Setup program's SETUP.1ST file for registration.

To create a .VBR file, go to the Components tab of Project Properties, which is accessed from the Project menu. This will bring up the screen shown below. By clicking the Remote Server Files check box, a .VBR file will be created during compiling of the program. This file needs to reside in the same folder where your project file resides (.VBP extension) so that Package and Deployment Wizard can use it later. It is important to remember that this option is only available in the Enterprise edition of Visual Basic.

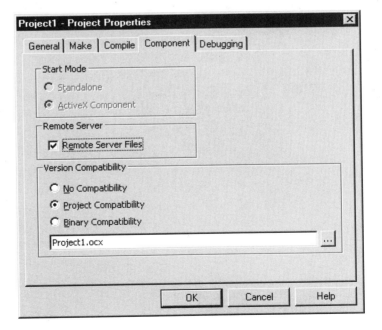

After setting this option on the server component's package, you also have to create two packages with the Package and Deployment Wizard. One package will be the client's setup program, the second will be the server's setup program.

Configuring DCOM on a Client Computer and on a Server Computer

Before an application implementing DCOM can be used on a client or server computer, you have to set certain application properties. If you are running a server application, security settings need to be set; on a client application, the location of the server needs to be configured. If DCOM isn't configured on the client computer and the server computer, the application won't function.

While reading the following sections, remember that a client doesn't necessarily mean a workstation, and a server doesn't necessarily mean a network server. A client in this case means a computer running the client portion of a DCOM application; a server computer is a machine running a server application. Either of these can run on a Windows 95/98, Windows NT Workstation, or Windows NT Server machine.

To configure these, the DCOM Configuration Properties dialog box is used. Unlike other dialog boxes you're familiar with, this one isn't accessed from a menu or command button. You must click your Windows Start menu, click Run, and type **dcomcnfg**. Before using this program, however, you must determine whether your operating system is configured correctly to run the program.

To use DCOM Configuration Properties, you first need to set your computer to use User-level security, which allows you to specify users and groups who have access to resources on your computer. This is different from Share-level security, in which you set a password for each resource on a computer. To set a Windows 95/98 computer to User-level access, you need to open the Network applet in Control Panel, and click on the Access Control tab. Here, click the User-level access control option, and enter the location from which your computer should obtain a list of users. Click OK and the Authenticator Type dialog box will appear. From the list box, select whether a Windows NT Server or a Windows NT Domain authenticates accounts on the network. Check with your network administrator to confirm which one your network is part of. Click OK and files will be copied to your system. To complete this, you will be required to restart your system.

exam
ⓦatch
Remember that you must have User-level access control to run the DCOM Configuration Properties dialog box. If you have Share-level security on your computer, you won't be able to start it.

You need to have File Sharing enabled on your computer to switch to User-level security. If you receive a message stating you need to enable this, first switch back to Share-level security, and then go to the Configuration tab of the Network applet. On this tab, click the File and Print Sharing button, and a dialog box will appear. Check the I want to be able to give others access to my files check box, and then click OK. Go back to the Access Control tab and redo the steps in the previous paragraph.

When you run the DCOM Configuration Properties dialog box, the screen shown below will appear. The Applications tab displays a listing of applications that can be configured. The Default Properties tab is used to enable DCOM on the computer you're configuring and to set default communication properties. For DCOM to be enabled, the Enable Distributed COM on this computer check box must be checked on this tab. Finally, the Default Security tab is used to edit default access permissions. It is from this tab that you can configure who is allowed to access applications.

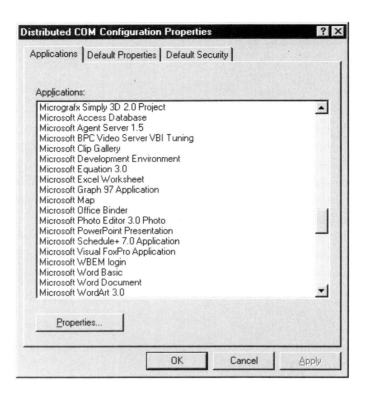

Configuring DCOM on a Client Computer

When applications that implement DCOM are run on a client computer, you must specify the server application that needs to be started. The client computer needs to know where the server application is located.

To do this, first select an application from the Applications tab of the DCOM Configuration Properties dialog box. Clicking the Properties button will bring up a property dialog box for that particular application. It is here that you will configure DCOM for your client computer.

The dialog box that appears has three tabs: General, Location, and Security. The General tab shows information on the application that consists of its name, local path, and the type of application. The Security tab allows you choose between default access permissions for the application or custom permissions that allow you to edit who can use the application. The Location tab is used to specify where you want the application to run.

You can choose to run it: on the computer you're configuring, where the data is located, or on another computer that you specify. In most configurations, specifying the location of the server application is all that's required to configure a client computer.

Configuring DCOM on a client computer

1. Open the Network applet in Control Panel. In the listing "The following network components are installed," check to see that "File and Print Sharing for Microsoft Networks" appears. If this does not appear in the listing, click the File and Print Sharing button. When the dialog box appears, click the I want to be able to give others access to my files check box. Click OK to close the dialog box.

2. Click on the Access Control tab of the Network applet. Ensure that the User-level access control is selected. If it isn't, select this option and enter the name of a server that has a listing of users and groups for your network or domain. Click OK and the Authenticator Type dialog box will appear. Select whether you are authenticated by a NT server or domain. Check with your network administrator for this information.

3. Exit the Network applet.

4. Click Run on the Start menu. Type **dcomcnfg** and click OK to open DCOM Configuration Properties.

5. Select an application listed on the Applications tab, and then click the Properties button.

6. Click the Location tab, and select where you want this application to run. Click OK to save your settings and exit.

Configuring DCOM on a Server Computer

When applications that implement DCOM are run on a server computer, security information for the client application needs to be set. This includes setting a user account that has permissions to start and access the application, and user accounts that are allowed to run it.

To set this information, first select an application from the Applications tab of the DCOM Configuration Properties dialog box. Clicking the Properties button will bring up a property dialog box for that particular application, (as discussed in the previous section). It is here that you will configure DCOM for your server computer.

The Security tab is where you can set permissions for that particular application. Clicking the Edit Default button will bring up the Access Permissions dialog box. Here, you can add and remove users. Clicking the Add button enables you to add user or group accounts. You can select the Grant Access or Deny Access option in Add Access Permissions to set user or group permissions.

CERTIFICATION OBJECTIVE 11.04

Planning and Implementing Floppy Disk- or Compact Disc-Based Deployment

Floppy disks and CD-ROMs are the most common ways to deploy an application. Floppy disks have long been the traditional method of getting an application to the end user. In recent years, CD-ROMs have become the most common method. This is largely due to the drop in writeable CD-ROMs (which allow you to write information to compact discs) and the popularity of CD-ROMs. Not only do they hold more information, they're more convenient. The end user isn't plagued by requests to change disks, which can be a big headache when you consider the size of modern applications.

Just as vinyl record albums have given way to CD-ROMs, the same is beginning to happen to floppies. Despite this, it is an oversight to not include floppy-disk deployments for your applications because there are still many computers out there that don't have CD-ROMs installed in them. And, of course, you want to deploy to CD-ROMs for workstations that don't have floppy disk drives. This is often seen in settings in which security is an issue; management doesn't want to risk users copying sensitive materials to floppies. As you can see, there are users who will benefit from your deploying to both forms of media.

Floppy Disk-Based Deployment of a Distributed Application

Deploying to floppy disk starts in the Package portion of the Package and Deployment Wizard. The reason you start in the Package portion is because deploying to floppy disk requires that you package your application to multiple CAB files. This is done through the Cab Options screen shown in Figure 11-4.

The Cab Options screen allows you to bundle your application to multiple CABs or a single CAB file. Selecting this option enables the Cab Size property, which has sizes that range from 720 KB to 2.88 MB. What you choose as your CAB size is determined by the size of your blank floppies. For example, if you were using double-density disks, you would

Cab Options screen of the Package and Deployment Wizard

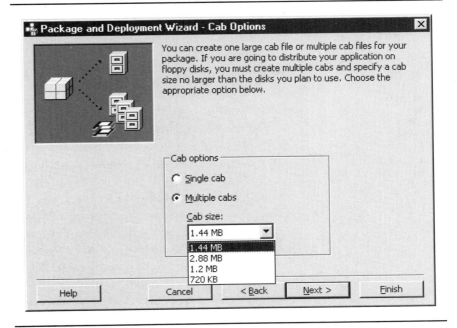

select 720 KB. If you had disks that had a capacity of 1.44 MB, you would select that. When deploying to floppy disks, you must have disks that are all the same size. You aren't able to mix and match, because you can only select one size from the list box.

You must use floppies of the same capacity for floppy disk deployment. The Cab Options screen will only package the multiple CAB files to one size. The CAB size can't be larger than the disks you use.

Once the application has been packaged to multiple CABs, you can go into the Deploy portion of the Wizard. Once you've selected your package from the Select Package list box on the Package and Deployment Wizard's main screen, click the Deploy button. The Wizard will analyze your package and go to the first screen of the Deploy portion. Click Next to go to the screen that allows you to choose your deployment method.

This screen allows you to choose how you want to deploy your application. Because you packaged your application to multiple CAB files, an option for floppy disk deployment will appear. If this option doesn't appear, you've most likely packaged to a single CAB file. To rectify this, return to the Package portion and repackage the application as multiple CABs.

Clicking the Next button will bring you to a screen that only appears for floppy disk deployment. Here, you can select which floppy drive will be used for deployment. If you have a single floppy drive, only one drive will appear in the list box. The Format before copying check box allows you to have each disk formatted before files are copied. It is wise to check this option because the deployment requires blank, formatted disks. If you have existing data on a disk or a disk isn't formatted, the deployment will fail.

You should always check the Format before copying check box. Even if you're using boxes of new "preformatted" floppies, it's not uncommon to come across unformatted floppies. I've had experiences with entire boxes of premium brand preformatted floppies that were unformatted, and one box that had data already on it! I've also experienced problems with the formatting of preformatted disks, causing errors to occur. Save yourself the frustration, and choose to format.

Upon reaching the final screen of the Deploy portion, you are given the option of naming and saving the settings of your session to a script. As mentioned previously, you can rename, duplicate, or delete this script through the Manage Scripts portion of the Package and Deployment Wizard. Clicking the Finish button on this screen will begin transferring files to the floppy disks.

Compact Disc-Based Deployment of a Distributed Application

Deploying to compact disc is similar to folder deployment, which is covered next. In most cases in the real world, you would actually use folder deployment for CD-ROM deployment. This is because few programmers are privileged enough to have a boss willing to have CD-ROM burners attached to every programmer's workstation. As such, you would use folder deployment, and then transfer the files afterwards to CD-ROMs.

CD-ROM burners are also called writeable CD-ROMs. The CD-ROMs you're familiar with allow you to read from a compact disc. CD-ROM burners can be used to read and also write information to CD-ROMs. To write your application to writeable CD-ROM, ensure that you have a blank CD-ROM in your CD-ROM burner, and use Package and Deployment Wizard to package and deploy the application.

In most cases, you would select to package your application to a single CAB file. This is done from the CAB Options screen of the Package Wizard. Although you can package to multiple CAB files, this is generally not required. Due to the storage capacity of compact discs, packaging to a single CAB file is the better and proper choice.

Depending on the CD-ROM burner you use, you can deploy your application with the Package and Deployment Wizard. To deploy your application in this way, select CD-ROM from the Deployment Method screen and follow the instructions that follow.

Planning and Implementing Network-Based Deployment

Network deployment doesn't start with the Package and Deployment Wizard or Visual Basic 6.0. It starts with determining whether you have the proper permissions or rights. If you don't have access to a network folder, you won't be able to deploy to it. In addition, you will need to find out if users who will install your application have the proper permissions or rights to the folder. They won't be able to access it otherwise. To find this information, check with your network administrator.

on the
Job

Although you can browse the network to see if you have access to a folder, it doesn't necessarily mean that others have access to it. The network administrator needs to set up access for users and groups who will install your application.

Once you've established access to a folder, you're ready to use the Package and Deployment Wizard. Generally, during the Package portion of the Wizard, you will package the application as a single CAB file. This doesn't mean you can't package to multiple CAB files, but single CAB is usually used for network deployment because of a hard drive's capacity for storage. Because there are fewer files, it also saves the end users from being confused by a large group of CAB files as they try to search for the file to start the installation.

Once you've packaged the application, click the Deploy button. The first screen will display a list box showing scripts for previous deployments. If you've never saved a script or if it's your first time using the Wizard, only one script will appear. Select the script you wish to use, and click Next.

The Deployment Method screen allows you to select the way in which your package will be deployed. Select Folder from the list, and click Next to view the Folder screen. The Folder screen (illustrated in Figure 11-5) allows you to select a local or network folder for deployment. The folder field allows you to type in the path of the folder to use for deployment. Below this is a Windows Explorer-style tree, through which you can find the folder you wish to use. To display a different drive's information in this pane, select it from the DriveBox. To create a new folder, click the New Folder button, then enter a name for the folder.

To deploy to a network, click the Network button. Here, you will see a dialog box showing a tree of your network. Browse through this dialog box to find the network computer you wish to attach to. Then navigate to an existing folder or click the New Folder button to create a new folder (if your permissions allow you to).

Depending on the network you're on and how your computer is configured, you may also be able to switch to a network drive using the DriveBox. This allows you to navigate the tree of folders and select the folder to deploy to.

FIGURE 11-5

The Folder screen allows you to select a local or network folder

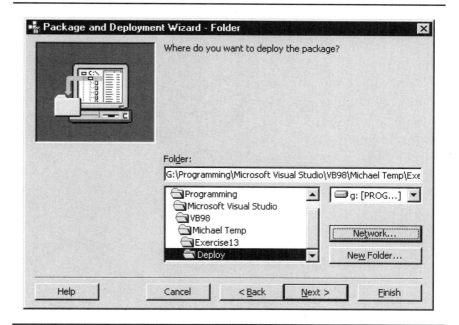

Clicking the Next button will bring you to the final screen. Here, you can name the script that will contain the settings chosen in this session. Clicking the Finish button will initiate the deployment and transfer the files to the network folder.

Packaging and Deploying for Network Deployment

Note: In this exercise, we will first create an application that we will then package and deploy. Save this application to disk because it will also be used for an exercise in the next chapter.

1. In Visual Basic 6.0, start a new Standard EXE project. From the File menu, select New Project, and then choose Standard EXE.

2. Add a data control to the form. In the Properties window, select the DatabaseName property. Click the button that appears with an ellipsis next to it, and then find and select the Nwind.mdb file from your hard disk.

3. In the Properties window, select the RecordSource property. When the list box appears, select Products.

4. Add a TextBox to the form. In the Properties window, select the DataSource property. When the list box appears, select Data1.

5. In the Properties window, select the DataField property. When the list box appears, select ProductName.

6. Save your project to a folder on your hard disk. Press the F5 key to run your program and see that it works. Toggle through the records by clicking the navigation buttons on the Data control. When you've established that it functions properly, end the program, and exit Visual Basic.

7. Start the Package and Deployment Wizard from the Windows Start | Programs menu. Click the Browse button and select the project you just created.

8. Click the Package button. Because we haven't compiled this application, a message box will appear stating this. Click the Compile button to compile your application. When it's finished compiling, the first screen will appear. Select Standard Setup Package and click Next.

9. The Package Folder screen will appear. Accept the default folder and click Next. When a message box appears asking to confirm the creation of a Package directory, click Yes to create the folder and continue.

10. Because we've created a database program, the DAO Drivers screen appears. As we are using an Access database, select "Jet 2.x : Jet 2.x" from the Available Drivers pane. Click the right arrow button to move this driver to the included drivers pane. Click Next to continue.

11. On the Included Files screen, click the Add button. Browse your hard disk for the Nwind.mdb database file we used for our project. This will add the database to our package, so end users can use it after installing. Click the Next button.

12. On the CAB Options screen, select the Single CAB option, and then click Next.

13. On the Installation Title screen, enter a title that will appear when your application is installed.

14. On the Start Menu Items screen, click on your project's group folder from the Start Menu Items pane, and then click Properties. Enter a name for the folder and click OK. After doing this, click on the application icon in the Start Menu Items pane and click Properties. Enter a more meaningful name for your application. This will appear on the end user's Start menu when the application is installed.

15. Click Next to accept the default values for the remaining screens and click Finish. Your application will be packaged.

16. From the main menu of the Package and Deployment Wizard, click Deploy. The project you just packaged will be analyzed and the first screen will appear. Accept the default script and click Next.

17. On the Deployment Method screen, select Folder, and then click Next.

18. On the Folder screen, click the Network button. This will bring up a dialog box that allows you to browse your network for a folder. After selecting the folder to deploy to, click OK to return to the Folder screen, and then click Next.

19. On the last screen, click the Finish button to deploy your package to the network folder.

QUESTIONS AND ANSWERS

I want to configure DCOM on a client computer. Where do I do this?	Use the DCOM Configuration Properties dialog box to configure DCOM on client and server computers.
How do I start the DCOM Configuration Properties dialog box? I can't find it anywhere!	Select Run from the Start menu, and type **dcomcnfg**. This will start DCOM Configuration Properties, which has a file name of DCOMCNFG.EXE
The floppy disk deployment method doesn't appear when I use the Deploy portion of Package and Deployment Wizard. Why?	If you packaged your application to a single CAB file, this method of deployment won't be offered. You must repackage your application as multiple CAB files, and then return to the Deploy portion and choose Floppy Disk.
There isn't a network deployment method offered on the Deployment Method screen. What do I do?	Select Folder as your deployment method. When you reach the Folder screen, click the Network button and select a network folder to deploy to.

CERTIFICATION SUMMARY

Package and Deployment Wizard provides a convenient way to create an installation program and deploy it to floppy disks, CD-ROMs, or network folders. In using the Wizard, you simply follow the instructions provided to package and deploy an application.

Distributed applications, including those that implement DCOM and COM, require information to be written to the Windows Registry. This information can be written and read programmatically, through self-registering files, or by editing various files. By registering information to the Registry, your application will run properly.

DCOM server and client computers require configuration before they can properly run applications that implement DCOM. To configure such computers, the DCOM Configuration Properties dialog box is used.

TWO-MINUTE DRILL

❑ Before using the Package and Deployment Wizard to package an application, you should first compile it.

❑ Creating a setup program is done through the Package portion of the Wizard.

❑ A CAB file is a setup file that contains .INF files, OCX files, and other files your application depends on to run.

❑ If you plan to deploy your application to CD-ROM, to a network or local folder, or over the Internet, you should have your files packaged to a single CAB. If you plan to deploy your package to floppy disk, you should choose multiple CABs.

❑ Dependency files have the extension .DEP, and contain information about an application or component's runtime requirements.

❑ The SETUP.1ST file created during the Package portion of Package and Deployment Wizard can determine how files are registered.

❑ The Registry key in SETUP.1ST can be edited to indicate that a file doesn't need to be registered, is self-registering, or contains information for the Registry.

❑ During the Package portion of the Wizard, a file called ST6UNST.EXE is added. This is the application-removal utility, and will install in the \Windows or \Winnt directory.

❑ When applications that implement DCOM are run on a client computer, you must specify the server application that needs to be started.

❑ Remote server files (also called remote support files) have the file extension .VBR and contain information required by the Registry to run ActiveX servers on remote computers.

SELF TEST

1. You start the Package and Deployment Wizard, and try to package an application that hasn't been compiled yet. What will happen?

   A. The Package and Deployment Wizard will display a message informing you of this, then shut down

   B. Nothing will happen; you'll have to shut down the Wizard, reopen Visual Basic, and compile the project from there.

   C. The Package and Deployment Wizard will display a message informing you of this, and give the option to compile from here

   D. The Package and Deployment Wizard will automatically compile it for you, without any user interaction

2. You want to compile a project called **MyProject**, which is part of a project group. How will you compile MyProject into an executable file?

   A. Select Make MyProject.exe from the File menu

   B. Select MyProject from the Project menu, and then select Make MyProject.exe from the File menu

   C. Select the project group from the Project window, and then select Make MyProject.exe from the File menu

   D. Select MyProject from the Project Window, and then select Make MyProject.exe from the File menu

3. You are packaging an Internet application with the Package and Deployment Wizard. When you reach the Cab Options screen, how will you package the application?

   A. Single Cab
   B. Multiple Cab
   C. Dual Cab
   D. Multi Cab

4. You are packaging an application that you plan to deploy on floppy disk. When you reach the Cab Options screen of Package and Deployment Wizard, how will you package the application?

   A. Single Cab
   B. Multiple Cab
   C. Dual Cab
   D. Multi Cab

5. You reach the Installation Title screen of the Package and Deployment Wizard. Where will information typed on this screen appear when the application is installed?

   A. It will appear as menu item and group titles in the user's Start menu

   B. It will change the name of the Setup file to what you have set on this screen

   C. It will display on-screen during the installation process

   D. It won't appear until after installation, and users can access the information through the Help menu

6. A user installs your application and a COM component can't be found. What will happen?

    A. The operating system will stop the installation

    B. All hard drives will be searched for the missing file

    C. The installation will skip the missing file and continue

    D. The Visual Basic Run time Library will produce a "File not found" message

7. Which files contain information about the directories created during installation; Registry entries that were created and modified; and self-registered .DLL, .EXE, or .OCX files?

    A. Unwise.log

    B. Install.log

    C. St6unst.log

    D. Vb6unst.log

8. What does the Registry key $(TLBRegister) represent in the Setup.1st file?

    A. The file is a type library and is to be registered as such

    B. The file is a self-registering DLL file

    C. The file is a self-registering EXE file

    D. The file is a remote support file (also referred to as remote server file)

9. Which of the following best defines what user-level access control (user-level security) is?

    A. A password must be set for each resource

    B. Allows you to specify users and groups who have access to resources

    C. A password must be set for each printer

    D. Allows you to specify domains and servers used for authentication

10. You are configuring DCOM on a client computer. Because the computer is running a client application, what must you specify in your configuration?

    A. The user account that will have access to start the application and user accounts that have permissions to run it

    B. The location of the server application that will be accessed or started

    C. The location of the client application that will be accessed or started

    D. The user account of the person who configured DCOM on that computer

11. What must you have to deploy to compact disc?

    A. CD-ROM

    B. Writeable CD-ROM

    C. Network access

    D. A computer running NT Server

12. You have deployed to a network folder. Users who want to install the application complain that they can't find the folder you said the install program was in. You check your computer, and find that the install program is there. What is most likely the problem?

A. You forgot to configure DCOM on the client computer

B. You forgot to configure DCOM on the server computer

C. You don't have proper permissions or rights to access the folder

D. You've lost your mind from overwork, and forgot to deploy the application

E. Other users or groups don't have proper permissions or rights to access the folder.

13. You have decided to run DCOM Configuration Properties to configure DCOM on a computer. How will you start this program?

A. From the Package and Deployment Wizard, click the DCOM button

B. From the Package and Deployment Wizard, select DCOM from the View menu

C. From Visual Basic, select DCOM from the View menu

D. From the Start menu, click Run and type **dcomcfng** to start the program

14. You are using the Package and Deployment Wizard to deploy to the network. What will you select as your method of deployment from the Deployment Method screen of the Deploy portion?

A. Network

B. Network Folder

C. Folder

D. Network Deployment

15. You are using DCOM Configuration Properties, and you select an application from the list and click the Properties button. A dialog box appears with several tabs. Which tab shows information on the application that consists of its name, local path, and the type of application it is?

A. General

B. Location

C. Security

D. Advanced

16. You are using DCOM Configuration Properties, and you selected an application from the list and clicked the Properties button. A dialog box appears with several tabs. Which tab allows you to choose between default access permissions for the application and custom permissions that allow you to edit who can use the application?

A. General

B. Location

C. Security

D. Advanced

17. You are using DCOM Configuration Properties, and you selected an application from the list and clicked the Properties button. A dialog box appears with several tabs. Which tab specifies where you want to run the application?

A. General

B. Location

C. Security

D. Advanced

18. Which of the following functions allow you to write information to the Windows Registry?

A. GetSettings

B. SaveSettings

C. Property Let

D. Property Get

19. Which of the following contain information about an application or a component's runtime requirements?

A. Dependency files

B. SETUP.1ST files

C. SETUP1.lST files

D. DEP.lST files.

20. You have decided to edit the Access Permissions for certain users of an application. In Add Access Permissions, which access permissions can you set for users or groups? (Choose all that apply.)

A. Grant Access

B. Read and Write

C. Full

D. Deny Access

21. During installation, where will the application-removal utility be installed?

A. The application directory

B. The common files directory

C. The shared files directory

D. The /Windows or /WinNT directory

22. What can you do to rename, delete, and duplicate package and deployment scripts that were created during Package or Deploy sessions?

A. Click the Manage Scripts button on Package and Deployment Wizard's main screen to open a dialog box for these purposes

B. Select Manage Scripts from the File menu of the Package and Deployment Wizard to open a dialog box for these purposes

C. Click the Manage Scripts button on the Deployment method screen of Package and Deployment Wizard

D. Click the Scripts button on the Package and Deployment Wizard's main screen to open a dialog box for these purposes

23. You want to create a setup program for your application. What will you use to do this?

A. Deploy portion of Package and Deployment Wizard

B. Package portion of Package and Deployment Wizard

C. Compiling the project in Visual Basic 6.0

D. Make Setup Program menu item on the File menu of Visual Basic 6.0

24. Which of the following functions allow you to read information from the Windows Registry?

    A. SaveSettings

    B. ReadSettings

    C. GetSettings

    D. Get

25. You are deploying to compact disc. Unfortunately, the Package and Deployment Wizard doesn't recognize that a writeable CD-ROM is attached to your computer. How can you still deploy to compact disc?

    A. Select Floppy Disk deployment and select the drive for your writeable CD-ROM rather than a floppy drive

    B. Select Network deployment and select the drive for your writeable CD-ROM.

    C. Select Folder deployment, and then after deploying to a local or network folder, transfer the files manually to compact disc.

    D. None of the above

26. What kind of access control must you set a computer to in order for it to run DCOM Configuration Properties?

    A. User-control

    B. Share-control

    C. NT Server authenticated

    D. NT Domain authenticated

27. What does the Registry key $(Remote) represent in the Setup.1st file?

    A. The file is a type library, and is to be registered as such

    B. The file is a self-registering DLL file

    C. The file is a self-registering EXE file

    D. The file is a remote support file (also referred to as remote server file)

28. Which determines the files that should be removed during an uninstall of your program? When executed, which file will remove all files, directories, and other items that were logged during installation?

    A. UNINSTALl.EXE

    B. ST6UNST.COM

    C. ST6UNST.EXE

    D. UNWISE.EXE

29. You want to compile a Standard EXE project named "MyProject." Which menu item on the File menu in Visual Basic 6.0 will you select to do this?

    A. Make

    B. Make Project

    C. Make MyProject

    D. Make MyProject.exe

30. Using Package and Deployment Wizard, you decide to package to multiple CAB files. The Cab Size list box becomes available when you chose this option. Which CAB sizes can you choose from this list box? (Choose all that apply.)

A. 1.44 MB

B. 2.88 MB

C. 1.2 MB

D. 720 KB

31. What must you have enabled on your computer in order to set User-level access control?

    A. File sharing

    B. Print sharing

    C. Share-level access

    D. A list of users set on your local hard disk

32. You are configuring DCOM on a server computer. Because the computer is running a server application, what must you specify in your configuration?

    A. The user account that will have access to start the application, and user accounts that have permissions to run it

    B. The location of the server application that will be accessed or started

    C. The location of the client application that will be accessed or started

    D. The user account of the person who configured DCOM on that computer

33. The GetSettings and SaveSettings functions access entries under which key in the Windows Registry?

    A. HKEY_CURRENT_USER\Software\ VB and VBA Program Settings

    B. HKEY_CURRENT_CONFIG\Softw are\VB and VBA Program Settings

    C. HKEY_LOCAL_MACHINE\Softwar e\VB and VBA Program Settings

    D. HKEY_CURRENT_CONFIG\Softw are\VB

34. You have decided to deploy to floppy disks. When you enter the Deploy portion of the Package and Deployment Wizard, "Floppy Disk" doesn't appear on the Deployment Method screen. What is most likely the reason for this?

    A. Deploy doesn't allow for floppy disk deployment

    B. You forgot to choose Floppy Disk deployment in the Package portion of the Wizard

    C. You forgot to package to multiple CAB files in the Package portion of the Wizard

    D. You forgot to package to a single CAB file in the Package portion of the Wizard

35. What information do the registry keys in the SETUP.1ST file indicate?

    A. The location of the Windows Registry

    B. The key in which to store information in the Windows Registry

    C. Whether a file is self-registering, contains information for the Registry, or doesn't need to be registered

    D. File location information for the Windows Registry

36. You are preparing to configure DCOM on a computer. The kind of security used on the computer requires that you enter a password for each resource. What kind of security is

this, and what will happen when you try to open DCOM Configuration Properties?

A. User-level, and DCOM Configuration Properties will open

B. User-level, and DCOM Configuration Properties will fail to open

C. Share-level, and DCOM Configuration Properties will open

D. Share-level, and DCOM Configuration Properties will fail to open

37. You are packaging an IIS application with the Package and Deployment Wizard. Which Packaging Type will you select in the Package portion of the Wizard?

A. Standard Setup Package

B. Internet Package

C. IIS Package

D. Web Package

38. You plan to package and deploy a Standard EXE project to a network folder. In the Package portion, you reach the Package Folder screen of the Wizard. What does this screen allow you to specify?

A. A network folder where your application will be deployed

B. A folder where your application will be bundled into a package

C. The location where the application to be packaged resides

D. The location of files to be added to the package

39. You are using the Package portion of Package and Deployment Wizard. The DAO Drivers screen fails to appear as you go through the Wizard. Why?

A. You failed to add Data Access Objects to your package

B. The Package portion has determined which drivers to include and doesn't require interaction

C. Your application doesn't contain any Data Access Objects

D. The DAO Drivers screen only appears in the Deploy portion

40. You reach the Shared Files screen of the Package portion of Package and Deployment Wizard. If your application has been packaged, deployed, and installed by the end user, who then decides to uninstall the application and what will happen to the files listed on this Shared Files screen? (Choose the best answer.)

A. Files that are shared files will be uninstalled

B. Files that are shared files are never uninstalled

C. Files that are shared files won't be uninstalled until every application using them is removed

D. Files that are shared files will need to be manually removed

MICROSOFT CERTIFIED SOLUTION DEVELOPER

12

Maintaining and Supporting an Application

Thism chapter deals with issues related to maintaining and supporting an application. As you'll see, these issues include implementing load balancing, dealing with errors, and deploying an application update. By the end of this chapter, you'll be able to fix existing errors in an application, prevent future errors, and get your updated application to the end user.

Implementing Load Balancing

Think of the last time you moved. You probably had a few friends help carry your stuff to a truck or to your car. Imagine that you decided to have one friend carry all of your belongings while the others stood idly by. What would happen? Aside from losing a friend, that person would slow down from performing all the tasks. While your friend was carrying one load, other items would pile up. In addition, chances are that the life spans of the idle friends would be longer than the one you're overworking. It would be wiser to balance the load evenly between all of your friends.

The same concept applies to load balancing in computers. *Load balancing* involves techniques that spread tasks among processors. Rather than bogging down one processor with all the tasks, you can distribute them among all of the processors. Balancing the load across all processors saves tasks from being queued for execution on one processor.

When a program is loaded into memory and prepared for execution, it's called a *process*. A process is started with a single "thread" of execution, but it can create additional threads. A *thread* is the actual code being executed. It's a sequence of execution in a computer, to which the computer schedules CPU time. In Win16 programs (Windows 3x and Windows for Workgroups), applications used a single thread, while Win32 (Windows 9x and Windows NT) allowed applications to use more than one thread. When a process is single-threaded, code can be executed for only one thread at a time. COM deals with this by "serializing" requests, so that requests are queued and processed one at a time.

Visual Basic 5.0 Service Pack 2 introduced apartment-model threading. This model provides the analogy that the thread is an apartment and objects are the apartment tenants. Just as you are unaware of what your neighbors are doing in an apartment building, objects in a thread are unaware of objects in other threads. The Professional and Enterprise editions of Visual Basic 6.0 include the capability of using apartment-model threading.

To extend this apartment analogy, imagine that everyone in your apartment building had access to one thermostat. Obviously, conflicts would arise when one person tried to turn up the heat, while another tenant tried to lower the temperature. This is similar to conflicts that threads had when they tried to access the same global data. To eliminate the conflict of two threads using the same data, the apartment model provides each thread with its own copy of global data. Because each contains its own copy of global data, objects can't use this data to communicate with objects on other threads.

e x a m
Ⓦ a t c h

Apartment-model threading is considered a new feature of Visual Basic 6.0, even though it first appeared in Visual Basic 5.0 Service Pack 2. An important feature of apartment-model threading is that each thread contains its own copy of global data.

With Visual Basic 6.0, you can implement apartment-model threading or single threading, in which all objects of a component are contained in a single thread. You can set the threading model for ActiveX DLL, ActiveX EXE, and ActiveX control projects, regardless of whether or not they provide a user interface. In previous versions of Visual Basic, you couldn't take advantage of multiple threading without suppressing visual elements like Forms and controls. Visual Basic 6.0 allows you to use apartment-model threading on projects containing Forms, UserControls, UserDocuments, and ActiveX designers. Setting the threading model for a project is done from the General tab of the Project Properties dialog box, which is accessed from the Project menu. The screen shown in Figure 12-1 displays the General tab.

FIGURE 12-1

General tab of the Project
Properties dialog box

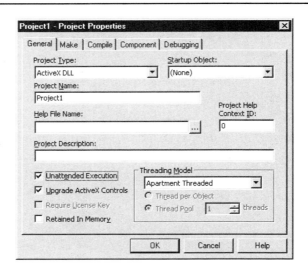

Depending on the type of project you're using, different areas of this
screen may be disabled. ActiveX DLL projects have the "Thread per
Object" and "Thread Pool" options disabled because it is an in-process
server component, that has threads furnished and managed by client
applications. These disabled settings are the same for ActiveX controls. For
an ActiveX DLL or ActiveX control, you are able to specify through the
Threading Model list box whether a project is "Single Threaded" or
"Apartment Threaded."

ActiveX EXE projects have this Threading Model list box disabled, but
the "Thread per Object" and "Thread Pool" options are enabled. The
Thread per Object option creates each new object on a new thread.
Selecting the Thread Pool option limits a component to a fixed pool of
threads. By selecting this option, you can specify the number of threads in
the pool. Specifying a thread pool of one makes the project single-threaded;
increasing the number of the thread pool makes your project
apartment-threaded. By using these options, you can control how your
out-of-process server manages threads.

The Unattended Execution check box allows you to specify whether a
component can run without user interaction on network servers. This
option suppresses anything that requires user intervention, such as message
boxes and dialog boxes. Also, checking this option doesn't affect the

threading model. You don't have to set a project for Unattended Execution to select a setting for the Threading Model, which was a requirement in previous versions of Visual Basic.

Using multiple threads on multiple processors can dramatically improve the performance of an application, but it can actually decrease performance on a computer with a single processor. When a component is single threaded, requests are *serialized*, which means that they are queued and processed one by one. When apartment threading is used, the threads must contend for the processor's attention. This means that the processor has to spend time switching between threads and the perceived time to complete the task increases. When dealing with processes that take a relatively equal amount of time, it is actually better to use single threading.

Multiple threading works well on a single processor when a mixture of long and short tasks is being processed, or when there is time blocked by tasks such as file I/O. While a computer is reading and writing a file to a hard disk, the processor can work on other threads that make the application appear to run faster. By the same token, when long and short tasks are being processed, performance increases because a long task isn't holding up shorter tasks that are waiting for the processor's attention. Although multiple threading will always increase performance on machines with multiple processors, this is not always the case with single-processor computers.

Fixing Errors and Taking Measures to Prevent Future Errors

To err is human. To forgive, divine.

This quote represents basic error handling for human relations. It doesn't matter whether it's an error in logic, a misspoken word, or an action that went wrong. When an error occurs, you need to deal with it.

The same premise applies to computers. Similar to these human errors, there are three kinds of computer errors: logic, syntax, and runtime. When one of these errors occur, you need to implement a course of action to deal with it. This is what error handling is all about.

Logic errors occur when your code executes without syntax or runtime errors, but the results aren't what you expect. One example of a logic error is to put the wrong e-mail address in a hyperlink. It will run without syntax or runtime error, but the e-mail will be sent to the wrong address. Another common logic error that crops up deals with adding a percentage to a variable. For this example, suppose you want to add 10% to a variable that has a value of 100. The correct way of doing this is to multiply the variable by 1.1, to return 110. However, many programming students make the mistake of multiplying the variable by .1, resulting in an answer of 10. The program runs correctly, but the logic error returns a result that wasn't intended.

Logic errors are corrected by testing the application; run the program, input information, and pay attention to what the program returns for the answers. You can also compile "beta" versions of the application, which are pre-released versions of your program. This preliminary release can be used by people who act as "beta testers." As they find errors, they can report them back to you. When you or your beta testers find an error, you must then look through your code to find where the logic errors occurred, and then edit the code to fix the error.

A syntax error results from incorrect use of the programming language, and it is the computer equivalent of tripping over your own words. When you mistype a keyword or fail to close multi-line commands (such as forgetting to put "End If" at the end of an If statement), you will experience a syntax error during compilation. To fix this error, you have to change the offending code or the program won't compile.

Visual Basic 6.0 comes with a syntax error-checking feature, which allows syntax errors to be caught as you mistype them. As shown in Figure 12-2, the Auto Syntax Check can be enabled or disabled from the Editor tab of the Options dialog box, which is accessed from the Tools menu. When enabled, Visual Basic will check syntax when you move away from a line of code. For example, let's say you typed the following code:

```
Dam x As Integer
```

Because the keyword "Dim" is incorrectly spelled, a syntax error will occur when you move your cursor off of this line. To inform you that the error has occurred, Visual Basic 6.0 will display a message box that brings the error to your attention.

FIGURE 12-2

Editor tab of Visual Basic
6.0 Options dialog box

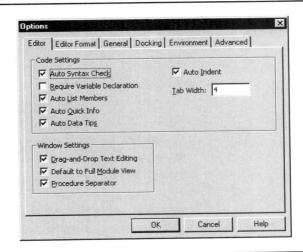

The Auto List Members feature of Visual Basic 6.0 can also aid you with syntax errors. Auto List Members can be enabled or disabled from the Editor tab in the Options dialog box, which is accessed from the Tools menu. With this feature enabled, a list box appears as you type your code, and displays all possible members for what you're typing. For example, if you typed **Dim y As** in the Code Window, a listing of members would appear, showing App, Integer, String, and everything else that y could be declared as. By listing these possibilities, the chance of mistyping a member decreases, which protects you from making syntax errors.

on the

Job

The Auto List Member feature in Visual Basic 6.0 saves you from trying to remember every member of every object in Visual Basic, which would be an impossible task at best. Before this feature, you had to refer to Visual Basic's Help documentation, buy lengthy reference books, and fumble through the pages looking for what you wanted. Auto List Member saves you from these trials by handing them to you on the fly. It is recommended to have this feature on, especially when you first start programming.

Unlike logic and syntax errors, runtime errors are the only kind of errors that can't be completely prevented when an application is distributed. Runtime errors occur when an invalid action is attempted by a command.

To illustrate a runtime error, let's say you create an application that uses a database on a server. In your program, a setup screen asks for the path and filename of the database. If the user incorrectly types the path or filename of the database, or the server or network goes down, a runtime error will result. Obviously, such an error is beyond the control of the programmer. There is no way to determine that a server or network will go down, or that a user might type the wrong path to a file. However, by adding code to handle such errors, runtime errors can be dealt with when they occur.

When you are designing a project and run it, runtime errors will cause Visual Basic to present you with a message box. This message box, as shown in Figure 12-3, can provide up to four different courses of action.

The first of these buttons is the Continue button, which allows an application to continue running with the error. Because the program continues to run with errors, clicking this button can produce unpredictable results. This button is disabled if a fatal error has occurred.

The next button is End, which stops the program and returns you to design mode. By clicking this button, you end the application and lose any information processed up to the point where your error occurred.

The next button is the Debug button, which is selected by default. Clicking this button will break the program at the line that caused the error, causing the application to run in single-step mode (explained later). In most cases, you will choose this button over the others because it brings you directly to where the problem exists.

Finally, the Help button is used to view information (when available) about the error your application has experienced. While the message box itself provides the error number of a runtime error and a brief description of the error, the Help button can provide detailed information about common errors.

FIGURE 12-3

Visual Basic 6.0 Runtime
Error Message

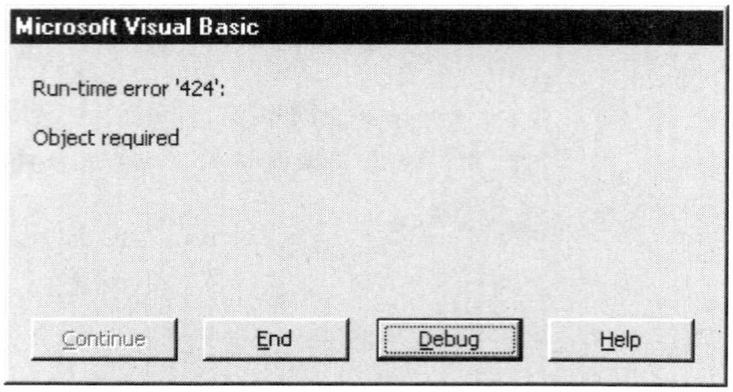

Microsoft Visual Basic

Run-time error '424':

Object required

Continue   End   Debug   Help

If you experience a runtime error in a compiled program, the message box you see will look significantly different from the one shown in Figure 12-3. As is shown in the following illustration, such a message box provides basic information and no recourse to deal with the error. The message is meant to tell the end user that an error has occurred, the error number, and a brief description of the error. This information is almost useless to the end user, but it is useful when a programmer is testing his or her application.

These default runtime error messages are cryptic at best to the end user, and can be somewhat frustrating. If the error occurs in a distributed program, it is just enough to: a) let the user know an error has occurred, and b) make him feel like an idiot. To avoid leaving a user dumbfounded by a message that is meaningless, you should implement your own error messages into an application.

Error Trapping

Before covering how to implement code that handles errors and adding custom error messages, it is important to have Visual Basic 6.0's error-handling settings properly configured. These settings appear on the General tab of the Options dialog box, which is accessed from the Tools menu. In configuring these settings, you are specifying how Visual Basic will deal with errors that are encountered in the design environment.

As is seen in Figure 12-4, the Error Trapping section of the General tab allows you to determine how Visual Basic handles errors. The first option offered is Break on All Errors, which causes Visual Basic to break on any runtime error it encounters. If this option has been set, any error-handling code you've implemented will be ignored. This option should be set if you're searching for where errors are occurring, so the code causing the error can be fixed.

The second option shown in the Error Trapping section is Break in Class Module. This is the default setting, meaning that it was the setting when your project was created. As its name somewhat suggests, this setting only comes into full effect when your project runs code in class modules.

FIGURE 12-4

General tab of Options

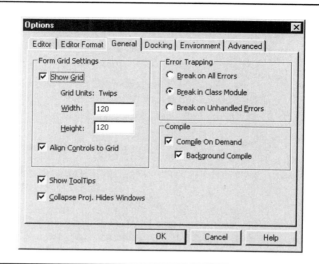

You can think of this option as forcing Visual Basic to break where a problem really exists. When code in your application calls code in a class module, it will break in the class's code. With the other options, if an unhandled error exists in a class module, it will break at the code that called the Class. When an unhandled error exists outside of the class module, this setting will treat it the same as Break on Unhandled Errors.

It is important to use this setting when you are creating an application that deals with ActiveX servers. This option causes Visual Basic to break in the ActiveX server's code, rather than passing the error back to your client application. As such, using this setting can save you considerable time trying to track down the source of an error.

The third setting in Error Trapping is Break on Unhandled Errors. Once you've created error-handling routines, you can test them to see if they actually work. If a runtime error occurs and error handling exists, Visual Basic allows the error handler to deal with the error. If there is no error handler for the offending code, Visual Basic will break at the error.

As mentioned earlier, if Break on Unhandled Errors has been set and an error occurs in a class module, Visual Basic breaks at the code that called the class module. You should use this setting only when you are testing error handlers that you've created.

FROM THE CLASSROOM

Application Maintenance and Support

I suggest that you have a comfortable level of understanding of the differences between single-threaded and multi-thread applications. The conceptual difference between a thread and a process has often confused students. Remember that a thread represents the actual code under execution. In Visual Basic 6, a single-thread application is actually an apartment-thread application using only one apartment. Also starting with Visual Basic 6, the suppression of visual elements is no longer necessary in order to support multi-threaded applications.

Threading issues carry different limitations based on the type of application project. For example, ActiveX DLLs (also known as in-process servers) cannot use the Thread Pool or Thread per Object choices, because thread assignment is handled by the client application within whose process space the DLL is sharing or running.

Supporting an application also involves dealing with the different types of errors that can occur, so be aware of the classifications: syntax, run-time, and logic errors. Full knowledge and experience in using the Err object should also be considered worthwhile,

not only for the exam, but also for general knowledge in proper debugging techniques.

No knowledge of debugging would be complete without being aware of the various error handler routine techniques, including the use of resume, resume next, and the various "On error" variations. Knowing the subtle differences in the use of these key phrases will prove necessary for a question or two.

Of course, application maintenance always has the possibility of including issuing application updates. It would be wise to recognize the difference in screens provided by the Package and Deployment wizard when performing an application upgrade rather than a full application deployment. Consider under what conditions the DAO driver screen may appear.

Finally, for the exam, be aware of the options for types of deployment, and the resulting media deployment options that will be presented, including the necessity of a valid URL and web server write-access.

—By Michael Lane Thomas,
MCSE+I, MCSD, MCT, A+

Writing Code that Traps Errors

The first step in dealing with an error is to trap it. This means implementing code that determines that an error has occurred, and then passes the error to a routine that deals with it. Once you've set your trap, it remains enabled until the procedure ends or the error trap is disabled.

You can enable an error trap with the On Error statement, which establishes error handling in your code. When an error occurs, the On Error statement detours execution to a specified place in your program, depending on what you've typed after the words "On Error."

The first detour we'll cover is redirecting an error to a labeled error-handling routine. This is seen in the following example of code:

```
On Error GoTo MyHandler
    'Code with error appears here
Exit Sub

MyHandler:
    'Error handling code appears here
```

In this example, the first line of code states that if an error occurs, execution should be detoured to a label called "MyHandler." Typing a name ending with a colon creates a label (":"), while code following the label deals with the error.

As shown in the previous example, the words "Exit Sub" appear at the end of your code and before the error-handling routine. This keeps the error-handling code from being processed each time the procedure is run. You don't want this error handler from running when it isn't intended to run.

Exit Sub provides a means for the procedure to exit when no error occurs. Without it, code will continue to be processed, causing the error handler to run even when no error has occurred.

There will be times when you won't wish to redirect execution to a label. Instead, you may want to skip over a line containing an error and resume processing on the next line. This is commonly used for inline error handling, discussed later, where errors are dealt with immediately after they occur. To instruct your program to resume execution on a line following one that caused an error, you can use the following code:

```
On Error Resume Next
```

This line of code is also useful when you expect errors that don't affect the remaining code. An example of such an occurrence is when you create a loop that goes through controls on a Form. Let's say you have a Form that asks users to input the URLs of servers on the Internet. Because URLs are traditionally lowercase, you can create a loop that moves through the Text property of every control on the Form and converts any uppercase text to lowercase. Because labels don't have a Text property, you can expect a runtime error each time a label is encountered. By adding On Error Resume Next before the loop, such errors are ignored. The loop skips over this control and converts the next control (assuming it has a Text property) to lowercase.

As mentioned earlier, an error trap will remain enabled until a procedure ends or the error trap is disabled. To disable an error trap, you must type the following code into a procedure:

```
On Error GoTo 0
```

This is useful when one procedure calls another procedure. In such a case, you may want to disable a previous error trap so that only the error handling in the called procedure is used.

Errors are handled in a *call stack* or *calling chain*. When one procedure calls a second procedure that has no error handling, the error is passed back to calling procedure. Let's say that Procedure 1 calls Procedure 2, which has no error handling but experiences an error. Procedure 2 will pass the error to Procedure 1; if Procedure 1 has an error handler, it will deal with the error. If it doesn't have an error handler, Visual Basic will display a message box and end the application.

The Err Object

The Err object is used to determine what error has occurred, the source application that caused the error. It also provides a brief description of the error encountered. You can use this object to implement the error handing that deals with specific errors in specific ways. Rather than having error code that deals with all errors the same way, the Err object allows you to implement code that deals with problems on an error-by-error basis.

Err has three properties that are regularly used in error handling. The first of these is Number, which contains an Integer value that represents the last error encountered. Visual Basic 6.0 has a number of codes representing trappable errors. When a trappable error occurs in Visual Basic, the appropriate code is passed to Number property. This allows you to determine which error has occurred, so code that specifically deals with the error can be run. To view a full listing of error codes available, look at the heading called "Trappable Errors" in Visual Basic's Help.

While Err.Number contains a number representing the last error occurred, the second property, Description property, can be used to view brief information about an error. Err.Description has a String value and allows you to display information about the last error that occurred.

Err.Source is used to determine the application that caused an error. This is useful when creating programs that work with other applications. If you create an ActiveX client application, you can use Err.Source to discover if an error resulted in the client or server application.

To clear the values contained in the Err object, you can use the Clear property. Err.Clear resets the value of Err.Number to 0, so that information about a previous error doesn't linger. If an error occurred and was dealt with, failing to clear the Err object could cause the error to be dealt with again. Your code might think this is a recent error, rather than one that's already been taken care of. To avoid this problem, Err.Clear can be used to reset the Err object.

In addition to helping your code deal with errors, the Err object can also be used to cause errors. The third property, Raise property of Err, is used for testing error-handling routines by causing errors to occur. To illustrate its use, the error code "71" is applied to Err.Raise, causing a "Disk Not Ready" error:

```
Err.Raise 71
```

If you were to place this line of code in your application, an error would result, enabling you to see if your error-handling routine deals with the error properly.

exam

ⓦatch

The Err object, its properties, and methods are fundamental to error handling, and it is important you understand what each does for the Microsoft exam. Be sure to review its properties and methods before going into the exam.

Once you've used the Err object to determine which errors occurred and have written code to deal with the error, you need to provide a way to exit the error handler. This can be done with one of three uses of the "Resume" statement:

```
Resume
Resume Next
Resume line or label
```

The first of these returns execution to the statement that caused an error. Execution returns to where the error originated so that an operation can be completed after the error has been corrected. Resume Next is used to return execution to the line immediately following the one that caused the error. This allows a program to skip over a problem line of code to continue the remaining code in a procedure. Finally, Resume, followed by a line or label, is used to resume execution on a specific line or a place where you've labeled a section of code. This allows you to control where the processing resumes.

EXERCISE 12-1

Error Handling

1. Start a new Visual Basic project. From the File menu, select New Project, and then choose Standard EXE.

2. Add a CommandButton to your form. Change its caption to "Error", and in the Click event add the following code:

```
On Error GoTo MyHandler
Dim intErr as Integer

intErr = InputBox ("Enter Error Number", "My Error",
"71"
```

```
Err.Raise (intErr)

Exit Sub

MyHandler:
MsgBox "Error: " & Err.Number & " has occurred in " &
Err.Source _
& ". Error was " & Err.Description

Resume Next
```

3. Press F5 to run the program. Click the command button. When the input box appears, enter an error code (detailed under the "Trappable Errors" section in Visual Basic Help) or accept the default error. Notice that the error is raised and passed to the error handler, which displays a message box detailing the error has occurred.

When creating error handlers, it is important to use the Err object to determine which error has occurred, and then use conditional execution to deal with the error based on the value of Err.Number. This allows you to deal with specific errors in specific ways.

Using a Select Case structure, an If…Then or If…Then…Else block, you can perform actions based on the error that has occurred. By comparing the value of Err.Number, you can then have the code that deals with particular errors execute. This is seen in the following code:

```
Private Sub cmdSave_Click()
On Error GoTo MyHandler
CommonDialog1.ShowSave
MyHandler:
If Err.Number = 0 Then
    'No error has occurred
ElseIf Err.Number = 58 Then
    MsgBox "That File Already Exists"
    Resume
Else
    MsgBox "Error:  " & Err.Description
End If
Err.Clear
End Sub
```

In reviewing this code, we see that when a CommandButton is clicked, a common dialog box is used to present a Save As dialog box. If an error occurs, the error is passed to the error handler, which determines a course of action based on the value of Err.Number. As it is passed through the error handler, it first sees whether the value of Err.Number is 0. If the value equals 0, nothing happens because 0 indicates that no error has occurred. If the Err.Number has a value of 58, this indicates a "File Already Exists" error, and execution returns to the line that presents the user with the Save As dialog box. If neither of these conditions is met, the Else section of code is executed. By using conditional execution with error handling, you can deal with specific conditions on an individual basis.

Conditional execution can be combined with inline error handling, which is used to deal with an error immediately after it occurs. The following example of code is identical to the last example, except that it uses inline error handling with a Select Case structure:

```
Private Sub cmdSave_Click()
On Error Resume Next

CommonDialog1.ShowSave

Select Case Err.Number
Case 0:
    'Do Nothing
Case 58:
    MsgBox "File Already Exists"
Case Else:
    MsgBox "Error:  " & Err.Description
End Select

Err.Clear
CommonDialog1.ShowOpen

End Sub
```

When this code executes, a Save As dialog box is displayed just as it was in the previous example. The "On Error Resume Next" statement is used to have the next line of code processed when an error occurs, which causes a Select Case structure to be run. Because the error is dealt with immediately, labels aren't used to identify error-handling code. Likewise, Resume statements aren't required because code is processed line-by-line.

When the end of the error handler is reached, Err.Clear is used to reset the Number property of the Err object. This is important in inline error handling because there are no Resume statements used to reset the Err.Number to 0. Failing to reset Err.Number could cause problems if this procedure called another procedure that had its own error handling. This would create a "ghost" error and cause the called procedure's error handler to deal with it.

As you create error-handling routines, you will often find that such code is used in several places. For example, a procedure that opens or closes a file can appear on a toolbar, as a menu item, or on another control. You can save yourself significant time in coding and decrease the amount of code in an application by creating a standard Function that contains error-handling code, and can be invoked as needed.

As is seen in the following example, a Function is used for error handling. This Function returns a Boolean value to the calling code that indicates whether the function succeeded or failed. By using this standard Function to determine if an error occurred and deal with errors as they happen, we can save significant time and space by invoking it from other places in our code.

```
Private Sub Command1_Click()
Dim strName As String
Dim blnSuccess As Boolean

strName = InputBox("Enter Application Filename")
blnSuccess = FuncOpen(strName)

MsgBox "Result opening " & strName & " was " & strSuccess

End Sub

Function FuncOpen(strName As String) As Boolean
On Error Resume Next
Shell strName

Select Case Err.Number
Case 0:
```

```
    FuncOpen = True
Case Else:
    FuncOpen = False
End Select

End Function
```

This code is basically a more elaborate version of the Run command located on the Start menu. It uses a CommandButton to open an input box when clicked. This input box requests the user to enter the filename of the application they wish to open. The filename is assigned to the variable strName, which is passed to FuncOpen. If the filename is valid (such as CALC.EXE), the application is started and no error occurs. This means that the value of Err.Number is 0 and the value of True is returned to the calling code. Because success has occurred, a message box displays to show this. If our program is unable to run a program, it returns a value of False to the calling code and a message box displays to show failure.

In reviewing this code, you'll notice that most of it resides in the Function. By reusing this code for error handling, there are fewer chances for logic and syntax errors because we're not rewriting the same error-handling routine throughout the application. This will also make our application smaller because it results in less code existing in the application.

By implementing centralized error handling, you can use yet another style of handling errors. This involves creating a primary error handler, which tells procedures how to deal with problem code. When an error is experienced, the Err.Number is passed to a central error-handling routine. This routine analyzes the value of Err.Number and then informs the calling procedure how to process the error. As is seen in the following example, centralized error handlers don't completely free you from adding error-handling code to a procedure, but they minimize the amount of code needed in each and every procedure in your application.

```
Private Sub Command1_Click()
On Error GoTo MyHandler
Dim blnSuccess As Boolean

Shell InputBox("Enter Application Filename")

Exit Sub
```

```
MyHandler:
blnSuccess = ErrHandle(Err.Number)

If blnSuccess = False Then
    Resume Next
ElseIf blnSuccess = True Then
    Resume
End If

End Sub

Function Errhandle(ErrNum As Integer) As Boolean
Select Case ErrNum
Case 53:
    Result = MsgBox("Program Not Found. Try Again?",
vbYesNo)
Case 5:
    Result = MsgBox("Program Not Found. Try Again?",
vbYesNo)
Case 0:
    Result = vbNo
Case Else:
    MsgBox "Error " & ErrNum & ":  Unloading"
    Unload Form1
End Select

If Result = vbYes Then
    ErrHandle = True
ElseIf Result = vbNo Then
    ErrHandle = False
End If

End Function
```

In the preceding example, we are dealing with yet another application that's similar to the Run command on the Windows Start menu. Code has been added to a command button, which displays an input box when clicked. The input box accepts the filename of an application that the user wishes to open. If an error results, because a user entered an invalid filename, an error handler called MyHandler is used. MyHandler passes the error to the centralized error handler called ErrHandle, which analyzes the error code.

The centralized error-handling routine called ErrHandle uses the value of the error code to determine a course of action. It decides whether the user gets another shot at entering an application name, if other code in the calling procedure should continue processing, or if the application should end. If it decides that the user should be asked for another application filename, it presents a message box consisting of a Yes and a No button. Clicking Yes results in a value of True being passed to the calling code, a Resume statement to be processed, and the input box to be redisplayed to our user. If the No button is clicked, a False value is returned to the calling code, a Resume Next statement is processed, and the operation is cancelled.

As you review the error-handling code, you'll notice that the Resume Next and Resume statements only appear in procedures containing the On Error statement. If these statements are placed in a procedure without the On Error statement, an error will always result. This is why some error-handling code has to appear in the calling procedure.

When Errors Occur in Error-Handling Routines

It is quite possible to experience an error in an error handler. When this occurs in centralized error-handling routines and in error handlers that are called, the error is passed back up to the calling procedure, which gives the calling procedure a chance to deal with the error. If the procedure doesn't have an error handler to deal with the error, the application displays a message and quits.

This is similar to what occurs when an error handler isn't called, but it is part of a procedure. When there is no calling procedure, the application displays a message and ends.

There are two ways of dealing with errors that occur in error handlers. The first is inane, while the second is highly recommended. It is possible for your error handler to invoke another procedure that contains error handling. This means that you could create an error handler for your error handler. If you were worried about this error handler experiencing problems, you could invoke another error handler to deal with that. This could go on until one of two things happen: you get fired for writing so much redundant code or your boss ships you off for a brief stay at the Betty Ford Clinic.

The second way to deal with errors in error handlers is straightforward: be careful. It is important to keep error-handling routines simple and to spend time visually checking the error handler for possible mistakes. The more redundant, unnecessary, and elaborate your code is, the greater the possibility of runtime errors. Remember that this code deals with errors, and as such can mask the fact that errors are occurring. By taking the time to visually check and test your error-handling routines, you will avoid errors from cropping up in them.

CERTIFICATION OBJECTIVE 12.03

Deploying Application Updates for Distributed Applications

If you think updates aren't important, remember that you're working with version 6.0 of Visual Basic. As you work with your creation, new features may pop into your mind and nasty bugs may appear in your application. When this happens, it's time to deploy an update of your program.

Deploying an update is the act of transferring an updated application to distribution media, such as floppy disks, folders, or a Web site. It is almost identical to deploying a full application, except for certain differences that need to be kept in mind.

Before you can deploy an application, you must first package it. Here is where some real differences between updates and full applications come into play. Remember that when the end user installs the update, any files included with a package overwrite those from a previous version. This can cause serious problems if your application uses a database file. Let's say your application uses an Access database, which you included with your full installation. By including a blank database with your update, this empty file will overwrite the database that the end user already has on his or her drive. This means any information the user has been storing in the file will be lost when the upgrade is installed.

Differences between packaging an update and a full application first appear in the Package and Deployment Wizard's DAO driver screen. This screen only appears when you are packaging applications that access data, as in our previous example of an application that uses an Access database. If your application doesn't use such files, you won't see this screen.

The DAO driver screen, shown in Figure 12-5, allows you to choose which Data Access Object drivers to include with the package. If you are packaging an update for an application recently created with Visual Basic 6.0, you probably won't need to include any of the files listed. However, if you are releasing an update for an application created with a previous version of Visual Basic, or an update for a full install that used older drivers, you will need to select which drivers to include with your update. If you're unsure which drivers are newer than the full install, select all that appear on this screen to be included with your update.

The Included Files screen, shown in Figure 12-6, is also used for packaging application updates. This screen allows you to select additional files to add to the package. If your application calls other executables or uses

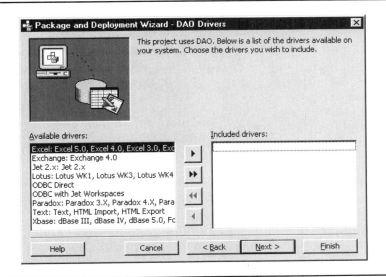

FIGURE 12-5

DAO Drivers screen of the Package and Deployment Wizard

FIGURE 12-6

Included Files Screen of the
Package and Deployment
Wizard

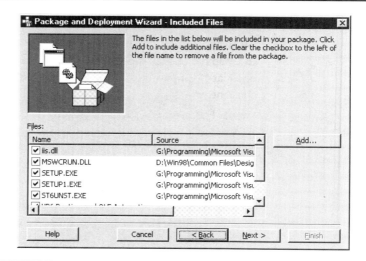

database files, this is where they are added to a package. Also listed here are
files that are installed into the Windows System directory. As mentioned,
you should add only the files you want to replace in the full installation
package of your application. Remember that you're creating an update
package, not a full installation, so you should include only files that have
been updated or are newer than those in the full installation package.

The remaining screens are identical to what was covered in Chapter 11,
in which we packaged and deployed a full installation of a program. When
you reach the Start Menu Items and Install Locations screens, you should
use the same locations that were used for the full installation of your
application. Doing so will result in a warning, informing you that this will
overwrite previous installations. However, because this is the purpose of
deploying an application update, this warning is nothing to be concerned
about. If anything, it lets you know that you've done your job of packaging
an application update correctly.

Packaging an Application Update

Note: This exercise assumes that you have already completed the exercise in Chapter 11 that deals with packaging and deploying a full version of an application. If you haven't completed that exercise, do so before starting this one.

1. From the Visual Basic folder in your Start menu, open the Package and Deployment Wizard. In Select Project, enter the path and filename of the project you created and distributed as a full installation in Chapter 11. Click the Package button, and then choose Compile.

2. When the wizard appears, select Standard Setup Package, and then click Next. A screen will appear that allows you to determine where the Package will be created. Accept the default and click Next. A message box may appear, asking if you want it to create a folder that it can work in or choose another folder. Accept this, so it can create the working folder.

3. The application we created and packaged in Chapter 11 was a database package, so the next screen we see is the DAO Drivers screen. Because we are packaging a recent update of a Visual Basic 6.0 application, these files have already been included with the full installation. As such, we don't need to include any of them with the update. Click Next to continue.

4. The Included Files screen allows you to choose which files to include with your package. Our application is a recent update, so we can deselect all of the Windows system files listed. Because the end user already has an existing database file, there is no need to include it with our package.

5. The next screen allows you to determine whether the application should be packaged as multiple CAB files (which are used for floppy distribution) or a single CAB file (which is best for network and Internet deployment). Select Single CAB and click Next to continue.

6. Accept the defaults for the following screens. You can either click Next for the remaining screens or click Finish.

Now that you've packaged your update, you're ready to deploy it with the Package and Deployment Wizard. To deploy the package, click Deploy on the main screen. When the wizard loads, the first screen you'll see contains a list of scripts for packages that were previously created. Click Next to accept the default entry in this list and go to the Deployment method screen.

Depending on the number of CAB files you created in the Package portion, the deployment methods available to you will vary. If you selected Multiple CABs during the package portion, you will be given the options of Floppy Disk, Folder, and Web Publishing. If you packaged to a single CAB file, you are given the options of Folder and Web Publishing. This is packaging to a single CAB file that won't fit on a floppy disk. The deployment method you choose here will determine which screens are viewed when clicking Next.

If you packaged to multiple CAB files and selected Floppy Disk, the next screen gives you the option of choosing which floppy drive the wizard is to deploy to. If you only have one drive installed on your machine, the drop-down box on this screen gives the impression that you still have a choice, but will contain only one entry. To ensure that floppies are formatted before files are copied to them, you should check the "Format before copying" check box. This will keep the wizard from failing if it encounters an unformatted disk, or one that already contains data. You must have formatted, blank floppies for this deployment to work.

If you selected Folder as your deployment method, the next screen allows you to choose a local or network folder to deploy to. On this screen, you can type the full path of a folder, or select a drive and folder through the Drive and Directory boxes. If you'd like to deploy to a new folder, clicking the New Folder button allows you to enter the name of your new directory. The Network button can be used for deploying your application update to a network folder. This brings up a Browse for Folder dialog box that looks and functions like the Windows Network Neighborhood. If you have proper permissions, you can browse your network and select a folder that is located on a server or workstation.

If you selected Web Publishing as your deployment method, the next screen displays a list of files included in the package. Unchecking a check box beside a filename means that the file won't be deployed. Clicking Next from this screen brings up "Additional Items to Deploy." As its name suggests, here you can choose additional files or folders to deploy with your package. Clicking Next brings you to the Web Publishing Site screen, which requires you to enter a valid URL. To publish to this site, you must have valid permissions on the Web server you enter here.

After working through the screens of the respective deployment methods, you must click Finish to start deploying your application update. If you decide not to deploy at the present time, you can click Cancel at any time. Once Finish has been clicked, though, the wizard begins deployment based on the settings you choose for that session.

EXERCISE 12-3

Deploying a Distributed Application Update

1. From the Package and Deployment Wizard's main screen, click Deploy.

2. Accept the default entry on the Package to Deploy screen and click Next.

3. From the Deployment Method screen, select Folder. Click Next.

4. Click the Network button. When the Browse for Folder dialog box appears, browse through your network until you find the folder you wish to deploy to. You must be connected to a network and have proper permissions to the folder for this to work. Click Next.

5. Click Finish and your application update is deployed to the Network folder.

CERTIFICATION SUMMARY

Load balancing involves spreading tasks across multiple processors on a computer. By setting a project to use single threading or apartment-model threading, you can set an application to use a single thread or multiple threads. Using apartment-model threading allows you to spread tasks across processors.

There are three types of errors you'll encounter in programming: logic, syntax, and runtime. Logic errors are dealt with by testing your program and then fixing any errors encountered. Syntax errors result from improperly using the Visual Basic language. Using the features available in Visual Basic 6.0, and then correcting errors that VB 6.0 brings to your attention can catch syntax errors. Runtime errors need to be trapped and dealt with by error-handling routines. To implement error handling, you should be familiar with the settings for Error Trapping available in Visual Basic 6.0, know how to trap errors, and be able to write code that deals with errors.

Package and Deployment Wizard is used to package and deploy application updates. The Package portion allows you to set the files that will be included with an update package. The Deploy portion allows you to determine how and where a package will be deployed.

TWO-MINUTE DRILL

- ❑ *Load balancing* involves techniques that spread tasks among processors.

- ❑ When a program is loaded into memory and prepared for execution, it's called a *process*.

- ❑ In Win16 programs (Windows 3x and Windows for Workgroups), applications used a single thread, while Win32 (Windows 9x and Windows NT) allowed applications to use more than one thread.

- ❑ Using multiple threads on multiple processors can dramatically improve the performance of an application, but it can actually decrease performance on a computer with a single processor.

- ❑ Visual Basic 6.0 comes with a syntax error-checking feature, which allows syntax errors to be caught as you mistype them.

- ❑ You can enable an error trap with the On Error statement, which establishes error handling in your code.

- ❑ The Err object is used to determine what error has occurred, the source application that caused the error, and provides a brief description of the error encountered.

- ❑ When creating error handlers, it is important to use the Err object to determine which error has occurred, and then use conditional execution to deal with the error based on the value of Err.Number.

❑ It is important to keep error-handling routines simple and to spend time visually checking the error handler for possible mistakes.

❑ Deploying an update is the act of transferring an updated application to distribution media, such as floppy disks, folders, or a Web site.

❑ If you selected Multiple CABs during the package portion, you will be given the options of Floppy Disk, Folder, and Web Publishing. If you packaged to a single CAB file, you are given the options of Folder and Web Publishing.

SELF TEST

1. Which of the following is a program that can be loaded into memory and prepared for execution?

   A. Thread

   B. Process

   C. Apartment

   D. Task

2. Which of the following must not be provided in a Visual Basic 6.0 project if apartment-model threading is to be used?

   A. UserControls

   B. UserDocuments

   C. Forms

   D. ActiveX Designers

   E. None of the above

3. Which of the following has its threads furnished and managed by client applications?

   A. In-process server

   B. Out-of-process server

   C. Standard EXE

   D. ActiveX EXE

4. How do you specify whether an ActiveX EXE is single threaded or apartment threaded? (Choose all that apply.)

   A. In the Threading Model section of the General tab of Project Properties, increase the Threading Pool to a value greater than one

   B. In the Threading Model section of the General tab of Project Properties, use the Thread per Object option

   C. In the Threading Model section of the General tab of the Project Properties dialog box, specify in the list box whether the project is "Single Threaded" or "Apartment Threaded"

   D. In the Threading Model section of the General tab of Project Properties, set the Threading Pool to a value of 1

5. You want to create a hyperlink that connects to http://www.odyssey.on.ca/~mcross. You are tired when you enter the URL and mistakenly enter Microsoft's Web site, http://www.microsoft.com. What kind of error has occurred?

   A. Logic

   B. Runtime

   C. Syntax

   D. Internet

6. A user attempts to save a file to his floppy drive, but forgets to insert a floppy disk. What kind of error will result?

   A. Logic

   B. Hardware

   C. Syntax

   D. Runtime

7. During the Package portion of using Package and Deployment Wizard, you chose to package your application to a single CAB file. When you deploy this application, which of the following deployment methods will be available to you? (Choose all that apply.)

   A. Floppy Disk

   B. Network

   C. Folder

   D. Web Publishing

8. You have decided to deploy your application to floppy disks, but you're not certain whether data exists on the floppies you're using for the deployment. What can you do?

   A. Do nothing because any existing data is automatically erased

   B. Do nothing because floppies are always formatted before the copying of files

   C. Check the Format before copying check box in the Deploy portion of Package and Deployment Wizard

   D. Check the Format before copying check box in the Package portion of Package and Deployment Wizard.

9. Which of the following can cause an error to occur in an application?

   A. Err

   B. Err.Number

C. Err.Raise

D. Err.Call

10. Which of the following thread models has each thread containing its own copy of global data?

   A. Win16 threading

   B. Win32 threading

   C. Single threading

   D. Apartment-model threading

11. What kind of error does the following line of code produce?
```
Dam x As Integer
```

   A. Logic

   B. Syntax

   C. Runtime

   D. Booboo

12. Which of the following specifies that a component can run without user interaction on network servers?

   A. Unattended ActiveX

   B. ActiveX Enable

   C. Unattended Execution

   D. Suppress User Interface

13. A procedure with error handling calls another error-handling procedure, which experiences an error. What will happen?

   A. The error will be passed to the calling procedure, which can then deal with the error

   B. An error message will be displayed and the application will quit

C. An error message will be displayed and the error will be passed to the calling procedure

D. The error handler that experiences the error will deal with its own error

14. A procedure without error handling calls an error-handling procedure. The error-handling procedure experiences an error. What will happen?

A. The error will be passed to the calling procedure, which can then deal with the error

B. An error message will be displayed and the application will quit

C. An error message will be displayed and the error will be passed to the calling procedure

D. The error handler that experiences the error will deal with its own error

15. An error handler that is part of a procedure experiences an error. It hasn't been called by any other procedure. What will happen?

A. The error will be passed to another procedure, which can then deal with the error

B. An error message will be displayed and the application will quit

C. An error message will be displayed and the error will be passed to a procedure that has error handling

D. The error handler that experiences the error will deal with its own error

16. You have implemented inline error handling in a procedure. What will reset the Number property of the Err object to 0? (Choose all that apply.)

A. Resume

B. Resume Next

C. Err.Clear

D. On Error GoTo 0

17. Procedure 1 calls Procedure 2. Procedure 1 has an error-handling routine. Procedure 2 experiences an error, but has no error handling. What will happen?

A. An error message will result and the application will quit

B. Procedure 2 will attempt to deal with the error

C. The error will be passed to Procedure 1, which will try dealing with the error

D. Procedure 2 will automatically fail and execution will return to Procedure 1

18. You set Error Trapping to Break in Class Module. An error occurs outside of the class module. What will happen?

A. Visual Basic will break in the class module

B. Visual Basic will break where the unhandled error occurs

C. Visual Basic will ignore the error until it has been set to a different Error Trapping option

D. Visual Basic will display an error message and end the program

19. You have implemented error handling and want to see whether your routine works properly. What will you set Error Trapping to, to determine that all errors are handled?

    A. Break in Class Module

    B. Break on All Errors

    C. Break on Handled Errors

    D. Break on Unhandled Errors

20. How do you specify whether an ActiveX DLL is single threaded or apartment threaded?

    A. In the Threading Model section of the General tab of Project Properties, increase the Threading Pool to a value greater than 1

    B. In the Threading Model section of the General tab of Project Properties, use the Thread per Object option

    C. In the Threading Model section of the General tab of Project Properties, specify in the list box whether the project is Single Threaded or Apartment Threaded

    D. ActiveX DLLs can only be single threaded

    E. ActiveX DLLs can only be apartment-threaded

21. During the Package portion of using the Package and Deployment Wizard, you chose to package your application to multiple cab files. When you deploy this application, which of the following deployment methods will be available to you? (Choose all that apply.)

    A. Floppy Disk

    B. Network

    C. Folder

    D. Web Publishing

22. Which property of the Err object is used to determine which application has caused an error?

    A. Number

    B. Source

    C. Application

    D. App

23. Which of the following is used to disable an error trap?

    A. Err.Clear

    B. Resume

    C. Err.Disable

    D. On Error GoTo 0

    E. On Error Clear

24. Which of the following are valid uses of the Resume statement? (Choose all that apply.)

    A. Resume

    B. Resume Next

    C. Resume Previous

    D. Resume *line*

    E. Resume *label*

25. You have implemented error handling to determine whether any errors exist in your code. To do this, all error-handling routines will have to be ignored. What will you set Error Trapping to?

    A. Break in Class Module

    B. Break on All Errors

C. Break on Handled Errors

D. Break on Unhandled Errors

26. Look at the following message box that displays when an error occurs. What does this tell you about the program?

A. The project hasn't been compiled

B. The project has been compiled

C. The project contains no objects

D. The project has experienced a logic error

27. The value of the Err object's Number property is 0. What does this signify?

A. A critical error has occurred

B. A fatal error has occurred

C. A nasty error has occurred

D. No error has occurred

28. Which of the following are valid labels for an error handler?

A. Err

B. MyError:

C. OnError

D. ThisIsAHandler

29. Which of the following provides a means for a procedure to exit when no error occurs?

A. End Sub

B. Exit Sub

C. Exit When Err=0

D. Exit ErrorHandler

30. How do you specify whether an ActiveX control is single threaded or apartment threaded?

A. In the Threading Model section of the General tab of Project Properties, increase the Threading Pool to a value greater than 1

B. In the Threading Model section of the General tab of Project Properties, use the Thread per Object option

C. In the Threading Model section of the General tab of Project Properties, specify in the list box whether the control is Single Threaded or Apartment Threaded

D. ActiveX controls can only be single threaded

E. ActiveX controls can only be apartment threaded

31. A procedure experiences an error, but its error handler deals with it. This procedure then calls another procedure, which then experiences and deals with the same error. What is most likely the reason for this?

A. On Error Resume Next wasn't implemented

B. Exit Sub wasn't used

C. The Number property of Err wasn't reset

D. The value of Err.Number was mistakenly set to 0

32. You are creating an ActiveX client application. What Error Trapping option should you choose?

    A. Break on All Errors
    B. Break on Unhandled Errors
    C. Break in Class Module
    D. Break in ActiveX server

33. You are working on a program that hasn't been compiled. When you run the project, an error message appears, notifying you of a runtime error. Four buttons appear on this message box. Which will you click to take you to the line of code that caused the error?

    A. Continue
    B. Break
    C. Debug
    D. End

34. You have created a procedure that adds sales tax to an amount, but instead of adding sales tax, you find that it is subtracting it. What kind of error has occurred?

    A. Syntax
    B. Logic
    C. Runtime
    D. Governmental

35. Which of the following features in Visual Basic 6.0 can aid in preventing syntax errors or catch them as they occur? (Choose all that apply.)

    A. Auto List Members
    B. Spell Check
    C. Auto Syntax Check
    D. Syntax Checker

36. How can logic errors be found and corrected in a Visual Basic application?

    A. Setting Auto Logic Check on the General tab of Options
    B. Testing the application, discovering the errors, and correcting the code
    C. Having others tell you they've discovered a logic error
    D. Using the Logic Check tool that comes with Visual Basic 6.0

37. An unhandled error occurs in a class module. Which of the following Error Trapping options will break at the line that calls code in the class module? (Choose all that apply.)

    A. Break on All Errors
    B. Break on Handled Errors
    C. Break in Class Module
    D. Break on Unhandled Errors

38. Which of the following will establish error handling in your code? (Choose all that apply.)

    A. On Error GoTo ErrorHandler
    B. On Error Resume Next
    C. On Error GoTo 0
    D. On Error Resume

39. Checking the Unattended Execution check box on the General tab of Project Properties will do which of the following to a project?

    A. Enable the Threading Pool so you can specify a fixed number of threads used by the project

    B. Enable the Thread per Object option

    C. Enable the Threading Model

    D. Suppress anything in the project that requires user interaction

40. Which of the following has the capability to use apartment-model threading? (Choose all that apply.)

    A. Visual Basic 5.0 Service Pack 2 Enterprise Edition

    B. Visual Basic 6.0 Standard Edition

    C. Visual Basic 6.0 Professional Edition

    D. Visual Basic 6.0 Enterprise Edition

Object
Reference

The following is a listing of controls, objects, and collections available in Visual Basic 6.0. For your convenience, it has been split into three sections: Controls, Data Report Designer, and Objects and Collections. Each entry includes an example of syntax (where applicable) and a description for each object, collection, and control. The way to read this listing is (when applicable) shown in the following example:

Object	Syntax (where applicable)	Description

Due to the number of objects, collections, and controls in VB, it is impossible to show the properties, methods, and events for every entry. For further information on properties, methods, and events of a control, object, or collection, refer to the Language Reference in VB's Help.

Controls

Object	Syntax	Description
ADO Data Control		Allows connection to a database, using ADO.
Animation		Allows you to create buttons that display animation files when clicked.
CheckBox	CheckBox	Used for selecting a single item or option that isn't related to other items. This control displays an X when selected.
ComboBox	ComboBox	Control with the combined features of a Textbox and ListBox control.
CommandButton	CommandButton	Appears as a push button on a form, and is used to begin, end, or interrupt processes.
CommonDialog	CommonDialog	Set of dialog boxes for common uses, such as opening, saving, printing, and so on.
CoolBar	CoolBar	Uses the Bands Collection to create toolbars that are configurable and similar to those found in Internet Explorer.
Data Control	Data	Allows access to databases using Recordset objects.
DataCombo	DataCombo	This is a data-bound combo box, which is automatically populated by a data source field.

Object	Syntax	Description
DataGrid	DataGrid	Displays a series of rows and columns that can be manipulated. These rows and columns represent the records and fields from a recordset.
DataList	DataList	This is a data-bound list box, which is automatically populated by a data source field.
DataRepeater	DataRepeater	Container that allows you to scroll through other data-bound controls.
DateTimePicker	DTPicker	Provides a drop-down calendar and a formatted time/date field.
DBCombo	DBCombo	Data-bound combo box. Combined features of a text box and list box that is populated with a field from a Data control.
DBList	DBList	Data-bound list box. List box that is populated with a field from a Data control.
DirListBox	DirListBox	Used to display directories and paths that the user can access at runtime.
DriveListBox	DriveListBox	Used to display drives that are currently available at runtime
FileListBox	FileListBox	Used to list files in a directory during runtime.
FlatScrollBar	FlatScrollBar	Two-dimensional scrollbar.
Frame	Frame	Used to group controls, such as option buttons, into a related grouping.
HscrollBar	HScrollBar	Used to add horizontal scroll bars.
Image	Image	Used to display graphics. This control uses fewer system resources than the PictureBox control.
ImageCombo	ImageCombo	Picture-enabled version of a combo box, which allows list items to have graphics associated with them.
ImageList	ImageList	Used as a repository for graphics, which can then be assigned to other controls.
Label	Label	Used to display text that is not changeable by the user. Often used to relate information to a user about another control's purpose.
Line	Line	Used to add horizontal, vertical, and diagonal lines to a form.

Object	Syntax	Description
ListBox	Listbox	Contains a listing of items from which the user can select.
ListView	ListView	Used to display items. Four different views of items are available with this control.
MAPIMessages	MAPIMessages	Creates mail-enabled MAPI applications.
MAPISession	MAPISession	Used to establish a MAPI session.
Masked Edit		A masked edit control acts like a text box with masked input and formatted output capabilities.
Menu	Menu	Used to display custom menus.
Microsoft Internet Transfer Control		Allows you to implement HTTP and FTP protocols into an application.
MonthView	MonthView	Calendar interface for setting date information.
MSChart	MSChart	Used to create a chart.
MSComm	MSComm	Allows you to implement serial communications into an application.
MSFlexGrid	MSFlexGrid	Displays read-only data in a grid format.
MSHFlexGrid	MSHFlexGrid	Displays read-only data in a grid format. It is used to display data in a hierarchical fashion.
Multimedia MCI Control		Media control interface that allows recording and playback of multimedia files.
OLE Container		Allows you to insert objects that will appear on your form. These can be linked objects, objects that are inserted and displayed at runtime, or objects that bind the control to a Data control.
OptionButton	OptionButton	Used to turn options on or off. Generally used in groups for related options in which only one can be on or off.
PictureBox	PictureBox	Used to display graphic images. If the control isn't large enough to show the entire image, it will clip the image.
PictureClip		Allows you to crop or clip an area of a bitmapped image and display the cropped image in forms or picture boxes.

Object	Syntax	Description
ProgressBar	ProgressBar	Shows the progress of a task by filling in a bar with colored chucks.
RichTextBox	RichTextBox	TextBox-type control with advanced formatting options. With this control, you can enter, access, and edit text.
Shape	Shape	Graphical control that can be displayed as a rectangle, square, oval, circle, rounded rectangle, or rounded square.
SSTab	SSTab	This control provides tabs that are similar to those seen in VB's Options. Each tab can contain other controls, and only one tab can be active at a time.
StatusBar	StatusBar	Bar divided up with up to 16 Panel objects. Used to display status information, date/time information, and so on in panels contained in the StatusBar.
SysInfo	SysInfo	Used to respond to system messages.
TabStrip	TabStrip	This control provides tabs that are similar to those seen in VB's Options. Each tab can contain other controls, and only one tab can be active at a time.
TextBox	TextBox	Allows users to enter, edit, and delete text at runtime, through a field. Text can also be entered at Design time through the control's Text property.
Timer	Timer	Allows execution of code to occur at regular time intervals.
Toolbar	Toolbar	This object contains the Button objects that make up a toolbar. Clicking on the Button object will execute code associated with it.
TreeView	TreeView	Allows viewing information of a hierarchical tree format. This format is similar to that seen in Windows Explorer.
UpDown	UpDown	Used with a "buddy" control, the UpDown control has a pair of arrows used to increment and decrement values. The values affected are in the buddy control.
VScrollBar	VScrollBar	Used to add vertical scroll bar.

Data Report Designer

The following list of controls, objects and collections deals specifically with the Data Report Designer. They are listed in their own section to avoid confusion with other objects, collections and controls in VB, which have similar or identical names.

Object	Syntax	Description
DataReport	DataReport	Represents the Data Report Designer.
Error	RptError	Used to return details on runtime errors.
Function Control	rptFunction	Used to display calculations using built-in functions at runtime.
Image Control	rptImage	Used to display graphics.
Label Control	rptLabel	Used to display text that is not changeable by the user.
Section	Section	Used to represent a section of Data Report Designer.
Sections Collection	Sections	Collection of section objects.
Shape Control	Shape	Graphical control that can be displayed as a rectangle, square, oval, circle, rounded rectangle, or rounded square.
TextBox Control	rptTextBox	Used to display text from a database at runtime. This control is data-bound.

Objects and Collections

Object	Syntax	Description
AddIn	AddIn	This object returns information about an add-in to other add-ins. One such object is created for every add-in listed in Vbaddin.ini.
AddIns Collection	AddIns	Accessed through the VBE object, this returns a collection of add-ins that are listed in the Vbaddin.ini.

Object	Syntax	Description
AmbientProperties		Allows access to ambient properties of a container object.
App	App	Allows you to access information about the application, such as its name, title, path, and so on.
AsyncProperty		Contains the results of AsyncRead methods, and is passed to the AsyncReadComplete event.
Axis	Axis	This object is used to represent the axis on a chart.
AxisGrid	AxisGrid	Object used to represent the area surrounding the axis on a chart.
AxisScale	AxisScale	Object used to set how chart values are placed on the axis of a chart.
AxisTitle	AxisTitle	Object used to represent the title of an axis on a chart.
Backdrop	Backdrop	Object used to represent shadows or patterns that appear behind items on a chart.
Band		Represents one band in the Bands collection.
Bands Collection	*object*.Bands.Count *object*.Bands(Index)	Collection that represents bands on the CoolBar control. Each band is a region that can contain a caption, image, and child control.
Binding	Binding	Part of the Binding collection. This object represents the binding of a property of a data consumer to a data source field.
Binding Collection	BindingCollection	Made up of Binding objects, this allows you to bind a data consumer to a data provider.
Brush	Brush	Used to specify the fill type of an element on a chart.
Button		Represents a single button on a toolbar.
ButtonMenu	ButtonMenu	Represents a menu that drops down from a button object on a toolbar.

Object	Syntax	Description
ButtonMenus Collection	ButtonMenus	Used to represent a collection of ButtonMenu objects.
Buttons Collection	*toolbar*.Buttons(Index) *toolbar*.Buttons.Item(Index)	Collection of Button objects which are accessed by their index number (which start at 1, rather than 0).
CategoryScale	CategoryScale	Used to represent the scale of a category axis.
Clipboard	Clipboard	Used to access the Windows Clipboard.
CodeModule	CodeModule	Represents the code of a component.
CodePane		Represents a code pane; can be used to manipulate text residing in the code pane.
CodePanes Collection		A collection of CodePane objects, which contains all active code panes in the VBE object.
Collection	Collection Dim *collection name* As New Collection	Used to organize related items into a collection, so it can then be referred to as one object.
Column		Part of the Columns collection, this object is used to represent a column in the DataGrid control.
ColumnHeader		Part of the ColumnHeaders collection, this object contains heading text of the ListView control.
ColumnHeaders Collection	*listview*.ColumnHeaders *listview*.ColumnHeaders(Index)	Collection used to hold ColumnHeader objects, which contain the heading text of the ListView control.
Columns Collection	Columns.Item Columns.Item(Index)	Contains Column objects, which are used to represent a column in the DataGrid control.
ComboItem	*object*.ComboItem	Contains list items of the ImageCombo control. This object can contain and display text or image items.
ComboItems Collection	*object*.ComboItems(Index)	The collection contains ComboItem objects, which contain items in the list portion of the ImageCombo control.

Object	Syntax	Description
CommandBar	CommandBar	Object that can contain other Commandbar objects, which act as button or menu commands.
CommandBarEvents		An event is triggered by this object when the command bar is clicked.
CommandBar Collections		Collection that contains all Commandbar objects in a project.
ContainedControls Collection	ContainedControls(Index)	Collection for accessing controls that are contained within other controls.
ContainedVBControls Collection		Collection that represents VBControl objects.
Control	Control Dim x As Control	The control object is the class name for internal controls in VB.
Controls Collection	*object*.Controls(Index) *object*.Controls.Count	Elements accessed by the Index represent controls in a component.
Coor	Coor	Used in charts, it defines the floating x and y coordinate pair.
DataBinding	DataBinding	There is a Databinding object for each property of a component that is Bindable. This allows you to bind a property to a database.
DataBindings Collection		Collects and makes available all bindable properties.
DataGrid	DataGrid	A series of rows and columns that represent a virtual matrix; it contains the data points and labels for MSChart control.
DataMembers Collection	DataMembers	Collection made up of data members for a data source.
DataObject	DataObject	Contains data being transferred to and from a component source to a component target.
DataObject (ActiveX)	DataObject	A data container for transferring data from a component source to a component target.

Object	Syntax	Description
DataObjectFiles Collection	*object*.DataObjectFiles	A collection of strings containing the property for the files type of DataObject.
DataObjectFiles Collection (ActiveX)	*object*.DataObjectFiles(Index)	Represents all filenames used by the DataObject.
DataPoint	DataPoint	Used to describe attributes of a single data point on a chart.
DataPointLabel	DataPointLabel	Contains the label for a data point on a chart.
DataPoints Collection	*object*.DataPoints(Index)	Collection of data points for a chart.
DEAggregate	DEAggregate	Used to define an aggregate field in DECommand.
DEAggregates Collection	DEAggregate(Index)	Collection of DEAggregate objects.
Debug	Debug	Used to send output to the Immediate window during a debugging session.
DECommand	DECommand	Contains Design time properties of ADO Command objects.
DECommands Collection	DECommands(Index)	Elements accessed through the index represent each DECommand object in the DataEnvironment.
DEConnection	DEConnection	Contains Design time properties of ADO Connection objects.
DEConnections Collection	DEConnections(Index)	Elements accessed through the index represent each DEConnection object in the DataEnvironment.
DEExtDesigner	DEExtDesigner	Top-level container of the Data Environment and provides a container for related DEConnection and DECommand objects.
DEField	DEField	Contains Design time properties of ADO Field objects.
DEFields Collection	DEFields(Index)	Elements accessed through the index represent each DEField object in the DECommand.

Object	Syntax	Description
DEGroupingFields Collection	DEGroupingFields(Index)	Elements accessed through the index represent each DEGroupingField object in the DECommand.
DEParameter	DEParameter	Contains Design time properties of ADO Parameter objects.
DEParameters Collection	DEParameters(Index)	Elements accessed through the index represent each DEParameter object in the DECommand.
DERelationCondition	DERelationCondition	In a relation hierarchy, this object defines relation conditions between parent and child Command objects.
DERelationConditions	DERelationConditions(Index) DERelationConditions.Count	Elements accessed through the index represent each DERelationCondition object in the DECommand.
DHTMLPage	DHTMLPage	Connects events between VB runtime and Dynamic HTML (Hypertext Markup Language) object model.
DHTMLPageDesigner		Object that represents the DHTML Page Designer.
Dictionary	Scripting.Dictionary	Stores items of any data type, which are accessed with a unique key. Can contain data key, item pairs.
Drive		Used to access a drive or network share properties at runtime.
Drives Collection	Drives	Provides read-only information on all available drives, including floppy and CD-ROM.
Err	Err	Used to return information on runtime errors.
EventInfo	EventInfo	Controls assigned to VBControlExtender can raise event information, which is then contained in this object.
Events		Provides properties that return event source objects. These can notify you of changes in VB for Applications environment.

Object	Syntax	Description
EventParameter	EventParameter	Used to represent parameters of a control event.
ExportFormat	ExportFormat	Used to determine attributes of text that's exported from the Data Report.
ExportFormats Collection	ExportFormats	Collection of ExportFormat objects.
Extender	Extender	Contains properties of controls that are controlled by a container object.
File		Used to access file properties.
FileControlEvents	FileControlEvents	Represents VB events that support file control.
Files Collection	*object*.Files	Represents File objects in a folder.
FilesSystemObject	Scripting.FilesSystemObject	Used to access the file system of a computer.
Fill	Fill	Used to determine the backdrop of an object in a chart.
Folder		Used to access folder properties.
Folders Collection		Collection of Folder objects.
Font	Font	Contains information to format text.
Footnote	Footnote	Contains text that is displayed beneath a chart.
Form	Form	Interface on which other controls are placed. Form objects are windows in an application.
Forms	Forms(Index)	Represents loaded forms in an application.
Frame	Frame	Contains information about the frame surrounding a chart.
Global	Global	Enables access to global (application-level) properties and methods.
HyperLink		Used to jump to a URL or HTML document.

Object	Syntax	Description
IDTExtensibility Interface	Implements IDTExtensiblity	Used to manage add-ins, and contains methods and properties of connected add-ins.
Intersection	Intersection	The point where two axes cross on a chart.
Label	*axis*.Label	Used to describe a chart axis.
Labels Collection	*axis*.Labels(Index)	A group of axis labels for a chart, which are accessed through the Index of the Labels object.
LCoor	LCoor	Used for long integer y and x coordinate pairs.
Legend	Legend	Used for chart legends, which explain what elements of a chart represent.
LicenseInfo	LicenseInfo	Represents ProgID and license key of a control.
Licenses Collection	Licenses	Collection of LicenseInfo objects, which represent ProgID and license key information about a control. Required when adding licensed controls to a Controls collection.
Light	Light	Used to represent light source lighting up a 3D chart.
LightSource	LightSource	Used to represent light source lighting up items in a 3D chart.
LightSources Collection	*object*.LightSources(Index)	Collection of LightSource objects.
LinkedWindows Collection		Comprised of Window objects, this contains all of the linked windows in a linked window frame.
ListImage		Contains a bitmapped image for use in other controls.
ListImages Collection	*imagelist*.ListImages *imagelist*.ListImages(Index)	Grouping of ListImage objects.

Object	Syntax	Description
ListItem		Contains text, and an index of an icon (that is, a ListImage object).
ListItems Collection	*listview*.ListItems *listview*.ListItems(Index)	Collection of ListImage objects, containing text and an associated index of an icon (that is, a ListImage object).
ListSubItem	ListSubItem	Used to access a subitem in a ListView control. Can only be created at runtime, using the Add method.
ListSubItems Collection	ListSubItems	Collection of ListSubItem objects. Used to access a subitem in a ListView control. Can only be created at runtime, using the Add method.
Location	Location	Used to represent the position of text-based items (title, legend) on a chart.
Marker	Marker	Used to identify a data point on a chart.
MDIForm	MDIForm	A multiple document interface form is an interface that can contain child windows.
Member	Member	Represents the properties and attributes of members. Properties are code-based, while attributes are type library-based.
Members	Members	Collection of module-level code members.
Node		Refers to an item that contains text and image, in a treeview control.
Nodes Collection	*treeview*.Nodes *treeview*.Nodes(Index)	Elements accessed through the index represent each Node used in a treeview control.
OLEObject		Represents an object inserted in a RichTextBox control.
OLEObjects Collection	*object*.OLEObjects(Index) *object*.OLEObjects.Item(Index)	Collection of OLEObject objects. Elements accessed through the index represent each OLEObject.
Panel		Represents a single panel in a status bar.

Object	Syntax	Description
Panels Collection	*statusbar*.Panels(Index)	Collection of Panel objects. Elements accessed through the index represent each Panel object in a status bar.
ParentControls Collection	ParentControls(Index)	Used to access the controls contained in another control container. Elements accessed through the index represent each ParentControl.
Pen	Pen	Reference to pattern and color used in the lines or edges on a chart.
Picture	Picture	Allows you to manipulate graphics assigned to an objects Picture property.
Plot	Plot	Used as a representation of the area on which a chart resides.
PlotBase	PlotBase	Represents area beneath a chart.
Printer	Printer	Allows communication with a printer.
Printers Collection	Printers(Index)	Used to access information on available printers.
Properties Collection	Properties	Used to return control or collection properties.
Properties Collection (VBA Add-in Object Model)		Used to represent object properties.
Property		Used to represent object properties of objects visible in the Properties window.
PropertyBag		Contains information that needs to be saved and restored across invocations of an object.
PropertyPage		Object used to create ActiveX Property pages.
Rect	Rect	Used to define coordinate locations.
Reference		Used as a representation of a project or type library.

Object	Syntax	Description
References Collection		Collection of all Reference objects, representing sets of references in a project.
ReferencesEvent		When references are added and removed from projects, this object is a source of events, and it is returned by the ReferencesEvent property.
RepeaterBinding	RepeaterBinding	Represents a component's bindable property.
RepeaterBindings Collection		Using the RepeaterBindings property, you can return collection references.
Screen	Screen	This object refers to the entire Desktop in Windows, and allows you to manipulate forms based on their placement on the screen.
SelBookmarks Collection	SelBookmarks	For each row selected in the DataGrid control, a bookmark is contained in the SelBookmarks collection.
SelectedControls Collection	SelectedControls(Index)	Elements are referenced through the index, allowing access to each selected control on an object.
SelectedVBControls Collection	SelectedVBControls	Returns selected controls on a component.
SelectedVBControlsEvents	SelectedVBControlsEvents	Returns events supported by selected controls.
Series	Series	Used both as a representation of data points on a chart, and as an item in the SeriesCollection collection.
Series Collection	Series(Index)	Collection of chart series.
SeriesCollection Collection	SeriesCollection(Index)	Returns information on a series in the Series collection.
SeriesMarker	SeriesMarker	Used to describe markers that identify data points in a chart series.
SeriesPosition	SeriesPosition	Refers to the location of a chart series in relation to other series. If all series have the same position, they are stacked.

Object	Syntax	Description
Shadow	Shadow	Contains information on a shadow's appearance on a chart element.
Split		Used as a representation of a split in a DataGrid control.
Splits Collection	Splits(Index) Splits.Item(Index)	Collection of Split objects in a DataGrid.
StatLine	StatLine	Contains information on how a chart's statistic lines display.
StdDataFormat	StdDataFormat	Allows data formatting as data is read and written to a database.
StdDataFormats Collection		Collection containing StdDataFormat objects.
StdDataValue	StdDataValue	Used after StdDataFormat does formatting, this object returns and sets values.
Tab		A tab in the Tabs collection of the TabStrip.
Tabs Collection	*tabstrip*.Tabs(Index) *tabstrip*.Tabs.Item(Index)	Elements accessed through the index represent each Tab used in a TabStrip control.
TextLayout	TextLayout	Used as a representation of the positioning and orientation of text.
TextStream	TextStream.*property* TextStream.*method*	Enables application to have sequential access to a file.
Tick	Tick	This object is a marker that indicates division of an axis on a chart.
Title	Title	Used for the title text on a chart.
UserControl		Base object that's used for creating ActiveX controls.
UserDocument		Used like a Form object in creating ActiveX documents. Base object that's used for creating ActiveX documents.
ValueScale	ValueScale	Scale used to display a value axis in a chart.

Object	Syntax	Description
VBComponent		Used as a representation of a component (class or standard module) in a project.
VBComponents Collection		Collection of VBComponent objects. Represents the components used in a project.
VBComponentsEvents	VBComponentsEvents	Represents events occurring when objects are added, deleted, activated, renamed, or selected in a project.
VBControl	VBControl	Used as a representation of component controls.
VBControlExtender	VBControlExtender	Used when dynamically adding controls to Controls collection.
VBControls Collection	VBControls	Collection of all components on a form.
VBControlsEvents	VBControlsEvents	Represents source of events occurring when objects are added, deleted, activated, renamed, or selected in a project.
VBE		Root object in VB for Applications, under which all other objects and collections reside.
VBForm	VBForm	Used to return a component in a project.
VBNewProjects Collection		Represents all new projects.
VBProject		Represents a project.
VBProjects Collection		Represents all open projects.
VBProjectsEvents	VBProjectsEvents	Represents source of events occurring when objects are added, deleted, activated, or renamed in a project.
View3D	View3D	Used to represent a charts 3D orientation.
VtColor	VtColor	Represents a chart's drawing color.
VtFont	VtFont	Represents the font used in a chart's text.
Wall	Wall	Used in a 3D chart, this object represents the planar area that depicts the y axis.

Object	Syntax	Description
WebClass	WebClass	WebClass objects are part of an IIS application and reside on the Web server. They intercept HTTP requests so that appropriate VB code can be processed. WebItems contained in this object are then sent to the browser.
WebClassError	WebClassError	Returns what error occurred when processing a FatalErrorResponse event.
WebItem	WebItem	Represents Web items such as HTML documents.
WebItemProperties	WebItemProperties	Collection of user-defined properties. These are contained in this object, and are associated with particular WebItems.
Weighting	Weighting	Represents one pie's size in relation to another in a chart.
Window	Window	Represents a window.
Windows Collection		Collection containing all permanent or open windows.

MICROSOFT CERTIFIED SOLUTION DEVELOPER

A

Self Test
Answers

Chapter 1 Answers

1. You are attempting to install Microsoft Transaction Server on a Windows 98 machine, and receive the following message: "Setup library mtssetup.dll could not be loaded or the function MTSSetupProc could not be found." What is most likely the problem?

   A. Microsoft Transaction Server doesn't run on Windows 98 (you must use Windows 95.)

   B. Microsoft Transaction Server will only run on Windows NT Server 4.0 or higher.

   C. Microsoft Transaction Server will only run on Windows NT Workstation 4.0 or higher.

   D. DCOM hasn't been enabled on the computer.
   D. When you receive this message while attempting to install Microsoft Transaction Server on a Windows 9x machine, it indicates that you didn't enable Distributed COM before attempting the installation.

2. Which of the following is an attribute of a control or object that can be manipulated programmatically or through a window at Design time?

   A. Event

   B. Property

   C. Method

   D. Form
   B. A property is an attribute of a control or object. It can be manipulated programmatically or through a window at Design time.

3. Which of the following features of a transaction determines that if any of the processing steps in the transaction fail, the transaction is aborted, and the data is rolled back to its previous state?

   A. Acidity

   B. Atomicity

   C. Consistency

   D. Durability

   E. Integrity
   B. Atomicity ensures that either all of the steps in a transaction succeed, or nothing happens. If any of the processing steps in the transaction fail, the transaction is aborted, and the data is rolled back to its previous state.

4. Which of the following serves as a middle-tier platform for running components?

   A. MTS Explorer

   B. Application Programming Interfaces (APIs)

   C. Resource Dispensers

   D. MTS runtime environment
   D. The MTS runtime environment serves as the middle-tier platform for running components.

5. Which of the following is proper use of commenting code? (Choose all that apply.)

    A. Dim x As Integer REM My Comment

    B. Dim x As Integer 'My Comment

    C. REM My Comment

    D. 'My Comment
    B, C, D. REM can be used at the beginning of a line to comment code. An apostrophe (') can be used at the beginning or within a line to comment code.

6. You are attempting to install Visual Basic 6.0 on a Windows 98 machine that has 12 MB of memory. The installation fails. Why?

    A. Visual Basic 6.0 won't run on Windows 98 because you need Windows NT 4.0 or higher, or Windows 95.

    B. You require 32 MB of RAM.

    C. You require 16 MB of RAM.

    D. You require 16 GB of RAM.
    C. Visual Basic 6.0 requires 16 MB of RAM for Windows 95 or Windows 98. 32 MB of RAM is required for Windows NT Workstation.

7. You are using MTS Explorer on an NT Server 4.0 machine, and want to add a computer to the Computers folder. Which of the following methods will allow you to add a computer? (Choose all that apply.)

    A. Right-click the Computers folder, and then select New and Computer

    B. Select the Computers folder, and then click the Create new object icon in the right pane toolbar

    C. Select the Computers folder, open the Action menu in the left pane, and select New

    D. None of the above. There is no Computers folder in MTS Explorer.
    A, B, C. Each of these methods will work. D is incorrect because MTS Explorer is being used on an NT Server machine. Windows 9x installations don't have Computers folder.

8. You have decided to declare a variable that will contain a user's first name. Which of the following data types is the best to declare this variable as?

    A. Integer

    B. Variant

    C. String

    D. Text
    C. Although you could declare this variable as a variant, it would take more storage space than the better choice of string.

9. Which tier of the application model is associated with the user interface?

    A. User services

    B. Business services

    C. Data services

    D. Middle-tier services
    A. User services is associated with the user interface, which presents data to the end user.

10. You have declared a variable called intNum with the data type of integer. How will you assign a value of 13 to this variable?

    A. Dim intNum As Integer

    B. 13=intNum

    C. intNum=13

    D. Dim intNum As 13
       C. The way to assign a value of 13 to a variable called intNum is with the following code: intNum=13.

11. Which event is used to save information, unload forms, and perform any other tasks required when the class ends?

    A. Load

    B. Initialize

    C. Terminate

    D. End

    E. Unload
       C. Terminate is the event used to save information, unload forms, and do any other tasks required when the class ends.

12. Which of the following is used for managing and deploying components?

    A. VSS Explorer

    B. MTS Explorer

    C. VSS Admin utility

    D. MTS Admin utility
       B. MTS Explorer is used for managing and deploying components.

13. Which of the following can be used to assign values to a property? (Choose all that apply.)

    A. Dim

    B. Property Set

    C. Property Let

    D. Property Get
       B, C. Property Set and Property Let both assign values to a property. Property Get is used to return the value of a property; Dim is used to declare variables.

14. Which of the following keeps a record of changes made to your source code?

    A. Visual Studio

    B. Visual SourceSafe

    C. Microsoft Transaction Server

    D. Microsoft SourceCode
       B. Visual SourceSafe keeps a record of changes made to your source code.

15. You have exported a package and notice that a subdirectory named Clients has been created on your server computer. Inside this subdirectory, you find an executable. Executing it, you find that it has overwritten and removed settings from the Windows Registry for the server application you just exported. What must you do to restore these settings?

    A. Shut down MTS Explorer and restart it

    B. Shut down the package and restart it

C. Reinstall MTS on your server machine

D. Use Add/Remove Programs to remove the application, and then delete and reinstall the package in MTS Explorer
D. Using the client executable overwrites and removes settings for the server package from the Registry. As such, you must use Add/Remove Programs to remove the application, and then delete and reinstall the package in MTS Explorer.

16. You need to create a new account so a user can save changes to the source code of a database. What tool will you use to create the account?

A. VSS Explorer

B. MTS Explorer

C. VSS Admin utility

D. NT Admin utility
C. Accounts are created with Visual SourceSafe's (VSS) Admin utility.

17. You are installing the Enterprise Edition of Visual Basic 6.0. How much disk space is required for the full installation?

A. 48 MB

B. 80 MB

C. 128 MB

D. 147 MB
D. A full installation of Visual Basic 6.0 Enterprise Edition requires 147MB of free disk space.

18. Which of the following refers to concurrent transactions not being able to see another when they are running?

A. Atomicity

B. Concurrency

C. Consistency

D. Isolation

E. Durability
D. Isolation keeps concurrent transactions from seeing that other transactions are running. This keeps the other transactions from seeing the partial or uncommitted results of the other transactions.

19. You are using MTS Explorer and find that the Roles, Role Membership, and Users folders are missing. What is most likely the problem?

A. Installation of MTS has failed, so you must remove MTS and reinstall

B. You are using MTS on a Windows NT 4.0 machine

C. You are using MTS on a Windows 95 machine

D. You have Hide Roles selected on the View menu
C. You are using MTS on Windows 95. Because administration on this platform doesn't support security properties and roles, you won't be able to see the Roles, Role Membership, and Users folders in MTS Explorer.

Chapter 2 Answers

1. You specify CTRL-X as a shortcut key for a menu item called Exit. This menu item appears under the File menu. What effect will creating the shortcut key have on the menu?

    A. The x in Exit will be underlined.

    B. Exit will appear in bold.

    C. CTRL-X will appear beside the menu item.

    D. It will have no effect on the menu item.
    C. Specifying a shortcut key for a menu item will list the shortcut key next to the menu item.

2. You have added a menu item to your menu system. When naming this menu item, what prefix should you use?

    A. mnu

    B. menu

    C. m

    D. alt
    A. The standard prefix for menu items is mnu.

3. You have decided to have a large number of menu items with the same name. How can you do this?

    A. Use the Index field to set a value starting at zero, and going up to 32,768.

    B. Use the Index field to set a value starting at zero or one, and going up to 32,767.

    C. Use the Index field to set any value.

    D. You can't have different menu items with the same name.
    B. To have multiple menu items with the same name, use the Index field to set a value starting at zero or one, and going up to a value of 32,767.

4. Which of the following events are associated with a menu item?

    A. Click

    B. Dragdrop

    C. GotFocus

    D. KeyUp
    A. Menu items only have one event associated with them—Click.

5. What are the possible values of the Checked, Enabled, Visible, and WindowList properties?

    A. True

    B. False

    C. Checked

    D. Unchecked
    A, B. The Checked, Enabled, Visible, and WindowList properties have a Boolean value. This means it can only have a value of True or False.

6. What will the following line of code do?
    `Dim x As Integer`

    A. Declare a variable named x as an integer.

    B. Declare an array named x that contains integer elements.

    C. Create a runtime error.

D. None of the above.

A. Using the Dim keyword, this line of code declares a variable, called x, that is of the Integer data type.

7. Which of the following lines of code will load the first menu item in a menu control array?

A. mnuItem(0)

B. mnuItem()

C. mnuItem

D. Load mnuItem(0)

E. Load mnuItem(1)

D, E. A menu in a menu control array is loaded using the Load keyword. Because an array can start with either one or zero, both D and E are correct.

8. Of the properties associated with command buttons, which are the most commonly manipulated ones during runtime via code?

A. Caption

B. Name

C. Enabled

D. Text

A, C. Caption and Enabled are the most common properties manipulated at runtime. Name cannot be changed at runtime, while Text isn't a property associated with command buttons.

9. You have decided that you want information displayed in a text box to appear on several lines. Which property

will you set, and what value will you set the property to?

A. Set Text to True

B. Set Text to False

C. Set MultiLine to True

D. Set MultiLine to False

C. Setting MultiLine to True will allow text in a text box to appear over several lines, rather than on a single line.

10. You have configured a text box to display text over several lines. Unfortunately, some of the data is disappearing below the bottom of the text box. What will you configure to see data below the bottom of the text box, and how will you configure it?

A. Set ScrollBars to True.

B. Set ScrollBars to False.

C. Set ScrollBars property to either Vertical, Horizontal, or Both.

D. Nothing, it will always allow you to view all data contained.

C. Changing the ScrollBars property to Vertical, Horizontal, or Both will allow the user to scroll through all data contained in the text box.

11. You want to change what appears in a label at runtime. Which syntax will you use to change this value?

A. `label.Text = new text`

B. `label.Text = "new text"`

C. `label.Caption = "new caption"`

D. *label*.Caption = *new
caption*
C. The correct syntax to change what appears in a label at runtime is: *label*.Caption = "*new
caption*". Failing to enclose the new value in quotes will cause a runtime error, as VB will assume you want to place the contents of a variable in the Caption property (unless the new caption is a single word that happens to coincide with an existing variable).

12. You want to assign code that responds to a specific control event. Which window will you use?

   A. Project
   B. Code
   C. Event
   D. Object
   B. Code is assigned to an event procedure through the Code window.

13. You have added a CommonDialog control to a form, and want to use it to invoke a dialog box in which users can specify printer options. What syntax will you use to invoke such a dialog box?

   A. CommonDialog.ShowOpen
   B. CommonDialog.PrintOptions
   C. CommonDialog.ShowPrinter
   D. CommonDialog.ShowPrint
   C. To invoke a dialog box for printing and specifying printer options, use the syntax CommonDialog.ShowPrinter.

14. You want to add a custom control to a project. How will you add the control so it appears on the Toolbox from which you can then add it to a form?

   A. Select Components from the Project menu, then select the control from the list.
   B. Select Project Properties from the Project menu. Click the Components button, and select the control from the list.
   C. Select Components from the View menu, then select the control from the list.
   D. Select Components from the Add menu, then select the control from the list.
   A. Custom controls are added by selecting Components from the Project menu, then selecting the control from the list.

15. You want to add a control to a form that can act as a repository for images. You will then call the images you need for other controls through code. Which control will you add to act as a storehouse for graphics?

   A. GraphicList
   B. ImageList
   C. ListView
   D. Image
   B. The ImageList control acts as a repository for images, which can be called for use in other controls.

16. You have typed text into the Text property of a panel in the StatusBar control. When you run the application, this text doesn't appear in the status bar. Why?

   A. The Text property hasn't been set to sbrText.

   B. The Style property hasn't been set to sbrText.

   C. The text should have been typed in the Key property.

   D. The Alignment property hasn't been set.
   B. If the Style property hasn't been set to sbrText, any textual information typed in the Text property won't appear at runtime.

17. You have added a two command buttons named cmdAccess to a form, and given them Index numbers of zero and one, respectively. At runtime your code adds the following buttons to the array: cmdAccess(2), cmdAccess(3), and cmdAccess(4). Which of these will you be able to remove programmatically using the Unload statement?

   A. cmdAccess(2), cmdAccess(3), and cmdAccess(4)

   B. cmdAccess(2), cmdAccess(3), and cmdAccess(4)

   C. cmdAccess(3) and cmdAccess(4)

   D. cmdAccess(0), cmdAccess(1), cmdAccess(2), cmdAccess(3), and cmdAccess(4)
   B. You are only able to remove the controls you added to an array at runtime with the Unload statement. cmdAccess(0) and cmdAccess(1) were created in Design mode, and thereby can't be removed at runtime. Therefore, you can only remove cmdAccess(2), cmdAccess(3), and cmdAccess(4).

18. A text box is grayed out and doesn't accept any input. Why?

   A. The Enabled property is set to True.

   B. The Enabled property is set to False.

   C. The Disabled property has been set.

   D. The control has no code associated with it.
   B. When the Enabled property of a control is set to False, it will appear grayed out and won't accept any input.

19. Of the following Form events, which will be triggered first?

   A. Activate

   B. Load

   C. Initialize

   D. GotFocus
   C. Initialize is the first event triggered in a form. It is triggered when a Form is created in an application.

20. You want to add a control to a form that will display a list of items as icons. Which control will you add to a form?

   A. ImageList

   B. ListView

   C. Toolbar

D. Statusbar
B. ListView allows four different views for viewing items, including viewing them as small or large icons.

21. When can you set the DataSource of a data consumer in VB?

   A. Runtime

   B. Design mode

   C. Any time

   D. Never. It must be done in the database application
   C. You can set the DataSource at anytime—in Design mode or programmatically at runtime.

22. A VB project uses help files for displaying online assistance. How many of these files can a project point to and use at any given time?

   A. One

   B. Two

   C. Unlimited

   D. As many configured in Project Properties
   A. A project can only use one help file at a time.

23. A user attempts to invoke help for an object that has its HelpContextID set to zero. What help will be displayed to the user?

   A. Context-sensitive help for that control will be displayed.

   B. No help will be displayed.

   C. Help for the container or parent object will be displayed.

D. An error will result.
C. When the HelpContextID is set to zero, there is no context-sensitive help for that particular object. If a user attempts to access context-sensitive help for the object, then Help for the container or parent object will be displayed.

24. Which object can provide the error number, a description of the error, and the source of an error encountered?

   A. Err

   B. Error

   C. ErrNum

   D. ErrHandler
   A. The Err object has three important properties, which can provide the error number, a description of the error, and the source of an error encountered.

25. An error occurs on line 10 of a procedure, and the error is passed to an error-handling routine. Resume Next is used to return execution to the original procedure. Where will execution resume?

   A. 10

   B. 11

   C. Execution will resume in the next called procedure

   D. It will exit the procedure
   B. Resume Next will return execution to the line following the one that caused the error. In this case, it will resume on line 11.

26. An error occurs on line 10 of a procedure, and the error is passed to an error-handling routine. Resume is used to return execution to the original procedure. Where will execution resume?

    A. 10

    B. 11

    C. Execution will resume in the next called procedure

    D. It will exit the procedure
       A. Resume will return execution to the line that caused the error. In this case, it will resume on line 10.

27. An error occurs on line 10 of a procedure, and the error is passed to an error-handling routine. No Resume statement is used in the error handler. Where will execution resume?

    A. 10

    B. 11

    C. Execution will resume in the next called procedure

    D. It will exit the procedure
       D. If no Resume statement is used, the procedure will exit.

28. You want to implement error-handling code that will deal with an error on the line in which it occurs. Which of the following will cause a line that causes an error to be skipped, and execution to continue on the next line?

    A. On Err Resume Next

    B. On Error Resume Next

    C. On Err Resume

    D. On Error Resume
       B. On Error Resume Next will cause a line of code causing an error to be skipped, and execution to resume on the line follow the one that caused an error.

29. You want to configure the OLEServerBusyTimeout so that a request is sent to an ActiveX server indefinitely. What will you set this property to so that this occurs?

    A. A value greater than 10,000

    B. A value greater than 86,400,000

    C. True

    D. False
       B. By setting the value of OLEServerBusyTimeout to a value greater than 86,400,000 a request will be sent indefinitely.

30. A user presses the F1 key to invoke context-sensitive help for an object. The value of the HelpContextID is an invalid number. What happens when the user presses F1?

    A. Help is searched, and help for the closest related object is displayed.

    B. Help for the container or parent object is displayed.

    C. The request for help is ignored.

    D. A message explaining that an error has occurred is displayed
       C. If an invalid number has been placed in the HelpContextID, no help

for that object can be found. As such, the request for help is ignored.

31. Which of the following can be used in your code to cause an error to occur?

   A. Error.Raise

   B. Raise

   C. Err.Raise

   D. None of the above.
   C. Err.Raise is used to cause an error to occur. It is used to test code by raising a specific error, and thereby test error handling.

32. You want to change the message text that appears in a dialog box, which is displayed when a request has been received but hasn't been serviced yet. Which property of the App object will you change?

   A. OLEServerBusyMsgText

   B. OLEServerBusyMsg

   C. OLERequestPendingMsgText

   D. OLERequestPendingMsg
   C. OLERequestPendingMsgText is a property of the App object. By changing its value, you can change the message text that appears in the Request Pending dialog box.

33. What kind of object does an ActiveX document use to allow you to command buttons, text boxes and other controls that will display in a browser?

   A. Form

   B. UserDocument

   C. Document

   D. Hyperlink
   B. UserDocuments are similar to forms and allow you to add controls that appear in the ActiveX document displayed in a browser.

34. Which of the following lines of code will disable an error handler?

   A. On Error GoTo Null

   B. On Error GoTo 0

   C. On Error Exit

   D. On Error Err
   B. On Error GoTo 0 will disable error handling.

35. Which of the following is a valid label for an error handler?

   A. Err

   B. ErrHand

   C. MyErr

   D. MyErrHandler
   C. By adding a colon to an end of a name, you can create a label for an error handler.

36. Which property would you set to cite a specific topic for What's This help?

   A. WhatsThisHelp

   B. WhatsThis

   C. WhatsThisID

   D. WhatsThisHelpID
   D. WhatsThisHelpID is used to specify the ID number used to access a specific help topic for What's This help.

37. Which of the following lines of code will remove a control in a control array from a form?

    A. Unload cmdArray(1)

    B. Del cmdArray(1)

    C. Load cmdArray(1)=False

    D. Unload cmdArray(1)=True
    A. Unload followed by the name of the control in a control array (in this case, cmdArray(1)) is used to remove a control.

38. You have Internet Explorer version 2 installed on your computer and find you can't display information from an ActiveX document within it. Why?

    A. ActiveX documents can only be displayed in containers like Microsoft Binder.

    B. ActiveX documents can only be displayed in version 3 or higher of Internet Explorer.

    C. ActiveX documents can only be displayed in browsers like Windows Explorer.

    D. ActiveX documents can only be displayed in version 5 or higher of Internet Explorer.
    B. ActiveX documents can only be displayed in Internet Explorer version 3 or higher.

39. Which of the following occurs when there are no enabled or visible controls on a form?

    A. GotFocus

    B. Activate

    C. Focus

    D. Enable
    A. GotFocus occurs when there are no enabled or visible controls on a form.

40. Which of the following occurs when all variables in a form have been set to Nothing?

    A. LostFocus

    B. Terminate

    C. Deactivate

    D. Unload
    B. Terminate is an event that occurs when all variables in a form have been set to Nothing.

Chapter 3 Answers

1. What property of COM objects gives them the ability to be reused in any other COM-compatible development environment?

    A. Encapsulation of Source Code

    B. A standard set of binary interfaces

    C. Versioning

    D. Object Manager
    B. A standard set of binary interfaces. By implementing a standard set of binary interfaces that all COM-compatible clients understand, COM is able to support any COM-compatible client, regardless of the development environment that

was used to create the client and the component.

2. What type of component would be best suited for implementing a special text box, that could be dropped on a Web page, to display images stored in a proprietary format?

A. ActiveX EXE Document

B. ActiveX DLL code component

C. ActiveX EXE code component

D. ActiveX control.

   D. ActiveX control. Although an ActiveX document can also be used in a Web browser, the only type of ActiveX component that can be used inside of a Web page is an ActiveX control.

3. You are developing a component that will be used to provide spell-checking services to the client through calls to methods and properties of the component. The specification requires that your component work with both 16- and 32-bit clients. Which type of component would be best?

A. ActiveX DLL Document

B. ActiveX DLL code component

C. ActiveX EXE code component

D. ActiveX control.

   C. ActiveX EXE code component. ActiveX Code components are best-suited for providing non-visual services to clients, and only out-of-process (EXE) components can be used without regard to the bitness

of the client because it does not have to run in the same thread as the client.

4. Which of the following project types will run inside Microsoft Binder?

A. ActiveX EXE Document

B. ActiveX DLL code component

C. ActiveX EXE code component

D. ActiveX control

   A. ActiveX EXE Document. ActiveX documents were originally included in Visual Basic with the idea that they would be used in Microsoft Binder, although they are more often used in Internet Explorer in real-world use.

5. Which of the following is a benefit of having a component running in the process space of the client?

A. Speed

B. Safety

C. Freedom from bitness considerations

D. Security

   A. Speed. The main reason to use in-process (DLL) components is to eliminate the need for expensive calls across process boundaries that must use Marshalling.

6. How does VB use the Project Description field on the Project Properties dialog box?

A. It is used as the default name for instances of that object in the client project

B. It is used in the Components or References dialog box to identify an ActiveX Component.

C. It is returned by the ProductName property of the App object provided by Visual Basic.
B. It is used in the Components or References dialog box to identify an ActiveX component. Be sure to provide a meaningful project description to make your component easier to locate in either the Components or References dialog box.

7. If you were designing a text-editing ActiveX control that exposed a font property, where should the font property be stored when the component is unloaded?

A. In the Registry

B. In an INI file

C. In the PropertyBag object of the client

D. In the PropertyBag object of the ActiveX control
C. In the PropertyBag object of the client. The PropertyBag of the client is used for persistent storage of properties of a component that are set at design time.

8. Which event should you use to set the default values to the properties of an ActiveX control?

A. InitProperties

B. ReadProperties

C. InitializeProperties

D. GetDataMember
A. InitProperties. The InitProperties event fires when an ActiveX control is first added to a client form.

9. How can you make Visual Basic fire the InitProperties, ReadProperties, and WriteProperties for the objects created from a standard class module in a component?

A. Class modules cannot use these events

B. Set the PersistData property to **Persistable**

C. Set the DataBindingBehavior property to **SimpleBound** or **ComplexBound**

D. Set the persistable property to **Persistable**

E. Both B and C
D. Set the persistable property to **Persistable**. The Persistable property of a class module will force events to be fired for an object to allow the initialization, loading, and saving of property values.

10. While testing an ActiveX control, you create a test project in the same project group as your control. The control appears in the toolbox of the test project, but it is disabled. What is wrong?

A. The control is not registered

B. The control is open in Design view in another window

C. The control does not expose any public properties

D. ActiveX controls cannot be debugged from within the same project group
B. The ActiveX control becomes disabled in the toolbox of all projects in the group, while the UserControl object of the ActiveX control is open in Design view.

11. When does the Initialize event fire for an ActiveX control?

   A. When the control is added to the host form from the toolbox

   B. When the hose form containing the control is opened

   C. When the host form sets a property of the control
   A. Because an ActiveX control actually is running in Design view, the initialize event is fired as soon as it is added to a host form.

12. Which type is the central type of object in an ActiveX document project?

   A. Class module

   B. Form

   C. UserControl

   D. UserDocument
   D. The UserDocument is the central type of object in an ActiveX document type project.

13. What is the proper syntax in an ActiveX document named to cause the container application to replace the current document with another document?

   A. UserDocument.Hyperlink.Navigate "c:\fullpath\Otherdocument.doc"

   B. UserDocument.URL = "c:\fullpath\Otherdocument.doc"

   C. UserDocument.Navigate "c:\fullpath\Otherdocument.doc"

   D. UserDocument.Document = "c:\fullpath\Otherdocument.doc"
   A. The Navigate method of the hyperlink object is used to change documents in the container application.

14. An in-process ActiveX document project named "MyAXDoc," containing one UserDocument object named "UDoc1," is compiled. What is the name of the file that is opened in the container application to view the object?

   A. MyAXDoc.DLL

   B. UDoc1.EXE

   C. MyAXDoc.OCX

   D. MyAXDoc.vbd
   D. When compiled, this project will create a MyAXDoc.DLL file and a UDoc1.vbd file. The VBD file is the one you open in the container application to see that particular UserDocument object.

15. How do you stop an execution from pausing while testing an ActiveX document project?

   A. Press the Pause button in Visual Basic

   B. Press CTRL-BREAK

   C. Press the stop button in the browser window

   D. Press the stop button in Visual Basic

E. Any of the above

F. Both A and B

   F. Either the Pause button or the CTRL-BREAK key combination will stop the execution of the code on the current line.

16. How are dependent objects instantiated by the client application?

    A. Through calls to CreateObject

    B. Through calls to GetObject

    C. Using the New Keyword

    D. They must be accessed through the properties and methods of a root level object in the component that creates them

    E. Both A and B

       D. Dependent objects are accessed through calls to the root object and are normally instanced as PublicNotCreatable so that they may not be created directly by the client.

17. Which of the following instancing options is appropriate for a root object in an ActiveX DLL project?

    A. Private

    B. PublicNotCreatable

    C. MultiUse.

    D. SingleUse

       C. Both Single and MultiUse are used with classes set up to be root objects in a component so that the client application can create objects from those classes, but SingleUse instancing

cannot be used in components that run in-process.

18. Which instancing type allows the client to create multiple objects from a single instance of the component?

    A. MultiUse

    B. SingleUse

    C. Private

    D. PublicNotCreatable

       A. MultiUse instancing allows the component to use the same instance of the component to create multiple objects. SingleUse instancing creates a new instance of the component for each object that is created by the client.

19. How are one-to-many relationships modeled in an object hierarchy?

    A. Using properties that expose arrays

    B. Using properties that expose collection objects

    C. Using multiple root objects.

    D. Using multiple inheritance

       B. Properties that expose collection objects are used in these situations. Object creation functionality is commonly exposed to the client through an Add method of the root object's collection property.

20. What problems can circular references in an object model cause?

    A. Recursive function calls

    B. Compile errors

    C. Runtime errors

D. Objects that cannot be destroyed
D. Circular references can cause serious trouble if not torn down correctly, leaving objects in memory that cannot be accessed from the client application.

21. What is the term used to describe a function call that requires the caller to wait for the execution of that function to complete before returning control to the caller?

A. Blocking

B. Asynchronous execution

C. Call-backs

D. Freezing
A. Blocking or synchronous execution describes this behavior.

22. Which of the following statements about a process is untrue?

A. A process is an executing piece of code

B. A process can be either 16- or 32-bit, but not both

C. A process can contain multiple threads

D. Only one process per processor can execute a command at a time
A. A thread is the actual executing code. The process is the virtual space in which it executes.

23. In a data consumer, how do you map the local properties to the data provided by the data provider?

A. Using the glue method of the DataConnector object

B. Using the Add method of the DataBindings collection

C. By naming the properties to the field names exposed by the data provider

D. By referencing the properties of the data provider class from within the properties of the data consumer and copying the values over to local storage
B. The DataBindings collection is used to map properties in the data consumer to data fields exposed by the data provider.

24. What does the data parameter return from the GetDatamember routine in a class built as a data source that has its datasource set to 1-vbDataProvider?

A. A DAO record set object

B. An OLEDB data source object

C. A two-dimensional variant array

D. An ADO record set object
D. An ADO record set object is expected unless the datasource property is set to "2-vbOLEDBProvider, when an OLEDB data source object is expected.

25. Which of the following instancing options, when used for a class in an ActiveX DLL project, allows methods and properties of a class to be accessed without first creating an instance of that object?

A. MultiUse

B. GlobalMultiUse

C. PublicNotCreatable

D. GlobalSingleUse
   B. Both GlobalMultiUse and GlobalSingleUse provide this behavior, but only GlobalMultiUse can be used in ActiveX DLL projects.

26. How would you limit the number of threads used for objects in an ActiveX EXE project?

    A. Mark the process to run with "Unattended Execution"

    B. Use the Thread Per Object setting

    C. Use the Thread Pool setting.

    D. Check the App.ThreadId property in the object code
       C. The Thread Pool setting allows you to limit the number of threads used to create objects from a component. The Thread Per Object setting, on the other hand, lets each instance get its own thread, regardless of how many threads that works out to be.

27. When VB executes the statement CreateObject ("EXCEL. APPLICATION"), how does VB know what interfaces are supported by the application object of Excel?

    A. It looks up the ClassID that is stored in the Visual Basic Project File, looks up the ClassID in the Registry to find the location of EXCEL.EXE, and asks EXCEL.EXE about its interfaces using the Iunknown interface.

    B. It looks up the AppID in the Registry to find the ClassID of EXEL.APPLICATION, uses the

ClassID to find EXCEL.EXE, and finally asks EXCEL.EXE about its interfaces using the Idispatch interface.

    C. It uses the ClassID to get the AppID from the Registry to look up the interfaces that are also stored in the Registry.

    D. It looks up the AppID in the Registry to find the ClassID of EXEL.APPLICATION, then uses the ClassID to find EXCEL.EXE, and finally asks EXCEL.EXE about its interfaces using the IUnknown interface
       D. AppId is used to convert "EXCEL.APPLICATION" from a user-friendly string to a ClassID. ClassID is used to find the location of the component from the Registry. The component itself uses IUnknown to expose its interfaces.

28. Which of the following commands can be used to register the out-of-process server COMPONENT.EXE?

    A. Regsvr32 COMPONENT.EXE

    B. Regsvr32 /U COMPONENT.EXE

    C. COMPONENT.EXE

    D. Regsvr COMPONENT.EXE
       C. EXE-type components register themselves when you run their executable file.

29. What model does a Web published database fit?

    A. One-tier

B. Two-tier

C. Three-tier

D. None of the above
C. Three tiers: the database server, the Web server, and the client browser.

Chapter 4 Answers

1. What are three benefits of Microsoft Transaction server? (Choose all that apply.)

   A. Scalability

   B. Ease of programming

   C. Reduced method invocation overhead

   D. Robustness
   A, B, D. MTS aids in the scalability and robustness of distributed applications while making programming easier. Because it intercepts calls to components (and they run out-of-process), MTS cannot reduce the method invocation overhead.

2. Durable data is managed by:

   A. Shared Property Manager

   B. Resource Managers

   C. Distributed Transaction Coordinator

   D. ODBC Resource Dispenser
   B. Resource Managers manage durable data; Resource Dispensers manage non-durable data. The Shared Property Manager and the ODBC Resource Dispenser are Resource Dispensers. The DTC manages transactions.

3. Which two protocols for Resource Managers allow MTS to manage transactions?

   A. ODBC Compliance protocol

   B. OLE Transactions protocol

   C. Distributed Transactions protocol

   D. X/Open XA protocol
   B, D. OLE Transactions protocol and X/Open XA protocol for Resource Managers allow MTS to manage transactions. The other two are fictitious protocol names.

4. A customer's address is durable data. True or false?

   A. True

   B. False
   A. True. A customer's address is an example of durable data.

5. Packages can contain which of the following objects? (Choose all that apply.)

   A. Roles

   B. Hyperlinks

   C. Components

   D. Interfaces
   A, C, D. Packages can contain roles, components, and interfaces. The MTS Explorer hierarchy includes some hyperlinks, but they do not belong to packages.

6. What kinds of packages run within the client process?

   A. Library packages

B. Server packages

C. No packages run within the client process under MTS

D. All packages run within the client process under MTS
    A. Library packages in MTS run in the client process.

7. Role-based security is available for which kind of packages?

   A. Library packages

   B. Server packages

   C. No packages

   D. All packages
      B. Only MTS server packages are compatible with role-based security.

8. A role serves what purpose?

   A. Determines who can access a package or its component

   B. Determines in which user context the components in a package will be run

   C. Determines under which process a component will run

   D. Roles serve no necessary function in MTS
      A. A role is a collection of users; it determines who can access a package, a component, or an interface.

9. Roles can contain which of the following? (Choose all that apply.)

   A. Windows NT permissions

   B. Windows NT groups

   C. Windows 95/98 users

D. Windows NT users
   B, C. Windows NT users and groups make up roles.

10. Which entities can be protected by role-based security? (Choose all that apply.)

    A. Files in NTFS partitions

    B. Packages

    C. Components

    D. Interfaces

    E. Methods
       B, C, D. Individual methods cannot be protected by role-based security. Files in NTFS partitions can be protected by NT security, but not by role-based security.

11. What kinds of machines can run client applications that access MTS?

    A. Any platform with a Java Virtual Machine

    B. Any platform with DCOM support

    C. Windows for Workgroups and above

    D. Only Microsoft Windows NT
       B. As long as the client machine runs an operating system that includes DCOM support, it can access MTS.

12. Exporting a package generates which files? (Choose all that apply.)

    A. A file named <PACKAGE NAME>.PAK

    B. A copy of all of the files associated with the components in the package

C. A self-installing setup file called SETUP.EXE

D. A self-installing setup file in the "Clients" folder called <PACKAGE NAME>.EXE

A, B, D. The .PAK file is the package file, and will be accompanied by a copy of all of the files associated with the components in the package. The setup file has the same name as the package, has an .EXE extension, and is placed in a folder named "Clients."

13. From where is MTS installed?

A. Windows NT Workstation CD-ROM

B. Windows NT Server CD-ROM

C. Microsoft Management Console CD-ROM

D. Windows NT Options Pack
D. MTS is installed from the Windows NT Options Pack.

14. Which of the following are components of MTS? (Choose all that apply.)

A. Microsoft Distributed Transaction Coordinator

B. Microsoft SQL Server

C. Microsoft Message Queue Server

D. Transaction Server Executive
A, D. SQL Server and MSMQ are separate products from MTS. The DTC and the Transaction Server Executive are part of MTS.

15. In an MTS application, business rules are implemented by:

A. SQL Server stored procedures

B. Resource Managers

C. Resource Dispensers

D. Client applications

E. ActiveX components
E. ActiveX Components are used to implement business rules in an MTS application.

16. An MTS server process may host how many components?

A. MTS server processes do not host components

B. One

C. Thirty-two

D. Any number

E. It depends on the platform running MTS
D. MTS server processes can host large numbers of components

17. Resource Managers work in conjunction with which elements of MTS?

A. MTS Explorer

B. Distributed Transaction Coordinator

C. Resource Dispensers

D. OLE Transaction Manager
B. The DTC and Resource Managers work together to manage transactions. The OLE Transaction Manager is a fictitious entity.

18. Which of the following are MTS Resource Dispensers? (Choose all that apply.)

A. Shared Property Manager

B. X/Open XA

C. OLE Resource Dispenser

D. ODBC Resource Dispenser
A, D. The Shared Property Manager and the ODBC Resource Dispenser are MTS Resource Dispensers. X/Open XA is a transactional protocol, and there is no such thing as the OLE Resource Dispenser.

19. MTS provides rollback facilities in which circumstances?

   A. Only transactions involving a single database

   B. Transactions involving multiple databases, only if the code handles the commit or rollback after each database access

   C. Transactions involving multiple databases, only if the databases support certain transaction protocols

   D. Explicit rollback support is only provided for MSMQ transactions
   C. MTS can manage transactions that span multiple Resource Managers (that include databases) if they implement either X/Open XA or OLE Transactions protocols.

20. In what circumstances do you access variables through the Shared Property Manager?

   A. To provide access to properties to components with lower security levels

   B. To retain properties after the machine is shut down

   C. To share properties with in-process COM servers

   D. To access common non-durable variables
   D. The Shared Property Manager allows objects to share non-durable data that will be lost if the machine is shut down.

21. The Microsoft Management Console is also used to manage which application?

   A. Windows Explorer

   B. Internet Explorer

   C. Internet Information Server

   D. Windows NT Control Panel
   C. The MMC is also used to manage IIS.

22. MTS Explorer can display packages from which computers?

   A. Any computer on the network running MTS

   B. Any computer on the network with DCOM support

   C. Any computer on the network running Windows for Workgroups or above

   D. Only the local computer
   A. The MTS Explorer can display packages from any accessible computers that are running MTS.

23. If you add a role to a package, but all users can still access its components, what is the most likely cause?

   A. Authorization checking has not been enabled on the package

   B. No users have been added to the role

C. You do not have permissions to administer declarative security

D. The users all have administrative privileges

A. Until authorization checking is enabled on a package, role-based security will not be active.

24. If you add a role to a package and no users can access its components, what is the most likely cause?

A. Authorization checking has not been enabled on the package

B. No users have been added to the role

C. You do not have permissions to administer declarative security

D. The users all have administrative privileges

B. If an empty role is added to a package, no users can access that package.

25. Role-based security which is administered through the MTS Explorer is known as:

A. Programmatic security

B. Administrative security

C. Declarative security

D. Server-level security

C. Declarative security is administered via the MTS Explorer, while programmatic security is managed from code. There is no such thing as administrative security or server-level security.

26. Trace messages can hinder runtime performance. True or false?

A. True

B. False

A. True. Trace messages can affect performance and should be used cautiously.

27. To restrict access to an interface to certain users, a role should be added to the following:

A. The Roles folder of an interface

B. The Roles folder of a method

C. The Role Membership folder of a component

D. The Role Membership folder of an interface

D. Interface access is protected by roles in the Role Membership folder of the interface. There is no such thing as a Roles folder for an interface or method.

28. You are required to configure a component that must write data to a log table in the database. These database writes must exist within a transaction, but if they fail, they should not affect any transactions that other components are involved in. What level of transaction support should you configure for the component?

A. Requires a transaction

B. Requires a new transaction

C. Supports transactions

D. Does not support transactions

B. By forcing the component to always start a new transaction, it will not participate in any transaction that the component which called it may be involved in.

29. Components may be imported from:

    A. A list of in-process servers installed on the local machine

    B. A list of ActiveX controls installed on the local machine

    C. A list of all COM components on any computer on the network

    D. Components cannot be imported into MTS

    A. To import components, they must have been already installed on the local machine. Only in-process servers are compatible with MTS.

30. The interfaces and methods can be browsed in the MTS Explorer for the following:

    A. All components

    B. No components

    C. Components that were installed with Component Wizard

    D. Components that were imported with Component Wizard

    C. Only components that were installed by the MTS Explorer Component Wizard, not those that were imported, are capable of displaying their interfaces and methods within MTS Explorer.

31. Components can be dragged and dropped between packages within MTS Explorer. True or false?

    A. True

    B. False

    A. Components can be moved between packages by dragging and dropping within MTS Explorer.

32. What is the default authentication level for package security?

    A. None

    B. Administrator

    C. Packet

    D. Packet integrity

    C. Packet is the default authentication level for packages. There is no such thing as Administrator-authentication level.

33. When importing an existing package, you have the option of also importing the following:

    A. Components belonging to the package

    B. Roles belonging to the package

    C. NT users saved within the package

    D. Transaction statistics belonging to the package

    C. It is optional to import any NT users that may be saved with the package. Components and roles will automatically be imported as part of the package, and transaction statistics do not belong to packages.

34. When a new package is created it contains the following:

    A. The default MTS component

    B. An empty component

    C. Components inherited from its parent

    D. No components

D. A new package does not contain any components. There is no such thing as a default component or an empty component, and packages do not have parents to inherit anything from.

35. The package identity determines the following:

    A. The NT user account under which the components will run

    B. The name of the package

    C. The text that comes before the dot in component names for that package

    D. The CLSID of the package
    A. The package identity is a user account under which components will run. Packages do not have CLSIDs.

36. Process isolation is provided by library packages. True or false?

    A. True

    B. False
    B. False. Because library packages run within the client application process, they do not provide process isolation.

37. MTS trace messages are logged by the following:

    A. The DTC

    B. The SDLC

    C. The MTS Executive

    D. Resource Managers
    A. The Distributed Transaction Manager is the source of trace messages. SDLC is a communications protocol, not an element of MTS.

Chapter 5 Answers

1. Which of the following are uses of ObjectContext object?

   A. Declares that the object's work is complete

   B. Prevents a transaction from being committed, either temporarily or permanently

   C. Instantiates other MTS objects and includes their work within the scope of the object's transaction

   D. All of the above
   D. ObjectContext is useful for all these jobs.

2. Which is best way to create an MTS object?

   A. Create the object using New word

   B. Create the object by calling CreateInstance method

   C. Create the object by using CreateObject method

   D. None of the above
   B. Even though we can create MTS objects using either New or CreateObject, the object does not inherit its context from the caller, so it cannot participate in the transaction, even if its transaction attribute is set to Requires a transaction or Supports transactions. If CreateInstance is used to create an MTS object, that object can participate in the existing transaction and it inherits its context from the caller.

3. Which of the following functions would notify MTS that the transaction is over?

   A. SetComplete, SetAbort

   B. EnableCommit, DisableCommit

   C. All of the above

   D. None of the above
      A. ObjectContext provides two methods, SetComplete and SetAbort, to notify MTS of the completion status of the work performed by the object.

4. Which of the following functions enable the object to be active throughout the transaction?

   A. SetComplete, SetAbort

   B. EnableCommit, DisableCommit

   C. All of the above

   D. None of the above
      B. ObjectContext provides two methods, EnableCommit and DisableCommit, to enable an object to remain active in a transaction while performing work over multiple method calls.

5. Which of the following is true?

   A. When the root object calls either SetComplete or SetAbort method the transaction ends

   B. Any object created in part of the transaction calls either SetComplete or SetAbort method the transaction ends

   C. If either EnableCommit or DisableCommit is called by the root object. the transaction ends

   D. None of the above
      A. Whenever the root object calls either the SetComplete or SetAbort methods, the transaction ends (remember that the objects created as part of the same transaction will not have any effect on the transaction lifetime, even if they call SetComplete or SetAbort). Even if the root object calls EnableCommit or DisableCommit, the transaction does not end. So to acquire the information needed from the client, it can keep the transaction alive by using the EnableCommit or DisableCommit methods.

6. Which of the following is the default method called in transaction on an object?

   A. EnableCommit

   B. DisableCommit

   C. SetAbort

   D. SetComplete
      A. If an object does not call SetComplete, SetAbort, EnableCommit, or DisableCommit, MTS treats the object as if it called EnableCommit. EnableCommit is the default status for an object unless it specifies otherwise.

7. Which of the following statements is true?

   A. A stateful object remembers state over multiple method calls

   B. A stateless object does not keep track of the state at all

C. A stateful object impacts the scalability of the application

D. All of the above
D. State stored in MTS objects is also called local state; properties are a good example. An object can have properties that store the information and also have methods that retrieve or update these properties. The object exists and keeps this information until the client releases it. An object that maintains state internally over multiple method calls like this is called a stateful object. However, if the object doesn't expose properties, and instead the values of the properties (state) are passed each time a method call is made, it is a stateless object. Stateless objects do not remember anything from previous method calls. Stateful objects often require server resources such as memory, disk space, and database connections, which impact the scalability of the application.

8. The Shared Property Manager consists of which of the following objects?

A. SharedPropertyGroupManager

B. SharedPropertyGroup

C. SharedProperty

D. All of the above
D. The Shared Property Manager consists of SharedPropertyGroupManager, SharedPropetyGroup, and SharedProperty objects.

9. Which of the following methods create and return a reference to a new shared property group?

A. CreateInstance

B. CreatePropertyGroup

C. Group

D. All of the above
B. The CreatePropertyGroup method creates and returns a reference to a new shared property group. Group method returns a reference to an existing shared property group and CreateInstance creates an MTS object.

10. SharedPropertyGroup consists of which of the following methods and properties?

A. CreateProperty, CreatePropertyByPosition

B. Property, PropertyByPosition

C. All of the above

D. None of the above
C. SharedPropertyGroup consists of CreateProperty and CreatePropertyByPosition methods, and Property and PropertyByPosition properties.

11. Which of the following statements are correct?

A. SharedProperty object consists of one property: Value

B. After creating a shared property, can work on it through the SharedProperty object

C. All of the above

D. None of the above
C. SharedProperty has one property, Value, and we work with it through the SharedProperty object after creating the property.

12. Which of the following is the best way to handle errors?

A. Terminate the transaction calling SetAbort on the root object

B. Report the error back to the client in a well-defined manner by calling Err.Raise method.

C. All of the above

D. None of the above
C. The best way to handle an error situation is to terminate the transaction so that this error does not corrupt data, and report it to the client so that user has an idea about what happened or what caused the error.

13. While debugging MTS components, what do you have to keep in mind?

A. You should not add components to an MTS package while it is being debugged

B. You should not export a package while one of the MTS components is being debugged

C. All of the above

D. None of the above
C. You should not add components or export a package while you are in debugging MTS components because they lead to unexpected results.

14. Windows NT Event Log is useful for which of the following?

A. To verify the internal errors that are recorded in the event log

B. To trace messages issued by Distribution Transaction Coordinator

C. All of the above

D. None of the above
A. Distribution Transaction Coordinator is used by MTS to manage transactions, whereas Windows NT Event Log is used to check the internal errors that occurred while performing a transaction.

15. Which of the following statements are true about improving efficiency of MTS objects?

A. By minimizing the number of hits required to use objects

B. By avoiding generation of events

C. By making objects apartment-threaded

D. All of the above
D. All are the best practices to write MTS components. They reduce the network round trips, increase scalability of the application, and approach simultaneous client requests.

Chapter 6 Answers

1. Universal Data Access eliminates

   A. commitment to a single vendor's products

   B. expensive and time-consuming movement of data into a single data store

   C. Both of the above statements are correct.

   D. None of the above.
   C. The whole concept of UDA is in eliminating the commitment to single vendor's products and expensive and time-consuming movement of data into a single data store.

2. ADO automatically adjusts itself to the functionality of the data provider.

   A. True

   B. False
   A. ADO automatically adjusts itself, depending on the functionality of the data provider. Consider Microsoft Excel and SQL Server. Excel gives a limited scope for database functionality; whereas SQL Server is pure database engine. ADO automatically adjusts itself to provided database functionality.

3. What is required to access a database through ADO?

   A. Recordset Object

   B. Connection Object

   C. Either Connection or Recordset object

   D. None of the above.
   C. You can open a Recordset automatically if you execute a command on the Active Connection object. It is also possible to access a data source without explicitly opening a connection (through a Recordset object).

4. Which of the following are true statements?

   A. Using Connection, Recordset, and Field objects, we can access a data source.

   B. Without explicitly opening a Connection object, it is possible to access a data source with a Recordset object.

   C. Both of the statements are correct.

   D. Neither statement is correct.
   C. You can access a data source successfully with Connection, Recordset, and Field objects. It is possible to open a connection through a Recordset object without opening the connection explicitly, and we can create a recordset by executing a command on the Active Connection without creating a Recordset object explicitly.

5. Properties is a collection to handle the collection of parameters of Connection, Command, Recordset, and Field objects. Which of the following methods is useful to extract the Property of that particular object?

   A. Item

   B. Value

C. Both of the above.

D. None of the above

A. You can retrieve a property value by using the Item method, either by the name or its ordinal position. Because Item is the default method in the ADO collection, you can simply omit it.

6. Which of the following is true?

A. Connection Events are issued when transactions on a connection begin, are committed, or are rolled back; when Commands execute; and when Connections start or end.

B. Recordset Events are issued to report the progress of data retrieval; when you navigate through the rows of a Recordset object; when you change a field in a row of a recordset, change a row in a recordset, or make any change in the entire recordset.

C. Only A is correct.

D. Both A and B are correct.

D. In ADO 2.0, event-based programming is introduced and the Connection Events and Recordset Events are supported in it.

7. What is ADO known for?

A. Ease of use

B. Programmable cursor sets

C. Ability to return multiple resultsets from a single query

D. All of the above.

D. ADO is a flexible and adaptable programming standard to access data

for all client/server or Web-based data retrieval applications.

8. You can control the transaction by using which of the following?

A. BeginTrans

B. CommitTrans

C. RollbackTrans

D. All of the above methods through the Connection object

D. You can control the transactions by using the BeginTrans, CommitTrans, and RollbackTrans methods through the Connection object.

9. What is used to retrieve a particular field value in a row? (Choose all that apply.)

A. ! operator

B. ~ operator

C. Field object

D. A and C

D. You could use either the ! operator or a Field object to retrieve the information from a row in a recordset.

10. We can open a DSN-less Connection, too.

A. True

B. False

A. You can open a DSN-less Connection through ADO. The main concept of the UDA is that it supports both traditional and non-traditional data sources and ADO is one of the core components of UDA. Total ADO is dependent upon OLEDB; it does not care about whether the data provider is traditional data source or not.

11. Because the Errors collection is only available from the Connection object, you need to initialize ADO off of a connection object.

   A. True
   B. False
      A. This is true.

12. What are the advantages of the three-tier design over traditional two-tier or single-tier designs? (Choose all that apply.)

   A. The added modularity makes it easier to modify or replace one tier without affecting the other tiers.
   B. Separating the application functions from the database functions makes it easier to implement load balancing.
   C. None of the above.
   D. Both A and B are correct.
      D. The three-tier system has these two as advantages over two-tier or single-tier applications.

13. To open a recordset you can use which of the following? (Choose all that apply.)

   A. Execute method on either Connection or Command object
   B. Open method on Recordset object
   C. None of the above
   D. Both A and B are true
      D. You can open a recordset by executing the Execute method on

either the Connection or Command object, or by executing the Open method on the Recordset object.

14. With the Execute Direct method, you execute already prepared SQL statements to access data. With the Prepare Execute method, you create SQL statements on the fly by using user input and execute these statements to access data.

   A. True
   B. False
      A. That statement is true.

15. By using stored procedures to execute a query on a database, you are allowing the RDBMS to cache those SQL queries.

   A. True
   B. False
      A. True

16. The stored procedures on Microsoft SQL Server have the following capabilities in returning the data:

   A. One or more result sets
   B. Explicit return value
   C. Output parameters
   D. All of the above.
      D. The SQL Server has all the above capabilities in returning the data by using stored procedures.

17. How do you execute a stored procedure from the Command object? (Choose all that apply.)

A. Simply set the CommandType property to adCmdStoredProc

B. Simply set CommandText to the name of the stored procedure

C. None of the above

D. Both A and B are correct
D. Just setting CommandType property of the Command object to the constant adCmdStoredProc and setting CommandText to the name of the stored procedure allows you to execute the stored procedure instead of a SQL query.

18. If you use the Refresh method, it causes ADO to make an extra trip to SQL Server to collect the parameter information.

A. True

B. False
A. If you use the Refresh method, it causes ADO to make an extra trip to SQL Server to collect parameter information. Instead, create Parameter Collections to reduce the network trips.

19. By setting CursorLocation property of Recordset object to this value, you can create a client-side cursor.

A. adUseNone

B. adUseClient

C. adUseServer

D. None of the above
A. Set the Recordset's CursorLocation property to adUseClient to create a client-side cursor.

20. Server-side cursors do not support the execution of queries that return more than one result set.

A. True

B. False
A. This avoids the scrolling overhead associated with the cursor and enables the cursor driver to manage each result set individually.

21. To open a dynamic cursor, set the CursorType property of Recordset object to this:

A. adOpenDynamic

B. adOpenStatic

C. adOpenReadOnly

D. adOpenKeyset
A. By setting CursorType property to adOpenDynamic, you can create a dynamic cursor.

22. What is the difference between a dynamic cursor and a keyset cursor? (Choose all that apply.)

A. By using a dynamic cursor, you could see all the changes, including additions and deletions made by other users.

B. By using a keyset cursor, you could see all the changes, including additions and deletions made by other users.

C. None of the above.

D. Both A and B are correct.
A. With a keyset cursor, you cannot see the additions and deletions made

by other users, except for the changes to existing data.

23. By setting what LockType property of a Recordset object we can create a read-only locked cursor:

   A. adLockReadOnly

   B. adLockPessimistic

   C. adLockOptimistic

   D. adLockBatchOptimistic
      A. Use adLockReadOnly to create a read-only lock.

24. Transactions are necessary whenever your application performs longer database insertions or changes because the user may lose network connectivity or abort the applications. You can roll back to the original status and hence will not lose any data.

   A. True

   B. False
      B. Transactions are more useful or sometimes necessary to make a lot of changes at once.

25. A disconnected recordset is a useful way to return data to a client that will be used for a long time, without tying up the MTS server and database server with open connections.

   A. True

   B. False
      A. A disconnected recordset contains a recordset that can be viewed and updated, but it does not carry with it

the overhead of a live connection to the database.

26. The UpdateBatch method creates a separate SQL query for each changed record to modify in the database while it is being called.

   A. True

   B. False
      A. The UpdateBatch method on the recordset object creates a separate SQL query for each record to modify in the database while it is being called.

Chapter 7 Answers

1. How do you define a local variable while programming in Transact-SQL?

   A. DECLARE #*var* int

   B. DECLARE ##*var* int

   C. DECLARE @*var* int

   D. DECLARE @@ *var* int
      C. You define a local variable in Transact-SQL by preceding the variable with one "@" sign. You define a global variable by preceding the value with two "@" signs.

2. What kind of join would you employ if you wanted to display data from two different tables in which there are entries in the first table but not in the second table? (Choose all that apply.)

   A. Inner join

   B. Left join

C. Right join

D. Cross join

B, C, D. You could either use a left join or a right join to join two different tables that contained entries in the one table but not the other. A left join would join the second table with the first table mentioned in the query, while a right join would join the second table with the first. You could also use a cross join, which will join all rows from one table to all rows in the other table. However, the result set will be much larger than what you would really need. An inner join would join two tables that may not have any row in common with the other table but which will have at least one row in common with a third table.

3. What happens if, in the process of execution, there is an error within a stored procedure?

A. The procedure will finish but return an incomplete result set

B. The procedure will finish but nothing will be returned

C. The procedure will be halted and return an incomplete result set

D. The procedure will be halted and nothing will be returned

D. When the Server encounters a problem in a stored procedure, the procedure will be halted and nothing will be returned.

4. How can you write a simple query that will look for a condition?

A. By using the WHERE clause

B. By using the IN keyword

C. By using the HAVING clause

D. By using the IF statement

A. You can have your query search for a value in a simple query by using a WHERE statement. Answer B would be correct except for the fact that IN is an operator and not a keyword. I know, this is sort of a trick question but not totally unlike what you might see on a Microsoft test.

5. Which of the following is true of a query? (Choose all that apply.)

A. A query can retrieve data from different databases

B. A query can retrieve data from different tables

C. A query can retrieve data from different rows

D. A query can retrieve data from different fields

A, B, C, D. A query can retrieve data from different databases, tables, rows and fields. The query looks in tables and rows and applies the query to fill in the fields of the result set.

6. Which kind of join would you employ to retrieve data from two tables that do not have any rows in common?

A. Inner join

B. Left join

C. Right join

D. Cross join

A. An inner join allows you to join the designated rows from two tables together, even if they may not have any rows in common with each other. By using rows, the two tables may have rows in common with a third table.

7. Which of the following are global variables that are connection-specific? (Choose all that apply.)

A. @@idle

B. @@error

C. @@connections

D. @@spid

B, D. The global variables @@error and @@spid are connection-specific global variables. The global variables @@idle and @@connections are server-specific global variables.

8. In what manner may a local variable be used? (Choose all that apply.)

A. Within a stored procedure

B. Within a WHERE statement

C. Within a subquery

D. Within a JOIN statement

A, B, C. You can place a local variable within a subquery, a WHERE statement, and a stored procedure. You may also place a local variable within a trigger.

9. What is a parameter used for when running a stored procedure? (Choose all that apply.)

A. To guide the procedure to look for a certain row

B. To guide the procedure to look for a certain table

C. To guide the procedure in filling in a global variable

D. To guide the procedure in filling in a local variable

A, D. A parameter is used in conjunction with a stored procedure to allow the stored procedure to determine the value of a local variable. When a local variable is declared within a stored procedure, a parameter can assign the value of the variable.

10. Which is true of a global variable? (Choose all that apply.)

A. They can be used within stored procedures

B. They can be changed by running a stored procedure

C. They can be used by local variables

D. You create one by preceding the variable by "@"

A, C. A global variable can be used within a stored procedure or a trigger. A global variable can also be used to provide the value for a local variable. A global variable is set by the system and cannot be changed by the user. A global variable cannot be changed, not even by running a stored procedure though a local variable can be.

11. How many subqueries can you nest in a query?

A. four

B. eight

C. sixteen

D. thirty-two
   C. You can nest up to 16 subqueries in a query.

12. Which of the following are characteristics of SQL Server? (Choose all that apply.)

   A. Provides centralized administration of databases

   B. Provides data security

   C. Provides data integrity

   D. Provides data storage

   A, B, C, D. Microsoft SQL Server allows for the centralized administration of databases, provides data security by only allowing access to authorized users, provides data integrity by ensuring that two users don't try to update the data at the same time, and provides for the storage of data on a dedicated server that can reduce your network traffic.

13. How may you run a group of queries? (Choose all that apply.)

   A. Through a batch

   B. Through a join

   C. Through a stored procedure

   D. Through a query
   A, C. You may run multiple queries as part of a batch or as part of a stored procedure. You may also run a series of subqueries nested within a query.

14. Which global variable would you use to display an error number?

   A. @error

   B. @@error

   C. @error_number

   D. @@error_number
   B. A global variable is preceded by two "@" signs, while a local variable is preceded by one "@" sign. There is no variable called "error_number."

15. Which of the following are valid methods for declaring multiple local variables?

   A. DECLARE @*var1* int @*var2* char(20)

   B. DECLARE @*var1* int, @*var2* char(20)

   C. DECLARE @*var1* int DECLARE @*var2* char(20)

   D. DECLARE @*var1* int, DECLARE @*var2* char(20)
   B. You can declare multiple variables by entering the variables on the same line, separated by a comma.

16. Which of the following data types can be used when declaring a local variable? (Choose all that apply.)

   A. char(20)

   B. varchar(20)

   C. integer

   D. money
   A, B, D. The data types CHAR, VARCHAR, and MONEY are used in declaring local variables. If you wished to create a variable of the integer type,

you would need to use INT instead of integer.

17. Which of the following services are part of the Application Model in the Microsoft Solution Framework? (Choose all that apply.)

   A. Business services

   B. Data services

   C. Network services

   D. User services
      A, B, D. The Application Model consists of business services, data services, and user services.

18. Which of the following are valid groups of operators? (Choose all that apply.)

   A. arithmetic operators

   B. comparison operators

   C. conversion operators

   D. logical operators
      A, B, D. Arithmetic operators, comparison operators, and logical operators are valid groups of operators. There is no class called conversion operators, but there is a group of conversion functions.

19. Which of the following support SQL? (Choose all that apply.)

   A. Access

   B. dBase

   C. Oracle

   D. SQL Server
      A, B, C, D. All of the above products support SQL.

20. Which of the following are global variables?

   A. @error

   B. @idle

   C. @spid

   D @version
      None. Another trick question. Did you notice that there is only one "@" sign before the variables? Had there been two "@" signs before the variables, all of them would be correct. Again, it's important to pay close attention to the questions because some of the questions you may see on the certification tests will be very misleading.

Chapter 8 Answers

1. Which of the following is not an advantage of the three-tier architecture?

   A. Application scalability

   B. Reduced reliance on SQL Server security

   C. Application security designed around business roles

   D. Increased usage of database connection pooling
      B. Reduced reliance on SQL Server security. Although SQL Server security is implemented differently under the three-tier architecture, it is still the means for securing SQL Server and plays a vital role.

2. Which of the following are the two types of security under MTS?

   A. Users and groups

   B. Users and roles

   C. Declarative and programmatic

   D. Component and objects
      C. Declarative and programmatic. Declarative security is applied at the component or interface level through the MTS Explorer. Programmatic security is "in the code" applied by the developer and utilized at runtime.

3. Which of the following statements are true about declarative security under MTS?

   A. It cannot be used under Windows 95

   B. It cannot be enabled or disabled

   C. Developers use the IsCallerInRole method to implement it

   D. It is defined through the NT User Manager for Domains
      D. It cannot be used under Windows 95. Declarative security is built upon NT user authentication mechanisms, so it cannot be used by components running on a Windows 95 platform.

4. Which of the following statements are true about programmatic security under MTS?

   A. It relies on SQL security

   B. It can be enabled or disabled

   C. Developers use the IsCallerInRole method to implement it

   D. It is defined through the NT User Manager for Domains

   C. Developers use the IsCallerInRole method to implement it. Programmatic security is always available in an MTS server package environment, and may be used by MTS components, regardless of whether they are accessing SQL databases.

5. To use MTS security in your VB application, you must set a reference to which resource?

   A. None, VB will take care of it automatically at runtime

   B. The Microsoft Transaction Server Security Library

   C. The VB Common Controls Type Library

   D. The Microsoft Transaction Server Type Library
      D. The Microsoft Transaction Server Type Library. There is no such thing as The Microsoft Transaction Server Security Library. The Type Library contains all the MTS exposed objects and interfaces for the VB programmer.

6. Which of the following errors will cause the caller's identity to be lost to MTS security, thereby making IsCallerInRole useless?

   A. Forgetting to set the package's identity in MTS Explorer

   B. Using the VB CreateObject function to instantiate another component

   C. Forgetting to call IsSecurityEnabled first thing in the program

D. Calling a utility function in a common .bas file
B. Using the VB CreateObject function to instantiate another component. Only the CreateInstance Method of the MTS ObjectContext object is "context aware" and will preserve the caller's identity (and other security information) for a new object. Calling IsSecurityEnabled once to establish the presence of an MTS security environment is a good idea, but it has no affect on maintaining caller identity.

7. Which of the following are not a place where roles may be applied to enforce security?

   A. Components

   B. Interfaces

   C. Database tables

   D. Any point in the code of a component
   C. Database tables. Tables are secured by database user names (which are mapped to NT user names), not roles.

8. Component A in Package 1 is calling Component B in the same package. Which of the following describes how the roles must be set up to allow this to happen?

   A. The same roles must be assigned to both components Role Membership folder

   B. The Interface being called in Component B must have the same role assigned as the calling Interface in Component A

   C. The identity of Package 1 must be in the same role as Component A

   D. Nothing
   D. Nothing. Components within the same MTS package implicitly "trust" one another and no role checking is performed.

9. Which of these best describes the MTS term OriginalCaller?

   A. The NT end user who initiated the transaction or process that is running in MTS

   B. The identity of the MTS package that the caller is executing in

   C. The identity of the MTS component that created (instantiated) the current one

   D. The user in the Adminstrator role of the system package
   A. The NT end user who initiated the transaction or process that is running in MTS. The OriginalCaller will be maintained as long as all components instantiate each other using the CreateInstance method of the MTS ObjectContext object.

10. If authorization checking is disabled at the package level, and enabled at the level of Component A, which of the following statements is true?

   A. Callers of Component A must be present in the Role Membership folder under the component

   B. Programmatic security is disabled for the package

C. Any other component in the Package calling A will fail

D. Declarative security is disabled for all components in the package, including Component A

D. Declarative security is disabled for all components in the package, including Component A. The settings on individual components have no effect when the containing package security is disabled. Programmatic security cannot be disabled.

11. After all the roles for a particular MTS package have been defined and authorization checking enabled, what else must be done to complete the configuration of MTS security?

A. Assign an identity to SQL Server so the components can access it

B. Assign NT users and/or groups to the various roles

C. Make the user ID assigned as the package identity part of the Domain Administrators group

D. Be certain the MTS role names appear in at least one NT group

B. Assign NT users and/or groups to the various roles. There must be at least one valid NT user or group assigned to a newly created MTS role, or no one will be able to access the package.

12. Which of the following is the preferred mode for SQL Server security?

A. Roles

B. Mixed

C. Integrated

D. Standard

C. Integrated. Because it uses NT authentication mechanisms, administration is simpler and users have to deal with only one login.

13. The right to perform operations on SQL tables is granted to which of the following?

A. MTS roles

B. SQL Server logins

C. Any NT user ID in the SQL Users group

D. Any domain user

B. SQL Server logins. These logins may be created from NT users and groups (in integrated or mixed security), but they are still SQL logins internally in SQL Server.

14. Which of the following is not an advantage of SQL stored procedures?

A. Centralized administration of SQL queries

B. Simplified SQL security management

C. Better performance

D. Support for more types of clients

D. Support for more types of clients. Client support in terms of SQL security is determined by the security mode. The other three answers are all advantages of stored procedures.

15. For SQL Standard security mode authentication, which property does the

developer need to set in order to provide the login info to SQL?

A. ConnectionString on the ADO Connection object

B. IsCallerInRole property

C. IsSecurityEnabled property

D. DSN parameter
   A. ConnectionString on the ADO Connection object. B and C are not properties, and DSN is one part of the ConnectionString information required.

16. In the three-tier architecture, where is user database auditing best performed?

A. In the Data Access (lowest) tier

B. In the Business (middle) tier

C. In the (top) tier

D. A and B
   D. A and B. The Data Access tier runs using the MTS Identity of the Business tier components, so it is not always possible to differentiate between end users at that point (although the MTS GetOriginalCaller method can help). User tier services do not call the database directly.

17. In SQL Server mixed-mode security and a trusted connection, which of the following describes the order of authentication attempts?

A. Integrated, then standard

B. Standard only

C. MTS Roles, then integrated

D. Integrated only
   A. Integrated, then standard. When using a trusted connection, SQL Server compares the component's SQL login name to the component's network user name. If they match, or if the supplied login name is blank or spaces, SQL Server uses the Windows NT integrated login rules (integrated security). If this is not true, then standard security rules are applied to any values for the user ID and password supplied by the component.

18. Which method can be used in your code to return the ID of the caller that initiated a particular application process independently of the running component's identity?

A. GetOriginalCallerName on the application context object.

B. GetOriginalCallerName on the security object.

C. IsCallerInRole

D. GetUserID
   B. GetOriginalCallerName on the security object, which is attached to the application security context (GetObjectContext().Security.GetOriginalCallerName()).

19. What kinds of components can take advantage of MTS programmatic security?

A. Any component with a pointer to the MTS application context object.

B. Any MTS component

C. Any MTS component installed in a server package

D. Any MTS component installed in a library package

C. Any MTS component installed in a server package. Components in a library package do not have programmatic security available.

20. What should you remember about the system package in MTS?

A. It is necessary to assign a valid NT user to the Administrator role before doing anything else with security

B. The system package is only necessary at MTS installation, and can be deleted after it is complete

C. The NT user Administrator is the only one that can open this package

D. User components requiring a high degree of security should be placed in the system package

A. It is necessary to assign a valid NT user to the Administrator role before doing anything else with security. Failure to do so can render the MTS Explorer unusable.

Chapter 9 Answers

1. Which of the following occurs when one application communicates directly with another?

A. Asynchronous communication

B. Message queuing

C. Message passing

D. Clustering

C. When one application communicates directly with another, it is called synchronous communication or message passing.

2. Which of the following is a hierarchical database management system?

A. DB2

B. AS/400

C. IMS

D. SQL

C. Information Management System (IMS) is a hierarchical database management system. It also provides transaction management services and data communication services.

3. You need to access data located on an IBM database. Which of the following will you have your applications interact with to achieve this?

A. SQL Server

B. SNA Server

C. Cluster Server

D. IBM Server

B. Microsoft SNA Server enables client workstations to access the data and applications that reside on mainframes.

4. Which of the following would you use to copy relational data between mainframe databases and SQL Server databases?

A. COMTI

B. OLEDB/DDM

C. ODBC

D. Host Data Replicator
   D. Host Data Replicator allows access to relational databases located on mainframes, and is used to copy relational data between mainframes and SQL Server databases.

5. Which of the following is an example of MOM: Message Orientated Middleware?

   A. Cluster Server

   B. Microsoft Transaction Server

   C. NT Server

   D. Microsoft Message Queue Server
      D. Microsoft Message Queue Server is an example of Message Orientated Middleware. This type of software allows applications to communicate with one another through message queues.

6. You are creating an application that accesses data from the mainframe. You require user defined data types in this application. Which of the following will you use to access the mainframe data?

   A. ODBC

   B. ODBC/DRDA

   C. DCOM

   D. Host Data Replicator
      C. DCOM allows you to create user-defined data types of any complexity for your application.

7. Which of the following is used to obtain the machine identifier of a computer?

A. MSMQQuery

B. MSMQQueue

C. MSMQIdentity

D. MSMQApplication
   D. MSMQApplication is used to obtain the machine identifier of a computer.

8. Which of the following objects would you use to create, open, and delete queues?

   A. MSMQQueue

   B. MSMQQueueInfo

   C. MSMQCreate

   D. MQMQQueueProp
      B. MQQueueInfo is used to create new queues, and open or delete existing queues.

9. Which of the following can be used to extend transactions from NT Server to mainframe environments using Microsoft Transaction Server (MTS)?

   A. COMTI

   B. DB2

   C. SNA Transaction Component

   D. OLEDB/DDM
      A. COMTI can extend transactions from NT Server to mainframe environments using Microsoft Transaction Server (MTS).

10. Which of the following is also known as asynchronous communication?

   A. Message passing

   B. Message queuing

   C. Message clustering

D. Message quelling

B. Message queuing is also known as asynchronous communication.

11. Which of the following is a relational database management system developed by IBM

A. DB2

B. IMS

C. SQL Server

D. Access

A. DB2 is an IBM relational database management system.

12. What do the letters "SNA" stand for?

A. Simple Network Application

B. Systems Network Architecture

C. Simple Network Architecture

D. Super Network Application

B. SNA is an acronym that stands for "Systems Network Architecture." This is a complex, proprietary network architecture developed by IBM.

13. You are creating an application that accesses data from the mainframe. You require support for Automation data types and embedded structures. Which of the following will you use to access the mainframe data?

A. ODBC

B. DCOM

C. Automation Data Replicator

D. Host Data Replicator

B. DCOM also supports embedded structures and Automation data types

14. Which of the following would you use to manipulate the properties of to define the label and body of a message?

A. MSMQLabel

B. MSMQBody

C. MSMQQueue

D. MSMQMessage

D. MSMQMessage is used to define MSMQ messages, such as the label and body of a message.

15. Which of the following would be used to determine if messages are delivered, depending on whether certain conditions are met? (Choose all that apply.)

A. SNA Server

B. Microsoft Cluster Server

C. Microsoft Message Queue Server

D. Microsoft Transaction Server

C, D. Microsoft Message Queue Server can be integrated with Microsoft Transaction Server, so that certain conditions must be met before a message is delivered. If messages are made part of MTS transactions, their delivery depends on the success or failure of a transaction.

16. Which of the following are features of using the ODBC driver to access data from a mainframe? (Choose all that apply.)

A. Scrollable cursors

B. Synchronous calling

C. No transaction support

D. Use of stored procedures
A, D. The ODBC driver provides scrollable cursors, full transaction support, use of stored procedures, array fetch and update, and asynchronous calling.

17. You are installing Microsoft Message Queue Client on your computer and choose Independent Client as the mode of installation. Where will the message store reside with this installation?

    A. Local hard drive
    B. MSMQ Server hard drive
    C. A mainframe
    D. Site Controller
    A. Independent Clients have a message store located on the local hard drive.

18. Which of the following best defines a server cluster?

    A. An NT Server that is accessed and managed as a single system
    B. Two or more NT Servers that are accessed and managed as a single system
    C. Three or more NT Servers that are accessed and managed as a single system
    D. A network segment that is accessed and managed as a single system
    B. Clustering is when two or more NT Server machines are accessed and managed as a single system.

19. You want to create a program that manages a Microsoft Cluster Server. When you attempt to make a reference to the appropriate API, you notice that the API isn't included with Visual Basic 6.0. Why not, and how can you remedy this?

    A. Cluster API doesn't come with Visual Basic 6.0 or Visual Studio 6.0. It must be installed through the Microsoft Cluster Server SDK.
    B. Cluster Automation Server API doesn't come with Visual Basic 6.0 or Visual Studio 6.0. It must be installed through the Microsoft Cluster Server SDK.
    C. The NT Option Pack needs to be installed for the API to appear.
    D. Visual Basic 6.0 hasn't had all Data Access Objects installed. Install the DAO objects from the installation disk.
    B. Cluster Automation Server API doesn't come with Visual Basic 6.0 or Visual Studio 6.0. It must be installed through the Microsoft Cluster Server SDK.

20. Which of the following is used for notification of message arrivals?

    A. MSMQApplication
    B. MSMQMessage
    C. MSMQEvent
    D. MSMQQueue
    C. MSMQEvent is used for the notification of message arrivals.

21. A user plans to send a message with your application, which uses Microsoft Transaction Server. The receiver of the message has turned off her computer and gone home for the day. What will happen when the user sends the message?

    A. The message will be returned to the sending user

    B. An error message, stating the message is undeliverable, will appear to the sending user

    C. The message will be stored on a mainframe's database until the receiver reads the message from the database

    D. The message will be stored in a queue, until the receiver reads the message from the queue
       D. Messages from sending computers are stored in a queue. Messages will stay in the queue until the receiving computer is ready to read the message.

22. Which of the following APIs can you use for cluster server programming with Visual Basic 6.0?

    A. Cluster API, for enabling a resource DLL or application to communicate with the Cluster Service and cluster database

    B. Resource API, for enabling Cluster Service to communicate through Resource Monitor with a resource

    C. Cluster Automation Server API, which gives an application the capability to manage clusters

    D. Cluster Administrator Extension API, which allows context menus and Property Pages to be integrated into Cluster Administrator
       C. Cluster Automation Server API, which gives an application the capability to manage clusters.

23. Which components are parts of SNA Server? (Choose all that apply.)

    A. OLEDB/DDM Provider

    B. Component Object Model Transaction Integrator (COMTI)

    C. OLE Provider

    D. Host Data Replicator (HDR)

    E. Component Object Model Integrator (COMI)
       A, B, D. OLEDB/DDM Provider, COMTI, and Host Data Replicator are components of SNA Server.

24. You are installing Microsoft Message Queue Client on your computer and choose Dependent Client as the mode of installation. Where will the message store reside with this installation? (Choose all that apply.)

    A. Local hard drive

    B. MSMQ Server

    C. Site Controller

    D. On a mainframe
       B, C. Dependent Clients use the message store of an MSMQ Server or Site Controller.

25. Which of the following objects is used to send a message to a specific queue?

    A. MSMQMessage
    B. MSMQEvent
    C. MSMQQueue
    D. MSMQQueueInfo
       A. MSMQMessage is used to send a message to a specific queue.

26. You have installed the Microsoft Cluster Server SDK on your computer. When you open references from the Project menu in Visual Basic 6.0, you notice that the MS Cluster Type Library doesn't appear in the listing of Available References. Why not, and how will you fix this?

    A. The SDK hasn't registered MSCLUS.DLL with the system registry. Use REGSVR32 to register this file.
    B. Visual Basic hasn't registered the SDK. Reinstall Visual Basic.
    C. Visual Basic hasn't registered the SDK with the system registry. Use REGSVR32 to register the SDK.
    D. The MS Cluster Type Library isn't included in the Microsoft Cluster Server SDK.
       A. If the MS Cluster Type Library does not appear in the Available References listing, the SDK hasn't properly registered MSCLUS.DLL with your system registry. Use the system registry program REGSVR32 to register this file.

Chapter 10 Answers

1. You need to compile an executable that will run on computers housing either an Intel 80x86 or a Motorola 68000 processor. Which compiler option should you select to ensure that your application will run?

    A. The Compile to Native Code option in the Compile tab of the Project Properties dialog box
    B. The Compile to P-Code option in the Compile tab of the Project Properties dialog box
    C. The Platform Portability option in the Link tab of the Project Properties dialog box
    D. Intel 80x86 and Motorola 68000 from the Portability list in the Link tab of the Project Properties dialog box
       B. Compile to P-Code is correct. This option creates code that can be run on any machine where a VB translator is present. Native code will run only on the family of processors it is created for. There is no Platform Portability option or Portability list.

2. When a *Break When Value Changes* condition triggers the program to transition to Break mode, where will the program break?

    A. The line before the value is changed
    B. The line where the value is changed
    C. The line after the value is changed

D. Assembly code does not correspond to VB code line by line

C. The line after the value is changed. However, if a breakpoint were used instead of a *Break When Value Changes* expression, the program would break on the line where the value is changed, but before the line is executed.

3. Which of the following allows programmers to dynamically change the value of a variable while an executing program is in Break mode? (Choose all that apply.)

A. The Immediate window.

B. The Locals window

C. The Watch window

D. The Call Stack window

A, B, C. The Immediate window, the Locals window, and the Watch window all enable programmers to dynamically change variable values in Break mode. The Call Stack window only displays static information.

4. The Immediate window can be used for which of the following? (Choose all that apply.)

A. Calling procedures

B. Displaying values of local variables

C. Moving the *current statement indicator*

D. Setting variable values

A, B, D. The Immediate window can be used to call procedures and to display and set the values of any variables not just local ones. The

current statement indicator cannot be moved in the Immediate window.

5. Which functionally does the Watch window provide that the Immediate window does not?

A. The capability to display the values of global variables

B. The capability to change the value of a variable

C. The capability to execute a procedure

D. The capability to trigger breaks

D. The capability to trigger breaks. Both the Immediate window and the Watch window are used to display and change variables. Only the Immediate window enables programmers to execute procedures.

6. The Debug object can be used to do which of the following? (Choose all that apply.)

A. Determine the level of the executing function in the call tree

B. Send output to the Immediate window

C. Dynamically set watch expressions

D. Suspend execution of the program where it resides

B, D. Send output to the Immediate window and suspend execution of the program it resides in. No objects can determine the call tree level or dynamically set watch expressions.

7. Which of the following will appear in the Locals window? (Choose all that apply.)

   A. All variables within the current scope of the function that is executing

   B. All variables within the current class of the executing function

   C. Me

   D. Variables declared in the current functions
   C, D. Variables declared in the current function and the Me structure appear in the Locals window, even if other variables are within the function's scope. To determine values of variables within the local scope, you should set watch expressions in the Watch window.

8. Which of the following CANNOT be performed in Break mode?

   A. Moving the *current statement indicator* to a different function

   B. Executing procedures in an order other than that of the normal execution flow

   C. Changing a variable's values

   D. Toggling breakpoints
   A. Moving the *current statement indicator* to a different function. You can move the *current statement indicator* to an executable line of code within the same function, but never to a different function.

9. On the following fragment of code, which error will eventually occur?
   ```
   Dim x As Integer
   ```

```
While 1
  x = x + 1
Wend
```

   A. Stack overflow

   B. Segmentation fault

   C. Subscript out of range

   D. Overflow
   D. Overflow. An overflow error (error 6) will be triggered when trying to write a value to x that is larger than x's allocated space in memory.

10. The #If conditional compilation directive can be used for which of the following?

    A. Including specific fragments of code in an executable and excluding others

    B. Triggering breaks

    C. Printing information into the Immediate window

    D. Checking for stack violations
    A. Including specific fragments of code in an executable and excluding others. It cannot be used for any of the other choices.

11. While in Break mode, which of the following CANNOT be performed?

    A. Adding another watch expression

    B. Undoing the last line of code that was executed

    C. Moving the *current statement indicator*

    D. Editing the source code
    B. Undoing the last line of code that was executed. This cannot be accomplished anywhere in Visual Basic.

12. What are some of the effects of defining the context in which a watch expression is to be evaluated? (Choose all that apply.)

    A. Increased speed at which your program executes

    B. Eliminating breaks that occur in functions that you're not interested in working with

    C. Decreased speed at which your program executes

    D. Alleviating ambiguity if more than one variable in your code has the same name

    A, B, D. Increased speed at which your program executes, eliminating breaks that occur in functions you're not interested in working with, and alleviating ambiguity if more than one variable in your code has the same name.

13. When the Debug object generates output using the print method, where is the output sent?

    A. stderr

    B. The console window

    C. The Immediate window

    D. The Watch window

    C. The Immediate window.

14. What advantages does p-code hold over native code? (Choose all that apply.)

    A. P-code is usually smaller than native code

    B. P-code can run on different platforms, provided that a VB interpreter is present

    C. P-code provides better performance than native code

    D. P-code is easier to read than native code

    A, B. P-code is usually smaller than native code and can run on different platforms, provided a VB interpreter is present. P-code usually performs slightly worse than native code because of the additional interpretation step, and both would be nearly impossible to read.

15. What effect will *step into* have if it is used when the program is in Break mode at the following line of code ? (Choose all that apply.)

    ```
    x = MyFunction
    ```

    A. The program will resume execution until another breakpoint is encountered

    B. The Call Stack window will have another function on top and the Locals window will have a new set of variables

    C. A dialog box will prompt you for a return value for MyFunction and assign it to x

    D. Execution will resume and pause again on the first executable line in MyFunction

    B, D. The Call Stack window will have another function on top, the Locals window will have a new set of variables, and execution will resume and pause again on the first executable line in MyFunction. Answer A could refer to the Continue command and answer C refers to nothing.

16. What attributes are NOT possessed by the *Break When Value Is True* expression?

    A. It allows you to break when the value of a variable becomes false

    B. It only breaks when expressions are true within the current scope of the context specified in the watch expression

    C. You must remove the expressions before you distribute the program

    D. It allows you to break when the value of a variable becomes true
    C. You must remove the expressions before you distribute the program. The expressions are not part of the executable, rather they are part of the project workspace. Thus, when you build your executable, the watch expressions are omitted. You can check to see if a variable is false by evaluating an expression that equates to False, such as (val = False). When the value of val becomes false, the expression becomes true and triggers a break.

17. When CONST_VAL = 1 is specified on the Make tab of the Project Properties window, CONST_VAL = 2 is specified on the command line used to compile the application, and #Const CONST_VAL = 3 appears in the source code of your program before any #If statements, what will the value of CONST_VAL be when it is evaluated by an #If statement?

    A. 1

    B. 2

    C. 3

    D. 6
    C. 3. The precedence order is #Const, then command line, then Make tab of the Project Properties dialog box. Keep in mind that the #Const must be declared before it is referenced in the source code.

18. What is the relationship between the Watch window and the Locals window?

    A. The Watch window is capable of displaying anything that the Locals window can display

    B. The Locals window is capable of displaying anything that the Watch window can display

    C. Only the Watch window can change the value of a variable

    D. Only the Locals window can change the value of a variable
    A. The Watch window is capable of displaying anything that the Locals window can display, including Me. You cannot add variables to the Locals window, and it will not display any value that has not been declared within the currently executing function and Me. Both windows allow you to change variable values.

19. Which Visual Basic debugging tool can be used to trigger a break?

    A. The Immediate window

    B. The Watch window

    C. The Locals window

    D. The Call Stack window

B. The Watch window can be used to trigger a break if either a *Break When Value Is True* or a *Break When Value Changes* is employed.

20. Before you enable the *Assume no Aliasing* compiler option, which of the following should you verify?

    A. No variable will over extend its allotted memory space

    B. Your program does not spawn multiple threads

    C. Your computer does not provide common registers

    D. No more than one variable name references a single value in memory
    D. No more than one variable name references a single value in memory. Aliasing is the process of taking all variable names that point to a single space in memory and giving them the same alias. If you allow the compiler to assume no aliasing, when X and Y both reference a single memory space, VB might copy X to a register and change Y n the meantime. When VB copies X back from the register, it overwrites any changes that should have been made on it, but instead were made to Y and are now lost.

21. You are sure your program performs no floating-point comparisons. Which of the following can you enable?

    A. Remove Safe Pentium™ FDIV Checks

    B. Allow Unrounded Floating Point Operations

    C. Remove Floating Point Error Checks

    D. A and C
    B. Allow Unrounded Floating Point Operations. Floating-point numbers maintain a higher precision than specified. When comparing two values that should be equal, the higher precision might cause them to evaluate as unequal if they are not rounded to the proper precision.

22. What will happen when you *step over* the following line of code when your program is in Break mode?

    `x = MyFunction`

    A. The line will be skipped and no assignment will be made to x

    B. The line will be skipped and a marker in the Locals window will indicate that x possibly has an incorrect value

    C. The line will be executed normally and pause at the first executable line directly below it

    D. The line will execute but no assign will be made to x
    C. The line will be executed normally and pause at the first executable line directly below it. The line will only be skipped if you move *the current statement indicator*.

23. When you enable the *Remove Referential Integrity Checking* compiler option, you must first ensure which of the following?

    A. All variable names correspond to an existing and accessible location in memory

B. No variable values will exceed their allotted space in memory

C. If you are using DAO, RDO, or ADO to access a database, no foreign keys can exist

D. This option does not exist
   D. This option does not exist. Referential integrity is when every foreign key field in a database can be dereferenced to a primary key. This option, however, does not exist anywhere within Visual Basic.

24. When declaring multiple constants in the Make tab of the Project Properties dialog box, what character is used as a delimiter?

A. A space

B. A colon

C. A semicolon

D. A comma
   B. A colon. The colon is also used to delimit constants declared on the command-line compilation statement. However, only one constant can be declared in a single #Const directive.

25. Which of the following describes the Call Stack window?

A. It displays the call stack with the currently executing function at the top of the list

B. It displays the call stack with the currently executing function at the bottom of the list

C. It displays all functions started but not finished, with the exception of the currently executing function

D. It enables you to move the call stack pointer
   A. It displays the call stack with the currently executing function at the top of the list. Nothing allows you to move the call stack pointer except natural execution of the program.

26. Which of the following would be a good reason to create a project group?

A. Debugging multithreaded programs

B. Debugging ActiveX controls

C. Debugging Standard EXEs

D. Debugging code written in Visual C++ or Visual J++
   B. Debugging ActiveX controls. There's no reason to create a project group for any of the other choices.

27. Which of the following DLL Base addresses is valid?

A. &H100000 (in hexadecimal)

B. &H1004000 (in hexadecimal)

C. &H10040000 (in hexadecimal)

D. &H0128000 (in hexadecimal)
   C. &H10040000 (in hexadecimal). Answer A is wrong because all DLL base addresses must be between &H1000000 (16,777,216 in decimal) and &H80000000 (or 2,147,483,648 in decimal). Answer B is wrong because addresses must be in increments of 64K, meaning that in hexadecimal the last four digits must all be zeros. Answer D is wrong on both of these counts.

28. Not selecting the *Remove Safe Pentium™ FDIV Checks* compiler option does which of the following?

    A. Prevents you from formatting a disk drive at the application level

    B. Catches and corrects floating-point errors caused by a flaw in the Pentium chip

    C. Allows your program to share the processor with other processes ,as long as they are on the Pentium Platform

    D. Allows applications to check the processor it is running on to see whether it is a member of the Pentium family
    B. Catches and corrects floating-point errors caused by a flaw in early Pentium chips. (All the other choices are a product of my imagination.)

29. While in Break mode, what is the most efficient way to return to the line that called the currently executing function?

    A. Step Over
    B. Step Up
    C. Step Out
    D. Set a watch expression on the return value of the calling function
    C. Step Out. Step Over will only execute the next statement and will not return from the function. Step Up does not exist. Setting a watch expression on the return value of the calling function would work if the calling function is part of an

assignment statement, but it's not as efficient as Step Out.

30. Which of the following attributes describes the *current statement indicator*?

    A. It cannot be moved

    B. It can be moved to another executable line of code within the currently executing function

    C. It can be moved to another executable line of code within the currently executing class module

    D. It can be moved to another executable line of code within the currently executing program
    B. It can only be moved to another executable line of code within the currently executing function.

31. Which of the following are correct statements about the #Const directive?

    A. A #Const statement must be provided both a name and a value

    B. You must declare a #Const statement in the Make Tab of the Project Properties dialog box

    C. If an #If directive attempts to evaluate a constant that is assigned a value by a #Const directive positioned below it, a compilation error will occur

    D. You must declare a #Const statement in the file that it is to be used
    A. You must provide both a name and a value to a #Const expression. You can set constants in the Make tab of the Project Properties dialog box, but

this does not require #Const. If an #If directive does not recognize a constant, it will be evaluated as zero (or False). The #Const can be included in another file that is part of the project, such as a common .bas module, but the compile must compile that module first if the value is to be used.

32. Which of the following will creating a project group enable you to do.

    A. Bind two projects together

    B. Work with different projects from the same development environment instance

    C. Organize folders to make use of common libraries

    D. Include multiple files in a single instance of the development environment
    B. Work with different projects from the same development environment instance. Project are never bound; they can always be loaded separately even after being included in project groups. Projects themselves house multiple files, so project groups are not required to do this. Answer C doesn't make sense.

33. Which of the following would not increase the speed of numeric computations?

    A. Selecting the *Assume No Aliasing* compiler option

    B. Selecting the *Remove Integer Overflow Checks* compiler option

    C. Selecting the *Allow Unrounded Floating Point Operations* compiler option.

    D. Selecting the *Remove Array Bounds Checks* compiler option
    D. Selecting the *Remove Array Bounds Checks* compiler option has no effect on numeric computations. All the other choices will increase execution performance slightly, but at the risk of unexpected side effects.

34. Which of the following optimizations can you take advantage of when compiling a program into p-code?

    A. Optimized for Fast Code.

    B. Optimized for Small Code.

    C. Either A or B.

    D. P-code can not be optimized.
    D. P-code can not be optimized. The optimizations mentioned apply to native code only.

35. Which scenarios will produce the OpSys variable to equate to "Window 98" given the following code? (Choose all that apply.)

    ```
    #If WinCE
     OpSys = "Windows CE"
    #Else
     OpSys = "Windows 98"
    #End If
    ```

    A. If WinCE is not defined

    B. If WinCE is equal to False

    C. If WinCE is set to 1 in the Make tab in the Project Properties dialog box and set to 0 as an argument when compiling from the command line

D. If WinCE is set to −1

A, B, C. If WinCE is not defined, is equal to False, or is set to 0 when compiling from the command line. The command line constants override the Make tab on the Project Properties dialog box. −1 resolves to true, which will invoke the else clause.

36. The *current statement indicator* marks the currently executing line of code. What are some of its characteristics? (Choose all that apply.)

   A. It can be moved in a drag-and-drop fashion

   B. It cannot be moved

   C. It is represented by a yellow arrow

   D. It is only visible when the call stack window is visible

   A, C. It can be moved in a drag-and-drop fashion, and it is represented by a yellow arrow when in Break mode. The *current statement indicator* is visible whenever a program is in Break mode. This includes code executed from the immediate window.

37. What effect will selecting the *Remove Safe Pentium™ FDIV Checks* compiler option have?

   A. It will have no effect on machines that do not require it

   B. It will increase performance slightly on all machines

   C. It will cause a program to crash if it is run on a DEC Alpha machine

   D. It will cause major problems for programs running on Pentium platforms with this flaw

   B. It will increase performance slightly on all machines including the DEC Alpha. It does not cause major problems; in fact, the division error made by these chips is so insignificant to everyday users that the chip was on the market for months before the flaw was discovered.

38. Which of the following CANNOT be used to trigger Break mode?

   A. Debug.Assert 0

   B. CTRL-BREAK

   C. Using the Break keyword

   D. Creating a breakpoint by clicking in the margin indication bar

   C. Using the Break keyword. Visual Basic does, however, provide and Stop keyword that can be used for this purpose. Keep in mind that Debug.Assert ensures that its expression is true. It only breaks when the condition resolves to false. CTRL-BREAK is a shortcut for the Pause command. Breakpoints always trigger breaks.

39. Which of the following can be used when testing an ActiveX control?

   A. Microsoft Internet Explorer 4.01

   B. A project group containing both the ActiveX control project and the standard EXE project

   C. A and B

D. The only way to test an ActiveX control is by using the Active Test program
C. Both Microsoft Internet Explorer 4.01 and a project group containing both the ActiveX control project and the standard EXE project can be used to debug an ActiveX control. Debugging a control in Internet Explorer 4.01 is much the same as anywhere else. You set breakpoints and run from the VB development environment.

40. Which of the following is NOT an attribute of the #Const compiler directive in Visual Basic?

A. A constant's value may be used as part of the conditional expression of a Visual Basic while loop

B. Constant declarations must provide both a name and a value

C. Constants will be evaluated as zero if they are referenced before they are declared

D. Once a constant's value is defined it can not be changed or redefined
A. A constant's value cannot be used as part of the conditional expression of a Visual Basic while loop. It will generate a "Variable not defined" compilation error. Unlike C++, VB constants must provide both a name and value. Constants will be evaluated as zero or false if they are referenced before they are declared. And although you can override constants declared on the command line or in the Make tab

of the project properties dialog box, once you define a #Const it cannot be changed.

Chapter 11 Answers

1. You start the Package and Deployment Wizard, and try to package an application that hasn't been compiled yet. What will happen?

A. The Package and Deployment Wizard will display a message informing you of this, then shut down

B. Nothing will happen; you'll have to shut down the Wizard, reopen Visual Basic, and compile the project from there.

C. The Package and Deployment Wizard will display a message informing you of this, and give the option to compile from here

D. The Package and Deployment Wizard will automatically compile it for you, without any user interaction
C. If you haven't compiled a project and start the Package portion of the Wizard, a message box will appear informing you the project is compiled. The Compile button on this message box gives you the option to compile from here.

2. You want to compile a project called **MyProject**, which is part of a project group. How will you compile MyProject into an executable file?

A. Select Make MyProject.exe from the File menu

B. Select MyProject from the Project menu, and then select Make MyProject.exe from the File menu

C. Select the project group from the Project window, and then select Make MyProject.exe from the File menu

D. Select MyProject from the Project Window, and then select Make MyProject.exe from the File menu

D. If a project you want to compile is part of a project group, you must first select the project from the Project window. You then use the Make command from the File menu. In this case, you would choose Make MyProject.exe from the File menu.

3. You are packaging an Internet application with the Package and Deployment Wizard. When you reach the Cab Options screen, how will you package the application?

A. Single Cab

B. Multiple Cab

C. Dual Cab

D. Multi Cab

A. If you are packaging an Internet application, you should choose to package as a single CAB file.

4. You are packaging an application that you plan to deploy on floppy disk. When you reach the Cab Options screen of Package and Deployment Wizard, how will you package the application?

A. Single Cab

B. Multiple Cab

C. Dual Cab

D. Multi Cab

B. When deploying to floppy disk, you must select packaging to multiple CAB files.

5. You reach the Installation Title screen of the Package and Deployment Wizard. Where will information typed on this screen appear when the application is installed?

A. It will appear as menu item and group titles in the user's Start menu

B. It will change the name of the Setup file to what you have set on this screen

C. It will display on-screen during the installation process

D. It won't appear until after installation, and users can access the information through the Help menu

C. The Installation Title screen has a field that allows you to type in a string. Information typed in this field will appear when the user installs the application.

6. A user installs your application and a COM component can't be found. What will happen?

A. The operating system will stop the installation

B. All hard drives will be searched for the missing file

C. The installation will skip the missing file and continue

D. The Visual Basic Run time Library will produce a "File not found" message
D. When a user installs your application and a COM component can't be found, Visual Basic Run time Library produces a "File not found" message.

7. What files contain information about which directories were created during installation; Registry entries that were created and modified; and self-registered .DLL, .EXE, or .OCX files?

   A. Unwise.log

   B. Install.log

   C. St6unst.log

   D. Vb6unst.log
   C. St6unst.log contains information on which directories were created during installation; Registry entries that were created and modified; and self-registered .DLL, .EXE, or .OCX files

8. What does the Registry key $(TLBRegister) represent in the Setup.lst file?

   A. The file is a type library and is to be registered as such

   B. The file is a self-registering DLL file

   C. The file is a self-registering EXE file

   D. The file is a remote support file (also referred to as remote server file)
   A. The Registry key $(TLBRegister) represents a type library, and is to be registered as such.

9. Which of the following best defines user-level access control (user-level security)?

   A. A password must be set for each resource

   B. Allows you to specify users and groups who have access to resources

   C. A password must be set for each printer

   D. Allows you to specify domains and servers used for authentication
   B. User-level security allows you to specify users and groups who have access to the resources on your computer.

10. You are configuring DCOM on a client computer. Because the computer is running a client application, what must you specify in your configuration?

   A. The user account that will have access to start the application and user accounts that have permissions to run it

   B. The location of the server application that will be accessed or started

   C. The location of the client application that will be accessed or started

   D. The user account of the person who configured DCOM on that computer
   B. Client applications need to have the location of the server application that will be accessed or started specified.

11. What must you have to deploy to compact disc?

   A. CD-ROM

B. Writeable CD-ROM

C. Network access

D. A computer running NT Server
   B. To deploy to compact disc, you require a writeable CD-ROM. You cannot deploy to compact disc with a standard CD-ROM.

12. You have deployed to a network folder. Users who want to install the application complain that they can't find the folder you said the install program was in. You check with your computer, and find that the install program is there. What is most likely the problem?

   A. You forgot to configure DCOM on the client computer

   B. You forgot to configure DCOM on the server computer

   C. You don't have proper permissions or rights to access the folder

   D. You've lost your mind from overwork, and forgot to deploy the application

   E. Other users or groups don't have proper permissions or rights to access the folder
      E. If you can "see" the installation program in a network folder, but other users of the network cannot, they most likely don't have proper permissions or rights to the folder.

13. You have decided to run DCOM Configuration Properties to configure DCOM on a computer. How will you start this program?

A. From the Package and Deployment Wizard, click the DCOM button

B. From the Package and Deployment Wizard, select DCOM from the View menu

C. From Visual Basic, select DCOM from the View menu

D. From the Start menu, click Run and type **dcomcfng** to start the program
   D. To start DCOM Configuration Properties, click Run on the Start menu, and then type **dcomcnfg**.

14. You are using the Package and Deployment Wizard to deploy to the network. What will you select as your method of deployment from the Deployment Method screen of the Deploy portion?

   A. Network

   B. Network Folder

   C. Folder

   D. Network Deployment
      C. To deploy to a network folder, select Folder from the Deployment Method screen.

15. You are using DCOM Configuration Properties, and you select an application from the list and clicked the Properties button. A dialog box appears with several tabs. Which tab shows information on the application that consists of its name, local path, and the type of application it is?

   A. General

   B. Location

C. Security

D. Advanced

A. The General tab shows information on the application that consists of its name, local path, and the type of application it is.

16. You are using DCOM Configuration Properties, and you selected an application from the list and clicked the Properties button. A dialog box appears with several tabs. Which tab allows you to choose between default access permissions for the application or custom permissions that allow you to edit who can use the application?

    A. General

    B. Location

    C. Security

    D. Advanced

    C. The Security tab allows you choose between default access permissions for the application or custom permissions that allow you to edit who can use the application.

17. You are using DCOM Configuration Properties, and you selected an application from the list and clicked the Properties button. A dialog box appears with several tabs. Which tab will you use to specify where you want to run the application?

    A. General

    B. Location

    C. Security

D. Advanced

    B. The Location tab is used to specify the location of where you want to run the application.

18. Which of the following functions allow you to write information to the Windows Registry?

    A. GetSettings

    B. SaveSettings

    C. Property Let

    D. Property Get

    B. SaveSettings is used to save settings to the Registry.

19. Which of the following contain information about an application or a component's runtime requirements?

    A. Dependency files

    B. Setup.lst files

    C. Setup1.lst files

    D. Dep.lst files

    A. Dependency files (.DEP extension) contain information about an application or a component's runtime requirements.

20. You have decided to edit the Access Permissions for certain users of an application. In Add Access Permissions, which access permissions can you set for users or groups? (Choose all that apply.)

    A. Grant Access

    B. Read and Write

    C. Full

D. Deny Access

A , D. The Add Access Permission dialog allows you to select Grant Access or Deny Access for setting a user or group's permissions

21. During installation, where will the application-removal utility be installed?

    A. The application directory

    B. The common files directory

    C. The shared files directory

    D. The /Windows or /WinNT directory
    D. The application-removal utility, St6unst.exe, is installed into the /Windows or /WinNT directory

22. What can you do to rename, delete, and duplicate package and deployment scripts that were created during Package or Deploy sessions?

    A. Click the Manage Scripts button on Package and Deployment Wizard's main screen to open a dialog box for these purposes

    B. Select Manage Scripts from the File menu of the Package and Deployment Wizard to open a dialog box for these purposes

    C. Click the Manage Scripts button on the Deployment method screen of Package and Deployment Wizard

    D. Click the Scripts button on the Package and Deployment Wizard's main screen to open a dialog box for these purposes
    A. Clicking the Manage Scripts

button on the Package and Deployment Wizard's main screen opens a dialog box that allows you to rename, delete, and duplicate package and deployment scripts created during Package or Deploy sessions.

23. You want to create a setup program for your application. What will you use to do this?

    A. Deploy portion of Package and Deployment Wizard

    B. Package portion of Package and Deployment Wizard

    C. Compiling the project in Visual Basic 6.0

    D. Make Setup Program menu item on the File menu of Visual Basic 6.0
    B. The Package portion of Package and Deployment Wizard is used for creating setup programs for your application.

24. Which of the following functions allow you to read information from the Windows Registry?

    A. SaveSettings

    B. ReadSettings

    C. GetSettings

    D. Get
    C. GetSettings is used to read information from the Registry.

25. You are deploying to compact disc. Unfortunately, the Package and Deployment Wizard doesn't recognize that a writeable CD-ROM is attached to

your computer. How can you still deploy to compact disc?

A. Select Floppy Disk deployment and select the drive for your writeable CD-ROM rather than a floppy drive

B. Select Network deployment and select the drive for your writeable CD-ROM.

C. Select Folder deployment, and then after deploying to a local or network folder, transfer the files manually to compact disc.

D. None of the above
C. If you don't have access to a writeable CD-ROM, or if the Package and Deployment Wizard doesn't recognize it, use Folder deployment. After deploying to a local or network folder, transfer the files to compact disc manually.

26. What kind of access control must you set a computer to for DCOM Configuration Properties to run?

A. User-control

B. Share-control

C. NT Server authenticated

D. NT Domain authenticated
A. To use DCOM Configuration Properties, you must set your computer to use User-level access control.

27. What does the Registry key $(Remote) represent in the Setup.lst file?

A. The file is a type library, and is to be registered as such

B. The file is a self-registering DLL file

C. The file is a self-registering EXE file

D. The file is a remote support file (also referred to as remote server file)
D. The Registry key $(Remote) represents a remote support file (also called a remote server file) and is to be registered as such.

28. Which determines the files that should be removed during an uninstall of your program, when executed will remove all files, directories, and other items that were logged during installation.

A. UNINSTALl.EXE

B. ST6UNST.COM

C. ST6UNST.EXE

D. UNWISE.EXE
C. ST6UNST.EXE reads the log file and determines all files that should be removed. When executed, it will remove all files, directories, and other items logged in the ST6UNSTt.LOG.

29. You want to compile a Standard EXE project named "MyProject." What menu item on the File menu in Visual Basic 6.0 will you select to do this?

A. Make

B. Make Project

C. Make MyProject

D. Make MyProject.exe
D. To compile a project, you would select the menu item that says "Make," followed by your project name, and (in the case of a Standard EXE project) an EXE extension. In

the case of a Standard EXE project named MyProject, the menu item would read "Make MyProject.exe."

30. Using Package and Deployment Wizard, you decide to package to multiple CAB files. The Cab Size list box becomes available when you chose this. What CAB sizes can you choose from this list box? (Choose all that apply.)

   A. 1.44 MB

   B. 2.88 MB

   C. 1.2 MB

   D. 720 KB
   A, B, C, D. The CAB size list box allows you to choose from 1.44 MB, 2.88 MB, 1.2 MB, or 720 KB CAB sizes.

31. What must you have enabled on your computer to set User-level access control?

   A. File sharing

   B. Print sharing

   C. Share-level access

   D. A list of users set on your local hard disk
   A. File sharing must be enabled on your computer to set User-level security.

32. You are configuring DCOM on a server computer. Because the computer is running a server application, what must you specify in your configuration?

   A. The user account that will have access to start the application, and user accounts that have permissions to run it

   B. The location of the server application that will be accessed or started

   C. The location of the client application that will be accessed or started

   D. The user account of the person who configured DCOM on that computer
   A. Server applications need the following: the user account that will have access to start the application and user accounts that have permissions to run it.

33. The GetSettings and SaveSettings functions access entries under which key in the Windows Registry?

   A. HKEY_CURRENT_USER\Software\ VB and VBA Program Settings

   B. HKEY_CURRENT_CONFIG\ Software\VB and VBA Program Settings

   C. HKEY_LOCAL_MACHINE\ Software\VB and VBA Program Settings

   D. HKEY_CURRENT_CONFIG\ Software\VB
   A. GetSettings and SaveSettings access Registry entries under HKEY_CURRENT_USER\Software\VB and VBA Program Settings.

34. You have decided to deploy to floppy disks. When you enter the Deploy portion of the Package and Deployment Wizard, "Floppy Disk" doesn't appear on the Deployment Method screen. What is most likely the reason for this?

A. Deploy doesn't allow for floppy disk deployment

B. You forgot to choose Floppy Disk deployment in the Package portion of the Wizard

C. You forgot to package to multiple CAB files in the Package portion of the Wizard

D. You forgot to package to a single CAB file in the Package portion of the Wizard

C. If you don't package to multiple CABs in the Package portion, Floppy Disk deployment won't be an option in the Deploy portion.

35. Registry keys in the Setup.lst file indicate what information?

A. The location of the Windows Registry

B. The key in which to store information in the Windows Registry

C. Whether a file is self-registering, contains information for the Registry, or doesn't need to be registered

D. File location information for the Windows Registry

C. The Registry key in Setup.lst can indicate that a file doesn't need to be registered, is self-registering, or contains information for the Registry.

36. You are preparing to configure DCOM on a computer. The kind of security used on the computer requires that you enter a password for each resource. What kind of security is this, and what will happen when you try to open DCOM Configuration Properties?

A. User-level, and DCOM Configuration Properties will open

B. User-level, and DCOM Configuration Properties will fail to open

C. Share-level, and DCOM Configuration Properties will open

D. Share-level, and DCOM Configuration Properties will fail to open

B. Share-level security requires you to set a password for each resource on a computer. If you have this level of access on a computer, DCOM Configuration Properties will fail to open.

37. You are packaging an IIS application with the Package and Deployment Wizard. What Packaging Type will you select in the Package portion of the Wizard?

A. Standard Setup Package

B. Internet Package

C. IIS Package

D. Web Package

B. When packaging an internet application, such as an IIS application, select Internet Package as the Packaging Type

38. You plan to package and deploy a Standard EXE project to a network folder. In the Package portion, you reach the Package Folder screen of the Wizard. What does this screen allow you to specify?

A. A network folder where your application will be deployed

B. A folder where your application will be bundled into a package

C. The location where the application to be packaged resides

D. The location of files to be added to the package
B. The Package Folder screen allows you to set where the application will be bundled into a package.

39. You are using the Package portion of Package and Deployment Wizard. The DAO Drivers screen fails to appear as you go through the Wizard. Why?

A. You failed to add Data Access Objects to your package

B. The Package portion has determined which drivers to include and doesn't require interaction

C. Your application doesn't contain any Data Access Objects

D. The DAO Drivers screen only appears in the Deploy portion
C. If your application doesn't contain Data Access Objects, the DAO Drivers screen won't appear.

40. You reach the Shared Files screen of the Package portion of Package and Deployment Wizard. If your application has been packaged, deployed, and installed by the end user, who then decides to uninstall the application and what will happen to the files listed on this Shared Files screen? (Choose the best answer.)

A. Files that are shared files will be uninstalled

B. Files that are shared files are never uninstalled

C. Files that are shared files won't be uninstalled until every application using them is removed

D. Files that are shared files will need to be manually removed
C. The shared files, which are listed on the Shared Files screen, will only be removed if every application using the file is removed from the end user's system.

Chapter 12 Answers

1. Which of the following is a program loaded into memory and prepared for execution?

A. Thread

B. Process

C. Apartment

D. Task
B. A process is a program that's been loaded into memory and prepared for execution.

2. Which of the following must NOT be provided in a Visual Basic 6.0 project if apartment-model threading is to be used?

A. UserControls

B. UserDocuments

C. Forms

D. ActiveX Designers

E.   None of the above
E. Ulike previous versions of
Visual Basic, Visual Basic 6.0 allows
you to use apartment-model threading
on projects containing all of these
user interfaces

3.   Which of the following has its threads
furnished and managed by client
applications?

A.   In-process server

B.   Out-of-process server

C.   Standard EXE

D.   ActiveX EXE
A. An in-process server component,
which has threads furnished and
managed by client applications.

4.   How do you specify whether an ActiveX
EXE is single threaded or apartment
threaded? (Choose all that apply.)

A.   In the Threading Model section of the
General tab of Project Properties,
increase the Threading Pool to a value
greater than one

B.   In the Threading Model section of the
General tab of Project Properties, use
the Thread per Object option

C.   In the Threading Model section of the
General tab of the Project Properties
dialog box, specify in the list box
whether the project is "Single
Threaded" or "Apartment Threaded"

D.   In the Threading Model section of the
General tab of Project Properties, set
the Threading Pool to a value of 1

A, D. When an ActiveX EXE project
has its Threading Pool set to 1, it is
single threaded. When the Threading
Pool is set to a value greater than 1, it
is apartment threaded.

5.   You want to create a hyperlink that
connects to http: www.odyssey.
on.ca/~mcross. You are tired when you
enter the URL and mistakenly enter
Microsoft's Web site, http://www.
microsoft.com. What kind of error
has occurred?

A.   Logic

B.   Runtime

C.   Syntax

D.   Internet
A. This is an example of a logic error.
Although a valid URL was typed in, it
was not the URL you intended. Such
an error won't produce a runtime or
syntax error, but will return
unintended results.

6.   A user attempts to save a file to his floppy
drive, but forgets to insert a floppy disk.
What kind of error will result?

A.   Logic

B.   Hardware

C.   Syntax

D.   Runtime
D. This is an example of a runtime
error. The command to save results in
an invalid action because there is no
floppy to save to.

7. During the Package portion of using Package and Deployment Wizard, you chose to package your application to a single CAB file. When you deploy this application, which of the following deployment methods will be available to you? (Choose all that apply.)

   A. Floppy Disk

   B. Network

   C. Folder

   D. Web Publishing
   C, D. Selecting single CAB during the package portion give the options of Folder and Web Publishing during the Deploy portion.

8. You have decided to deploy your application to floppy disks, but you're not certain whether data exists on the floppies you're using for the deployment. What can you do?

   A. Do nothing because any existing data is automatically erased

   B. Do nothing because floppies are always formatted before the copying of files

   C. Check the Format before copying check box in the Deploy portion of Package and Deployment Wizard

   D. Check the Format before copying check box in the Package portion of Package and Deployment Wizard.
   C. Floppies can be formatted before files are copied to them by checking the Format before copying check box

in the Deploy portion of Package and Deployment Wizard

9. Which of the following can cause an error to occur in an application?

   A. Err

   B. Err.Number

   C. Err.Raise

   D. Err.Call
   D. Err.Call will generate an error because it is an invalid command.

10. Which of the following thread models has each thread containing its own copy of global data?

    A. Win16 threading

    B. Win32 threading

    C. Single threading

    D. Apartment-model threading
    D. Apartment-model threading has each thread containing its own copy of global data.

11. What kind of error does the following line of code produce?
    ```
    Dam x As Integer
    ```

    A. Logic

    B. Syntax

    C. Runtime

    D. Booboo
    B. This line of code shows an improper use of the Visual Basic language, with a keyword being misspelled. It is an example of a syntax error.

12. Which of the following specifies that a component can run without user interaction on network servers?

    A. Unattended ActiveX

    B. ActiveX Enable

    C. Unattended Execution

    D. Suppress User Interface
       C. The Unattended Execution check box allows you to specify whether a component can run without user interaction on network servers.

13. A procedure with error handling calls another error-handling procedure, which experiences an error. What will happen?

    A. The error will be passed to the calling procedure, which can then deal with the error

    B. An error message will be displayed and the application will quit

    C. An error message will be displayed and the error will be passed to the calling procedure

    D. The error handler that experiences the error will deal with its own error
       A. When an error handler is called and it experiences an error, that error is passed to the calling procedure. If, as in this case, the calling procedure has its own error handler, it will attempt to deal with the error.

14. A procedure without error handling calls an error-handling procedure. The error-handling procedure experiences an error. What will happen?

    A. The error will be passed to the calling procedure, which can then deal with the error

    B. An error message will be displayed and the application will quit

    C. An error message will be displayed and the error will be passed to the calling procedure

    D. The error handler that experiences the error will deal with its own error
       B. If a calling procedure doesn't have an error handler and it calls an error handling procedure that experiences an error, the application displays an error message and quits.

15. An error handler that is part of a procedure experiences an error. It hasn't been called by any other procedure. What will happen?

    A. The error will be passed to another procedure, which can then deal with the error

    B. An error message will be displayed and the application will quit

    C. An error message will be displayed and the error will be passed to a procedure that has error handling

    D. The error handler that experiences the error will deal with its own error
       B. When an error handler is part of a procedure and it experiences an error, the application will display an error message and quit.

16. You have implemented inline error handling in a procedure. What will reset

the Number property of the Err object to 0? (Choose all that apply.)

A. Resume

B. Resume Next

C. Err.Clear

D. On Error GoTo 0
C. Resume statements aren't used in inline error handling and On Error GoTo 0 is used to disable error trapping (not to reset Err.Number). The only choice that applies here is Err.Clear.

17. Procedure 1 calls Procedure 2. Procedure 1 has an error-handling routine. Procedure 2 experiences an error, but has no error handling. What will happen?

A. An error message will result and the application will quit

B. Procedure 2 will attempt to deal with the error

C. The error will be passed to Procedure 1, which will try dealing with the error

D. Procedure 2 will automatically fail and execution will return to Procedure 1
C. Errors are passed up the calling chain so that they can be dealt with by error handling in calling procedures.

18. You set Error Trapping to Break in Class Module. An error occurs outside of the class module. What will happen?

A. Visual Basic will break in the class module

B. Visual Basic will break where the unhandled error occurs

C. Visual Basic will ignore the error until it has been set to a different Error Trapping option

D. Visual Basic will display an error message and end the program
B. When an error occurs outside of a class module and Error Trapping is set to Break in Class Module, Visual Basic will break where the unhandled error occurs.

19. You have implemented error handling and want to see whether your routine works properly. What will you set Error Trapping to in order to determine that all errors are handled?

A. Break in Class Module

B. Break on All Errors

C. Break on Handled Errors

D. Break on Unhandled Errors
D. After creating error-handling routines, you can test them to see if they actually work by setting Error Trapping to Break on Unhandled Errors.

20. How do you specify whether an ActiveX DLL is single threaded or apartment threaded?

A. In the Threading Model section of the General tab of Project Properties, increase the Threading Pool to a value greater than 1

B. In the Threading Model section of the General tab of Project Properties, use the Thread per Object option

C. In the Threading Model section of the General tab of Project Properties, specify in the list box whether the project is Single Threaded or Apartment Threaded

D. ActiveX DLLs can only be single threaded

E. ActiveX DLLs can only be apartment-threaded
C. You can specify through the Threading Model list box whether an ActiveX DLL project is Single Threaded or Apartment Threaded.

21. During the Package portion of using the Package and Deployment Wizard, you chose to package your application to multiple cab files. When you deploy this application, which of the following deployment methods will be available to you? (Choose all that apply.)

A. Floppy Disk

B. Network

C. Folder

D. Web Publishing
A, C, D. Selecting Multiple CABs during the package portion will give the options of Floppy Disk, Folder, and Web Publishing during the Deploy portion.

22. Which property of the Err object is used to determine which application has caused an error?

A. Number

B. Source

C. Application

D. App
B. Err.Source is used to determine the source of an error.

23. Which of the following is used to disable an error trap?

A. Err.Clear

B. Resume

C. Err.Disable

D. On Error GoTo 0

E. On Error Clear
D. On Error GoTo 0 is used to disable an error trap

24. Which of the following are valid uses of the Resume statement? (Choose all that apply.)

A. Resume

B. Resume Next

C. Resume Previous

D. Resume *line*

E. Resume *label*
A, B, D, E. Resume, Resume Next, and Resume *line or label* are valid uses of the Resume statement.

25. You have implemented error handling to determine whether any errors exist in your code. To do this, all error-handling routines will have to be ignored. What will you set Error Trapping to?

A. Break in Class Module

B. Break on All Errors

C. Break on Handled Errors

D. Break on Unhandled Errors
B. To ignore error handling and break on all errors, set Error Trapping to Break on All Errors.

26. Look at the following message box that displays when an error occurs. What does this tell you about the program?

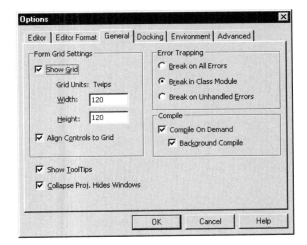

A. The project hasn't been compiled

B. The project has been compiled

C. The project contains no objects

D. The project has experienced a logic error
B. This type of message box appears when a program has been compiled and contains no custom messages with which to display information.

27. The value of the Err object's Number property is 0. What does this signify?

A. A critical error has occurred

B. A fatal error has occurred

C. A nasty error has occurred

D. No error has occurred
D. When the value of Err.Number is 0, no error has occurred.

28. Which of the following are valid labels for an error handler?

A. Err

B. MyError:

C. OnError

D. ThisIsAHandler
B. A label is created by following a name with a colon (":"). The only one that does this is MyError:.

29. Which of the following provides a means for a procedure to exit when no error occurs?

A. End Sub

B. Exit Sub

C. Exit When Err=0

D. Exit ErrorHandler
B. Exit Sub provides a means for the procedure to exit when no error occurs.

30. How do you specify whether an ActiveX control is single threaded or apartment threaded?

A. In the Threading Model section of the General tab of Project Properties, increase the Threading Pool to a value greater than 1

B. In the Threading Model section of the General tab of Project Properties, use the Thread per Object option

C. In the Threading Model section of the General tab of Project Properties, specify in the list box whether the control is Single Threaded or Apartment Threaded

D. ActiveX controls can only be single threaded

E. ActiveX controls can only be apartment threaded
    C. You can specify through the Threading Model list box whether an ActiveX control is Single Threaded or Apartment Threaded.

31. A procedure experiences an error, but its error handler deals with it. This procedure then calls another procedure, which then experiences and deals with the same error. What is most likely the reason for this?

A. On Error Resume Next wasn't implemented

B. Exit Sub wasn't used

C. The Number property of Err wasn't reset

D. The value of Err.Number was mistakenly set to 0
    C. This is most likely the result of Err.Number not being reset. When the Number property of Err isn't cleared, this kind of problem can occur when your procedure calls another procedure that has its own error handling. By not resetting Err.Number, a "ghost" error is created, which results in the called procedure's error handler attempting to deal with it.

32. You are creating an ActiveX client application. What Error Trapping option should you choose?

A. Break on All Errors

B. Break on Unhandled Errors

C. Break in Class Module

D. Break in ActiveX server
    C. Break in Class Module should be used when dealing with ActiveX servers. This option causes Visual Basic to break in the ActiveX server's code, rather than passing the error back to your client application.

33. You are working on a program that hasn't been compiled. When you run the project, an error message appears, notifying you of a runtime error. Four buttons appear on this message box. Which button will you click to take you to the line of code that caused the error?

A. Continue

B. Break

C. Debug

D. End
    The Debug button takes you to where the error occurred. This allows you to fix the error without ending the program.

34. You have created a procedure that adds sales tax to an amount, but instead of adding sales tax, you find that it is subtracting it. What kind of error has occurred?

A. Syntax

B. Logic

C. Runtime

D. Governmental

B. This is an example of a logic error. Although the program functions properly, it is producing unexpected results.

35. Which of the following features in Visual Basic 6.0 can aid in preventing syntax errors or catch them as they occur? (Choose all that apply.)

A. Auto List Members

B. Spell Check

C. Auto Syntax Check

D. Syntax Checker

A, C. Auto List Members lists all members of an object and aids in preventing syntax errors. Auto Syntax Check catches syntax errors as they occur by warning you of them when you move off the code, causing an error.

36. How can logic errors be found and corrected in a Visual Basic application?

A. Setting Auto Logic Check on the General tab of Options

B. Testing the application, discovering the errors, and correcting the code

C. Having others tell you they've discovered a logic error

D. Using the Logic Check tool that comes with Visual Basic 6.0

B. Although having others tell you they've found an error is a valid way to

discover logic errors, it does nothing to fix them. The only choice that covers finding and correcting logic errors is testing the application, discovering the errors, and correcting the code.

37. An unhandled error occurs in a class module. Which of the following Error Trapping options will break at the line that calls code in the class module? (Choose all that apply.)

A. Break on All Errors

B. Break on Handled Errors

C. Break in Class Module

D. Break on Unhandled Errors

A, D. Break on All Errors and Break on Unhandled Errors will break at the line that calls code in a class module, rather than breaking at the line in the module that caused the problem. Break in Class Module causes Visual Basic to break at the line that caused the error in the class module, while Break on Handled Errors doesn't exist.

38. Which of the following will establish error handling in your code? (Choose all that apply.)

A. On Error GoTo ErrorHandler

B. On Error Resume Next

C. On Error GoTo 0

D. On Error Resume

A, B. You can use the On Error statement to establish error handling in your code. Specifying the label of an error handler (such as ErrorHandler), or using On Error Resume Next can do this.

39. Checking the Unattended Execution check box on the General tab of Project Properties will do which of the following to a project?

 A. Enable the Threading Pool so you can specify a fixed number of threads used by the project

 B. Enable the Thread per Object option

 C. Enable the Threading Model

 D. Suppress anything in the project that requires user interaction
 D. Unattended Execution suppresses anything in the project that requires user interaction, such as message and dialog boxes.

40. Which of the following has the capability to use apartment-model threading? (Choose all that apply.)

 A. Visual Basic 5.0 Service Pack 2 Enterprise Edition

 B. Visual Basic 6.0 Standard Edition

 C. Visual Basic 6.0 Professional Edition

 D. Visual Basic 6.0 Enterprise Edition
 A, C, D. Apartment-model threading was introduced in Visual Basic 5.0 Service Pack 2. Both the Professional and Enterprise editions of Visual Basic 6.0 have the capability to use apartment-model threading.

MCSD
MICROSOFT CERTIFIED SOLUTION DEVELOPER

B

About the CD

This CD-ROM contains a browser-based testing product, the *Personal Testing Center*. The *Personal Testing Center* is easy to install. Just click Setup and you will be walked through the installation. The Personal Testing Center program group will be created in the Start Programs folder.

Test Type Choices

With the *Personal Testing Center*, you have three options in which to run the program: Live, Practice, and Review. Each test type will draw from a pool of over 500 potential questions. Your choice of test type will depend on whether you would like to simulate an actual MCSD exam, receive instant feedback on your answer choices, or review concepts using the testing simulator. Note that selecting the Full Screen icon on Internet Explorer's standard toolbar gives you the best display of the *Personal Testing Center*.

Live

The Live timed test type is meant to reflect the actual exam as closely as possible. You will have 90 minutes in which to complete the exam. You will have the option to skip questions and return to them later, move to the previous question, or end the exam. Once the time has expired, you will automatically go to the scoring page to review your test results.

Managing Windows

The testing application runs inside an Internet Explorer 4.0 browser window. We recommend that you use the full-screen view to minimize the amount of text scrolling you need to do. However, the application will initiate a second iteration of the browser when you link to an Answer in Depth or a Review Graphic. If you are running in full-screen view, the second iteration of the browser will be covered by the first. You can toggle between the two windows with ALT-TAB, you can click your task bar to maximize the second window, or you can get out of full-screen mode and arrange the two windows so they are both visible on the screen at the same time. The application will not initiate more than two browser windows, so you aren't left with hundreds of open windows for each Answer in Depth or Review Graphic that you view.

Saving Scores as Cookies

Your exam score is stored as a browser cookie. If you've configured your browser to accept cookies, your score will be stored in a cookie named History. If you don't accept cookies, you cannot permanently save your scores. If you delete the History cookie, the scores will be deleted permanently.

Using the Browser Buttons

The test application runs inside the Internet Explorer 4.0 browser. You should navigate from screen to screen by using the application's buttons, not the browser's buttons.

JavaScript Errors

If you encounter a JavaScript error, you should be able to proceed within the application. If you can't, shut down your Internet Explorer 4.0 browser session and re-launch the testing application.

Practice

When choosing the Practice exam type, you have the option of receiving instant feedback as to whether your selected answer is correct. The questions will be presented to you in numerical order, and you will see every question in the available question pool for each section you chose to be tested on.

As with the Live exam type, you have the option of continuing through the entire exam without seeing the correct answer for each question. The number of questions you answered correctly, along with the percentage of correct answers, will be displayed during the post-exam summary report. Once you have answered a question, click the Answer icon to display the correct answer.

You have the option of ending the Practice exam at any time, but your post-exam summary screen may reflect an incorrect percentage based on the number of questions you failed to answer. Questions that are skipped are counted as incorrect answers on the post-exam summary screen.

Review

During the Review exam type, you will be presented with questions similar to both the Live and Practice exam types. However, the Answer icon is not present, as every question will have the correct answer posted near the bottom of the screen. You have the option of answering the question without looking at the correct answer. In the Review exam type, you can also return to previous questions and skip to the next question, as well as end the exam by clicking the Stop icon.

The Review exam type is recommended when you have already completed the Live exam type once or twice, and would like to determine which questions you answered correctly.

Questions with Answers

For the Practice and Review exam types, you will have the option of clicking a hyperlink titled Answers in Depth, which will present relevant study material aimed at exposing the logic behind the answer in a separate browser window. By having two browsers open (one for the test engine and one for the review information), you can quickly alternate between the two windows while keeping your place in the exam. You will find that additional windows are not generated as you follow hyperlinks throughout the test engine.

Scoring

The *Personal Testing Center* post-exam summary screen, called Benchmark Yourself, displays the results for each section you chose to be tested on, including a bar graph similar to the real exam, which displays the percentage of correct answers. You can compare your percentage to the actual passing percentage for each section. The percentage displayed on the post-exam summary screen is not the actual percentage required to pass the exam. You'll see the number of questions you answered correctly compared to the total number of questions you were tested on. If you choose to skip a question, it will be marked as incorrect. Ending the exam by clicking the End button with questions still unanswered lowers your percentage, as these questions will be marked as incorrect.

Clicking the End button and then the Home button allows you to choose another exam type, or test yourself on another section.

MICROSOFT CERTIFIED SOLUTION DEVELOPER

C

About the
Web Site

Access Global Knowledge Network

As you know by now, Global Knowledge Network is the largest independent IT training company in the world. Just by purchasing this book, you have also secured a free subscription to the Global Knowledge Network Web site and its many resources. You can find it at: http://access.globalknowledge.com

You can log on directly at the Global Knowledge site, and you will be e-mailed a new, secure password immediately upon registering.

What You'll Find There

The wealth of useful information at the Global Knowledge site falls into three categories:

Skills Gap Analysis

Global Knowledge offers several ways for you to analyze your networking skills and discover where they may be lacking. Using Global Knowledge Network's trademarked Competence Key Tool, you can do a skills gap analysis and get recommendations for where you may need to do some more studying. (Sorry, it just might not end with this book!)

Networking

You'll also gain valuable access to another asset: people. At the Access Global site, you'll find threaded discussions, as well as live discussions. Talk to other MCSD candidates, get advice from folks who have already taken the exams, and get access to instructors and MCTs.

Product Offerings

Of course, Global Knowledge also offers its products here, and you may find some valuable items for purchase—CBTs, books, or courses. Browse freely and see if there's something that could help you take that next step in career enhancement.

D

Conventions

Like anything that's been around a while, there are conventions that apply to good programming. Conventions are a standardized way of doing things, and they often make things much easier in programming. They affect the structure and appearance of code, making it easier to read and maintain. There are naming conventions, coding conventions, and constant- and variable-naming conventions. These conventions allow a programmer to look at the work of another, and help him or her in determining what is going on in code.

Coding Conventions

When you're programming, you should follow certain conventions in your code. This includes the placement of variables and the structure of the code itself. When you declare variables, you should always place them at the top of a procedure. You can place your variables anywhere before they are used, but you should always put them at the top. That way, any changes can easily be made by looking for them at the top of a procedure. You always know where to find them.

A good example of the usefulness of placing variables at the top of your code is declaring a variable that represents minimum wage. Because minimum wage changes every few years, you should declare the minimum wage variable at the top of your code and assign a value to it. When the minimum wage changes, you don't have to search through your code to change the variable. It is always at the top of the procedure. In such an example, your code might appear as follows:

```
Private Sub WrkWeek()
Dim curAnswer, curMinWage As Currency
Dim intHours As Integer
curMinWage = 6.85
Hours = 40
    curAnswer = curMinWage * intHours

    MsgBox curAnswer
End Sub
```

This example shows several things in addition to where to declare variables and assign values to them. First, it shows the importance of using meaningful names. By looking at intHours and curMinWage, you can automatically tell what they represent. While you could have used names like x, y, and z for variables, these names don't explain much about their purpose. This also applies to naming procedures. By using a name like WrkWeek, you can determine that this probably has something to do with a work week.

The example shown above also displays the use of spacing in your code. Visual Basic version 6 ignores white space, the spacing in your code where nothing appears. As such, indenting code and adding blank spaces to separate parts of code (by pressing ENTER), is ignored by VB. Though the compiler ignores the white space, its presence makes it considerably easier for programmers to read.

While a procedure or function should always deal with one task (such as calculating your paycheck or opening another form), you will always have parts of code that deal with different things. For example, declaring variables and code that deals with those variables are two different parts of code. You should leave a blank line between such items. If your code does different tasks, such as running a loop and displaying a message box, you should separate the code with blank lines. By doing this, your code becomes significantly easier to read.

You should also indent your code to show different tasks in your code. For example, using nested IF...THEN statements can be confusing if they are bunched together. If parts of the code are indented, it becomes easier to read. Compare the following example, and you can see the difference:

```
If x < y then                      If x < y then
If z>x then                            If z>x then
Msgbox "z is greater than y"               Msgbox "z is greater
End if                         than y"
Msgbox "x is less than y"              End if
End if                         Msgbox "x is less than y"
```

By indenting the lines of code, you can easily see which End If applies to which If statement. You can also see what code applies to which

IF…THEN statement. Indenting code organizes it so that you can read it much easier.

If you have lines of code that are particularly long, stretching past the width of your code window, you should split the line of code across two or more lines. This is done with the line continuation character. This character is a space followed by an underscore; it makes your code easier to read while not affecting its performance. The following is an example of a single line of code, split across several lines with the line continuation character.

```
txtMyText.Text= "This is my line " _
& "that is split across several lines " _
& "of code."
```

While one statement should appear on each line of code, it should also be mentioned here that you can put several lines of related code on the same line. This is done by using a colon (:) to indicate a separation between each statement. The following example shows how this is done:

```
Label1.Caption = "Hello World": Label1.BackColor = vbRed
```

This shows two related statements, separated by a colon. When VB reads this, it will recognize this as two different statements.

In addition to conventions that affect the appearance of your code, you should also use comments in your code. Comments can be placed in code by beginning your sentence with an apostrophe ('). Comments can be placed alone on a line or at the end of a line of code. If you are placing the comment on a line by itself, you can also use the REM statement, which is short for remark. The REM statement is way of making comments that goes back to the early days of programming and is still used today. The following shows examples of comments in action:

```
REM This starts my program
Dim x As Integer 'This declares x as an integer
'The following line displays x
txtMyText.Text=x
```

In addition to showing how comments are used in code, this example also shows how they should not be used. You should avoid commenting code that is obvious (that is, stating that "this starts my program") and commenting everything occurring in your code. Another bad example is explaining that a variable is being declared. Try to code with other programmers in mind. Ask yourself, "Will this be obvious to another programmer?" If the answer is no, then comment it. In addition, keep in mind that while a chunk of code makes sense to you now, it may not be so clear to you six months or a year from now. Commenting code avoids such problems.

on the job *A colleague of mine experienced a particularly funny example of bad commenting. He was working on some code written by a person who no longer worked for the company. While working on the code, he came across the comment "Don't touch this. It's important!" Since the code was being upgraded, he had to spend extra time determining if the code was still "important" or was now obsolete. Unfortunately, it was a particularly long and elaborate piece of code. I say this example is funny, because it happened to him, not me. It does illustrate the need to be straight to the point and explain things properly when writing comments.*

Object-Naming Conventions

Naming conventions allow you to look at an object and determine what it is. Rather than having to guess if MyLine is a label, text box, or whatever, you should be able to look at an object's name and determine what it is. This is done by adding a prefix to the object's name to specify its type.

Table D-1 below lists prefixes commonly used for controls in VB version 6. You should use these when naming objects in VB.

Table D-2 shows the prefixes for Data Access Objects (DAO). You should use these prefixes whenever naming DAO objects.

Control	Prefix	Example
3D Panel	pnl	pnlPanel
ADO Data	ado	adoData
Animated button	ani	aniEnter
Check box	chk	chkBold
Combo box, drop-down list box	cbo	cboListing
Command button	cmd	cmdExit
Common dialog	dlg	dlgOpen
Communications	com	comModem
Control (used within procedures when the specific type is unknown)	ctr	ctrControl
Data	dat	datData
Data-bound combo box	dbcbo	dbcboOrders
Data-bound grid	dbgrd	dbgrdMyGrid
Data-bound listbox	dblst	dblstEmployee
Data combo	dbc	dbcLastName
Data grid	dgd	dgdBooks
Data list	dbl	dblCost
Data repeater	drp	drpDatRep
Date picker	dtp	dtpDatPic
Directory listbox	dir	dirDirect
Drive listbox	drv	drvSource
File listbox	fil	filFile
Flat scroll bar	fsb	fsbScroll
Form	frm	frmMain
Frame	fra	fraOptions

TABLE D-2	Control	Prefix	Example
Standard Prefixes for Object Naming Conventions	Gauge	gau	gauStatus
	Graph	gra	graIncome
	Grid	grd	grdOutcome
	Hierarchical flexgrid	flex	flexPublisher
	Horizontal scroll bar	hsb	hsbMove
	Image	img	imgMyPic
	Image combo	imgcbo	imgcboPicture
	ImageList	ils	ilsMyImage
	Label	lbl	lblFirstName
	Lightweight check box	lwchk	lwchkMyBox
	Lightweight combo box	lwcbo	lwcboAuthor
	Lightweight command button	lwcmd	lwcmdEnter
	Lightweight frame	lwfra	lwfraSave
	Lightweight horizontal scroll bar	lwhsb	lwhsbHorBar
	Lightweight listbox	lwlst	lwlstPrice
	Lightweight option button	lwopt	lwoptGross
	Lightweight text box	lwtxt	lwoptFirst
	Lightweight vertical scroll bar	lwvsb	lwvsbHigh
	Line	lin	linMyLine
	Listbox	lst	lstCustomer
	ListView	lvw	lvwTitles
	MAPI message	mpm	mpmMessage
	MAPI session	mps	mpsSession
	MCI	mci	mciVideo

Control	Prefix	Example
Menu	mnu	mnuFile
Month view	mvw	mvwMonth
MS Chart	ch	chMyChart
MS Flex grid	msg	msgFlexGrid
MS Tab	mst	mstTab
OLE container	ole	oleFiesta
Option button	opt	optCanada
Picture box	pic	picMyPic
Picture clip	clp	clpPicClip
ProgressBar	prg	prgDataRate
Remote Data	rd	rdRemDat
RichTextBox	rtf	rtfDetails
Shape	shp	shpMyShape
Slider	sld	sldSlideBar
Spin	spn	spnOutHere
StatusBar	sta	staMyStat
SysInfo	sys	sysMem
TabStrip	tab	tabTeStrip
Text box	txt	txtFirstName
Timer	tmr	tmrTest
Toolbar	tlb	tlbFunctions
Treeview	tre	treDirect
UpDown	upd	updDirection
Vertical scroll bar	vsb	vsbMyBar

DAO Object	Prefix	Example
Container	con	conMyCont
Database	db	dbCustomer
DBEngine	dbe	dbeVaroom
Document	doc	docMyDoc
Field	fld	fldFirstName
Group	grp	grpMarketing
Index	ix	idxGender
Parameter	prm	prmMyPara
QueryDef	qry	qryTopSales
Recordset	rec	recMyRec
Relation	rel	relFinance
TableDef	tbd	tbdPublishers
User	usr	usrMyUser
Workspace	wsp	wspMyWork

Variable-Naming Conventions

In addition to objects, you should also use naming conventions for variables. This will allow you to identify easily the data type of your variable. In doing so, you can avoid improperly matching data types and mismatching errors. An example of such an error would be trying to multiply a Boolean data type called Answer by a integer named Amount. By using the prefixes of variable-naming conventions, you would rename these to intAmount and blnAnswer. In doing so, you would know their data types and avoid such an error. Table D-3 lists the standard prefixes.

When using prefixes, I can't stress enough that you should give your variable a meaningful name. Renaming a variable called x to intx may

Data Type	Prefix	Example
Boolean	bln	blnYesNo
Byte	byt	bytOutaCrime
Collection object	col	colComics
Currency	cur	curMoola
Date (Time)	dtm	dtmBDate
Double	dbl	dblStarVal
Error	err	errOopsy
Integer	int	intAge
Long	lng	lngDistance
Object	obj	objMyAffection
Single	sng	sngUnattached
String	str	strName
User-defined type	udt	udtCustomer
Variant	vnt	vntMyVar

follow the naming convention, but it hardly gives an accurate indication of what the variable is for. You should always try to name the variable something that indicates what it is being used for.

Using meaningful names is equally important when naming procedures, functions, and objects. You should try to determine what something is being used for, and name it accordingly. It is also wise to show the scope of a variable as being modular or global by prefixing them with the letters *m* and *g*, respectively. By doing this, you can automatically determine if a variable is modular or global.

While it may seem difficult trying to remember the methods and prefixes of conventions, they are well worth learning and using. In the long run, they will save you a substantial amount of time. It is easier to take a moment to look up a prefix in the tables contained in this appendix than to spend considerably more time searching through code to figure out the data type of a variable.

E

The MCSD
Career Center

Y ou might be tempted to think that your work is finished once you have achieved your MCSD certification. Nothing could be further from the truth. Now that you have the certification, you need a job that is going to provide opportunities to use your certification. You might also look for a job that will allow you to obtain additional certifications. Finding that job can be difficult if you don't know where to look or what to look for.

The MCSD "Help Wanteds:" Planning Your Attack

Looking at the title of this section, you might think you were going to war. Well, it's not quite as bad as that, but a job-hunting campaign, like a military campaign, should have a strategy. Many people start with the attitude that if you have no idea what you're looking for, then you won't be disappointed with what you find. There's probably some truth in that, but I would add that you probably won't find the job that's right for you, either.

I also like to use the analogy of courtship when explaining the importance of having a strategy for your search. If you've never stopped to think about your perfect mate, then chances are you don't really know what you're looking for. If you go ahead and get married anyway, you could find yourself in a marriage that is going to lead to a messy divorce or many years of unhappiness.

Getting fired or quitting a job isn't as bad as getting a divorce, but it's not much fun. In my career I've had good and bad jobs, jobs that have gone from good to bad, and jobs that have gone from bad to good. I've been hired, fired, and I've "moved on to other opportunities" (I quit). All of these changes required decisions from me, and a lot of thought had to go into those decisions.

In the next few pages I'm going to try to help you develop a job search strategy. Since I am both a certified professional and a technical recruiter, I'll try to give you a little insight from both sides of the table.

(✍)
recruiter
@dvice

Before talking to a headhunter or recruiter, put together an information packet that includes a resume, a cover letter, a skills list, a project list, and maybe even references. The more information you provide, the easier it will be for a headhunter or recruiter to place you.

The Job Search

We begin with the job search. Time seems to be the biggest factor for most folks when it comes to looking for a new job. How long is this going to take? That's a tough question. The answer depends on the market, on the type of job you are looking for, and your personal situation.

The ideal situation to be in when searching for new job is to have a job you already like. That might not make sense at first, but think about it for a minute. If you don't feel like you have to leave your current job, you aren't going to feel as much pressure to take a less than optimal new job. You will spend more time learning about new opportunities and educating yourself about what you're getting into.

With more time, you may broaden your search and consider areas or industries that you might not have considered under a time crunch. You'll feel better about holding out for a higher salary or a better signing bonus. Most importantly, you will not be rushed into a decision that is going to shape the rest of your life. You will have time to decide what you want, and then to develop a strategy for how you are going to get it.

Incidentally, recruiters love to find people who are under the gun, because they know that they can get these people on board faster and at a lower cost. However, a manager will recognize that this type of person may not be around for long, because the person may be getting into a job he isn't suited for. Remember that recruiters make recommendations, but it's managers who make decisions.

If you happen to find yourself "between jobs" at the moment, don't sweat it. If you are certified, or are getting certified, the jobs are out there. There has never been a better time to be an out-of-work Microsoft Certified Professional. If you need to convince yourself of this, find the latest salary survey from *MCP Magazine*. Believe me, you will feel better about your situation. Just relax and take some time to focus on your strategy. Then implement that strategy.

If you aren't currently in a job, you may actually have an advantage over someone who does have a job. You have an abundance of one of the world's most limited resources—spare time!

Networking 101

You have heard someone say, "It's not what you know, but whom you know." There is some truth in that. Networking has two big benefits for you if it's done right. The first benefit is contacts. The second benefit is association.

The contacts benefit is fairly straightforward, so we'll talk about that in a second. Let's talk about associations first, since it might not be so obvious. One very common method of networking is to join professional groups like software user groups. Even if you don't attend the meetings, you can tell people that you're a card-carrying member of the XYZ group.

If the XYZ group has a reputation for being a very technical and prestigious group, chances are your value just went up in the mind of the recruiter. By the way, you are also demonstrating the capacity to be social. Most recruiters aren't interested in even the most technically proficient people if they can't relate to other people.

Let's say for a moment that you did join a users group or any type of social organization, and you actually attended the meetings. Whom might you meet there? Well, you might meet me or one of my fellow recruiters. That could prove helpful.

You might also meet directors, project managers, senior technical leads, or entrepreneurs. All of these people are always on the lookout for talent—it's ingrained in them. Every time they meet someone new, the question they ask themselves is "Could I use this person?"

If you can prompt someone to ask that question about you, and answer "yes," then you have probably just found yourself a job. At a minimum, you have gained recognition from an influential person inside the organization. That puts you about a light-year ahead of your competitors who are answering ads from the Sunday paper.

(🖐)
**recruiter
@dvice**

Make yourself a list of questions before going into an interview. You don't even have to memorize them. Take notes, and press for information if you aren't satisfied with the answers. Remember that you are interviewing the company just as much as they are interviewing you.

Using Placement Services

I have mixed feelings about placement services. I think placement services are excellent vehicles for finding entry-level positions. If you have just finished your MCSD, then a placement service might be a good choice for you.

However, if you've had your MCSD for a while, or if you already have a lot of industry experience, then be careful of placement services. Most services make their money by doing a volume business. You register with the service, and the service attempts to place you in the first job request they receive for which you are qualified.

Placement services rarely take the time to investigate the jobs into which they are placing people. Many times the placement services get their list of job positions right out of the newspaper. Many of the opportunities that you will find through placement services are temporary staffing positions.

This might be just what you need to build a resume. However, for an experienced individual looking for a full-time position as a senior technical lead, listing a number of temporary staffing positions on your resume may do you more harm than good.

If you choose to use a placement service, consider using one of the nationwide services like Kelly Technical Services or AeroTek. I have been impressed in the past with the speed at which these services have filled positions, and with the quality of applicants that these services attract. Also, if you are willing to travel, the nationwide services may be able to find you a specific type of job.

To sum it up, my advice on placement services is not to discount them. Just make sure that the type of job you are looking for is the type of job that the service fills on a regular basis.

Going Online

By now, I hope I don't need to tell you that you can find a wealth of information on the Internet. This includes company marketing information, securities exchange information, and recruiting information. Almost all of the Fortune 500 companies, and many of the smaller ones, provide a way to submit resumes either through an e-mail address or through a Web form.

If you submit your resume through e-mail, be sure that you clearly indicate what file format it's in. Pick something common like RTF format or Microsoft Word 6.0/95 format. When you submit your resume via e-mail, you can be reasonably sure that someone is going to print it out and read it.

When e-mailing resumes you need to plan for the least common denominator. All your high resolution color graphics, watermarks, and textures may look great at home, but when printed on the high-volume laser printer at the recruiter's office, they become distracting. Guess what happens to resumes that are distracting and hard to read. That's right—straight in to the trash. I've thrown away dozens of resumes because they were just too much work to read.

When submitting your resume via an online form, you need a slightly different strategy. Think key words. There's a good chance that all of the information you are entering is being stored in a database. At some point, someone is going to run a query against that database that goes something like this, "Show me all of the MCSDs with at least TWO YEARS WORK EXPERIENCE and CERTIFIED on Visual Basic."

You've got to get as many keywords as you can into the information you are entering in the database. That way, your name will come up more often. As you can imagine, trying to maximize keywords can lead to some pretty hilarious text, but it works. It also demonstrates that you understand how computer systems work. That isn't lost on recruiters

If you happen to be just what a company is looking for, then submitting your resume online might be a good idea. However, it's been my experience that submitting a resume online isn't much better than mailing in a resume to the attention of the personnel director.

I'm not fond of this method, because it lacks a certain personal touch. Also, you really have no idea who is receiving your resume. It might be someone in the personnel department at a company, or it might be someone at a placement office that has the contract for the company you are interested in.

Whenever I submit my resume, I always identify the job I'm looking for, then I find out who is responsible for filling that position. This often requires a little inside knowledge. Try to find someone in the organization who will give you an exact job title and the name of a manager responsible for filling that position.

An excellent source for this type of information is ex-employees. Most will be more than happy to give you the inside scoop. They will probably also be willing to tell you what to look out for. Finding an ex-employee and taking him or her out to lunch may be one of the best investments you ever make.

After a personal contact, such as a phone call or a lunch appointment, I then submit my resume to that person. That person then becomes my sponsor. He or she passes my resume on to whoever needs to see it, hopefully with some positive remarks. That is a level of personal contact that just can't be achieved through an online submittal process.

Getting the Advice of Peers

Once you have identified a company that you want to work for, you need to get the lay of the land. You need to gather intelligence. Try to make some contacts within the company, and try to meet some people who have interviewed with the company before. This is usually easier said than done, but you can get some really valuable information.

Ask around. You might just get lucky and find someone who has successfully, or unsuccessfully, done what you are trying to do. Try to figure out what works and what doesn't. Be careful, though. If you start asking too many questions, you might tip your hand to either a vindictive supervisor or a coworker planning on interviewing for the same position you are. Know who your friends are.

Now is the right time for you to make a friend at the company you are interested in. There is nothing better than inside information. Find someone who is willing to check the internal postings a couple of times a week, or someone who knows someone.

This might be easier than you think. Many companies are now offering finders fees for technical talent. If an employee submits someone's resume, and the candidate is eventually hired, that employee may have earned a bonus of a few thousand dollars. You would be amazed how many "friends" you'll have if you have the potential of putting a few thousand dollars in their pocket.

The Interview

So far, so good. You've been granted an interview. This is no time to forget about your strategy! On the contrary, now is the time to redouble your efforts. This may be your only face-to-face interaction with the company of your dreams. You've got to make a good impression, and you are going to be limited in the amount of time you have to do that.

Try to ask pointed questions that demonstrate that you know programming. For example, you might ask a technical interviewer about their applications and languages being used. Find out whether the company has a 100 percent 32-bit desktop, and whether the Y2K issue is presenting any problems.

All of these are great questions if you are talking to a technical interviewer. These are not appropriate questions if you are talking to someone from the human resources department, or a senior non-technical manager. If you're talking to a vice president or a senior manager, don't talk technical, talk business. Ask whether the company has done a Total Cost of Ownership (TCO) analysis, and if so, what were the results. Ask what the acceptable Return on Investment (ROI) is for a capital project.

If you aren't comfortable with these questions, stick to something simpler like asking what projects are in the works for improving productivity, improving reliability, or reducing support costs. These are the issues that business people wrestle with every day. If you want to relate to these folks, you've got to speak their language, and you've got to talk about things that they care about.

When answering questions, give direct, concise responses. If you don't know an answer, admit it, then offer your best guess. Guessing is acceptable, as long as you identify your answer as a guess. Don't ever try to pass yourself off as something you are not. A technical interviewer will smell a phony as soon as the answers start to stink.

Working with a Headhunter

As someone looking for a job, I loved working with headhunters. As a recruiter, I hate competing with them. So for the purpose of this discussion, I'm going to try to think like someone looking for a job.

The really nice thing about headhunters is that most of them are paid a finder's fee that is a percentage of the salary of the person hired. Consequently, the more money you make, the more money your headhunter makes. This is one of the few situations in life where your agent's best interests are truly your best interests. Also, most headhunters don't get paid at all unless they fill a position. They work fast, usually with remarkable results.

There are some things to watch out for, though. There are people out there calling themselves career consultants, or even headhunters. They want you to pay them a few hundred dollars to build a resume and to tell you what your ideal job is.

First, you don't need someone to tell you what your ideal job is. You should be able to figure that out on your own. Second, if these people even have a placement service, you would be amazed how many times your ideal job just happens to be the position they are trying to fill. Third, there are too many good recruiters and headhunters out there who don't charge you a dime. You should never, ever pay someone to find you a job! Now give me a second to get off my soapbox...

I guess I get so excited about this topic because I know some really good headhunters who do excellent work. When they make a placement, the company is happy, the employee is happy, and the headhunter makes a little money. But there are always a few who give the rest of the recruiting industry a bad name, because they've taken clients' money and left them in the same job, or a worse job.

Headhunters often specialize in a particular type of job, location, or industry. If you are looking for something specific, ask around and find a headhunter who has concentrated on that area. Not only will this person know what is going on in her specialty, she can help tailor your presentation to that area. That's the real benefit. Think of these specialists as insiders for hire—only you're not paying the bill!

Even if you don't need a specialist, before you contact a headhunter, try to narrow down your goals. Headhunters aren't in the business of being career counselors. They are in the business of finding you the job you're looking for. That's not to say that they won't help you. On the contrary, they will probably give you a great deal of attention. But only you know what you want.

Put together a professional-looking resume listing every skill you have. Also put together a cover letter that details what type of job you are looking for, what kind of salary and benefits package you need, and any other interesting bits of information about yourself. This is the documentation that is going to catch the eye of a headhunter.

Your headhunter will then probably take you out to lunch, and the two of you will have a chat. By the time you're ordering dessert, you will probably have defined your job requirements even more precisely. You may also leave with a list of things to do. The list might include making enhancements to your resume, researching companies, and maybe even scheduling an interview.

On the other hand, the headhunter may tell you point blank that you just aren't qualified for what you want to do, and that there is no way he or she could place you in the job you're looking for. That's hard to hear, but it's probably an honest assessment.

Remember that headhunters only make money if you make money. If a headhunter tells you that you're not qualified, you need to decide whether to continue pursuing this job with another headhunter, or to look for another job for which you are better suited.

My advice is to swallow your pride, open your mind, and see what the headhunter has to say. Chances are, he's going to have some ideas that you might not have considered. At a minimum, you should be able to find out why you aren't qualified and what you need to do to get qualified for the job of your dreams.

One final thought on this topic. A lot of people worry that a headhunter is going to rush them into a job that they won't enjoy, just so the headhunter can get paid. Well, in the first place, you're the decision-maker. Only you can decide whether or not to take a job.

Second, a growing trend in the industry is that headhunters don't get paid their full commission until the client has held the job for more than six months. I like this trend because once again, your best interests dovetail with the headhunter's. There's little incentive for a headhunter to put you in a job you're not going to enjoy.

Working with headhunters has been a very positive experience for me. Some of the best jobs I've ever had have come through headhunters. If you find one you like, they are an excellent resource for taking your career where you want it to go.

Preparing for the Interview

Start with a little research. You need to be able to talk intelligently about the company you are interviewing with, the industry the company is in, and how you can help the company achieve its goals. At a minimum, you should check out the company's Web site and learn its mission statement, objectives, and goals. You need to demonstrate that you know where this company wants to go and how they are planning to get there.

You can also check out one of the online investment firms to gather information, if the company you're researching is publicly traded. Know what the financial status of the company is. Know whether there are any planned mergers or acquisitions.

You should also try to get a feel for the technology being used in the company. This information could be a little more difficult to obtain than financial information; you may need to find an insider. Be careful of making any recommendations about technology during an interview. After all, you don't want to tell someone how to do his job or step on someone's toes. You might, however, be able to identify some troublesome areas that your skills could ease.

Acing the Interview

I wish I could give you a nice, simple formula for ensuring success in an interview. If one exists, I haven't found it, and I don't know anyone who has.

By definition, an interview occurs when two or more people get together for the purpose of filling a job. When you get two people together, there exists the possibility for conflict. Unfortunately, you can do everything right and still have a lousy interview simply because your personality clashed with the personality of the person doing the interviewing.

One of the things that you might consider doing is buying a couple of books, audio tapes, or videos about interviewing or personal selling. There are lots of tapes on how to sell, and quite a few about interviewing. All of them will give you some ideas for building a personal relationship with someone in a very short amount of time.

Try to avoid obvious gimmick techniques like commenting on something you see in the person's office. I was on a sales call one time with a junior sales representative who made the mistake of complementing a manager about the large fish he had mounted on the wall. The manager looked right at the rep and said, "I hate that damn fish. My boss goes on all of these company-sponsored fishing trips, spends a fortune, and then decorates our offices with his stupid fish." The sales call was over before it even began.

This may sound like a cliché, but be yourself. Don't put on airs; don't try to be something you aren't. Most people are not good actors, and most recruiters can spot a performance very quickly. When a recruiter interviews you, he or she wants to get a sense of who you are—not just what you know. Don't make it hard on the recruiters by putting on a show.

When being interviewed, you should appear confident about yourself and your abilities. Practice showing confidence by standing in front of a mirror and "introducing yourself" a few times. Tell your mirror image how happy you are to have an opportunity to interview for the position. Then briefly explain to yourself what your qualifications are and why you would be a good fit for the position. (But avoid telling yourself that you are the *best* candidate for the position. You never know that, and you might be setting yourself up for feeling "robbed" if you're not eventually hired.) Finally, ask yourself a few questions about the job and your own plans, and then answer them. Try this technique. I guarantee it will be the toughest interview you ever have.

Now let's talk for a moment about interview etiquette. I've never seen a formal guide to interview etiquette, but there is certainly an informal set of expectations.

For example, most recruiters are tolerant of a candidate being ten minutes late. Five minutes early is preferable, but ten minutes late is acceptable. Beyond ten minutes, your chances for a successful interview begin to drop precipitously. If you are going to be more than ten minutes late, you definitely need to call, and you can probably expect to reschedule your interview.

Another piece of etiquette involves who speaks first in the interview. Once introductions are made, and everyone is comfortable, the interviewer will ask the first question. That question may be followed by another series of short-answer "warm-up" questions, or the interviewer may ask a more open-ended question.

Open-ended questions are designed to give the person being interviewed an opportunity to talk openly or to bend the conversation towards a topic he or she wants to discuss. Recognize the different types of questions and respond appropriately. If you speak out of turn or fail to answer appropriately, you are running the risk of annoying the interviewer and having your interview cut short.

Incidentally, if the interviewer asks you a trick question, and it's obvious that it is a trick question, call him on it. Let him know that you're not afraid to call a donkey a donkey. Most interviewers will appreciate this and probably accord you a little more respect as a result.

Following Up on the Interview

Always follow up on an interview. This can be done with a simple thank-you card or a phone call.

You're trying to accomplish several things with the follow-up: refreshing the memories of the decision makers (who may have interviewed numerous candidates), projecting a positive impression, and demonstrating interest and eagerness to work for this company.

Don't worry about looking desperate; you are more likely to come off as confident and professional. Never worry about following up an interview with a phone call to check the status of your application. In many companies, the people doing the interviewing are also the people doing real work. Interviewing is not their primary responsibility. Consequently, applications sometimes slip through the cracks. It may be up to you to keep the ball rolling by continuing to call and ask questions. You might get hired through persistence alone.

(✋)
**recruiter
@dvice**

Never stop looking for your perfect job. You should test the waters and go out on an interview or talk to a headhunter once every six months. High-tech industries change rapidly, and with that change comes a myriad of new opportunities.

Glossary

access key   A keystroke combination that allows a program to be activated.

Active Serve Pages (ASP)   A scripting environment in which the processing of scripts takes place on an IIS or Web server.

ActiveX   A way to package components for delivery in Web browsers or other software using COM. OLE, which is also built on COM, is a subset of ActiveX.

ActiveX Controls   Technology for creating UI elements for delivery on the Web.

ADO (ActiveX Data Objects)   Enables client applications to manipulate and access data in a server (through any OLE DB provider). ADO supports key features for building Web-based and client-server applications.

Advanced Data TableGram Format   A proprietary data storage format from Microsoft.

Application Programming Interfaces (APIs)   Sets of commands used in an application to request services performed by the operating system.

Application Server   A component with a dual identity. It can be run like any standard EXE-type application, and can be used by a client as an OLE server.

ASCII   An acronym for American Standard Code for Information Interchange. It uses numbers ranging from zero to 255 to represent keyboard characters: numbers, letters, and special characters such as ! @ # $ % ^ & * ( ).

asynchronous processing   Processing that goes through several steps to complete a task. It allows the client to perform other tasks before returning earlier results.

authentication   The logon process; it includes verifying the correct username and password.

availability   The capability of a program to handle failures.

binding   The control is linked or tied to a data source, so it can access the data contained within it.

Binding Collection   Works as a link between the consumer and the source, allowing information from the source to be passed to the consumer. Using the Binding Collection allows you to bind data during runtime.

Bitness   The status of a process, whether it is 16-bit or 32-bit.

Boolean Value   A value of True or False. Boolean values must be one or the other.

Bound Mode   The property of an object when it is linked to a data source. (See also **binding**.)

Break Mode   Allows the user to examine, debug, reset, step through, or continue the execution of an application.

call-back   An application makes a call to a function or method, and goes about its business. When the external function has completed the task, it calls the application back by calling a function in the client designated to answer it.

call stack   The chain of procedures; the order in which code and procedures are executed.

calling chain   (See **call stack**.)

CD key A code that comes with the installation package of software. Many installation processes require a valid CD key to be input before continuing the installation.

Change Event An event coded to indicate that a change has occurred in a control.

class modules Allow you to add custom object variable types to a VB project. Classes are templates that are used to create objects. They are the start for building COM components.

Code Window The window in VB that allows you to input and view the code making the application you're developing.

Command Object One of the three main ADO objects; it defines commands and parameters and can execute commands against Connection objects.

comments Insertions into code that are not compiled, but provide explanation and clarification. They begin with an apostrophe.

Component Object Model (COM) A standardized specification module that can be reused without modification in many different applications.

conceptual design The process of identifying an application's requirements.

concurrency The locking method for a cursor. Concurrency types include read-only, optimistic, batch optimistic, and pessimistic.

condition compiling Allows you to create one project that deals with all versions of your application.

Connection Object   One of the three main objects of ADO; it establishes connections with data sources, manages transactions, and reports errors from the underlying OLE DB components.

constant   A data value that does not change. Constants are resolved when the application compiles.

controls   Items that make up the user interface.

constraints   Business logic that is enforced by the database server by limiting data input, ensuring referential integrity.

cross-process components   Another term for out-of-process components.

cursor   The result set of an application connecting to a database to process rows of data. Cursors can be client-side and server-side, and are further broken down to static, forward-only, dynamic, and keyset.

Data Access Object (DAO)   An application programming interface that is independent of the database management system. Uses the Microsoft Jet engine.

Database Management System (DBMS)   Software tool that organizes, modifies, and analyzes information stored in a database.

Data Consumer   A class that can be bound to an external data source.

Data Environment Designer   A feature of Visual Basic that provides an interactive design environment for creating programmatic data access during runtime. Data Environment objects can leverage drag-and-drop to automate creation of data-bound controls.

Data Form Wizard   A wizard in Visual Basic that allows you create forms quickly from a template.

Data Grid A control that provides a direct exposure to all of the data defined by the data control in a spreadsheet format.

Data Report Designer A feature of Visual Basic that quickly and easily allows simple reports to be created and integrated with the Data Environment Designer.

dead code Unused code in an application. It should be removed before compiling. This does not include comments.

dependent objects Objects created by using the methods exposed by externally-creatable objects.

deployment stage A phase of application design in which decisions are made about how components are or aren't distributed across the network.

Design Time The operation mode of Visual Basic while an application is being created. You build the components and set the properties of your application in this mode.

DHTML Page Designer A feature of Visual Basic that allows you to design and create HTML documents without a previous knowledge of HTML.

documentation A few common examples of documentation include recording the objectives of your application and describing what different aspects of your application do, and creating flow charts. Documentation can be utilized in later stages of design and in the creation of Help documentation.

DSN (Data Source Name) A term for the collection of information used to connect an application to a particular ODBC database.

Dynamic HTML (DHTML) Used for developing Web pages. DHTML allows Web page authors to dynamically change the elements of an HTML document. With DHTML you can add, delete, and modify what appears on a Web page.

Early Binding Method   In the variable declaration, telling the compiler in advance what type of object it will reference.

error handling   The part of a program that deals with errors in the rest of the program to prevent a full system crash. It involves checking the error, handling the error in some way, and exiting the error handler.

error trapping   Writing code that allows the program the chance to correct an error, or offering the developer a chance to correct it.

event   Action that is recognized by an object.

exposed object   An object (such as a control in a different program) that your program can "see."

extensibility   Allows an application to go beyond its original design.

externally creatable objects   Top-level objects exposed by a component to the client.

forms   Basic building block of a VB application. Containers in VB that contain other objects and controls.

general declarations section   The section of code in which you declare and define general variables.

Globally Unique Identifier (GUID)   A 128-bit number that is guaranteed to be unique across time and space.

Graphics Method   Performs runtime drawing operations; used for animation and simulations.

help files   Files that contain organized information about the application in use to help users who are having trouble or want to learn more.

hierarchical cursor   A feature that allows you to create record sets that contain child record sets embedded as fields within the parent records.

HyperText Markup Language (HTML)   A standardized programming language to create Web documents and some Help files.

HTML Help   Application help files that are created in HTML. They have the file extension .CHM.

HTML Help Workshop   Allows you to create new HTML files, import existing HTML documents, and compile them into the format used for Help.

Hungarian Notation   A set of standard prefixes for items in code (for example, MNU, TXT).

Immediate Window   One of the Debug windows; it lets you type code that responds as if it were directly in your code.

Initialize Event   Initializes any data used by the class, and can be used to load forms used by the class.

inline error handling   Inserting code where an error is likely to occur in order to allow the program to skip over it to the next item without interruption.

in-process servers   Loaded into the process space and share memory with the client application; consequently, are able to exchange information with the client more quickly than out-of-process servers.

instancing   A property used to designate classes as available to the client (public) or for internal use only (private).

integer   A variable type that requires a number.

Late Binding Method   Object variables are not declared with a specific class name. Instead, the variables are declared as type "Object." This method is used to provide the flexibility of accessing different types of objects with the same reference.

ListBox   Fields that display a list of various objects you select by clicking.

Locals Window   A Debug window that allows you to monitor the value of any variables within the current procedure's scope.

logical design   Phase of development that involves taking logical design information; this is where a system actually evolves.

logic error   A code executing without a syntax or runtime error, but producing unintended results.

Menu Editor   A tool that allows you to implement menu-based navigational aids in the program under development.

method   Action that an object can perform.

Microsoft Data Access Components (MDAC)   A package of technology components intended to implement Universal Data Access. The version 2 release included OLE DB 2, ADO 2 (including an updated RDS), and ODBC 3.5.

Multiple Document Interface (MDI) Environment   The MDI environment contains child windows, which are contained in a single parent window.

multitiered application   An application that has its functionality broken out into components that are each tasked with a particular aspect of using the application.

Microsoft Jet Engine   A proprietary database engine from Microsoft.

Object Browser   Used to quickly look up information on classes exposed by components, but cannot be used with components that do not expose type libraries. It allows you to view the classes, events, methods, properties, and constants in a project.

Object Linking and Embedding (OLE)   Obsolete form of COM objects; replaced by ActiveX.

Object-Oriented Programming (OOP)   System of programming that permits an abstract, modular hierarchy featuring inheritance, encapsulation, and polymorphism.

OLE Automation   Another term for the interaction among ActiveX components.

OLE DB   This specification model provides a standard definition of data access methods for data sources.

OLE Server   Another name for an ActiveX server.

Parent Property   A property used to reference the parent object that contains it.

permissions   Allowable actions taken by users (such as read-only, write, update, and delete).

persistent graphic   A method that stores output in memory and retains the graphic during screen events.

physical design   Design phase that takes the business objects and services identified in the logical design and maps them to software components.

pointer   A reference to an address in memory where the object lives.

Private Variable   A variable that is released when the routine in which it is defined terminates.

programmatic interface   The properties and methods used to access the functionality of a software component.

Project Group   A setting in Visual Basic that allows you to work and test multiple projects at the same time.

Project Window   A window that allows you to navigate through the forms and modules that make up the application you're working on.

property   Attribute of a control or object.

Property Get   Procedure executed when the calling code reads the property.

Property Let   Procedure used for non-objects, such as variables.

property procedures   Procedures that allow you to execute a procedure when a value is changed or read, to have a property constrained to a small set of values, or to expose properties that are read-only.

Property Set   Procedure used when setting the value of an object property.

Public Variable   A variable defined with the Public keyword; it is available to all procedures and functions, not just the ones in which they are defined.

Query Builder   A tool to automatically generate grammatically correct SQL queries from simple parameters defined by the developer.

record set   Representation of all records in a table, or the result of a query.

Recordset Object   One of the three main ADO objects; it provides methods to manage and manipulate result sets of information, in both immediate and batch modes.

referential integrity   A method with which an RDBMS ensures that the proper references exist between key values, thus maintaining the validity of relationships.

roles   Sets of database users.

runtime   The time during which an application is loaded into memory and running.

runtime error   An error that occurs during the execution of a program, causing the program to halt. Runtime errors occur when a command attempts to perform an invalid action.

scalable   Capability to be expanded to meet future needs.

scope   The scope of a variable is the area in which other parts of code can be aware of an object or variable.

server cluster   Two or more Windows NT Server machines that are accessed and managed as a single system.

Services Model   A conceptual model for designing a program that organizes your application's requirements into specific services.

Shape Command Language   Part of ADO that provides data-shaping functionality. The commands allow you to define a hierarchy based on record relations, parameters, or aggregate function groupings. The syntax used by the Shape language is relatively complicated, and you should refer to the online help for more information about the syntax.

shortcut key   Shortcut keys allow a user to access a menu item at any time.

Single Document Interface (SDI) Environment   When this option is used, windows can be moved anywhere on the screen, and will remain on top of other applications. (The user can see other open applications or the Windows desktop in the background.)

splash screen   The initial screen that is displayed when an application is started.

standard modules   Containers for procedures and declarations commonly accessed by other modules. There is only one copy of the module's data at any given time; a standard module's data exists for the life of the program.

stored procedures   Stored procedures are the code modules of SQL Server that give the database designer full programmatic control over data.

string   Group of characters not longer than 255 characters.

synchronous processing   A client making a method call that's blocked until the call returns.

syntax error   An error that results from incorrect use of the programming language.

Terminate Event   Associated with a class module; occurs when the object variable is set to nothing or goes out of scope. Used to save information, unload forms, and handle any other tasks required when the class ends.

Toolbox   The main tools window tools in Visual Basic. You can use it to drag controls onto your form, and you can customize it with new objects.

ToolTips   The little labels that appear over buttons when the mouse rests on an item for a moment without clicking.

triggers   Triggers fire when an update, insert, or delete happens on a table; they consist of Transact-SQL and can perform any number of tasks in response to a data change.

Twips   A unit of measurement equal to 1/20 of a point (about 1,440 twips per inch). Twips are screen-independent, and allow the placement and proportion of items to appear the same on multiple screens.

Type Library   Dictionary of classes and interfaces supported by a component.

Universal Data Access   An initiative by Microsoft to allow applications to access information from any location, regardless of where or how it is stored.

variable   Used to temporarily hold values during a program's execution.

variant   Data type; a variable that can hold any type of data.

versioning   The capability of a COM component to remain compatible with clients using older versions of the component, while allowing the developer of the component to further enhance the component.

Viewport   The screen area used to display an ActiveX document in a container application.

Visual Component Manager   A new feature of Visual Basic 6.0 that manages a large number of separate components in an application, and provides a way to find the needed components when the time comes to reuse them in applications.

Visual Data Manager   A component of Visual Basic that allows you to view the actual data underlying the data source.

Visual SourceSafe (VSS)   A component of Visual Basic that keeps a record of changes made to source code.

Visual Studio 6   A suite of programs that includes Visual Basic 6.0.

Watch Window   A Debug window that allows you to specify which expressions to watch, and returns information about their values as your program runs.

What's This Help   Help files that are context-sensitive and allow a user to get help on a specific item by pressing an access key.

Windows Explorer   A tool that comes with Windows 95 and Windows 98; allows the user to navigate the file system easily.

wizard   An easily followed series of steps that guide you through a particular process.

INDEX

N

S

Custom Corporate Network Training

Train on Cutting Edge Technology   We can bring the best in skill-based training to your facility to create a real-world hands-on training experience. Global Knowledge Network has invested millions of dollars in network hardware and software to train our students on the same equipment they will work with on the job. Our relationships with vendors allow us to incorporate the latest equipment and platforms into your on-site labs.

Maximize Your Training Budget   Global Knowledge Network provides experienced instructors, comprehensive course materials, and all the networking equipment needed to deliver high quality training. You provide the students; we provide the knowledge.

Avoid Travel Expenses   On-site courses allow you to schedule technical training at your convenience, saving time, expense, and the opportunity cost of travel away from the workplace.

Discuss Confidential Topics   Private on-site training permits the open discussion of sensitive issues such as security, access, and network design. We can work with your existing network's proprietary files while demonstrating the latest technologies.

Customize Course Content   Global Knowledge Network can tailor your courses to include the technologies and the topics which have the greatest impact on your business. We can complement your internal training efforts or provide a total solution to your training needs.

Corporate Pass   The Corporate Pass Discount Program rewards our best network training customers with preferred pricing on public courses, discounts on multimedia training packages, and an array of career planning services.

Global Knowledge Network Training Lifecycle   Supporting the Dynamic and Specialized Training Requirements of Information Technology Professionals

- Define Profile
- Assess Skills
- Design Training
- Deliver Training
- Test Knowledge
- Update Profile
- Use New Skills

College Credit Recommendation Program   The American Council on Education's CREDIT program recommends 53 Global Knowledge Network courses for college credit. Now our network training can help you earn your college degree while you learn the technical skills needed for your job. When you attend an ACE-certified Global Knowledge Network course and pass the associated exam, you earn college credit recommendations for that course. Global Knowledge Network can establish a transcript record for you with ACE, which you can use to gain credit at a college or as a written record of your professional training that you can attach to your resume.

Registration Information

COURSE FEE: The fee covers course tuition, refreshments, and all course materials. Any parking expenses that may be incurred are not included. Payment or government training form must be received six business days prior to the course date. We will also accept Visa/MasterCard and American Express. For non-U.S. credit card users, charges will be in U.S. funds and will be converted by your credit card company. Checks drawn on Canadian banks in Canadian funds are acceptable.

COURSE SCHEDULE: Registration is at 8:00 a.m. on the first day. The program begins at 8:30 a.m. and concludes at 4:30 p.m. each day.

CANCELLATION POLICY: Cancellation and full refund will be allowed if written cancellation is received in our office at least six business days prior to the course start date. Registrants who do not attend the course or do not cancel more than six business days in advance are responsible for the full registration fee; you may transfer to a later date provided the course fee has been paid in full. Substitutions may be made at any time. If Global Knowledge Network must cancel a course for any reason, liability is limited to the registration fee only.

GLOBAL KNOWLEDGE NETWORK: Global Knowledge Network programs are developed and presented by industry professionals with "real-world" experience. Designed to help professionals meet today's interconnectivity and interoperability challenges, most of our programs feature hands-on labs that incorporate state-of-the-art communication components and equipment.

ON-SITE TEAM TRAINING: Bring Global Knowledge Network's powerful training programs to your company. At Global Knowledge Network, we will custom design courses to meet your specific network requirements. Call 1 (919) 461-8686 for more information.

YOUR GUARANTEE: Global Knowledge Network believes its courses offer the best possible training in this field. If during the first day you are not satisfied and wish to withdraw from the course, simply notify the instructor, return all course materials, and receive a 100% refund.

In the US:

CALL: 1 (888) 762-4442

FAX: 1 (919) 469-7070

VISIT OUR WEBSITE:

www.globalknowledge.com

MAIL CHECK AND THIS FORM TO:

Global Knowledge Network

Suite 200

114 Edinburgh South

P.O. Box 1187

Cary, NC 27512

In Canada:

CALL: 1 (800) 465-2226

FAX: 1 (613) 567-3899

VISIT OUR WEBSITE:

www.globalknowledge.com.ca

MAIL CHECK AND THIS FORM TO:

Global Knowledge Network

Suite 1601

393 University Ave.

Toronto, ON M5G 1E6

REGISTRATION INFORMATION:

Course title _____

Course location _____ Course date _____

Name/title _____ Company _____

Name/title _____ Company _____

Name/title _____ Company _____

Address _____ Telephone _____ Fax _____

City _____ State/Province _____ Zip/Postal Code _____

Credit card _____ Card # _____ Expiration date _____

Signature _____

LICENSE AGREEMENT

THIS PRODUCT (THE "PRODUCT") CONTAINS PROPRIETARY SOFTWARE, DATA AND INFORMATION (INCLUDING DOCUMENTATION) OWNED BY THE McGRAW-HILL COMPANIES, INC. ("McGRAW-HILL") AND ITS LICENSORS. YOUR RIGHT TO USE THE PRODUCT IS GOVERNED BY THE TERMS AND CONDITIONS OF THIS AGREEMENT.

LICENSE: Throughout this License Agreement, "you" shall mean either the individual or the entity whose agent opens this package. You are granted a non-exclusive and non-transferable license to use the Product subject to the following terms:

(i) If you have licensed a single user version of the Product, the Product may only be used on a single computer (i.e., a single CPU). If you licensed and paid the fee applicable to a local area network or wide area network version of the Product, you are subject to the terms of the following subparagraph (ii).

(ii) If you have licensed a local area network version, you may use the Product on unlimited workstations located in one single building selected by you that is served by such local area network. If you have licensed a wide area network version, you may use the Product on unlimited workstations located in multiple buildings on the same site selected by you that is served by such wide area network; provided, however, that any building will not be considered located in the same site if it is more than five (5) miles away from any building included in such site. In addition, you may only use a local area or wide area network version of the Product on one single server. If you wish to use the Product on more than one server, you must obtain written authorization from McGraw-Hill and pay additional fees.

(iii) You may make one copy of the Product for back-up purposes only and you must maintain an accurate record as to the location of the back-up at all times.

COPYRIGHT; RESTRICTIONS ON USE AND TRANSFER: All rights (including copyright) in and to the Product are owned by McGraw-Hill and its licensors. You are the owner of the enclosed disc on which the Product is recorded. You may not use, copy, decompile, disassemble, reverse engineer, modify, reproduce, create derivative works, transmit, distribute, sublicense, store in a database or retrieval system of any kind, rent or transfer the Product, or any portion thereof, in any form or by any means (including electronically or otherwise) except as expressly provided for in this License Agreement. You must reproduce the copyright notices, trademark notices, legends and logos of McGraw-Hill and its licensors that appear on the Product on the back-up copy of the Product which you are permitted to make hereunder. All rights in the Product not expressly granted herein are reserved by McGraw-Hill and its licensors.

TERM: This License Agreement is effective until terminated. It will terminate if you fail to comply with any term or condition of this License Agreement. Upon termination, you are obligated to return to McGraw-Hill the Product together with all copies thereof and to purge all copies of the Product included in any and all servers and computer facilities.

DISCLAIMER OF WARRANTY: THE PRODUCT AND THE BACK-UP COPY OF THE PRODUCT ARE LICENSED "AS IS." McGRAW-HILL, ITS LICENSORS AND THE AUTHORS MAKE NO WARRANTIES, EXPRESS OR IMPLIED, AS TO RESULTS TO BE OBTAINED BY ANY PERSON OR ENTITY FROM USE OF THE PRODUCT AND/OR ANY INFORMATION OR DATA INCLUDED THEREIN. McGRAW-HILL, ITS LICENSORS, AND THE AUTHORS MAKE NO GUARANTEE THAT YOU WILL PASS ANY CERTIFICATION EXAM BY USING THIS PRODUCT. McGRAW-HILL, ITS LICENSORS AND THE AUTHORS MAKE NO EXPRESS OR IMPLIED WARRANTIES OF MERCHANTABILITY OR FITNESS FOR A PARTICULAR PURPOSE OR USE WITH RESPECT TO THE PRODUCT. NEITHER McGRAW-HILL, ANY OF ITS LICENSORS, NOR THE AUTHORS WARRANT THAT THE FUNCTIONS CONTAINED IN THE PRODUCT WILL MEET YOUR REQUIREMENTS OR THAT THE OPERATION OF THE PRODUCT WILL BE UNINTERRUPTED OR ERROR FREE. YOU ASSUME THE ENTIRE RISK WITH RESPECT TO THE QUALITY AND PERFORMANCE OF THE PRODUCT.

LIMITED WARRANTY FOR DISC: To the original licensee only, McGraw-Hill warrants that the enclosed disc on which the Product is recorded is free from defects in materials and workmanship under normal use and service for a period of ninety (90) days from the date of purchase. In the event of a defect in the disc covered by the foregoing warranty, McGraw-Hill will replace the disc.

LIMITATION OF LIABILITY: NEITHER McGRAW-HILL, ITS LICENSORS NOR THE AUTHORS SHALL BE LIABLE FOR ANY INDIRECT, SPECIAL OR CONSEQUENTIAL DAMAGES, SUCH AS BUT NOT LIMITED TO, LOSS OF ANTICIPATED PROFITS OR BENEFITS, RESULTING FROM THE USE OR INABILITY TO USE THE PRODUCT EVEN IF ANY OF THEM HAS BEEN ADVISED OF THE POSSIBILITY OF SUCH DAMAGES. THIS LIMITATION OF LIABILITY SHALL APPLY TO ANY CLAIM OR CAUSE WHATSOEVER WHETHER SUCH CLAIM OR CAUSE ARISES IN CONTRACT, TORT, OR OTHERWISE. Some states do not allow the exclusion or limitation of indirect, special or consequential damages, so the above limitation may not apply to you.

U.S. GOVERNMENT RESTRICTED RIGHTS: Any software included in the Product is provided with restricted rights subject to subparagraphs (c), (1) and (2) of the Commercial Computer Software-Restricted Rights clause at 48 C.F.R. 52.227-19. The terms of this Agreement applicable to the use of the data in the Product are those under which the data are generally made available to the general public by McGraw-Hill. Except as provided herein, no reproduction, use, or disclosure rights are granted with respect to the data included in the Product and no right to modify or create derivative works from any such data is hereby granted.

GENERAL: This License Agreement constitutes the entire agreement between the parties relating to the Product. The terms of any Purchase Order shall have no effect on the terms of this License Agreement. Failure of McGraw-Hill to insist at any time on strict compliance with this License Agreement shall not constitute a waiver of any rights under this License Agreement. This License Agreement shall be construed and governed in accordance with the laws of the State of New York. If any provision of this License Agreement is held to be contrary to law, that provision will be enforced to the maximum extent permissible and the remaining provisions will remain in full force and effect.